TO

BARB

Second Edition

The Evolution of Economic Thought

By

W. E. KUHN, PhD
Professor of Economics
University of Nebraska

Published by

SOUTH-WESTERN PUBLISHING CO.
Cincinnati   Chicago   Dallas
New Rochelle, N.Y.   Burlingame, Calif.

H26

38078

This volume owes its origin to the author's dissatisfaction some years ago with the then existing textbook literature. As pointed out in the Preface to the First Edition, it aims at the achievement of a limited set of high-priority objectives, which in the order of relative importance are:

(1) To acquaint students with the best minds that have exerted themselves on economics as a body of scientifically developed propositions.

(2) To show in which specific subject matter areas the leading thinkers have set their landmarks. In giving an intelligible account of what these thinkers accomplished, names are associated primarily with *topics*, and only secondarily with schools of thought.

(3) To distinguish clearly, by spatial separation, between positive contributions to the ever-growing mass of theoretical insights and the external circumstances which propelled the contributors on their chosen paths.

Those who value the distinction between economic thought and economic theory may note that the book is oriented toward the more circumscribed of these categories: it addresses itself to *scientific* economic thought.

It has *not* been the author's design to unroll before the reader the screen of economic history which nurtured and conditioned the minds of the all-time greats in economics. Without some background knowledge of the developments which in Western Europe led to the downfall of feudalism and later of mercantilism, and which ushered in the Industrial Revolution as well as numerous political revolutions, an attempt to appreciate the problems to which economists have addressed themselves from time to time will be largely fruitless.

The organization of the material is based on the premise that in the long sweep of history value and distribution theory (microeconomics) has been the "warp and woof" of the subject matter of our science. Under this heading are covered new conquests relative to the nature of production and exchange and of the relation between factor returns and prices of produced goods, insights that are not inherently bound up with the economic organization of a particular group. The first seven chapters are devoted to the explication of advances in value and distribution theory.

Little had been done prior to the 1930's to explore the interrelationships of such aggregates as a nation's income, consumption, saving, and investment. Although Keynes attacked with indefatigable zeal the problem of how to maintain a proper balance between these magnitudes, thus sparking a lively professional debate, there are no grounds for slighting the long labors of nineteenth-century writers, resulting in the frontiers of economic knowledge being repeatedly pushed back. There is still some danger that contemporary historians of economic thought become so engrossed with recent macroeconomic exploits that all pre-1930 contributions to economic theory appear to have been only "preparatory" in nature. The author, while prepared to use them as tools, has attempted to keep in proper perspective the analytic advances of the last thirty-five years. Yet because the Keynesian Revolution has continued to inspire much empirical work, and to sharpen the thrust toward technique which has been the hallmark of modern economics, an entirely *new* chapter (9), "Extensions of Keynesian Macrotheory," has been incorporated into this edition. It emphasizes as much the quality of recent work in the Keynesian tradition as it does the profile of great economists, in full recognition of how difficult it is to draw a line between singularly outstanding and merely very competent personalities. The author awaits with some suspense the hardening of this body of thought, the ripening of historical judgment on the most recent epoch.

Theory in the fields of money and banking, international trade, business cycles, public finance, and labor had, until well into the twentieth century, been developed, if at all, largely on the periphery of value and distribution theory. Even more, it had to await the evolution of certain capitalistic (or anticapitalistic) institutions, and it has been somewhat less "pure" *qua* theory. But it constitutes today a set of indispensable building blocks for the adroit economist. The singling out and separate treatment of the above topics are merely a matter of educational convenience — a learning device and an expedient for reference purposes — and students who do not rebel against the customary organization of material found in the "Principles" text may welcome the suggestion that they proceed likewise in the study of the evolution of economic thought.

Again, in resurveying the full landscape, some hard decisions had to be made. The following *additions* to material in Part III, "Complementary Avenues of Theoretical Advance," are worthy of note. Chapter 11 highlights, in the new edition, some features of recent work in monetary theory by Patinkin, Gurley and Shaw, Tobin, and Friedman. Chapter 13 lets Harry G. Johnson "stand" for much of what has served to flesh out international trade theory during the last two decades. Chapter 16 has been enriched by a section entitled "Liberal Socialism" to suggest that the dust has now nearly settled over the theory-oriented "isms" controversy carried on by such ideological torchbearers as von Mises, Lange and Taylor, and von Hayek. Wherever weighty extensions were made, chapter summaries have been adapted to the expanded format. Likewise, Biographical Notes of still living economists have been brought up to date. What may be viewed as a supersummary, Chapter 17's "Reorientation and Overview," has been rounded out to accommodate the antecedent chapter expansions.

Just when, it may be asked, can a leading economist be said to have been elevated to the top echelon of his fraternity? Can he, while still living, be ranked among the select few of the highest stature, those who have given economics a decisive impetus or a new direction? Certainly, while a fraternal consensus is still in the process of being formed, this must remain a matter of bold judgment. In this matter the author continues to prefer erring on the conservative rather than the liberal side. As indicated in the Preface to the First Edition, it is to enhance the prospects of lasting retention of the panorama that, generally, only the towering peaks have been illuminated. In order to bring peak performances into still sharper focus, not only are some important names left out, but an attempt has been made to show by what lines of reasoning theorists have arrived at their major conclusions. That they were not isolated in developing a particular body of truths, that their scientific ideas were filiated in time and place, are some related hoped-for insights to be gained by the reader. With direct quotation held to a minimum, this book serves to bridge the gap between many a standard text listing in somewhat disconnected fashion the principal contributions of major (and often minor) writers and the book of readings introducing broad and sometimes indiscriminate selections of source material with only a few threads of evaluative commentary.

In order to inject still more clarity, whenever in this text a name appears in the exposition for the first time, the appropriate number refers the reader to a Biographical Note at the end of the chapter. Study of these notes is indispensable for those who want to judge the doctrinal significance of a writer in his temporal and spatial environment. Reference to biographical data appears in boldface in the name index.

For a bird's-eye view of the panorama, the Summary at the end of each chapter will suffice. For a close-up of the landscape, it will be necessary to traverse the trails — still shortcuts — marked out in the body of the text. For a mastery of the terrain which their authors covered, there is as yet no substitute for studying the original writings, to the more important of which reference, with suggested chapter priorities, is made in the Recommended Readings for each chapter.

The author hopes to win additional converts to the principle that it is wiser for the undergraduate student with an economics major to know a limited number of creative writers fairly well than to have a vague idea, a smattering of knowledge, about a great many of the lesser greats. He also trusts that the additions to his previously quite slender gallery of postwar commanding figures will not be judged rash at such a time in the future when the sifting and evaluating process has reached a point of near-finality — when economists dare to talk with as much assurance about the theoretical advances of the 1950's and 1960's as they did a generation ago, after the Keynesian splash, in assessing neoclassicism (in the traditional meaning of the term).

Certainly, reader reaction to the first edition suggests that the topical approach, which accords with the principle of the division of labor that has governed the more recent evolution of economics, is gaining in favor. One may venture the guess that it will have become *the* accepted procedure of historians of economic theory a few decades hence. The reason for this conjecture is the almost certain proliferation of professional work into still more outlying areas of investigation, a line of development characterized by such already established specialties as the economics of education, the economics of the "health industry," etc.

The author wishes to express gratitude to his colleagues at the University of Nebraska, Wallace Peterson, Theodore Roesler, and Tom Iwand, for suggestions that have benefited this revision.

W. E. KUHN

TABLE OF CONTENTS

ix

Since 1954, year of the posthumous publication of J. A. Schumpeter's *History of Economic Analysis* (under the editorship of his widow, Elizabeth Boody Schumpeter), the science of economics has been enriched by an English language reference work in which schools and streams of economic thought are discussed with rare comprehensiveness, insight, and clarity. The *History*, written primarily for professional economists and social scientists, testifies to such immense scholarship as few writers can ever hope to attain. All the same, there is a continuing need to provide students of economics with a guide in which the historical accretions to the major strands of economic theory are straightforwardly recorded. To help fill that need, following lines of organization[1] that few textbooks have chosen to adopt, is the modest aim of this book.

Economic thought is as old as the history of man making a living by utilizing the scarce resources provided him by nature. Economics as a science is much younger. Just where to draw the line between informal, unfettered thought and rigorous, disciplined theory nobody knows. In this book, the treatment of major branches of economic theory is based partly on artificial and partly on natural distinctions, distinctions that are the result of conventions on the one hand and of unplanned development of organized economic activity on the other.

If no one can assert with persuasive finality just when economics became an independent science, a case has nevertheless been made for the thesis that the emancipation of economic from other social thought occurred during the second half of the eighteenth century. This proposition is supported by at least two historical facts.

First, soon after the middle of that century, there emerged in France an intellectual leader who began to look upon the realm of economic activity from a new and abstract angle. His reflections led him to conceive of a national economy as an organic whole consisting of harmoniously interrelated parts. This man had been — by no means coincidentally — a medical doctor in the service of France's royal household; his name was François Quesnay. His dedication to finding the laws that govern the production and circulation of wealth in an organized human society led him to construct a diagram, called *Economic Table* (1758), which dimly reflects his economic philosophy. A group of ardent disciples, known to posterity as the *Physiocrats*, began to gather

[1]The claim that a topical arrangement destroys the "conceptual unity" of a theorist's contribution is untenable. Scarce are pretwentieth-century economists whose work(s) may be said to constitute, or be comparable to, a mathematical-type model.

1

around Quesnay and to render assistance in the task of dispersing "the light." While the master and his disciples were certainly not lacking in enthusiasm, their insights were colored by metaphysics and centered in what they called the "Natural Order," which, if not rejected outright, can at most be accepted on faith. All the same, the Physiocrats did bring into the open elements which, through judicious selection, could be combined into an independent discipline.

Second, to this task the Scotsman Adam Smith addressed himself on the eve of the Industrial Revolution in England, and the result of his labors was the famous *Wealth of Nations* (1776). With great determination and patience, and paying due regard to many predecessors with whom the Physiocrats had not been concerned, Smith so competently effected this task that later generations have deigned to call him the father of economic science. Hyperbolic though such statements may be, Smith was a successful professor of moral (social) philosophy who, upon finding that no one — not even his illustrious countryman David Hume — had yet undertaken the task of weaving the many loose strands of thought into a strong fabric, went at it with the deliberation to which leisure and financial security are highly conducive. Ingeniously, Smith combined the assembling of many partial truths with the branding of falsehoods, often unmasking erroneous theories as products of self-seeking and misinformation.

Self-seeking in the economic realm need not, as Smith was perhaps the first to recognize, run counter to the common good; but, lest the former degenerate into iniquitous practices, certain objective conditions (competition, free access to markets, etc.) must be met. Smith knew that they were not fulfilled in his time, but he hoped England would eventually approximate them. Today, when it is occasionally said of people that they advocate a return to Adam Smith, they are subtly and perhaps insidiously accused of being enemies of the greatest good for the greatest number, the implication being that Smith, in effect, wrote for a vested-interest group composed of businessmen clamoring to be left to their own devices. Few of those who join in making such a glib charge realize that Adam Smith was careful to hedge with a number of provisos his pronouncements concerning the most beneficial course of action. Only grossly uninformed persons can claim, besides, that Adam Smith's views of the role of government in economic life were meant to apply to all times and all places.

Liken, if you will, economic theory to an eighteenth-century sailing vessel. After Smith had retraced the past and charted the future course of the ship which was to sail for several decades (the *classical* period) under the flag of free-enterprise political economy, the pace of economic development accelerated, especially in England. Although those outraged by the misery and degradation of the working class under the English factory system, sometimes aggravated by flagrant employer abuses, fired many torpedoes against it during the first half of the nineteenth century, the vessel remained seaworthy. Malthus and Ricardo took command of it in the early decades, Senior and John Stuart Mill in later ones. A number of shipmates—Say in France and McCulloch in England, to mention only two — labored on behalf of the English captains. In the New World, they were more or less ably assisted by others. Thus was spread what appeared to later generations as the "gospel" of the Classical school, whose primary field of active research was value and distribution theory.

When John Stuart Mill, a phenomenal mind with deep roots in the utilitarian philosophy of Jeremy Bentham (a contemporary and friend of his father, James Mill), proceeded to restate the classical theory in terms that would make the ship well-nigh impregnable in the mid-nineteenth-century political battles, it appeared to him that for all practical purposes nothing remained to be added to its armor. The bulk of his educated contemporaries probably agreed with Mill that he had accommodated enough of the criticisms of Socialists and advocates of social reform to give classical theory the appearance of a felicitous blend of stability and flexibility.

Indeed, few had heard as yet the name of the German Karl Marx, who in 1848 had written the *Communist Manifesto* in collaboration with Friedrich Engels. Nor were many then aware that a Frenchman, Cournot, had opened up vistas for the services of mathematics in the development of a theory of market structures; Cournot, in fact, became the "father" of a long line of mathematical economists. Nor, finally, were they aware that another German, Gossen, was about to state (he did so in 1854) certain laws which showed how "want satisfaction" can be maximized by taking into consideration the utility provided by small increments to the stock of an economic good. We see, then, that just when the Classical school was getting ready to rest on its past accomplishments, having already weathered many a storm, new approaches to the study of political economy and the economic system to which it conformed were being sought. Of these, the one taken by the *Marginalists* (Marginal Utility school) was solidified during some two or three decades prior to the turn of the century.

Jevons, Menger, and Walras — these are the names of a famous trio of teachers and writers who a little less than one hundred years ago succeeded in formulating, independently of each other, a set of new doctrines by taking an approach radically different from (early) classicism. Walras, a French mathematician, opened the door to general equilibrium analysis, which attempted to present an overall view of the economy in precise, yet abstract, terms. He also originated the Lausanne school of thought, which shortly before the turn of the twentieth century found its main spokesman in Walras' successor at the University of Lausanne, the Italian Pareto. Pareto's legacy has in turn inspired such midtwentieth-century luminaries as Hicks in England and Samuelson in the United States.

Without Menger, there probably would never have arisen an Austrian school. His compatriots von Wieser and von Böhm-Bawerk, both some ten years younger, freely acknowledged their indebtedness to the founder of the branch of economic theory which pursued into its finest ramifications the problem of the pricing of productive factors on the basis of the utilities of final goods.

Jevons, laboring in England where Mill — the last of a series of illustrious writers adhering to a classical cost theory of value — remained an authority for years after his death in 1873, faced an uphill struggle in trying to break new ground. Jevons died in his prime, before he was able to gather a following. It was under his countryman Marshall, who was fortunate enough to see the ripening of the fruits of his sustained endeavors, that England more or less regained its authority as the home of the world's leading economic theorists. By that time, the closing years of the nineteenth century, a synthesis of the cost and marginal utility theories of value and distribution suggested itself to enlightened and cosmopolitan minds. No one succeeded like Marshall did in combining what was of enduring value in both the "old" and "new" theory into a "third way," which came to be called *neoclassicism*. Marshall's fame was greatly enhanced by his accomplishments in the way of forging additional tools of analysis.

Although, at the turn of this century, several nations not mentioned so far had produced first-rate economists — J. B. Clark in the United States and Knut Wicksell in Sweden being perhaps most representative of the geographical diversification of talents — England maintained a position of at least informal leadership in our science. To illustrate, the first welfare economist of some renown — A. C. Pigou — was an Englishman, as was J. M. Keynes, the man whose unorthodox views stirred up commotion in the ranks of the profession. To Keynes, the impact of economic ideas upon public policy was a *fait accompli*, which might as well be utilized to best advantage for the common good.

Keynes was also an assiduous builder of conceptual tools, which is why his name has come to be mentioned with a degree of confidence among the all-time greats. Let us note a point — it will be made again — which, in the author's opinion, bears repeating. Keynes' arrival on the scene has often been heralded as marking the end of an era whose great achievement was an ever more refined analysis of the behavior of the individual within the economy. But it is safe to say that *macroeconomics* has not by any means superseded microeconomics. Keynes' emphasis on enlarged understanding of the processes of the modern economy as a whole was merely overdue, having been largely neglected since Quesnay's days.

With the spread of economic teaching during the second half of the nineteenth century, economists in many countries set up their own professional organizations. The American Economic Association, for example, was born in 1885 under the initiative of a group of young men, many of whom had studied in Germany. There they had often come under the tutelage of the founders of the so-called *Historical school* — Roscher, Hildebrand, and especially Knies — whose members rebelled, in differing degrees, against established economic theory and method, including both the English (classical) and the Austrian varieties. This is why American economic thought for at least three quarters of a century has been more empirical and less deductive in its general orientation than perhaps the bulk of European economic thought. It has also been *institutional* to a large extent; that is, it has tended to focus on legal forms and modes of thought, as well as on quantitative, statistical work. We will encounter some prime examples of American leadership in this field. It began roughly in the first quarter of this century after Veblen, the bold innovator and eccentric satirist, had made his undignified appearance on the scene of American economics. It was reflected in the work of Fisher, Mitchell, and Commons, who will be discussed in the chapters dealing with monetary, business cycle, and labor theory respectively.

The United States has also become the main breeding ground for *econometricians*, a brand of researchers who, impressed by the profusion of quantitative data on many economic problems, see the greatest promise for advance in a judicious blending of economic theory, statistics, and mathematics. They embrace a problem-oriented approach to the expansion of theoretical horizons. They have drawn much inspiration from Keynes who, in the face of the worst depression the world had ever experienced since economics became a science, in his *The General Theory of Employment, Interest, and Money* (1936) adopted a national income approach. This work barely suggested new lines of advance, but it nevertheless set the stage for much of the ensuing effort.

With the rise of the United States to economic leadership after World War I, this country became something of a magnet for leading economists of the Old World. Particularly people who were "brought up" under members of the Austrian Trio (see Chapter 4) and/or have helped to solidify the Austrian contribution to the evolution of economic thought found congenial working conditions in this country; Schumpeter, von Mises, von Hayek, von Haberler, and Machlup have perhaps been as illustrious in the United States at various times during the last three or four decades as they were in Europe before emigrating to this country.

Out of the cross-fertilization of ideas, some pursued inductively and others deductively, have come significant theoretical advances. They have placed this country in a position of unexcelled attraction for students from all over the world. Many from Latin America, Asia, and Africa have come here with the firm belief that a thorough knowledge of economics is perhaps the most important stepping-stone to success in efforts to launch their countries, or help them along, on the path to self-sustaining growth.

RECOMMENDED READINGS

Ashley, W. J. *An Introduction to English Economic History and Theory*, 2 vols. London: Longmans, Green & Co., Ltd., 1888–1893. It covers roughly the second half of the Middle Ages.

Bland, A. E., P. A. Brown, and R. H. Tawney. *English Economic History; Select Documents*. New York: The Macmillan Company, 1915.

Cunningham, William. *The Growth of English Industry and Commerce in Modern Times*, 2 vols. Cambridge: Harvard University Press, 1890, 1892.

Heaton, Herbert. *Economic History of Europe*. New York: Harper & Row, Publishers, 1936.

Laski, H. J. *Political Thought in England from Locke to Bentham*. New York: Holt, Rinehart & Winston, Inc., 1920.

Lipson, Ephraim. *Introduction to the Economic History of England*, 3 vols. New York: The Macmillan Company, 1929–1931. This work deals with the Middle Ages and mercantilism.

Mantoux, Paul J. *The Industrial Revolution in the Eighteenth Century; an Outline of the Beginnings of the Modern Factory System in England*. New York: Harcourt, Brace, & World, 1928. Rev. ed. London: J. Cape, 1961.

Pirenne, Henri. *Economic and Social History of Medieval Europe*. New York: Harcourt, Brace, & World, Inc., 1937.

Robertson, H. M. *Aspects of the Rise of Economic Individualism*. New York: The Macmillan Company, 1933.

VALUE AND DISTRIBUTION THEORY

From Aristotle to Smith

In the records of the ancient world of Greece and Rome, we generally find only a somewhat sketchy summary treatment of economic affairs. From the modern point of view, the Greek legacy is much more meaningful and deserving of our attention.

ARISTOTLE[1]

Aristotle's power of analytical thinking justifies his being ranked among the founders of the core of the subject matter of economics. This far-ranging Greek philosopher put forth the fundamental proposition that every commodity may be viewed from two angles: whether it serves to satisfy a want directly, its proper use, as when shoes are worn; or whether it serves to satisfy a want indirectly, as when shoes are exchanged for something else. This latter, improper use — in contrast to the former — lends itself to abuse because it may lead to an accumulation of goods exceeding the necessities of life

Several distinctions flow from this dichotomy: (1) that between *value in use* and *value in exchange;* (2) that between true or genuine wealth, to which there is a limit set by nature, and unnatural wealth, the acquisition of which is, broadly speaking, unlimited, being regulated only by the greater or lesser cupidity of man in his capacity as an economic agent[2]; (3) that between the requirements of domestic economy, or finance in the good sense of the term, and what exceeds these requirements, or finance in the bad sense.

Distinctions (2) and (3) are scientifically of little import, as they imply value "judgments" and presuppose a theoretical ideal concerning the stratification of wants in society as well as the means to their satisfaction (crude welfare economics). The first, however, has become the

---

[1]See Biographical Note A.

[2]Perhaps a note of caution is in order here. Aristotle does not seem to suggest that possession of an article as a means of exchange is unnatural per se. Obviously men may exchange, as in primitive barter, without being engaged in the art of moneymaking, the target of Aristotle's strictures.

basis of an imposing structure of thought, gaining in complexity right down to our day.

Aristotle himself took another decisive step forward by reasoning that value in exchange is *derived* from value in use. Their common denominator is human wants. Commodities differ not only in their ability to satisfy these wants (utility), but also in the ease with which they can be readied for human consumption (cost of production). Hence, anticipated Aristotle with keen insight, value is not a quality inherent in a commodity, but something dependent upon two factors: utility and cost of production. He thus set forth the rudiments of two theories of value whose reconciliation still defied the efforts of writers during the first century of economics as an independent science, well over two millennia later. The key distinction between capital goods and consumer goods does not appear in Aristotle's writings.

MEDIEVAL THOUGHT

The centerpiece of the medieval writers' contribution to modern value doctrine was their theory of a *just price*. Their chief attention in considering the cost of production of a commodity was focused on labor cost, as goods were made mostly in the home — either to be consumed there or to be sold in a local or regional market. Again they clearly perceived that value is not something absolute and objective, inherent in the goods produced for sale, but something dependent on men's wants. However, neither the need of any one consuming individual nor the cost of production of any one individual producer could be the determining elements of value, but rather these were to be found in the common estimate of the whole group of interrelated buyers and sellers as to the social utility of the products exchanged. Consequently, the just price was the objective resultant of many subjective valuations and productive efforts. Being based on estimates, it could not be stated with absolute exactness; nor could it be exempt from modification by external circumstances, such as the urgency of need of the buyer or the loss which the seller would incur in parting with a good. The "margin," revealed by consideration of the special situation in which the parties to an exchange transaction found themselves, was to be largely governed by the fundamental idea of the Middle Ages that no one should take advantage of another, always heeding the Golden Rule.

The principle of the *just wage* logically arises as a corollary, or special case, of the canon of the just price. Certainly the laborer's wages could not be the sole element in the determination of prices;

but inasmuch as the craftsman worked with his own tools in his own home or shop, the value of his investment (the economic significance of the capital furnished by him) could be but vaguely gauged. The rate of remuneration of a seller of handicraft products was therefore largely one based on personal services performed. In addition, according to the ethico-religious standards of the Middle Ages, the rendering of these services should enable the ordinary worker to derive enough to live decently in that station of life to which he was destined by an inscrutable Providence.

The other main corollary of the just-price dogma was the *prohibition of usury*. Although the term was used by *St. Thomas Aquinas*[3] and others in a much broader sense than that of pure interest or even gross interest, its main field of application was nevertheless the making of "profits" out of loans. But while Aristotle had condemned this practice in accordance with his highly inadequate view of the proper functions of money, conceived by him merely as a means of exchange (see Chapter 10), the exponents of scholastic thinking were soon confronted with the need of realizing that such a narrow concept was at odds with the development of embryonic commercial capitalism in parts of Europe (see Chapter 16). What in their line of thinking strikes the modern student of economic thought as increasingly anachronistic must, however, be viewed in the context of ethical principles that some seven hundred years ago could not have been thrown overboard without undermining the whole structure of medieval philosophy. As a result of the lag in the intellectual superstructure relative to the mode of production, to borrow Marxian concepts, the principle became so riddled with exceptions that in time it was almost relegated to the status of a dead letter. With a view to preserving equity and fairness, it was constantly adapted to new needs. Major illustrations showing the gradual separation taking place between legitimate interest on the one hand, illegitimate usury on the other, are: the lender could prove that because of his loan he had suffered a definite loss; he could demonstrate that he had missed an opportunity for profit in an alternative investment; he could attest that he had undergone the risk of not being repaid; and, in a contract stipulating the return of money on a certain date, he could show that he was at a disadvantage if, by virtue of not being repaid on time, he had been unable to utilize investment opportunities following the maturity date of the loan. In all such cases, a special charge was legitimate.

---

[3]See Biographical Note B.

Though none of these concessions involve the suspension of the prohibition of payment of money for the use of money pure and simple (economic, or pure, interest), they nevertheless pave the way for the modern approach to the analysis of the interest phenomenon.

WRITERS IN THE MERCANTILIST PERIOD
[ABOUT 1500–1750]

Under this label falls a group of writers, to be encountered again in Chapter 12, who had little inclination to devote themselves to the important but abstruse topic of value. In the main no novel ideas were produced in the field until well into the seventeenth century, after the prime of the Mercantilists. Their notions concerning rent and profits remained embryonic. They developed a theory of *low wages* in terms of a nation's competitive interest in low production costs, stressing the desirability of keeping in check wage earners' aspirations for a bettering in their level of living. Whereas, in general, the "legitimacy" of interest taking was granted, only a faint awareness of the relation between interest and the productivity of capital was in evidence. When, with the growth of industry, manufacturing became the chief concern of economic thinkers and exchange was relegated to a secondary position in their analytical framework, it was no longer possible to insist that exchange value arises primarily or solely in commerce. The stage was gradually being set for a group of men to occupy a prominent position as anticipators of the main currents of thought embodied in the Classical school, men who were able to overcome the intellectual limitations set by their mercantilist environment.

Petty[4]

The first to reformulate and expand a still tenuous set of principles inherited from the Middle Ages was Petty. In his *Treatise of Taxes and Contributions* (1662), he set forth interesting elements of a theory of *interest* and a theory of *rent*. As to the former, he distinguished two principal cases: (1) the one in which the lender may call in his loan at any time he wishes; and, (2) the case in which the borrower can choose when (and where) to repay. In the first of these contractual arrangements, interest is not justified as the borrower is under the imminent necessity of having to tap an alternate source of finance in order to satisfy his creditor, who presumably is suffering no disadvantage as

---

4See Biographical Note C.

long as he can reattain at a moment's notice the full control over the funds lent. In the second case, the cards are turned around, so to speak, with all the potential advantages accruing to the borrower, who consequently should pay something (interest) for their enjoyment.

Petty also devotes some reasoning to the issue of the maximum and minimum rate of interest to be paid or received. The minimum interest, he argues, surely can never be less than the rent on land derived from the investment of an equal capital, for the security of an investment in land is indubitable. As to the maximum, it will depend on the risks involved, but it may in no case be equivalent to more than the principal itself. Furthermore, any part of the interest payment exceeding the remuneration from an equal investment in land may be viewed as an insurance premium measuring the size of the risks involved. In conflict with this, though grossly one-sided, was Petty's fundamental doctrine that the value of commodities is determined by the quantities of *labor* embodied in their production, thus making labor time the common denominator of all values. But labor theories of value did not come to full fruition until two centuries later.

Hume[5]

Hume also deserves a place in the pre-classical history of value theory, not so much for what he added to accepted doctrine but for revealing a serious pitfall of thinking. In his *Discourse of Interest* (1752) he opposes the common fallacy of ascribing the lowness of the *interest rate* to a plenty of money. Illustrating his point that the causal nexus is much more complex, he cites England's development since the discovery of the Indies, a period during which prices rose about four times; but, he adds, ". . . it is probable gold and silver have multiplied much more: But interest has not fallen much above half."[6]

Hume credits three circumstances with high interest rates: (1) great demand for borrowing, (2) a small supply of loanable funds, and (3) great profits arising from commerce. By segregating the third component from the first, where it obviously belongs, he obscures his awareness of the interdependence of profits and interest, yet appears to suggest the fact that the demand for loanable funds is a derived demand and that the profits earned by business are to a substantial extent conditioned by the use of capital.

---

[5]See Biographical Note D.

[6]Arthur Eli Monroe, *Early Economic Thought* (Cambridge: Harvard University Press, 1924), p. 312.

Cantillon[7]

Cantillon, the first systematic thinker comparable in his perspective to the exponents of classical economics, was also the first to note that the quantity and quality of *natural resources*, along with the quantity and quality of human labor, are components of the *intrinsic price* (value) of finished goods. This novel emphasis on natural resources became in the approach of the Physiocrats a one-sided weapon in the pursuit of class interests, and thus in the short run probably did more harm than good. He also noted that *market price* may well deviate from intrinsic price. Failing to define the latter, he went as far as saying: "There is never any variation in the intrinsic value of things. . . ."[8] At any rate, Cantillon's outstanding contribution is to have pointed out the *interaction of value and market price* as the regulatory mechanism in an otherwise unregulated system. It constitutes the embryo of a theory which was to occupy the center of the classical system of economics. In one respect Cantillon did even better than some of the theorists who succeeded him: he realized that for the producers to adjust their productive resources in response to a change in price takes a certain length of time.

Further pursuing Petty's idea that there are various types and *rates of interest* in a nation and that these rates vary with the degree of risk incurred by the lender, he pointed out that the wealthiest and most solvent entrepreneurs pay a rate equal to that on a real estate mortgage loan, where — presumably — safety is 100 percent. He thus brought into focus the criterion of *credit standing* as an important element conditioning the rate actually paid. He also enriched economic analysis by demonstrating that high prices do not necessarily mean high interest rates, and vice versa. He shows convincingly that the market rate of interest follows its own laws, that is, a statistical correlation between interest rates and commodity prices should not tempt one to think that there is a causal interconnection between the two variables.

Finally, he developed the *capitalization-of-rent* concept in noting that the ruling rate of interest in a state seems to serve as a basis and guide for the prices at which land is bought and sold.

---

[7]See Biographical Note E.

[8]Philip C. Newman, Arthur D. Gayer, and Milton H. Spencer (eds.), *Source Readings in Economic Thought* (New York: W. W. Norton & Company, Inc., 1954), p. 71. This piece of speculative reasoning was ideally suited for the purposes of Marx's labor theory of value. An unproven tenet, it eventually undermined his own complicated system of thought, as it conflicted with the evidence of common-sense facts and observations (see Chapter 16).

PHYSIOCRATS

Quesnay[9]

With the arrival on the scene of the Physiocrats, many an isolated observation of earlier writers was incorporated in the system which this first school in economics worked out under Quesnay's leadership. But systems of thought frequently achieve internal consistency only at the expense of a flexibility dictated by observational reality. For example, whereas Petty had allowed for a wide margin between the maximum and minimum rates of interest possible, though without convincingly demonstrating the validity of the upper limit, Quesnay arbitrarily postulated that in the "natural order" the *interest rate* can never be higher than the rate of return derived from the use of land by the investment of money capital (of an equivalent amount). Cases to the contrary Quesnay branded as injustices to the natural order and drew a practical but quite "un-physiocratic" conclusion. He stated, in effect, that if this upper limit is not observed by the parties to a contract involving the advancement of loanable funds, the sovereign should pass laws to prevent such violation of the natural state of things.

Turgot[10]

In this respect Turgot, the most enlightened and least subservient writer of the group, also known as "Economists," proved to have greater insight. Advocating the free formation of interest rates, he reasoned that, since these rates only reflect the prevailing *land rent,* a person with loanable funds could not for long derive a higher return by offering them for purposes of investment in capital goods; for by that very action he would make them relatively scarcer in the market of buyers and sellers of land. With a falling price for land — its productiveness being taken as a datum — rent would rise. This process would continue until rent and interest are once again equalized. Turgot thus came close to a formulation suggestive of the classical theory of economic equilibrium.

Yet Turgot did not see that the rent of land and the interest rate on loanable funds are simultaneously and mutually determined. One still encounters between the lines the physiocratic bias to the effect that the rate of interest is essentially derived from land rent. Nevertheless, Turgot showed that the price of a piece of land, like the price of any other commodity, is determined by the forces of supply and demand.

---

[9]See Biographical Note F.
[10]See Biographical Note G.

Furthermore, if in fact the rate of return which a capitalist will demand in making loans to productive enterprises outside agriculture is higher than the rent on land, this does not invalidate the observations relative to the above-mentioned equalization process. An investment in land being virtually riskless, while investments in other forms call for administrative routines and skills as well as worries and risk-taking on the part of the lender, the two types of return will rarely justify equality of remuneration per unit of investment. While Turgot is open to criticism for having neglected the risk factors associated with real estate purchases, he must be credited with unusual sagacity in his analysis of the principal considerations entering the minds of alert persons weighing various investment opportunities.

Perhaps most important from the point of view of detached economic reasoning is not the fact that Turgot called to the attention of his readers many objective reasons which justify the lender's demand for the payment of interest but that he assessed a subjective element: the owner of funds, by virtue of his very ownership right in them, can dispose of his funds in any way he wants and can "set" the price accordingly. For lending at interest, in his view, is simply a transaction in which the lender is a person who sells the use of his money, whereas the borrower is a person who buys this selfsame use. It is thus a transaction analogous to the sale and purchase of the use of a piece of land by landlord and tenant.

Finally, Turgot performed some pioneering work in the field of analyzing the *exchange process*. Recognizing that individual valuations of goods differ greatly, he found that if each exchange act is considered by itself, there will be as many subjective exchange ratios as there are individual valuations; but as soon as several buyers and several sellers confront each other in a market, a uniform exchange ratio will be constituted. It will lie somewhere between the greatest quantity and the smallest quantity of a good that the various potential buyers and sellers are willing to exchange for a given quantity of another good. In addition, trading will bestow on each commodity a market value relative to all other commodities.

GALIANI[11] AND CONDILLAC[12]

We return now from the pricing of factor services, of which the Physiocrats showed considerable awareness, to that of produced goods.

---

[11]See Biographical Note H.
[12]See Biographical Note I.

There are two more writers whose contributions to nascent economics in the third quarter of the eighteenth century mark milestones on that devious path which the development of our science was to take before its core, value theory, was a well-rounded whole. Galiani and Condillac furnished indispensable elements for the structure, but, like Cantillon's brilliant treatise, their work remained stillborn for about one hundred years. Also, as with Cantillon's, their writings were not addressed to a large readership; and, the true gems of the early insights of powerful minds hide behind unpretentious presentation.

Galiani, "boy wonder" of a kind, in his *On Money* (1750), developed a series of propositions anticipating, in particular, the *Austrian school*, to which we will turn in Chapter 4. He recognized, among other relationships, the interdependence between the price of a good and the quantity of it consumed; the different consumer and producer reactions, in the case of different goods, to changes in the quantities supplied and demanded of them (what Marshall came to call "elasticity"); the effects of unequal distribution of wealth and income on the quantities of goods consumed (a price fall makes available to the poorer classes goods they formerly could not afford); the principle of diminishing utility coupled with the fact that the utility of additional doses of a good may become zero or even negative; the fact that the rate of interest serves to accomplish equality in exchange of present for future goods; and a number of "minor" principles. Indeed, an impressively rich array of penetrating observations to be considered by a beginning student of the principles of our science!

Condillac, in his *Commerce and Government* (1776), basically hews in the same vein, but instead of mainly illustrating principles he explicitly states them in a form that is both clear-cut and easily remembered. Examples: The value of things grows relative to their scarcity and diminishes relative to their abundance. Value may become zero when a thing becomes superabundant. A future want does not give a thing the same value as a present want. A thing does not have value because it costs something, but it costs something because it has value. (Notice that only the first half of this statement is correct if the term value is conceived broadly.) In exchange, things do not have an absolute price; they have a price only in terms of the estimate of their worth that we form at the moment when we make an exchange. If the degree of scarcity or abundance could always be precisely foreknown, one would be in a position to determine the true value of everything. Value and price must not be confounded: price presupposes value, but value does not presuppose price.

There are several reasons why things do not have an absolute price, some of which had already been stated by Turgot. Condillac provides the important addendum that competition among buyers and sellers may be absent, may be slight, or may be great. He is clearly cognizant of the price-lowering effect of competition.

Finally, Condillac points out that in trade one always gives something of less (subjective) value for something of more value; hence it is wrong to say that in exchange one simply gives value in return for equal value. More significant than the Frenchman's clarification of concepts is his proof that traders enhance the mass of wealth in the sense of the sum total of subjective utilities.

ADAM SMITH[13]

We have seen that prior to the publication of Smith's standard work, the *Wealth of Nations* (1776), writers on economic matters had relatively simple views as to what determines the price of commodities. The most enlightened were aware of its dependence on their scarcity or abundance relative to their utility, or — as was stated without deeper probing — on the proportion which the supply of commodities bears to their demand. No real effort was made to trace the effects of reproducibility and competition. Smith showed that, and elaborated why, these are very important considerations when allowance is made for time lapsed in the process of production. Specifically, and most importantly, he revealed that the average *market price* of reproducible commodities over an extended period of time, when competition is allowed to operate without restraint, corresponds to their average *necessary price*, that is, to their average cost of production. This was a breakthrough, and its attainment is by no means less remarkable because Smith's analysis of the elements which enter into the necessary price of commodities was less than perfect.

Smith was anxious to find a commodity which, being itself produced in large quantities and in only slightly changing proportions, would serve better than any other commodity as a *standard of value* though it might be inferior to others as a medium of exchange. He correctly suggests that corn (the English word for grain) qualifies for this purpose inasmuch as it is the principal staple of food; and the number of consumers will, at least on a level of development where the human diet is little diversified, rise or fall proportionally to variations in its quantity. The merit of this insight is scarcely abridged by the

---

[13]See Biographical Note J.

fact that corn did not by any means constitute the entire subsistence of the laborer and his family and that its abundance or scarcity cannot, therefore, exclusively determine population growth or decline.

Finally, Smith's authority greatly helped to standardize the *terminology* in value theory. What he called *value in use* (use value) is still meant to denote the utility of some particular object; his *value in exchange* (exchange value) still generally means the power of a particular object to purchase other goods in exchange. With a couple of striking examples — water, diamonds — he demonstrates how the two can greatly differ one from the other.

The Core of Smith's Value Theory

His distinction between the *natural rates* of the components of the real price of commodities and the *market rates* of these components, which in turn are reflected in the natural and market prices of commodities, has given pause to many generations of economists because these relationships have been recognized as focal and crucial. If a commodity sells at a price which just barely covers the natural rates of wages, profit, and rent, that is, the rates resulting from the employment of the factors of production under ordinary or average circumstances of the society at a given time and place, then it sells at its natural price. ". . . When the price of any commodity is neither more nor less than what is sufficient to pay the rent of the land, the wages of the labor and the profits of the stock employed in raising, preparing, and bringing it to market according to their natural rates, the commodity is then sold for its natural price."[14] The actual (market) price at which a commodity is sold may, however, be above or below its natural price. It is above the natural price if the quantity brought to market falls short of the effectual demand (at the natural price), and, as a consequence, some or all of the component parts of the price must rise above their natural rates, with the further consequence that in time the supply of the factors of production will increase. It is below the natural price if the quantity brought to market exceeds the effectual demand (at the natural price), and in turn some or all of the factors will be underpaid, which induces their owners to reduce their supply and consequently causes the supply price to rise. As a result of the upward and downward adjustments in factor supplies, the prices of all commodities continually gravitate toward their natural prices, or what Smith calls the central price of each.

[14] Adam Smith, *An Inquiry into the Nature and Causes of the Wealth of Nations*, ed. Edwin Cannan (New York: The Modern Library, Random House, Inc., 1937), p. 57.

Smith's distinction between the *real* and *nominal prices* of commodities is equally fundamental, although, with further advances in economics, they in time no longer corresponded with the exact meanings given them by Smith. In his analysis, the former was the price of commodities expressed in terms of labor, the latter their price expressed in monetary terms. Today the first mode of expression is obsolete because the labor theory of value has been long discarded as too narrow; but the second continues to be recognized as useful.

According to the labor theory of value, goods exchange for equal quantities of labor as the only true standard of value, that is, as the only standard by which we can compare the values of different commodities at all times and places. Why has Smith's dichotomy between the money price and the real price of commodities, as based on the labor theory of value, failed to arouse more than passing interest among the bulk of economists grappling with the problem of finding an ultimate standard of value? Largely because in practice, as Smith himself seems to suggest, it is only possible to measure the value of things in terms of some other commodity used as a standard. Corn or a metal such as silver readily suggest themselves, but both have their advantages and disadvantages. In the long run ("from century to century," according to Smith), corn is a superior measure because the quantities of labor required to produce a certain quantity of it will be more nearly the same than the quantities of labor required to command a certain quantity of silver. But in the short run ("from year to year"), silver is a better measure because the same quantities of it are more nearly equal to a given quantity of labor. Though this analysis is defective, because neither is labor itself exactly measurable nor is it used without the assistance of other productive factors, it points up a perennial economic problem: whatever we use in practice as a gauge of value is less than perfect.

Lastly, if it were not for the elements of time and place, the difference between the real and the nominal price of commodities would be academic; for at a given time and place a given quantity of a commodity as expressed by its price, whether in terms of a metallic or some other standard, enables us to obtain a quantity of some other commodity, again as expressed by its price, however measured. But through time the prices of these commodities vary in different proportions; whatever is used as money to serve as a standard of value is no longer an exact measure of the real exchangeable value of all commodities. Hence the real price of things, that nebulous something for which economists have hunted in vain, differs from their money price over time.

In discussing the component parts of the price of commodities, Smith lists several important factors accounting for variations in the *value of labor services*, hence in wage rates: the relative agreeableness of a job; the relative difficulty and expense of acquiring certain skills; the relative constancy of employment; the degree of trust reposed in the holder of a job; and, the probability of success in employment. He seems to have been dimly aware even of what in recent decades has come to be referred to as quasi-rent, noting that the superior value of the produce of excellent talents may be more than the compensation that can reasonably be expected for the time and effort spent in acquiring them.

From Price Theory to Distribution Theory

Much more weighty from the point of view of the need for fitting together a skeleton of basic economic theory was Smith's clear statement of this cardinal principle of value and distribution: that in any advanced society the price of every commodity immediately or ultimately resolves itself into its component parts, which he recognized as wages, rent, and profit. There is still a lack of perception with respect to the shares of "profit" represented by interest on the one hand and compensation for the risk of loss on the other.[15] While there are a few rare cases in which rent is not a component part of the value of a finished good (for example, fishing in the seas), and still less frequent ones in which "profits" are also absent (for example, gathering of nature-made consumer goods without the aid of capital and on land not privately owned), in general all three of Smith's factorial shares play a part in the production of commodities.

Smith observes that what is true of every particular commodity taken alone must also hold for the total of all the commodities composing in their entirety the annual produce of every country. "The whole of what is annually either collected or produced by the labour of every society . . . is in this manner originally distributed among some of its different members. Wages, profit, and rent, are the three original sources of all revenue as well as of all exchangeable value. All other revenue is ultimately derived from some one or other of these."[16]

He also brings out the fact that the three sources of income are apt to be confounded when they belong to the same person. A landlord may well farm part of his own estate, combining with it his own labor

---

[15]Smith reserves the term "interest" for revenue derived from "stock" by the person who, rather than employing it himself, lends it to another.

[16]Smith, *op. cit.*, p. 52.

and capital; yet he may well call his entire income profit and neglect the fact that only a portion represents profit and that the rest comprises rent and wages (compensations later to become tagged "implicit").

Smith anticipates Ricardo and others in his discussion of the relationship of the factorial shares in the long run. Whereas rent and wages rise with the prosperity and fall with the decline of a society, "profits" tend to move in opposite directions; they tend to be high in relatively poor and low in relatively wealthy countries. It might be added that Smith did not yet recognize the underlying causal connections of relative scarcity and abundance of factor supplies.

Lending — Principle and Qualification

One more topic to be mentioned that reveals Smith's limitations as a child of his time, despite his generally progressive outlook, concerns lending at interest. He clearly draws the distinction between loans made for productive purposes and those extended to increase consumption purchases, but the value judgments he attaches to it are unfortunate because they reflect a narrow view of the possible economic effects of the two types of transactions. For Smith, loan funds used "as a capital" are advantageous because they result in the employment of productive laborers and an increase in total wealth. Used for immediate consumption, they dissipate "in the maintenance of the idle, what was destined for the support of the industrious."[17] In the latter case, repayment of principal and payment of interest involve alienation of, or encroachment upon, some other source of revenue, and hence are economically disadvantageous, according to Smith. It is readily seen that at least two crucial observations escaped the author of the *Wealth of Nations*, to the detriment of his analysis: (1) the employment effect of consumption expenditures, regardless of whether funds are spent for goods or for personal services; and, (2) the fact that the necessity to pay off debt obligations may spur on the borrower to enhance his productive efforts in order to procure the additional income necessary to maintain his consumption level.

However, in discussing various other aspects of a loan transaction, Smith rightly stresses that what is fundamentally transferred is not the money but the command over goods and services, the things money can purchase. Looked at from this perspective, the loan is the assignment by the lender to the borrower of the right to a portion of the annual output of goods and services.

[17]*Ibid.*, p. 333.

Particularly lucid is Smith's elaboration of the causes of why the interest rate that must be paid for the use of loanable funds diminishes with an increase in their supply. There are hints of the Law of Variable Proportions and references to the competition between capitalists for profitable outlets for their funds, to the competition of employers for additional workers to produce and operate the capital goods newly created, and to the effects of the process on wages and profits.

Lastly, Smith rounds out the earlier contributions to the discussion of why the *prohibition of interest-taking* by governmental regulation is not only useless but harmful. Instead of preventing it, such a policy stimulates "usury," he points out. It does so by forcing the debtor to pay not only for the lender's sacrifice in foregoing present consumption but also for the risk of detection and penalty which the latter incurs by accepting a compensation for his services. Ghosts of the notorious medieval church ban were now finally laid to rest.

Observations on Rent

Generally, Smith's views with respect to the rent on land are not much more, and in a few instances are even less, advanced than those of his predecessors. For example, he laid down as a universal principle that all land which yields food must simultaneously also yield rent; yet it is known that in the early stages of a country's economic development, when the best lands are still for the taking and when a given quantity of labor may yield the greatest possible quantity of food, no rent is paid. Closer scrutiny would also have led him to the conclusion that, notwithstanding some elements which make the owner of land a monopolist of sorts, the price of its produce is not influenced by the payment of rent but may make its payment possible and necessary.

On the other hand, he exposes the erroneousness of the view that rent is merely a return, in the form of interest or profit, on capital investments made by the landlord for the purpose of improving the land. He admits that such elements occasionally may be a part of what is commonly called rent, but adds that rent is also demanded from, and can be paid by, the tenant using unimproved land — let alone the fact that the tenant himself sometimes invests capital on land cultivated by him.

Smith correctly states that rent is proportioned "to what the farmer can give" and that this payment in turn depends on the relation between the price at which farm products can be sold in the market and their cost of production. Only if the former exceeds the latter so that there results a "surplus" can rent be paid, and this will in turn depend on the demand for the products. Most significant perhaps is his statement concerning the different way in which rent — as contrasted with wages and profit — enters into the composition of the price of different commodities: "High or low wages and profit, are the causes of high or low price; high or low rent is the effect of it."[18]

Moreover, Smith stresses the two basic rent-determining factors: fertility and location ("situation"). He points out that, assuming the same degree of fertility (and, hence, cost of cultivation), land in the neighborhood of a town enjoys a cost advantage since its distance from the market, which bears on the transportation costs for its produce, is relatively smaller.

Finally, he recognizes that the rent on improved land, such as land used for the raising of corn, "regulates" the rent on unimproved land, such as pasture land for beef raising; but the causal connections are not as rigid as he construed them to be.

SUMMARY

Aristotle was probably the first to distinguish between *value in use* and *value in exchange*. He recognized that the latter is derived from the former and that value is not inherent in a commodity but is dependent on utility and cost of production.

The medieval writers, foremost St. Thomas Aquinas, set forth the concept of the *just price*, a price based on estimates as to the social utility of goods exchanged, as well as its corollaries, the *just wage* and the *prohibition of usury*. The course of economic development gradually undermined the force of this taboo, and the many concessions made furnished in turn the elements of a more realistic approach to the analysis of the interest phenomenon.

While the writers during the period of mercantilism granted the legitimacy of lending at interest, they showed little awareness of the relation between the payment of interest and the productivity of capital. Petty viewed the *risk factor* as the principal element explaining variations in interest rates.

Cantillon may be regarded as a precursor of classical theory in his explanation of the interaction of value (cost of production) and market price of a good as a regulatory mechanism in a free-market system. Turgot was aware of the tendency in such a system for the rate of return from the investment of loanable funds to be equal — assuming equality

---

[18]*Ibid.*, p. 146.

of risk — in the various uses to which such funds can be put, and he looked upon the rent on land as the basic regulator. While he moved a step ahead of his contemporary Quesnay, who saw a need for governmental action in case interest rates should exceed their *natural* level, Turgot, still under the spell of the Physiocratic school, overemphasized the role of land as a determinant of the rate of return from capital investments. He also did some pioneering work in analyzing valuation aspects of the exchange process.

Both Condillac and Galiani in their economic thinking were well in advance of their times. Their brilliant work anticipated many insights on which the Austrian school was to capitalize about a century later, but their immediate impact on the development of economic thought was small.

Adam Smith advanced value theory by pointing out the effects on the price of goods of reproducibility and competition and, given these assumptions, the equality of average cost of production and average market price in the long run. His authority was instrumental in standardizing the terminology in value theory. He recognized that there is no one commodity or service that serves perfectly as a standard by which to express the value of other goods and services at all times and places. He also stated this fundamental principle of value and distribution theory: in any advanced society, the price of commodities resolves itself into wages, rent, and "profit," which are its component parts.

While he did not perceive of the scarcity of the factor land as a necessary prerequisite for the payment of rent, he did demonstrate the analytical need for conceiving of this factorial payment as distinct from interest and profit. He accounted for variations in the value of labor services by enumerating most of the elements that play a role in producing such variations. In discussing lending transactions, Smith recognized the importance of the interpersonal transfer of power to purchase a portion of the goods and services produced by the economy; failed to grasp the potentially wealth-creating effects of borrowing for consumption purposes; and called attention to the futility of legal prohibitions to charging interest on loans.

BIOGRAPHICAL NOTES

A.—*Aristotle.* Of the trio of Greek thinkers — Xenophon, Plato (the spokesman for Socrates), and Aristotle — who in their writings during the fourth century B.C. were more concerned with economic questions than were other ancient literary greats, Aristotle displayed the keenest and most far-reaching mind. While they all deserve mention in a history of economic thought, Aristotle's scientific method, characterized by a deep respect for fact and a striving for utmost accuracy, has proved the most fruitful in the building of a body of scientific knowledge. Living from 384 to 322 B.C., he was the last of the famous trio (Xenophon: 444 to 354 B.C.; Plato: 427 to 347 B.C.). Aristotle in his formative years became much indebted to Plato, to whom he remained attached in friendship despite some sharp ideological differences — manifested mainly in their opposing views concerning the feasibility of a community of property and a community of wives. Aristotle's views on matters economic remained more influential through the centuries, reaching the prime of their acceptance in the Middle Ages, specifically as building blocks for St. Thomas Aquinas' imposing system of thought.

Although he molded the dogmas of the medieval Catholic church, it would be preposterous to visualize Aristotle primarily as an early economist. There was in his time no special branch of the social sciences dignified by the name "economics," yet the Greek word *oikonomia* (management of the household) represents the core term of the vocabulary of what more than two thousand years later became "political economy"; it was Alfred Marshall who — some one hundred years later still — made the term "economics" stick.

Three points merit emphasis in this brief survey. First, taking all knowledge as his province, Aristotle was primarily a grand organizer of scientific thought, a philosopher, political scientist, historian, and "economist" in one. Second, to Aristotle as to the other Socratic thinkers, economic problems were moral problems in the sense that they distinguished between proper and improper economic modes of action, viewed in terms of the desirability to erect the most perfect polity, the ideal state. This normative strain has deeply colored almost all subsequent economic thought up to the intellectual liberation borne out of the Enlightenment. Third, although economic development was still very limited in ancient Greece, some basic economic processes that are essentially timeless, such as the division of labor and the valuation of goods and services, lent themselves to analysis, and it is here that the Socratic thinkers could make a genuine contribution of a scientific nature. Aristotle was anything but an armchair philosopher. As tutor of Alexander the Great, he traveled far and wide; and, upon his return to Athens, where he had been a student of Plato in his early years, he founded his own school of philosophy, the Lyceum.

Of primary interest to the historian of economic theory is the first book of Aristotle's *Politics* as well as the *Nicomachean Ethics*. Although neither of these works is devoted to purely economic questions, Aristotle posed in them a multitude of economic problems that served as a point of departure for an untold number of thinkers of later ages.

B.—*St. Thomas Aquinas* (1225–1274) represented the most highly developed form of a basic point of view that characterized the entire period of the Middle Ages. This was the view of a human society being held together and made meaningful by a system of mutual obligations and services, in which each member occupied a place appropriate for him in the light of his natural endowments and the circumstances of his environment. In the "give and take" of mutual support — a characteristic of the feudal society — he would find his raison d'être in this earthly world, which was only a stepping stone to the other (invisible) world, life after death. It was the office of the Catholic church to guide through its teachings all human relationships in order to strengthen the realization of the members of society that they were merely preparing for eternal salvation in the hereafter.

In their turn, the exponents of Catholic medieval thought, the Schoolmen or scholastic philosophers, drew from two main sources: the teachings of Aristotle and those of Christianity. The latter were based on two distinct, but related, contributions: the Bible and the writings of the church fathers. The two principal sources presumably yielded identical, or at least not contradictory, answers to the questions of the time; and it is valid to say that St. Thomas (also known as the Angelic Doctor) attempted a synthesis, or fusion, of Christian doctrine and the Aristotelian legacy.

In essence, medieval economic thinking had in common with that of the Socratic period the view that economic activity was regarded as simply one phase of all human activity and thus subject to a general moral code. It differed from its Greek predecessor in postulating that the present world is but a preparation for the hereafter. Nevertheless, in both cases economic considerations were bound to be less significant than in a world in which the art of moneymaking, more generally that of increasing material wealth, is sanctioned as legitimate in its own right.

Although he was aided by many others in building up and refining the union of Christian theology and Aristotelian logic, St. Thomas' writings, which cover almost every facet of human relations, are more representative of the best efforts of scholasticism than are any other works of the time.

Born near Naples, Italy, St. Thomas entered the Dominican Order at the age of seventeen. His early promise induced encouragement by his superiors, who sent him to the then greatest Schoolman, Albertus Magnus. Under this teacher, he studied first in Cologne, and then in Paris, where he obtained his doctorate in 1257; and subsequently, he enhanced his reputation as a first-rate teacher at various European seats of learning. Extraordinary industry, terminated by his premature death in 1274, is attested to by some sixty works from his pen, of which the *Summa Theologica* is by far the outstanding and most frequently consulted one. Its Part II, dealing with the nature and consequences of human action, especially the "Questions" addressed to what constitutes fraud in buying and selling, what is usury, and why is it sinful, is most relevant for the economist concerned with canonistic doctrine in general — the rules worked out by the logical jurists with a view to regulating evils they felt could not be entirely prevented.

C.—*Sir William Petty* (1623–1687) was one of the most remarkable figures in the history of economic thought and certainly the outstanding one among the group of men that have been variously classified as forerunners of economic liberalism, founders of political economy, and exponents of the reaction against mercantilism (for mercantilist views, see

Chapter 12). The more eminent included such people as Barbon, North, Hume, Child, Cantillon, and Boisguillebert, and most of these we will meet again.

Among them Petty, who had the most variegated career — physician, shipbuilding experimenter, surveyor of lands in Ireland, professor of music as well as of anatomy, cofounder of the British Royal Society, and landowner — has been considered both the founder of statistics and the founder of the labor theory of value. (Certain authors, such as Roll, call him "the founder of political economy," no less; this is also the impression he made on Marx. See Eric Roll, *A History of Economic Thought*, 3d ed. [Englewood Cliffs: Prentice-Hall, Inc., 1956], p. 100.)

Petty acquired his most lasting claim to fame as an early advocate of empiricism in the field of numbers, weights, and measures (statistics), which he proposed to substitute for "comparative and superlative Words, and intellectual Arguments." (C. H. Hull [ed.], *The Economic Writings of Sir William Petty* [2 vols.; London: Cambridge University Press, 1899], I, 244.) The modern offshoot of economic science known as econometrics is indebted to Petty as one of its pioneers. He was much in advance of his time, not only in the methodology of economic study but also as an economic theorist. While his writings do not present an integrated view of economic society, such as was to be offered in the next century by Cantillon, Quesnay, and Smith, he tackled a diverse number of unexplored economic problems for which he proposed (administrative) solutions; but some of them, such as the labor theory of value, led later researchers into blind alleys. However, his keen spirit of inquiry, coupled with his eminently practical bent, more than made up for certain weaknesses, such as the lack of systematic arrangement of subject matter and the one-sidedness of his value theory. He generated his quantitatively impressive output for the most part during the last quarter of his life, although some of his scientific labors were not published until after his death. We will note briefly the following of Petty's works:

A *Treatise of Taxes and Contributions* (1662) may, as the title suggests, be regarded as an early analysis of principles of public finance, dealing with the sources of public revenue, the types of public expenditures, and the best way of getting maximum "mileage" out of funds temporarily diverted from private circulation.

The *Verbum Sapienti* (1664) treats his views on money and capital and shows a high degree of sophistication in his presentation of the nature and sources of wealth — in refreshing contrast to seventeenth century Mercantilists.

The *Political Anatomy of Ireland* (written in 1672, but not published until about twenty years later) was largely a result of his part in a land survey of Ireland, which was to be the basis for redistribution of lands to those of Cromwell's soldiers who had helped to suppress the Irish rebellion.

In his *Discourses of Political Arithmetic* (written in 1678 and published in 1690 or 1691), he defended his unusual (statistical) approach to economic inquiry, showed how data should be collected and compiled, and displayed unprecedented acumen in building bridges between factual research on the one hand, theoretical analysis on the other.

The *Quantulumcumque Concerning Money* (written a few years before his death, but not published until the mid-1690's) reveals how far he had moved away from the crude views of the Bullionists, a group which advocated placing an embargo on bullion exports and legally regulating both interest and exchange rates. In the manner of Oresme (see Chapter 10), he also took sharp issue with those who would resort to debasement of coins as a means of increasing public spending powers.

D.—*David Hume* (1711–1776) was a contemporary and close friend of Adam Smith who always held his twelve-years-older compatriot and fellow Scotsman in very high regard. Whatever he added to the forthcoming emancipation of our science, Hume was not an economist first and foremost, but rather a philosopher, political scientist, and historian. Yet a glance at the titles of his major published works is likely to induce an underestimation of Hume's contribution to economic analysis, for they appeared as *Treatise of Human Nature* (1739), *Political Discourses* (1752), and *History of Great Britain* (1761). As a matter of fact, the *Discourses* deal with political economy as much as they are concerned with political science, and they contain a number of essays ("Of Money," "Of Commerce," "Of Interest," "Of the Balance of Trade," "Of Taxes," "Of Public Credit") that either embody felicitous restatements of earlier, especially British, doctrines or, on occasion, sparkle with flashes of originality.

On this latter point we cannot be absolutely certain, for we do not know whether Cantillon's *Essay* (see Biographical Note E), which was published in 1755 but written at least twenty years before, had or had not come to Hume's knowledge. At any rate, one cannot overlook some pronounced similarities in the argumentation of the two men, and if they arrived at their conclusions independently, both must be credited with valuable new insights, especially in the fields of foreign trade and money.

Furthermore, in view of the broad sweep of Hume's intellectual horizon, coupled with the fact that he was never in business for any great length of time, his performance as an analyst of contemporary economic problems is an impressive one. There are, indeed, good grounds for assuming that he could have equaled Adam Smith's feat had he set himself the task of weaving the various loose strands of economic knowledge together into a strong fabric. As it was, he left the combining and systematizing to his receptive compatriot and admirer Smith, contenting himself with the fame he had acquired in his other scientific capacities and with the rewards he had earned in the 1760's as a member of the British diplomatic service. To the end of his days Hume remained an influential member of Edinburgh's intellectual elite — he had in 1752 been appointed librarian of the Faculty of Advocates in Scotland's capital — in a milieu which proved no less congenial for the author of the *Wealth of Nations*.

E.—*Richard Cantillon* (1680–1734) was one of those luminaries in the history of economic thought who, through a quirk of fate, were deprived of their just fame during their lifetime. The scanty biographical record suggests that Cantillon was a banker of Irish descent who spent several years in France and established business connections in the principal cities of the European continent. He was acquainted with John Law (1671–1729), the Scottish-born financier and France's minister of finance for a few years, who advocated the replacing of specie in circulation with batches of paper money and went to extremes in an attempt to stimulate business activity. Cantillon was fully aware of the flimsiness of Law's money and land-bank schemes and was able to take advantage of his promotion of the Mississippi Bubble by speculating on the "bear" side of the market before the bubble burst, thereby incurring the ill will of the reckless financier, who successfully ordered him to leave France. (For a more complete biographical sketch of Law, see Chapter 10, Biographical Note D.)

Cantillon may also have known some of the Physiocrats. They were familiar with the only work that survived his death (he was assassinated by a discharged manservant who subsequently set fire to Cantillon's house). The *Essay on the Nature of Commerce in General* was originally written in English and then translated by the author into French for the use of friends, notably the Marquis de Mirabeau in whose *L'Ami des Hommes* (1756) many of Cantillon's ideas reappear. But the *Essay* was not published in that language until 1755. Its abstract character and close reasoning did not favor an enthusiastic reception, and while some physiocratic writings explicitly acknowledge a debt to Cantillon, his work was quickly forgotten. Thus matters remained until 1881, when W. Stanley Jevons (see Chapter 3) discovered a copy of it, was struck by the maturity of Cantillon's views, and in glowing tones pointed out to his contemporaries its great merit as the first systematic exposition of economics in the history of the science. (While Petty had already discussed most of the leading ideas presented in the *Essay*, Cantillon was able to tie these and other strands of thought together into a coherent whole.)

There can be no doubt that Cantillon had risen well above the typical mercantilist views of his era. In some respects he was already ahead of the Physiocrats, who at the time of his death had been scarcely heard of as yet. For example, some of their work was retrogressive inasmuch as Cantillon had already made clear that land cannot be regarded as the sole source of wealth, though it is its ultimate source in the sense that human labor could not exist in the absence of a natural resource base.

As substantiated in the text, perhaps the most valuable notion of Cantillon was that of the self-regulating nature of the price mechanism (cost, supply, demand, and price), including the automatic mechanism that distributes the monetary metals internationally.

F.—*François Quesnay* (1694–1774) was the leader of a group of devoted followers, known in their own time mainly as the Economists and later as the Physiocrats (the term "physiocracy" was first used by Dupont de Nemours in a book published in 1768). With Quesnay began the era of schools and systems of economic thought, and thanks to a coincidence of historical circumstances, the first school in economics also became the most tightly knit, the most undeviating, and in at least one respect the most extreme that ever united the believers in a gospel accepted blindly from a master.

Quesnay's writings, found in two articles in the *Encyclopédie* ("Farmers," 1756; "Grain," 1757) and the famous *Economic Table* (*Tableau economique*, written for King Louis XV in 1758), would have made a rather slender volume had Quesnay himself combined his sparse writings under a single cover, perhaps with a view of putting out a best seller. As a matter of fact, the synthesis was accomplished by his disciples, the younger members of the esoteric circle. With the sole exception of Turgot, they all wrote with a foremost endeavor to divine the master and interpret him as uncritically and faithfully as possible.

Perhaps this is due to the exalted position held by Quesnay as the court physician of Madame de Pompadour and later of Louis XV, a position based on thorough medical training, plus the fact that he was in his sixties when he was first heard from as a proponent of economic doctrines. A less mature age would have made him susceptible to a lesser degree of trustworthiness, precluding his instantaneous acceptance with an influential group of well-educated intellectuals. Yet had it not been for his great originality of thinking, it would still be doubtful whether Quesnay could have so completely swayed France's intelligentsia. Add to this that Quesnay consistently emphasized the natural order of things, *l'ordre naturel*, which not only appealed to the prevalent thinking of the enlightenment type but, since it came from a man whose previous career had given him special insight into life and death processes, carried added persuasion. In his previous publications in the field of medicine, he had evinced a great faith in the healing powers of nature, and his knowledge of the circulation of blood in the human body supported his analogies in the realm of the social order.

In any case, this first attempt to analyze the flow of income (goods and money) on a macroeconomic basis was not devoid of a touch of genius. It showed what a consistent application of the scientific methods of isolation and abstraction could lead to, and by revealing the weaknesses of this approach it also suggested alternative paths for advancement. Furthermore, in his single-mindedness of purpose, Quesnay foreshadowed other grandiose ventures into system building — such as Marx's — which, by logically tracing out the consequences of one basic premise, enriched the economic discussion and challenged thinking along more refined and balanced lines. Quesnay's premise — that land was the only source of the economic surplus and that agriculture alone was productive — was rooted in his upbringing; he came from peasant stock and spent the first seventeen years of his life on the family estate near Paris. Of Quesnay's converts, Mirabeau the Elder, who with others attended a series of meetings sponsored by Quesnay and productive of that zealous spirit characterizing the group, was the most ardent propagator of physiocratic doctrine. He was effectively seconded by Du Pont de Nemours, Mercier de la Rivière, and — in a more independent fashion — Gournay, as well as by others of lesser importance.

Turgot stands apart — not in Quesnay's shadow. It is perhaps not accidental that as the only other Physiocrat with more than one truly original idea, and who was not particularly anxious merely to broaden the footsteps of a blindly revered master, Turgot was also highly successful — up to a point — in his professional career (see following note).

G.—*Anne Robert Jacques Turgot* (1727–1781) spent the bulk of his adult life in government service and was virtually the only Physiocrat who during his public career could put some of the new doctrines to a practical test.

Unfortunately, he was not allowed to follow through with his reform ideas, and this accounts at least in part for the decline of the school's reputation in the last quarter of the eighteenth century.

Turgot's life was an outstanding illustration of a case in which exceptional ability is coupled with the necessary courage to hurt vested interest groups in order to promote the greater public good. These vested interests could be contained up to a certain point, but when they were forced to make major adjustments for the sake of a more viable economy, they conspired and coalesced into an effective lobby, threatening to undermine the social order unless left undisturbed. Such were the circumstances faced by Turgot toward the end of his brief (1774–1776) tenure as comptroller general (mainly minister of finance) of France under Louis XVI, who succumbed to a wave of protests hurled against his able and forceful finance minister and dismissed him at a most critical turn in the country's history.

Yet Turgot merely had been putting into practice on a nationwide basis the reforms that had proved a great success when, from 1761–1774, he had experimented with them as the intendant (general administrator) at Limoges, in a poverty-stricken district of France. For example, he had abolished on a regional basis the corvée (forced labor on public works); overhauled the tax collection system; provided for grain-handling facilities; worked for greater freedom in domestic trade; and improved educational and occupational opportunities, especially by abolishing the craft guilds.

He studied theology at the Sorbonne and became prior there at the age of twenty-two but left that position three years later for civil service, which included tours of inspection and a judgeship. This thorough training greatly strengthened his qualifications for the administrative job at Limoges, from which he was launched into the prestigious but fleeting position as comptroller general. No sooner had he been moved to the sidelines than his successful reform measures were revoked and the *ancien régime* was back again on the road toward bankruptcy, moving downhill at an accelerating pace.

Turgot's published works include his *Eulogy of Gournay* (to whom the phrase *laissez faire, laissez passer, le monde va de lui-même* is usually ascribed), *Values and Moneys*, and *Reflections on the Formation and Distribution of Riches*. The last-named work, written in 1766 but not published until 1769–70, contains not only Turgot's exposition of the fundamentals of political economy as conceived by the Physiocrats, but also most of the principles developed by him as an independent thinker.

H.—*Ferdinando Galiani* (1728–1781) was one of a fairly long series of Italians, beginning with Davanzati in the sixteenth century, who occupied themselves with developing principles of a theory of value.

Educated for the church, he attained the rank of monsignor, but like Turgot, he spent most of his life in the service of his government. As secretary to, and later head of, the Neapolitan Embassy in Paris (1759–1769) he had access to the salons of the cultural elite in the metropolis. Gifted with sparkling esprit and biting critical acumen, he soon became an admired conversationalist and was thus able to project himself into the limelight. However, he was not always fair in his attacks and one of his books, *Of Money* (written in Italian, entitled *Della Moneta*, 1750), remained anonymous until some thirty years later. In this brilliant study, he manifested an understanding of certain hitherto neglected economic relationships, an understanding no economist was able to surpass until about a century later. This contribution to the literature of economic thought deserves to be read as much for the ideas concerning the relativity which, in view of the variability of man and society in time and place, attaches to a given policy, as for the devastating arguments designed to sweep away confused thinking in the more technical domains of economics. His command of the historical method, combined with his profound comprehension of European economies in operation, gave his book extraordinary persuasive power. It might well have served as an antidote against the tendency, most pronounced in the first half of the nineteenth century, of claiming universal validity for practical principles that were relevant to a given situation in England, for instance, but irrelevant to France or Holland. When in 1770 the *Dialogues on the Grain Trade*, written in French under the title *Dialogues sur le commerce des blés*, was published, Galiani resided in London, but he later returned to Italy to accept an appointment as a member of the supreme board of trade in Naples. The *Dialogues* are an undisguised attack directed against the theories of the Physiocrats whom the author ridiculed as political doctrinaires enamoured with the building of an abstract system bare of the elements of reality. He thereby provoked a none-too-effective counterattack by the journalistic talent of the sect. After that, the physiocratic movement never fully regained its prestige and on balance declined during the remaining years of the eighteenth century.

I.—*Etienne Bonnot* (*Abbé*) *de Condillac* (1714–1780), a clergyman and philosopher, is another example of a writer whose ideas matured during the physiocratic era but were generally well in advance of most of the physiocratic and many of the classical doctrines.

In contrast to Galiani, with whom he shared a burning interest in clarifying the relationships between utility, scarcity, and value, he had one foot still firmly planted on physiocratic ground. Perhaps as a Frenchman he was constitutionally not quite capable of the foreigner's detachment and perspective when dealing with home-grown ideas that were then still very much in vogue. His *Commerce and Government Considered One in Relation to the Other* appeared in the same year as Smith's

Wealth of Nations. It constituted a restatement of Galiani's utility theory and thus considered value as the central problem and unifying core of political economy. What was still missing, however, in the Galiani–Condillac structure of thought was the notion of the *margin*, which was not developed until well along in the nineteenth century. It may be a matter of speculation to what extent Condillac recognized that his utility approach was clearly incompatible with the physiocratic dichotomy of productive and sterile labor and with what amounted to a denial that value could be created in the process of exchange. The fact is that Condillac, perhaps at the pain of some unresolved scruples, avoided an open break with his illustrious countrymen, in whom even an Adam Smith found much to be admired.

J.—*Adam Smith* (1723–1790) was born the posthumous son of a customs official in Kirkcaldy, Scotland, and spent most of his life in that country, primarily in Kirkcaldy, Glasgow, and Edinburgh. Other places with which he became closely acquainted through extended stays were Oxford, London, Paris, and Toulouse. Raised fatherless, but in comfortable circumstances, by his deeply revered mother, Smith entered Glasgow College at the early age of fourteen. After three years, during which he devoted himself principally to mathematics and philosophy, he accepted a scholarship for study at Balliol College, Oxford. The six Oxford years (1740–46) Smith was inclined to consider as relatively barren, since his host school, suffering from academic anemia, did not sustain the intellectual challenge he had received at Glasgow.

However, Smith was already an independent reader — he favored Greek and Latin classics — and after a period of semi-idleness, he fully recovered from the Oxford anticlimax of his student years when in 1748 he began to give public lectures on English literature at Edinburgh. Three years later he probably had forgotten his earlier disappointment; at the age of only twenty-eight he was appointed professor, first of logic and then of moral philosophy, at Glasgow College. (Since Oxford had not seen fit to bestow the ordinary honor of a doctor's degree upon him, Glasgow made amends in 1762 by offering him a doctor of laws degree.) There followed thirteen years of intense work which greatly accelerated the maturing of views Smith had first embraced as a student under Francis Hutcheson, professor of philosophy. Incidentally, the latter also influenced Smith's friend Hume.

Undoubtedly, Smith's grasp of economic problems was greatly strengthened by his association with Glasgow's businessmen — merchants, manufacturers, bankers — with whom he attended a weekly discussion club.

In 1759 the first edition of the *Theory of Moral Sentiments* was published, his only work in book form besides the *Wealth of Nations*. (Both underwent many editions until 1790, the year of their author's death.) The *Theory of Moral Sentiments* fortified and spread Smith's reputation as a philosopher and soon led to his being invited to accompany as tutor, on prolonged travels in Western Europe, a young Scottish aristocrat, the Duke of Buccleuch.

The book's tenor is not, as some superficial observers have been inclined to conclude, at odds with the *Wealth of Nations*. On the contrary, the two works supplement each other closely and merely deal with different parts, II and IV, of Smith's very broadly conceived lectures on moral philosophy. His course was divided into natural theology, ethics, justice (jurisprudence), and expediency (such political regulations as were calculated to increase the wealth and power of the state).

Briefly, the *Theory of Moral Sentiments* deals with the formation in the minds of the individual members of society of shared moral sentiments, which develop into regulators of their conduct. Human beings in association cannot help but sympathize, through imaginative sharing, with each other's feelings and impulses, and out of such experiences their consciences form and become the ultimate standards by which to judge their own actions as well as those of their fellows. Smith used the term "sympathy" in a broad sense, connoting "fellow feeling." It cannot, therefore, be equated with benevolence (though the latter is part of it), and it is not inconsistent with self-interest as a principal motivating force for individual attitudes and actions. Fellow feeling results from the reflection in the spectator's psyche of other persons' apparent feelings and is possible only through a successful, that is, imaginative, identification of the self with those of other persons. On the degree of concord of feelings depends, in turn, the spectator's measure of approval (or disapproval) of the actor's conduct.

Unfortunately, Smith's intention, as indicated in his first book, of also writing on "the principles of natural justice" never materialized, and all we have to go by, in an attempt to guess what the author already had in mind, is a copy of a student's notes of Smith's course of lectures on "Justice, Police, Revenue, and Arms," the last three parts of which became, with amendments and supplements, his *Wealth of Nations*.

This work was started at about the time (1764) he had settled down in France with the young duke, ward of the then Chancellor of the Exchequer. Their leisurely stays at Toulouse and Paris afforded Smith relief from classroom and administrative drudgery while at the same time providing him with new stimuli, including acquaintance with some of the leading Physiocrats, such as Turgot and Quesnay. The stipend he received in addition to travel expense payments freed him from the necessity to seek employment or to depend on the royalties from a new book. The unwonted atmosphere of financial security, coupled with a meditative pace of work, was most conducive to the proper ripening of a fruit which he did not feel ready to harvest until 1776, even though upon return to Scotland toward the end of 1766 he did not resume teaching. According to the terms of the previous offer, the £300 a year stipend was converted to a pension for life in the same amount when Smith had completed his tutorial tasks. Most of the time between 1770 and 1776 was taken up by rewriting and revising the first draft of the *Wealth of Nations;* for negotiations with the publisher and for the finishing touches on his magnum opus, Smith stayed in London after 1773.

The last twelve years of his life saw him back in public service, in the unlikely (for an advocate of free trade) but lucrative position of Commissioner of Customs of Scotland in Edinburgh. This employment, while further cushioning his existence with material comforts, left him sufficient leeway to keep the *Wealth of Nations* up to date.

He also had the rare satisfaction that accompanies the translation of an author's work into several foreign languages, although Smith did not live long enough to see one of its principal offshoots, J. B. Say's *Treatise on Political Economy*, take firm root on French soil. Three years before his death, Glasgow College honored its most famous alumnus and teacher by appointing him Lord Rector. In spite of the fact that ample and extraordinary distinction had been bestowed upon him, Smith seems to have retained a humble attitude, as witnessed by the fact that a week before his death he ordered all unfinished manuscripts — approximately sixteen volumes — destroyed!

Questions for Review and Research

1. What distinctions flow from Aristotle's dichotomy between the proper and improper uses of a commodity?

2. According to the medieval (scholastic) writers, how was the "just price" to be ascertained at any given time and place? Which element of cost did they consider as most important?

3. What difference, if any, is there between St. Thomas Aquinas' concept of usury and what we refer to as net and gross interest?

4. Did the Mercantilists have a wage theory? Explain.

5. What areas of value and distribution theory did Petty emphasize in his *Treatise of Taxes and Contributions*? What did he consider as the common denominator of all value?

6. Who was the main anticipator of classical doctrines of value and distribution theory? When and where did he live, and in which book did he set forth his main ideas?

7. In Quesnay's "natural order," what puts a ceiling on the interest rate? Did Turgot agree with him on this score? Explain. In what respect(s) did Turgot's analysis leave something to be desired?

8. Were Galiani and Condillac Physiocrats? Were they precursors of Adam Smith in the sense that Cantillon was a precursor?

9. Explain Smith's pathbreaking distinction between the market price and the necessary price of reproducible commodities.

10. Why, according to Smith, was corn a superior commodity in serving as a standard of value?

11. What did Smith recognize as the component parts of the price of every commodity? From the modern point of view, which component was "missing"?

12. How did Smith's views on lending at interest differ from those of (a) the Scholastics? (b) twentieth-century economists?

Recommended Readings

Heimann, Eduard. *History of Economic Doctrines, an Introduction to Economic Theory.* New York: Oxford University Press, 1945. Chapter I, "Problem and Method," pp. 3–21.

Letwin, William. *The Origins of Scientific Economics.* London: Methuen and Co., Ltd., 1963. Garden City, N.Y.: Doubleday & Company, Inc., 1964. Chapter 5, "Sir William Petty: Political Arithmetic," pp. 123–157.

Monroe, Arthur Eli (ed.). *Early Economic Thought.* Cambridge: Harvard University Press, 1924. Chapter I, "Aristotle," pp. 1–29; Chapter III, "St. Thomas Aquinas," pp. 51–77; Chapter IX, "Sir William Petty," pp. 199–220; Chapter XI, "Richard Cantillon," pp. 245–277; Chapter XII, "Ferdinando Galiani," pp. 279–307; Chapter XIII, "David Hume," pp. 309–338; Chapter XIV, "François Quesnay," pp. 339–348; Chapter XV, "Anne Robert Jacques Turgot," pp. 349–375.

Smith, Adam. *An Inquiry into the Nature and Causes of the Wealth of Nations,* edited with an introduction, notes, marginal summary, and an enlarged index by Edwin Cannan and an introduction by Max Lerner. The Modern Library. New York: Random House, Inc., 1937. "Introduction," pp. v–x; "Editor's Introduction," pp. xxiii–lvi.

Book I, "Of the Causes of Improvement in the Productive Powers of Labour, and of the Order According to Which Its Produce Is Naturally Distributed Among the Different Ranks of the People": Chapters I–III, pp. 3–21; Chapters V-IX, pp. 30–98; Chapter X, pp. 99–118; Chapter XI, pp. 144–174.

Book II, "Of the Nature, Accumulation, and Employment of Stock": "Introduction," pp. 259–261; Chapter I, pp. 262–269; Chapters III and IV, pp. 314–340.

2

VALUE AND DISTRIBUTION THEORY

From Say to John Stuart Mill

We have seen that the so-called Classical school found its first representative in the person of the Scotsman Adam Smith. About a quarter century after Smith's pathbreaking work had come off the press, France, which had produced the first school of the fledgling science of economics, reverberated with the echoes of what a few decades later in Germany came to be called "Smithianism." But, in contrast to the German reaction, there was little contempt in the words of Adam Smith's first and principal French spokesman, Jean-Baptiste Say.

JEAN-BAPTISTE SAY[1]

Opinions are divided on whether Say, the first college professor of economics on the European Continent, was in the main merely an interpreter and systematizer of Smith's doctrines, or whether he deserves an independent place in the history of economic theory — as an eclectic who formed a bridge between Turgot on the one hand, Cournot and Walras on the other. There can be no doubt, however, that the tenor of Say's writings was basically Smithian; but since he regarded economics as a positive science, they reflect a greater detachment from any inherent urge to establish practical precepts for the wise statesman. Certainly, little good can come from a dispute over whether Say was merely the most eminent of Smith's continental disciples or whether he was a systematizer in his own right of pre-classical economic views. Say did bring order and method into the statement of economic principles. They were presented to the reading public with fewer digressions, in a more compact form, and with an additional touch of elegance. Lucidity and transparency of style were perhaps Say's principal fortes.

For what will have to be presented under the heading of value theory Say is seldom remembered outside the history of economic

---

[1]See Biographical Note A.

thought. His popular acclaim rested mainly on what has come to be known as Say's Law, which will be discussed in connection with the early contributions to a theory of business fluctuations (see Chapter 14). For many decades to come, Smith's triple division of the subject matter into production, distribution, and consumption of wealth was found to provide a convenient topical organization for textbook writers, including Say. But, Say restored the balance between agriculture, manufactures, and commerce as equally important segments of a national economy, his primary emphasis on manufacturing helping to offset the physiocratic bias as reflected in Smith's treatment of agriculture.

Say's dissent from Smith in his view of *immaterial* products must be regarded as a distinct analytical step. By including the latter in a broader definition of wealth, the Frenchman rounded a turn and bridged a gap between physiocratic and modern economic doctrine, but he overshot the mark by stretching the wealth concept to cover all talents, natural or acquired. Say sensibly stipulated that the classification of something as wealth presupposes that it be measurable because otherwise political economy would not be a positive science. Yet, as far as talents are concerned, he overlooked that in every country a considerable amount of them are not subject to regular exchange or valuation; hence they certainly cannot be quantified as part of a country's total wealth.

Say, furthermore, correctly observed that in the case of immaterial goods, or services, consumption necessarily coincides with production. He was adamant in stating that *all activities that create utilities*, as evidenced by the ability of goods and services to command a price in the market, *are productive*. But he added the warning that there are limits to the productivity of labor incorporated in immaterial products: where such labor does no longer augment the utility, and thereby the value, of a product, it has become unproductive. To illustrate, laws could be rendered increasingly intricate so as to give more and more lawyers an abundance of work in expounding them, but such a practice would be no less absurd than to spread a disease with a view of providing more work for physicians.

In pushing the idea of cost of production as the basis of exchange value into the background, Say followed the tradition of Galiani and Condillac as exponents of a wholly psychological theory of value; he, too, looked to human wants for the origin of value. By assigning this idea a prominent place in his theoretical structure, he not only counteracted the staying power of physiocratic thought, but actually accelerated emancipation from "the school."

He deduced as a logical corollary the fact that *the value of the means of production derives from the value of the end products* to which they contribute. Since the prices of all factors depend on the prices of their products, in the final analysis factor prices depend on consumer demand. Specifically,

> . . . it is obvious that the current value of productive exertion is founded upon the value of an infinity of products compared one with another; that the value of products is not founded upon that of productive agency, as some authors have erroneously affirmed; and that since the desire of an object, and consequently its value, originates in its utility, it is the ability to create the utility wherein originates that desire, that gives value to productive agency, which value is proportionate to the importance of its cooperation in the business of production, and forms, in respect to each product individually, what is called, the cost of its production.[2]

It appears that Say groped for an equilibrium analysis of the economic process but, lacking the necessary mathematical equipment, was unable to give it full expression. Nevertheless, his analysis points toward Walras (Chapter 3), and he is therefore sometimes regarded as one of the founders of the modern equilibrium approach.

The foregoing has implied that Say was less one-sided than Smith in accounting for the factors responsible for the creation of value. Whereas Smith had, in effect, ascribed the power of producing values almost exclusively to the labor of man, Say made it clear that, in addition to the industry of man, value is also derived from the agents known as *nature* and *capital*. This broader perspective enabled Say to avoid attributing a disproportionate influence to the division of labor and to bring into full relief the uses made of the powers of nature and of machinery in the production of wealth.

Not the least of Say's merits was his establishment of some clear-cut *definitions*, which even today are fully as useful for economic analysis as when they were framed. One of them is that of production as the "creation, not of matter, but of utility"; there can be "no actual production of wealth, without a *creation or augmentation* [emphasis added] of utility."[3] This broad definition enabled him to drive home his main point — directed primarily against the Physiocrats, but to a lesser extent also against Smith — namely, that the powers of expanding and multiplying wealth within the reach of communities are much less confined than had previously been imagined. He also introduced the

---

[2]Jean-Baptiste Say, *A Treatise on Political Economy,* translated from the 4th ed. by C. R. Prinsep (Philadelphia: J. B. Lippincott Co., 1854), p. 287.
    [3]*Ibid.,* pp. 62–63.

term "entrepreneur," which became a fixture in the vocabulary of economists. He drew the distinction between the capitalist, the lender of funds, and the entrepreneur, the agent who combines land, labor, and capital in business enterprises, who stands at the center of the productive process, who anticipates the presumed needs of consumers, thereby incurring a risk, and who serves as the connecting link between product and factor markets.

THOMAS ROBERT MALTHUS[4]

The contributions to the body of value theory of this representative of the second generation of English classical economists can be most conveniently discussed under two subheadings.

Definition of Wealth and of Productive Labor

Malthus agreed with Say that wealth should include only those objects the increase or decrease of which is susceptible to being stated in numerical terms. He found the most useful line of demarcation between wealth and nonwealth to be that which separates material from immaterial things. On the surface, he may thus appear to have taken too narrow a view of the fund which constitutes a nation's economic well-being. But closer inspection shows that he made his decision only after careful reasoning led him to the conclusion that once we desert matter in the definition of wealth, there is no logical boundary line which is both distinct and capable of being applied consistently. To illustrate, ". . . if the gratification and information derived from a lecture on chemistry . . . are to be considered as wealth, in consequence of a specific sum being paid for attendance, why should the taste and information acquired by a larger outlay in foreign travels be refused the same title."[5]

Aware that Smith's distinction between productive and unproductive labor — the former being confined to the application of human effort to material objects, that is, to wealth — is artificial, if not offensive, Malthus substitutes the term "personal services" for "unproductive labor." They designate those kinds of labor or industry which, not realizing themselves on objects which can be valued and transferred without the presence of the person instrumental in their creation,

---

[4]See Biographical Note B.

[5]T. R. Malthus, *Principles of Political Economy* (2d ed.; New York: Augustus M. Kelley, Publishers, 1951), p. 32.

cannot be entered into an estimate of national wealth. With this modification, Malthus removed the stigma attached to an unfortunate term, but without sacrificing one of Smith's basic conceptual distinctions. We will see later, however, that he was not a blind advocate of accumulation as justified per se; he shows that saving, pushed to excess, can destroy the motive to production.

Nor does he underrate the crucial importance for future prosperity of *some* personal services, such as education. These are so necessary to the production and distribution of wealth that the skills acquired by their recipients will be ultimately realized in the value of material objects. Hence capital employed in education must be considered as maintaining productive labor and is in line with Malthus' definition of capital as "that portion of the stock or (sic!) material possessions of a country which is kept employed with a view to profit in the production or distribution of wealth."[6] In sum, although the capacity of certain personal services to stimulate the production of wealth cannot be gainsaid, in Malthus' definition of wealth they do not *directly* contribute to its creation.

Measurement and Meaning of Value

We have seen in the last chapter that Smith had come to this conclusion: whatever we use in practice as a gauge of value is less than perfect. Malthus agreed, but pointed out the importance of reducing potential sources of error or confusion by always making clear the exact meaning in which the term is used. He thus came to distinguish three kinds of value: (1) *value in use* — the intrinsic utility of an object, whether it be a free good or an economic good; (2) *nominal value in exchange* — defined as the value of commodities estimated in the precious metals; (3) *intrinsic value in exchange* — the power of purchasing arising from intrinsic causes, that is, the estimation in which a commodity is held as a result of the desire to possess and the difficulty of obtaining possession of it. In still other words, Malthus refers to the estimation in which a commodity is held as determined by the state of supply and demand. Notice the broadening of the concept "intrinsic," which in Cantillon's use was equivalent to Smith's "necessary" price. Malthus acknowledges that the *permanent* prices of the bulk of all commodities bought and sold are determined by their ordinary cost of production, that is, ordinary wages, profits, and rent expended in their production. But he is anxious to give greater emphasis to the

---

[6]*Ibid.*, p. 37.

influence of "the higgling of the market." In this connection he distinguishes between the market prices of raw products and those of manufactures, and points out that the former are almost always different from what they would have been if cost of production had exclusively regulated them. Even in the case of manufactures (where existing market prices coincide more frequently with the cost of production), an alteration in the relationship of demand to supply may for some time quite overshadow the influence of production cost. This cost, furthermore, influences the price of a manufactured product only inasmuch as meeting production cost is a necessary condition for continued supply — a hint at the distinction between reproducible and nonreproducible commodities.

Malthus' emphasis on the *interdependence of supply and demand,* as the price-determining factors not only of finished products but also of the productive agents, marks him as a more detached student of the basic forces of value determination than is true for any of his contemporaries in the English tradition and as another link, à la Say, between the Galiani-Condillac type of reasoning and the further work applied to the utility theory of value in the second half of the nineteenth century. Unfortunately, Malthus' advance in economic reasoning on this front went largely unnoticed — perhaps because he had made a name for himself in other scientific pursuits, but probably also because he was primarily thought of as a member of the Classical school from which few creative insights that would modify a labor or a cost-of-production theory of value were expected.

In the same vein, it is interesting to note Malthus' critical attitude toward Smith on account of the latter's representation of the *profits* of capital as a deduction from the produce of labor. He inflicted another, but not very effective, blow on the prevailing labor theory of value by pointing out that these profits — a term still denoting a mixture of interest and profits in the modern sense — are estimated in exactly the same way as the contribution of the worker who receives wages, namely by what is necessary in the existing state of society to encourage the application of the factor capital to a particular type of production. He shows that in neither a primitive nor a more advanced stage of society has price been determined or measured by the relative quantities of labor employed in the production of goods. This insight was largely lost on his contemporaries.

Furthermore, if it is not even at the *same* place and time that the relative values of different commodities could be measured by the differing amounts of labor which they have cost in production, how much less could labor be *the* price-determining factor of commodities traded at *different* places and in different periods of time. In contrast to labor, money does at least measure the rate at which commodities exchange for each other at a given place and time, although money, too, fails as a measure of the relative values of commodities over time and space.

While it is thus impossible to find a measure for the purchasing power of things *in general,* we can measure the relative purchasing power of *two particular objects* by merely comparing their respective money prices. Malthus concludes that it is futile to use the term value, or value in exchange, by itself: we always ought to mention specifically the articles in the purchase of which incomes are chiefly spent.

Finally, it comes as no surprise that Malthus should have taken Smith to task for having stated that corn is a better measure of value "from century to century" than money (because Smith believed the relation of corn to labor to be more constant than that between labor and any other commodity). In a historical example cited by Malthus, after the lapse of fifty or sixty years a given quantity of wheat came to represent little more than half the original quantity of labor, that is, a day's labor came to purchase nearly twice as much wheat at the end of that period.

The Formation of Rent

Malthus defined rent as "the excess of the value of the whole produce, or if estimated in money, the excess of the price of the whole produce, above what is necessary to pay the wages of the labour and the profits of the capital employed in cultivation. . . ."[7] As the *primary cause* of the excess referred to in the definition, he considered the productivity of the soil over and above the quantity of necessaries of life required for the maintenance of agricultural workers. The *other causes* adduced include the tendency of the necessaries of life to create their own demand via an increase in the number of mouths to be fed, clothed, sheltered, and the comparative scarcity of fertile land.

Certainly these were the most enlightened views on the subject up to that time. Even the second of the three causes, while it has not been in evidence for some time in the relatively wealthy regions of the world, is still a powerful factor in keeping down the levels of living of many underdeveloped countries.

---

[7]*Ibid.,* p. 136.

What Malthus did not foresee, and could not have foreseen, was the possibility that under favorable technological conditions improvements in agriculture might completely swamp the tendency of the population to "take up the slack" created by a rapidly increasing output of food and raw materials — the agricultural "revolutions" the end of which is not in sight as yet. As a consequence of many powerful innovations in the cultivation of land, the *Law of Diminishing Returns*, which Malthus implied and for which Ricardo furnished the intellectual justification, could never operate for very long on a *given* level of production possibilities. Consequently, the fact that agriculture is typically an industry subject to diminishing returns — emphasized by orthodox British economics throughout most of the nineteenth century — was of little relevance for the long-run population growth of the *Western* world. However, although the consequences of the law, which Malthus thought threatened mankind in general, have been postponed if not forestalled by the technologically more advanced peoples, Malthus' theory of the dilemma posed by the discrepancy between the natural trend of population growth on the one hand and the expansion of the food base on the other hand has still been true as a broad statement of tendency.

DAVID RICARDO[8]

Adam Smith had attempted to show that in the earlier stages of society, when land had not yet been appropriated and capital accumulation was practically unknown, the exchangeable value, or the relative worth of commodities, depended exclusively on the quantities of labor necessarily required to produce them.

The core and principal legacy of Ricardo's efforts in the field of value theory consists in elevating this principle to general validity; that is, he tried to demonstrate that the value of commodities is determined in *all* stages of society by the quantity of labor required for their production. He did this by means of a series of assumptions which, if granted, lead by logical necessity to Ricardo's conclusions. His method of reasoning is deduction of the highest order and reflects his mathematical cast of mind, although he used few mathematical symbols. But such a method lacked the balance provided by frequent testing of hypotheses against observational reality and thus tended to convey to political economy the flavor of an armchair philosophy, lacking in close contacts with the ever-changing world — from which a

[8]See Biographical Note C.

good theory must draw its fundamental strength. In fact, to the twentieth-century reader Ricardo appears as the epitome of that branch of nineteenth-century classical economics which showed a one-sided orientation towards finding immutable laws of a cosmopolitan scope.

Secondly, Ricardo, in full awareness and with a sense of mission, switched the engine of analysis onto a different track. Whereas from mercantilism onward the exponents of previous currents of economic thought — including Smith and his early interpreters — had somehow or other been concerned with the ways and means by which organized human society could enhance its material wealth (for whatever ultimate purpose), the Ricardian branch of the Classical school shifted its attention to problems of *distribution* of the national product. The shares accruing to the factors of production were now beginning to be viewed as subject to immanent laws working out inexorably within a framework of premises considered as basically unalterable — not affected by the dynamics of economic evolution. Thus the stage was set for a more rigid methodological approach, which unnecessarily delayed adaptation of the existing body of knowledge to changing circumstances, especially those of a technological nature.

If Ricardo's shortcomings in time conclusively demonstrated that economics cannot be cast within an artificial mold forged from a limited set of related hypotheses, his approach nevertheless enlarged the scope for fruitful investigation. It was eventually superseded by more flexible thinking on the problems of distribution, these latter being viewed merely as a necessary complement to the theory of production.

Perhaps the greatest stumbling block to a reasonably full understanding of Ricardo's main work, the *Principles of Political Economy and Taxation* (1817), lies in the *lack of system* exhibited in this book. Its perusal in the order in which the materials were presented is bound to lead the novice into many blind alleys. From these, however, he can now be rescued without too much trouble.[9] Even so, a reader of Ricardo in the original is bound to be baffled by the faulty arrangement of paragraphs, which confirms the impression that the work went to press before it was finished — as in fact it did, at the urging of Ricardo's friends who may have mistaken obscurity for depth. It is less clear why Ricardo should have consented to a second and third edition without any attempt at recasting the text as a whole, or at least at eliminating its main literary defect: desultoriness.

---

[9]Reference is directed to such guides as are provided in E. C. K. Gonner's introductory essay, "Ricardo's Political Economy," in David Ricardo, *Principles of Political Economy and Taxation* (ed. Gonner; London: George Bell, 1891), and especially Oswald St. Clair, *A Key to Ricardo* (New York: Augustus M. Kelley, Publishers, 1957).

When, at the end of his sustained efforts, a determined student sees the various pieces of the puzzle fall into place, he comes away with a more favorable impression. He may well have discovered a hidden bond of unity among the disjointed parts, all of which were designed to illumine a set of principles which were clearly established in Ricardo's own mind, and which concern the modes in which the rewards for productive services are proportioned in the long run.

The Conceptual Framework — Partly an Exercise in Terminology

If, as indicated above, *the ratio in which commodities exchange for one another is to be regulated by the amount of labor realized in them*, we would surely expect Ricardo to conceive of labor in an unusually broad sense. This, indeed, he did. To illustrate, in making allowance for different degrees of skill and intensity of effort, he grants that one hour of one type of labor may be worth many hours expended in the performance of another type. More important, labor may be *indirect*, that is, incorporated in the prior manufacture of capital goods which are presently contributing to the manufacture of those consumer (or capital) goods whose exchangeable value is to be explored. In viewing (fixed) capital as so much compressed labor, however, Ricardo overlooked that there is no common denominator for comparing, in value terms, the result of labor performed in the past with that of labor performed in the present.

Like Smith, Ricardo recognized that the relations of *demand and supply* determine the market price of all commodities at a given time. But underlying the accidental and temporary causes influencing this price, there is, according to Ricardo, a permanent cause which, in the absence of these short-run disturbances, would lead to a *normal* ratio of exchange. This is the "cost of production," conceived of as the total of all labor costs, broadly interpreted, and it is equated to *value*.

Our next observation concerns the fact that an increase in the total of a country's commodities need not involve an increase in the labor absorbed in producing them, and consequently does not necessarily entail an augmentation of value. It *does* involve an increase in *real* value, or riches possessed by the community; but exchange value, which merely denotes a ratio, may remain unaffected (and will remain unaffected if value has not changed).

By the same token, inventions which facilitate production will change the degree to which separate commodities partake of real value. In other words, since value (as distinguished from real value) of a commodity depends not on its aggregate abundance or aggregate scarcity but rather on the facility or difficulty encountered in its production, riches are not closely related to value at all.

By now, the question may have occurred to the reader: Does Ricardo distinguish between price and value? The answer is yes, but the distinction is not of any fundamental import. It is superficial in that it rests only on the fact that when we compare goods with money we speak of their prices, and when we compare them with one another we speak of their respective, or relative, values. Hence market price and market value mean essentially the same thing.

The *relationship between exchange value and real value* becomes clear when it is realized that a commodity's ratio of exchange relative to other commodities also depends on the degree to which that commodity, as compared with other commodities, is possessed of real value. This, of course, is tantamount to saying that the relative worth of a commodity is an expression of its relative scarcity — utility being taken for granted. Ricardo views the cost of production, the "foundation" of value, as regulating exchange value, but we know, of course, that the causal nexus, far from being a one-way street, is quite complicated. While not overlooking *demand*, he did not devote a great deal of attention to it because he did not believe that, except for nonreproducible commodities such as rare paintings, it exercises more than a temporary influence upon price.

In looking for something in the nature of a general *standard of value*, Ricardo had even less "success" than Smith. We have already seen why neither "corn" nor the precious metals can satisfactorily serve in this capacity; it remained for Ricardo to show that, contrary to Smith's and Malthus' conclusions, not even *labor* qualifies for the performance of this task. Why? Because the amount of labor which can be obtained in exchange for a particular commodity does not necessarily match the amount employed in its production. This Ricardo does not attempt to prove, but neither would it be possible to prove the opposite. Not only is it practically impossible to reduce the various degrees of skill to the level of unskilled labor, but also the labor incorporated in capital goods produced in the past, and contributing to presently produced goods, is not strictly comparable to labor incorporated in similar capital goods produced today.

Even *if* we excluded the exertion of capital and confined ourselves to present labor, and *if*, for the sake of simplicity, we assumed this actual labor to be homogeneous in nature, it does not follow that we can use the reward of labor as a standard of value, since reward is not necessarily in proportion with productive contribution. This latter point Ricardo failed to make sufficiently clear.

While all of the foregoing may be considered as only preparatory to what Ricardo had to say regarding the laws according to which the distribution of value is regulated, it is precisely this latter analysis whose validity may be questioned. For, within his framework of categories, Ricardo is led to the conclusion that, regardless of the productiveness of human energy, the crucial question is one of distribution of *value* only rather than one of distribution of *riches*. Thus, in his own view, it makes no difference how large an absolute quantity of commodities is obtained by capitalists, landowners, and laborers, since this quantity is, by definition, not indicative of the rate of rent, profit, and wages. In other words, he does not ask how the total riches produced are divided, but how total value—this abstract concept of a sum of exchange ratios — is divided.

Remember that, according to Ricardo, value differs from riches in that it depends not on abundance but on the difficulty (facility) of production. The distinction may become somewhat clearer by reference to one of his examples:

> Suppose with a given capital the labour of a certain number of men produced 1,000 pair of stockings, and that by inventions in machinery, the same number of men can produce 2,000 pair . . .; then the value of the 2,000 pair of stockings . . . will be neither more nor less than that of the 1,000 pair of stockings before the introduction of machinery; for they will be the produce of the same quantity of labour. . . . By constantly increasing the facility of production . . . we not only add to the national riches, but also to the power of future production.[10]

The Treatment of Rent

We recall that at the root of Ricardo's treatment of value lies the "law," weakened by uneasy qualifications, that commodities exchange according to their cost of production, as determined by the amount of effort going into their production. The question arises as to whether the payment of rent, which in physiocratic view rests on the bounty of nature, invalidates this "law."

Ricardo does not believe that it affects the question of exchange value at all, because that value is being determined, in the long run, by the relative quantities of labor supplied under the most *unfavorable* circumstances. In other words, identical commodities are not always

[10]J. R. McCulloch (ed.), *The Works of David Ricardo* (London: John Murray, 1871), pp. 165–166.

produced by the same amount of labor. But "the exchangeable value of all commodities . . . is always regulated, not by the less quantity of labour that will suffice for their production under circumstances highly favorable . . .; but by the greater quantity of labour necessarily bestowed on their production by those . . . who continue to produce them under the most unfavorable circumstances; . . . the most unfavorable under which the quantity of produce required, renders it necessary to carry on their production."[11]

Ricardo assumes that if in the process land of increasingly lower degrees of fertility is taken into cultivation, rent arises (or increases) on lands of higher quality:

> Thus suppose land — No. 1, 2, 3 — to yield, with an equal employment of capital and labour, a net produce of 100, 90, and 80 quarters of corn. In a new country, where there is an abundance of fertile land compared with the population, and where therefore it is only necessary to cultivate No. 1, the whole net produce will belong to the cultivator, and will be the profits of the stock which he advances. As soon as population had so far increased as to make it necessary to cultivate No. 2, from which 90 quarters only can be obtained after supporting the labourers, rent would commence on No. 1; for either there must be two rates of profit on agricultural capital, or ten quarters, or the value of ten quarters must be withdrawn from the produce of No. 1, for some other purpose. Whether the proprietor of the land, or any other person, cultivated No. 1, these ten quarters would equally constitute rent; for the cultivator of No. 2 would get the same result with his capital, whether he cultivated No. 1, paying ten quarters for rent, or continued to cultivate No. 2, paying no rent. In the same manner it might be shown that when No. 3 is brought into cultivation, the rent of No. 2 must be ten quarters, or the value of ten quarters, whilst the rent of No. 1 would rise to twenty quarters; for the cultivator of No. 3 would have the same profits whether he paid twenty quarters for the rent of No. 1, ten quarters for the rent of No. 2, or cultivated No. 3 free of all rent.[12]

Furthermore, according to Ricardo, the total value (read: sum of all costs of production) remaining after the payment of rent is divided among the forces engaged in production. If, due to a *general rise in productivity*, the remuneration for each effort of each productive agent goes up, as measured by a larger amount of necessaries, comforts, and luxuries available to the owners of productive agents, has total value been increased as a result? Not in Ricardo's scheme; all that has taken place is an increase in riches. In his own words, ". . . the wealth of a

---

[11]David Ricardo, *Principles of Political Economy and Taxation*, ed. Gonner (London: George Bell, 1891), p. 50.

[12]McCulloch, *op. cit.*, p. 36.

country may be increased in two ways: it may be increased by employing a greater portion of revenue in the maintenance of productive labour — which will not only add to the quantity, but to the value of the mass of commodities; or it may be increased, without employing any additional quantity of labour, by making the same quantity more productive — which will add to the abundance, but not to the value of commodities."[13] This leads to the paradoxical conclusion that, allowing for the fact that an increase in the social dividend need not be a direct result of nature's bounty, an increase in riches is possible without an increase in effort on anybody's part.

In sum, effort always "receives" the same value, regardless of the amount of commodities which may be its reward. While the cogency of the argument is beyond question if we accept Ricardo's definition of value, in the light of everyday language, and especially in the light of what became standard professional terminology, the practicality of Ricardo's usages may be questioned.

Division of Value between Labor and Capital

Assuming with Ricardo that all labor, including the effort embodied in capital, can be estimated in terms of simple labor units, we are prepared for a further conclusion of his: that if at any time a greater share in the value (sum total of cost of production) be assigned to any group of labor units, this increased share will be subtracted from the value apportioned to others. Specifically, how will value be divided between labor and capital?

Here Ricardo has been frequently misinterpreted, although — considering that rent does not constitute a cost of production in his analysis — he was only stating a truism when he said that profits depend on real wages, that is, on the number of days' work necessary to obtain the number of pounds annually paid to the laborer. At this juncture, we need to realize again that most classical writers recognized only three factorial payments: wages, profits, and rent. Consequently, with rent being a datum not entering cost of production, whatever of total value will not accrue to direct labor will have to accrue to capital (indirect labor), and vice versa. Ricardo never asserted that wages and profits cannot grow together as far as the *amount* of commodities which their shares can purchase are concerned. He was only interested in the *relative* payments that can be made to the productive agents, labor and capital. Just as it is impossible for two commodities simultaneously to

---

[13]Ricardo, *op. cit.*, p. 263.

become more valuable one relative to the other, so it is likewise *impossible for labor to obtain a larger share of total value without capital experiencing a diminution of its share, and vice versa.*

Long-Run Tendencies in Distribution

If the account so far has given the impression that Ricardo is interested only in static equilibrium, it becomes imperative to retouch it: he is also anxious to discover the forces which in the long run control the division of value among the two variable agents of production. Here the most important relationship investigated is that between *wages and population.* Specifically, harking back to Malthus, who did not have much of a wage theory but was concerned about the tendency for population growth to outrun the growth in food supply,[14] Ricardo asserts that there exists a tendency for population to increase with an increase in real wages, that is, the quantity of food, necessities, and conveniences received by the laborer. However, he does not consider the natural price of labor, the "price which is necessary to enable labourers one with another to subsist and perpetuate their race without either increase or diminution,"[15] as absolutely fixed and constant. His explanations support the conclusion that there must be a floor under wages if labor is to maintain its relative importance among the factors of production, but that there is no definite ceiling, except that the tendency for labor to increase in importance will become more pronounced in proportion as its remuneration rises above what is necessary to maintain the accustomed level of living. Since this level, according to Ricardo, could never rise far above subsistence, the range between ceiling and floor must be rather narrow. It bears repetition that the share of total value accruing to the owners of capital as profit will vary in accordance with the quantitative variations in the share accruing to labor. And it may vary not only as measured in value, but also as measured in commodities.

But the crux of the matter is Ricardo's thought that with the progress of society the *natural price of labor has a tendency to rise secularly because of the ever greater difficulty of producing food.* He did not consider improvements in agriculture or the opening of new sources of food supply abroad as capable of permanently checking the tendency to a rise in the price of necessaries, though that tendency might be counteracted temporarily. He also asserted that the natural price of all

---

[14]See Biographical Note B.

[15]Ricardo, *op. cit.*, p. 70.

commodities, with the exception of raw produce and labor, tended to fall, since the rise in the natural price of raw materials from which manufactured goods are fashioned would be more than offset by improvements in machinery, organization of labor, and skills — hence, the *tendency of profits to fall* in the long run.

In sum, the long-run tendencies visualized by Ricardo all center about the Law of Diminishing Returns from land, which may be said to dominate the economic position and to govern the fortunes of all classes. The *laborers*, owing to their lack of foresight, will tend to multiply in proportion to the means available for their subsistence, and are thus destined to remain perpetually poor. Surely, since the cost of the means of subsistence is bound to rise, their money wages will have to rise too, but since the latter are merely keeping pace, the laborers will not be any better off in the long run. The *capitalists*, owing to the continually rising price of the laborers' food, will see the rate of profit upon their capital continually fall. The *landlords*, through no doing of their own but rather thanks to the niggardliness of nature (which has furnished mankind with only a limited quantity of first-grade land), will grow wealthy, for every extension of cultivation to inferior land brings them an increase in rent.

The Law of Diminishing Returns will cease to bring about these distributional consequences only when it ceases to operate, that is, when it becomes impossible to cultivate lower-grade land because its yield will not suffice to replace the expense of cultivation, including a profit for the capitalists who made the advances. When that state of things has arrived, population, rents, as well as the rate of profit on capital, will become stationary.

NASSAU WILLIAM SENIOR[16] AND JOHN STUART MILL

Senior's work may be regarded as another stepping stone between Adam Smith and John Stuart Mill or, alternatively, as the third leg of a tripod balancing the weights carried by the contributions of Malthus and Ricardo. Joint consideration with Mill is suggested by Senior's own conviction — accentuated later by Mill — to the effect that those inferences of political economy relating to the nature and *production* of wealth are universally true, whereas inferences relating to its *distribution* are likely to be affected by the specific institutions of particular countries, hence are true only in a relative sense.

---

[16]See Biographical Note D.

Haunted by an uneasiness over an ever more confounding economic terminology — with terms being increasingly used merely to suit the particular needs of a given writer — Senior saw as one of his principal tasks the search for a consistent *nomenclature*. In this uninspiring effort, he probably spent a disproportionate amount of energy, creating the impression that the ascertainment of facts by close observation was no longer the principal task of economic science. If only economists could be made to speak a uniform language which, furthermore, would correspond as closely as possible to ordinary usage, the principal difficulty of the science would be removed.

This sort of unification, while bound to enhance the layman's respect for the stature of a body of knowledge, can of course be only a subsidiary concern of the creative scientist. Nor was it Senior's only concern, whatever his critics may have alleged to the contrary. In fact, effort aimed at the unification of the science in a *substantive* sense was far from negligible. The result of this endeavor was the presentation of economic theory in the light of a presumed need for the setting up of certain basic empirical postulates, from which a series of deductions could be drawn. This method was by no means new — Ricardo had used it implicitly — but Senior was probably the first to demonstrate its strengths and weaknesses by unabashedly placing it in the center of his edifice of thought.

Senior's Four Postulates

Senior believed that the facts on which general economic principles rest may be stated in a few elementary propositions. These premises he viewed as the combined result of observation and common sense ("consciousness"); as axioms they would not call for proof. He presented them as follows:

(1) That every man desires to obtain additional Wealth with as little sacrifice as possible.
(2) That the Population of the world, or, in other words, the number of persons inhabiting it, is limited only by moral or physical evil, or by fear of a deficiency of those articles of wealth which the habits of the individuals of each class of its inhabitants lead them to require.
(3) That the power of Labour, and of the other instruments which produce wealth, may be indefinitely increased by using their Products as the means of further Production.
(4) That, agricultural skill remaining the same, additional Labour employed on the land within a given district produces in general a less proportionate return, or, in other words, that though, with

every increase of the labour bestowed, the aggregate return is increased, the increase of the return is not in proportion to the increase of the labour.[17]

Considering the stage that value theory had reached by the mid-1830's, how shall we assess this attempt at providing an axiomatic basis for the apparatus of economic analysis? The first proposition, above, is merely the economist's version of a broader heuristic principle: means, in the natural order of things, are economized in the attainment of ends, since the former are limited but the latter are boundless. It does not mean that wealth, though it is a *sine qua non* for human existence, hence the object of a universal desire, is the principal end of human striving. As competing objectives, Senior lists power, distinction, leisure, love for friends, the public good. Money, being abstract wealth, serves more satisfactorily than anything else in the pursuit of the most diverse objectives. Senior's reason for stating such self-evident truths is that they constitute "the ultimate fact beyond which reasoning cannot go, and of which almost every other proposition is merely an illustration."[18]

The remaining propositions are readily recognized, especially by those familiar with Malthus' *Essay*, as restatements of principal tenets of earlier classical writers. The statement concerning the limitation on the population "by moral or physical evil" evokes Malthus' "vice and misery," the two most powerful checks; the "fear of a deficiency" of basic necessities is reminiscent of the same author's prudential restraint, that preventive check in whose operation Malthus had only limited confidence. Senior thus helped to entrench the teaching of Malthus' *Essay* still more firmly in what had already become a system of economic orthodoxy.[19]

Proposition (3) harks back to Smith's stress on the central role of capital accumulation, which is in turn encouraged by division of labor, the foundation of an increase in the powers of labor. The concluding proposition is an improved version of Ricardo's statement of the Principle of Diminishing Returns, improved in the sense that the stipulation of no change in the techniques of production is made explicit. In his subsequent elaboration of the principle, Senior was very emphatic about an alleged tendency toward increasing returns in manufactures, but he did not recognize that he was concerned with cases that were not, strictly speaking, comparable. He wrote:

---

[17]Nassau W. Senior, *An Outline of the Science of Political Economy* (New York: Holt, Rinehart & Winston, Inc., 1939), p. 26.
[18]*Ibid.*, p. 28.
[19]See Biographical Note B.

The advantage possessed by land in repaying increased labour, though employed on the same materials, with a constantly increasing produce, is overbalanced by the diminishing proportion which the increase of the produce generally bears to the increase of the labour. And the disadvantage of manufactures in requiring for every increase of produce an equal increase of materials, is overbalanced by the constantly increasing facility with which the increased quantity of materials is worked up.[20]

He evidently means by "materials" in the first case a fixed factor of production, natural agents; in the second, a variable factor, capital. Now it is clear that the factor proportion land/labor must continuously change to the disadvantage of labor as with a rising population, agricultural skill remaining the same, land will yield less and less per unit of labor. On the other hand, capital, in the long run, has tended to increase more rapidly than labor power; hence, in manufacturing, where land is usually negligible as a factor of production, there has been a tendency for the returns from labor applied to capital to rise relatively fast. Since Senior minimized the possibilities of technological progress in agriculture, while giving it ample play in manufacturing, in a comparison of the returns of a unit of *labor* from land with those of a unit of *labor* from capital he could not fail to arrive at the one-sided conclusion mentioned above. Unfortunately, it was to constitute a stumbling block in the advance of theory for the next several decades. Had he formulated the idea into another postulate, one to the effect that, in the long run, technological progress in agriculture tends to lag behind technological progress in manufacturing and is not able to overcome the effects of the Law of Diminishing Returns, the corollary of proposition (4) would not have remained unchallenged for so long.

Senior's Rearrangement of the Factors of Production

In his discussion of the instruments of production, Senior ventured forth with an innovation apt to shed new light on the *role of capital*.

He first defined the primary instruments of production, labor and natural agents. The former consists of "the voluntary exertion of bodily and mental faculties for the purpose of production,"[21] the latter of "every productive agent so far as it does not derive its power from . . . man."[22] He substituted the term "natural agents" for land in order to

---

[20]Senior, *op. cit.*, p. 83.

[21]*Ibid.*, p. 57.

[22]*Ibid.*, p. 58.

"avoid designating a whole genus by the name of one of its species,"[23] certainly a step in the right direction.

The reason for introducing the term "abstinence" must be sought in his endeavor to get at the very foundation of an increase in the powers of labor and of the other instruments that produce wealth. The mere combination of labor and natural agents results either in the production of consumer goods or of capital goods, hence is not a distinguishing criterion for capital. But capital formation does call for the abstention from the unproductive use of natural agents, regardless of whether such conduct is, or is not, motivated by conscious preference for remote rather than immediate results. Since the term "capital" designates a certain category of articles of wealth, while it is desirable to identify a principle which *underlies* the production of that type of wealth, the expression "abstinence" — which Senior used for want of a better term — has obvious advantages. If we accept his reasoning as valid, capital still continues to serve as a secondary or derivative productive agent, but it occupies a different place. It now no longer merely presupposes the effective combination of labor and natural agents, but in addition calls for the employment of a distinct human faculty: temporary renunciation of the command over economic goods that could be used to yield direct satisfaction. In Senior's view, this *delay of enjoyment* is the crucial element underlying capital formation; while it is distinct from labor and the agency of nature, without its concurrence capital could not come into existence.

Senior, despite his misgivings concerning the new term, stressed the connotation of sacrifice and may thus not have been aware that sacrifice need not be involved in the case of *all* "abstainers" (people who save rather than consume). More important, when Senior pointed out that abstinence stands in the same relation to profit as labor does to wages, he seems to have overlooked the fact that the rate of return resulting from the use of materials in the production of remote goods may have very little relation to the quantity of immediate pleasures foregone, but will depend on how effectively unconsumed wealth can, at a given stage of technological knowledge, be used in the production of future goods. Nevertheless, Senior deserves recognition for having made unmistakably clear that, of the various means by which man can rise on the scale of well-being, abstinence is the most potent.

In conclusion, we may state that since Senior, along with the sacrifice of the capitalist, also stressed the *disutility of labor*, his analysis

---

[23]*Ibid.*, p. 59.

of the cost of production, viewed in subjective rather than objective terms, appears as rather unique.

Introduction to Mill[24]

John Stuart Mill's original contributions to value theory are scattered through various chapters of Book III, "Exchange," of his *Principles of Political Economy* (1848). Book IV, entitled "Influence of the Progress of Society on Production and Distribution," contains some dynamic aspects of the problem of distribution, as distinguished from the analysis of a static society in the preceding Books. While in Book IV we witness a fertile mind speculating on possible economic trends in a developing economy that may eventually become stationary, this part of the *Principles* is less rewarding for those merely in search of elaborations of specific components of the existing body of value theory.

Viewed as a whole, the *Principles* is mainly *a treatise on production and distribution,* as viewed from a midnineteenth-century perspective. Senior's conclusion to the effect that the laws of production differ from those of distribution in that the latter are (at least in part) of man's making whereas the former are not, is stressed by Mill in his "Preliminary Remarks" as well as in subsequent passages; but it is not formally reflected in the organization of the broad sweep of materials that constituted Mill's restatement of classical doctrine.[25]

Although progress in arrangement is clearly in evidence, especially as compared to Ricardo's and Senior's principal works, Mill, despite orderly presentation, still left room for further improvement, especially since he did not provide a subject matter index to ease the chore of investigating his treatment of specific problems. Stylistically, the *Principles* are imbued with a charm reminiscent of Smith.

---

[24]See Biographical Note E.

[25]It must be readily granted that the Senior/Mill distinction has merit, but as stated by Mill it is obviously too sharply drawn. The laws of production are at least in part a result of the organization of production, that is, while they may be viewed as immanent in the myriad of possibilities in which factors of production can be combined, they achieve relevance only in proportion as man learns to shape and control these factors and to uncover new facets of their interaction.

It was to Mill's credit, however, that he pointed out the following: Man's power to decide through statutes and usages the modes of distribution of wealth in society, his power of deciding by *what* institutions society shall be governed, is not identical with arbitrary determination of *how* these institutions shall work. "The Conditions on which the power they possess over the distribution of wealth is dependent . . . are as much a subject for scientific inquiry as many of the physical laws of nature." (John S. Mill, *Principles of Political Economy* [New York: Longmans, Green & Co., Inc., 1891], p. 14.)

Problems of Production

Mill was concerned about the fact that the Physiocrats, and to a lesser extent Adam Smith, had created and supported the impression that natural agents in some occupations contribute more to the final value of a product than they do in others, and that, consequently, human labor is responsible for a smaller or larger portion, respectively, of that product. Mill pointed out that it is *impossible to evaluate the contribution to a final product of any one necessary factor of production*, because, in the absence of that factor, the product would simply not have come into existence. No doubt the contributive shares of the various productive agents in the value of a given commodity may differ, but, as long as any one of these agents is indispensable, the final product is just as much the result of that one agent as it is the result of others.

The venerable problem of *what types of labor are productive or un-productive* should, in Mill's view, be reduced to one of mere language and classification. What we produce, or intend to produce, is always utility. Labor can never produce matter, but at best rearrange the particles of matter; it never creates objects, but merely brings about such a rearrangement of the material properties of an object that the object becomes (more) suitable for consumption. By the same token, the act of consumption involves no destruction of matter, but only the appropriation of qualities of an object which fitted it for the purpose of being consumed. So far so good! Unfortunately, however, this insight did not lead Mill into Say's track. It will be recalled that Say held the view that all labor which produces utility should be accounted productive. Mill, in fact, placed himself in the anomalous position of asserting that the work of surgeons, legislators, teachers, and the like, is certainly productive of utility, but is not productive per se! Why?

In his view, *production involves the idea of a result that is tangible*, or that may at least later be reflected in something tangible. Hence, only those utilities "fixed and embodied in outward objects" and those "fixed and embodied in human beings," but not those "consisting in a mere service rendered," can be said to have issued from productive labor. Only labor which produces wealth can be called productive per se. Furthermore, services which create utility only while they are being performed are not susceptible to accumulation, and things must lend themselves to being stored (like the skill implanted by a teacher in his pupil) if they are to be classified as wealth. In conclusion, according to Mill *labor should be considered as productive if, and only if, it is employed in creating permanent utilities*, regardless of whether these are embodied in animate or inanimate objects. The practicality of this usage of the term "productive" may well be questioned. How, for example, are we to judge whether in a given case the utility received survived the act of rendering it or expired with the act? By Mill's criterion, the labor of a musical performer or actor would not be productive because it presumably does not result in new occupational skills. But, it may be countered, the temper and disposition of an educated audience may well be different (from what they would have been without the enjoyment of the performance) long after this audience has left the concert hall or theater. The delayed but lasting effects of the enjoyment of artistic skills may well enhance the productive endeavors of people whose whole outlook on life is favorably affected by the availability of such intellectual pleasures.

Mill's classification also suffers from the fact that the portion of wealth that is manifested in human skills rather than in material objects — both being likewise the result of productive labor — is incapable of being measured. Despite such shortcomings, Mill's wrestling with a shopworn problem should not be discarded as fruitless; it is only through the reassessment of alternatives that we arrive at clearer conceptions of the merits of a given terminology.

Mill also applied the same dichotomy to *consumption*. An unproductive consumer is one who contributes nothing directly or indirectly to production. On the other hand, even a productive laborer may engage in unproductive consumption, as when, for example, his consumption does not result in "keeping up or improving . . . health, strength, capacities of work, or in rearing other productive labourers,"[26] when it is rather focusing on "pleasures or luxuries." An elusive distinction again!

Mill made an original contribution in working out a *theory of joint cost*, treated by him as one of the "peculiar cases of value." Two goods, such as coke and coal gas, have a joint cost of production in that they are both products of the same operation and the outlay is incurred for the sake of both together. Total production cost would be the same if one of the end products were not in demand at all. Assuming that there is a market for both of them, is the value of each commodity relative to the other a function of cost of production? No, says Mill. Yet cost of production does determine their joint value, because, in the long run, the proceeds from the sale of both must repay the expenses incurred in their production (including what is now called a normal profit).

---

[26]John Stuart Mill, *Principles of Political Economy, with Some of Their Applications to Social Philosophy* (New York: Appleton-Century-Crofts, 1866), I, 80.

If cost of production does not determine their individual prices but only the sum of their prices, what principle regulates the ratios of these prices? For equilibrium to be attained, it is necessary that both commodities sell at prices for which the quantities of each produced will be sold. Hence, Mill argues, it is the law of demand and supply, according to which the quantity demanded of a commodity varies with its price and the price must be such that the quantity demanded equals the quantity supplied, that furnishes the explanation of the repartition of the proceeds from the sale of the two commodities. If, for example, at a given set of prices cost of production is fully covered, and purchasers can be found for the entire output of commodity B (say, gas) but only for less than the entire output of commodity A (say, coke), it will be necessary to lower the price of A in order to sell it all. But at this lower price, Mill assumes, revenue from A will be smaller and, hence, total revenue will no longer be sufficient to cover joint cost of production. It therefore becomes necessary to raise the price of commodity B, which in turn calls for a contraction of output. This trial-and-error process will go on until prices become "stationary," that is, until the joint effect of the price rise of B and of the price fall of A is the purchase of so much less of B and so much more of A that there is now a market for the entire output of B and A. In sum: "When, therefore, two or more commodities have a joint cost of production, their natural values relatively to each other are those which will create a demand for each, in the ratio of the quantities in which they are sent forth by the productive process."[27]

Refinements of Distribution Theory

In the chapter treating "Of Profits," Mill, after having endorsed Senior's term "abstinence," the remuneration of which are the profits of the capitalist, proceeds to show that only a part of these gains is an equivalent for the use of capital itself. This portion, which can only be estimated, is what a borrower would pay in the market for loanable funds. This *interest component of profits* corresponds to the remuneration which a person can earn by abstaining from immediate consumption and offering funds to others to be used for productive purposes. Mill is careful to point out that the remuneration for mere abstinence is identical with interest only in those instances where a borrower is

---

[27]John S. Mill, *Principles of Political Economy* (New York: Longmans, Green & Co., Inc., 1891), p. 345.

solvent, where funds are advanced on "such security as precludes any appreciable chance of losing the principal."[28]

The *size of the differential* between the rate of profit and the rate of interest, which may be considerable, depends on two elements: risk, and the work of the owner of funds associated with the superintendence of their employment. Mill assumes that the person who supplies the bulk of the funds by which the operations of industry are carried on also controls them. "To exercise this control with efficiency, if the concern is large and complicated, requires great assiduity, and, often, no ordinary skill. This assiduity and skill must be remunerated."[29]

In sum, *out of the gross returns from capital three claims must be met:* that which arises from the sacrifice imposed by waiting; that which constitutes an indemnity for risk incurred; and that based on the time, effort, and skill involved in superintendence. Mill goes on to separate the cases in which these compensations are paid to the same person — which presumes that the firm has not borrowed and is in the form of an individual proprietorship — from those in which they are paid to different persons; he explores various combinations in the arrangement of claims. On the whole, he effected a much more acute analysis of business practices than any of his predecessors.

One questionable feature remains. Mill did not consider the remuneration for risk incurred but rather the managerial wages of the entrepreneur, as the residual element in gross profits. He treated the former merely as an insurance premium, susceptible of being estimated by actuarial methods. He viewed the necessary remuneration for abstinence, conditioned by the effective desire for accumulation, as highly variable and found even wider variations in the compensation for risk. However, at a given time and place, "that portion of profit which is properly interest, and which forms the real remuneration for abstinence" (what is now known as "pure" or "net" interest) is the same regardless of how the funds have been employed. Mill failed to perceive the analytic difference between the risk element included in the gross interest return on borrowed funds and the residual risk factor borne by the entrepreneur. In his exposition, the two are mingled.

A further advance lies in his recognition of the fact that the process of *equalization of returns from the different employment of funds* does not necessarily involve their actual withdrawal from existing investments. It may well be that new investment capital is simply not attracted to businesses whose chances of profit are considered inferior to those in

---

[28]*Ibid.*, p. 245.
[29]*Ibid.*

other employments. In a rapidly developing society, in particular, new accumulations of capital merely direct themselves to the more thriving industries and thereby prevent the employment of capital from remaining more profitable in some occupations as compared with others. This highly realistic insight may be viewed as a corrective to the impression conveyed by earlier writers of an instantaneous mobility of capital. A sort of balance in the distribution of capital between more profitable and less profitable employments is restored *gradually;* expectations of profit tend to a common average and may oscillate around it.

Lastly, Mill conceives the *rate of profit as determined by three circumstances,* or variables, of which the cost of labor is a function: the efficiency of labor, the actual wage expenditures incurred, and the varying costliness of the articles which the laborer consumes. For practical purposes, it is most important always to distinguish clearly between wages and the cost of labor. The cost of labor may frequently be very high where wages are very low and vice versa, as Mill demonstrated by examples drawn from contemporary experience. This discussion is a marked improvement over that of Ricardo who, in suggesting that the rate of profit moves in inverse proportion to wages, may in his own mind have equated wages with the cost of labor while failing to bring out this point in his writings.

SUMMARY

Say, the popularizer of Adam Smith on the European Continent, held a balanced view of the elements that account for the value of commodities. Production to him was essentially the creation of utility; and any labor that contributes to this end, including that which exhausts itself in rendering direct services to consumers, was therefore productive. He was vividly aware of the strategic role of the entrepreneur as a factor of production in all branches of economic activity and elevated manufacturing to parity with agriculture. He recognized that the value of factor services depends ultimately on the value of final products as judged by buyers.

Malthus reserved the term "wealth" for material things and substituted the term "personal services" for Smith's "unproductive labor." He allowed for the indirect contribution to wealth of personal services, citing education as an example of the means by which the productive power of labor could be enhanced. He stressed that the intrinsic value in exchange of commodities was a result of the estimation in which a commodity is held in consequence of a set of supply and demand conditions and saw the permanent prices of most commodities as determined by their ordinary cost of production. He showed that profits are not a deduction from the produce of labor but are explained by scarcity of the factor capital. His explanation of rent was more advanced than that of any of his predecessors, although in assuming that an increase in the supply of the means of subsistence would be almost automatically followed by a correspondingly increased demand for them, he failed to anticipate the effects of a technological revolution in agriculture that, at least in the Western world, failed to produce an equally impressive population explosion.

Ricardo, in spite of the obstacles he encountered in the pursuit of his efforts to find a universally valid law of value, remained loyal to his belief that, in all stages of economic development, the exchange value of commodities is determined by the quantity of labor, past and present, required for their production. Such a conclusion could only be upheld by means of a series of assumptions, many of which are too far removed from reality to serve as useful tools of economic analysis. Ricardo's results revealed at once the promise and the pitfalls of the method of abstracting from real-world behavior, the strength coupled with weakness of a powerful logic divorced from empirical encumbrances. In seeking to enlarge the economic horizon, Ricardo concentrated on problems of distribution of the national product. Rent, which does not enter into value (cost of production), is essentially the result of the fact that equal amounts of labor or capital applied to different grades of land yield different products. Since the exchange value of agricultural commodities in the long run always is regulated by the relative quantities of labor supplied under the most unfavorable conditions of cultivation, rent appears as a differential return from land superior in quality to land the product of which just pays for the cost of labor and capital applied to it. Ricardo considered the shares of value accruing to labor and capital as mutually determined, that is, the larger the portion absorbed by labor, the smaller the portion remaining for capital. Since the Law of Diminishing Returns from land will require a long-run rise in money wages (the natural price of labor rises as the price of the means of subsistence goes up) in order merely to maintain labor's accustomed level of living, and since rent inevitably absorbs an ever larger share of national product, profits, as another share of this product, tend to decline in the long run. For the natural price of all commodities, except that of agricultural raw materials and labor, tends to fall as a result of technological progress and improved economic organization. Thus, in the final analysis, the Law of Diminishing Returns is made to carry the whole burden of a gloomy outlook for a capitalistic economy operating within a framework of pure competition.

Senior was justifiably concerned about the fact that the lack of a common terminology not only impeded the fruitful intercourse among economists themselves but also was responsible for the gap between popular and professional usage of terms which tended to alienate the layman seeking to broaden his understanding of economic matters. Fortunately, this academic economist and social reformer did not exhaust his energies in defining terms and interpreting those used by his predecessors and contemporaries; he also contributed to the substance of economic theory. Overly impressed by the need to stake out the boundaries of economic investigation, he stated four propositions or postulates from which, he held, all useful principles could be derived through a process of pursuing their implications by reasoning. It was not the lack of observed facts that impeded the progress of our science, but the slowness in drawing from them correct conclusions. However, Senior's four postulates did not open up any new vistas; they were merely elaborations of principles that had already been stated. He established an artificial dualism between manufacturing and agriculture, viewing the former as operating under conditions of increasing returns and the latter, decreasing returns. This line of reasoning, though influential in the subsequent history of economic thought, was faulty in that it was based on the comparison of fundamentally dissimilar factor constellations. His introduction of the term "abstinence" shed light on the fact that, in general, capital accumulation is not possible without sacrifice, and that the pain involved in foregoing present satisfactions, just as the pain caused by labor services, must be rewarded if people are to be induced to incur it. As an explanation of interest, however, this innovation was not sufficient, as will become clear in Chapter 3.

John Stuart Mill brought the body of classical theory to a level of perfection and refinement that remained unequaled. He incorporated in it the best of Smith and his successors and, optimistically, thought that he had completely explored and clarified once and for all the laws of value. But, before the end of his life, value theory was in a state of fundamental transformation, as will be shown in the following chapter. If it were not for this fact, Mill's restatement might still stand as a paragon of enlightened reasoning in political economy; for charm and clarity of expression, the *Principles* will always remain a masterpiece. As to specifics, Mill made it clear that it is impossible to attribute to any one factor of production a definite share in the value of an end product, inasmuch as in the absence of its contribution that end product could not have been produced.   Less fortunate were his attempts at classifying labor as productive or unproductive depending on whether it was or was not fixed and embodied in outward objects or in human beings; in this regard, Say had shown more discernment when he considered all labor productive which created or added to utility.   Mill's theory of joint cost was a piece of sophisticated analysis that proved his creative ability in a field he himself considered as offering little scope for originality.   In distinguishing between abstinence, risk, and labor services as constitutive elements of profits, and in showing the varying roles these elements may play under varying circumstances of investment, Mill performed a distinguished service of elaboration and clarification, but he failed to view remuneration for risk as the residual element in the compensation earned by the capitalist.   His treatment of the way in which a balance in the distribution of funds tends to occur between more or less profitable employments was more realistic than that of his predecessors, as was also his broader view of the relationship between profits and labor costs, of which wages are only one cause.

Finally, much of the confusion that afflicts students of classical value theory hinges on a fine distinction which suggests that the idea of a measure of value must not be confounded with the idea of a regulator or underlying principle of value.   When Ricardo wrote that the value of a thing is regulated by quantity of labor, he did not mean the quantity of labor for which the thing will exchange, but the quantity required for producing it.   By contrast, when Smith and Malthus said that labor is a measure of value, they did not mean the labor by which the thing is made, but the quantity of labor for which it will exchange, or the value of the thing estimated in labor (rather than, say, a precious metal or "corn").

BIOGRAPHICAL NOTES

A.—*Jean-Baptiste Say* (1767–1832), a member of a French Protestant family returned from exile around the middle of the eighteenth century, had a varied career as soldier, editor, statesman, businessman, college professor, and writer. He survived the Revolution of 1789, the Directorate, the Restoration, and the Revolution of 1830.

After Smith's *Wealth of Nations* had been translated into French in 1779, Say felt the need for a more logical, systematic, and orderly presentation of the main principles of the budding science. Out of subsequent efforts in this direction arose his principal work, published in 1803 under the title *A Treatise on Political Economy;* it went through many editions before, and some after, the author's death, was translated into several languages, and found perhaps its most lucrative foreign market in the United States, where it served as a standard textbook for decades. Before the first edition had come off the press, Say had accepted a position in the government of Napoleon. Since some of the findings in the *Treatise* tended to discredit governmental policy, Say was urged to revise the book, but this he stoutly declined. As a consequence, he had to resign his position in the Tribunate.

He then established himself as a cotton-spinning manufacturer, and in this capacity for about ten years (until 1813) enjoyed the advantage of getting firsthand knowledge of what he was writing about, which may have lent the revised editions of the *Treatise* a new air of authenticity.

In 1819, when he joined the faculty of the Conservatory of Arts and Crafts, he became the first academic teacher of political economy on the European Continent. During the last two years of his life, he enjoyed an even more prestigious position as professor of political economy at the College of France in Paris. By that time, a new generation of classical French economists had completed their training, and they did much to give added luster to the name of the founder of French classical economics. This tribute was well deserved, for Say, not satisfied with the *Wealth of Nations* as a model, had both criticized its weaknesses and enlarged upon it with notable originality.

Say's other works, *A Catechism of Political Economy* (1817) and *A Complete Course in Practical Political Economy* (1828–29), contained few ideas — beyond those already expressed in his standard work — that might have further enhanced his stature.

B.—*Thomas Robert Malthus* (1766–1834) was the son of a country gentleman and lawyer of comfortable circumstances. First as a tutor, then as a benevolent counselor, the elder (Daniel) Malthus took an active part in his son's mental and spiritual growth. Robert's distinguished years as a student of theology, classical languages, and mathematics began in 1784 at Cambridge, from which he graduated four years later. Although he had taken holy orders, he preferred to stay at Cambridge nine more years and did not become a parish minister of the Church of England until 1797.

By that time, he had been thoroughly aroused by the utopian ideas held by Godwin (*An Enquiry concerning Political Justice,* 1793) and Condorcet (*Sketch of the Progress of the Human Spirit,* 1795), both of whom proclaimed the gospel of the perfectibility of man through the development of his reasoning powers, a process which, in time, would allow cessation of reproduction and virtually lead to immortality of man!

The immediate cause for Malthus' breaking into print with a set of views that shocked the literary world in short order was a friendly argument with his father, who — perhaps in part to bring out the best in his son's debating skill — had taken the side of the two idealistic philosophers. At any rate, young Malthus overnight became an anonymous celebrity with his *Essay on the Principle of Population, as It Affects the Future Improvement of Society, with Remarks on the Speculations of Mr. Godwin, M. Condorcet, and Other Writers.* Published in 1798, this pamphlet-size booklet had the effect of a bombshell.

Partly in order to be better prepared to stand his ground in the storm of vituperations hurled against this allegedly misguided clergyman, the author subsequently undertook empirical research on the continent of Europe and, in 1803, was ready with a much enlarged, better grounded, and more carefully expressed set of views, published under his own name. If his critics had hoped to be able to silence this heterodox population theorist, they were bitterly disappointed, for the work went through four more editions before Malthus' death. Since it lies on the margin of economics, it is not further discussed in the body of this text. His fundamental thesis — that man's procreative powers are at odds with the powers of the earth to supply him with his means of subsistence — has retained much plausibility to the present day, at least in some of the most densely populated countries of the world hovering, decade after decade, on the margin of subsistence.

Moral (prudential) restraint, which Malthus had recommended in the second edition as a preventive check to inordinate population growth, might perhaps take the sting out of the previously mentioned positive checks — famine, disease, war, and the like. However, on the whole, this preventive check has remained a rather tenuous link in the chain of factors keeping world population within bounds. Malthus himself did not expect too much of it, and it is no wonder that economics came soon to be known as the dismal science (Carlyle).

In the meantime, Malthus had been appointed professor of political economy and modern history at a new college of the East India Company at Haileybury, where young men were trained for service abroad. He taught at this small institution with acclaim from 1805 until his death almost thirty years later. (Setting a fair example of "moral restraint," he did not marry until 1804, and his offspring numbered only three.)

In 1811, he began a friendship with David Ricardo and subsequently engaged in a lively correspondence and much oral exchange through visits with the famous financier-turned-writer. Although the two started from different premises and looked at current problems from different points of view, thus never arriving at essentially the same conclusions, their differences did not disturb the spirit of cordiality in which each tried to enlighten the other.

On hindsight, it may strike us as unfortunate that Ricardo's system in effect won the day, thereby channeling economic thought along lines somewhat devoid of strong empirical foundations. For years to come, the scales remained unbalanced with an overload of abstractions — reasoning from just a few, not well verified hypotheses — but Keynes, more than a century later, gave Malthus, whose penchant for induction was shared by few fellow economists, his due as a realistic observer of forces making for disequilibrium (see Chapter 14).

Today Malthus' *Principles of Political Economy Considered with a View to Their Practical Applications* (1820) enjoys recognition equal, if not superior, to Ricardo's main work. Many now would consider it the more fruitful of the two principal alternative developments that Smith's *Wealth of Nations* underwent at the hands of economists of the next generation.

Malthus also took an active part in Britain's economic policy controversies toward the end of the Napoleonic Wars. He stated his views on questions of the day in a number of pamphlets, in one of which he argued — contrary to Ricardo — for restricting the importation of foreign corn. Though he never saw public service in the manner of Smith and Ricardo, and though he took no active part in the intellectual ferment produced by Bentham and the Philosophical Radicals, he was always much concerned with the "greatest good of the greatest number," his recommendations of restraint in supporting the indigent with public funds notwithstanding. His stature as a truth-loving, indefatigable scholar was never questioned by those equally sincere and gifted and is attested to by his role as co-founder of the Political Economy Club in 1821 and of the Royal Statistical Society in 1834.

C.—*David Ricardo* (1772–1823), born in London, was the son of a Jewish stockbroker of Spanish descent who migrated from Holland to England and made a name for himself in the financial community. The elder Ricardo was able, perhaps not without pressure, to interest his son in a similar career, for at the early age of fourteen, after only a rudimentary commercial education, David became actively involved as an assistant in his father's business. However, in his capacity as a faithful servant to an authoritative elder, he could not give free reign to his ambitions. He vigorously asserted the independence of his own mind when, contrary to his father's wishes, he gave up the Jewish faith at the age of twenty-one and married a Quakeress. The consequent domestic estrangement made it necessary for him to strike out on his own; and with some help from other members of the Stock Exchange, whose admiration he had won by his extraordinary professional ability and strength of character, he was able to jump the initial financial hurdles.

By the age of twenty-five, this young business genius had already accumulated a considerable fortune; and he could now begin to devote himself to broader intellectual pursuits, initially in the field of science and beginning in 1799 — when he first came across a copy of Smith's *Wealth of Nations* — in the field whose cultivation was to bring him permanent fame.

It was not until ten years later that he ventured into writing for publication. *The High Price of Bullion, a Proof of the Depreciation of Bank Notes* brought him immediate acclaim. In these letters to a newspaper, expanded in 1810 into a tract bearing the same title, Ricardo demonstrated that, rather than gold having appreciated in value, the notes of the Bank of England had depreciated in value and that this depreciation was measured by the premium charged for gold. When in 1811 Ricardo hurled his devastating *Reply to Mr. Bosanquet's Practical Observations on the Report of the Bullion Committee* against a gentleman who had great experience as a merchant but lacked in clear perception of basic monetary principles, he expertly defended the conclusions of a parliamentary committee of inquiry in what was perhaps the hottest economic controversy of the day. While Ricardo had not himself been a member of the study committee, his earlier publication had already established the canons which pervaded the Report. We will return to the divisive controversy in Chapter 10.

Having further enhanced his fortune as a financier for the British government during the Napoleonic Wars, he retired in 1814 from active business and settled down to the life of a country gentleman. Three years later the unfinished draft of his only book, *Principles of Political Economy and Taxation*, went to the publisher's. It has ever since been known as one of the most abstractly reasoned works in economics. Like Malthus' *Principles*, it aimed at — but did not quite achieve — a comprehensive view of the subject matter of our science, and developed in a different direction, based on critical analytical refinements, many of Smith's trains of thought. Unlike Smith's contributions, however, Ricardo's theory of value and distribution, the body of his work, did not abound in homespun historical illustrations but was addressed to the professional economist rather than the reader with a general education. Nevertheless, feeding on the interest of a group of ardent disciples, it went through two more editions before Ricardo's death six years later. It found in James Mill, father of John Stuart, the most deeply devoted editorial assistant, and in J. R. McCulloch the least critical propagator of the doctrines expounded within its covers. It also added zest to a friendly controversy in writing between Ricardo and Malthus, who had known each other since about 1811; but few of Malthus' critical suggestions convinced Ricardo of the need to reformulate his statements. In the famous Corn Laws Controversy that raged in England especially between 1813 and 1815, each of the two "stuck to his guns," with Ricardo steadfastly advocating the gradual freeing of the import trade in corn and Malthus, viewing high rents as the best possible evidence of a nation's true prosperity, arguing no less earnestly for protection of British agriculture.

Ricardo elaborated his free-trade position especially in pamphlets published in 1815 and 1822; the later one entitled *On Protection to Agriculture* was perhaps the most persuasive of his minor writings. Strangely enough, he took this liberal position despite the fact that he had become proprietor of an estate and, hence, would seem to have been tempted to advocate policies beneficial to the maintenance of high rents from land. Tempted he may well have been, but he did not hesitate to lay bare the self-interest of landed proprietors as in conflict with higher interests. His pleas for the promotion of the public good, even when it was at odds with policies advocated by his own class, testify to the sincerity of his singular quest for truth. They made him ideally suited to become a politician (without party affiliation) during the last four years of his life.

He served with distinction as a member of the House of Commons, overcoming in time the initial paralyzing doubts about his effectiveness as a speaker and public servant. His modestly given advice was highly regarded in parliamentary circles, and his eagerness to enrich the pamphlet literature with proposed solutions to everyday economic problems never ceased.

Before succumbing to a painful ear infection in his fifty-second year, he counted among his friends not only the ubiquitous Malthus, McCulloch, and James Mill, but also Jeremy Bentham, spiritual head of the Philosophical Radicals, and the Frenchman J. B. Say. Though never an academician himself, Ricardo had been fully accepted as a keen scientific thinker whose acumen matched the best that had been produced in Britain's halls of learning.

D.—*Nassau William Senior* (1790–1864) was the first English economist to occupy an endowed chair of political economy. In his early twenties, he had studied law at Oxford; he graduated with an M.A. degree in 1815. Admitted to the bar in 1819, he found that law practice did not best suit his physical and mental disposition. After doing "postgraduate" work in political economy, he was honored by the appointment to the newly established Drummond Chair at Oxford for the 1825–1830 period. By the rules governing its occupancy, he was not eligible for a consecutive term but was returned to it in 1847. After the expiration of his second appointment, he was retained as a professor of political economy at Oxford until his death.

In the 1830's and 1840's, he earned the gratitude of the public-spirited for his performance as a Master in Chancery (member of a court of equity) and as an investigator on various royal commissions. Producing a respectable quantity of factual research, he was instrumental in shaping the recommendations for an amendment to the Poor Law (1834) and for legislation dealing with factory conditions, the situation of hand-loom weavers, and education. Much of his thought on economic matters is thus buried in blue books, and this largely explains why in his time he was looked on primarily as a reformer.

Work as a professional economist culminated in his *An Outline of the Science of Political Economy*, first published in article form in the *Encyclopedia Metropolitana* in 1836, revised in 1850. Reminiscent of Ricardo's *Principles*, the arrangement of materials in this slender volume leaves much to be desired, the lack of organization reflecting the fact that appeal to a large readership most certainly was not a motivating factor in its composition. However, the work bears numerous traces of subjective originality and, in contrast with the writings of James Mill and J. R. McCulloch, refreshes the reader by the absence of doctrinaire orthodoxy.

The flexibility of Senior's outlook was enhanced by his frequent travels abroad, financed by a modicum of independent means. This widening of horizons was manifested by acquaintanceship with some of the more eminent of continental thinkers, including J. B. Say. In fact, Senior's emphasis on utility as a value determinant may well have been inspired by this early expounder of the French brand of classical doctrine. Much of the remainder of his mental makeup was due to the formative influence of an Irish Archbishop, Richard Whately, Senior's tutor. A few aberrations borne out of sloppy reasoning, coupled with glib generalizing by careless contemporary readers, tended to give Senior the undeserved reputation of standing for a doctrinaire laissez-faire policy. Apparently he has never been forgiven for having stated that a reduction of daily working hours in cotton mills by one eleventh would be disastrous because it would wipe out profits completely — assuming profits to be 10 percent, he argued that they were all generated during the last hour of the working day!

However, such slips hardly affected John Stuart Mill's receptive and close attention to, and reinterpretative use of, what Senior had poured into the mold of his *Outline*. And many decades later, Senior's stature was immeasurably enhanced by the discovery and subsequent publication (1928) in two volumes, entitled *Industrial Efficiency and Social Economy*, of a large batch of his manuscripts. In recent decades he has thus emerged as a much more mature thinker than his contemporaries were prepared to view him; his powers of critical analysis were probably second to none among the classical economists.

E.—*John Stuart Mill* (1806–1873) was one of the chief intellectual figures of the nineteenth century, a mental athlete who could be claimed as one of their great by more than one school or discipline. That he was a builder of bridges between many branches of the social sciences, and that he was equally at home in philosophy and associationist psychology, enhances his overall stature, even though it be granted that such a broadly sweeping intellect was unlikely to churn the depths of all the seas he set out to explore. "Lack of originality" has been an epithet with which economists perhaps more often than political scientists and sociologists have tagged him, yet this would have happened less often had Mill (1) not modestly brushed off the possible expectations of his readers that they were about to follow a bold adventurer into uncharted territory, (2) presented his economic views in a less voluminous work than the *Principles*, in which the strands of original thinking would have stood out more conspicuously, (3) seemed to be less in a hurry. Covering over one thousand pages, the *Principles*, more extensive than the *Wealth of Nations*, was committed to paper within the incredibly short period of about eighteen months and during off-hours from a full-time job.

What were some of the prerequisites for the attainment of a mind whose springs were so tautly wound? First and foremost, he had been the guinea pig in a rare and almost frightening educational experiment. When his father, James Mill, was still a free-lance writer without certain prospects for a materially comfortable existence, yet had embarked upon a siring spree the like of which made a shamble of Malthus' modest hopes for the inculcation of a sense of prudential restraint, he seems to have channeled his life's ambitions into a process of force-feeding his firstborn child, John. Already a convert to Bentham's utilitarian philosophy, James viewed domestic education as a fertile field for testing the workability of some of the ideas of the group headed by Bentham, who shortly became known as the Philosophical Radicals. In pursuit of "truth," the father mercilessly exposed the star of his hopes to a daily routine paced frantically with the study of Greek and Latin, mathematics and ethics, all this about five to ten years ahead of customary programs of learning. At the age of thirteen, John Stuart was called upon to assess his father's understanding of political economy as distilled from Ricardo: the older Mill, having expounded his ideas, depended on his precocious son for written accounts of his daily "lectures." Through this process of sifting and evaluating grew the body of a book by James Mill, which in 1821 was published under the title *Elements of Political Economy.*

In the meantime, largely on the strength of his *History of British India* (1817), James Mill had secured a position with the East India Company, and in 1823 he managed to draw his son into the services for this prestigious concern. The years just prior to accepting what became a lifetime position — John Stuart remained with the company until its dissolution as a semiprivate enterprise in 1858 — saw him as a visitor to France and a student of law. The time spent across the English Channel molded young Mill into a lifelong friend of the institutions of his host country; after his death in 1873, his body was interred in Avignon, as had been his wife's, whom he survived by fifteen years.

As a member of the Benthamite circle, John Stuart first became a full-fledged adherent and active propagator (through articles in the Westminster Review) of the creed. But, in 1829, he underwent a serious mental crisis — compared in his autobiography to a religious conversion — that shook him loose from foundations too artificially and rigorously planted for permanent comfort. Filial piety prevented him from breaking openly with Utilitarianism until after 1836, the year of his father's death. But even after he finally could breathe more freely, and in the wake of a decline of Philosophical Radicalism in the late 1830's, he was unable to jettison all of the doctrinaire cargo. He remained a firm believer in the blessings of liberalism and free competition, albeit the waves of socialist criticism that had begun to ruffle the ocean of orthodox political economy with the ominous rumblings of Sismondi (see Chapter 14), Rae, and Lauderdale never receded.

The forces that pulled Mill in different directions became stronger in time — his intellectual curiosity and honesty prevented him from closing his mind to influences alien to his own edifice of thought. Among these environmental forces, the most powerful was that of Harriet Taylor, whom, after a platonic friendship of more than twenty years, while her first husband still lived, he married in 1851. His strange blend of reformist attitudes, coupled with a penchant toward socialism, were reflected in his publications during the remaining quarter of his life.

Mill, prior to his marriage, had already made a name for himself with his splendid *System of Logic* (1843) and his *Essays on Some Unsettled Questions of Political Economy* (1844). The *Principles of Political Economy* (1848), intended as an up-to-date Smith, but in reality a readable, graceful, and delightful Ricardo, with the broadness of scope that characterized the *Wealth of Nations,* raised him to a pinnacle of fame and went through many editions during Mill's lifetime. It was far from replaced, though made more vulnerable, by Jevons' *Principles of Political Economy,* published in 1871 (see Chapter 3). Like Ricardo, Mill gave substance to his concern for the public good by serving in the English Parliament, namely, from 1865 to 1868. Living in line with the high moral tone that issued from his literary output, his life was outwardly uneventful but was pervaded by an inner vitality and glow that still radiates its charm on his readers.

Questions for Review and Research

1. What do you know about the life of Smith's first and principal spokesman and interpreter on the European Continent? What relations, if any, are there between this man's specific creative contributions to political economy and his career?
2. Give Say's views of the categories of (a) "productive" activities and (b) wealth.
3. Was Say merely restating Smith's findings in describing the factors responsible for the creation of value? Explain.
4. Why did Malthus substitute "personal services" for Smith's "unproductive labor"?
5. What are the three kinds of value distinguished by Malthus and the meanings he attached to each?
6. How did Malthus define rent? Does this definition differ in important respects from Ricardo's rent concept?
7. What is the principal legacy of Ricardo's contributions to value theory? Was Ricardo more interested in problems of production or distribution?
8. According to Ricardo, what is the normal ratio of exchange between two commodities?
9. Why, in Ricardo's view, was it impossible for labor to obtain a larger share of total value without capital experiencing a diminution of its share and vice versa?
10. State in your own words Senior's Four Postulates.
11. What are the names of the principal works in value and distribution theory written by Malthus, Ricardo, Senior, and J. Stuart Mill? When was each of them published?
12. Explain J. Stuart Mill's distinction between (a) productive and unproductive labor and (b) productive and unproductive consumption.

Recommended Readings

Malthus, Thomas Robert. *Principles of Political Economy, Considered with a View to Their Practical Application,* 2d ed. New York: Augustus M. Kelley, Publishers, 1951. "Introduction," pp. 1–19; Chapter I, "Of the Definition of Wealth and of Productive Labour," pp. 21–49; Chapter II, "On the Nature, Causes, and Measures of Value," Sections 1–6, pp. 50–122.

Mill, John Stuart. *Principles of Political Economy, with Some of Their Applications to Social Philosophy,* 5th ed., 2 vols. New York: Appleton-Century-Crofts, 1866.
    Volume I: "Preliminary Remarks," pp. 17–42.
        Book I, "Production": Chapter I, "Of the Requisites of Production," pp. 45–52; Chapter III, "Of Unproductive Labour," pp. 71–82.
        Book II, "Distribution": Chapter III, "Of the Classes Among Whom the Produce Is Distributed," pp. 301–305; Chapter IV, "Of Competition and Custom," pp. 306–313.

Book III, "Exchange": Chapter I, "Of Value," pp. 535–543; Chapter II, "Of Demand and Supply, in Their Relation to Value," pp. 544–554; Chapter III, "Of Cost of Production, in Its Relation to Value," pp. 555–561; Chapter VI, "Summary of the Theory of Value," pp. 588–593.
Volume II: Book III, "Exchange (cont.)": Chapter XVI, "Of Some Peculiar Cases of Value," pp. 120–125.

Ricardo, David. *The Principles of Political Economy and Taxation.* Everyman's Library. New York: E. P. Dutton & Co., Inc., 1912. Chapter 1, "On Value," pp. 5–32; Chapter 2, "On Rent," pp. 33–45; Chapter 5, "On Wages," pp. 52–63; Chapter 6, "On Profits," pp. 64–76; Chapter 20, "Value and Riches, Their Distinctive Properties," pp. 182–191; Chapter 21, "Effects of Accumulation on Profits and Interest," pp. 192–200; Chapter 30, "On the Influence of Demand and Supply on Prices," pp. 260–262; Chapter 31, "On Machinery," pp. 263–271.

St. Clair, Oswald. *A Key to Ricardo.* New York: Kelley & Millman, Inc., 1957.

Say, Jean-Baptiste. *A Treatise on Political Economy; or the Production, Distribution, and Consumption of Wealth,* translated by C. R. Prinsep, 2 vols. London: Longman, Hurst, Rees, Orme, and Brown, 1821.
Volume 1:
Book I, "Of the Production of Wealth": Chapters 1–13, pp. 1–135.
Volume 2:
Book II, "Of the Distribution of Wealth": Chapters 7 and 8, pp. 91–164.
Book III, "Of the Consumption of Wealth": Chapters 1–5, pp. 221–274.

Senior, Nassau W. *An Outline of the Science of Political Economy,* 1st ed. London: William Clowes and Sons, Ltd., 1836. "Introduction," pp. 1–5; "Nature of Wealth, "pp. 6–25; "Statement of the Four Elementary Propositions of the Science," pp. 26–86.

VALUE AND DISTRIBUTION THEORY

From Cournot to Walras

EARLY CONTRIBUTIONS TO MARGINAL ANALYSIS

We will now catch a glimpse of the workshop of some pioneers in marginal analysis: two Frenchmen, two Germans, and an Englishman. With varying success, they all strove for the utmost in precision, and they foreshadowed much of present-day work in economics.

Cournot[1]

The French classical tradition, which had been firmly established by Say and his followers, toward the middle of the nineteenth century acquired a new orientation that is best illustrated by the quality of Cournot's work. His brilliant and original mind laid the foundation for the mathematical treatment of the processes of exchange and thus contributed to freeing political economy from the utilitarian and laissez-faire policy implications of the main body of writings that were published between 1776 and 1848. Be it noted that mathematics provided a new *method*, rather than serving as the intellectual focus of a new school, a fact which is fully appreciated by those who hold that the work of the professional economist should be limited to an analysis of the exchange process.

In his *Researches into the Mathematical Principles of the Theory of Wealth* (1838), Cournot set himself a modest goal, namely, to restate a number of economic relationships that were particularly well suited to treatment in terms of *functions*. He did not aim either at the discovery of new principles or at the reformulation of rules of policy. The core of his labors is found in Chapters 4–10, which deal with the demand function, the theory of monopoly and that of perfect competition, as well as the cases of duopoly, bilateral monopoly, and oligopoly. While his

---

[1]See Biographical Note A.

approach was that of *partial equilibrium analysis*, he was not blind to
the theoretical desirability of taking the entire economic system under
analytical purview; some thirty-five to forty years later, the first fruits
of the more comprehensive mathematical approach left their imprint
in the general equilibrium system of Walras who is counted, with
Jevons and Menger, as one of three principal founders of the Marginalist school.

In order to appreciate Cournot's performance, it is necessary to
realize that practically no *theory of monopoly* had existed before him.
In laying the foundations, the Frenchman pointed out that the demand
function and, consequently, the total and marginal revenue functions
are data for the monopolist. Revenue functions can be confronted
with total and marginal cost functions; the latter, in contrast with the
former, may be at least in part subject to control by the monopolist,
since in some cases he may be able to choose among several plants of
varying efficiency. Cournot derived the important proposition that
present gain would be maximized if the monopolist set a price at which
marginal revenue equals marginal cost.

Cournot also recognized that a monopolist's cost structure may be
more favorable than that of a purely competitive industry and that
the determinacy of monopoly price is of a nature different from that
which pertains to competitive price: the competitive seller has to
accept the ruling price, the monopolist seeks the one price at which he
maximizes his revenue, either in the short or in the long run. Cournot
does not seem to have glimpsed the problems posed by price discrimination, which later came to be recognized as a foremost aspect of a
monopolist's strategy. Below is a sample of Cournot's approach.

. . . . suppose that a man finds himself proprietor of a mineral spring
which has just been found to possess salutary properties possessed by
no other. He could doubtless fix the price of a *liter* of this water at 100
francs; but he would soon see by the scant demand, that this is not the
way to make the most of his property. He will therefore successively
reduce the price of the liter to the point which will give him the greatest
possible profit; *i.e.* if $F(p)$ denotes the law of demand, he will end, after
various trials, by adopting the value of p which renders the product
$pF(p)$ a maximum, or which is determined by the equation

$$(1) \qquad F(p) + pF'(p) = 0.$$

The product $\quad pF(p) = \dfrac{[F(p)]^2}{-F'(p)}$

will be the annual revenue of the owner of the spring, and this revenue
will only depend on the nature of function F.

To make equation (1) applicable, it must be supposed that for the value of p obtained from it, there will be a corresponding value of D which the owner of the spring can deliver, or which does not exceed the annual flow of this spring; otherwise the owner could not, without damage to himself, reduce the price per liter as low as would be for his interest were the spring more abundant. If the spring produces annually a number of liters expressed by $\triangle$, by deducing p from the relation $F(p) = \triangle$, we necessarily obtain the price per liter which must finally be fixed by the competition of customers.[2]

To illustrate Cournot's mathematical symbolism, assume the following demand schedule, where p = price of a commodity, $F(p)$ = x = quantity demanded of that commodity:

p	$F(p)$
8	0
6	1
4	2
2	3
0	4

The demand function can then be expressed by the equation $F(p) = x = 4 - \frac{p}{2}$, and its first derivative will be $F'(p) = x' = -\frac{1}{2}$.

The monopolist will seek to maximize his total revenue $(xp) = R$. By substitution

$$R = px = p\,F(p) = p\left(4 - \frac{p}{2}\right) = 4p - \frac{p^2}{2}.$$

Since profit is maximized where marginal revenue $(R') = 0$, we have to find the value of p where $R' = 0$. Since $R' = dR/dp = 4 - \frac{2p}{2} = 4 - p$, this is the case where $p = 4$. At $p = 4$, $F(p) = 2$, and the monopolist will maximize his revenue if he sells 2 units at a price of 4. Before inserting these values into Cournot's equations, note the transposition of (1). If $F(p) + pF'(p) = 0$, then $F(p) = -pF'(p) = p[-F'(p)]$. Hence $p = \dfrac{F(p)}{-F'(p)}$.

Multiplying this expression by $F(p)$, we get Cournot's equation

$$pF(p) = \frac{[F(p)]^2}{-F'(p)}.$$

Substituting the above values into Cournot's equation (1), we get

$$2 + 4\left(-\tfrac{1}{2}\right) = 2 - 2 = 0$$

[2]Augustin Cournot, *Researches into the Mathematical Principles of the Theory of Wealth*, translated by Nathaniel T. Bacon (Reprints of Economic Classics: New York: Augustus M. Kelley, Publishers, 1960), pp. 56–57.

and verifying his expression for maximum revenue

$$4 \, (2) \; = \; \frac{[2]^2}{- \, (\, - \frac{1}{2})} \; = \; \frac{4}{\frac{1}{2}} \; = \; 8.$$

We note that the next higher (6) and the next lower (2) price in the above demand schedule, total revenue would be only 6.

Instead of taking the case of perfect competition as his starting point (as is customary today in introducing students to various market structures), Cournot began his treatment of price and output determination with monopoly and worked through duopoly to perfect competition. In the case of *two sellers*, he assumed that one duopolist set the quantity sold and stood back to observe the price reaction, supposing that the rival's output was independent of his own. This action would, in turn, necessitate an output adjustment on the part of the second duopolist, an adjustment based on his requirements for profit maximization. But this would call for a revision of output plans by the first of the two sellers. Thus, through a process of *trial and error*, the duopolists would eventually arrive at output-price combinations which would call for no further adjustments, since neither seller could improve his profits by departing from his position.

Incidentally, on Cournot's assumptions such a determinate equilibrium would also be the end result in the case of *oligopoly*; but such a solution, because it necessitates the stipulation of very restrictive assumptions, has been deemed impractical by later investigators of the problem, especially by Edgeworth.[3] On the other hand, Cournot was not blind to the fact that the output of maximum profit for the sellers depends on the elasticity of demand for the good in question. Despite its shortcomings, the Cournot model remained a part of modern oligopoly theory.

We should note that the permanent place occupied by Cournot in the history of value theory does not stem from any specific contribution to utility theory as such. He was simply not concerned with the relation between exchange value and utility. To conclude that he did not think that the utility assigned to different goods by different consumers had anything to do with the formation of exchange value would be clearly inadmissible, however. Rather, he saw his mission in a refinement of the technical apparatus of our science. Undoubtedly he succeeded in

---

[3] Edgeworth, an English mathematical economist of the late nineteenth century, will be discussed briefly in Chapter 6.

demonstrating that there was a definite place for the use of mathematical symbols in economic analysis, that it was possible to express market relations in a series of equations, in brief that certain economic laws, or at least hypotheses, could be formulated more elegantly in mathematical language.

Von Thünen[4]

Johann Heinrich von Thünen, a German landowner and farmer during much of the first half of the nineteenth century, was a highly original and truly remarkable thinker. There is something refreshingly unique about him, for he arrived at his theories in the course of actually *experimenting* with the variables whose interrelationships he explored, manifesting a singularly profound understanding of the relation between theory and facts. His foremost claim to fame rests on the up-to-then full statement of the *marginal productivity theory of the factors of production.*

His starting point was Ricardian, although his conclusions were much broader with respect to both rent and other factorial shares. Following Ricardo — but perhaps without having read the latter's *Principles of Political Economy and Taxation* — he was aware of the differences in cost of production of agricultural commodities resulting from use of lands of differing fertility and location. He saw that some lands lend themselves to being cultivated intensively, whereas others pay for the cost of production of produce only if cultivated extensively. He viewed the optimum intensiveness of cultivation as the result of two independent conditions: the physical quality of the land and its proximity to a market in which its output can be sold. At the same time, he recognized that different types of produce are not equally well suited to extensive or intensive cultivation; those that are bulky in relation to value are more costly to transport than their opposites. Furthermore, some do not lend themselves to lengthy transportation because of their perishability.

The Beginnings of Location Theory.—Thünen's merit was not so much to have been cognizant of all these conditions and variables as to have constructed an *analytic model* in which they could be logically related and which would demonstrate the locations required for most economical operation of major branches of agriculture. Discussion of the implications of the model absorbs most of the space of the first volume (1826) of his *The Isolated State in Relation to Agriculture*

---

[4]See Biographical Note B.

and Political Economy. He stipulated the following assumptions, which are basic for an understanding and judicious use of his conclusions:

(1) A town is located in the center of a fertile plain bordered by a wilderness.

(2) All land between the central market and the unexplored periphery is of homogeneous quality.

(3) There are no obstacles to, or special facilities for, transportation which would give some of the cultivated land a locational advantage over other cultivated land.

(4) There is no trade with the "outside" world.

Under these conditions, what will be the pattern of land use? Thünen answered that it will be reflected in a series of concentric rings around the town as illustrated below.

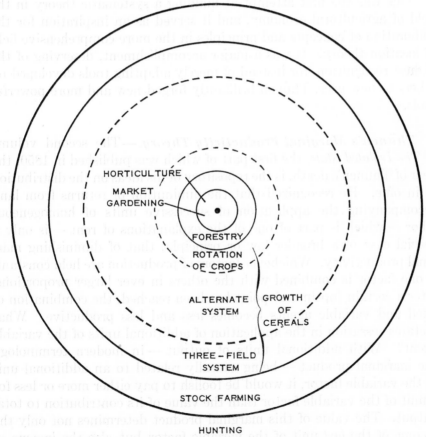

HORTICULTURE

MARKET
GARDENING

FORESTRY

ROTATION
OF CROPS

ALTERNATE   GROWTH
SYSTEM   OF
                 CEREALS

THREE – FIELD
SYSTEM

STOCK FARMING

HUNTING

THÜNEN'S "ISOLATED STATE"

(A graphic presentation of his theory of agricultural location.)

Commodities that are perishable, that do not tolerate heavy transportation cost, or lend themselves to intensive cultivation, will be grown near the consuming market; those governed by the opposite conditions will tend to be grown at a relatively long distance from it. In accordance with such considerations, market gardening and horticulture will be concentrated in the innermost circle, which is enveloped by a zone of *sylviculture* (intensive cultivation of forests to supply the town with building materials and fuel). Moving outward into the next concentric ring, we find the growth of cereals to be most advantageous, but subdivisions appear according to the need to vary cultivation between crop rotation, alternation between crops and pasture, and a three-field system. The fourth ring-shaped zone is given over primarily to stock raising; any land beyond will be good enough only for hunting.

This was the first attempt at building a systematic theory in the field of agricultural economy, and it served as an inspiration for the elaboration of concepts and principles in the more comprehensive field of location theory. It was a major accomplishment, deserving of the highest recognition, for instead of merely adapting tools developed by others to new uses, Thünen brilliantly forged new and more powerful tools.

Thünen's Marginal Productivity Theory.—The second volume of *The Isolated State*, the first part of which was published in 1850, the year of Thünen's death, is the repository of his ideas on the distribution of income. He recognized that the diminution of returns from land accompanying the application of successive units of homogeneous labor — which is part of one of the explanations of rent — is only a special case of a broader law or principle: that of diminishing marginal productivity. Whichever factors of production are held constant, if one factor is combined with the others in ever larger proportions, after a certain (optimum) point has been reached, the combination of fixed and variable agents becomes less and less productive. What dictates cessation in the application of additional units of the variable agent? With additional units of output — in modern terminology the marginal product — being causally related to an additional unit of the variable factor, it would be foolish to pay either more or less for a unit of the variable factor than the value of its contribution to total output. The value of this marginal product determines not only the income of the *last* unit of the variable factor but also the income of any other unit of that factor. For just as under conditions of competition there can be only one price for the homogeneous units of any finished good, so there can be only one price for the use of homogeneous units of the factors labor and capital. Thus, wage rates and interest are determined by the marginal productivity of labor and capital.

One of the corollaries of his productivity theory of distribution baffled Thünen. On the one hand, justice demanded that workers of equal skill receive equal wages — wages equal to the marginal revenue product. On the other hand, all workers except the marginal one (which could be any one!) contributed more to total output than did the latter, for *if* fewer workers were used, the marginal product would be inevitably greater. Thünen concluded that there is an unavoidable element of exploitation if labor is paid according to the marginal productivity theory of wages. Coping lengthily with this problem, he eventually came up with a formula for what he called the natural wage: $w = \sqrt{ap}$, where a is the amount spent by wage workers for subsistence, p the net value of the national product, and w the total payroll. Paying the natural wage would allow the owner of the business to retain enough to continue his operations while, at the same time, giving the worker a stake in the enterprise, permitting him to benefit from a rise in productivity. It should be noted that this profit-sharing formula does not embody Thünen's theory of the "market wage," but it reflects his efforts to get at something better than the result produced by the market. It is to his credit that he put the idea into practice and left the world with the will that the formula be engraved on his tombstone as a monument to his sincere convictions.

Gossen[5]

Hermann Heinrich Gossen was the *first to apply the concept of the margin to utility* and has been considered as the real founder of the modern theory of value. He worked out his ideas in a book published in 1854 under the title *Development of the Laws of Exchange among Men and of the Consequent Rules of Human Action*. He was disturbed by the fact that the laws of exchange had not been reduced to mathematical exactness, and he did not hesitate to apply the apparatus of mathematics to his analysis of the laws of human conduct. Influenced by Bentham's[6] utility calculus, he started with the assumption that rational human beings strive to bring about an optimum balance between utilities and disutilities. He developed two fundamental or primary *laws* and a third one that is merely corollary to the other two.

---

[5]See Biographical Note C.
[6]See Biographical Note D.

The first law rests on the interchangeability of the units of a given good: since one unit is rated like any other unit, including the marginal, the reduction in total utility resulting from the removal of a unit is equivalent to removing the marginal unit. Then, in view of the principle of diminishing marginal utility, any unit of the remaining stock of the good will have a higher value; this simply means that marginal utility is a decreasing function of the stock: the greater the latter, the smaller the former. Since the amount of additional enjoyment derived from the consumption of a good decreases with each additional unit consumed, *marginal utility decreases until it becomes zero at the point of satiety.* In the coordinate plane, with the y-axis representing utility and the x-axis representing quantity, the utility (demand) curve will slope downward from left to right.

Gossen's second law denotes the fact that *a rational consumer will try to maximize total enjoyment derived from a number of goods* that compete for his satisfaction. Maximization is attained *by equalizing the increments of satisfaction or utility derived from these goods.* In other words, the last (marginal) units of money spent on different consumer goods must provide an equal amount of utility; otherwise, the allocation of income to consumer purchases will not be optimal. Putting it still another way, the intensity of desire for different goods, complete satisfaction of which is not possible because of limited resources, must be equal at the point where consumption is discontinued, that is, must occur at a uniform level of want satisfaction.

The third law, no innovation, merely states that *a good has subjective or use value when the quantity supplied is smaller than the quantity needed for complete satisfaction* (satiety). Again, as more units are supplied, the subjective value of each additional unit decreases and eventually becomes zero.

By combining the strands of thought expressed in his "laws," he succeeded better than any of his predecessors in showing that value depends entirely on the relation between the subject and the object, that there is no such thing as absolute value in the external world.

Gossen was an anticipator of insights that matured fully in the 1870's, mainly in the work of Jevons, an Englishman, and Menger (Chapter 4), an Austrian. For example, Jevons went on to show in detail what was merely sketched by Gossen when he pointed out that the pain or disutility accompanying human exertion must be set against the enjoyment for which labor creates the means. Consequently, man can enhance his total enjoyment so long as the increase in enjoyment made possible by the marginal product of labor is greater than the pain inflicted in the creation of that product. In his classification of goods, Gossen foreshadowed what became almost an obsession on the part of members of the Austrian school. His distinction between consumer goods, goods of the second class, and goods of the third class is not particularly logical: he defines second-class goods merely as those consumer goods that are incapable of supplying enjoyment unless they are used jointly with others (later to be called complementary goods), and those of the third class as goods used in the production of other goods; yet here were the germs for an imputation theory that absorbed much of the mental energy of the Austrians.

JEVONS[7]

We now turn to the first among the three principal founders of marginalism, an Englishman with a sensitive temper who strove for early recognition that he felt was unduly withheld from him. His writings display a prickly quality and a sense of aggrieved justice, but they also reflect rare honesty in attributing priorities. Filled with a missionary spirit, Jevons tended to overemphasize the differences between the "new doctrine" and the tenor of the still lingering Smith-Ricardo-Mill school, to which he had somehow to accommodate himself in order to avoid being ignored as an outsider. The uncomfortable necessity, however, of adjusting to the prevalent intellectual climate only enhanced his eagerness to demonstrate by his writings the clean break which he believed the somewhat novel opinion, that "value depends *entirely* [emphasis added] upon utility,"[8] constituted.

There is no doubt that, like the anticipators of the Marginalist school, he started at the pole opposite from that to which the Classicists had been drawn. Jevons regarded labor as neither the origin nor the cause of value but as an indirect determinant of it, working through variations in supply, which in turn would influence what he called the *final degree of utility* (the utility of the last unit). Since he regards the latter as the only *direct* determinant of value, he in effect tones down the construction which the somewhat pointed adjective "entirely" at first suggests. Jevons cannot be dismissed as an upside-down version of Marx, who with his emphasis on labor as the *sole* determinant of the value of commodities was much more radical (see Chapter 16). While Jevons was anything but oblivious or ignorant of the work of the

---

[7]See Biographical Note E.

[8]W. Stanley Jevons, *The Theory of Political Economy* (3d ed.; London: The Macmillan Company, 1888), p. 1.

anticipators, there runs through the two editions published during his lifetime of *The Theory of Political Economy* — a third edition was supervised by his widow in 1888, six years after his death — the unshakable conviction that all the work he undertook in pure theory after 1862 was merely an elaboration of conclusions firmly and distinctly arrived at when he was twenty-seven. At that time he presented a paper entitled "Notice of a General Mathematical Theory of Political Economy" before the Statistical and Economic Section of the British Association for the Advancement of Science. Jevons strikes the reader as a somewhat uneven genius always in a hurry. New brilliant insights might well have evolved from his youthful vision had not an untimely death cut short his crammed labors.

Given to exaggeration, Jevons claimed that his theory of economics was "purely mathematical in character"; in fact, while he did not shun the liberal use of symbols and formulas of the calculus, his principal work is interwoven with many passages stated in ordinary English. Methodologically, Jevons took a less abrupt turn than his friend and correspondent Walras (see page 90), and many portions of his work are thus well within the comprehension of a cultured nonspecialist.

Jevons describes his theory as "the mechanics of utility and self-interest."[9] Fully cognizant of the fact that deduction without empirical verification is a halfway house, he frankly admits that his theoretical structure is still in need of being fleshed out with numerical data drawn from the everyday world of exchange. But holding no less strongly that "correct theoretical notions" must precede the collection of commercial statistics, he has no misgivings about presenting to the world, for what it is worth, a novel apparatus. Should the latter prove faulty and incomplete in the light of facts not yet statistically established, Jevons would gladly see it subjected to whatever refinements are called for by a more intimate union between theory and the "reality of life and fact."

Aware of the fact that the language employed by Bentham, whom we recall as a friend of James Mill and David Ricardo, may lend itself to misapprehension, Jevons nevertheless makes the *pleasure-pain calculus* the underlying basis of his reasoning. If we allow Benthamite terminology to be broadened to mean that "any motive which attracts us to a certain course of conduct"[10] be called pleasure, and that "any motive which deters us from that conduct"[11] be called pain, there can,

---

[9]*Ibid.*, p. 21.
[10]*Ibid.*, p. 24.
[11]*Ibid.*

according to Jevons, no longer be any quibbling over Bentham's dictum that "nature has placed mankind under the governance of two sovereign masters — pain and pleasure."[12] While it cannot be the economist's task to deal with any but "the lowest rank of feelings," to assign a proper place to the pleasures and pains associated with the provision of the ordinary wants of men is a task worthy of the best effort.

Jevons' Utility Calculus

Abstracting from some of Bentham's dimensions of pleasure or pain as either irrelevant to the solution of economic problems or beyond quantification, Jevons limits himself to the circumstances of *intensity* and *duration*. "Every feeling must last some time; while it lasts it may be more or less acute and intense."[13] How can we cope with the difficulty that the intensity of feeling changes all the time? For the sake of simplicity, we may assume that the intensity changes at regular intervals, say after every minute, but remains constant in between. It is then possible to represent the quantity of feeling during every minute by a rectangle whose height, proportional to intensity, is measured along the *y*-axis, and whose base corresponds to equal time units, say minutes.   Diagrammatically, the aggregate quantity of feeling thus appears as the aggregate area of all the rectangles plotted in the *xy*-plane. If the intervals of time are chosen to be infinitely short, that is, if intensity is treated as varying continuously, it becomes possible to represent the variation of feeling in a curve falling from left to right, whose decreasing slope conforms to the assumption that intensity is gradually evening out. The total quantity of feeling generated during any given time is then measured by the area bounded by the two axes, the declining curve, and a line perpendicular to the *y*-axis.

Jevons then proceeds to introduce *pain as the negation of pleasure*. Assuming that the two are bound together, a decrease in pain is the equivalent of an increase in pleasure, and vice versa, so that the problem becomes one of maximizing, in the direction of pleasure, the algebraic sum of a series of pleasures and pains. This implies that we must avoid any action or object which results in a negative balance, one characterized by an excess of pain over pleasure. If a given activity is accompanied first by great pleasure and little pain but subsequently by increasingly less pleasure and increasingly more pain, a point will

---

[12]*Ibid.*, p. 26.
[13]*Ibid.*, p. 29.

be reached where an increment of positive feeling will be just counter-balanced by an increment of negative feeling, where pleasure and pain increments are just equal and their algebraic sum is zero. This is the point at which the activity must stop if the balance of pleasure is to be maximized.

If it be accepted that economics is to rest on the laws of human enjoyment, these laws not being developed by any other science, then J. Stuart Mill, according to Jevons, must have been dead wrong in excluding from economics considerations dealing with the consumption of wealth. This, he seems to suggest, should have been obvious to anybody who is willing to concede that *consumption is the objective of production*, rather than vice versa. Just as a manufacturer cannot afford to disregard the needs and tastes of his customers if he is to survive in the world of business, neither can economics afford to dispense with a correct theory of consumption.

Distinction between Final Degree of Utility and Total Utility

Jevons blames the failure to distinguish between the two concepts indicated in the subtitle for much of the confusion in contemporary economic literature. It is the *final degree of utility* — the utility of the last increment consumed, or the next increment about to be consumed — which *is of concern in ordinary commercial transactions*. Total utility or enjoyment derived by a person from the consumption of a commodity cannot be computed, although it might be interesting to estimate it. Nevertheless, little gain would be derived for economic analysis from such an undertaking. It is the little more or little less, the balancing at the margin, which is of the essence from the standpoint of maximizing utility. "The final degree of utility is that function upon which the Theory of Economics will be found to turn,"[14] except that in the case of certain commodities available in abundance, such as water, the final degree of utility under normal circumstances approaches zero and thus becomes economically irrelevant. It may be these very commodities, however, whose total utility is so infinitely great that we could not exist without them.

Jevons exhibits some inconsistency when he fails to draw a distinction between the final degree of utility derived from a commodity in one single consumption act and that resulting from repeated consumption acts taking place at different times. Perhaps the proper distinction is implied, since in the first case the satisfaction of a specific physical

---

[14] *Ibid.*, p. 52.

want is alluded to, whereas in the second case he refers to a general nonphysical type of enjoyment. However, the lack of comparability of the two does not become clear in the text: "All our appetites are capable of satisfaction or satiety sooner or later. . . . It does not follow . . . that the degree of utility *always* [emphasis added] sinks to zero. This may be the case with some things . . . such as foods, water, air, etc. But the more refined and intellectual our needs become, the less are they capable of satiety. To the desire for articles of taste, science, or curiosity, when once excited, there is hardly a limit."[15] Is there? Certainly, the capacity of a person to absorb scientific knowledge at any one time is subject to hardly less stringent physical limitations than is the capacity of his stomach to absorb food, even though this latter limit will be reached much more quickly than the former. Jevons' examples thus blur over some qualitative differences in want patterns. If the reader be inclined to shrug off the criticism as unfounded because Jevons deals only with variations in the degree of utility of *commodities* as a function of their quantity, he may want to know that by "commodity" the author understands "any object, substance, action, or service, which can afford pleasure or ward off pain."[16] Incidentally, since an object gains access to the rank of a commodity by virtue of possessing the abstract quality called utility, Jevons suggests "discommodity" as the term by which to signify "anything which we desire to get rid of."[17] This suggestion has itself suffered the fate that befalls Jevons' "discommodities" — as an example he mentioned ashes. Fortunately, a more enduring existence has been enjoyed by the *abstract notion* signifying discommodities, the notion of disutility.

Jevons further developed an economic principle which, along with several others, had already been stated in a rudimentary form by Gossen. In the instance of a commodity which is capable of two or more different uses, each of them associated with the creation of utility, a person will have maximized his advantage if, at any given moment, no change in the distribution of the commodity among different uses would yield him more pleasure. This is the same as saying that any small increment of the commodity would enhance total utility as much in one use as in another, or that the final degrees of utility in the two uses are equal. Jevons then takes an additional step by pointing out that *the number of uses capable of yielding utility* is not fixed, but *may itself vary*, depending on the relative abundance or scarcity, at any

[15]*Ibid.*, p. 53.
[16]*Ibid.*, p. 38.
[17]*Ibid.*, p. 58.

given time, of the commodity in question. Illustrative of such cases would be barley, which may be used for bread, feeding cattle, or producing alcohol. A crop failure might so limit the quantity of barley available for different purposes that only its most urgent use, that of serving as staple food for humans, would be justified economically. That is, the final degree of utility of barley, even when barley is used for bread only, would still be higher than the final degree of utility of barley when converted into alcohol, however small a quantity were turned to this secondary use. In such a case, the final degree of utility of a commodity in one employment would exceed that in any other.

Theory of Exchange

From the theory of utility, Jevons in logically compelling fashion developed a theory of exchange. Whereas his use of the new concept of a *trading body* — which may be an individual or an aggregate of individuals appearing in a market as buyer(s) or seller(s) — proved to be of only limited usefulness, this portion of his book brings into relief several insights which became part of the economist's "stock-in-trade" in later decades. His *law of indifference*, according to which "in the same market, at any moment, there cannot be two prices for the same kind of article,"[18] presupposes perfect homogeneity of all portions of a given commodity, so that potential buyers are entirely indifferent as to which particular units of the stock they acquire. In the absence of defective credit on the part of the purchasers and barring any imperfections in the latter's knowledge of the market, merchants who arbitrarily charge different prices for equal and uniform portions of a commodity would not be able to sell the higher-priced portions.

In exchanging one commodity for another, *two trading bodies* (one, for example, possessing only corn and the other only beef) *will continue to trade until the ratio of exchange reflects the ratios of the final degrees of utility of these commodities* in the estimation of the traders. To stop before this point has been reached would be tantamount to foregoing the maximum possible benefit from trade; to go beyond it would involve a sacrifice of utility. Alternatively, the point of equilibrium can be defined as the point at which the parties find the (final) utility gained just equal to the (final) utility lost from trading the two commodities at the established ratio of exchange, or as the point at which an infinitely small additional amount of commodity exchanged will cause neither gain nor loss of utility, at which a net gain would be converted into a net loss in the process of exchange.

---

[18]*Ibid.*, p. 91.

Now since two commodities are seldom exchanged in a ratio of one unit of X for one unit of Y, that is, the quantities exchanged tend to be unequal (say, one pound of silk exchanges for three pounds of cotton), the final degrees of utility of the commodities will also be unequal. For if they were equal, it would be advantageous to continue the exchange. Equilibrium is attained only when "a person procures such quantities of commodities that the final degrees of utility of any pair of commodities are inversely as the ratios of exchange of the commodities."[19] Nevertheless, a person would distribute his income so that the utility of the final increments of all commodities acquired is equalized. Certainly this distribution would vary greatly among different individuals, even if all of them conducted their affairs as economic men. Moreover, if we take into consideration the disutility of parting with commodities (or money) possessed in exchange for the commodities demanded, the following will define the equilibrium condition: a person will have expended his income to greatest advantage when the algebraic sum of the quantities of commodity received and parted with, respectively, *each multiplied by its final degree of utility*, is zero.

The following illustration may help to make clear the meaning of Jevons' equilibrium condition. Assume that an individual spends his income on only one commodity, that his income is sufficient to acquire any amount of the commodity with a final degree of utility which is still positive, and that the inverse relationship between the amount of money income not spent and the final degree of utility of money is determined by a complex of price and income expectations. Assume also that the price of the commodity remains constant as the individual buys more or less of it and that the final degree of utility of money does not change continuously but only as money is spent in ten units or multiples thereof. As long as the final degree of utility of the commodity acquired is positive, the product of the quantity bought and the final degree of utility will yield a positive number; and as long as

Commodity Acquired (+Utility)				Money Parted with (−Utility = Disutility)				Algebraic Sum of (4) and (8)
Price per Unit	Quantity Bought	Final Degree of Utility	Product of (2) × (3)	Amount Spent	When Deprived of Units	Final Degree of Utility	Product of (5) × (7)	
(1)	(2)	(3)	(4)	(5)	(6)	(7)	(8)	(9)
$10	1	30	+30	$10 (−)	1–10	1	−10	+20
10	2	20	+40	20 (−)	11–20	2	−40	0
10	3	12	+36	30 (−)	21–30	3	−90	−54
10	4	6	+24	40 (−)	31–40	4	−160	−136

---

[19]*Ibid.*, p. 139.

the final degree of utility of money increases as the individual parts with more and more of it, the product of the two (indicating negative utility, or disutility) will increase as spending increases, yielding negative numbers.

When only one unit is bought, necessitating the spending of $10, the positive product on the "acquisitions side" of 30 exceeds the negative product on the "outlay side" of 10 by 20 units; but when two commodity units are bought, the positive product of 40 is just matched by the negative product of 40, thus meeting Jevons' equilibrium condition. (The purchase of 3 or more units would progressively tip the balance more and more on the disutility side.)

In conclusion it may be fitting to return to our starting point and take note of the advance which the theory of the origin of value underwent at the hands of Jevons. After having demonstrated that labor can never be the cause of value but at best only a "determining circumstance," Jevons presents his conclusions concerning the relationships between cost of production, supply, utility, and value as follows:

> Cost of production determines supply.
> Supply determines final degree of utility.
> Final degree of utility determines value.[20]

WALRAS[21]

Léon Walras, though spared the utter professional disregard that befell Gossen, shared with him the fate of the pioneer with a vision who — being decades ahead of his contemporaries — meets with general indifference or skepticism. *The revolutionary quality of Walras' pregnant ideas was not fully appreciated until well into the twentieth century*, and his work still stands at the back of much outstanding present-day research.

While usually grouped together with Jevons and Menger as a codiscoverer of the marginal utility concept, Walras' place in the history of economic thought is not adequately characterized by this association. His foremost claim to fame rests on his espousal of *general equilibrium analysis*, of whose mathematical formulation he was truly the founder. Instead of focusing on particular segments of the economy, Walras attempted to take the economic structure in its entirety into his powerful intellectual grip. In developing what has come to be known

---

[20]*Ibid.*, p. 165.
[21]See Biographical Note F.

as the general equilibrium approach, Walras as much as designed a new engine of analysis, more sophisticated, more demanding of rigorous reasoning, but reflecting his unperturbed confidence that mathematics can and must be harnessed for the purpose of making economics a pure science, akin to the natural sciences. In pursuit of this aim, he developed a *system of equations* showing the interdependence of the various functional parts of the economic system, hoping that some day econometrics would make it possible to fill these equations with statistical content so as to render the functional relationships empirically meaningful.

For a long time, Anglo-American economists with mathematical skills but lacking reading proficiency in French were debarred from full access to Walras' magnum opus, the *Elements of Pure Economics*, a work whose first edition was published in two parts in 1874 and 1877 respectively. An excellent English translation of it by Professor William Jaffé was completed in 1954. Since then, the members of the economics fraternity with foreign language deficiencies have been in a position to subject the Walrasian system to firsthand scrutiny.

Outline of the Walrasian System in Nonmathematical Terms

This system of pure economics is, in essence, the theory of the *determination of all prices under an assumed regime of perfectly free competition.* It is also a theory of social wealth, by which Walras means the sum total of all material and immaterial things which can be priced because they are scarce.

His most fundamental distinction is that between *capital goods* or durable goods, and *income goods* or nondurable goods; the former can, while the latter cannot, be used more than once. He includes in capital goods not only produced goods employed in further production but also land and personal faculties. Income goods, on the other hand, encompass not only consumer goods but also raw materials and the services of capital goods. Depending on whether the latter have direct or indirect utility, they are called *consumer services* or *productive services.* Consumer services are thus akin to consumer goods, and productive services belong in the same class as raw materials.

The diagram shown on page 92 may help to clarify the heterodox and complex Walrasian scheme of classifying goods and services.

Having made these distinctions, Walras sees the determination of prices as the joint result of transactions summarized under four partial theories. The determination of the prices of consumer goods and services is explained by the *theory of exchange.* The *theory of production* deals with the determination of prices of raw materials and productive services. The *theory of capitalization* is concerned with the determination of the prices of fixed capital goods, while the determination of the prices of circulating capital goods is the object of the *theory of circulation*. Let us discuss each of these theories briefly.

If the only market is that in which consumer goods and services are bought and sold, we can visualize the approach toward an equilibrium position to occur in successive steps. In the Walrasian model, the prices of consumer goods and services are "cried" (as by an auctioneer) until the quantities offered and the quantities demanded by the various parties are exactly equal for each of the various goods to be traded. One of these goods would serve as the *numéraire*, that is, as the standard in terms of which all exchange ratios are stated.

If next we allow for the fact that consumer goods are products resulting from a combination of productive services or from their application to raw materials, we enlarge our vista and introduce the market considered by the theory of production. In this market, profit-seeking entrepreneurs act as buyers of productive services from, and as sellers of finished products to, landowners, workers, and capitalists. Strictly speaking, this market should be imagined as consisting of a products and a services segment. Again Walras assumes that prices are "cried" at random until there is achieved equality between the sale of factor services and finished products. Equilibrium will be achieved only when entrepreneurs have no reason to expand or contract output, that is, when the selling price of the products is equal to the cost of productive services (including a normal profit) involved in their production. As in the market for consumer goods, prices for productive services and raw materials will rise whenever "demand exceeds supply" and fall whenever "supply exceeds demand."

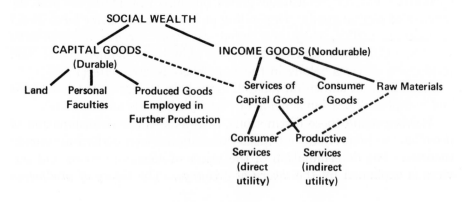

The theory of capitalization further expands the framework of analysis by posing the problem of capital formation. If certain landowners, workers, and capitalists save and demand new capital goods in the amount of their savings, and if there are entrepreneurs who produce new capital goods instead of raw materials or consumer goods, savings and capital goods will be exchanged against each other in a certain ratio. This ratio will depend on the prices of the consumer and productive services yielded by the capital goods, as determined in turn by the theory of exchange and the theory of production. As before, manufacturers of new capital goods will be guided by the relationship between the selling price of their output and its cost of production, equilibrium being attained when these are equal. The *rate of income*, that is, the sum total of the discounted future returns from capital goods, enables us to calculate not only the price of newly manufactured fixed capital goods, but also the price of old fixed capital goods, such as land, capital goods proper, etc.

To find the price of circulating capital, Walras views such capital as rendering a "service of availability," either in kind or in money, the latter making possible the inclusion of the "desired cash balance." The supply of such services of availability is looked upon as coming exclusively from capitalists, and the demand as coming in part from landowners, workers, and capitalists and in part from entrepreneurs, in conformity with Walras' distinction between consumer services and productive services. He thus shows that the current prices of services of availability of circulating capital are determined just as are the prices of all other services.

So far we have stated only *one condition of market equilibrium,* namely, that for each and every commodity the aggregate quantity demanded is equal to the aggregate quantity offered. The *second condition* is that each party to the exchange attain maximum utility from it. Maximum utility is attained only when each party to the exchange demands and offers commodities in such quantities that upon completion of the exchange the *raretés* of these commodities are proportional to their prices. By *rareté* Walras means the intensity of the last want satisfied, which is a decreasing function of the quantity consumed. It corresponds to Jevons' final degree of utility.

It is important to note that in the Walrasian system all the problems of exchange, production, capital formation, and circulation are determinate problems because the number of equations entailed, though extremely large, is exactly equal to the number of unknowns.

A Minuscule Illustration in Nonmathematical Terms

Presenting an overall framework of the price and output interrelationships for the economy as a whole, including both commodities and factors of production, general equilibrium analysis aims at a mathematical demonstration that all prices and quantities produced can adjust to levels which are mutually consistent. Although, being static, this analysis does not provide a framework for actual price determination over time, we may still gain a more concrete flavor of it by dropping a stone, as it were, into the calm pool of a perfectly equilibrated economic system and watching at least the initial ripples.

Assume that, as a result of crop failure in a major producing country, the *price of coffee rises* by 50 percent. Assuming for a moment that everything else remains unchanged except for the reaction of the final consumer, a smaller quantity of coffee will be bought, and, depending on their demand elasticities, final buyers will have either more or less purchasing power to be spent for other commodities. Even with such a partial equilibrium approach, the aggregate schedule of personal savings and the aggregate demand schedules for various commodities would have to be redrawn. And this would be the first step toward general equilibrium analysis.

With tens of millions of European households preferring *café au lait* (perhaps in half-and-half proportions) to black coffee for breakfast or supper, the demand for the complementary good, milk, will drop off — although by less since milk, as contrasted with coffee, will serve as an ingredient for many solid foods, in addition to being drunk (without the admixture of coffee) by many children. But consider the further ramification that the demand for the substitute good, tea, will rise, perhaps causing its price to rise; or that people will substitute a free good, such as water, if substitution is to take place at all. With demand for coffee being highly (or perfectly) elastic, they would in this case spend (much) less on beverages. At the same time, their demand for a nonrelated food item, or a completely nonrelated item such as gasoline, might rise. If the production of gas were subject to increasing or decreasing costs as output expands, consumer purchases might be damped or further stimulated. If they happened on a large enough scale, these changes in the markets of consumer goods would be paralleled by changes in the demand for factor services, whose owners might be forced to shift their employment. Less labor, for example, might be employed on coffee plantations and on dairy farms, in the shipment and processing of coffee and milk, etc.; but additional hands would be called upon to grow tea and to process and market it. The above implies not only that labor services somehow associated with the production and sale of gasoline would also be affected, but, further, that land use and the employment of capital would shift in many places, perhaps making some of the latter obsolete while at the same time necessitating the production of other (new) capital goods. Changes in the demand for and supply of workers in various industries would affect, if only slightly and at several removes, wage demands and wage offers, and some of these might induce the substitution of capital for labor, or vice versa — quite independently of the changed demand for "directly affected" capital goods.

To trace through, in purely theoretical terms, the effects on the economic system of a single disturbance — a supply-caused change in the price of coffee — would already call for the use of a very great number of equations, worthy of processing by the most advanced model of electronic computers on the market.

Conclusion

Before leaving Walras, we may raise the question: In what respects did Walras' work resemble that of Jevons and Gossen, and in what respects did it differ from theirs? Without attempting to give an exhaustive answer, we may point out that the facets of similarity include the large-scale use of mathematics (including the differential calculus), the professed intention of making economics an abstract science rather than a complete social science, and the central place accorded to marginal utility. The points of difference are highlighted by these: Whereas Jevons and Gossen had examined economic equilibrium in specific sectors of the economy, Walras attempted to present an overall view of it, that is, he offered a theory of equilibrium for the economy as a whole. Even if he had proceeded less far, for example, if he had left out of consideration the markets other than that of the exchange of consumer goods, he would still have transcended Gossen and Jevons by virtue of making his analysis of market exchange applicable to any number of commodities, rather than just two.

The proof of the *functional interdependence of demand, supply, and price in all markets and their ultimate determination by rareté, or marginal utility*, gives the Walrasian system a brilliant comprehensiveness.

SUMMARY

The French mathematician Cournot took monopoly as his starting point for the development of various models of partial equilibrium.

In his *Researches into the Mathematical Principles of the Theory of Wealth* (1838), he restated a number of economic relationships in terms of functions. He was only incidentally concerned with the relation between exchange value and utility, which captivated the attention of the Austrian school. Nor was he actively interested in the reformulation of the rules of economic policy, which formed an integral part of the classical system. However, he realized that relations in the market could be viewed as purely formal relations in a series of functional equations. Unfortunately, the results of his treatment of the problems of price determination under conditions of pure competition, monopoly, and duopoly remained neglected for decades.

The German landowner and farmer — and economist by avocation — von Thünen was one of the most fertile thinkers that ever graced the economic profession. He became most famous for his model of *The Isolated State*, which constitutes the bulk of the first volume (1826) of his work dealing with theoretical economic questions. In it he logically related a number of variables derived from the two basic ones of natural productivity and location. In genuinely original strokes he fashioned new tools of analysis. After his death, he became recognized as the principal founder of the marginal productivity theory of the distribution of factor earnings, having laid the broad base which gave impetus and direction to the work of an American economist, J. B. Clark (see Chapter 5). Unlike the latter, he did not believe that the market rate of wages was validated by ethics, and he devised a formula for the natural (just) wage which allotted to the worker more than his subsistence minimum.

Gossen, the anticipator of the modern theory of value, was a tragic figure in the history of economic thought. His *The Development of the Laws of Exchange among Men and of the Consequent Rules of Human Action* (1854) exercised no influence in his own lifetime and remained completely ignored until it was rediscovered in the 1870's. Jevons, seconded by Walras, went out of his way to resurrect the work of the obscure German pioneer. It stated in original fashion certain rules of human conduct and was based on a combination of utilitarianism, a consumption approach, and use of the mathematical method. Gossen's "laws" rest on the assumption that the aim of all human conduct is to maximize enjoyment. He specifically examined the manner in which enjoyment proceeds with increasing consumption and, in the process, arrived at the propositions which are known as Gossen's first and second laws. The rest of his work, including a classification of goods, was largely an elaboration of these laws.

Jevons in his *The Theory of Political Economy* (1871) managed to combine the various strands of earlier utility analysis into a comprehensive theory of value, exchange, and distribution; and this feat constitutes his unique, though by no means his only, contribution to pure economic theory. His strictly utilitarian approach is reflected in the central principle that value is entirely dependent upon utility. Whereas the classical theory of value had been objective in the sense that it referred to the whole of society's economic activity, Jevons started with individual, subjective wants and, with the help of Bentham's hedonistic philosophy, erected a structure of thought which could serve as an alternative to the classical theory. He clearly distinguished between total (individual) utility and final degree of utility, and he explored in detail the implications of Gossen's second law. Passing on to exchange, he showed that in equilibrium marginal utility for each party will be proportionate to price. Elaborating the concept of subjective valuations, he employed the notions of commodity, discommodity, law of indifference, and trading body. In this he was not entirely successful; in particular, he failed to recognize the analytical differences between isolated exchange and competitive exchange. His extensive use of the concept of disutility of labor as a determinant of supply — labor being defined in purely subjective terms — manifests his debt to Senior and other late classical writers.

Walras drew still more heavily on the mathematical tool kit with which his countryman Cournot had already probed into the phenomena of exchange. He was the first — and for decades the only — economist to incorporate the various functional parts of the economy into an all-embracing system of equations, in which the prices of all goods and services, including those of the factors of production, are in a formal sense uniquely determined. Cournot had merely paved the way for the theory of general equilibrium in his demonstration of the functional interdependence of prices and demand. In his *Elements of Pure Economics* (1874, 1877), Walras discussed price determination under four partial theories: exchange, production, capitalization, and circulation. He employed the term *rareté* to denote the intensity of the last want satisfied; it corresponds to Jevons' final degree of utility. Exchange is based on the desire to equalize *raretés*. By using the notion of a price called by a hypothetical auctioneer, he demonstrated how, in the process of competition, the equilibrium price is achieved through a series of successive approximations. In equilibrium the ratios of the *raretés* of various commodities must be equal to the ratios of their prices. Although the practical application of general equilibrium theory still presents immense problems, both because of the virtually infinite number of equations to be solved simultaneously and the difficulty of obtaining the necessary data for the equations, the brilliance of Walras' theoretical feat cannot be denied.

BIOGRAPHICAL NOTES

A.—*Antoine Augustin Cournot* (1801–1877) was an eminent French philosopher, teacher, and administrator, and generally has been considered as the founder of mathematical economic analysis.

After a few years in the classroom, first at the *Ecole Normale Supérieure,* later as professor of physics at the University of Lyon (1834), he became Rector of the Academy of Grenoble in 1835, Inspector General of Studies in 1838, and Rector of the Academy of Dijon in 1854. His principal works, those that brought him widespread recognition, are concerned with probability theory and epistemology. His *Researches into the Mathematical Principles of the Theory of Wealth* (1838) remained unnoticed for many years; they are a by-product of his cultivation of broader interests. Nevertheless, the lack of attention which the work encountered must have been disappointing to the author. He subsequently proceeded to simplify the presentation, by skipping many purely mathematical demonstrations, in his *Principles of the Theory of Wealth* (1863), and in a still more elementary version entitled *Summary View of Economic Doctrines* (1876). However, it was not until Jevons, in the second edition of his *The Theory of Political Economy* (1879), paid glowing tribute to Cournot's pioneering work that the far-reaching implications of his original theories were recognized. Had this service, prompted by Jevons' integrity and sense of fair play, been denied him, Cournot's place in economics might have remained as nondescript as that occupied by Gossen.

B.—*Johann Heinrich von Thünen* (1783–1850), with his *The Isolated State in Relation to Agriculture and Political Economy,* was an isolated example of a mind almost perfectly balanced between the inductive and deductive methods of investigation, a mind which was constantly and urgently drawn to the formation of broad laws or principles, but also a mind that shied away from binding statements before having assembled a sufficiently comprehensive stock of empirically ascertained facts.

Descendant of an old feudal family, he was born in the Grand Duchy of Oldenburg. Deprived of his father in early childhood, he expected to take over the paternal estate after having secured a thorough grounding in the practical and theoretical labors pertaining to farming. At the age of sixteen, he attended an agricultural college near Hamburg, and only four years later had already conceived the outline of *The Isolated State,* the ingenious model that imbued his restless intellect during the remainder of his life. Two semesters spent in 1803–04 at the University of Goettingen contributed little to the enlargement of his horizon. Having sold his family estate, he married in 1806 and for a few years, haunted by the adversities of war and poor harvests, worked the mediocre soil of a leased estate. In 1810 he managed to buy a sizable piece of land in Mecklenburg. He thenceforth devoted himself in painstaking labor, interrupted by spells of ill health, to the exploration of the problems which he encountered as a practicing farmer. Not content to accept traditional precepts at face value, he wrested a wealth of newfangled research data from his agricultural experiments.

By 1826, von Thünen was able to overcome his misgivings about the response which so completely different a book as his might evoke from an unprepared public. As it was, the first edition of *The Isolated State* appealed only to an esoteric circle, but the revised edition, published in 1842, gained him widespread recognition. During the rest of the 1840's, his estate became a place of pilgrimage for those who sensed the originality of a mind anxious to share hard-won enlightenment.

In 1850, shortly before his death, he was induced to publish, as the first part of a second volume, his researches on the natural wage in relation to the rate of interest and to rent of land. The rest of his rich scientific legacy was published by one of his friends and pupils in 1863; it constituted Part 2 of the second volume and the third volume of *The Isolated State*. The latter dealt mostly with principles for the determination of rent, optimal periods of land rotation, and forest management.

C.—*Hermann Heinrich Gossen's* (1810–1858) tragic fate would have hardly become the subject of attention by economists had not Jevons made it a *cause célèbre*. Born in southwest Germany, Gossen as a young man was active in government service. He retired in 1847 and began to devote himself to economic problems. His only work, a volume of less than three hundred pages entitled *The Development of the Laws of Exchange among Men and of the Consequent Rules of Human Action*, found a publisher in 1854 but scarcely caused a ripple in the literary world. Acutely disappointed and smarting under the apparent rebuff — he had hoped to gain the fame of a Copernicus — the author shortly before his death four years later withdrew the unsold stock (almost the entire printing) and ordered it to be destroyed.

Some twenty years later, his name was rescued from oblivion by an English scholar who, guided by a German bookseller's catalog, succeeded in 1878 in unearthing a copy of the book. Brought to Jevons' attention, it ceased to be an utter failure when, in the preface to the second edition (1879) of his *The Theory of Political Economy*, Jevons generously and emphatically gave credit to Gossen for having completely anticipated him in all essentials.

Aided by the praise bestowed upon it by Walras, the book was reprinted in 1889. But it has never been translated into English — nor has it ever much appealed to readers with mathematical disabilities or to those who are chilled by pretentiousness. However, Gossen's pioneering feat in a largely unmapped territory has gained him a permanent place in the history of economic doctrines — thanks to the miraculous rediscovery in the 1870's.

D.—*Jeremy Bentham* (1748–1832) was born in London and trained for the practice of law, but he devoted most of his adult life to the study of problems related to the welfare of man. A retiring and eccentric person, he failed to make a political career for himself. (See also Chapter 2, Biographical Notes C and E.)

E.—*William Stanley Jevons* (1835–1882), one of the main pillars of English economic thought in the nineteenth century, stands chronologically between J. Stuart Mill and Alfred Marshall. His straightforward but crude marginalism contrasts strongly with Mill's refined but multicolored classicism; in confluence with the latter, it becomes submerged in Marshallian neoclassicism before the turn of the century.

Born in Liverpool, the son of an iron merchant, Jevons attended University College, London, from 1851 to 1854, when straitened financial circumstances in his family forced an interruption of his studies. Whereas in the early 1850's he had concentrated on the natural sciences, during the next five years he immersed himself in the theory and practical problems of political economy. Always an introvert, he spent these years in a sort of solitary confinement in Australia, mainly as an assayer of the mint in Sydney, a busy place following the gold discoveries on the down-under continent. These formative years were filled with sustained mental activity based on empirical and deductive research. Upon his return to England via the United States, he resumed his work at University College and in 1863 graduated with an M.A.

In the preceding year, Jevons, to his own satisfaction and that of a later generation, had already proved his promise as a scientist with a paper, "Notice of a General Mathematical Theory of Political Economy," read before the British Association for the Advancement of Science. His reputation grew with the publication in 1865 of the statistical study, *The Coal Question*. In 1866, at the age of thirty-one and a year before his marriage, he became Cobden Professor of Political Economy at Owens College, Manchester, and in 1876 accepted a call to his Alma Mater, to resign only four years later for reasons of health. Death by drowning at a bathing resort in 1882 cut short his promising career.

The second half of his life was filled with restless activity: civil servant, writer, reader of papers before learned societies, and teacher. His numerous extracurricular duties detracted from his effectiveness in the classroom; always on the go, he had little time to devote to improving his lecture presentation, which was not one of his fortes in the first place.

Yet, a steady stream of publications, covering a wide range of subjects, bear testimony to his fertile mind. His pioneering work in mathematical statistics was geared to an attempt at devising a method for forecasting business fluctuations, which he related to the rhythms he had, as a student of meteorology, observed in natural phenomena. (He computed correlations between sunspot frequencies, precipitation, agricultural output, and the ups and downs of general business activity.) His short pamphlet, *A Serious Fall in the Value of Gold* (1863), the outgrowth of immense labors, constitutes a masterpiece of empirical-deductive research and opened up entirely new vistas for the study of secular movements and the construction of index numbers. Refined, amplified, and placed in broader perspective, this type of work bore additional fruit, of which his *On the Variation of Prices and the Value of the Currency since 1782* may be mentioned as representative. The wide range of his interests and competence is attested by his *Pure Logic* (1863) and *The Principles of Science* (1874).

Undoubtedly his greatest contribution to the body of economic thought was his *The Theory of Political Economy*. Published in 1871 (2d ed., 1879), it did not make a mark commensurate with its intrinisic merit, and when Jevons died he left no school of disciples dedicated to improving upon his fundamental notions and to giving finish to his work in pure theory.

F.—*Marie-Esprit Léon Walras* (1834–1910), as far as pure theory is concerned, has been considered the greatest economist of all times by at least one twentieth century economist who was a giant in his own right: J. A. Schumpeter.

The external circumstances preceding the achievement by this Frenchman of his pioneering feats, however, were by no means propitious. Born in a provincial town of France in 1834, Léon did have the good fortune of being the son of an economist of some stature, Auguste Walras, who in his work, *On the Nature of Wealth and the Origin of Value* (1831), anticipated certain essential ideas of the Marginalists. Aside from this, Léon had few foundations on which to build except Cournot's work, *Researches into the Mathematical Principles of the Theory of Wealth*. Like Jevons, he remained unaware of Gossen's insights until he had substantially worked out by independent research the fundamental principles of marginal utility analysis. Had it not been for Jevons' rediscovery of Gossen and also correspondence with Jevons, Walras might never have learned about their common precursor. His academic start was singularly inauspicious. While in his late teens, he twice failed to pass the competitive examination for entering the *Ecole Polytechnique*; and, in 1854, he had to content himself with admission to the *Ecole des Mines* where, without any deep commitment, he studied engineering for less than one year.

His Bohemian tastes induced him to turn to literature and try free-lance writing, but little came of it. His only novel, published in 1858, was a rather distinct failure. Persuaded by his father to bear down on an intensive study of economics, Walras' fortunes began to improve when, in 1860, he was permitted to read a paper at an international congress on taxation held in Lausanne, Switzerland. Though gaining only fourth place in the prize competition sponsored by the canton of which Lausanne is the capital, he deeply impressed a member of the audience, Louis Ruchonnet, who later became chief of the department of education of the Canton of Vaud. In this capacity, he invited Walras in 1870 to become the first occupant of a newly founded chair in economics at the Faculty of Law of the Academy of Lausanne.

The twenty-two years preceding his retirement in 1892 were Walras' chief period of creative activity, crowned by the publication in 1874 and 1877 of the two parts of his *Elements of Pure Economics*. His *Studies in*

Applied Economics (1898) dealing with practical economic problems; his *Studies in Social Economics* (1896), in which he addressed himself to social ethics and advocated a land-nationalization scheme; and his *Autobiography* (1908), published in the *Giornale degli Economisti*, were of secondary importance and a hindrance rather than a help to gaining recognition. Of an entirely different nature than the *Elements*, the quality of these other writings appears as doubly wanting when placed alongside his superb achievement.

The *Elements* certainly would not have been possible without the peace and security provided him by his teaching position at Lausanne. The appointment to the Lausanne chair was by no means a foregone conclusion considering the fact that Walras had not received any academic preparation in economics at all! As a matter of fact, he was for the most part self-taught. The twelve years between his abandonment of a literary career and the call to Lausanne were marked by continuing disappointments, a period of confrontation with the hard facts of the business world — at one time he was managing director of a bank for cooperatives that later failed.

Although France withheld recognition from him during practically all his life, he never gave up his French citizenship. In regard to the French Academy of Moral and Political Sciences, before whom in 1873 he read, without the slightest success, a memoir explaining the principle of a mathematical theory of exchange, he remarked: "I grieve for this learned body, and I venture to say that after the double misfortune of awarding a prize to Canard and slighting Cournot, it might, in its own interest, have profited by this opportunity to establish its competence in economics a little more brilliantly." See *Elements of Pure Economics*, translated by William Jaffé (Homewood, Illinois: Richard D. Irwin, Inc., 1954), p. 44.

Although Walras did not gather a ring of disciples around him, he was convinced at the turn of the century that the doctrines conceived by him in the 1870's had gained wide acceptance. However that may be — and the evidence suggests that his professional contemporaries remained mostly indifferent or hostile — he was permitted to pick his own successor when he resigned his chair at Lausanne 1892. It was this man, Vilfredo Pareto, rather than Walras, who became responsible for making Lausanne the center of a school. Its influence, however, was for the most part confined to Italy, Pareto's native country.

Questions for Review and Research

1. What is the distinction between partial equilibrium analysis (Cournot) and general equilibrium analysis (Walras)? Does the use of mathematics have anything to do with it?

2. What objective did Cournot pursue in his *Researches*? When was this work published?

3. According to Cournot, how does a monopolist have to proceed in order to maximize his present gain?

4. Did Cournot deny the existence of a link between utility and exchange value? Explain.
5. In what sense was Thünen more creative and original than any of his contemporaries in the field of political economy?
6. Demonstrate the Ricardian points of departure of Thünen's marginal productivity theory of the factors of production.
7. State the principal assumptions underlying the model by which Thünen developed the foundations of an agricultural location theory.
8. Explain the first two of Gossen's three laws.
9. Who was largely responsible for securing a permanent place for Gossen in the history of economic thought?
10. What is Walras' system of "pure economics" in its essence?
11. What is meant by "final degree of utility"? Which of the three principal founders of marginalism used this term?
12. From whom did Jevons derive his pleasure-pain (utility-disutility) calculus? Which dimensions of pleasure (pain) did he consider as most relevant for economic analysis?

Recommended Readings

Cournot, Augustin. *Researches into the Mathematical Principles of the Theory of Wealth* (1838), translated by Nathaniel Bacon. Reprints of Economic Classics. New York: Augustus M. Kelley, Publishers, 1960. "Preface," pp. 1–5; Chapter I, "Of Changes in Value, Absolute and Relative," pp. 18–28; Chapter V, "Of Monopoly," pp. 56–66; Chapter VII, "Of the Competition of Producers," pp. 79–89.

Jevons, William Stanley. *The Theory of Political Economy*, 4th ed. London: Macmillan & Co., Ltd., 1911. Chapter 1, "Introduction," pp. 1–27; Chapter 2, "Theory of Pleasure and Pain," pp. 28–36; Chapter 3, "Theory of Utility," pp. 37–74; Chapter 4, "Theory of Exchange," pp. 75–166.

Newman, Philip C., Arthur D. Gayer, and Milton H. Spencer (eds.). *Source Readings in Economic Thought*. New York: W. W. Norton & Company, Inc., 1954. The selection "The Isolated State," by Johann Heinrich von Thünen, pp. 320–330.

Spiegel, Henry William (ed.). *The Development of Economic Thought*. New York: John Wiley & Sons, Inc., 1952. The selection "Walras on Gossen," pp. 470–488.

Stigler, George J. *Production and Distribution Theories*. New York: The Macmillan Company, 1941. Chapter II, "William Stanley Jevons," and Chapter IX, "Léon Walras."

Walras, Léon. *Elements of Pure Economics, or the Theory of Social Wealth*, translated by William Jaffé. Homewood, Illinois: Richard D. Irwin, Inc., 1954. "Preface to the Fourth Edition," pp. 35–48; Part I, "Object and Divisions of Political and Social Economy," Lessons 1–4, pp. 51–80.

VALUE AND DISTRIBUTION THEORY

From Menger to Böhm-Bawerk

Well before the end of the nineteenth century, there arose a school of Austrian economists whose principal achievements were personified in three names: Menger, von Wieser, and von Böhm-Bawerk. They so analyzed utility as to base a comprehensive theory of value upon subjective elements. In applying their reasoning to the valuation of the factors of production, they were most successful in developing a theory of capital and interest.

MENGER[1]

Carl Menger, the *founder and early leader of the Austrian school of economics*, approached the problems of value theory without utilizing the mathematical tools that were so heavily relied upon by the other two principal founders of marginal utility theory. His crowning achievement, *Principles of Economics*, was published in 1871, *before* he had embarked on an academic career as professor of political economy at the University of Vienna. This book was intended as the first of four volumes which would constitute a comprehensive, self-contained system, but due to unanticipated demands on his attention he actually never completed more than the first (fundamental) part of the project. Nevertheless, the *Principles* stands as a landmark, no less impressive in its way than the Walrasian and Jevonian building blocks for twentieth-century economic thought. It is the foundation on which his pupils and colleagues — among the latter especially von Wieser and von Böhm-Bawerk — erected the impressive theoretical structure which students of this century recognize as the Austrian contribution to economics, essentially complete at the turn of the twentieth century. Since the Austrians added more to the body of pure economic theory than any other "school," and since Menger's

---

[1]See Biographical Note A.

104

basic theories serve as the foundation on which almost the entire edifice of Austrian economics was built, no apologies need be made for a treatment of seemingly disproportionate length.

Most of Menger's original ideas can be found in the first five chapters of his *Principles*, especially Chapter 3 on "The Theory of Value." In 1950, they were finally made accessible to a wider circle of economists when, after a delay of almost eighty years, at long last an English translation of the *Principles* was published. It compensates for its late appearance because the style is much more elegant than that of the German original.

Preliminaries

Menger's most basic distinction is that between goods directly capable of satisfying human needs and those contributing only indirectly to want satisfaction. The former he called "goods of the first order," the latter "goods of a higher order." Higher-order goods, in turn, are divided into those of the second, third, fourth order, and so on, depending on the closeness of their relationship to first-order goods. In Menger's classification, consumer goods are first-order goods; capital goods, as well as productive services of factors other than capital, carry the higher "index numbers." Example: While bread, fully produced, is a first-order good, the flour, salt, and other ingredients of bread are of the second order; the grainmills, wheat, rye, and labor services joined in the production of flour are of the third order; and the land, agricultural tools or machinery, and labor services of farmers used in growing and harvesting bread grain are goods of the fourth order. Obviously, the order of a good has no inherent property — the farmer's labor services may be devoted to the baking of bread as well as to growing of marketable crops. It merely serves as an expository device.

There are two laws governing the *goods-character*, or status as goods, of higher-order goods. First, this character is possessed only by those goods that can be successively transformed into goods of a lower and, finally, first order. But, to make this transformation possible, we usually need to have command of "complementary" goods of a higher order. It is not sufficient that a person have command of the ingredients of bread, of the appliances necessary for the production of bread, and of the labor services bringing the ingredients and appliances into a productive relationship. Unless he has the fuel for heating the baking oven, he does not have the effective power of utilizing all the other goods of the second order at his command, and the latter will lose their goods-character — certainly with respect to the need for bread, though not necessarily with regard to other first-order goods. Hence "the goods-character of goods of second order is dependent upon complementary goods of the same order being made available to men with respect to the production of at least one good of first order," and by extension "the goods-character of goods of higher order is directly dependent upon complementary goods of the same order being available with respect to the production of at least one good of the next lower order."[2] This by no means exhausts the list of prerequisites for the establishment of the goods-character of things. It is not only necessary that we be able to transform goods of the third into goods of the second order, but, in subsequently transforming the latter into goods of the first order, we must also be able to command all necessary complementary goods of the second order. Similar considerations apply to the successive transformation of goods of a higher-than-third order into (eventually) first-order goods.

Second, as a corollary, the goods-character of higher-order goods *may* be lost if goods of the first order lose that character. The reason for the "may" is that new needs satisfied by new first-order goods may supplant needs satisfied by the former first-order goods; but, if the already existing higher-order goods can be transformed into the new first-order goods, the goods-character of these higher-order goods will not be lost. Consequently, the character of goods as goods of higher order is merely *derived from* the goods-character of lower-order goods. To put it differently, complementary goods of a second order may be susceptible to different combinations, with the result that they can be transformed into a variety of first-order goods. Means of production may thus stand in only a loose, or indirect, causal relationship to the satisfaction of human needs. Regardless of whether goods can be placed in direct causal connection with the satisfaction of human needs (first-order goods), or manifest only an indirect relationship (second-order goods), the goods-character of things will be lost upon the disappearance of the (ultimate) needs they have served to satisfy. This effect will take place only if the goods of the first as well as of higher orders serve the satisfaction of not more than *one* need — which in reality is the exception rather than the rule. In the example of tobacco, if people should suddenly lose their taste for smoking, not only stocks of finished tobacco products, but also the raw tobacco leaves and the equipment

---

[2]Carl Menger, *Principles of Economics* (Glencoe, Illinois: Free Press, 1950), p. 60.

used exclusively in the processing of tobacco would lose their goods-character. However, land and agricultural implements previously used in the cultivation of tobacco would retain their goods-character inasmuch as they could be turned to the cultivation of crops which, after processing, would still serve to satisfy human needs. This would be true also of nonspecialized machinery which, if no longer needed for the manufacture of tobacco products, could be put to work in the manufacture of other goods satisfying human needs.

Menger, in contrast to his predecessors, lays stress on the *time* element involved in the transformation of goods of higher order into first-order goods. The actual time lapsed will obviously differ according to the nature of the case, and particularly according to the number of stages that a good will traverse before attaining the status of a good of first order. This becomes clear if one compares, for instance, the growing of an oak forest with the production of certain foods and beverages, assuming that in both cases the entrepreneur has control over all the land, labor services, tools, and so forth, required for the attainment of the end product.

Whereas Adam Smith had regarded division of labor as the central factor in the *economic progress* of mankind, Menger views this principle as only one, and certainly not the most important, cause of that progress. The Austrian places the progressively increasing employment of goods of higher order at the center of an explanation of the growing quantity of goods available for human consumption. It appears that Menger exaggerated the extent of Smith's neglect of the accumulation of capital as a factor in economic progress; nevertheless, the Scotsman had failed to describe the intimate relationship between the specialization of labor on the one hand and capital accumulation on the other.

Menger's discussion of the *requirements for goods of various orders* led him to the important principle that we can *utilize* quantities of goods of higher order in the production of given quantities of goods of lower order (including, eventually, first-order goods) only if we can simultaneously command the complementary quantities of the other goods of higher order. Likewise, our *requirements* for particular goods of higher order are geared to the availability of complementary quantities of the corresponding goods of higher order. Finally, goods of higher order cannot be or become economic goods, as distinguished from free or noneconomic goods, unless they are or become suitable for the production of *some* economic good of a lower order. This implies, furthermore, that goods of a lower order are not economic goods because the goods employed in their production displayed economic character *before* the beginning of the production process. The relationship is rather inverse. As proof Menger adduces the fact that man, "... who is himself the point at which human economic life both begins and ends,"[3] experiences needs for goods of the first order, with goods of a higher order being largely *dependent* on the progress of his economic activity.

Menger's Theory of Value

The analytical core of Menger's theory of value consists of his views on the nature of value, the subjective and objective determinants of the measure of value, and the problem of imputation.

Nature of Value.—It is the activity called economizing, arising whenever the requirements for a good in a time period are greater than the quantity of it available in that period, which is the core of the phenomenon called value. In this case, the available quantity of the good cannot be diminished without causing one or several specific needs to be either no longer provided for or to be satisfied less completely than was previously possible. If, therefore, the satisfaction of human needs is dependent on the availability of each *partial* quantity of the good in question, and if the economizing man becomes aware of this quantitative relationship, the good acquires for him the significance which is generally called value. *Value is not an inherent property of goods, but merely the relative importance that we attribute to economic goods in the satisfaction of our needs.*

Since the requirements for noneconomic goods are always smaller than the quantities available, at least a portion of the total supply of these goods is not related to unsatisfied human needs. This portion could be lost or destroyed without in any way diminishing the satisfaction of human needs. From this, it follows that no one single unit of a noneconomic good is indispensable for need satisfaction, and, consequently, definite quantities of noneconomic goods have no value for us.

Menger differs with those economists who held that although noneconomic goods have definitely no exchange value, they still have use value. He regards exchange value and use value as coordinate concepts, both subordinate to the general concept of value. Since an economizing individual cannot under ordinary circumstances attribute value to, say, a cubic foot of air, then neither does this quantity of air possess any use value.

---

[3] *Ibid.*, p. 108.

In this connection Menger also makes an unorthodox *distinction between utility and use value.* In his singular terminology, a thing may have utility although it has no use value. He views utility as a purely abstract relation between a species of goods and a human need rather than as a relation between concrete units of a good and that need. Therefore, noneconomic goods, such as air, do have utility although (under ordinary circumstances) no use value. As he applies the term, something has utility as soon as the *total* available quantity is capable of satisfying our needs, as would certainly hold true for the noneconomic good, air. Thus, the concept utility does not have a psychological content, but is a purely objective concept. Although Menger is not familiar with the term "marginal utility"— while nevertheless fully aware of the relation designated by it — it would be correct to say that he regarded the presence of total utility as quite compatible with the absence of marginal utility, the relationship which characterizes the nature of noneconomic goods. While utility is a prerequisite of goods-character in general, use value in addition presupposes a scarcity relationship between the thing and the need for it, hence is embodied only in economic goods. *Both economic and noneconomic goods possess utility, but only the former also possess use value.*

The value property is, of course, predicated upon human knowledge that want satisfaction depends upon the control of a good or of a certain quantity thereof. It is immaterial whether men are in error about the degree to which a good contributes to their want satisfaction; thus, we may encounter the phenomenon which Menger refers to as *imaginary value.* Also, changes in the relative availability of goods to satisfy human needs may give rise to value where there was none before, and vice versa: as far as individuals are concerned, noneconomic goods may become economic in character, and economic goods may become noneconomic, the dividing line between the two being fluid. Since value is always ". . . a judgment economizing men make about the importance of the goods at their disposal for the maintenance of their lives and well-being,"[4] it is entirely subjective in nature; objectification of the value of goods Menger regards as erroneous.

Subjective Factors Determining the Measure of Value.—In discussing differences in the magnitude of importance of various satisfactions, Menger distinguishes between those satisfactions on which men depend for the maintenance of their lives and those that merely

---

[4]*Ibid.*, p. 121.

determine their well-being in a greater or lesser degree. What is more, men with their limited resources try to satisfy the more urgent before they attempt to satisfy the less urgent wants, but they may combine the more complete satisfaction of the more pressing with the less complete satisfaction of their less pressing wants. (The adjective "complete," as used here, merely refers to total satisfactions; it does not refer to the degree of satisfaction at the margin.) Each concrete act of satisfaction has, furthermore, a different significance for them according to the degree of satisfaction that they have already reached. For purposes of illustration, Menger introduced ten hypothetical commodities and assigned to each a scale of the importance of different satisfactions yielded by successive equal additions to the amount of the commodity consumed. Presumably these satisfactions are based on successive expenditures of equal amount of some other resource, say money. He arranged these data as follows:

COMMODITIES

	I	II	III	IV	V	VI	VII	VIII	IX	X
	10	9	8	7	6	5	4	3	2	1
	9	8	7	6	5	4	3	2	1	0
	8	7	6	5	4	3	2	1	0	
	7	6	5	4	3	2	1	0		
	6	5	4	3	2	1	0			
	5	4	3	2	1	0				
	4	3	2	1	0					
	3	2	1	0						
	2	1	0							
	1	0								
	0									

(UNITS OF SATISFACTION)

Source: Carl Menger, *Principles of Economics* (Glencoe, Illinois: Free Press, 1950), p. 127.

Commodity I serves the satisfaction of a more urgent want than do commodities II, III, etc., because the expenditure of the first unit of another (not specified) resource yields 10 units of satisfaction, as against 9 in the case of commodity II, 8 for commodity III, and so on. But it is also evident that an individual expending three resource units on commodity I, and nothing on commodity II, would fall short of maximum want satisfaction, because in this case his total satisfaction (10 plus 9 plus 8 = 27, in column I) is less than the total satisfaction obtained if he had spent only two resource units on I (yielding 10 plus 9 = 19) and one resource unit on II (yielding 9), giving him a total of 28 units of satisfaction. Only if he had at least four units of spendable resources at his disposal would the purchase of a third unit of I be economically justifiable; but with four resource units he might, without changing the net result, spend two units on I, one unit on II, and one unit on III; or two units on I, two units on II, and nothing on III; rather than three units on I, one unit on II, and nothing on III. It is evident that by Menger's assumptions in the case of an individual with four or five resource units the spending pattern is indeterminate, and that only the possession of at least seven resource units would justify the purchase of a fourth portion of commodity I (yielding 7 units of satisfaction).

If the scale in column I expresses the diminishing importance, to a hypothetical individual, of the satisfaction of the need for food, and if column V expresses the diminishing importance to him of the satisfaction of his need for tobacco, it is clear that up to a certain degree of completeness the satisfaction of his need for food has precedence over the satisfaction of his need for tobacco. Only after he has satisfied his food need up to the point at which the importance of this satisfaction is measured by the figure 6, does the consumption of tobacco begin to have the same importance to him as further satisfaction of his need for food. In other words, if the need for food and tobacco were the only needs competing for his limited resources (if the needs that can be satisfied by the other eight of the ten commodities in the table were nonexistent), and if at the same time he had only, say, four resource units at his disposal, he would expend all of his resources on food and nothing on tobacco, because the last unit spent on food would have the importance of seven units of satisfaction, whereas the first unit spent on tobacco would yield only six units of satisfaction. Only with command over five or more resource units would it become necessary for this individual to allocate his resources *between* food and tobacco, namely, in such a way as to bring the satisfactions derived from these commodities into equilibrium. (We note that with five resource units he might either spend all of them for food — 10 plus 9 plus 8 plus 7 plus 6 = 40 units of satisfaction — or four units on food and one on tobacco — 10 plus 9 plus 8 plus 7 = 34, plus 6 = 40 units of satisfaction.) Thus, with the progressive satisfaction of his need for food, a stage will be reached at which he deems further acts of satisfaction of the need for food of lesser importance than the first acts of satisfying his need for tobacco.

Although the numbers in the table were chosen by Menger merely for the purpose of facilitating the demonstration of a complex problem, he thereby succeeded in shedding light on a phenomenon to which earlier economists had devoted relatively little attention: *the weighing of the relative importance of his needs by the economizing individual.* It remained for later economists to make the assumptions underlying Menger's model explicit — for example, the indispensable requisite that the satisfaction from the consumption of each commodity listed in the table is independent of the amount of consumption of the other commodities. This would be the case if one and only one commodity were suitable for the satisfaction of each need. In the example used, the ten distinct commodities must be opposite ten concrete (independent) needs.

Objective Factors Determining the Measure of Value.—To illustrate the fact that in ordinary life there are usually quantities of goods standing opposite a complex of human needs — rather than there being so many single goods capable of satisfying so many single concrete needs — Menger visualizes an *individual farmer* who has just completed a rich harvest of *wheat.* His dependence on this grain varies with respect to various *types* of satisfaction. Menger lists six, and in the order of their relative importance they are: maintenance of the farmer's family's life until the next harvest, preservation of health, continued operation of the farm (use of a portion of wheat as seed-grain in the following year), production of luxury beverages (beer, whiskey), fattening of cattle, and feeding of pets. The striking fact is that, although the various portions of the available supply of wheat serve to satisfy needs of greatly differing importance, the bushels of wheat used for subsistence have no higher value (per bushel) than the bushels used for the manufacture of luxury beverages, or even than the bushels used for growing another wheat crop during the next season, *if* the total wheat supply is composed of homogeneous units. This is so because *no particular satisfaction is dependent on any one particular portion of the total supply;* although, when the total supply is relatively small, needs of lesser importance may not be satisfied at all, or all needs may be satisfied less completely.

As a result of their propensity to maximize total satisfactions from a good that can be used for the (partial) satisfaction of several different kinds of needs of varying importance, economizing men will allocate their supply of the good so that all needs are satisfied up to an equal degree of importance. Because an individual would by all means want to satisfy his more important needs before satisfying the less important ones, if he were deprived of one unit of a given quantity of a good he would sacrifice the satisfaction that has the *smallest* importance to him.

From this, Menger derived the illuminating principle that the value of a given unit of a quantity of a good is measured by the importance to the individual of the satisfaction of least importance. This is tantamount to saying that ". . . of all the satisfactions secured by means of the whole quantity of a good . . ., only those that have the least importance to him are dependent on the availability of a given portion of the whole quantity."[5] Such was Menger's cumbersome mode of expressing the now familiar idea that the value of a unit of a good is measured by its "marginal utility," a term first used in Germany (*Grenznutzen*) and coined by von Wieser.

Menger also pursues the question of how differences in the quality of goods influence their value and shows how a smaller quantity of a higher-quality good may yield the same total satisfaction as a greater quantity of a lower-quality good.

The Problem of Imputation.—The most difficult problem encountered by Menger — one which he did not bring to a satisfactory solution — was: What principle determines the value of goods of higher order? He devoted a great deal of effort to showing the error in the reasoning of the classical writers, who argued that "products" have value because the productive agents employed in their manufacture have value, instead of arguing that the value of the services of goods of a higher order was derived from the value of goods of the first order.

But what about the value of these goods which, after all, must be produced before they can be sold? Menger reasons that in the absence of an actual value it must be the *prospective*, or expected, value of goods of the first order that determines the value of goods of a higher order employed in their production. "Hence goods of higher order can attain value . . . only if . . . they serve to produce goods that we expect to have value for us."[6] Also, since the *prospective* value of goods of lower order often deviates from the value of such goods *in the present*, the value of the goods of higher order cannot be measured by the current value of goods of lower order. Hence the connection between the value of goods of first order in the present and the value of currently used goods of higher order that serve in the future production of first-order goods may be extremely loose.

Menger then shows that the aggregate present value of all the *complementary goods of higher order* that are required for production

[5]*Ibid.*, p. 132.

[6]*Ibid.*, p. 50.

of a good of first order must be equal to the prospective value of the latter. It is important that the computation of these complementary quantities of goods of higher order include not only the services of land, the raw materials, labor services, machines, tools, and so forth, but also the entrepreneurial services (bringing together all the other goods of higher order) as well as the interest payments ("services of capital").

The valuation of *individual goods of higher order* hinges on our ability to vary the proportions in which the various complementary goods of higher order can be combined in the production process. Menger simply transfers the principle that regulates the value of goods of first order to the economizing individual to the valuation of higher-order goods. Just as the value of a particular consumer good is equal to the importance which the individual attaches to the satisfactions he would have to forego if he were deprived of it, so the value of a given quantity of a particular good of higher order is equal to the importance of the satisfactions made possible by that portion of the (final) product that would not have been produced in the absence of the given quantity of the good of higher order. After considering several possible cases and making explicit the underlying assumption that the available goods of higher order are employed most economically, Menger synthesizes his findings in the following *general law:* ". . . the value of a concrete quantity of a good of higher order is equal to the difference in importance between the satisfactions that can be attained when we have command of the given quantity of the good of higher order whose value we wish to determine and the satisfactions that would be attained if we did not have this quantity at our command."[7] The import of this somewhat cumbersome statement can be assessed more fully if we realize the corollary principle; namely, that ". . . the value of a good of higher order will be the greater (1) the greater the prospective value of the product if the value of the other complementary goods necessary for its production remains equal, and (2) the lower, other things being equal, the value of the complementary goods."[8] Menger thus came close to formulating a marginal productivity theory.

Conclusion

Impressive though Menger's structure of thought was at the time it made its appearance, it nevertheless exhibits serious *gaps*, some of which were closed in the neoclassical synthesis developed by Alfred Marshall

[7]*Ibid.*, p. 165.
[8]*Ibid.*

(see Chapter 6). Menger neglected to consider problems of production under so-called increasing, constant, and decreasing cost conditions; more generally, he failed to explain the role of cost of production in the valuation process. His theory of price is fragmentary, though its scope was expanded relative to the classical body of thought by his inclusion of new ideas on price formation under monopoly and under bilateral competition.

Finally, the Austrian occupies a place of honor in the history of economic thought not only for his superior performance and moral victory in the *Methodenstreit* (see Biographical Note A), but also because he evinced a degree of consistency and strict adherence to the requirements of a comprehensive system which was probably unrivaled in the economic writings of the nineteenth century.

THE OTHER MEMBERS OF THE "AUSTRIAN TRIO"

In the writings of the early 1870's by Jevons, Walras, and Menger, the *subjective theory of value* had been clearly sketched in all the important fundamentals. There appear differing emphases, but no egregious contradictions exist between their individual contributions to the body of economic theory: they all saw in what Wieser in 1884 for the first time called "marginal utility" the concept that governs, directly or indirectly, all valuation processes. *Still lacking were a well-rounded theory of the marginal productivity of the factors of production and a reconciliation of the subjective with the objective or cost theory of value*, as inherited from the Classical school. To bridge the first of these gaps, two Austrian writers, Friedrich Freiherr von Wieser and Eugen von Böhm-Bawerk, labored diligently in the 1880's and 1890's. Before turning to their writings in the remainder of this chapter, we will pause to cast a glance at what lies further ahead in our study of value and distribution theory.

John Bates Clark, the first world-famous American economist, was also much concerned with problems of marginal productivity (see Chapter 5).

To reconcile the subjective with the objective (cost) theory of value, an Englishman, Alfred Marshall, made the foremost of his research endeavors (see Chapter 6). In a sense, his *Principles of Economics*, published in 1890, constitutes the capstone on an edifice which braved all the winds of controversy for the better part of the following half-century, that is, until John Maynard Keynes in the 1930's was able to show that the assumptions underlying the Marshallian structure were not sufficiently broad to explain the dynamics of economic change (see Chapter 8).

Marshall became the founder and principal exponent of the Neoclassical school, whose principles subtly and skillfully combined all the major findings of objective and subjective analysis of economic value. His *Principles* exhibits all the marks of a sovereign and seasoned thinker. He was second to few in handling the indispensable mathematical tools, although for the sake of making economics more "popular" he shunned a conspicuous display of his masterful command of mathematical language.

Keynes, not satisfied with the impressive feats of neoclassicism, broke out of a framework which had become too confining for his heterodox disposition. Beginning in the 1930's, he blazed a trail on which congregated during the next couple of decades such a large following that it shortly became the most frequently traveled highway, not always free from congestion.

Friedrich von Wieser[9]

Though not one of his pupils, Wieser had the good fortune of being called to occupy Carl Menger's Vienna chair when the latter resigned it in 1903. While still a professor of economics at the University of Prague, Wieser in his *Natural Value*, published in 1889, arrived at all of the essential conclusions yielded by his theory of value. Two concepts in particular have been associated more closely with his name than with that of any of his contemporaries: *imputation* and *opportunity cost*. But the powers of his original mind have encompassed a scope much broader than is suggested by a couple of catchwords. We will confine our attention as much as possible to those aspects of his value theory which represent a notable advance over the received body of doctrine.

General Observations.—The *explanation of value* is viewed by Wieser essentially as the explanation of valuation processes engaged in by economizing individuals, something "to which practical life gives its entire assent."[10]

What gives goods their value is the satisfaction of wants; however, not all things that satisfy wants have value, only those that are scarce

---

[9]See Biographical Note B.

[10]Friedrich von Wieser, *Natural Value* (New York: Kelley & Millman, Inc., 1956), p. 6.

in relation to wants. Wieser discusses material and nonmaterial, continuous and intermittent wants, and the extent to which Gossen's law of the satiation of wants applies in each case, with varying scales of satiation. In a manner reminiscent of Menger, he shows how the maximum of total enjoyment in the satisfaction of wants can be attained only if the separate branches of expenditure are adequately weighed against each other, with the boundary lines being fixed in each case by the general circumstances of individual wealth. He warns against a too literal interpretation of Jevons' rule to the effect that, in order to maximize satisfaction, it must be possible for individuals to attain the same level of marginal utility in every branch of expenditure. It militates against a common-sense observation to insist that every addition to income must be laid out equally in every branch of expenditure. Want satisfactions are not infinitely divisible, hence *a given addition to income may not permit a proportionate increase of expenditures all along the line.* As Wieser puts it: ". . . the receptive power of one want is great, that of another comparatively small . . ."[11] Therefore, the economic employment of money (or other goods with many possible uses) does not call for the attainment in every employment of the same (lowest possible) marginal utility; maximization of want satisfaction requires only that the use of resources in a given employment has not necessitated the loss of a higher utility in some other employment.

It is extremely rare that goods are valued singly and by themselves — a painting by a great master being representative of the rare cases; rather, they are usually valued in connection with other similar goods belonging to the same stock. With this reminder, Wieser "prepares the ground" for the formulation of a *general law of value* in stating the proposition that in almost every case goods are acquired and used in parts; for, if it were otherwise, the law of marginal utility would not hold. According to this law, as stated by Wieser, the larger the supply of a good the smaller, *ceteris paribus,* will be the marginal utility and hence its value; or — with supply being given — the greater the need for a good the higher will be both its marginal utility and its value.

If there are only two units of a good, each unit has the value of the *second degree* in the scale of utility for that good. By the same token, one of three "entirely similar goods" has the value of the *third degree,* etc. We also note that in each case *any* one of the two or three units of the given supply has the value of the marginal unit, that is, the value of the second or third degree, respectively. If ". . . a poor man

---

[11]*Ibid.*, p. 15.

receives every day two pieces of bread, while one is enough to allay
the pangs of positive hunger, . . . neither of the two pieces . . . will
have that value which belongs to the allaying of positive hunger."[12]
From the fact that either of the two pieces has a value equal to the
second degree of utility, Wieser infers that jointly they have twice this
value. This observation holds true whenever we are concerned with
the valuation of goods in stock. It leads us to Wieser's general law of
value, namely, ". . . the value of a supply of similar goods is equal to the
sum of the items multiplied by the marginal utility."[13]

But beware of leaping to the conclusion that the use obtained from
a supply of economic goods — what Menger called their total utility —
is fully, or at all, represented in their (total) value. The need for caution
becomes clear when we realize what Wieser calls the *paradox of value,*
that *when total utility reaches its maximum, total value becomes zero!*
Such is the case when, as the point of superfluity is reached, the value
of the marginal unit has fallen to zero (when, therefore, the product of
marginal utility and the number of units of the good are zero). This
contradicts the commonly accepted view that value is an absolutely
desirable characteristic of goods, its mathematical expression being
the largest positive amount. In the absence of competing wants, it is
desirable that total enjoyment from the consumption of a given good
attain its maximum, and this is the case precisely when marginal utility
has dropped to zero.

Furthermore, the value of a *supply* of a given good must increase as
long as the increment of value accounted for by the utility of a *newly
acquired* unit is greater than what is lost through the reduction of value
which its addition causes to every unit of the good *already in stock;*
on the other hand, the value of the supply must decrease when the
former becomes smaller than the latter. We may thus contemplate an
"ascending" and a "descending" branch of the movement of value, or
value in the "upgrade" and value in the "downgrade." Over both,
total enjoyment (utility) will be on the "upgrade." Wieser illustrates
the principle in tables[14] shown at the top of page 119 which can be
combined as indicated.

Wieser thus discovered the interesting fact that *total value must be
zero in two diametrically opposed situations:* when the stock of a good
is zero, and when it is so great that an additional unit of the good
does not contribute anything to want satisfaction. "If we possess

---

[12]*Ibid.,* pp. 24–25.
[13]*Ibid.,* p. 25.
[14]*Ibid.,* pp. 28ff.

	0	1	2	3	4	5	6	7	8	9	10	11	
With	0	1	2	3	4	5	6	7	8	9	10	11	goods (units),
there will be	0	10	9	8	7	6	5	4	3	2	1	0	units of value per (unit of the) good.

Hence, there will be total enjoyment (utility) of 　 0 10 19 27 34 40 45 49 52 54 55 55 units of value, and

total value of 　 0 10 18 24 28 30 30 28 24 18 10 0 units

"Ascending" branch 　 "Descending" branch

nothing, there are no objects to value; if we possess everything, there is . . . no subjective inducement to an act of valuation. Only if we possess something . . . does the phenomenon of value appear. It presents itself with the first goods that come into our possession, and increases up to a certain culminating point from which it decreases, until, when superfluity is reached, interest is again completely withdrawn from the goods."[15]

Antinomies of Value and the Concept of Natural Value.—Wieser believed that households move almost entirely within the "ascending" branch of value, but he failed to make a convincing case for this claim. What he apparently refers to is the fact that the total exchange value of commodities usually increases with an increase in output, exceptions being those commodities for which the demand is relatively inelastic. In this light, at any rate, must be interpreted his reference to exceptionally favorable weather resulting in a bumper crop, when despite an augmentation in the amount of goods and of the enjoyment they provide their (total) value will decrease. In this case, we are confronted with an *antinomy between value and utility;* but, Wieser assures us, whenever there is such a conflict, "utility must conquer." He sees the greatest benefit of the distinction between utility and value in the fact that the latter greatly simplifies economic calculation. This is so because the value of a stock can be expressed merely as the *product* of stock and marginal utility, whereas utility can be expressed only as a *sum* composed of as many items as there are in the stock. This fact becomes of ever increasing importance as societies attain higher levels of economic development.

In addition to (subjective) *use value,* Wieser distinguishes between *exchange value in the subjective* and *exchange value in the objective sense.* The former is that value which sellers and buyers attach to goods on

---

[15]*Ibid.,* p. 31.

account of an anticipated act of exchange and is of the same nature as use value, varying according to personal circumstances. Exchange value in the objective sense is merely price, a definite amount of money required for the purchase of a good. Wieser realizes that objective exchange value, although dependent on valuations of personal interest, is basically *not* a fair representation of the individual valuations of the members of society; that is, while price is a social fact, it is not an indicator of the relative social importance of goods: high-priced luxuries are not indicative of a relatively higher *social* estimate of value than attaches to low-priced necessaries.

As *antinomy of exchange value*, Wieser denotes the fact that entrepreneurs are interested mainly in maximizing utility for themselves, while this interest may militate against the maximization of social utility. If by reducing the amount to be sold they can increase their returns, they will do so, and by the same token they find it to their advantage to turn free goods into economic goods. In order to mitigate the socially harmful effects of this antinomy, it is important that the market power of entrepreneurs be restrained. To make social utility the ruling principle of economic life, free competition must prevail, and, to the extent that this ideal cannot be attained, the economic order must be supplemented by appropriate government intervention.

Wieser calls *natural value* the "... value which arises from the social relation between amount of good and utility, or value as it would exist in the communist state.... In natural value, goods are estimated simply according to their marginal utility; in exchange value, according to a combination of marginal utility *and purchasing power* [emphasis added]. In the former, luxuries are estimated far lower, and necessaries, comparatively much higher than in the latter. Exchange value ... is ... a caricature of natural value...."[16] He goes on to show that even in a communistic state the factors of production would obtain value, that is, there would be a natural rent from land and a natural interest on capital, and so on. The only difference would be that rent and interest in a communistic state would accrue to the entire community instead of being sources of private income, but the economic-technical services of the factors in controlling production would remain. Wieser was cognizant of the fact, however, that the examination of natural value, a neutral phenomenon, cannot prove anything for or against economic orders. He was probably the *first to realize explicitly that there was nothing specifically capitalistic about the basic concept of value and the*

---

[16]*Ibid.*, pp. 60, 62.

concepts of cost and imputed returns, that these are rather elements of a general logic of economic behavior, applicable to other "isms" as well.

Principles of Imputation.—In view of the fact that production goods contain indirect (prospective, potential) utility and, inasmuch as they are not available in superfluity, must, therefore, receive value, we are confronted with the need to establish a relation between these goods and the value of their products — as Menger had already recognized. Because the value of production goods is measured by the value of their return, as reflected in the goods they help produce, *productive value is return value.* Return may assume different forms, but only the value of the "greatest possible return" can serve as a basis for the valuation of production goods. It is "the anticipated value of the anticipated return" which underlies the formation of productive value.

This proposition suffices only for the valuation of the cooperating factors of production *as a whole;* it does not explain their valuation *individually.* Is there a criterion making it possible to divide the whole return into its constituent parts, that is, to separate from the joint product the quotas of land, capital, and labor? Wieser finds the principle of solution in the *productive contribution of the factors.* The effectiveness of every productive factor depends on its combination with other productive factors. Certainly, if it were not possible to alter the relative proportions of the factors, it would not be possible to distinguish the specific effects of each of them. However, by taking into account all the important circumstances, such as the amounts of the products, their value, and the amounts of the means of production employed, we arrive at a number of *equations,* from which it is possible to make a reliable calculation of the importance of each single instrument of production.

Wieser assumes that the range of possible combinations is represented by the following three equations, where x, y, and z denote factors of production and the numerical values on the right-hand side denote the jointly acquired (or anticipated) returns:

$$x + y = 100$$
$$2x + 3z = 290$$
$$4y + 5z = 590$$

Solving these three equations with three unknowns simultaneously, we get $x = 40$, $y = 60$, and $z = 70$.

The number of individual equations to be taken into account will depend on the number of factor combinations — a huge number, indeed — carried out within the entire field of production. Since the total amount of productive wealth employed, as given on the left, must equal the total value of the return, as shown on the right, and since the number of equations is equal to the number of unknowns, we can attribute to each productive element a definite share in the total performance. It is the share in the return credited to the individual productive factor that Wieser calls its "productive contribution."

It goes without saying that *in practice* calculations can never be made as exactly as is suggested by the above set of equations. But, even though the sum of all the equations is never fully taken, we can arrive at useful results by what Wieser calls a "method of testing," that is, applying the values obtained in a given case to similar cases, making the necessary corrections. Fortunately, we do not have to calculate the whole mass of productive goods all at once. "The experience obtained while transferring now one, now another productive element, and watching the effect of each combination upon the value of the return, gives us sufficient information as to the amount with which the individual elements are bound up in the total return."[17]

The *difference between Menger's and Wieser's solutions* may now become clear. Whereas Menger, in an attempt to identify the return obtained from a particular production good, asked by how much total return would fall if an entrepreneur were to go without that good, Wieser traces the effects resulting if all production goods are actually employed according to plan. Whereas Menger was interested in the share of return dependent upon the cooperation of a single production good, Wieser is concerned with the productive contribution of each factor. Consequently, whereas in Menger's case, if a farmer loses his cart horse he loses only the value of the animal (as reflected in the diminution of return consequent upon his being forced to go without it), in Wieser's case he loses not only the value of the animal but something more, by virtue of a less effective combination of his remaining productive wealth — the other productive elements are robbed of a portion of their effect. In conclusion, Menger's method of imputation is no doubt simpler and clearer, but Wieser's is more realistic and perhaps more useful. For, if we concentrate upon productive contribution, rather than "share dependent upon cooperation," of production goods, we impute to them, as we should, a greater effect than they could obtain through their own powers. This treatment is justified by the fact that no production good could by itself produce anything; they all require the cooperation of others.

---

[17]*Ibid.*, p. 89.

Wieser's Opportunity Cost Concept.—In Wieser's analysis, marginal utility is not only the basic source of value, but it also sanctions cost, namely, cost viewed as social sacrifice. Since production not only creates, but also destroys, value, it should always be directed so as to achieve the best possible net result. This fact is of special importance in the case of production goods capable of more than one employment (cost goods) and where the different employments are not of equal economic efficiency. Obviously, at any given time such production goods cannot be devoted to more than one employment; if they are employed in the production of *A*, they are thereby withdrawn from the production of *B*, *C*, etc. The person considering a particular use of production goods should, therefore, have a clear idea of the value of all products (*B*, *C*, etc.) that cannot be produced if the production good is employed in the manufacture of *A*. The potential value of all "cognate" products must, therefore, be incorporated in the value of "common" economic factors of production.

Wieser thus arrives at a point of view from which *the use of production goods appears as an opportunity cost.* "To say that any kind of production involves cost simply implies that the economic means of production, which could doubtless have been usefully employed in other directions, are either used up in it, or are suspended during it,"[18] the latter being illustrated by unconsumable land. Production goods, except those to which attaches a natural monopoly (monopoly goods), always receive their value from the marginal product produced. Therefore, the measure for estimating costs is always their productive marginal utility after all of their possible economic employments have been considered. Cost goods, which Wieser calls "parent goods of the great productive relationships, within which they act as combining forces and equalizers of value,"[19] can be illustrated by unskilled labor, since it is in evidence in a great many different kinds of employment.

Eugen von Böhm-Bawerk[20]

Böhm-Bawerk, third member of the great Austrian triumvirate, did his share — and probably more than the other two — to give Vienna an international reputation for outstanding work in the field of economic theory. While still in the plenitude of his powers, he was more firmly tied down in public service than was the case at any time with Menger and Wieser. Nevertheless, we are indebted to him for a massive

---

[18]*Ibid.*, p. 175.
[19]*Ibid.*
[20]See Biographical Note C.

critical study of interest theories as they evolved historically, and a *detailed exposition of his own interest theory*. Both publications resulted from his sustained efforts during the decade of the 1880's. The first has been translated under the title *Capital and Interest*, the second under *The Positive Theory of Capital*. Neither of these labels is indicative of the true scope of his investigations: *Capital and Interest* is a painstaking and minute review of the explanations of interest proffered from ancient times to the last quarter of the nineteenth century; *The Positive Theory of Capital* envisages the whole economic process and represents a broad theory of the formation of value and price with special emphasis on the nature and conception of capital, its role as an instrument of production, and the source and rate of interest.

The Role of Capital.—Among the countless meanings which the word *capital* had been given by writers on economic subjects, two stand out distinctly: capital as an instrument of production and capital as a source of interest. As a tool in the production process, it helps to make labor more effective in wresting wealth from land; as a source of individual income, it competes with other claimants for a share in the distribution of the national product. The author is much concerned with a glib generalization that emerged during the evolution of economic thought: that interest is nothing but payment for one of the factors of production, namely, the compensation received by capital for its economic contribution. Certainly, when capital serves as an instrument of production, it is capable of producing, and usually does produce, interest; but only a portion of all the interest payments is attributable to the services rendered by capital as an instrument of production. Objects bearing interest, such as a dwelling house, are not by themselves indicative of the productive powers of capital. It is merely an historical accident that two distinct classes of phenomena, presenting distinct scientific problems, are so closely linked together by the same name. There is *no inherent parallelism between the powers of capital as a productive agent and its powers as a bearer of interest.*

One of the principal objectives of Böhm-Bawerk's labors was to show the superiority of *indirect* (roundabout, capitalistic) methods of production over *direct* methods. This superiority manifests itself in two ways: a greater end result can be obtained with a given amount of labor; goods can be obtained that would not be produced if we had to rely on nature and labor alone. He did more than any of his predecessors and contemporaries to establish this as a fundamental proposition in the theory of production: ". . . every roundabout way means

the enlisting in our service of a power which is . . . stronger . . . than the
human hand; every extension of the roundabout way means an addition
to the powers which enter into the services of man, and the shifting
of some portion of the burden of production from the scarce and costly
labour of human beings to the prodigal powers of nature."[21]

Since the distinction between production from hand to mouth and
production which employs circuitous methods is so fundamental,
Böhm-Bawerk calls the products that come into being in the course
of the roundabout process "intermediate products," and capital which
serves as a means to the socio-economic acquisition of goods "social
capital," or "productive capital." On the other hand, capital in the
general sense of the term is merely "a group of Products which serve as
means to the Acquisition of Goods."[22] He refers to the parent conception, "acquisitive capital," also as "private capital." This usage enables
him to retain the *double relation of the word "capital,"* its relation to
acquisition of interest on the one hand and to production on the other.
But he emphatically excludes the personal means of acquisition (labor)
from the conception of capital, in contradistinction to Menger, whose
"goods of higher order" cover the productive services of labor. Böhm-
Bawerk also excludes land, despite the fact that it has some features
in common with "produced" means of production.

He delimits the contents of social capital to include improvements
of land, productive buildings, productive utensils, productive animals,
raw and auxiliary materials, finished consumption goods (as long as
they remain in the hands of producers), and money. Except for money,
Böhm-Bawerk's use of the term social capital is thus practically identical with the terms "producers' goods" or "capital goods," as these
are employed today. His inclusion of money, but exclusion of debts
and other kinds of claims, is somewhat inconsistent. He recognizes that
the latter "are not capital, because they are not real goods,"[23] but
"representative . . . of real goods,"[24] while denying this property to
money itself.

In harmony with his definition, *private capital* covers all forms of
social capital and, in addition, consumption goods employed in the
acquisition of other goods, such as apartment houses.

The adoption of *capitalistic methods of production,* harnessing allies
from the stores of natural powers, is *attended by both advantages and*

---

[21]Eugen von Böhm-Bawerk, *The Positive Theory of Capital* (London: Macmillan
and Co., Ltd., 1891), p. 22.

[22]*Ibid.,* p. 38.

[23]*Ibid.,* p. 71.

[24]*Ibid.*

disadvantages. Its principal advantage is that, with an equal expenditure of labor and valuable natural powers, roundabout methods of production produce more and/or better goods than could be obtained by direct production. Its main disadvantage is the sacrifice of time, one of the "ground pillars" of the theory of capital.

What significance attaches to *differences in stages and degrees of roundabout production* relative to the output of final products? Mainly that the lengthening of the roundabout process, while permitting an increase in total output, does not permit it to grow in the same proportion. At work here is the principle of diminishing returns, but with a difference. The length of the process of production can be "measured" (a euphemistic term!) by the *"average* [emphasis added] period which lies between the successive expenditure in labour and uses of land and the obtaining of the final good."[25] In proportion as production becomes more roundabout or capitalistic, (1) the proportion of a year's productive powers consumed within the same year will fall, (2) the proportion of intermediate products maturing only later into finished goods will rise, and (3) the time at which intermediate products have matured will become more remote. Also, the more capitalistic a community, the more will it draw, during any given year, on productive powers created relatively long ago. The fact that a country rich in capital can to a large extent utilize productive powers of the past has two further consequences: to satisfy its present needs for consumption goods, it does not have to draw so much on new productive powers of the present; it can, therefore, utilize a large proportion of its current productive power for investment in still more roundabout methods of production, which will enhance future output.

Value.—Only a few new insights were gained by Böhm-Bawerk when he addressed himself to the task of interpreting relations of subjective value; more rewarding was his probing in the area of objective value.

As to *subjective value,* he makes more explicit Menger's and Wieser's distinctions drawn in connection with the gradation of wants. As we have seen, this gradation or ranking may refer either to *kinds* of wants or to *degrees* of wants (concrete individual feelings of want). Kinds are illustrated by Böhm-Bawerk as wants for food, clothing, housing, recreation, etc.; concrete feelings of want, by the degrees of intensity with which particular types of satisfaction are craved. In the gradation of concrete wants, we encounter a great deal more variation than in the scale of kinds of wants. Wants of various kinds "cross and intersect

---

[25]*Ibid.*, p. 90.

each other,"[26] as he expresses one of Menger's important findings. Consequently, while the most important concrete wants of the genus (kind) "subsistence" are higher up in the scale of utilities than the most important concrete wants of the genus "housing," less important concrete wants of the "subsistence" type may be "overpassed" by the most important concrete wants of the "housing" type. It thus happens that "the bottom members of the highest class"[27] are "overpassed by the top members of the lowest class."[28] Provided that our wants are divisible, that is, susceptible of piecemeal satisfaction, the value we attribute to goods is always based on the gradation of concrete wants rather than on the gradation of kinds of want. In the felicitous language used by the author, ". . . the more important kind [of want] is marked off from the less important only by the fact that, to some extent, its head rises higher than the others, while its base stands on the same level as all the others."[29]

Böhm-Bawerk echoes his compatriots in answering the question: *What determines the value of a good?* It is neither its greatest nor its average utility, but the least (marginal) utility which it will provide under a given set of economic conditions: ". . . the value of a good is measured by the importance of that concrete want, or partial want, which is *least urgent* among the wants that are met from the available stock of similar goods."[30] He boldly regards this proposition not only as the "keystone" of value theory, and of economic theory in general, but also as the "master key" to individual economic behavior relative to the acquisition of goods. He pursues in new directions some of the interesting and far-reaching *implications of this doctrine,* for example the fact that the marginal utility, and hence the value, of a good of one kind may be measured by the marginal utility of a good of another kind, the replacement good. In the case of goods affording different marginal utilities in different employments, the standard for valuing them is that employment which yields the highest marginal utility. (Who would price mahogany furniture at its value as fuel?) More generally, *we allocate a stock of a good among those concrete uses which are of most importance on our scale of utilities.* An example of Böhm-Bawerk's, slightly modified, will make the idea clear. If there are five opportunities for the employment of a good (indicated by the figures 10, 8, 6, 4,

[26]*Ibid.*, p. 141.
[27]*Ibid.*
[28]*Ibid.*
[29]*Ibid.*, p. 144.
[30]*Ibid.*, p. 148.

and 2 as measures of their relative importance) in one particular branch, and if in another branch there are also five opportunities (indicated by the figures 9, 7, 5, 3, and 1), a man possessing altogether 5 individual units of a good will allot them to the opportunities signified by 10, 9, 8, 7, 6, that is, to the employments affording the highest utilities. The marginal utility of the good, in this case 6, is higher than the marginal utility which would have resulted in the absence of competing employments — in which case it would have been either 2 or 1.

Again, *if a particular good affords a different marginal utility depending on whether it is employed in personal use or in exchange, it is the higher of the two which gives it its value.* "The scholar keeps his books, the bookseller sells his."[31] In this sense, both *exchange value* and *use value* are kinds of *subjective value*. Both are also related to *objective exchange value*. If the scholar becomes impoverished, and, therefore, sells his books, the subjective exchange value of his books will have become greater than their use value, while their objective exchange value (price) remains the same — unless scholars, generally, are in bad straits and flood the market with books. The marginal utility of money, or of other goods represented by money, has become greater than the marginal utility of the books as reflected in their use value. The example also shows that subjective exchange value is much more closely related to use value than to objective exchange value. Böhm-Bawerk recognized that, in an appraisal of the phenomena of value, *subjective exchange value is something entirely distinct from objective exchange value,* a fact of fundamental importance.

Price.—*Exchange* can take place only when persons put a different subjective value upon a commodity and upon its price equivalent, that is, when the buyer puts a higher estimate on the commodity than he does on the equivalent (money, or other goods) demanded by the seller, while the opposite relationship holds true for the seller. The more advanced the division of labor, the more numerous, generally, are the chances of opposing estimates and, consequently, the greater the opportunities of exchange. Also, the less value a person places on his own commodity (seller) or its price equivalent (buyer), and the greater value he places on the *quid pro quo*, the better the chances for exchange. These ideas Böhm-Bawerk applies to the cases of "isolated exchange," "one-sided competition," and "two-sided competition." Let us glance briefly at a typical situation of *two-sided competition*, where Böhm-

---

[31]*Ibid.*, p. 167.

BUYERS		SELLERS	
A_1 values a horse at £30 (and will buy at any price under)		B_1 values a horse at £10 (and will sell at any price over)	
A_2	28	B_2	11
A_3	26	B_3	15
A_4	24	B_4	17
A_5	22	B_5	20
A_6	21	B_6	21.5
A_7	20	B_7	25
A_8	18	B_8	26
A_9	17		
A_{10}	15		

Source: Eugen von Böhm-Bawerk, *The Positive Theory of Capital* (London: Macmillan Co., Ltd., 1891), p. 203.

Bawerk's analytical genius stands out most brilliantly. As illustrated above, he assumes that ten competitive buyers and eight competitive sellers, each with different subjective valuations, appear simultaneously in a horse market. Horses are assumed to be of equal quality, buyers and sellers to be fully informed about the conditions of the market and to pursue their self-interests as fully as possible. We are led to the following observations.

(1) It is obvious that A_1 could acquire a horse quite easily, since all of the eight sellers are willing to sell at a price less than £30. Certainly, seller B_1 could likewise get rid of his horse on satisfactory terms, since even the "least capable" buyer, A_{10}, would pay him £15, or £5 more than his asking price. In fact, because of the subjective valuations of the other buyers and sellers, neither buyer A_1 nor seller B_1 will have to trade at prices which in the *market* appear as rather unfavorable.

(2) At any price less than £15, the lowest bid price, the market could not be cleared, since all ten buyers would be willing to acquire a horse while only two sellers, B_1 and B_2, would be willing to part with their animals. If the price were raised to £16, A_{10} would no longer buy, but at the same time an additional seller, B_3, would find it advantageous to sell. However, at this price there would still be an excess of buyers over sellers, and the active competition of buyers and sellers would prevent this from becoming the market price.

(3) If the price were increased further, it would eventually have to reach a level at which the number of active buyers has fallen so much, and that of sellers has risen so much, that they will become equal. Indeed, if it should be raised beyond this level, the number of sellers

would begin to exceed the number of buyers, which — once again — would violate the best interests of all parties concerned.

What will be the *equilibrium price*? Is there a single price at which equilibrium will be attained?

(4) Böhm-Bawerk writes: ". . . at any price over £20, only six horses are demanded and five offered, the majority of buyers over sellers being thus reduced to one."[32] This statement is, strictly speaking, not correct, since at a price of, say, £23, which is "over £20," there would be only four buyers ($A_1 - A_4$), but six sellers ($B_1 - B_6$). What he apparently meant, as the context makes clear, is that at any price above £20 *but not exceeding £21* six buyers ($A_1 - A_6$) will confront five sellers ($B_1 - B_5$).

(5) To eliminate the one extra buyer without bringing in another seller, the price must rise above £21, but not as high as £21.5. At the latter price, the number of sellers (six) would exceed that of buyers by one. An exchange between A_6 and B_6 would be out of the question, since the highest price A_6 is willing to pay is £21, but the lowest price B_6 is willing to accept is £21.5. Hence, so long as the price is above £21 and below £21.5, the number of buyers and sellers will be equal; and final settlement is possible as they can all be satisfied simultaneously.

Böhm-Bawerk's analysis is not without fault. Actually, the conclusions arrived at here are not technically identical with the author's. It may well be asked why, if A_6 "values a horse at" £21, he would only pay for it a price *less* than £21, or why, if B_6 "values a horse at" £21.5, B_6 would be satisfied only with a price *over* £21.5. If we incorporate Böhm-Bawerk's inconsistency into the conclusion reached under (5) above, it would read (thus corresponding to the conclusion he *should* have reached): The relation favorable to settlement is one in which the market price is *no less than £21* and *no more than £21.5*, since, at these limits, A_6 and B_6 would still be excluded (under the odd assumptions criticized above). On the other hand, buyers $A_1 - A_5$ would be matched by sellers $B_1 - B_5$. In this view, as we contemplate once more the hypothetical reactions of buyers and sellers to bidding up the price from less than £15, the bidding of buyers against each other ". . . comes to an end, and the bargains *may* be concluded at the price of £21."[33] But if the sellers are shrewder than the buyers, the transactions may instead be concluded at a price as high as £21.5. Any price

---

[32] *Ibid.*, p. 205.
[33] *Ibid.*, p. 206.

within these limits, except £21.25, would be indicative of a superior judgment of market conditions by one or the other of the parties.

Analysis also reveals that *on both sides it is the "most capable" competitors that will come to terms*, that is, the buyers who place the highest subjective value and the sellers who place the lowest subjective value on the commodity to be traded. A_5 will be "successful" because, although he is not willing to bid as high as the other four successful buyers ($A_1 - A_4$), that is, is "less capable" than they are, his bid price of £22 is still higher than the price of £20 "asked" by B_5, the "least capable" of the successful sellers. This leads Böhm-Bawerk to conclude, somewhat anticlimactically, that the price cannot be higher than the valuation of A_5 (£22) nor less than the valuation of B_5 (£20), because otherwise either the fifth buyer or the fifth seller would certainly have been eliminated. Nor, as we have already seen, can it be higher than the valuation of B_6 (£21.5) and lower than the valuation of A_6 (£21), because otherwise the equilibrium would again be destroyed. We thus arrive at a seemingly incompatible *double* limitation on both the upper and the lower side. Böhm-Bawerk is quick to point out, however, that it is in effect the *narrower* pair of limits that matters. When, nevertheless, he concludes that "the market price is limited and determined by the subjective valuations of the two Marginal Pairs,"[34] using the plural form, he thereby indicates that sometimes it may be the valuations of the *last pair actually coming to terms*, rather than the valuations of the *pair just excluded*, as in the above case, that determine the price limits. (To visualize this other possibility, let the valuation of A_6 be £19 instead of £21, and the valuation of B_6 £23 instead of £21.5, with all other valuations remaining unchanged.)

Our final conclusion is that *the valuations of all unsuccessful competitors, except (possibly) the "most capable" among these*, in our case A_6 and B_6, have no effect on price whatsoever.

Interest.—It was intimated earlier that the *Positive Theory of Capital* is devoted to the exploration of the basic source underlying interest and to interest rate determination. Both are tied together by Böhm-Bawerk's propositions regarding the *valuation of present and future goods*. Much of this spadework done by Böhm-Bawerk was in the nature of new conceptualizations and numerical illustrations thereof, some of which did not survive close scrutiny by economists with a critical bent. But to have ventured some untenable doctrines can hardly detract from Böhm-Bawerk's overall performance: he broke

---

[34] *Ibid.*, p. 209.

new ground and left its fertilizing to others, thereby contributing no less to the advance of our science than did his successors.

The basic core of his interest theory centers around the proposition that *as a rule present goods are valued more highly than future goods of like kind and number*. It rests on the hypothesis that anticipated feelings of want are commensurate with presently felt sensations, that both of these are internally commensurable, and that future goods are also commensurable with one another as well as with present goods.

There are *three great causes* of differences in value between present and future goods. The *first* one arises from the fact that the circumstances of *wants and their provision differ with respect to present and future*. Such situations are frequent and are typically found when a person has undergone hardship and/or can look forward to being better provided for than he is at present.

The *second* one is accounted for by the fact that *people systematically underestimate future wants* and, consequently, the goods that serve to satisfy these wants. Such improvidence is especially noteworthy in the case of children and savages, but it is by no means negligible with adults and societies in an advanced state of development. It is exhibited under a variety of forms. Böhm-Bawerk attributes the reasons why future feelings have less control over our judgments and actions than do present feelings to "incompleteness of the imaginations we form to ourselves of our future wants"; to "defects of will," which may be coupled with quite adequate anticipations of future wants; and to "consideration of the uncertainty of life."[35] All of these behavioral patterns tend to reinforce the efficiency of the first cause for the different valuation of present and future goods: the difference in the provision of goods for the satisfaction of present and future wants.

The *third* of the great causes rests on the "technical superiority of present goods": *productive instruments available presently are on technical grounds superior to an equal amount of such instruments available only at a later time*, hence they have a higher marginal utility and value than the latter.[36] It is this last proposition which forms the main pillar of Böhm-Bawerk's interest theory. But all three causes together account for the fact that for a vast majority of men the subjective use value of present goods exceeds the subjective use value of the same goods in the future. The relation of subjective valuations is reflected in

---

[35]*Ibid.*, p. 257.

[36]This is so because capital goods already on hand are more useful than those not yet available, the time interval which must elapse before they generate finished goods being shorter than that which would elapse if these intermediate products were not yet available.

the market as a whole in a higher objective value (price) for present goods. Finally, since loans are but exchanges of present for future goods, the *interest paid* on them *simply reflects the "agio" (premium) of present over future goods.* "The borrower ... will ... purchase the money which he receives now by a larger sum of money which he gives later. He must pay an 'agio' or premium ..., and this agio is interest. Interest, then, comes in the most direct way, from the difference in value between present and future goods."[37]

However serious Böhm-Bawerk's aberrations may have been — they were probably exaggerated by grieved opponents — he was the first to make a study of the role of *time* in economic life an explicit foundation of production and particularly of capital theory, and by this contribution the labors of twentieth-century economists have been immeasurably enriched.

SUMMARY

Menger was the only one among the three principal founders of the marginal approach to value theory who did not employ the tools of higher mathematics. His exposition is therefore somewhat more long-winded and cumbersome, though by no means less lucid, than those of Walras and Jevons. His original ideas were consistently developed in the first five chapters of his *Principles of Economics* (1871). In contrast to that of Jevons, Menger's subjective theory of value betrays no allegiance to utilitarianism, or any other ethic or psychology. Somewhat like the classical writers, Menger views the behavior of the economy as merely the sum total of the behavior of the participating individuals. As did the German Gossen and the other leading Austrians, Menger laid great stress on the gradation of goods. He was also aware of the importance of complementarity for the determination of value. Although he did not use the term "marginal utility," he showed a full appreciation of the concept when he pointed out that the value of a given unit of a quantity of a good is measured by the importance to the individual of the satisfaction of least importance. He developed germs of a theory of (negative) imputation by making clear that the valuation of individual goods of higher order hinges on variations in the proportions in which complementary goods of higher order can be combined. The value of the former is measured by the importance of the satisfactions (in terms of final product) that would have to be foregone in the absence of (a given quantity of) the good of higher order.

---

[37] *Ibid.*, p. 286.

Two writers, von Wieser and von Böhm-Bawerk, have been mainly responsible for the maturation of a body of economic theory known as the Austrian school.   For the most part during the 1880's, they broadened and solidified the trail blazed by their countryman Menger.

Wieser, occupant from 1903 to 1922 of the Vienna chair of the stimulating Austrian pioneer in marginal analysis, developed his own ideas in a book called *Natural Value* (1889).   In it, he worked out patiently the fundamentals of value theory, as he had envisioned them in *Origin and Principal Laws of Economic Value* (1884).   The fertility of his mind is reflected in the concepts of "opportunity cost" (cost of production explained by indirect utility) and "imputation"; the grandeur of his conception of economic life is reflected in his reasoning about a communistic society, in which there is room for "natural value."   In natural value, goods are estimated according to their marginal utility, rather than according to a combination of marginal utility and purchasing power. (He thus realized that there is nothing specifically capitalistic about the basic concept of value.)

His "paradox of value" is a statement to the effect that total utility reaches its maximum when total value becomes zero, because marginal utility — a term coined by Wieser — has fallen to zero.   He also discovered the striking fact that total value must be zero both when there is no stock of a good and when the stock is so great that an additional unit cannot enhance total want satisfaction any further.   Closely akin are his views concerning the "antinomy" between value and utility. He clearly marked off the categories of subjective use value, subjective exchange value, and objective exchange value, recognizing that the latter, as reflected in price, is not an indicator of the relative social importance of goods.

In his theory of imputation, Wieser furnished an explanation of the value of the factors of production when their quantity is being varied, as distinguished from their valuation when they appear in a fixed combination.   He thus arrived at the notion of a factor's "productive contribution."

Böhm-Bawerk was a public servant during much of his life, but his performance as a teacher and writer was far from negligible.   He rendered his principal contributions to economic theory *before* devoting his energies to government service: both *Capital and Interest* (a historical analysis of interest theories) and *The Positive Theory of Capital* (a broad exposition of the formation of value and price) were produced when he was in his thirties.   No creative work comparable to these books came from his pen during the final decade of his life, when as a professor at the University of Vienna he was influential in shaping the minds of the next generation of Austrian economists.

Böhm-Bawerk was much concerned with capital in two distinct roles: as an instrument of production and as a source of interest. He showed, however, that the concept of interest covers more than the compensation received by the factor capital for its productive contribution in the economic process. Much of his work was devoted to the exploration of the superiority of indirect (roundabout) methods of production over direct ones. He attached more significance than did any of his contemporaries to differences in stages and degrees of roundabout production, in their relation to the output of final products.

In the field of subjective value theory, he pursued the implications of the gradation of wants according to kinds and degrees. In the case of goods affording different marginal utilities in different employments, he found that the standard for valuation is determined in that employment yielding the highest marginal utility. Böhm-Bawerk did spadework in applying subjective utility analysis to price formation under conditions of "isolated exchange," "one-sided competition," and "two-sided competition." His investigation of bilateral competition culminated in the proposition that the price level is determined and limited by the level of the subjective valuations of the two "marginal pairs."

Böhm-Bawerk's interest theory centers about the process of valuation of present and future goods. Differences in value between these were explained by three basic causes: differences in the (estimated) provision of wants in the present and future, the underestimation of future wants due to improvidence, and the technical superiority of present goods. By making the role of time an explicit foundation of production and capital theory, he paved the way for work with dynamic models and inspired the economics of the first American pure theorist of international stature: John Bates Clark (see Chapter 5).

BIOGRAPHICAL NOTES

A.—*Carl Menger* (1840–1921) — often misrepresented as Karl Menger, his son, who was responsible for the posthumous second edition of his father's *Principles* — was born the son of a lawyer in Galicia, which later became a part of Poland. After studying at the Universities of Vienna and Prague, he took his doctor's degree at the University of Cracow. Journalistic activities, followed by a brief career as a civil servant in the Austrian prime minister's office in the late 1860's and early 1870's, constitute the "institutional" background from which emerged that most carefully planned work which secured him a permanent place in the history of economic theory: *Grundsaetze der Volkswirtschaftslehre*, or literally, "Fundamental Propositions of Political Economy." (The English translation, *Principles of Economics*, by Dingwall and Hoselitz, was completed in 1950.)

On the basis of this profound piece of research, Menger was able to secure a lectureship at the University of Vienna and in 1873 the position of professor extraordinary. This was by no means a choice plum, because of the absence of a local tradition and the intellectual orientation of the future lawyers and civil servants who formed the bulk of his audience. He interrupted his work at Vienna for two years when, in 1876, he accepted an invitation to serve as tutor to the Crown Prince Rudolph, with whom he traveled through the greater part of Europe. Soon after his return to Vienna, he was offered the chair of political economy at the University, which he held from 1879 until his retirement in 1903. The last eighteen years of his life were spent in research and writing. Menger remained the venerated target of pilgrimages by younger scientists to his home.

His principal impact on economics was through succeeding generations of devoted disciples of similar calibre, who effectively utilized and built upon the foundations laid by the master.

Menger would have made a name for himself even if he had never remodeled the foundations of economics. His work in the field of money, which culminated in a long article "Money" in the first edition (1892) of the famous "Encyclopaedia of the Social Sciences" (*Handwoerterbuch der Staatswissenschaften*), stands out prominently, and so does the role he played as one of the principal contestants in the *Methodenstreit*, the "controversy over methods," which broke out after his publication in 1883 of *Inquiries into the Method of the Social Sciences, and Particularly Political Economy*. His main adversary, Gustav Schmoller, then Rector of the University of Berlin and leader of the Historical school, emerged more deeply battle-scarred; he was especially guilty of conjuring up imaginary differences for the mere purpose of defaming Menger. The latter was more than able to hold his ground, not without avoiding polemics in self-defense, however. This controversy, which centered upon the relative merits of the inductive and deductive methods of analysis, in the 1880's absorbed a great amount of Menger's mental energy. It partly explains why the planned sequence of his comprehensive project never advanced to the state of publication. It nevertheless served to clear the air by pointing out the limitations which strict adherence to inductive research, as advocated by Schmoller and his cohorts, was bound to encounter.

In 1900, Menger was honored by being appointed a life member in the upper chamber of the Austrian parliament, but he remained aloof from the political controversies of the day. His personal library was one of the most extensive that has ever been bestowed upon posterity by a thinker thoroughly at home in fields outside the area of his special competence; most of the collection is now deposited in the Tokyo University of Commerce. Not the least of his merits rests in the fact that, in contrast to Jevons and others, he was able to state a subjective theory of value free from the trappings of a hedonistic philosophy.

B.—*Friedrich Freiherr von Wieser* (1851–1926) was born in Vienna, scion of an aristocratic family with the conventional devotion to government service. His early interests focused on history, but at the age of seventeen he enrolled at the University of Vienna and embarked upon the course of study expected of members of his social class: jurisprudence. By the time of his graduation (1872), he nurtured a close friendship with a classmate, Eugen von Böhm-Bawerk, who later became his brother-in-law. During the next few years, Wieser gained some practical experience in the fiscal administration of Lower Austria.

Just before getting his law degree he had become acquainted with Menger's *Principles of Economics*. The new approach to problems of value theory by the then still obscure lecturer had definitely intrigued Wieser. Both he and Böhm-Bawerk in 1875 successfully applied for a traveling fellowship, entitling the recipients to pursue graduate work in economics in Germany, where the Historical school ruled supreme through the teaching and writing of such leaders as Roscher, Hildebrand, and Knies. In the spring of 1876, Wieser submitted a distinguished report to Knies' seminar at Heidelberg. It contained some of the basic ideas that were fully elaborated in works published in the 1880's, especially the earliest known version of the concept of opportunity cost. Although Menger, when confronted with the seminar paper, reacted something less than enthusiastically, he apparently thought much of young Wieser's scientific promise and helped his protégé to get a one-year extension of his travel grant.

Now armed with a broad knowledge of economics at the professional level, Wieser spent the years between 1877 and 1884 once again in the fiscal administration of Lower Austria. He continued his studies of economic literature, but notably without commitment to the method of the Historical school. In 1884, on the strength of a draft of several chapters of a proposed book, *Origin and Principal Laws of Economic Value*, Wieser managed to install himself as a lecturer at the University of Vienna. Shortly thereafter, at Menger's recommendation, he was able to secure a teaching position at the University of Prague. With the publication of the book, he had established his academic credentials.

Not satisfied with this accomplishment, he continued to focus on the subjective theory of value; and in 1889, after years of strenuous work, Wieser found a publisher for a definitive version of his earlier constructions. Entitled *Natural Value*, it subsequently became one of the classics in the field of value theory and was translated into English in 1893. Not only did this work immediately help Wieser climb another rung on the academic ladder — the University of Prague promoted him to the rank of full professor in 1889 — but it diffused the message of the Austrian school across international boundaries. And, no doubt, it enhanced Wieser's appeal as a potential successor to Menger's chair in Vienna.

In the fourteen years before the call could be extended to him, Wieser turned away from the heavy theoretical work which had begun to sap his strength. He started to occupy himself with what he felt were less ambitious problems, which he found mainly in the areas of public finance and economic policy. Having married in 1886, he also indulged more freely his artistic bent; in time his residence became a noted center of cultural life in Bohemia.

Before transferring back to Vienna in 1903, Wieser had resumed his research in economic theory. In his Vienna inaugural address, he demonstrated the applicability of the subjective theory of value to the problem of the value of money. He further expanded these ideas in writings published during the first few years as a teacher in Vienna.

His magnum opus — the only comprehensive-systematic work issuing from the Austrian school — turned out to be ill-timed, because its publication almost coincided with the outbreak of World War I in 1914. *Social Economics*, translated into English in 1927, more than his earlier works bore evidence of the wide range of his interests, and it abounded with fruitful points of departure for the further development of economic theory. It also contained an outline of Wieser's sociological theory. During the remaining years of his life (except for a wartime stint as minister of commerce in the last two cabinets of the Austro-Hungarian Empire), this broader field absorbed his spare-time energies almost exclusively — during the years 1922–1925 he held an honorary professorship at the University of Vienna. The final results of his wide-ranging sociological investigations were laid down in a work published just a few weeks before his death. *Das Gesetz der Macht*, a work of art rather than a dry treatise — and considered by the author as the capstone of his life's achievement — permanently established his reputation as a universal scholar.

C.—*Eugen von Böhm-Bawerk* (1851–1914), an exact contemporary of Wieser as far as the year of his birth and his studies at the University of Vienna were concerned, was survived by his "comrade-in-arms" by a span of twelve years, and by Menger, their mentor, who had been born in 1840, by seven years. Böhm-Bawerk thus lived a shorter life than the other principal champions of marginal utility theory, but a life no less conspicuous for single-minded devotion to duty both inside and outside the halls of learning.

Also born into a family of civil servants, his early interests indicated a predilection for science, but external factors favored a commitment to the study of law, which he took up at the University of Vienna in 1868. Reference has already been made in the preceding note to his friendship with Wieser dating from these years and—following the doctorate and a brief "hitch" in the ministry of finance — their common study tour of Germany (1875–1877), which brought the two young men into contact with the luminaries of the Historical school. Böhm-Bawerk's purely scientific interest in economic theory, an interest free from any reformatory zeal à la Marx, took definite shape in these years.

His fundamental ideas first appeared in a now little-known work published in 1881, on the strength of which he had been able to secure an instructorship at the University of Vienna the year before. But no sooner had he taken this hurdle than the University of Innsbruck beckoned, and for the time being this institution held more promise for his scientific career. Indeed, in 1881 he was promoted to the rank of professor extraordinary and only three years later to that of ordinary (full) professor. By no mere coincidence, this was also the year when the first volume of his work on capital and interest was published. Although it dealt with the history and criticism of interest theories, as indicated by its German title (*Geschichte und Kritik der Kapitalzinstheorien*), it was translated into English under the title *Capital and Interest*. (The translation was undertaken by an indefatigable Scotsman, William Smart of the University of Glasgow, who permitted himself to become the chief instrument for the spread of Austrian doctrine in the English-speaking world. *Capital and Interest* was completed in 1890, and other translations followed in short order.)

The *Positive Theory of Capital*, a towering achievement in a creative vein, was rushed through the press in 1889, the year in which Böhm-Bawerk accepted a call to serve in the ministry of finance. Apparently, he anticipated full-time absorption by his duties as a public servant and wanted to see the fruits of his relatively quiet academic years at Innsbruck harvested before conflicting demands on his time might impair the unity of the work of his most creative decade. At its beginning, he had married Wieser's sister, and this alliance proved of priceless value to the otherwise quite self-reliant social scientist.

During the long years spent in government employment (1889–1904), he served three times as minister of finance in the cabinet, having previously prepared a draft of the great Austrian tax reform which, much along the lines suggested by him, became law in 1896. In the 1890's, he found time for both offensive and defensive moves in the professional controversies of the time, but his sallies were always ennobled by a spirit of respect for his peers as well as for people of a lesser intellectual stature. He also maintained his peripheral academic relation by serving as a special lecturer at the University of Vienna, and in 1892 he became one of the cofounders of a German economic periodical.

When he returned to full-time academic life by accepting the position of ordinary professor at his Alma Mater in 1905, his creative force was spent; however, he continued to inspire a crop of pupils who later became famous economists, including the incomparable Schumpeter. The latter has dubbed his teacher the "Bourgeois Marx" because his model of the economic process parallels that of Marx. Nevertheless, he was anything but a disciple of Marx, as attested by his famous criticism of the Marxian system in a work published in German in 1896 and translated into English in 1898 under the title, *Karl Marx and the Close of His System*.

Questions for Review and Research

1. How are the works of the three principal founders of marginalism (subjective theory of value) related in time?
2. What is Menger's most basic distinction relative to want satisfaction?
3. Did Menger agree with Smith's dictum that the division of labor is the central element in the economic progress of mankind?
4. According to Menger, are noneconomic goods absolutely unrelated to the satisfaction of human needs? Explain.

5. Explain how, according to Menger, the more complete satisfaction of the more pressing wants is combined with the less complete satisfaction of the less pressing wants.
6. Explain the concept of "opportunity cost." To whom is it due?
7. Why did Böhm-Bawerk attach significance to differences in stages and degrees of roundabout production?
8. What did Wieser mean in writing about (a) the "antinomy" between value and utility? (b) the "antinomy" of exchange value?
9. With what two principal powers of "capital" was Böhm-Bawerk concerned? In his terminology, are the concepts of "private capital" and "social capital" mutually exclusive?
10. Briefly state Böhm-Bawerk's view of price formation under two-sided competition.

Recommended Readings

Böhm-Bawerk, Eugen von. *Capital and Interest,* translated with a preface and analysis by William Smart. New York: The Macmillan Company, 1890. "Translator's Preface," pp. v-xx; "Introduction: The Problem of Interest," pp. 1–10; Book VII, "Minor Systems": "Conclusion," pp. 421–428.

Menger, Carl. *Principles of Economics,* translated and edited by James Dingwall and Bert F. Hoselitz, with an introduction by Frank H. Knight. Glencoe, Illinois: The Free Press, 1950. Chapter I, "The General Theory of the Good," pp. 51–76; Chapter II, "Economy and Economic Goods," pp. 77–113; Chapter III, "The Theory of Value," pp. 114–174.

Schumpeter, Joseph A. *Ten Great Economists from Marx to Keynes.* New York: Oxford University Press, Inc., 1951. The biographical essay "Carl Menger (1840–1921)," pp. 80–90.

Stigler, George J. *Production and Distribution Theories.* New York: The Macmillan Company, 1941. Chapter VI, "Carl Menger"; Chapter VII, "Friederich von Wieser"; and Chapter VIII, "Eugen von Böhm-Bawerk."

Wieser, Friedrich von. *Natural Value,* edited with a preface and analysis by William Smart, translated by Christian A. Malloch. New York: Kelley & Millman, Inc., 1956. "Author's Preface," pp. xxvii-xxxvi; Book I, "The Elementary Theory of Value," pp. 3–36; Book II, "Exchange Value and Natural Value," pp. 39–66; Book III, Part I "The General Principles of Imputation," pp. 69–113.

5

VALUE AND DISTRIBUTION THEORY

The American Contribution

For many decades, while in England the classical theory of value and distribution rose to prominence under David Ricardo and his disciples, was refined and restated by John Stuart Mill, and finally challenged, if not dethroned, by the marginal utility theorists in the 1870's and early 1880's, American economic thought remained on the sidelines. The rapid expansion and settlement of this country, coupled with the spread of industrialization, did produce native problems and native attempts at their solution, but the new ideas did not shake the foundations of the imposing intellectual structure that had made political economy synonymous with liberalism of the classical (English) variety.

Daniel Raymond[1], the Careys[2], and John Rae[3] had espoused some unorthodox ideas relative to a number of aspects of political economy, including the principle underlying the formation of rent, the domestic benefits to be gained from protection against foreign competition, and the blessings that could be bestowed upon the citizens through governmental promotion of innovation and capital formation; but little of this thought measured up to standards of scientific theory. Exposition of economic doctrines did not get very far in the absence of chairs of political economy and manifested itself mainly in a somewhat slavish allegiance to the tenets that reigned supreme on the British Isles.

During the third quarter of the nineteenth century, the rumblings of a distant American voice became distinctly audible in European halls of learning. Being neither particularly shrill nor penetrating, it did not cause economic theorists in England and on the continent to perk up their ears. Henry George and Francis Walker, of different temperament but both public-spirited, had "sent out their feelers." While their

---

[1]See Biographical Note A.
[2]See Biographical Note B.
[3]See Biographical Note C.

ideas reached maturity, around the beginning of the fourth quarter of the nineteenth century, the one man who shortly was to make economics in America respected in the old countries had just completed his formal education in Germany under Karl Knies,[4] one of the early leaders of the German Historical school. John Bates Clark (see page 158) has claims to independent discovery of many principles incorporated in the marginal utility approach to value theory, although the period of gestation of his main ideas lagged by roughly a decade behind the economic banner years of 1871 and 1874.

HENRY GEORGE[5] AND FRANCIS A. WALKER[6]

What makes these two Americans noteworthy apart from their feats in the political and military arenas, for which they are principally known to the general historian? Very little as far as the new value theory is concerned. Yet *both effectively questioned certain time-honored assumptions of the Classical school,* and this indirectly helped to undermine the rather uncritical devotion which a lack of independent and forceful thinking had fostered in the United States.

Henry George, not an academic economist and treated somewhat sneeringly by the general run of economic professionals, performed a distinguished service by arousing public opinion to injustices in the distribution of income. He depicted land rent as the most egregious example of unearned increments and displayed some keen thoughts on the relation of wages to rent.

According to the classical "wages-fund" theory, wages are determined by the proportion between the number of laborers and the sum total set aside for the employment of labor. They tend toward a subsistence minimum, because workers frequently multiply more rapidly than capital expands. This theory, a concomitant of the Malthusian doctrine and one of the weakest buttresses of the classical edifice, George branded as false and a figment of the imagination. For one, there just is no fund specially set aside for the payment of wages. George believed that the classical writers were misled by the fact that wages are paid before the completion of the product to which workers have contributed. But, although the process of production may be long, the creation of value takes place *before* the product is ready for consumption. It is not necessary to put aside funds for the payment of

---

[4]See Biographical Note D.
[5]See Biographical Note E.
[6]See Biographical Note F.

wages because partly finished products are exchanged just as quickly as completely finished ones. Now if the latter remain unsold for some time, certainly the businessman is in need of funds; but this has nothing to do with his function as an employer of labor. If anybody, it is the worker rather than the employer who makes an advance, since the services of the former are utilized before they are paid for by the latter.

In the second place, a persistent increase in population does not reduce per capita wages but rather increases them. Despite the fact that human multiplication compels recourse to poorer soil, it expands the subsistence base, because the rise in productive powers more than compensates for the operation of the principle of diminishing returns. George went so far as to construe misery in new countries by a theory of underpopulation. But why, then, do we also observe misery in the most advanced nations? He finds the explanation for the seeming paradox in the *unequal distribution of the rapidly increasing wealth*. This points to the core of the problem of *Progress and Poverty*. Although wages do not come out of capital, there is a close connection between the two distributive shares of wages and interest. George shows that interest is, in a sense, derived from labor. Not only can labor services expended on land produce wealth without the aid of capital; but, by the very nature of things, labor must produce wealth before capital can come into existence. Since capital can always be augmented or diminished by devoting more or less labor to its production, interest is tied to wages; it is correlated with the movement of wages. In George's final analysis, wages and interest as factorial shares are affected not only by the increase in productive powers but by the increase in the rent from land. The rewards which the factors of labor and capital receive are governed by competition and thus limited to what they produce on no-rent land.

By way of comparison, George substituted for Ricardo's relation between capital and labor (where the one can gain in the long run only at the expense of the other) a new relation: between capital and labor on the one hand, and land on the other. As Teilhac has pointed out:

> By the intimate solidarity which he established between capital and labor . . . he [George] opposes himself at the same time to both Ricardian economics and Marxian socialism. Although he repudiates the Ricardian relation between wages and interest, he nevertheless adopts the Ricardian theory of rent.[7]

Among the leading critics of George was Francis A. Walker, who, although he seconded George in the attack on the wages-fund theory,

---

[7] Ernest Teilhac, *Pioneers of American Economic Thought in the Nineteenth Century*, translated by E. A. J. Johnson (New York: The Macmillan Company, 1936), p. 140.

segregated interest from profits in order to make the treatment of profits analogous to that of rent, as explained below. This new departure is revealed by a study of his *residual claimant theory of wages.* According to this theory of distribution, the shares of the product of industry *other than wages* are fixed, as it were, in their nature and amount. Consequently, the laborers receive all they help to produce minus the predetermined shares of rent, profit, and interest. Along Ricardian lines, Walker finds rent determined by the productivity of land superior to no-rent land. Rent (from supramarginal land) neither affects the price of agricultural products nor does it come out of the remuneration of agricultural workers. Interest, the remuneration for the use of savings, must be high enough to induce producers of wealth to save rather than to consume. Although it may vary according to the state of development of a society, in essence it is also predetermined.

Profits, the remuneration of the entrepreneur for setting into motion the complicated machinery of production, closely resemble rent from land. To begin with, Walker assigns great importance to the *entrepreneurial function.* He states that the qualifications for business are highly unequal and vary according to a wide range of ability. He distinguishes, quite arbitrarily, poor from moderately good, highly able, and rarely gifted (genius type) performers of this function. In close analogy to marginal (no-rent) land, Walker visualizes a margin of no-profit employers, people inadequately qualified who are scarcely "good" enough to stay in business and who derive from their "checkered careers" nothing beyond a "bare subsistence." Depending on how much above this level of performance other employers may rise in theirs, they will derive larger or smaller positive profits, with the most capable men earning the greatest rewards, just as the most fertile (and/or best situated) land fetches the highest rent. Barring restraints on competition, these profits would not, however, form a part of the prices of commodities. They would consist merely of wealth produced over and above what would have been created by industrial enterprises with the same labor force and capital but directed by no-profit employers.

With rent, interest, and profits deducted from the product of industry, the remaining portion of it represents the property of the laboring class, their wage remuneration for services performed. Walker believed that inasmuch as competition is permitted to work fully and freely, every form of technological progress accrues to workers by purely natural laws. It is only on account of their own neglect, the operation of inequitable laws, or strong social customs that they might remain deprived of part of their residual claim on the product of industry.

It is obvious that *Walker's theory of wages stands or falls with his theory of profits*, if we accept as basically correct his interpretation of rent and interest — the latter he failed to explain satisfactorily, viewing interest both as a remuneration of capitalists for having risked their capital in production *and* as a reward for abstinence. However fruitful his analytical innovation may have been from the point of view of the scientific need for continuously reexamining established categories, there still appears no more reason for applying the term "residual" to wages than for applying it to other factorial shares. Trite though it may be, the "truest" statement is still that each factorial share comprises all of the product which the other shares do not absorb.

JOHN BATES CLARK[8]

For all practical purposes, the United States was lacking a "master builder" of economic thought until J. B. Clark appeared on the scene. His assiduous scholarship during the years from 1886 to 1899 resulted in a penetrating work entitled *The Distribution of Wealth*. In addition, he was the first among American economists who came close to founding a school in the same sense that Quesnay in France and Ricardo in England had founded schools of thought. Both of these facts augured well for American economics as the twentieth century dawned. What Clark stated to be the purpose of *The Distribution of Wealth* was largely synonymous with the purpose of his lifelong devotion to economics: ". . . to show that the distribution of the income of society is controlled by a natural law, and that this law, if it worked without friction, would give to every agent of production the amount of wealth which that agent creates."[9]

Any theory of value and distribution must remain less than perfect if it fails to distinguish clearly between static and dynamic forces. It was Clark's signal service to point out at the start that his efforts were to be largely confined to *tracing economic laws under static* — what the classical economists called "natural"— *standards*. He thereby recalled the tremendous handicap under which the economist is condemned to work because he must abstract from the multitude of dynamic forces

---

[8]See Biographical Note G.
[9]John B. Clark, *The Distribution of Wealth* (New York: The Macmillan Company, 1931), p. v.

under which society actually operates. If it is possible to isolate the forces to which the prices of the factors tend at any time to conform, one of the most basic prerequisites for any study of changing phenomena has been met. It is in this endeavor that Clark displayed rare originality. He carried on the methodological tradition of the Classical school but without subscribing to its more narrow set of assumptions. There is only one pioneer to whose work Clark's is closely linked by primary focus: J. H. von Thünen, whose beacon Clark freely acknowledged. There are many whose works resemble Clark's in general approach, those of the Austrians being in the forefront. But there is at least one feature of Clark's performance that gives it a quality all its own: his elaboration of a difference between (permanent) *capital*, that is, an abiding fund of productive wealth, and particular instruments of production in the form of *capital goods*, which are productively consumed.

The Marginal Productivity Theory

According to Clark, the study of distribution involves the tracing to each of the productive factors that are combined in a wealth-creating process of the individual parts which these factors separately contribute to the joint result, and *the problem of distribution is to be solved by tracing the social product to its sources*. He contends that, where natural laws have their way, the shares of income attaching to each of the factors are equal to the actual products created by their services. In this view, the study of distribution resolves itself into an analysis of "specific production." For political as well as other reasons, the disposal of that part of the total product which is created by the laboring classes is the most critical issue. From this insight derives the practical importance of Clark's attempt to prove that under pure competition each producer, including the worker, receives the amount of wealth that he specifically creates, to prove that factorial products and shares coincide.

Clark contrasts personal with functional income distribution and concludes that the latter falls entirely within the field of economics, whereas the former does not. He points out that personal income is more often than not a composite of different functional shares — most typically illustrated by the entrepreneur who, in addition to coordinating the other factors, usually owns some capital and performs some labor services. From the point of view of individual members of society, functional distribution means the resolving of personal incomes into their functional parts according to the particular ways in which the

incomes were obtained.   Clark firmly believes that the grievances
arising between entrepreneurs and workers as a result of discrepancies
in their personal incomes can be proved to be either justified or lacking
substance, and, therefore, can be settled by a knowledge of the principles underlying functional distribution.   For "if each productive
function is paid for according to the amount of its product, then each
man gets what he himself produces."[10]   Hence, *whether or not workers
get what they produce is a question of fact, not one of ethics.*

If we are interested in how well various segments of the economy are
doing, we inquire into a type of income distribution that is intermediate
between functional and personal distribution.   "Group distribution,"
as Clark calls it, merely indicates how much a particular industry as
a whole gets, relative to other industries, and is mainly governed by the
market prices of the commodities produced by it.   However, these market prices in the long run will tend to conform to "normal" ("natural")
prices.   The latter are themselves a result of the distributive process.
They reflect that condition under which labor and capital produce (and
get) the same return in all industries in which they may be used, and,
therefore, have no incentive to leave one industry and enter another.
Thus, through many ramifications, Clark is led back to the law of
normal (natural) price that was already stated by Adam Smith.   Clark
considered the classical formulation as misleading because it focused on
the entrepreneur's, instead of on the social, point of view.   Clark's
analysis also suggests that prices are normal when group distribution is
in a natural state, that is, when there is neither overproduction nor
underproduction in the various industries.   In the contrary case,
workers and capitalists will move from industries in which product
prices are low to industries where they are high, and this will bring
prices into balance, that is, back to normal.   The interesting observation follows that "an influence that originates in distribution brings
about a state of social production in which exchange values are
normal."[11]   Never before had the *mutual interdependence of factor prices
and commodity prices*, of the phenomena of distribution and production,
been brought into clearer relief.

The classical economists were not fully aware of the implications of
what they called "natural" values.   Clark has been able to show that
natural commodity prices as well as natural factor prices are actually
equivalent to "static" rates, that is, the rates that would be realized in
a state of perfect competition, and in the absence of economic progress.

---

[10]*Ibid.*, p. 7.
[11]*Ibid.*, p. 19.

Unfortunately, Clark applies the term "static" when referring to the *differentiae specificae* of the stationary state; for him statics was simply the model of a stationary society and dynamics the model of evolutionary change. He failed to see that the term "statics" should be reserved to a particular *method* of dealing with economic phenomena, namely, that method which establishes relations between economic variables relating all to the same point or period of time, or which compares equilibrium positions at different points in time. It thus escaped him that by a "stationary" state is meant not a method but a certain *state of the object* to be analyzed, namely, an economic process that merely reproduces itself. (Both terms apply, of course, to nothing but methodological fictions.) As a result of this confusion, Clark makes the somewhat misleading distinction between "Social Economic Statics"[12] and "Social Economic Dynamics."[13] The first of these is concerned with the natural standards of commodity prices and rates for factor services as they would be achieved in a stationary state (what should be called the dynamics of the stationary state). The second deals not only with forces that would act if society were in a stationary state but also with influences acting as disturbances — changes in wants, modes of production, population — affecting the structure of society (what should be called the dynamics of an evolutionary state). Clark correctly pointed out that the action of the disturbing (evolutionary) forces cannot suppress the action of the ones operative in a stationary society; the latter still assure that actual values (commodity prices), wages, and interest are kept relatively near the natural rates. The difficulty, not fully recognized by Clark, is to construct a theory of the dynamics of the evolutionary state that can fully interpret the real world, a difficulty compounded by the fact that evolutionary forces constantly create new conditions in which natural values are themselves different from what they would be in a stationary state. By way of an illustration, the price of cotton cloth which would be its natural price at the time the fabric is made by hand is no longer its natural price when that fabric is made by machinery. But it is precisely because the forces that act in an imaginary stationary state continue to act in an evolutionary one that Clark is so anxious to establish the laws governing the former.

In working out his theory of the final productivity of factors of production, Clark is particularly concerned with the familiar question of *how the specific product of labor may be singled out.* He assumes that

---

[12]*Ibid.*, p. 29.
[13]*Ibid.*, p. 31.

an employer has a certain number of workers who perform tasks of different importance but are freely interchangeable. He then poses the questions of, first, how much an employer would lose if one of his men left him, and second, if it would make any difference whether the departing worker had performed a relatively more or a relatively less important task. Since the men are interchangeable, if the man who quits has been doing work that is indispensable the employer will put in his place the worker who previously performed the least important task. Consequently, the reduction of a work force by one unit of labor (one man) will always result in a reduction of output corresponding to the contribution of the marginal worker, the one who had performed the least needed work. Hence, "the *effective* importance to his employer of any . . . interchangeable men is measured by the *absolute* importance of the one that does the least necessary work."[14]

Where men are not completely interchangeable, this principle of effective productivity will still hold, by and large. If the work of a superior man, namely one who performs a very important function, has to be taken over by one somewhat less skilled, substitution will necessitate a loss of product greater than the value of the product of the marginal worker; and the difference between the actual loss and that caused by removing the marginal worker from his job and assigning him a more important task measures the degree in which the superior worker was "irreplaceable."

In the case of both perfect and less than perfect interchangeability, we must distinguish between a worker's absolute and his effective productivity. But only in the first case is the effective productivity of all men the same. For only with free interchangeability will the loss of output be the same regardless of whether a man doing indispensable work or one doing work of slight importance is removed from the establishment. The loss of a particular man's absolute productivity will be fully recovered by placing the man of least productivity into his job, and what the firm loses is represented by a man's effective productivity, which is the same for any possible arrangement of workers. If there are four men, A, B, C, and D, performing work of decreasing relative importance (which means that A's absolute productivity is greater than B's, B's greater than C's, and C's greater than D's) and if A quits, then A may be directly replaced by D, or B may move into A's place, C into B's, and D into C's. In either case the only work that remains undone is the least necessary. It follows that if a labor

[14]*Ibid.*, p. 103.

force is made up of freely interchangeable workers, the effective productivity of any one worker is equal to the absolute productivity of the marginal, the most dispensable, worker. *The wage of all workers is measured by effective rather than absolute productivity,* because as long as an employer can freely substitute men for one another, any one member of the work force is worth to him neither more nor less than the worker performing the least important task — who is worth to the employer only as much as his productive contribution adds to the firm's revenue. Clark is fully aware that inertia and friction may keep actual wage rates from ever attaining the theoretical standard; the important point is that if competition is allowed to work, it will cause wages to gravitate toward the level fixed by the product of the marginal worker.

Extending the scope of the inquiry, Clark further establishes that there is a tendency to *uniformity of pay for marginal workers of a given kind*, both as between several employers in the same industry and as between different branches of industry. As long as workers of a given kind and of uniform quality can be freely transferred from one field to another, their productive powers, and hence their wages, will be equalized at the margin of employment in the different fields. However, this equalization can take place *only if capital is freely transmutable*, that is, if it has unlimited power to employ varying amounts of labor. We are thus led to a final set of distinctions, one which is *uniquely* associated with the name of J. B. Clark.

(Social) Capital v. Capital Goods

While admitting that the effects of spending money on education and of spending it on nonhuman instruments of production may be quite similar, Clark rejects as inexpedient the practice of some classical writers to include acquired abilities of workmen in the stock of productive wealth.

Capital in the broadest sense, which is always *based* on concrete and material goods, may be viewed either as a fund whose distinctive attribute is its permanence or as specific means of production whose destiny it is to perish in the process of helping to produce other goods. The baffling fact now is that unless capital goods are "destroyed" (used), capital itself cannot be permanent! For if machines, tools, etc., were not used, they would ultimately become so antiquated that the potential value of their services would fall near zero, obsolescence having taken its toll. "Capital goods . . . not only *may* go to destruction but *must* be destroyed, if industry is to be successful; and they must do so, in order that capital may last."[15]

Another point of contrast is the perfect *mobility of capital* v. the substantial *immobility of capital goods*. Funds may be readily transferred from one industry to another through our monetary mechanisms (banks and stock market, among others), but a ship cannot be converted into a cotton mill. If ships wear out, the depreciation allowances can be used to build cotton mills instead of more vessels. Whereas the *form* of capital is subject to constant change, capital remains as a social fund, ready to migrate between different sets of material bodies. The practical importance of the dichotomy is illustrated by the owner of a business firm who, when questioned about his capital, speaks of it in terms of money. Assume that he has originally invested a sum of $100,000. This is embodied in very diverse concrete things, whose composition changes continuously during the life of the business as a going concern. But the owner thinks of the $100,000 as an abiding thing, as a stock of productive wealth worth $100,000. If thought of as actually embodied in concrete things, the $100,000 is no longer an abstraction, and it would be erroneous to presume that capital can live in a disembodied state. Rather capital lives by "transmigration," by shifting continuously from one set of material things to another. When we conceive of it in monetary terms, we merely mean a continuous succession of shifting goods always worth a certain number of dollars. According to Clark, the only exception to this rule that capital is a sum of wealth continuously transforming itself relates to the part of it that is invested in land. However, the exception holds true less frequently than Clark saw: while the irrigation canal, once built, will remain essentially unaltered, the seedcorn put into the ground will cast off its present body and take another.

Clark's distinction between capital and capital goods has further practical implications. Notice that in popular usage we speak of rent when we allude to the amount that a concrete capital good earns but of interest when we refer to the earnings of capital (as a permanent fund); the former is expressed as a lump sum, the second as a percentage. *Interest and rent thus bear the same relationship to one another as do capital and capital goods.* Furthermore, we can easily reduce interest to the form of rent, and vice versa; in fact, they merely describe the same income in two different ways. As Clark put it: "Rent is the aggregate of the lump sums earned by capital goods; while interest is

---

[15]*Ibid.*, p. 117.

the fraction of itself that is earned by the permanent fund of capital"[16] or interest "... is total rent, reduced to a percentage of total capital."[17]

Clark also clarifies the *significance of the concept of abstinence*, especially in relation to capital and capital goods. While abstinence merely amounts to taking our income in the form of capital goods instead of consumer goods, not all creation of capital goods calls for abstinence. Since worn-out capital goods can be replaced out of the sinking fund accumulated during their lifetime, replacement calls for no further act of abstinence. Such is only required when we start an entirely new series of capital goods, in other words, is confined to net capital formation; but the successors in the series of capital goods are virtually generated by the first act of abstinence. Since it *originates* new capital goods, abstinence must be credited with bringing about accretions to capital (the permanent fund).

Finally, with respect to Böhm-Bawerk's "period of production" we can say that it is related to capital goods rather than to capital, for the period of production is measured by the interval which lapses between the labor in making a concrete instrument of productive wealth (say, a hatchet fashioned by sharpening a stone) and the concrete fruits of that labor (say, in the form of firewood). Such capital goods, in Clark's view, renew themselves in an endless series of periods of production, but capital itself is timeless, has no periods; its continued life can be marked off only by using arbitrary calendar divisions. While raw materials mature into capital goods which later exhaust themselves and are replaced, capital as a permanent fund has no life cycle of its own. Since every addition to the quantity of (permanent) capital in existence adds less to the product of industry than did the preceding additions, it is when — *ceteris paribus* — the quantity of (permanent) capital increases that the interest rate falls.

This is in contrast to Böhm-Bawerk, who held that every addition to the average *length* of the period of production tends to reduce interest. In rebuttal Clark pointed out that if, with Böhm-Bawerk, we measure productive periods by the lifetimes of particular capital goods, they may be lengthened (by the goods being retained) or shortened (by the goods being discarded) without affecting the rate of interest; lengthening per se does not add to the *amount* of capital, a prerequisite for a reduction in the interest rate. On the other hand, if, with Clark, we measure productive periods by the duration of "true" capital, they are

---

[16] *Ibid.*, p. 124.
[17] *Ibid.*, p. 125.

endless. This, then, explains why Clark had little use for Böhm-Bawerk's period of production.

SUMMARY

Several economic thinkers on this continent had espoused unorthodox (opposed to the Classical school) ideas in the course of the nineteenth century, but their influence was not sufficient to establish a recognized American branch of value and distribution theory. The closest approximation to theoretical contributions of permanent validity is found in the works of Francis A. Walker and Henry George, both "activists" who left the stamp of their forceful personalities on contemporary economists. Many of these declined to take the latter seriously while to the former they may have accorded tribute too generously. *Progress and Poverty,* an all-time best seller among economic tracts, although not devoid of rigorous logic, was ignored or defamed by the kind of people who in 1885 elected Walker to the first presidency of the American Economic Association. Walker's supporters thus made up by professional recognition (denied to George) what Walker did not achieve in popular acclaim (won by George's *Progress and Poverty*) when he published his two books, *The Wages Question* and *Political Economy.*

In addition to their own positive contributions to the body of distribution theory — George by his analysis of rent as an unearned increment and Walker by his residual claimant theory of wages — both Americans rendered economic science a service by giving the already discredited wages-fund theory its coup de grâce. (Removal of impedimenta or scientific deadwood is sometimes no less worthy of recognition than a new discovery.)

J. B. Clark, the late nineteenth-century master builder in the field of value and distribution theory, rallied native economists to an awareness of the potential that lay in independent American research. In *The Philosophy of Wealth* (1885), he had established his credentials as a profound thinker; *The Distribution of Wealth* (1899) contains the fruits of his more mature scholarship. He viewed the problem of income distribution as that of tracing the social product to its sources and of proving that distribution is controlled by a natural law. This law, if it worked without friction, would give to every agent of production the amount of wealth created by it.

Clark made a hitherto much-neglected distinction between static and dynamic forces. He pointed out the need for the development of economic laws under (assumed) static conditions before a fruitful attack could be made on the more complicated problems of dynamic change. He distinguished between personal and functional income distribution and recognized only the latter as being entirely within the domain of economics. Group distribution, he pointed out, indicates how large a share of the total product is received by a particular industry. He brought into brilliant relief the mutual interdependence of factor prices and commodity prices, of the phenomena of distribution and production, and gave new content to the notion of natural (normal) price.

In working out his theory of the final productivity of the factors of production, he dealt at length with the question of how the specific product of labor, whose rising political influence he anticipated, could be singled out. He showed that the answer hinges in part upon the interchangeability of workers, which leads to a differentiation between absolute and effective productivity. Clark worked out a unique distinction between capital and capital goods, viewing the former as a fund with the attribute of permanence and the latter as specific means of production destined to be used up in the process of producing other goods. Finally, he found that the creation of new capital goods does not necessarily require a preceding act of abstinence.

BIOGRAPHICAL NOTES

A.—*Daniel Raymond* (1786–1849) has been recognized for having written the first American treatise on political economy. His *Thoughts on Political Economy* (1820) went through four editions but did not directly exert any significant influence on other economists.

A Baltimore lawyer, seeking diversion and relief from the tedium of legal study, he undertook to write a fairly comprehensive discourse on the subject which Adam Smith had made respectable. He impressed a limited group of friends, one of whom (Matthew Carey) offered five hundred dollars to support a chair of political economy at the University of Maryland if Raymond would accept an invitation to become its first occupant. Carey was not taken up on this offer.

Strongly influenced by Alexander Hamilton, Raymond felt that the tenor of Smith's thought could not be squared with experience in the American environment, and his doctrines reflect the contrast between American and European economic conditions. He denounced the Scotsman for the alleged identity between national and individual interest and proceeded to outline the basic difference between national and individual wealth: a nation's wealth will always rest on the productivity of its labor, but an individual can often support himself, or live luxuriously, on income derived from (inherited) property. Raymond held that Smith's failure to grasp the conceptual difference between the interests of a nation and those of individuals prevented him from arriving at an unbiased appreciation of the proper functions of the state.

A strong nationalist, he advocated the large-scale use of protective tariffs on imports competing with domestic production. He advised nations to consult their own interests only and pay no heed to conflicting interests of other countries. He held that full employment of national labor, to be promoted by government, is accomplished best by a monopoly of the home market. Some of Raymond's criticisms of Smith's purportedly erroneous views on the nature of wealth and on the duties of the state were also advanced in the writings of such European economists as Lauderdale and Sismondi.

B.—*Matthew Carey* (1760–1839), as an expositor of Hamiltonian economic ideas, achieved more publicity than Raymond. A fugitive emigrant from Ireland — he had served a prison term for being unsparingly critical of the British government — he enjoyed the esteem of Benjamin Franklin, for whom he had worked in Paris for a while. With a gift from another American friend he set himself up as a printer and book publisher in Philadelphia. Highly successful in this endeavor, he achieved additional fame for his humanitarian passion, for which he found an outlet in numerous projects of charity. A charter member of the Philadelphia Society for the Promotion of National Industry, he was a vigorous advocate of Henry Clay's American System, which eventually won the day. Most of his arguments for government intervention through protective tariffs appeared in pamphlet form, his eloquence being occasionally tainted by violent abuse.

His son, *Henry Charles Carey* (1793–1879), with only the bare bones of a formal education, in contrast to the elder Carey acquired more prestige among men of letters than among businessmen seeking government aid against foreign competition. With ready access to his father's book-publishing house, the sky was the limit in his efforts to acquire brilliance as a self-taught man. His business acumen helped him secure a fortune as junior partner of the firm between the ages of twenty-four and forty-two. Retired from moneymaking at the midpoint of his life, he had many decades left to devote to research and writing. His prolific authorship, betraying breadth rather than depth, is attested by some thirteen volumes, plus thousands of pages of pamphlet material and newspaper contributions. Never hesitant to offer advice on public policy, he exhibited extremely optimistic views in such works as *The Principles of Political Economy* (1837–1840), *The Past, the Present, and the Future* (1843), *The Harmony of Interests* (1850), and *The Principles of Social Science* (1858–1859).

He aimed at, but hardly reached, a Comtian integration of all the social sciences, in which accumulation of wealth takes a secondary place. In his views of practical policy he walked the whole gamut from doctrinaire free trade to ardent protectionism. He denied the existence of problems of wealth distribution, since the harmony of interests joining the participants in the economic process would prevent them from taking advantage of each other.

He meticulously searched for empirical evidence to prove Ricardo's theory of rent wrong and stated in no uncertain terms that its conclusions had been vitiated by Ricardo's erroneous assumption that the cultivation of land proceeds from the best soils to increasingly poorer ones. He became convinced that, contrariwise, first settlers everywhere have commenced the work of cultivation on the most barren soil. He denied no less vehemently the premises of Malthus' theory of population, poking fun at the latter's arithmetic and geometric ratios of food and population growth. Child of an environment with limitless natural resources that cried for development, the younger Carey's vision remained to his end that of an uncompromising optimist with unbounded faith in the plans of a benevolent Creator. Lacking in analytical skills, his contribution to economics was slender, but the much debated idea of a balanced development of agriculture, commerce, and industry had some merit. (For H. C. Carey, see also Chapter 17.)

C.—*John Rae* (1796–1872) — not to be confused with the John Rae who became the chief biographer of Adam Smith — was an emigrant from Scotland who had studied at Edinburgh but, subsequently, under the double strain of financial and matrimonial misfortune, sought greener pastures in the New World. He taught on the secondary school level both in Canada and in the United States, maintained his skills as a physician on a California-bound ship during the gold-rush days and as a medical agent on the Hawaiian Islands, and spent the last years of his erratic life in retirement on Staten Island as guest of a former pupil.

His colorful and somewhat frustrated career was marked by originality of thinking stemming from a wealth of ideas coupled with a distinct lack of analytical ability. His only workmanlike and striking achievement, the *Statement of Some New Principles on the Subject of Political Economy* (1834), stressed invention and the government intervention needed to stimulate inventive capacity as the true source of wealth. It took Adam Smith, to whose work Rae largely owed what little economic training he had, to task on various counts.

First, in regard to the division of labor, which in the *Wealth of Nations* is depicted as the principal inducement to invention, Rae inverts this order of events and regards the division of labor as dependent on the antecedent progress of invention. Second, he deemphasizes "dexterity" which, as machines take over more and more of the tasks requiring skill, tends to become obsolete. Third, he by and large equates private accumulation with mere acquisition and points to the limits beyond which individual accumulation cannot advance the national capital. And fourth, he denies, by inference, that there is a natural harmony between private and national interests. Rae evokes numerous instances — gambling, sharp bargaining, among others — where self-interest is not guided by an "invisible hand" to the promotion of larger ends.

If laissez faire fails to do a satisfactory job, the field is wide open for governmental promotion of invention, the category which takes the place of honor in Rae's scheme of things. In it, premiums, bounties, and import duties all perform significant auxiliary functions, and the infant-industry argument for protective tariffs is given its due. Many of H. C. Carey's ideas are foreshadowed in Rae's *New Principles*. His gentle scorning of vanity, luxury, and ostentation of riches was in a vein which Thorstein Veblen half a century later worked more deeply and sarcastically.

D.—*Karl Knies* (1821–1898), a professor at the University of Heidelberg for years, molded many young minds seeking enlightenment in Germany. His contribution to economic theory rests in the body of ideas known as the older branch of the German Historical school. (For additional information on Knies, see Chapter 17, Biographical Note F.)

E.—*Henry George* (1839–1897) was born and raised in Philadelphia in a fervently religious home which may have bestowed on him the missionary zeal that characterized his entire life. At the age of sixteen, he embarked as a sailor for Australia and India; upon his return two years later, he learned the printing trade. An avid reader of books obtained from free libraries, he soon heard news about a gold rush in California and, at the age of nineteen, secured a berth on a ship bound for the West Coast. Failing to make a fortune, or less, in the newly discovered gold fields, George sought and intermittently found work as a typesetter, but poverty continued to stalk him. He undertook a second, equally unsuccessful, attempt to strike it rich in gold mining. Floating about from one newspaper enterprise to another, he finally found a job that allowed him to advance rapidly through the positions of reporter, contributor, and editor. In 1867 he became one of the founders of the *San Francisco Post*, but this venture was disastrously affected by the panic of 1873.

His first published pamphlet, *Our Land and Land Policy*, was published in 1871. In it he outlined ideas fully worked out in *Progress and Poverty* (1879), an all-time best seller. The sensational success of this diagnosis of the economic ills of society coupled with a panacea (a single tax on the rent of land, reminiscent of the physiocratic prescription but more radical because confiscatory in nature) catapulted George to international celebrity.

In 1880 he left San Francisco for New York City and soon thereafter entered politics. As a candidate for mayor of New York City in the election of 1886, he narrowly lost, but he continued to enjoy the support of labor and socialist groups that had sponsored him. He ran for the same office again in 1897, only to die before the close of the campaign. His unfinished manuscript for a book entitled *The Science of Political Economy* was completed and published by his son in 1898.

Devoutly committed to the cause of social reform and justice, Henry George impressed millions of his contemporaries by sincerity and unflagging idealism in the face of adversity. His cause inspired many movements, but the actually accomplished land reforms attributable to his pleadings have been disproportionately few. What little recognition was given this self-taught economist by the profession, uneasy when stirred out of its complacency, was grudging and certainly not a fair measure of his analytical competence.

F.—*Francis Amasa Walker* (1840–1897) was born in Boston and graduated from Amherst College in 1860. His study of law was interrupted by the outbreak of the Civil War. He enlisted as sergeant major, saw action, was wounded in battle and confined to prison, and through a string of promotions had become brigadier general when he was mustered out of service. He then helped his father to write *The Science of Wealth*, published in 1866.

Soon Walker made himself available again for government service, first as superintendent of the census (1870), then as Commissioner of Indian Affairs (1871), and once more in the census (1880). Meanwhile he had accepted the first chair of political economy at the Sheffield Scientific School of Yale University, which he held — notably without previous academic training in the field he taught — from 1872 until 1881. He then accepted a call to become president of Massachusetts Institute of Technology, and remained associated with this institution during the remaining sixteen years of his life. Academic honors of many kinds were showered on him: he was vice-president of the National Academy of Science, held the presidency of the American Economic Association during the first seven years of its existence, and presided over the American Statistical Association for fifteen years. A man possessed of indefatigable industry, he contributed substantially to professional literature. His creditable performance in the field of general economics is manifested by the publication of *The Wages Question* (1876) and a textbook, *Political Economy* (1883), used on American college campuses for many years. His reputation was further enhanced by his work on money and currency policy.

Walker distinguished himself by vigorous espousal of definite views and by giving his fighting support to one side or the other in the controversies of the day. But his thinking was pervaded by a strong sense of fairness, and he avoided a doctrinaire belief in laissez faire.

G.—*John Bates Clark* (1847–1938) was born in Providence, Rhode Island, descendant of a long line of New England Yankees in whom the Puritan tradition, though tempered by time and the rapid transformation of the country, had remained strong.

He studied first at Brown University and then at Amherst, from which institution he graduated — with some delay caused by two interruptions on account of his father's ill health and death — in 1872. Encouraged by his teachers to think highly of his potential as a social scientist, he became one of the group of young Americans who did their graduate work under the direction of exponents of the Historical school in Germany. From 1872 to 1875 he studied at Heidelberg and Zurich, mostly under Professor Knies. Receptive to the lectures of this leader, he yet absorbed them with a selective mind — readily accepting those features which fitted in with his own ethical background but unhesitatingly rejecting the wholesale condemnation of the English Classical school, on which many German economists prided themselves. His own bent, furthermore, was theoretical rather than historical, and he was never to undertake the kind of empirical studies for which the German Historical school called.

Returning to the United States, he first joined the faculty at Carleton College — whose most brilliant student at the time was Thorstein Veblen — then moved to Smith College in 1881 and to Amherst in 1893. Only two years later he accepted a call to Columbia University and remained associated with this institution until his retirement in 1923.

In 1885 *The Philosophy of Wealth*, the first of his three principal works, was published. It was made up of a number of articles which had previously appeared in the *New Englander Magazine* and helped to establish his professional reputation as a forward-looking economist with strong ethical preferences. *The Distribution of Wealth*, an analysis of "social economic statics," followed in 1899. More than any of his other writings, it served to propel him to the front ranks of economists in the Western world. His *Essentials of Economic Theory* (1907), which dealt with "social economic dynamics," was a follow-up work, but in it he did not manage to push ahead as far as he had hoped.

In 1911 he became Director of the Division of Economics and History of the Carnegie Endowment for International Peace, which undertook objective studies of war and militarism.

One of the cofounders of the American Economic Association, Clark died as the "patron saint" of the young American branch of economics which during his lifetime had grown from colonial dependency to independence.

Questions for Review and Research

1. Summarize the American contribution to economic thought prior to the second half of the nineteenth century.

2. Were the first exponents of the marginal utility theory in the United States Henry George and Francis Walker? Explain.

3. Why was the "wages-fund" theory, which played a rather important role in the classical structure of thought, not discussed in previous chapters?

4. Elaborate on the connection(s), as viewed by George, between the wage share and the interest share in national income.

5. With what name is the "residual claimant" theory of wages most prominently associated? According to this theory, which factorial shares are predetermined?

6. Briefly discuss Walker's contribution to the theory of entrepreneurship.

7. What was the primary purpose pursued by J. B. Clark in writing *The Distribution of Wealth?* When was this pioneering book published?

8. J. B. Clark had a famous son, John Maurice. Check your library for any publications that have appeared under this name since World War I. Did the younger Clark's interests coincide with his father's?

9. Restate in your own words the Clarkian difference between "capital" and "capital goods."

10. Why did J. B. Clark attach great practical importance to a knowledge of the principles underlying functional distribution?

11. How did J. B. Clark further develop the classical analysis of "natural" commodity prices and "natural" factor prices?

12. Discuss J. B. Clark's distinction between "absolute" and "effective" productivity, and construct an illustrative example.

Recommended Readings

Clark, John B. *The Distribution of Wealth, a Theory of Wages, Interest, and Profits.* New York: The Macmillan Company, 1924. Chapter I, "Issues That Depend on Distribution," pp. 1–9; Chapter II, "The Place of Distribution within the Traditional Division of Economics," pp. 10–24; Chapter IV, "The Basis of Distribution in Universal Economic Laws," pp. 36–51; Chapter VII, "Wages in a Static State the Specific Product of Labor," pp. 77–94; Chapter IX, "Capital and Capital-Goods Contrasted," pp. 116–140; Chapter XI, "The Productivity of Social Labor Dependent on Its Quantitative Relation to Capital," pp. 157–172; Chapter XII, "Final Productivity the Regulator of Both Wages and Interest," pp. 173–187.

Dorfman, Joseph. *The Economic Mind in American Civilization,* 5 vols. New York: The Viking Press, 1946–49. Vol. 2, Chapters XXII, XXVIII, and XXIX; Vol. 3, Chapters IV, VI, and VIII.

George, Henry. *Progress and Poverty.* New York: Robert Schalkenback Foundation, Inc., 1945. "Introductory, The Problem," pp. 3–13.
Book I, "Wages and Capital," pp. 17–88.
Book III, "The Laws of Distribution," pp. 153–224.

Stigler, George J. *Production and Distribution Theories.* New York: The Macmillan Company, 1941. Chapter XI, John Bates Clark.

Walker, Francis A. *Political Economy,* 3d ed., revised and enlarged. New York: Henry Holt & Company, Inc., 1887.
Part II, "Production": Chapter IV, pp. 69–77.
Part III, "Exchange": Chapter I, pp. 78–111.
Part IV, "Distribution," pp. 187–258.

VALUE AND DISTRIBUTION THEORY

From Marshall to Wicksell

Jevons' *Theory of Political Economy* (1871) was full of brilliant new insights, but it did little more than unsettle the classical corpus of economic theory. We recall that the legacy of the Classical school was embraced without much questioning in English writing and teaching after John Stuart Mill's authority had remodeled it with an air of dogmatic finality.

ALFRED MARSHALL[1]

Marshall early recognized the promise of Jevons' innovations, but he was convinced that in the form in which these were presented to his contemporaries they would remain superimposed upon, rather than become integrated with, the work that had gone before. Products of haste, some of Jevons' propositions turned out on close examination to be both inaccurate and incomplete. Marshall's *mental disposition* was diametrically different from that of Jevons: deliberate and painstaking instead of rushing and tempestuous, cautious and conscientious rather than adventurous and heedless. Jevons had evinced a propensity to "throw the baby out with the bathwater." Marshall saw that there was much to be salvaged from the cargo of the Smith-Ricardo-Mill legacy. Many years before he ventured into print with his *Principles of Economics* (1890), Marshall had a clear conception of how subjective value theory could be fused with objective value theory. Refusing to be rushed by considerations of priority, he insisted on building an engine that would not only run but also be devoid of bugs and flaws and capable of sustained momentum. In this he succeeded as none of his predecessors had, with the possible exception of Adam Smith. It was unnecessary ever to revise the *Principles* in its fundamental organization and substance as the book successively went through eight

---

[1]See Biographical Note A.

editions during the remaining thirty-four years of Marshall's life and continued to gain acceptance and achieved its greatest sales success in the 1920's and 1930's.

Marshall was a *sovereign and awe-inspiring master builder* who easily outshone any of the other exponents of what came to be known as the Neoclassical school. Of it Marshall was truly the founder, although founding a school was never his intent. Possessed of the gift of synthesizing all the solid strands of thought that had been woven before, he was qualified to perform a feat comparable to Smith's a century earlier. Thoroughly trained in mathematics, however, he moved on a loftier plane than Smith, putting to excellent, though inconspicuous, use tools which the Scotsman had been able to get along without in the less complex world of the eighteenth century. In the process, Marshall's fertile mind grasped entirely new vistas. Great as was his scientific genius in blazing new trails, his principal merit — the one that makes him timeless — was a recognition that economics ". . . is not a body of concrete truth, but an engine for the discovery of concrete truth."[2] It is all the more remarkable how durable a set of truths his "engine" fashioned. For Marshall was ever on the alert to overhaul the analytic apparatus if this should keep it more serviceable for changing needs.

His economics, if not his name, still occupies substantial space in any balanced principles text. Marshall amply demonstrated that the subjective theory of value could not displace the objective (cost) theory of value. Today, past the midpoint of the twentieth century, it unfortunately still needs to be emphasized that macroeconomics of a Keynesian brand is not a substitute for microeconomics à la Marshall. Each of the two has a distinct place in economic analysis, and there is a need for skillful blending of the two analytical approaches rather than for reading microeconomics "out of court." Although Marshall is unique in his comprehensive grasp, we will, in keeping with the tenor of this book, confine our attention to those of Marshall's contributions that are marked by a substantial degree of subjective originality.

The Concept of Elasticity

Having paid tribute to the Law of Diminishing Utility, according to which a person's desire for a good diminishes — *ceteris paribus* (other things being equal) — with every increase in the amount of it in his

---

[2] J. M. Keynes, *Essays in Biography* (New York: Harcourt, Brace & World, Inc., 1933), p. 208.

possession, Marshall proceeds to explore the question of how rapidly this decline occurs. For, depending on the rate of decline of anticipated satisfactions, the price will have to be lowered by more or by less in order to induce a person to increase his purchases by a given amount. Hence, what Marshall calls *elasticity of demand is based on the elasticity of human wants*. If a given reduction in the price of a commodity induces a person to expand his purchases greatly, the elasticity of his demand is great; if the same price reduction causes only a small increase in purchases, elasticity will be small.

Not satisfied by a general statement of this sort, Marshall draws the line between "great" and "small" at the point of equality of the rates of quantity change and price change. For example, if a fall of 1 percent in price is accompanied by a rise of 2 percent in quantity demanded, elasticity will be 2; whereas if the same fall in price is reflected in a quantity increase of $\frac{1}{2}$ percent, elasticity will be $\frac{1}{2}$. It follows that if the price fall is just matched by the rise in quantity purchased, elasticity is 1 — the borderline case between "great" and "small" elasticity of demand. Marshall does not apply the term "inelastic" to those cases in which quantity changes less than price, but otherwise his presentation accords with modern usage. His diagrams show the (negative) slope of the tangent to the demand curve as indicative of the numerical coefficient of elasticity. It is no exaggeration to say that the widely used formula $e = \dfrac{dx}{x} : \dfrac{dy}{y}$ has been entirely due to Marshall. Without the aid of this tool, the theory of value and distribution could hardly have made much headway in the period since the turn of the twentieth century.

Marshall, always concerned with the interpretation of the world of reality, distinguishes between the *elasticity of individual demand and that of market demand for a commodity*, and within the former category between the elasticity of demand of *rich* men and *poor* men. He notes that elasticity tends to be great when a high-priced good, which has been out of reach for the bulk of the population, is being offered more cheaply. However, the closer we come to a situation in which all can afford to buy a great quantity (or, in some cases, all they care for), the more will elasticity of demand decline. In the extreme case where the level of satiety is reached by the great bulk of buyers, elasticity would approach zero.

A further variation is linked to the fact that there are some commodities the demand for which by the great mass of the population is easily satiated and other commodities for which their desire — always in relation to available purchasing power — is practically unlimited.

It follows that the coefficient of elasticity will remain higher when the price of the second group of commodities is gradually lowered than when the price of the first group is subjected to reductions. Prices can thus be conceived as high and low, respectively, in relation to the elasticity of demand for the commodities to which they are attached.

Marshall also shows how several *partial-demand curves*, representing the demand of rich, middle-class, and poor buyers, can be superimposed on each other in such a fashion as to make the total demand curve represent the aggregate of the partial demands. He points out that this aggregate demand retains elasticity over a larger price range than does the demand of any one individual in any of the different income classes.

Marshall incorporated the *availability of substitutes* into his analysis of elasticity of demand for a particular commodity. If the price of a commodity is raised slightly while that of a close substitute remains fixed, the demand for the former is highly elastic, that is, the quantity purchased falls greatly. Complementally, a slight fall in its price would considerably enlarge the quantity of it purchased, as it would largely displace its substitute.

Marshall also discusses the influence which *variety of use* exerts on the nature of demand elasticity. The greater the number of uses to which a particular commodity, such as water, is capable of being put, the more elastic the demand for it tends to be. Even though water be high priced, it will be used freely by all classes as "food" (for which use it is most urgently needed), but perhaps in only limited quantities for cooking and still more sparingly for washing, as far as the poorest class is concerned. At a lower price its use by the rich will not measurably increase, but the poor will find less need for economizing in its less important uses (cooking, washing); that is, while the overall demand for water by the rich is highly inelastic over any practical price range, demand by the poor will be predominantly price-elastic, whereas the structure of demand elasticity of middle-income groups would be intermediate.

In these and many other ways (for example, by tracing the effect of durability of goods on demand elasticity) Marshall uncovered a wealth of facets and ramifications of a concept whose importance, despite difficulties of statistical verification, can hardly be exaggerated. He was fully aware of disturbances caused by the element of time. We might note that these manifest themselves mainly in two ways: other things seldom remain equal over periods substantial enough to permit collection of adequate statistical data, and the full effects of a given cause are often felt long after it has ceased to operate.

Consumer's Surplus

This Marshallian concept is rooted in the fact that ordinarily the price paid for a good does not fully represent the benefit which its possession yields to the purchaser. In other words, the satisfaction obtained from it may well exceed that which is given up by parting with the purchasing power required for its acquisition. If so, the purchaser will reap a surplus satisfaction, the economic measure of which Marshall termed "consumer's surplus." It is represented by the excess of the price which a person *would be willing* to pay for a good (rather than go without it) over the price which he actually *has* to pay.

As "good instances" Marshall mentions matches, salt, newspapers, and postage stamps. This partial list indicates that two different types of goods are favorite candidates for yielding a consumer's surplus: those where quantity purchased does not enter into consideration — one newspaper will do, and unless its price is considerably higher than normal, it will continue to be bought regularly — and those for which demand elasticity is very small, that is, quantity purchased may vary only when price changes are large. In the latter case a considerable (though not large) price fall will not induce a rise in the quantity purchased, and consequently a consumer's surplus will arise with price reductions short of large. But we need not insist on a low degree of elasticity if we abandon the notion, as we should, that a consumer's surplus arises only in connection with the "last" unit purchased. However, if we concentrate on those cases where the number of units purchased varies considerably with price, so that even a small price change will affect the quantity bought, we have to look for the surplus as arising only on the intramarginal units rather than on all units.

In his *standard example*, Marshall allows elasticity to be great *or* small, depending on the particular price range considered. Translated into table form, his illustration appears as follows:

INDIVIDUAL DEMAND FOR TEA

Quantity Purchased (in pounds)	Price per Pound (in shillings)	Total Expenditures (in shillings)
1	20	20
2	14	28
3	10	30
4	6	24
5	4	20
6	3	18
7	2	14

Source: Adapted from Alfred Marshall, *Principles of Economics* (4th ed.; London: Macmillan & Co., Ltd., 1898), p. 200 ff.

If we assume that the buyer of tea acts rationally, the total enjoyment he expects to derive from the purchase of 1 pound at 20 *s.* must be as great as, but no greater than, that which he would obtain by spending 20 *s.* on other goods. At a price of 14 *s.*, regardless of whether he buys 1 or 2 pounds of tea, he will reap a surplus satisfaction of 6 *s.* For if he buys only 1 unit (for 14 *s.*) his surplus is 6 *s.*, because he would have been willing to pay 20 *s.* But if he buys 2 units (for 14 *s.* each), paying 28 *s.*, his surplus is also 6 *s.*, because only 1 of the 2 units was worth to him exactly the price he paid for it (14 *s.*), whereas he values the other unit at 20 *s.* Hence, by paying a total of 28 *s.* he gets satisfactions valued at $20 + 14 = 34$ *s.*

In a similar way, we can compute the consumer's surplus when the price falls to 10 *s.* The subjective utility of 3 pounds to the individual would be $20 + 14 + 10 = 44$ *s.* But when buying 3 pounds, he can get them at 10 *s.* per pound, or for a total outlay of 30 *s.*, which yields him a surplus of satisfactions valued at 14 *s.* The same result is obtained by answering the question of what would happen if, as the price drops from 14 *s.* to 10 *s.*, he continues to buy only 2 pounds. These 2 pounds, which would be worth to him 20 *s.* + 14 *s.* = 34 *s.*, could be had for 2 times 10 *s.* = 20 *s.*; hence, his surplus would amount to 14 *s.*

It can be shown that the surplus increases more rapidly as the elasticity of demand becomes less than one (when total expenditures begin to fall). For instance, at a price as low as 2 *s.* the individual would purchase 7 pounds, at a total cost of 14 *s.* But 7 pounds would be worth to him as much as 59 *s.* (20 *s.* + 14 *s.* + . . . + 2 *s.*), yielding a consumer's surplus totaling 45 *s.*

Marshall emphasizes that this surplus enjoyment is a *result of favorable external circumstances* over which the individual purchaser has no control. If, for example, tea were no longer available at any price, having previously been priced at 2 *s.* per pound, he would lose satisfactions equal to what he could have obtained by spending an additional 45 *s.* on such other commodities which would be worth to him no more than what he would have to pay for them, that is, commodities yielding no surplus satisfactions. Marshall did not take formal account of changes in the marginal utility of money because he did not think much of an attempt at adding together the total utilities of all commodities for purposes of estimating consumer's surplus. He also admitted that *any list of demand prices is quite conjectural except for a narrow range in the neighborhood of the customary price.* It follows that even the most careful estimates which economists might form of the total utility of a commodity are subject to a large margin of error.

Although the concept of consumer's surplus has proved operationally less significant than Marshall may have anticipated, it has served to underscore the fact that the marginal utility of a commodity is no indicator of its total utility to the purchaser. It has also served to stimulate a new type of investigation which under Pigou's[3] leadership has become known as *welfare economics.* Marshall himself emphasized that a pound sterling's worth of satisfaction to a poor man may be a great deal more than a pound's worth of satisfaction to a rich man, a fact which should be taken into more than passing consideration by governments raising revenue through taxation.

Factor Returns

Marshall recognized that there is a *general tendency for saving to be the greater the higher the rate of interest* but also that there are notable exceptions to this rule. He pointed out that some saving might conceivably occur even if interest were negative, just as some work would be done even if a penalty were attached to it. But in spite of the fact that people who aim at a predetermined income, to be available to them (or their families) at a predetermined future date, will save less when the interest rate is high than when it is low, a rise in rate paid for loanable funds still tends to increase the overall volume of savings, because it increases both the majority's desire to save and their power to do so.

Marshall believed that "the older economists" overestimated the wealth-increasing potential of a rise of interest income at the expense of wages, and that they underestimated the importance of the investment of resources in the education of children of wage workers. He sounded a modern note in saying "that from the national point of view the investment of wealth in the child of the working man is as productive as its investment in horses or machinery."[4]

In the course of his lengthy discussion of industrial organization, Marshall skillfully develops the novel concepts of *external economies* and *internal economies.* Both arise from an increase in the scale of production. Internal economies are achieved by individual firms whose resources enable them to improve the organization of their economic activities, the efficiency of management; these economies center about an ever more refined division of labor, brought about largely with the

[3]See Biographical Note B.

[4]Alfred Marshall, *Principles of Economics* (4th ed.; London: Macmillan & Co., Ltd., 1898), p. 316.

aid of machinery. External economies are dependent upon the general development of an industry, which in turn benefits the members of that industry; they center largely, though not exclusively, about the localization of industry. Among the special advantages of localized industries, Marshall mentions the development of hereditary skills ("the mysteries of the trade . . . are as it were in the air, and children learn many of them unconsciously,"[5]), the growth of subsidiary trades in the neighborhood, the use of highly specialized machinery, and the development of a local market for special skills. Generally speaking, the development of railroads, the printing press, and the telegraph have greatly contributed to the realization of external economies. Every cheapening of the means of transportation and communication, every new device promoting the free interchange of ideas between distant places by newspapers, trade and technical publications favors the enlargement of markets for the exchange of commodities and factor services.

An important source of economies of scale is derived from the use of specialized and expensive *machinery*. In certain branches of production, only large establishments can provide constant employment for such machinery; without the latter being put to regular use, it would not pay for itself over its lifetime. Hence small manufacturers, whose scale of operations does not permit them to buy the "best" in the market, must continue to have many things done by hand or by less efficient tools, and this mode of operations places them at a competitive disadvantage. On the other hand, there are "trades," such as cotton spinning, in which even factories of moderate size can take full advantage of the most efficient machines for every process, and in which larger-scale plants can gain no additional economy through the use of machinery.

Marshall also sheds light on the advantages accruing to large firms in buying and selling (quantity discounts, lower freight rates, advertising by more effective media) and advantages in being able to hire managers with exceptional natural abilities. On the other hand, he recognizes the limitations inherent in management of complex businesses: divided responsibility, the likelihood that messages get distorted on their long journey from top to bottom or vice versa, the difficulty of checking performance — in other words, what later came to be called managerial diseconomies of scale.

The upshot of his analysis, reminiscent of Senior, is that in those branches of production in which nature plays a minor part we observe

[5]*Ibid.*, p. 350.

the working of a *law of increasing returns* — the counterpart to the *law of diminishing returns* in agriculture. Accordingly, an increase of labor and capital provides, through improved organization, a return greater than in proportion to the increase in factor services used. Marshall contemplates the possibility that increasing returns (in manufacturing and the like) may overbalance decreasing returns (in agriculture and the like), but he draws no categorical conclusions. As a special case he mentions a *law of constant returns* — an increased output is obtained by factor services augmented in the same proportion. Much will depend on such things as the stage of economic development of a country, the living conditions of workers and the habits of life in general, and the incidence of wars. However, "in most of the more delicate branches of manufacturing, where the cost of raw material counts for little, and in most of the modern transport industries the law of increasing returns acts almost unopposed."[6]

Demand and Supply in Relation to Time

We are indebted to Marshall for an *extremely useful distinction in the analysis of demand and supply:* he pointed out that the nature of the causes which determine the equilibrium between the forces of demand and supply depends on the length of the period over which the market for a good is being considered.

A period may be so short that supply is limited to the stock already on hand. In a somewhat longer period, the supply is more or less influenced by the cost of producing additional quantities of the commodity. And in a still longer period, this cost of production — no longer dependent on a *given* supply of production agents — will be influenced by the cost of producing more or less of the productive agents themselves. The perceptive student will have recognized here the distinction between market periods — short run and long run — which have come to occupy a central place in even the most elementary discussion of the cost of production of goods and services.

When Adam Smith wrote about the "normal," or "natural," value of a commodity, he meant the one which economic forces tend to bring about in Marshall's "long run." However, economic forces would effectuate this (average) value only if real-world conditions were fixed for a period long enough to enable each of them to work out its full effect. The fact that the general conditions of life are never stationary prevents us from ever testing this normal-value hypothesis. Marshall

---

[6]*Ibid.*, p. 398.

suggests that the expenses of a *representative firm*, that is, one managed with normal ability and having normal access to economies of large-scale production, might serve as a standard for estimating normal production expenses; but the concept of the "representative firm" is itself too vague to get us very far.

What do we mean by an *increase (decrease) of normal demand or normal supply*? Marshall was careful to point out that such changes may be viewed in terms of their quantity components or price components, or both. Thus an increase in demand may mean that at each of several possible prices purchasers would take a greater quantity than before, or that for each of several possible quantities which they may buy they would be willing to pay a higher price. Similarly, an increase in supply may be interpreted as an increase in the amounts that would be offered for sale at each of several possible prices or as a fall in the prices at which each of several possible quantities would be offered for sale. Similar considerations govern the analysis of decreases in normal demand or normal supply.

Among the many factors accounting for an increase in demand, Marshall lists not only the familiar ones of changing tastes, changing wealth (income), and expanding markets, but also development of new uses for a commodity, and reduced availability of substitutes. Likewise, he enriches the discussion of changes in supply by listing not only technological advances, discovery of new sources, and the like, but also the granting of bounties and the imposition of taxes.

He then regarded the *effects of changes in demand in relation to conditions of constant, diminishing, and increasing returns:* a given increase in demand leaving price unaffected in the first case, raising it in the second, and lowering it in the third, with the quantity bought rising moderately in the first case, little in the second, and much in the third.

Marshall, genial mediator that he was, revealed the fruitlessness of the century-old dispute as to whether value is governed by cost of production or by utility by introducing the analogy of a *pair of scissors.* Just as it is futile to insist that the cutting of a piece of paper is effected by the blade which is moving when the other blade is held stationary, so it is pointless to claim that demand is all that matters once the cost of production of a good has already been incurred. The demand price will depend not only on the amount which buyers can afford to spend on it, but also on their ability to get a good like it at as low a price at some future time. This latter condition will depend on the causes which govern the supply of the good over time, and hence upon the cost of production. It is true, however, that the shorter the period we are concerned with, the greater will be the influence of demand on value (fixed stock of a perishable commodity), and the longer the period, the greater the influence of cost of production on value (commodities produced under constant returns).

In order to rule out the disturbing effects of causes which cannot be conveniently handled together, the economist must resort to the fiction of *ceteris paribus*. He thereby isolates those causes which allow him to arrive at statements concerning the effects of others. By narrowing the issue, he can handle it more exactly, but he can do so only at the cost of a lesser correspondence with real life. It is therefore mandatory, Marshall points out, that he be able to combine numerous partial solutions into a more or less complete solution, which is done by the method of *successive approximation*. "With each step of advance more things can be let out of the pound [called *ceteris paribus*]; exact discussions can be made less abstract, realistic discussions can be made less inexact than was possible at an earlier stage."[7]

Marshall, operating with the fiction of the *stationary state*, applies this procedure to the study of the influences exerted by the elements of time on the relations between cost of production and value and then contrasts the results obtained with those found in a *dynamic world*. In a stationary state, cost of production would govern value; there would be no reflex influence of demand, and normal price would never vary. In the real world, however, not only are volume, methods, and cost of production always mutually influencing each other, but they also modify, and are modified by, the nature and extent of demand. Hence, any simple formulation as to the relations between cost of production, demand, and value over time is likely to be specious.

Marshall carefully elaborates the implications for the distinction between *short run* and *long run*. In the short run, the stock of "appliances of production" is practically fixed, but the rate at which they are used varies with demand. Also, the larger the share of the appliances (read: fixed capital), the more prices can fall below their normal level (read: total unit cost of production) before reaching the level of prime cost (read: variable unit cost).[8]

Marshall points out that it is the fear of spoiling their markets that keeps producers holding out for a price considerably higher than that sufficient to cover their variable unit cost, although it would be temporarily worth their while to produce at a price barely covering the

[7]*Ibid.*, p. 439.

[8]Marshall used the terms "prime cost" and "supplementary cost" to indicate what is now usually referred to as "variable cost" and "fixed cost."

latter. "Thus, although nothing but prime cost enters *necessarily and directly* into the supply price for short periods, it is yet true that supplementary costs also exert some influence indirectly."[9]

Marshall warns that it may be unrealistic to assume that the profit-maximizing producer varies his output by single units or by small amounts. Due to *indivisibilities in production functions* — an expression not used by Marshall himself, although he clearly operates with this concept — it may be necessary to expand output considerably or else not at all: an entire new line may have to be added; one additional machine would be uneconomical if used only for small output increases. These facts of economic life tend to blur the precision of the theory of value, but they cannot be neglected by the economist who would keep abstraction within tolerable bounds.

In the long run, supply price will be governed by the incomes which can be earned by all investments of material and human capital, that is, these investments have time to be adjusted to the incomes which producers expect will be earned by them. In modern terminology: costs which were fixed in the short run have become variable. Some firms will leave the industry or adjust their plant scale, others will enter the industry or adjust their plant scale, but the long-run normal supply price will conceal such variations in the fortunes of individual firms.

Finally, the distinction between "short" and "long" periods is not drawn by nature but merely fills the need for isolation of certain variables. Any hard and fast line of division will be of no avail in the solution of practical problems.

Marshall barely hints at *secular price movements*. He attributes these to the growth of knowledge, population, and capital as it takes place over generations and affects conditions of demand and supply.

Marshall's Amendment of Classical Rent Theory

He sees nothing wrong with the classical doctrines that the price of agricultural produce is determined by the money cost of production on the margin of cultivation and that rent does not enter into cost of production. But he thought that the *classical economists did not go far enough, because they treated agricultural produce as a single commodity.* Marshall took into account the competition between different kinds of agricultural produce — say, wheat, oats, and barley — for the use of good land. In equilibrium all crops will have to yield the same net return to the outlay of labor and capital on the margin of cultivation,

[9]Marshall, *op. cit.*, p. 448.

with the marginal application contributing nothing to rent since it just pays for itself. While rent again is no element in the expenses of producing the marginal amount of the given crop (to which its price must conform), Marshall explained why *a statement to the effect that rent does not enter into the cost of production may be misleading when made with reference to a particular crop.*

Marshall observed that the net incomes derived from appliances for production made by man are in some way analogous to true rent. To bring their similarity to light, he coined the term "quasi-rent." The principal difference between such appliances on the one hand and land on the other is that their supply must be regarded as *temporarily* fixed, whereas the stock of land is *permanently* fixed. By "temporarily fixed" Marshall means that we may be considering periods of time too short to enable the supply of the appliances to respond to a change in the demand for them.

If, for instance, a sudden increase in the demand for a consumer good, say a textile fabric, calls for the installation of special machinery, and if this machinery will for a time yield an income greater than the difference between the proceeds from the sale of the consumer good and the outlays, including depreciation, incurred in production, the machinery may be said to yield a quasi-rent. Not until the stock of such machinery has been increased so that it will no longer yield a special scarcity return will quasi-rent have been eliminated. Marshall concludes that "when the causes which determine short-period fluctuations of production are under discussion, the net income derived from the investment of capital may be classed with rent proper: on the ground that it stands outside of the payments which influence producers to take such action as would increase the available supply within a short period."[10]

As can readily be seen, rent and quasi-rent have in common the fact that neither enters directly into the marginal cost of production.

VILFREDO PARETO[11]

The endeavor to make economics into an exact science was continued by Walras' handpicked successor to his chair at the University of Lausanne. The Italian Pareto had come to the social sciences via extended study and practice of mathematics and engineering. He was the *first to attempt a complete mathematical formulation of general equilibrium*

---

[10]*Ibid.*, p. 492.
[11]See Biographical Note C.

theory in terms of monopoly and collectivism, an extension of Walras' equilibrium analysis within a framework of pure competition. For this ambitious goal he laid the foundations in 1896–97 in a work (based on lectures at Lausanne) entitled *Cours d'Economie politique,* in which he emphasized the general interdependence of all economic quantities and the theoretical legitimacy of the concept of a determinate general economic equilibrium, much as Walras had done before him. He had hoped to be able to quantify his functional equations, but the fragmentary nature of historical statistics forced him to abandon this attempt.

He broke some new ground in his *Manual of Political Economy,* published in Italian in 1906 and translated into French three years later. In this work he took an entirely *new view of utility* by stating that utility is not measurable but has to be conceived in an ordinal sense, that is, in terms of a scale of preferences that can be deduced for each individual without assigning numerical values to his various utility functions. Pareto's theory of utility was objective in nature in that it called for no explanation as to why preferences had arisen.

He developed the new theoretical apparatus by the use of *indifference curves,* envisaged in an embryonic fashion by the English economist Francis Y. Edgeworth[12] and foreshadowed in an early work of the American economist Irving Fisher.[13] His construction of a theory of value on the basis of scales of preference takes as its point of departure an individual confronted with two goods, which for consumption purposes may be combined in various ways without a change in the total amount of utility derived from them. These quantitative combinations equally desired by the individual may be arranged on an indifference curve, to which Pareto assigned an index.

Another set of combinations of the same goods yielding higher total utility, but between which the individual would again be indifferent, can be depicted in a curve with a higher index number. In fact there is an infinite number of sets of quantitative combinations of equal total utility. By representing the resultant indifference curves in a horizontal plane we get an *indifference map* which, in the manner of a contour map, shows different levels of equal-satisfaction combinations.

A specific example presented in the *Manual* considers a man who, governed by his tastes only, has one kilogram of bread and one kilogram of wine. He would be willing to have only .9 *kg.* of bread provided he had 1.2 *kg.* of wine, or only .8 *kg.* of bread if he were to command 1.4 *kg.* of wine. Between these and other combinations he would not know how

---

[12]See Biographical Note D.
[13]See Biographical Note E.

to choose; it being a matter of indifference to him, he would be just as satisfied by one combination as by any of the others. Such an indifference *series* becomes an indifference *curve* if plotted on graph paper, where O is the origin and the X-axis measures, say, quantity of bread, and the Y-axis therefore measures quantity of wine. Any movement along a given indifference line, on which the quantities of the two goods change inversely, leads to combinations with the same index of *ophelimity;* any movement from one indifference line to another, that is, from one height above the plane represented by XOY to another height, will lead to combinations with a higher or lower index of ophelimity.

By using this new term, a substitute for utility as the motivating characteristic of an object of desire, Pareto wanted to set himself apart from the hedonistic utility theorists. He was not concerned with the psychological foundations of value but rather with the empirical facts of choice. As regards its misleading associations, he was also concerned about the fact that the term "utility" has a much narrower meaning in everyday speech than it does in economics. While morphine, in the former usage, does not have utility because it harms the addict, in political economy it does so because it serves to satisfy one of his needs — injurious or otherwise.

Nevertheless, Pareto's basic approach to the problem of value still has strong subjective overtones, as evidenced by the fact that he sees the poles of economic activity in *tastes* on the one hand and *obstacles* on the other.

Economic equilibrium, the main object of study of the *Manual*, exists when changes induced by tastes are restrained by the obstacles in the way to their realization. This is Pareto's way of stating the basic problem of economics: scarcity of resources relative to the limitlessness of human wants. There being an everlasting antagonism between men's tastes (desires) and the obstacles in the way of satisfying them, Pareto's analysis logically evolves as a study of tastes, a study of obstacles, and a study of the way in which these elements are combined so as to achieve equilibrium. It is thus a characteristic of equilibrium that at the moment it takes place the changes permitted by the obstacles are restrained by the tastes of man, or — what amounts to the same thing — that the changes permitted by his tastes are restrained by the obstacles.

Pareto's work is more than a revised version of Walrasian economics. While he arrived in part at the same conclusions as had his predecessor, he pointed out that the satisfaction derived by an individual from the consumption of a certain quantity of a good depends not uniquely on that quantity, but on the quantities of all economic goods consumed or at his disposal, and that in the construction of indifference curves it is not necessary to resort to the concept of cardinal utility. He also overhauled Walras' theory of production and capitalization and made quite a splash with his *"law" of the distribution of income*, according to which the inequality of income distribution shows a high degree of constancy for different times and countries, reflecting the natural and universal inequality of human ability. This last one has been a less durable contribution to economics than Pareto's pure theory.

KNUT WICKSELL[14]

Shortly before the turn of the twentieth century, a Swedish economist published in rapid succession three books in German that dealt with value and distribution theory and some of its applications. Wicksell's outstanding achievements were tardily recognized on the European Continent, and for several decades they received even less attention in English-speaking countries. Those relating to interest theory and the price level, which will be taken up in Chapter 11, found in J. M. Keynes an alert recipient, who used them as building blocks for parts of his own monumental structure. As an exact contemporary of Wieser, Wicksell found in the latter's interest theory a still unfinished product calling for future processing.

While he became the *founder of the so-called Swedish school*, Wicksell was *singularly open to outside influences*, especially the school of Vienna, the school of Lausanne, and the school of Marshall. Perhaps his greatest claim to fame rests on his *ability to perceive the common denominator of various economic systems and to integrate with his own work only the lasting contributions of his antecedents*. He thus became foremost a creative middleman exemplifying the element of continuity in the growth of economic theory as expressed by the leading Western European contemporary writers in their native language. His eclecticism was paired with a strong training in mathematics, giving his work much of the flavor exuding from the writings of Walras, Pareto, and Edgeworth.

The principal significance and the interrelations of the central propositions of value and distribution theory he presented most lucidly and architectonically in a two-volume work, whose English translation appeared in 1911 under the title *Lectures on Political Economy*. In *fusing the main teachings of Walras and the Austrians*, he was able to

---

[14]See Biographical Note F.

give to the philosophical depth and literary abstruseness of Menger and his followers some of the precision and elegance that adhere to the mathematical formulations of the Lausanne school. Wicksell's eminence as a masterful blender of streams of thought was rooted in the catholicity of his mind and was most conspicuous in his contribution to the part of production theory dealing with problems of capital and interest.

The Marginal Principle

In Exchange.—Wicksell recognized that the theory of value and price is germane not only to economies governed by a highly developed division of labor, but also to individual productive enterprises and households. There is a place for it where free competition reigns as well as under collectivism. For him the broadest principle arising out of the investigations of the second half of the nineteenth century was the "marginal principle," which governs every part of political economy: exchange, production, distribution, and capital. It serves as a connecting link between higher mathematics and economics and expresses the idea that given magnitudes are variables, whose rates of change must be regarded as new quantities.

Wicksell, in explaining the principles of marginal utility, takes as his starting point Adam Smith's thesis relating to the divergence between value in use and value in exchange, exemplified by water and diamonds. He then shows that, while for a buyer value in exchange can never be greater than value in use and for a seller value in exchange can never be less than value in use, the same thing may possess different degrees of utility for different persons. Consequently, the relative values in use can at a given time "be greater or less than the relative exchange values *for one or other of the exchanging parties respectively.*"[15]

Of the various possible degrees of value in use, that which determines the actual exchange value of a commodity is the degree of utility which it possesses at the time the exchange is effected, regardless of whether that utility arises from the present or future needs of the exchanging parties. This so-called *marginal utility of a commodity* corresponds to the least important of the needs satisfied by the *acquisition* of the commodity, which is, at the same time, the most important of the needs which are not satisfied if the commodity is acquired in lesser amounts. For each of the exchanging parties, in order that the

---

[15]Knut Wicksell, *Lectures on Political Economy* (London: Routledge & Kegan Paul, Ltd., 1934), I, 29–30.

marginal utilities of the commodities exchanged stand in the same relation as their common exchange value, it is also necessary that the
marginal utility of the commodity *surrendered* in exchange correspond
to the least pressing of the needs which — with exchange completed —
remains unsatisfied.

As long as the marginal utilities are not proportional to the exchange
values of both commodities, at least one of the parties will desire to
exchange further. This kind of analysis enables Wicksell to dispose of
the traditional dualistic concept of exchange value as requiring two
properties, utility *and* scarcity, since *marginal utility now represents a
synthesis of utility and scarcity.* "Marginal utility becomes the degree of
utility at which the consumption of a commodity must cease precisely
because of its *scarcity.*"[16]

Since to the rich man, who can fully satisfy practically all his needs,
all commodities must have a very much lower marginal utility than to
the poor man, it is immaterial to compare the relative marginal utilities
of the same thing to two different persons. What always is relevant to
comparison (by rich and poor alike) is the marginal utilities of *different*
commodities to the *same* individual. In a system in which income and
wealth were equally distributed, goods highly esteemed under a system
of unequal distribution would definitely fall in exchange value, though
their marginal utilities to different persons would still differ to some
extent because of differing tastes.

In the actual market exchange of goods between individual buyers
and sellers, the influence exercised by individual traders is usually quite
small, that is, they plan their economic behavior as if the exchange
value of the goods were predetermined. Nevertheless, the seller of, say,
agricultural goods, to be exchanged for various types of consumer goods
not produced on the farm, must regulate his offers and his demands
in such a way that (potential) consumption both of the goods given up
and of the goods received will (would) yield a marginal utility proportionate in each case to the *given* exchange value of the goods in question.
Since there are likely to be different unit prices for these goods, a comparison of the marginal utility of each good must involve a comparison
of *weighted* marginal utilities. Only when the latter are equal for the
various goods will exchange result in maximum satisfaction. Then the
last money unit spent on any of a number of goods acquired and the
last money unit's worth of any good retained for consumption must,
over a given period of time, bring the same amount of utility to the
transactor.

---
[16] *Ibid.*, p. 32.

As far as special cases are concerned, Wicksell shows that price determination for exchange between *two isolated individuals* is an indeterminate problem, that is, one that cannot be solved merely on the assumption that both parties are motivated by the profit-maximization incentive. The practical importance of the analogous case of bilateral monopoly between an organization of employers and one of employees, where the wage bargain will depend largely on the bargaining strength and shrewdness of the contracting parties, is obvious.

In an *open market governed by free competition*, on the other hand, an individual desiring to exchange goods will regulate the supply of his own goods and his demand for other goods in such a manner that the marginal utility of each commodity will be proportional to its price, that is, such that the weighted marginal utility is everywhere the same. Whatever the resulting price relationships may be, the combination of supply and demand, and the quantities of goods retained and acquired, will be determinate for each individual.

It is true, of course, that *concrete economic phenomena are much too complex to be adequately explained by the theory of marginal utility*, because such forces as mutual goodwill, philanthropy, social considerations, and the like, nearly always interfere with the quest for the greatest personal gain. These forces can be ignored, however, as long as we are satisfied with a first approximation to a scientific explanation of price formation in open markets, and so can the forces (such as habit and inertia) that cause economic friction. The most important practical objection to his theory of value Wicksell sees in the fact that the assumption of free competition can be only incompletely realized in actual life, and may fall far short of being realized.

In Production.—Wicksell applied the marginal utility theory to the explanation of production and made use of the marginal concept in explaining the returns to land, labor, and capital. Following Böhm-Bawerk, he regarded capital as produced means of production, or stored-up wealth, but went beyond the Austrian master by regarding *interest* as the *difference between the marginal productivity of saved-up labor and saved-up land on the one hand, and of current labor and land on the other*. Like Clark, he also viewed capital as a permanent fund and focused on time as the essence of capital theory. The marginal productivity of stored-up labor and land is greater than the marginal productivity of current labor and land, because the latter exist in relative abundance for the purposes for which they can be employed. Because saved-up labor and land are not adequate for the many purposes in which they have an advantage, there arises an opportunity-cost element in roundabout production which is expressed through the interest rate.

Since Wicksell, like Walras, always stressed the mutual interdependence of all elements in the determination of price, his interest theory is a component part of the equilibrium system of mutual dependence. The implications of this for the theory of the relations between money rates of interest, natural rates of interest, and movements in the general level of prices will be discussed in Chapter 11.

In conclusion it must be emphasized that Wicksell's work was more than mere synthesis: in many cases, his restatements of received doctrines were tantamount to independent analyses.

SUMMARY

Alfred Marshall was by far the most able exponent of the body of economic thought known as neoclassicism, and his influence, despite the recent vogue of Keynesian writing and teaching, still endures. Perhaps because he was the most cautious and methodical writer of all the giants in economic thought, his *Principles of Economics*, developed in a very deliberate fashion, withstood the test of close scrutiny through the many decades during which it has served both as a textbook in American and British classrooms and a reference work for the professional economist. Marshall did for his generation what John Stuart Mill had attempted for an earlier one: he brought up to date a science which was badly in need of integration and reconstruction at the hands of a master builder. For a couple of decades, the Classical school had been under fire, mainly from Jevons and the Austrians; Marshall showed how the "new work" had to be combined with, rather than substituted for, the old. This remarkable feat of getting economics back on a steady course, as it were, would not have been possible without Marshall's impressive display of analytical ability, and especially without his ingenuity in filling up a box of sorely needed economic tools.

He "settled" the controversy about the respective parts played by demand and cost of production in the determination of value by making clear the mutually dependent position and interaction of economic variables. He pointed out that equilibrium of supply and demand as a determinant of value is just as important in the commodity markets as in those for the factors of production. He elaborated the idea that substitution at the margin is meaningful not only between alternative objects of consumption but also between the factors of production. The explicit introduction of the element of time was due mainly to

Marshall, as was the relation of "long" and "short" periods to cost of production and selling price. The concepts of "prime cost" and "supplementary cost" and those of "external" and "internal" economies enabled Marshall to give additional precision to the theory of markets, prices, and the allocation of resources. He developed, on the basis of very little preliminary work, the notion of "elasticity," and coined the term "consumer's surplus" to represent the excess of the price which a person would be willing to pay for (units of) a good over what he actually does have to pay. This in turn helped to make clear that the marginal utility of a commodity is no indicator of its total utility to the purchaser. He further developed classical rent theory and broadened its scope by way of introducing the concept of quasi-rent.

Marshall had a superior command of mathematics and was the first to make generous use of diagrams in the service of economic analysis.

The endeavor to render economics an exact science was even more evident in the Italian Vilfredo Pareto, the successor to Léon Walras — founder of the so-called Lausanne school.

Pareto became the first to attempt a complete mathematical formulation of the theory of general economic equilibrium couched in terms of monopoly and collectivism as well as competition. He developed the apparatus of indifference curves and modernized it by divorcing it from considerations of cardinal utility. Although he never freed himself completely from utility concepts, he was able to give his economics a very mature statement in the *Manual of Political Economy*, which served as a point of departure for much twentieth-century refinement of general equilibrium analysis.

In his day, he was better known for his "law" of income distribution, according to which the distribution of income follows a certain pattern conditioned mainly by the inequality of natural endowments. Although it evoked critical discussion and has not withstood the test of time, Pareto established himself with this theorem as a pioneer econometrician.

Pareto's overall stature was enhanced by the fact that he had come to our science as a successful businessman and engineer with an extensive knowledge of industrial processes, rare in academic economists.

The Swedish economist Knut Wicksell was identified with the double task of adding technical improvements to the formulation of general equilibrium theory and of filling out and supplementing the bold literary outlines of marginal utility theory sketched by the Austrian school.

His peak achievement was the integration of the monetary and general equilibrium theory. Founder of the Swedish school, he was able, as no one before him except Marshall, to perceive the common denominator of various streams of value theory and, through brilliant eclecticism, to preserve what was durable in the contributions of antecedents with widely varying foci of interest. He not only raised the "marginal principle" to a broader conceptual level, but applied it to the explanation of production and factor returns in a dynamic world more successfully than the nonmathematical members of the Austrian school had been able to do. He concentrated especially on a more refined version of interest theory, which, in contrast to Böhm-Bawerk, he made a component part of an equilibrium system of mutual interdependence.

BIOGRAPHICAL NOTES

A.—*Alfred Marshall* (1842–1924) was born approximately at the halfway point in the span between John Stuart Mill's and J. M. Keynes' births. Son of a cashier at the Bank of England, whose wish it was that he be ordained in the Evangelical ministry, Marshall's early mental development was stressed by his father — somewhat in the manner of James v. John Stuart Mill.

At the age of nineteen, Alfred gained a scholarship for study at St. John's College, Oxford. Lo! he had his heart not so much in the classics and in Hebrew, in which his father sought to steep him, as in mathematics, which held a rare fascination for him. Beginning in 1864, with the financial support of a kindly uncle, Marshall was able to devote himself thoroughly to the study of mathematics at St. John's College, Cambridge. He intended eventually to become a molecular physicist. However, during his Cambridge study years, he came under the spell of a combination of metaphysical agnosticism, evolutionary progress, and utilitarian ethics which propelled his mind in a new direction: the solution of economic problems.

On the occasion of a trip to Germany in 1868 he came into contact with the works of German philosophers (Kant, Hegel) and economists (Roscher). Upon his return to St. John's, a special lectureship in moral science was established for him. From 1868 to 1877, as a fellow and lecturer reading widely as well as deeply, he laid the foundations for his future eminence as an economist. He seldom ventured into print during these years, and one of his lifelong idiosyncrasies had already become apparent: shying away from publication until he had convinced himself that an idea had fully matured. His frequent travels included a trip to the United States in 1875, which immeasurably broadened his perspective.

In 1877 he married a former pupil of his, Mary Paley, and in collaboration with her wrote his first book, *Economics of Industry*, published in 1879. During the rest of his life, he derived much intellectual and moral support from her unselfish devotion to his work.

Marriage forced the loss of his fellowship at Cambridge and led to his accepting a position as principal of, and professor of political economy at,

University College, Bristol. A siege of ill health was broken by the year (1881–1882) he spent in Italy, which gave him a welcome opportunity to advance with research for his magnum opus.

After a brief career (1883–1885) as lecturer in political economy at Balliol College, Oxford, Marshall returned to Cambridge, which had removed its restrictions on the marriage of fellows. His greatest work, *Principles of Economics*, now began to assume its final form; but it was not until after several long vacations devoted to painstaking reorganization of the material that he was ready to permit its publication (1890). The book became an instant success though it lacked the sensational touch, was sparing in its criticisms of predecessors, and — overly modest — did not make any claims to novelty or originality. Many economists have since believed that in *Principles* Marshall attempted to achieve a finality which, in view of the transitory character of economic facts, was hardly justified. Certainly, the progress of economics and the dissemination of its leading principles would have been faster — and thus Marshall's influence might have been greater still — had he been less scrupled by the dictates of scientific perfection.

The years from 1885 to 1890 had been the most active and productive of his life; in addition to his lectures and seeing *Principles* through its final stages, he was occupied by papers, addresses, and public testimony. During the remaining eighteen years as one of Cambridge's brightest stars, his pace, though slower, remained impressive. He had hoped in 1890 to publish soon a second volume of *Principles*, but there were too many competing demands on his time. His work as a member of the Royal Commission on Labor, 1891–1894, was only one, though the most extensive, of a series of services he rendered to the British government. He took an active part in the founding of the British Economic Association (later the Royal Economic Society) and in restructuring the curriculum of his Alma Mater. He had fought long to secure for economics an independent and more elevated status as a mental discipline. The high standards of scientific accuracy he brought to bear on it help to explain the success of these efforts, which, along with the rest, qualify him as the true founder of the Cambridge school of economics. It was through his pupils (Edgeworth, Pigou, Keynes, *et al.*), even more than through his writings, that he became the father of British economics for almost half a century.

When in 1908 he retired from the chair of political economy at Cambridge, he sought release from routine duties, lest the treasure of his mind's possessions remain largely untapped. As old age began to creep up on him, it became imperative that his waking hours be reserved almost exclusively for writing and the gathering in of the harvest of his prime. *Industry and Trade*, containing his best historical work, was at long last published in 1919. Some of the ideas expressed therein Marshall had carried with him for decades, and many of his contemporaries once again regretted their delayed embodiment in print. He had not been able to defy his temperament: one of caution coupled with highest standards. The book gives an able account of the forms of Western European capitalism at the turn of the twentieth century; again, it was a remarkable success.

With a great effort of will and determination, he proved equal to the task of composing one more book, *Money, Credit, and Commerce,* which was published in 1923 and included fragments which had been written as much as fifty years earlier. His plans to piece together an additional volume to be called *Progress: Its Economic Conditions* failed when death overtook the eighty-two-year-old in the summer of 1924.

B.—*Cecil Arthur Pigou* (1877–1959) was perhaps Marshall's most distinguished pupil. Carrying on in the Marshallian tradition, he became one of the pioneers of welfare economics, and he ranked as the leading British economist until challenged by J. M. Keynes.

C.—*Vilfredo Pareto* (1848–1923) was born in Paris, where his Italian father, a marquis, lived in self-imposed exile. As a result of a political amnesty, the Paretos were willing to return to Italy in 1858, and soon thereafter Vilfredo embarked upon the study of classical languages and mathematics. In 1869 he graduated from the Polytechnical School of the University of Turin with a thesis entitled "The Equilibrium of Solids," which already foreshadowed his later interest in the theory of economic equilibrium.

In the years following 1870, he gained experience as a railroad engineer and general manager of the Italian Iron Works, broadening his outlook with foreign travel. During this period he also gave vent, in numerous articles, to his antagonism against protectionism and state socialism and campaigned polemically against the militaristic tendencies of the Italian government.

Before he became acquainted with the work of Léon Walras, his frequent scientific speculations, largely sociological in nature, lacked a strong focus. His wrestling with the economics of Cournot, Walras, and Edgeworth gave birth to a series of articles along mathematical lines which he wrote for the *Giornale degli Economisti.* Having also published a critical and profound essay on the Marxian system, he subsequently endeared himself to Walras, who was happy to discover in Pareto a highly qualified disciple of his own doctrines. Thanks to Walras' support, the Italian successfully applied for the chair in economics at the University of Lausanne, Switzerland, which Walras vacated in 1892.

There follows a period of some thirteen years during which Pareto devoted himself passionately to the study and teaching of economic theory. In addition to numerous monographs, he published in rapid succession the *Lectures on Political Economy* (like most of his economic writings, not translated into English; French title *Cours d'Economie politique,* 1896–97), *Socialist Systems* (2 vols., 1900–02), and the *Manual of Political Economy* (Italian ed., 1906; French ed., 1909), one of the most erudite and elegant expositions of mathematical economics ever written. Failing health forced Pareto to accept a reduction in his teaching load and in 1907 to resign his chair in economics, although he taught some sociology for a few years thereafter.

His semiretirement in a shabby house full of cats on Lake Geneva was consecrated to the working out of a great treatise in sociology entitled

Trattato di Soziologia Generale, as important a contribution to a sister discipline as was his *Manual* to economics. A two-volume tome, the *Treatise* was published in Italian in 1916, in French in 1917, and in English (under the title *Mind and Society*) in 1935.

In 1917 a brilliant anniversary celebration bespoke his international outreach: an influential segment of the European academic community assembled in Lausanne to render homage to the great scientist on the eve of his seventieth birthday and of the twenty-fifth anniversary of his successorship to Walras' chair. Pareto also took a leaf from Walras in donating his comprehensive personal library to the institution which a quarter of a century before had opened its doors to him.

During the very last years of his life, he was immersed in a wave of extraordinary popularity in Italy, where it was believed that he was one of the main supporters of Mussolini's emergent fascism. As a matter of fact, independent-thinking Pareto remained on the sidelines, although he may well have expected from the new political leadership salvation from the social disorganization of prostrate Italy in the postwar period. Pareto, notwithstanding the senatorial rank conferred upon him, never embraced fascism, just as he had never identified himself with any other "isms."

D.—*Francis Ysidro Edgeworth* (1845–1926) was a pioneer in the use of mathematics in Britain. He considered himself a disciple of Marshall, but was much less influential in shaping neoclassical economics. His brilliance in the use of mathematical tools was already evident in his *Mathematical Psychics,* published in 1881. He was the first editor of the *Economic Journal,* the mouthpiece of the Royal Economic Society, and served in that capacity until his death. Much of his work was collected in his *Papers Relating to Political Economy* (1925).

E.—*Irving Fisher* (1867–1947), in a sense, was Edgeworth's counterpart in America as far as the development of mathematical techniques for the solution of economic problems is concerned. Educated both in the United States and in Europe, Fisher as editor of the English translation of *Researches into the Mathematical Principles of the Theory of Wealth* was instrumental in getting belated recognition for Cournot, the principal founder of the "mathematical school." He was associated with Yale University for almost half a century (1890–1935), and, in addition to a number of books addressed to the general public, wrote learned treatises devoted to the theory of capital and interest. It was in his *Mathematical Investigations into the Theory of Value and Price* (his Ph.D. thesis, published in 1892) that he anticipated Pareto's use of the indifference curve. For a detailed discussion of Fisher, see Chapter 11.

F.—*Johan Gustaf Knut Wicksell* (1851–1926) entered the arena of economic discussion relatively late in life, namely at the age of forty-one. His active interest in economics developed only after he graduated in philosophy and mathematics at the University of Uppsala in 1885. Before taking his doctorate in political economy at Uppsala in 1895, he studied for several years in France, Germany, Austria, and England.

His first important work immediately manifested his thorough mathematical training. Published in German in 1893, it was translated into English under the title *Value, Capital, and Rent*. There followed his *Studies in Finance Theory* (1896) and his *Interest and Prices* (1898), both also translated from their German original.

In 1900 he was appointed assistant professor of political economy at the University of Lund, where he held the chair of this discipline from 1904 to 1916.

In *Value, Capital, and Rent,* he had already supplied an outline solution to the main problems of the pure theory of value and distribution. More fully developed and further refined, it reappeared as the first volume (*General Theory*) of his *Lectures on Political Economy*, originally published in Swedish in 1901. His now famous theory concerning the relationship between the money rate of interest and the general level of prices found its definitive statement in the second volume (*Money*) of *Lectures on Political Economy*, published in its Swedish original in 1906.

Besides contributing to the theory of public finance, he was very articulate on the population problem, and, too forthright to conceal his somewhat radical neo-Malthusian inclinations, got himself into trouble (including a jail term) with governmental authorities. In the main, however, he led the life of a quiet, industrious, but retiring scholar.

He was a frequent contributor to professional periodicals, mainly those published in Swedish, German, and English, in that order.

Most of the older twentieth-century Swedish and Norwegian economists of renown got their economic foundations and much of their advanced training from Wicksell. They in turn helped to disseminate his teachings, giving momentum to the so-called Swedish school.

Questions for Review and Research

1. Contrast the mental dispositions of Jevons and Marshall. In what area(s) did their interests coincide?
2. Did Marshall erect his imposing structure of microeconomics primarily on the foundation of objective or subjective value theory? Explain.
3. What does Marshall mean when he uses the adjective "small" in referring to elasticity of demand?
4. According to Marshall, how does (a) the availability of substitutes and (b) the variety of uses influence the price elasticity of demand for a particular commodity?
5. Define or clearly describe the concept of consumer's surplus.
6. How is consumer's surplus related to welfare economics?
7. Search in the twentieth-century economics literature for references to welfare economics. Other than Pigou, were there any English pioneers in this new branch of our science? Has welfare economics displaced traditional (orthodox) economics?
8. Furnish applications of Marshall's concept of "external" economies.
9. In what context did Marshall use the famous "scissors' analogy"?

10. Explain how Pareto enlarged the tool box of economic analysis by his development of indifference curves and maps.
11. In Pareto's conceptual apparatus, what is economic equilibrium?
12. Do you think that Wicksell rendered economics a greater service by his technical innovations or by felicitously combining the contributions of the various schools contending for attention at the turn of the twentieth century? Substantiate your answer.

Recommended Readings

Marshall, Alfred. *Principles of Economics, an Introductory Volume*, 8th ed. London: Macmillan & Co., Ltd., 1930.
  Book I, "Preliminary Survey": Chapters I–IV, pp. 1–48.
  Book II, "Some Fundamental Notions": Chapters I–IV, pp. 49–82.
  Book III, "On Wants and Their Satisfaction": Chapter I, "Introductory," pp. 83–85; Chapter III, "Gradations of Consumers' Demand," pp. 92–101; Chapter IV, "The Elasticity of Wants," pp. 102–116; Chapter VI, "Value and Utility," pp. 124–137.
  Book IV, "The Agents of Production": Chapters VIII–XI, "Industrial Organization," pp. 240–290; Chapter XIII, "Conclusion. Correlation of the Tendencies to Increasing and to Diminishing Return," pp. 314–322.
  Book V, "General Relations of Demand, Supply, and Value": Chapter III, "Equilibrium of Normal Demand and Supply," pp. 337–350; Chapter V, "Continued, with Reference to Long and Short Periods," pp. 363–380; Chapter XII, "Equilibrium of Normal Demand and Supply, Continued, with Reference to the Law of Increasing Return," pp. 455–461; Chapter XIV, "The Theory of Monopolies," pp. 477–495; Chapter XV, "Summary of the General Theory of Equilibrium of Demand and Supply," pp. 496–503.
  Book VI, "The Distribution of the National Income": Chapter XI, "General View of Distribution," pp. 660–667.
Newman, Philip C., Arthur D. Gayer, and Milton H. Spencer (eds.). *Source Readings in Economic Thought*. New York: W. W. Norton & Company, Inc., 1954. The selection "Manual of Political Economy," by Vilfredo Pareto, pp. 477–488.
Schumpeter, Joseph A. *Ten Great Economists from Marx to Keynes*. New York: Oxford University Press, 1951. The biographical essay "Vilfredo Pareto (1848–1923)," pp. 110–142.
Stigler, George J. *Production and Distribution Theories*. New York: The Macmillan Company, 1941. Chapter IV, "Alfred Marshall," and Chapter X, "Knut Wicksell."
Wicksell, Knut. *Lectures on Political Economy*, edited with an introduction by Lionel Robbins. London: Routledge & Kegan Paul Ltd., 1934.
  Volume 1: "General Theory": "Introduction," pp. 1–11.
    Part I, "The Theory of Value": Chapters 1–5, pp. 13–83.
    Part II, "The Theory of Production and Distribution": Chapter 2, "Capitalistic Production," pp. 144–195.

VALUE AND DISTRIBUTION THEORY

Chamberlin and Robinson

A substantial portion of the literature on value theory since the late 1920's has been concerned with reformulations and elaborations which became necessary if the ubiquitous assumption of pure competition was to be dethroned. Many of the Marshallian concepts called for clarification and adaptation to changing economic practice. The *great debate on the Marshallian heritage,* which developed around the late 1930's, was evoked mainly by an article from the pen of Piero Sraffa.[1] Sraffa argued that the laws of returns, as stated by classical writers and modified by Marshall, should be expressed in terms which meet head-on the existence of conditions that are not purely competitive. Fired by a conviction that the practice of nonprice competition was no longer an exceptional or secondary phenomenon, he made a very successful beginning in sketching the outlines of a reformulated theory of market equilibrium; but the bulk of the impending work fell on the shoulders of Professors E. H. Chamberlin in the United States and Joan Robinson in England. Sraffa was able to show, for example, that in many situations, characterized by a large number of sellers who are able to realize some internal economies, sellers will attempt to secure and hold as large a share of the total market as possible by the continued expenditure of sales costs.

E. H. CHAMBERLIN[2]

In his *The Theory of Monopolistic Competition,* Chamberlin starts from a realization of the inadequacy of a neat theoretical distinction between competition and monopoly; he viewed the market phenomena as not *either* competitive *or* monopolistic but rather an intermixture of the two. The formulation of a theory of prices cannot, therefore,

---

[1]"The Laws of Returns under Competitive Conditions," *Economic Journal,* Vol. XXXVI (December, 1926), pp. 535–550. Sraffa was an Italian who studied under Marshall and later taught at Cambridge himself.

[2]See Biographical Note A.

stop at a clear definition of the two fundamental forces and their examination in isolation, but it must aim at their synthesis.

The middle ground, or twilight zone, between competition and monopoly had been explored to some extent by Cournot and Edgeworth — both had focused on duopoly and, in the process, had arrived at different solutions. But the case of "monopolistic competition" escaped their attention; they were not concerned with situations of many sellers offering differentiated products. Yet, in the world of reality most prices involve monopoly elements; and when businessmen merely speak of "competition," they think in terms of monopolistic rather than pure competition.

The *theory of pure competition,* heretofore so absorbingly dealt with, Chamberlin deemed of interest not so much because it is descriptive of particular markets, but mainly because it serves as *a useful point of departure for the analysis of monopolistic competition.* Chamberlin confined himself to pointing out those elements of the traditional model which allowed him to bring into clearer relief its contrast with monopolistic competition.

Monopolistic Competition

The interplay of monopolistic and competitive forces, previously referred to, is derived from *product differentiation.* Chamberlin regards a general class of product as ". . . differentiated if any significant basis exists for distinguishing the goods (or services) of one seller from those of another."[3] There arises immediately a dual dichotomy: Differentiation may be based on *actual* differences, or those which may be merely *imagined;* in the case of actual differences, differentiation may rest on certain *physical or legal characteristics of the product,* or it may relate to *conditions surrounding its sale.* Illustrative of the product characteristics are packaging, patents, and trademarks; of sale conditions, the seller's location, his methods of doing business, and the many intangible factors that make his firm the preferred choice of buyers. These two aspects of product differentiation are placed within such a broad framework that it becomes difficult to think of market relations lacking in differentiation. In their work, most of the earlier economists tended to draw a somewhat artificial line between a product that stood out distinctively in its general class, in which case it would be dealt with as governed by monopoly conditions, and a product that lacked such conspicuousness, which would make it part of a field of economic activity regarded as essentially competitive. Patents would typically fall

---

[3]Edward H. Chamberlin, *The Theory of Monopolistic Competition* (6th ed.; Cambridge: Harvard University Press, 1947), p. 56.

in the former class, trademarks in the latter. "All value problems are relegated to one category or the other according to their predominant element; the partial check exerted by the other is ignored."[4] This procedure was apt to create in the minds of readers a spurious antithesis, while in practice an intelligent analysis of price formation must account for both the forces of competition and those of monopoly. If monopoly is regarded as the antithesis of competition, it is possible to speak of pure monopoly only in the case where the supply of all economic goods is controlled by one seller, simply because all things are more or less imperfect substitutes for each other. On the other hand, pure competition would be said to prevail only where large classes of goods are perfectly standardized: here every seller is confronted with a competition of substitutes for his own product which is perfect. In all cases between these extremes, both competitive and monopolistic elements are always present and must be recognized for their relative importance. It follows that the *theory of pure competition fails to explain prices adequately as soon as a product is even slightly differentiated,* and a purely competitive price is not a normal price in the sense that actual prices tend (in the long run) to conform to it.

On the other hand, there are several reasons why it is inadmissible to describe the entire field of differentiated products in terms of perfect monopolies, that is, one monopoly for each seller. The main reason why the *theory of monopoly is inadequate* to describe many real-world situations is that it deals with the isolated monopolist facing a given demand curve for his product, whereas generally the competitive interrelationships of groups of sellers militate against taking the demand schedule for the product of any one of them as given. In other words, monopolistic competition addresses itself not only to the problem of an *individual* equilibrium, but also to that of the adjustment of economic forces within a *group* of competing monopolists. It differs from pure competition in that the market for each seller is no longer perfectly merged with those of his rivals; instead of describing a single large market of many sellers, monopolistic competition describes a network of related markets and brings into focus the monopoly elements arising from ubiquitous partial independence.

Implications of Product Differentiation for the Theory of Value

Whereas under pure competition the individual seller can sell as much as he pleases at the going price, under monopolistic competition

---
[4]*Ibid.,* p. 57.

his sales are circumscribed not only by *price,* but also by the *nature of his product* and by his *advertising outlays.*

As to price, he now no longer faces a horizontal demand curve. If he raises his price, the monopolistically competitive seller, like the pure monopolist, will have to sacrifice volume; if he lowers price, he will be able to sell a greater quantity. His profits may be increased by one or the other of these courses of action, depending upon both the elasticity of the demand curve for his product and upon its position relative to his unit-cost curve.

With reference to the nature of his product, the volume of sales of the monopolistic competitor will depend upon the manner in which he is able to "vary" his product from that of his competitors, where this variation may include much more than alterations in quality. With the possibility of differentiation present, sales will depend partly upon the skill with which the product is made to appeal to a particular group of buyers.

Finally, the volume of sales may be influenced by expenditures specifically directed to its enlargement. Since such expenditures will raise both the unit-cost curve and the selling price per unit, the monopolistic competitor will try to adjust this amount so as to render a maximum profit.

Both advertising expenditures and product differentiation are non-existent under pure competition; they are peculiar to monopolistic competition. Value theory, hitherto concerned only with price adjustment for a given product, must now also cope with the notion of "product equilibrium." Specifically, it must recognize that *price* adjustment is a relatively unimportant phase of the whole competitive process, while *product* adjustment may loom large. However, the equilibrium adjustment for the individual seller cannot be defined without reference to the availability of competing products *and* their respective prices, because the markets for goods which are substitutes for each other are closely interrelated. If he cannot adjust his price, equilibrium adjustment involves only his "product," and if the "product" is somehow set, he can only vary his price. But in many cases equilibrium adjustment involves variation in both. Chamberlin traces each type of adjustment in isolation and then proceeds to combine them. He demonstrates by various diagrams that the effect of monopoly elements on the adjustment of the individual seller typically makes for a higher price and a smaller scale of production than would be attained under pure competition, because the demand curve is now sloping rather than perfectly horizontal.

As far as *group equilibrium* is concerned, he proceeds in the same fashion. If there are excess profits for the typical producer, this means that the demand curve will intersect the cost curve. After an influx of new firms, the demand curve faced by the typical firm will shift downward and to the left, since total purchases (from all firms) must now be distributed among a larger number of sellers. If we assume cost curves to remain unaffected, this process will continue until the demand curve for each "product," that is, for the differentiated product of each seller, is tangent to its cost curve — which means that excess profits have been wiped out.

On the other hand, if there had been pure losses for the typical producer — that is, if the original demand curve had lain below the cost curve throughout the entire possible output range — the same final adjustment (tangency of demand curve to cost curve) would have been reached through an exodus of firms, the demand curve faced by the typical producer shifting upwards and to the right as total sales are shared by a smaller number of competitors. It should also be noted that, inasmuch as under monopolistic competition the movement of resources into or out of the industry reduces or raises profits to the level which would be attained under pure competition, the producer is no better or worse off. But since, under monopolistic competition, the demand curve is never tangent to the cost curve at the lowest point, the price will—given identical cost curves—inevitably be higher and the scale of production smaller than under pure competition, with the exact price differential depending on the strength of the monopoly elements.

Finally, the more elastic the demand schedule for the product of individual producers, the more will prices tend toward uniformity. But general price uniformity neither proves that competition is free from monopoly elements nor indicates the relative proportions of monopoly and competition in the admixture of a particular industry.

The Role of Production Costs and Selling Costs

The theory of monopolistic competition would be a halfway house, indeed, without recognition of the fact that *demands can be changed by advertising*. Costs incurred for this purpose are *the most prominent type of selling costs*. The latter are simply costs expended with a view to altering the position and/or shape of the demand curve for a product. Forces other than advertising that act upon sales volume, and consequently upon prices and profits, include the salaries of salesmen, window displays, demonstration of new goods, and premiums granted to middlemen.

If buyers had perfect knowledge as to goods and services offered, and if their wants were given, selling efforts would be of no avail. As a matter of fact, buyers may be in the dark with respect to both the existence of certain firms and the prices and qualities of goods offered. The dissemination of information will tend to alter their choices as to the means of satisfying their wants. Advertising by a firm may make the demand for its product more elastic, thus offering greater opportunities for price competition. But its effect also is likely to be a shift to the right of the demand curve for the advertised product, since it spreads knowledge of its existence and suggests the utilities it will provide to the purchaser. Of course, only truthful information will contribute to more effective want satisfaction; false or misleading advertising works the opposite effect.

In practice, the *distinction between advertising that alters the wants themselves and advertising that merely alters the channel through which existing wants are satisfied may be obscured.* For instance, if an advertisement merely displays the name of a particular trademark or manufacturer, the demand for the advertised product may be increased pari passu with the diminution of the demand for other nonadvertised brands.

Chamberlin introduces a convenient criterion by which selling costs can readily be distinguished from production costs. He does so by asking the question of *whether a particular cost does, or does not, alter the demand curve for a product.* This is the same as saying that costs of production create (form, place, time, etc.) utilities in order that demands may be satisfied, whereas costs of selling create and shift the demands themselves. It should therefore be immediately obvious that costs of production cannot be equated with the price of a good as it leaves the manufacturer, since costs incurred for transportation, storage, and the like are costs of production (adding utilities to the good itself) rather than selling costs (creating or shifting demand). The distinction between the two kinds of costs can also be stated by saying that ". . . those made to *adapt the product* to the demand are costs of production; those made to *adapt the demand* [emphasis added] to the product are costs of selling."[5]

The significance of the distinction to value theory is analogous to and intimately related to that between supply and demand, with costs of production increasing the former, costs of selling increasing the latter. Value theory had previously slurred over this distinction be-

---

[5] *Ibid.*, p. 125.

cause it reckoned all entrepreneurial outlays as costs of product, although only a portion thereof are of this nature. By taking demand as a datum and by counting all costs incurred as costs to meet this demand, production and selling costs were intermingled. The theory of pure competition, by neglecting selling costs — since they are at odds with the assumption of pure competition — fell considerably short of explaining the facts of economic life. Since under pure competition the number of firms is very large, and since each firm sells an indistinguishable product, not only would a large advertising expenditure by one firm have a very small effect on total demand, but its own sales gain would be a negligibly small fraction of this. Or, since under pure competition the market for any one seller is infinitely large, we can say that his advertising would be wasted: he can sell all he wants to without resorting to it.

What about the *curve of selling costs*? The net results of increasing advertising expenditure depend on both elements conducive to increasing returns and elements conducive to decreasing returns. Among the former are the need to overcome sales resistance by *repeated* assaults on the buyer's consciousness, and also economies of large-scale operations. Decreasing returns are explained by the fact that the best potential markets are exploited first and that added selling effort applied to any one group of potential buyers induces the sacrifice of continually more important wants. Forces favoring increasing returns tend to dominate their counterparts in the early stages, but tend to become submerged by forces working toward decreasing returns in the later stages. Translating these insights into diagrammatic form, Chamberlin obtains a curve of average selling cost per unit of product which, being a composite of all the forces, first falls, then reaches a minimum, and then rises, as we shift from a net balance of increasing returns to a net balance of decreasing returns. "The position of the curve and the exact point at which it turns upward will depend upon the nature of the 'product,' upon its price, and upon the competing substitutes which limit its market."[6] The problem of combining the curves of selling cost and of production cost can be resolved by a simple process of addition.

It can be seen now that under monopolistic competition in equilibrium prices are, as it were, two steps higher than under pure competition, assuming identical production cost curves. They are higher, in the first place, because selling costs must be added, and in the second place, because the demand curve is tipped from the horizontal, thus

---

[6]*Ibid.*, p. 136.

moving the point of tangency with a curve of combined cost of producing and selling to the left and upwards from the minimum point on the curve.

In relating monopolistic competition to the productivity theory of distribution, Chamberlin stated as his leading proposition that a sloping demand curve for the product of the individual firm reduces the remuneration of a factor of production below the value of its marginal product.

The Impact of Monopolistic Competition Theory

On the eve of World War II, a new approach to the empirical investigation of industries and markets gained ground, resulting before long in the emergence of the field of economic study known as "industrial organization." In essence, it was the application of the new, institutionally colored price theory, with its emphasis on marketing, to problems of concentration of economic power. As a consequence, most of the preexisting artificial barriers between theoretical and institutional studies of markets disappeared, the new empirical investigations being characterized by a distinct theoretical orientation. This meant a switch from the internal or industrial management view of a single firm's market performance to an external view of market performance of groups of firms, shedding light on market structures of industries, interindustry differences in structure, and — perhaps most significantly — associations between market structure and market performance. Thus *The Theory of Monopolistic Competition* advanced a construct which became the basis of an even more sophisticated classification of market structures.

The implementation of Chamberlin's basic construct was extremely important because of the great empirical relevance of business enterprises to the American economy, composed as it was (and is) of a mixture of pure and heterogeneous oligopolies, atomistic markets with product differentiation, and some markets approaching pure competition. Chamberlin's initial market classification, being substantially adequate, has not been replaced, merely fruitfully elaborated. It was especially by providing the major outlines of a theory of oligopoly that Chamberlin gave direction to further theorizing and subsequent empirical research. His identification of selling cost, product quality, and product variety as dimensions of market performance suggested a range of matters deserving empirical study beyond those involving price, production cost, and output. One of the first and most fertile minds to grasp the broad implications of the Chamberlin construct and classification of market structures and to suggest leads for research progress in the field of industrial organization has been Edward Mason, formerly at Harvard University.

One of the main contributions of welfare theory being its analysis of the allocation of resources under different market structures and comparison with the social optimum, the question arises whether monopolistic competition analysis has made as strong an impact on welfare economics. The answer is "probably not," mainly because monopolistic competition theory is partial, not general, equilibrium analysis and thus is not directly concerned with accounting for the *interrelationships among the outputs of the various industries.* If product differentiation has proved particularly resistant to general equilibrium analysis, the main reason is that there are no rigorous criteria by which one can recognize either an industry or a product.

While the analysis of product differentiation thus gives little aid to the economist assessing the allocation of resources among industries, the excess capacity theorem implicit in differentiation has important welfare consequences. Recall that since the elimination of excess profits requires tangency between a firm's average cost and revenue curves and since the demand curve has a nonzero slope under monopolistic competition, the equilibrium point must lie on a negatively inclined portion of the average cost curve — hence the firm could reduce its unit costs by increasing output. The validity of the welfare implications of the excess capacity theorem has been attacked on various grounds. It may be argued, for example, that we cannot take for granted, as Chamberlin did, that other things remain constant as output is varied; consequently, a small increase in output from its equilibrium level will not necessarily reduce average cost. (But one must be on guard against an opposite error. If a firm increases its advertising along with its production, and if as a result its unit costs rise, this does not mean that the initial equilibrium, however much less costly it may have been, was sufficiently large to yield minimum costs.)

It has also been said that it makes little sense to use the term "capacity" for the minimum point on a firm's average cost curve because in a world of specialized resources the equality of average cost and average revenue is either an accounting convention or is imposed on a firm by the capital market which constantly revalues specialized resources. Although this point may be valid, the excess capacity hypothesis remains unimpaired: if, as is likely, the weight of the evidence indicates that small firms with heterogeneous products compete each other's normal profits out of existence, then most firms are left so small a segment of the market that they must proceed at an uneconomically small scale of operation.   Granted this is not to say that too little will be produced by an *industry* (however defined) whose products are differentiated, since Chamberlin's excess capacity theorem is not a statement about the desirability of resource allocation among industries; it only says that the organization of an industry into too many firms is wasteful, impairing total welfare.   However, because of the social costs of standardization of products, reducing the number of firms may not mean a gain in welfare: with fewer firms producing differentiated outputs, the variety of goods available to the consumer falls.   Reorganization of the industry according to efficiency criteria, for example, by restricting the number of firms via a licensing system, may thus entail a net gain *or* a net loss.

While monopolistic competition analysis has enriched welfare economics little, Chamberlin's book has had a lasting impact on the habits of mind of economists and has permanently altered their point of view, leading them to recognize many different types of monopolistic elements and to speculate on their social consequences.

JOAN ROBINSON[7]

Several generations of eminent British economists received their training from Marshall or were imbued with the Marshallian aura. Among his disciples who held important academic chairs in Britain were Edgeworth, Pigou, and J. M. Keynes. But when the master resigned his chair at Cambridge in 1908, Joan Robinson—for nearly four decades a prolific writer — could scarcely have heard yet of the science of economics.

A Unique Double Coincidence

At almost exactly the same time — October, 1932 — Cambridge, Massachusetts (where Chamberlin launched the work discussed in the preceding section), was being paralleled by Cambridge, England: Joan Robinson, in her *The Economics of Imperfect Competition*, covered much the same general ground concurrently being covered by Chamberlin. Emotionally and intellectually more strongly bound to the tradition of Marshall (and Pigou), *Mrs. Robinson devoted comparatively greater attention to pure monopoly than to monopolistic competition.* She set out

---

[7]See Biographical Note B.

a highly sophisticated technical apparatus which made possible both an elegant refinement of price theory and an extension of the traditional theory of monopoly. Like Chamberlin, she stated the conditions of equilibrium in similar terms for all market situations, but she laid more stress than her American counterpart on the comparison of results — in terms of price, output, and the remuneration for factor services — to which each market situation leads. She stressed *positions* of equilibrium rather than the *processes* which bring it about.

Inspired by the earlier work of Professor Pigou, she also pursued some of the ramifications of her propositions in the realm of welfare economics, a commendable feat in view of the distressingly high level of abstraction at which she felt compelled to carry the argument. In contrast to Chamberlin, who paid a great deal of attention to the phenomenon of product differentiation through advertising, Mrs. Robinson rendered practically no homage to "institutionalism," which by the early 1930's had become quite fashionable.[8]

All in all, *as both Chamberlin and Robinson stress the joint influence of monopolistic and competitive elements in the determination of equilibrium, the upshot of their theory is much the same:* a statement of conditions of market equilibrium broad enough to make it equally applicable to competition, to monopoly, or to any intermediate situation; and the ample use of geometry for the purpose of shorthand expression.

It is because they have furnished a box of tools much sharper than those supplied from Marshall's "workshop" that Chamberlin and Robinson have greatly indebted themselves to midtwentieth-century analytical economists. It is for the latter to broaden the area within which these tools can work, that is, to provide new materials on which they can exercise their ingenuity. Enlisted in Mrs. Robinson's work is an impressive array of average and marginal revenue curves on the demand side and a no less impressive array of cost curves on the supply side.

Price Discrimination

Mrs. Robinson's essay in the technique of economic analysis, which, incidentally, does not claim to make a direct contribution to our knowledge of the real world, covers familiar as well as new ground. As already intimated, the technique deployed is one for studying equilibrium positions, with no reference being made to the effects of the passage of time, that is, no study being made of the process of moving from one equilib-

---

[8]See Biographical Note C.

rium position to another. It is difficult to pinpoint the areas in which she made "inventions," especially in view of the fact that, in the development of her ideas, she was always able to use other famous Cambridge economists (Professors Kahn, Shove, etc.) as her sounding board. With this reservation in mind, let us first explore the skeleton of the apparatus built for the analysis of price discrimination, a practice by no means negligible in today's business world. Methodologically, it appears as an outgrowth of monopoly equilibrium analysis and belongs within the same broad framework.

Price discrimination takes place when *the single seller of an article is able to dispose of it to different buyers at different prices.* This he can do only when, first, the different markets in which he is selling are so divided from each other that it is not possible to resell in a dearer market goods bought (from the monopolist) in the cheaper market, and second, customers residing in the dearer market are prevented from transferring themselves to the cheaper market (with a view to taking advantage of the lower price there).

Price discrimination presupposes some degree of *market imperfection* plus the above-mentioned capacity of an individual seller to divide his market into separate parts. But when market imperfection is slight, so that the demand curves faced by individual sellers are highly elastic, price discrimination cannot go very far. On the other hand, when there is no close competition between the various rival sellers, or when they can agree on policy, chances for successful price discrimination are much brighter. Furthermore, where there is no possibility whatsoever of transfer from one market to another, as for instance in the case of professional services, price discrimination becomes almost irresistible. Division of markets may be accomplished by the fact of wide geographical separation of the markets coupled with high transportation cost, and /or by tariff barriers. In the latter case, that is, when a seller is able to dispose of his article at a lower price in the export market, "dumping" takes place. Another principal case is that in which "several groups of buyers require the same service in connection with clearly differentiated commodities," as when ". . . a railway can charge different rates for the transport of cotton goods and of coal without any fear that bales of cotton will be turned into loads of coal in order to enjoy a cheaper rate."[9]

In the absence of natural barriers between groups of customers, price discrimination may be achieved by selling brands of a certain article

[9]Joan Robinson, *The Economics of Imperfect Competition* (London: Macmillan & Co., Ltd., 1933), p. 180.

(whose properties are much the same) as different qualities under names and labels which appeal to different income strata. By so doing, the monopolist puts himself in a position of selling substantially the same good at varying prices.

What determines whether it will be of advantage for the monopolist to charge different prices in the different markets? The answer is that the elasticities of demand in the separate markets must be unequal. In this case, total profit can be maximized by selling less in those markets in which the elasticity of demand is less (and hence the marginal revenue smaller) and selling more in those where the elasticity of demand is greater. The monopolist will therefore strive to adjust his sales in such a way that the marginal revenue obtained from selling an additional output unit is the same for all the markets. Profits will be maximized when the marginal cost of the *whole* output is equal to the marginal revenue in *each* of the separate markets.

Graphically, monopoly profits would be shown as the area which lies between the *aggregate* marginal revenue curve, obtained by summing up laterally each of the marginal revenue curves corresponding to their respective demand curves, and the marginal cost curve of the firm. In other words, by deducting from the area that lies between the aggregate marginal revenue curve and the x-axis the area that lies between the marginal cost curve and the x-axis, an area corresponding to total profits will emerge.[10]

A corollary of the above analysis is that if the demand curves of the separate markets were iso-elastic, that is, if at any price the elasticity of demand were the same in each market, there would accrue no advantage from price discrimination; if the marginal revenue curves in each market were equal, the prices would then also be equal.

In many cases, the *manner of dividing up the market* will be partly under the control of the monopolist, as when a railroad company, in setting up rate schedules, somewhat arbitrarily groups together the types of goods which are to be charged at various rates. It goes without saying that the manner of breaking up the market, inasmuch as it can be controlled, will largely determine the profitability of the monopoly. At any rate, the monopolist can no longer improve his position by further subdividing the total market once he has reached the point at which each submarket consists either of a single buyer, or else of a group of buyers whose elasticities of demand are the same. Each of these buyers or groups of buyers, as the case may be, will of

---

[10]Robinson, *op. cit.*, p. 183.

course be charged a different price, the highest price being charged in the least elastic market and the lowest price in the most elastic market.

As far as output is concerned, Robinson shows that in cases where the separate demand curves are straight lines discriminating monopoly output is equal to simple monopoly output; although, after discrimination is introduced, the quantity sold in some markets will decrease, whereas in others it will increase. Further complications arise when the concavities (convexities) of nonstraight-line demand curves differ.

Does society ever benefit from price discrimination? At first sight one might be inclined to answer this question in the negative, because the monopolist's excess profit would be higher under price discrimination than it is under monopoly with a one-price system (where it is already greater, and output is undesirably smaller, than it generally is under conditions of competition). But a closer look suggests a different result. Under a one-price system, if the average-cost curve lay above the demand curve throughout its length, clearly no profit could be made by producing any output. But, under price discrimination, if the average-cost curve lay at some point below the average-revenue curve, a profit could be made at an output corresponding to that point; and, provided discrimination was possible, that output would be produced. The rationale for allowing railroads to practice discrimination may thus be twofold: without it, the railroad might not be built, as this would be uneconomical; and price discrimination would not be objectionable since, after all, the average revenue earned by it cannot be greater than the average utility to consumers of railroad services. And, if average revenue (= average utility to consumers) should be greater than average cost, a net gain to society will result.

If, in contrast to the preceding case, some output would be profitably produced even if discrimination were prohibited, it is not possible to say whether or not customers would, on balance, benefit from it, as compared with their situation under a one-price monopoly. This is so because discrimination must always hurt those buyers for whom the price is raised and benefit those for whom it is reduced. To identify oneself with one or the other group of customers would militate against the difficulty of making intergroup utility comparisons, which cannot be resolved except by entering the domain of welfare economics.

Generally speaking, and barring a worse maldistribution of resources as between different uses, *price discrimination will be superior to simple monopoly in all cases when it leads to an increase in output,* by bridging part of the "output gap" between simple monopoly and pure competition.

Monopsony

On a scale of market structures, at the end opposite to that of monopsony — the situation where there is only one buyer of a given good — is perfect competition among buyers. We may recall that this requires that two principal conditions be met: that the number of buyers be so large that a change in the amount purchased by any one of them will not influence the price; and that sellers are indifferent as to whom they sell. Under perfect competition among buyers, marginal cost to the buyer — which is equated to marginal utility derived from the purchase — must be equal to the price of the commodity. The marginal utility curve for a buyer represents the amounts which he will buy at various marginal costs, and since the supply of the commodity is perfectly elastic to him, the marginal utility of each amount of the commodity will be equal to its price (= marginal cost). Finally, when competition among buyers is perfect, the market demand curve represents the marginal utility curve of the buyers as a group (the collective marginal utility curve), with each buyer acquiring of the total amount purchased such a portion that its marginal utility will be equal to the price.

Robinson correctly points out that it is far more realistic to postulate that competition among buyers be perfect than to postulate that competition among sellers be perfect, as Chamberlin's emphasis on monopolistic competition—leaving out monopsonistic competition—has already suggested. At any rate, it is a fact that in most ordinary markets there is usually a large number of buyers to each seller. However, there are also numerous examples of buyers whose purchases represent the whole or a large portion of the output of a commodity produced by an industry. We are here concerned only with monopsony, that is, cases where this output is produced by a *competitive* industry and where *all* of it is purchased by a single buyer or buying agency. We are ipso facto not interested in cases of oligopsony (several large buyers absorbing the output of a competitive industry) or of bilateral monopoly (monopsonists buying from monopolists).[11]

---

[11]*Heinrich von Stackelberg* (1905–1946), a German economist, explored these and other more complicated situations in a work with the title *Marktform und Gleichgewicht*. Translated as *Market Structure and Equilibrium*, this book was written and published within a year or two after the "Robinson-Chamberlin coincidence." Its author regarded the "pure" duopoly case as the central problem of monopoly theory and emphasized the interdependence of firms and the indeterminacy of price. The book foreshadowed the post-World War II application of the theory of games to economics.

Stackelberg was professor at the University of Berlin and later taught at the University of Madrid. Not accidentally — in view of his conclusion that the free play of forces will not result in economic equilibrium, and considering the environment in which he wrote — he developed a defense of authoritarian interventionism.

Under monopsony, as distinguished from perfect competition among buyers, marginal utility will no longer be equal to price — except in the rare case where the commodity is sold under conditions of constant supply price. But, as before, the amount purchased will have to be adjusted so that marginal utility is equal to marginal cost. If the average-cost (supply) curve of the sellers is rising, the amount purchased and sold will be priced at less than marginal cost; if it is falling, the price will be more than marginal cost for the amount traded. This follows from the fact that, if the industry supply curve is rising, the marginal cost curve, from the point of view of the monopsonist, will be rising even faster; whereas, a falling industry supply curve will be accompanied by a marginal cost curve to the buyer that drops more sharply.

The monopsonist has to pay the supply price of the output of the commodity he buys, and this is indicated on the supply curve (AC). But he will strive to make his marginal cost (MC) equal to his marginal utility, and since the latter is indicated by the demand curve (D), it is the intersection of the MC and D curves which indicates his optimum purchase. He will thus buy ON and pay NP. NM measures marginal

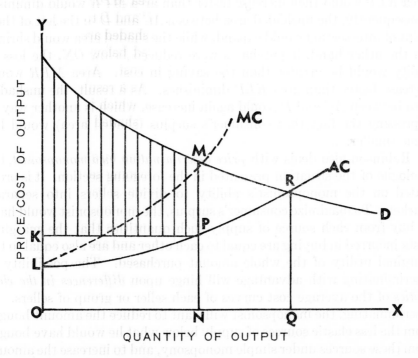

QUANTITY OF OUTPUT

Source: Adapted from Joan Robinson, *The Economics of Imperfect Competition.* London: Macmillan & Co., Ltd., 1933. Figure 66 (p. 220) and Figure 69 (p. 223).

cost and marginal utility where they are equal. Under perfect competition among buyers (or constant supply price), AC and MC would coincide from the individual buyer's point of view, and average cost would also be equal to marginal utility. Specifically, under constant supply price, the amount purchased under monopsony will be the same as under pure competition; whereas, under increasing or decreasing supply price, marginal cost to the monopsonist will not be equal to the price (AC) of the commodity; marginal cost will be higher or lower respectively. If marginal cost is higher, the monopsonist will buy less than the competitive amount (OQ in the foregoing diagram); and if it is lower, he will buy more.

The diagram can also be used to illustrate the Marshallian concept of the *consumer's surplus*. The monopsonist maximizes his surplus when he buys ON at the supply price NP. It is represented by the (shaded) area bounded by the Y-axis, the D curve, and lines MP and KP.

We know already that consumer's surplus must be at a maximum when marginal cost and marginal utility are equal. If an output greater than ON were purchased, marginal cost would exceed marginal utility. Area KLP would then increase faster than area MPR would diminish. Consequently, the unshaded area between AC and D to the left of their point of intersection would expand, while the shaded area would shrink. On the other hand, if purchases were reduced below ON, the loss of utility would be greater than the saving in cost. Area MPR would increase faster than area KLP diminishes. As a result, the unshaded area between AC and D would again increase, which is another way of expressing the fact that consumer's surplus (shaded area) would become smaller.

Robinson also deals with *price discrimination by a monopsonist*, the analogue of the situation presented in the foregoing section. It is predicated on the monopsonist's ability to divide sellers into separate markets. To maximize consumer's surplus, the monopsonist would have to buy from each source of supply such quantities that the marginal costs incurred in buying are equal to each other and are also equal to the marginal utility of the whole amount purchased. The possibility of discriminating with advantage will hinge upon *differences in the elasticities* of the average cost curves of each seller or group of sellers. In discriminating, the monopsonist will want to reduce the amount bought from the less elastic sources of supply below what he would have bought from these sources under simple monopsony, and to increase the amount bought from the more elastic sources, lowering in the former case, and raising in the latter, the price paid for the changed quantities. It is already evident that the analytical technique to be applied to discriminating monopsony is symmetrical to the one developed for discriminating monopoly, and we need not pursue Robinson's conclusions any further. It also goes without saying that the principles governing monopsony can be applied to purchases of both finished commodities and factors of production.

Conclusions

In comparing the relationships of monopsony and monopoly to perfect competition, Robinson concludes: ". . . the common-sense rule that the individual will equate marginal gains (whether of utility or revenue) with marginal cost, applies equally to monopsony, to monopoly, and to perfect competition."[12] This can be demonstrated as follows. Whereas the supply curve of a commodity is not perfectly elastic from the point of view of the single buyer under monopsony, it is perfectly elastic from the point of view of a buyer under pure competition. But, in both cases, the individual buyer equates marginal utility with marginal cost. The only difference is that under monopsony the price is *lower than* both marginal utility and marginal cost, whereas the competitive buyer pays a price *equal to* both marginal cost and marginal utility.

Furthermore, both the monopolist and the seller under purely competitive conditions equate marginal revenue to marginal cost. The only difference here is that under monopoly marginal revenue and marginal cost are both *less than* price; whereas marginal revenue, marginal cost, and price are all *equal* for the purely competitive seller.

By *placing the marginal principle in a broader context and showing its pervasive and utmost importance in economic analysis*, Robinson counteracted its one-sided application in most earlier economics textbooks to perfectly competitive conditions, showing also that the cases arising in perfect competition are only special cases of a general rule. Along with Chamberlin, she has admirably succeeded in breaking down the exaggerated distinction between analysis suitable to competition and analysis suitable to monopoly and in demonstrating that the *same system of ideas is equally applicable to the most diverse market structures*. While both Chamberlin and Robinson excel in clarity and elegance of style, the conciseness of presentation and logical rigor make Robinson's work the more demanding of the two.

---

[12]Robinson, *op. cit.*, p. 230.

SUMMARY

In 1926 Piero Sraffa wrote for the *Economic Journal* a pathbreaking article which opened the eyes of many students of value theory to the fact that this body of doctrine was urgently in need of being reformulated with a view to accommodating the ever-widening field of nonprice competition. The appearance of Chamberlin's and Robinson's books some six and seven years later — following a vigorously increasing interest that provoked additional articles in professional journals — marked the maturity of the new approach to value theory. The idea of partial competition had cropped up every now and then since Cournot; but it was not developed into a systematic set of market relationships, broad enough to embrace the hallowed theory of pure competition, until Chamberlin and Robinson, independent of each other, devoted themselves to this major task. While neither of the two works was comprehensive, they supplemented each other in important ways, staking out an extensive field for further professional cultivation. Each recognized the classical account of pure competition as a boundary rather than a typical case.

Robinson concentrated much of her energy on an ingenious analysis of the sorely neglected problems of price discrimination and monopsony, and, at the same time, after first having separately developed their outstanding properties, skillfully integrated the theories of competitive equilibrium and monopoly equilibrium. Chamberlin's study of partial monopoly centers around the concept of monopolistic competition and the successive positions of the demand curve of the firm as rival firms change their market policy. He emphasized that policy in semi-monopolistic markets depends on assumptions about the way in which rival firms will react to a change in price, "product," or advertising outlays. He clearly expounded the meaning of differentiation, the distinction between individual and group equilibrium and that between selling costs and production costs. His most specific contribution relates to the place assigned to selling costs in the theory of value and the diversity of conditions surrounding each producer.

Although not elaborated in the body of this chapter, it should be noted that both authors applied their principal findings in the intermediate area between pure competition and pure monopoly to the productivity theory of distribution, with particular emphasis on the demand for labor.

While Robinson occasionally strayed from her highly abstract reasoning into the realm of welfare economics, Chamberlin never ventured outside the strictly analytical territory. Both writers force-fully demonstrated that the general effect of partial monopoly is to restrict output and to raise price, but Robinson intermittently qualified her adverse appraisal, pointing out cases in which monopoly extends output and lowers price as compared with the competitive norm. Both authors, but especially Robinson, were concerned with the equilibrium positions as such, rather than the influence of time as a significant variable in the process of adjustment. Finally, while both were aware of the limitations of their tools — abstracting as they do from irrational behavior, imperfect knowledge, and the technological requirements — Robinson more than Chamberlin realized the unful-filled need to provide materials on which these new weapons of attack could be exercised.

One frequently overlooked contribution of the Chamberlin-Robinson doctrines is that they have made the major propositions emerging from Keynesian macroeconomic analysis more meaningful. It became natural and plausible to explain price rigidities and wage stickiness, which Keynes associated with underemployment equilib-rium, with reference to the fact that the world is not predominantly purely competitive. And reference to these doctrines helps to make analytical sense out of the dilemma that sustained full employment may be impossible to achieve without at least a creeping inflation. Moreover, to investigate the conflicting claims of demand-pull and cost-push theories of inflation without regard for the new micro appara-tus sketched in this chapter is to neglect a vital ingredient in the analysis.

BIOGRAPHICAL NOTES

A.—*Edward Hastings Chamberlin* (1899–   ) was born in La Conner, Washington. He received his B.S. degree from the University of Iowa in 1920, M.A. degrees from the University of Michigan in 1922 and Harvard University in 1924, and his Ph.D. from the latter institution in 1927. Two doctor's degrees *honoris causa* have been bestowed upon him by the Catho-lic University, Milan, and the Sorbonne in Paris, and an LL.D. degree by Boston College.

Since 1922 he has been at Harvard University where he was instructor from 1922 to 1929, assistant professor from 1929 to 1934, associate pro-fessor for the next three years, and has been full professor since 1937. Chamberlin was chairman of the Department of Economics from 1939 to 1943 and was appointed David A. Wells professor of political economy in 1951 (is now emeritus). He has repeatedly accepted invitations to appear as visiting professor or guest lecturer in European countries. In 1953 he received the Paul D. Converse Award of the American Marketing Associa-tion and in 1958–59 was a Guggenheim fellow.

He has been a member of various international agencies and institutes as well as numerous professional associations. He held vice-presidencies in the American Economic Association and the Catholic Economic Association and was editor of the *Quarterly Journal of Economics* from 1948 to 1958.

Among his numerous books, in addition to *The Theory of Monopolistic Competition* (published in its eighth edition in 1962), are the following: *The Impact of the Union* (1951), *Towards a More General Theory of Value* (1957), and *The Economic Analysis of Labor Union Power* (1958). He served as editor of the work, *Monopoly and Competition and Their Regulation*, which was published in 1954. In 1967 a book of essays in honor of Chamberlin (edited by Robert E. Kuenne) appeared under the title, *Monopolistic Competition Theory: Studies in Impact.*

B.—*Joan (Violet) Robinson* (1903–   ) is a Cambridge product, and one of the most prolific among the living economic authors trained in England during the first half of the twentieth century. Educated in London and Cambridge, she completed the Economics Tripos in 1925. Married the following year to E. A. G. Robinson, a famous economist in his own right, Mrs. Robinson became a Faculty Assistant Lecturer in economics at Cambridge University in 1931, a University Lecturer in 1937, a Reader in 1949, and has been a Professor at her Alma Mater since 1965. She has traveled widely as a visiting lecturer, thus strengthening her international reputation as a thoughtful student of the economics of a centrally planned economy.

The more famous among her publications include the following: *The Economics of Imperfect Competition* (1933), *Essays in the Theory of Employment* (1937), *Introduction to the Theory of Employment* (1937), *Essay on Marxian Economics* (1942, second edition, 1967), *The Rate of Interest and Other Essays* (1952), *The Accumulation of Capital* (1956, second edition, 1965), *Collected Economic Papers* (first volume, 1951; second volume, 1960; third volume, 1965), *Essays in the Theory of Economic Growth* (1962), *Economic Philosophy* (1962), and *Economics: An Awkward Corner* (1966, first American edition, 1967). Her articles have appeared in numerous journals, especially the *Economic Journal*, of which her husband became joint editor in 1944. Her devotion to spreading the "Keynesian revolution" has been exceeded by few of her native or foreign colleagues.

C.—Institutional economics is for the most part a native American product; and, among the many laborers in the field, *Thorstein Veblen* (1857–1929) distinguished himself both by his pioneering feats in this virgin territory and by his erratic and colorful personality. Rejected or treated indifferently by most of his colleagues, Veblen was more successful as a writer than a teacher and within the first quarter of the twentieth century produced nearly a dozen books and numerous essays. His pungent style and unorthodox views drew force from a highly developed critical acumen, to which his Norwegian heritage and upbringing in a frontier community in Minnesota contributed. His *The Theory of the Leisure Class* (1899) appeals as much to the philosopher of social institutions as it does to a person with more narrowly economic interests. *Thorstein Veblen and His America,* published by Joseph Dorfman in 1934, is a "must" for those who would penetrate more deeply this enigmatic and powerful mind. The reason why Veblen is not treated in the body of this text is that for all practical purposes his "cultural economics" does not constitute an addition to economic theory.

John R. Commons (1862–1945) and Wesley C. Mitchell (1874–1948) likewise occupy distinguished places in the institutionalist "hall of fame." Their more significant contributions to economic theory will be discussed in Chapters 17 and 14 respectively.

The interested reader looking for a concise introduction to the foundations of institutionalism is referred to Joseph Dorfman and others, *Veblen, Commons, and Mitchell Reconsidered. A Series of Lectures.* Berkeley: University of California Press, 1963.

Questions for Review and Research

1. How did Sraffa infuse new life into the established body of value and distribution theory?

2. Were Chamberlin and Robinson the first to explore the twilight zone between pure competition and monopoly?

3. How is it possible to systematize the presentation of the variety of cases suggested by the broad term "product differentiation"?

4. Read the prefaces of the books of Chamberlin and Robinson which were discussed in the text. Are there any hints as to how they regarded each other's work in the area cultivated by both of them?

5. What reasons are advanced by Chamberlin for the contention that both the theory of pure competition and the theory of monopoly are inadequate in describing the majority of real-world situations?

6. Does Chamberlin use any diagrams to illustrate price adjustment and product adjustment under monopolistic competition?

7. How are demand and cost curves related to each other if a pure loss is suffered by a producer throughout any conceivable output range?

8. Give four examples of selling costs, including the most prominent kind.

9. How, according to Chamberlin, can production costs be readily distinguished from selling costs?

10. Following Robinson, what are the prerequisites for successful price discrimination?

11. Why, as a rule, is marginal utility not equal to price under monopsony, although the two coincide under conditions of perfect competition among buyers?

12. Following Robinson's analysis, how can a price-discriminating monopsonist maximize consumer's surplus?

Recommended Readings

Chamberlin, Edward H. *The Theory of Monopolistic Competition, a Reorientation of the Theory of Value*, 7th ed. Cambridge: Harvard University Press, 1956. Chapter I, "Introduction," pp. 3–10; Chapter II, "Value under Pure Competition," pp. 11–25; Chapter IV, "The Differentiation of the Product," pp. 56–70; Chapter V, "Product Differentiation and the Theory of Value," pp. 71–116; Chapter VII, "Selling Costs and the Theory of Value," pp. 130–176.

Robinson, Joan. *The Economics of Imperfect Competition*. London: Macmillan & Co., Ltd., 1933. "Introduction," pp. 1–12.
Book I, "The Technique": Chapters 1–2, pp. 15–43.
Book II, "Monopoly Equilibrium": Chapter 3, pp. 47–59.
Book IV, "The Comparison of Monopoly and Competitive Output": Chapters 10–14; pp. 133–176.
Book V, "Price Discrimination": Chapters 15–16, pp. 179–208.
Book VI, "Monopsony": Chapters 17–19, pp. 211–231.

Shackle, G. L. S. *The Years of High Theory*. Cambridge: At the University Press, 1967. Chapter 3, "Sraffa and the State of Value Theory, 1926," pp. 13–21; Chapter 4, "Marginal Revenue," pp. 22–42; Chapter 5, "The New Establishment in Value Theory: (i) Mrs. Joan Robinson," pp. 43–60; Chapter 6, "The New Establishment in Value Theory: (ii) Edward Chamberlin," pp. 61–70.

"The Theory of Monopolistic Competition after Thirty Years," *American Economic Review*, Papers and Proceedings, Vol. LIV, No. 3, May, 1964, pp. 28–57.

CHAPTER

8

MACROECONOMICS

J. M. Keynes

In 1936, the year when the last countries of the world gave up their allegiance to the international gold standard and the curtain was rung down on an era in which international monetary cooperation successively deteriorated, an Englishman correctly predicted that his new book, if its message were to fall on receptive ears, would initiate a major break with the past. Symptomatically, Keynes[1] had long preached the gospel that continued adherence to the international gold standard in its traditional form constituted a fetter and that there was a crying need for its replacement by a superior monetary order. Consequently, he was called upon during the last few years of his life to contribute from his vast wealth of experience to the plans for international postwar monetary reconstruction; and he lived to see the day when such "new-fangled" institutions as the International Monetary Fund and the International Bank for Reconstruction and Development were ready to be launched on their generally successful careers.

A major controversy erupted once *The General Theory of Employment, Interest, and Money* (1936) came from the printing press; and, as if they had already been cued in on the impending battle between Modernists and Neoclassicists, Keynes' eager followers stood ready to hold their ground when the opposition began to return the fire.[2] There followed a period of continuous and animated skirmishing, but it was not until the end of the 1950's that a really powerful counterattack

---

[1] See Biographical Note A.

[2] Joan Robinson's *Introduction to the Theory of Employment* (London: Macmillan & Co., Ltd., 1937) performed valuable yeoman's services at a time when there was still the task of popularizing Keynes' teaching rather than countering the blows of an aroused opposition. By simplifying, condensing, and putting things in proper order, she greatly helped to accelerate the Keynesian victory.

in book-length form made the headlines.[3] For better or for worse, by that time the Keynesian message had seeped through many layers of academic teaching and research.

Now, in a less emotional environment, it is somewhat easier to glean the grain and separate it from the chaff. Nevertheless, no attempt will be made here to arrive at a final evaluation of Keynes' contribution to the body of macroeconomics and his inspiration of varied econometric research. Suffice it to say that Keynes toward the end of his life had mixed feelings about the impact of his own message. In an article published posthumously in the *Economic Journal*,[4] he deplored the trend that he had done so much to shape — to consider the "classical medicine" of freedom of trade as defunct. After having, for all practical purposes, jettisoned the classical theories on which he had been brought up and had held with firm conviction through a good part of his career, Keynes once more became cognizant and appreciative of their strong points — not to say their timeless content. But he did not live long enough to decelerate the momentum of a drive to translate Keynesian doctrine into practical policy. Much less circumspect than their master, some of his modern disciples have "gone all out" in their occasionally blind enthusiasm to replace private initiative with government planning and have thus promoted welfare statism in ways that Keynes himself might never have endorsed.

Undoubtedly, receptiveness for Keynesian theory was greatly enhanced by the lingering depression of the 1930's. Preoccupied as he was with its causes, Keynes worked within a framework of certain assumptions — perfect competition, fixed techniques of production, fixed capital coefficients — and analyzed the relations between the major aggregates but scarcely attempted to break down these aggregates into their respective component parts. It is therefore difficult, if not impossible, to explain in generally valid terms Keynes' antidepression policies; his followers have not been able to agree on the particular mix of monetary, fiscal, and other policies which Keynes would have recommended had he lived long enough to advise modern

---

[3]Henry Hazlitt, *The Failure of the New Economics* (Princeton, N.J.: D. Van Nostrand Company, Inc., 1959). The Keynesians now were so firmly in the saddle that they could afford to bypass this work or deal with it cavalierly. Although not free from weaknesses — for example, caviling, pedantry, and tediousness — it constitutes nevertheless a scientifically respectable piece of work. More important, it opened the door to a more varied and enlightened critical assessment (in one volume) of Keynes by his professional peers. See *The Critics of Keynesian Economics* (edited by Henry Hazlitt) under the Recommended Readings for this chapter.

[4]In a celebrated phrase, he speaks of ". . . how much modernist stuff, gone wrong and turned sour and silly, is circulating in our system. . . ." "The Balance of Payments of the United States," *Economic Journal* (June, 1946), p. 186.

governments on the implementation of "full" employment policies. It cannot be disputed, however, that at long last the problem of unemployment in industrially advanced countries has been placed in the forefront of economic discussion: the armaments race has made such large demands on our material and human resources that we cannot afford large-scale unemployment if at the same time we insist on a further continuous rise in the level of living. Few who hold dear the preservation of an essentially capitalistic economy differ with Keynes that, at least sporadically, something has to be done to keep the economic machine in good running order. The New Deal was at least superficially in harmony with the general pattern of Keynesian policies: deficit financing of public works and managed currency geared to artificially low interest rates were unmistakably weapons from the Keynesian arsenal.

In what follows, only those Keynesian tools that have been widely adopted and have become standard equipment of basic research and investigation will be discussed at any length. Since the *General Theory* was addressed to fellow economists and many portions of it are not easily intelligible to undergraduate students, a strongly selective approach commends itself. Even though not obvious, Keynes' basic ideas are quite simple, and much of posterity has regretted that he did not steer clear of laborious modes of expression. As far as personal emphases are concerned, rather than endorsing Keynes in his contention that the assumptions of the classical theory are applicable to the special case of full employment only and to view in this the most radical departure of the *General Theory*, the author believes that Keynes' most valuable and enduring feat has been the integration of monetary theory — tailored to modern developments — with the general theory of supply and demand.

THE PRINCIPLE OF EFFECTIVE DEMAND

Keynes' treatise on macroeconomic theory is not concerned with the distribution and the relative rewards of a *given* volume of employed resources among different uses but with the question of what determines the *actual employment* of the available resources. Nevertheless, he does not relinquish the classical assumption — in accord with the principle of short-run diminishing returns — that ". . . with a given organization, equipment and technique, real wages and the volume of output (and hence employment) are uniquely correlated, so that, in general, an increase in employment can only occur to the accompaniment of a decline in the rate of real wages."[5] Where Keynes parts company with his predecessors, including Marshall,[6] is on the question of whether individual saving acts will inevitably lead to parallel investment acts. He stresses the essentially different nature of these two activities and sets out to destroy the alleged nexus uniting decisions to abstain from present consumption with decisions to provide for enhanced future consumption. Motives underlying the one and motives underlying the other cannot be readily linked.

Keynes distinguishes between "factor cost" and "user cost" of a given employment and sets off user cost from the total income of an employer, the difference between user cost and total income being the net income of the entrepreneur. The aggregate supply price of the output resulting from a given amount of employment is equated with the entrepreneurial expectation of proceeds which will just make it worthwhile for him to offer that employment. Keynes emphasizes that both individual firm employment and aggregate employment depend on the amount of the proceeds which entrepreneurs expect from the sale of the output corresponding to that employment, with entrepreneurs endeavoring to maximize the excess of the proceeds over the factor costs.

In functional notation, if Z symbolizes the aggregate supply price of the output from employing N men and if D represents the proceeds expected by entrepreneurs from the employment of N men, then, if for a given value of employment (N) the expected proceeds (D) exceed the aggregate supply price (Z), entrepreneurs will have an incentive to increase employment beyond N and to continue doing so until it has reached a level at which Z has become equal to D. *Effective demand*, then, is the value of D corresponding to the volume of employment given by the point of intersection between the "aggregate demand function" and the "aggregate supply function." Much of the rest of the *General Theory* revolves around this principle of effective demand and consists of a thorough examination of the various determinants of the two functions.

The equilibrium level of aggregate employment is reached when employers as a whole have no inducement either to expand or to contract employment. It is Keynes' contention that, with a given propensity to consume, the equilibrium level hinges on the amount of

---

[5]John M. Keynes, *The General Theory of Employment, Interest, and Money* (London: Harcourt, Brace and Company, 1936), p. 17.

[6]Economists of the neoclassicist group are, somewhat arbitrarily, lumped together with the classical writers properly so called, thus obliterating such fundamental distinctions as that between the marginal utility analysts of the last third of the nineteenth century and writers like J. Stuart Mill and David Ricardo.

investment. But the chain of dependent variables is lengthened by the fact that the amount of current investment hinges, in turn, on what Keynes called the "inducement to invest"; and the latter, once more removed, depends on the schedule of the "marginal efficiency of capital" and on the interest rate structure.

The level of employment consistent with equilibrium (with equality between aggregate supply price and aggregate demand price) cannot be greater than full employment — but it may well be less than that. Keynes refers to the special relationship between the propensity to consume and the inducement to invest which is associated with full employment as an "optimum relationship" and blames the Classicists for having assumed the prevalence of this optimum condition. In Keynesian terminology, it exists, however, only when ". . . current investment provides an amount of demand just equal to the excess of the aggregate supply price of the output resulting from full employment over what the community will choose to spend on consumption when it is fully employed."[7]

When employment increases, the amount which the community can be expected to spend on consumption (D_1) out of its income will increase but not by so much as effective demand (D), because a portion of its increased income will be absorbed by new investment (D_2). Consequently, the gap between aggregate supply price (Z) of output and the amount spent by consumers on it (D_1) will become greater as the volume of employment increases, and vice versa. If the propensity to consume remains the same, employment cannot increase *unless* at the same time the amount devoted to new investment (D_2) increases; or, to paraphrase, if D_2 remains the same, employment cannot increase *unless* the propensity to consume (not just D_1) is increasing.

The Classicists, Keynes claims, always assumed the operation of some force which, with a given increase in employment, causes D_2 to rise sufficiently to fill the gap between Z and D.

Keynes believed that there is a tendency for the gap between a community's actual employment and full employment to widen as it grows richer. The challenge faced in finding sufficient investment opportunities is much harder to meet in a rich country than it is in a poor one. According to the principle of effective demand, the problem of oversaving for a rich community would be solved through a reduction of actual output. Eventually, its current income will have dropped so low that its surplus over consumption will once again correspond to the weakness of the inducement to invest. Also, when the opportunities

---

[7]Keynes, *op. cit.*, p. 28.

for further investment have become few, the interest rate will have to drop more for a sufficient number of those opportunities to be worth while exploiting — sufficient, that is, to bring the volume of savings seeking investment outlets into balance with investment demand.

This cursory survey has already revealed what Keynes would consider as principal gaps in the body of existing knowledge and where we would expect him to concentrate the exercise of his creative talents: the propensity to consume, the marginal efficiency of capital, and interest rate theory (with special regard to the role played by money).

Among the economists considered so far, Malthus was the only one who had instinctively grasped the importance of Keynes' principle of effective demand and the possibility of a demand deficiency; but, in spite of his premonition, he had not managed to communicate clearly the vagaries of demand. Keynes appears to consider it as something of a catastrophe for the development of economic thought and ipso facto for the development of public policy that Ricardo — who in effect considered it impossible for effective demand to be deficient in the long run — was able to prevail over Malthus as far as public response to their theories was concerned. In Keynes' view, economic science then acquired a flavor of unrealistic optimism which contrasts sharply with the appellation given it by Carlyle as the "dismal science."

Before we pursue the major ramifications of the principle of effective demand, we should take cognizance of two matters of definition. First, Keynes, bothered by the customary choice of units for measurement, makes use of only two fundamental quantity units: quantities of employment and quantities of money value. The unit in which he expresses the quantity of employment he calls "labour unit," and the money wage of a labor unit he labels "wage unit." Unfortunately, as abstractions these do not lend themselves to the solution of questions of economic policy; even their theoretical relevance has been seriously questioned, because they are based on the assumption of homogeneity in the supply of labor and require a weighting of skilled workers in proportion to their respective remuneration. Second, saving and investment are so defined as to make them equal (ex post). This follows from the identities

Income (= Value of Output)   = Consumption Expenditure plus Investment Expenditure, and

Income   = Consumption Expenditure plus Saving,

which are now usually written as $Y = C + I$, and
$$Y = C + S.$$

Clearness of mind on this matter is best reached, perhaps, by thinking in terms of decisions to consume (or to refrain from consuming) rather than of decisions to save. A decision to consume or not to consume truly lies within the power of the individual; so does a decision to invest or not to invest. The amounts of aggregate income and of aggregate saving are the *results* of the free choices of individuals whether or not to consume and whether or not to invest; but they are neither of them capable of assuming an independent value resulting from a separate set of decisions taken irrespective of the decisions concerning consumption and investment.[8]

It goes without saying that such special definitions may be given the above terms that as a result saving and investment are not necessarily equal. Keynes correctly notes that differences of usage arise for the most part out of the definition of investment or that of income, since there is almost complete unanimity as to the meaning of saving and of consumption expenditure. The reader is especially cautioned to realize that unintentional increments in the stock of unsold goods are part of total investment expenditure.

THE PROPENSITY TO CONSUME AND ITS COMPLEMENT, THE PROPENSITY TO SAVE

We recall that the aggregate demand function relates any given level of employment to the expected proceeds derived from consumption spending and investment spending when employment is at that level. Keynes divides the factors governing the first of these quantities into "objective" and "subjective" factors.

He deems it a sufficiently good approximation to consider both income and consumption in terms of wage units. Consequently, he feels free to define the propensity to consume as

$$C_w = f(Y_w), \text{ where}$$

C_w symbolizes the expenditure on consumption out of a given level of income in terms of wage units,

Y_w stands for the income in terms of wage units (corresponding to a level of employment N), and

f denotes the functional relationship between the two.

Objective Factors

Among the objective factors influencing the amount which the community spends on consumption, there are primarily two: the

---

[8]*Ibid.*, pp. 65–66.

amount of its income, and the principles on which the income is divided between the individuals composing the community. The first of these will be affected by changes in real income, windfall changes in capital values, changes in the rate of interest, and changes in expectations with regard to future income. Changes in fiscal policy as a deliberate instrument for a more equal distribution of income will have their effect on the second. For instance, income taxes can exert a very powerful leverage both by lowering the propensity to save on the part of the wealthy and by increasing the amount spent on consumption by the recipients of the redistributed tax funds.

Lest he be misunderstood, Keynes points out that the influence of the rate of interest is much more complex than the classical writers assumed. The latter, who generally regarded the rate of interest as the equilibrating factor between the supply of and demand for saving, believed that changes in consumption expenditures and in the rate of interest were negatively correlated, inasmuch as a fall in the interest rate resulting from a decrease in investment demand for loanable funds would appreciably increase consumption, and vice versa. The Classicists also visualized the possibility of a positive correlation between changes in consumption expenditures and the rate of interest: a decrease in consumption by increasing the supply of loanable funds would tend to depress the interest rate (and to encourage the demand for investment funds). In any case, the interest rate would bring about the adjustments necessary to return *total* spending to a high level.

Keynes, however, recognized that there are conflicting tendencies at work resulting, at least in the short run, in the rate of interest having but little direct influence on spending in either direction. (As we will see, the indirect influence may be quite noticeable: if a fall in the rate of interest leads to an appreciation in the prices of securities, thus resulting in a windfall gain, a person might well be encouraged to spend more than he would have otherwise.)

Although none of the factors mentioned is fixed, the principal variable upon which the consumption component of the aggregate demand function will depend is clearly income itself, that is, the volume of output and employment. This is what Keynes means by saying that the propensity to consume is a "fairly stable function."

In asking about the likely shape of the consumption function we are confronted, according to Keynes, with a *fundamental psychological law* which enjoys both inductive and deductive support. This has been often, but somewhat inaccurately, referred to as the *law of the diminishing marginal propensity to consume*. As a matter of fact, we must clearly distinguish between two distinct tendencies: that men are disposed to increase the amount of their consumption by less than a given increase in their income; and that men will, as a rule, spend a smaller *proportion* of income on consumption as their income increases. Whereas Keynes' fundamental psychological law refers to the more general (more inclusive) of these tendencies, it is only the second that falls under the law of the diminishing marginal propensity to consume. Its correlative is, of course, the law of the increasing marginal propensity to save. With respect to Keynes, he was merely impressed by the evidence that regardless of what the average propensity to consume is, it is extremely rare for a change in income (whether upward or downward) to be accompanied by an equal *absolute* change in consumption, that is, for the marginal propensity to consume to be equal to 1. In Keynes' own notation, $\triangle C_w$ is positive (negative) when $\triangle Y_w$ is positive (negative); but the former is smaller than the latter. Whether this holds true not only in the short run, with which Keynes was mainly concerned, but also in the long run, is still an open question. Several inductive studies that have been undertaken since the death of the master suggest that in the long run the *average* propensity to consume may rise — which does not really upset Keynes' conclusion, since it does not presuppose a *marginal* propensity to consume >1. Keynes only claimed that $\dfrac{\triangle C_w}{\triangle Y_w}$ is less than unity, which ". . . means that, if employment and hence aggregate income increase, *not all* the additional employment will be required to satisfy the needs of additional consumption."[9]

Just as the gap between income and consumption widens when both are rising, so that gap narrows when they both decline. It may even disappear if the fall in income goes far enough, a situation which will be reached when individuals and institutions use up financial reserves to cover what has become an excess of consumption spending over income. If this were not so, downward fluctuations in income could go to extreme lengths.

Keynes, in an interesting digression, emphasizes the heavy drag on the propensity to consume in circumstances when a community already possesses a large stock of capital. An overly large deduction may then have to be made from its income before we arrive at the net income available for consumption. Sinking funds (depreciation allowances) may thus withdraw spending power from the consumer while, at the same time, demand for expenditure on replacement has not yet come

---

[9]*Ibid.*, p. 97.

into play. It is, then, by virtue of the fact that financial provision for
the future is not paralleled by physical production for the future (investment spending) that financial prudence may diminish aggregate
demand and hence total employment.

> The greater, moreover, the consumption for which we have pro-
> vided in advance, the more difficult it is to find something further to
> provide for in advance, and the greater our dependence on present
> consumption as a source of demand. Yet the larger our incomes, the
> greater, unfortunately, is the margin between our incomes and our
> consumption.[10]

Thus Keynes summarizes the dilemma which, barring government
intervention, appeared to him to condemn rich countries to an amount
of unemployment sufficient ". . . to keep us so poor that our consumption falls short of our income by no more than the equivalent of the
physical provision for future consumption which it pays to produce
to-day."[11] Here we have the famous Keynesian underemployment
equilibrium. In view of the fact that current consumption is satisfied
partly by current production and partly by past production, the
Keynesian misgivings may be stated thus: We may no longer get
new capital investment to outrun capital disinvestment by an amount
sufficient to fill the gap between net income and consumption; and,
what is more, the former can only exceed the latter as long as *future*
expenditure on consumption is expected to increase. Hence, Keynes
concludes, any weakening in the propensity to consume must reduce
not only the demand for consumption goods but also for capital goods.

Subjective Factors

Keynes lists eight subjective motives leading individuals to save
and four leading governments and business corporations to do so.
Some of these have their counterpart in negative saving (dissaving) at
a later date. The variety of motives prompting individuals to withhold
income may be suggested by the catch words used by Keynes — pre-
caution, foresight, enterprise, avarice; a partial list of institutional
motives to saving comprises self-financing and liquidity. Since the
strength of these subjective motives varies greatly with the institutional
framework of a particular society, it is difficult to assess their overall
importance. However, they tend to change only slowly over time, and
Keynes takes them as data in his analysis. Also, believing that for the
most part objective factors tend to change little in the short run, he is

---

[10]*Ibid.*, p. 105.
[11]*Ibid.*

led to the conclusion that short-period changes in consumption do not depend on changes in the *propensity* to consume, although the *amount* spent on consumption will of course vary with the rate at which income is earned.

Changes in the rate of interest can be very deceptive. Keynes admits that a rise in the rate is likely to induce the community to save more *out of a given income*. However, he considers this a useless hypothesis, because the very rise in rate will tend to diminish investment. And this fall in investment will lead, via greater reductions in income, to a fall in both consumption and saving, so that eventually actual aggregate saving will be less rather than more. From the definitional equality between saving and investment it follows that, given the propensity to consume and the marginal efficiency of capital, incomes will have to fall by that amount which is required to decrease net saving by the same amount by which the rise in the rate of interest has decreased investment. This opens up rather dire vistas for the community as a whole: the more it will be induced by a rise in the interest rate to practice thrift, the greater the chances that it will wind up with fewer savings. Such a paradox of thrift condemns what has been traditionally regarded as a virtue to impotence, and worse. According to Keynes, in the absence of government intervention only one contingency could prevent this outcome: if the rise in the rate of interest were offset by a corresponding change in the demand schedule for investment.

The Multiplier

Keynes pays tribute to his countryman R. F. Kahn[12] for developing the concept of the multiplier. This, we may recall from our earlier training, is the ratio between the additional income created by a given increase in investment and that increase itself. For Keynes' purposes, it may be viewed also as the ratio between the total increase in employment and what he calls "primary employment," that is, the addition to employment resulting from the increased investment. If we know either the propensity to consume or the propensity to save — which together must always be equal to 1 in a closed economy and ignoring government — we can thus establish a precise relationship between aggregate income (employment) and the rate of investment. In Keynes' notation,

---

[12]See Biographical Note B.

$$\triangle Y_w = k \triangle I_w, \text{ where}$$

$\triangle Y_w$ is the increase in income in terms of wage units,

k is the investment multiplier, and

$\triangle I_w$ is the increment of investment.

In other words, the factor k indicates by how many times income will be greater than the investment increment.

$\dfrac{\triangle C_w}{\triangle Y_w}$ is the marginal propensity to consume; $1 - \dfrac{\triangle C_w}{\triangle Y_w}$ is the marginal propensity to save. If we let $1 - \dfrac{\triangle C_w}{\triangle Y_w} = \dfrac{1}{k}$, then by transformation $\dfrac{\triangle C_w}{\triangle Y_w} = 1 - \dfrac{1}{k}$. In other words, the multiplier is the reciprocal of the marginal propensity to save, or the reciprocal of 1 minus the marginal propensity to consume. Now since the reciprocal of $1 - \dfrac{\triangle C_w}{\triangle Y_w} = \dfrac{1}{1 - \dfrac{\triangle C_w}{\triangle Y_w}}$, it has become conventional to use the short-

hand expression $\dfrac{1}{1 - \dfrac{\triangle C}{\triangle Y}}$ when reference is made to the multiplier, k.

Assuming that the community will choose to consume, say, four fifths of an increment of income, the multiplier will be 5. *If* the employment multiplier is the same as the investment multiplier, and *if* we assume no reduction in investment elsewhere, the total employment generated by increased investment in a given industry will be five times the primary employment provided by the latter. In the rare event that the community should decide to save all of the increased income, the multiplier would be 1, and the increase in employment would be limited to the primary employment provided by the increased investment expenditure.

If the multiplier is greater than 1 and less than infinity, we can say that the effort of the community to consume part of its increased income will stimulate output and employment until the new (and higher) level of income provides an amount of saving sufficient to match the increased investment. In other words, intended saving, having "lagged," as it were, behind investment, will finally catch up with it.

Another generalization is that the closer the marginal propensity to consume is to unity, the greater the increase in total employment resulting from a (sustained) increment in investment, or the smaller will be the (sustained) increment in investment needed to fill the gap between actual employment and full employment — assuming in both cases that there is unemployment in the first place. An increase in investment after full employment has already been reached can only result in higher prices, not in increased aggregate real income, regardless of whether the marginal propensity to consume is large or small.

Keynes is aware that there may be a number of offsets, or leakages, so that the multiplier will be less than would be expected on the basis of the existing marginal propensities. Perhaps most important is the fact that for a country heavily dependent on foreign trade a substantial portion of the multiplier effect of the increased investment will benefit foreign, rather than domestic, employment. This follows from the fact that a portion of increased consumer spending will be directed to foreign-produced goods.[13] Consequently, a given fluctuation of investment will be associated with a much milder fluctuation of employment in countries in which foreign trade plays a large part, as compared with countries where it plays a small part. Also, we should note that, generally speaking and for various reasons, the multiplier is likely to be smaller, on the average, for a large increment in investment than it will be for a small increment.

THE MARGINAL EFFICIENCY OF CAPITAL

Since this concept often remains only vaguely understood even on the part of students who have completed the Principles course, it is necessary to dwell briefly on a couple of related notions.

Definitions

Keynes starts with the assumption that a man considers buying a capital asset (say, a machine). He expects to obtain a series of returns from selling its output, but he will incur running expenses in producing that output. The difference between the two, viewed as a series of annuities, is called the *prospective yield* of the investment. The *supply price* of the capital asset is ". . . the price which would just induce a manufacturer newly to produce an additional unit of such assets. . ."[14] Marginal efficiency of capital is the relation between these two concepts,

---

[13]The implications of the so-called foreign-trade multiplier were first fully elaborated in an excellent study by Fritz Machlup, *International Trade and the National Income Multiplier* (Toronto: The Blakiston Company, 1943). Machlup is one of the more famous economists who were educated in Vienna and emigrated to this country during their prime. In the United States since 1933, Machlup taught at Johns Hopkins University from 1947 to 1961. Since then he has been associated with Princeton University.

[14]Keynes, *op. cit.* p. 135.

that is, between the prospective yield (of one more unit) of a capital asset and the supply price (of one more unit) of it. It is important to view the marginal efficiency of capital as a rate of discount. There can be only one such rate which, if applied to the series of prospective yields, makes the sum of these discounted yields equal to the supply price of the capital asset. It is this rate, which equalizes (net) returns from the asset with the cost of the asset, that Keynes called the *marginal efficiency of capital.*

Let us note that we are dealing here partly with unknowns: the *expectation* of a series of yields; and, since the supply price is known, the rate of return *expected* from a (financial) investment in a newly produced capital asset. There will likely be two forces at work which jointly will tend to reduce the marginal efficiency of capital if there is an increased (real) investment in a given type of capital asset over a period of time. The first one derives from a decrease in prospective yield of the capital asset as more and more output is produced from it. The second one is related to short-run diminishing productivity; that is, as additional quantities of productive factors are called into service to produce the capital asset (machine), unit cost of production will rise, and so will the supply price of the asset.

For each type of capital we may construct a (hypothetical) schedule showing how its marginal efficiency is related to the size of investment in it. Since these potential investments are stated in monetary units, it will be possible to aggregate all the schedules previously obtained for the different types of capital — just as we add horizontally individual demands for a consumer good to obtain the market demand. The result will be a new schedule relating the amount of *aggregate* investment to the corresponding *generalized* marginal efficiency of capital. This Keynes calls the *investment demand schedule.* Notice its aggregative nature!

The last step is to bring the *current rate of interest* into the picture. It should be obvious that investment in any class of capital asset of which the marginal efficiency is greater than the interest rate would be advantageous. In terms of schedules, it would be the point of intersection of the investment demand schedule and the schedule of the market rate of interest which marks off the optimum amount of investment. Keynes is aware of the fact that in practice we are dealing with a structure of interest rates rather than a single rate, but he avoids this complication for the sake of keeping the exposition as simple as possible.

Changes in Investment Decisions

Now that the elements entering into entrepreneurial calculations of the net effect of investment decisions have been assembled and their relationship has become clearer, we need to bear in mind Keynes' warning that the marginal efficiency of capital depends on its prospective, not merely on its current, yield. Any future developments which either lower the cost of production of capital assets[15] or the price of output produced from these assets would tend to diminish the marginal efficiency of capital, inasmuch as they can be foreseen as probable. Contrariwise, the expectation of a rise in the general price level would tend to stimulate investment by raising the investment demand schedule. But if, in the face of the expectation of higher prices, the rate of interest were to rise pari passu with the marginal efficiency of capital, this expectation would of course produce no stimulating effect on investment. This observation brings home forcefully the fact that output stimuli will always derive from a favorable change of the marginal efficiency schedule *relative* to the interest rate schedule. It is conceivable, for example, that both may fall, but the interest rate schedule will fall more; an incentive to greater output of capital assets would then be provided. Finally, there may result some depressing effect from the expectation of a future fall in the interest rate. The lowering of the investment demand schedule would in this case reflect the expectation that the future output from capital assets produced today will have to compete with future output produced from future capital assets which, due to the lower interest rate, could "get along" with a lower rate of return.

These observations help to clarify a very intimate relationship between changes in the state of expectation and changes in the marginal efficiency of capital. The more volatile the former, the more subject to violent fluctuations will be the latter.

This account would be incomplete without mention of Keynes' distinction between two principal types of risk, both of which will tend to keep the volume of investment lower than it would be in their absence. The borrower's (entrepreneur's) risk is rooted in doubts in his own mind as to whether or not the contemplated capital asset will actually earn the yield for which he hopes. The lender's risk derives from the possibility of voluntary or involuntary default on the part of the borrower. The effect of these risks is cumulative by lowering, as it were, the marginal efficiency of capital on one hand and raising the

---

[15]Such lower priced equipment can be "content" with a lower price for its output.

actual rate of interest above the *pure* rate on the other. Keynes prefers to view the second risk as involving ". . . in part a duplication of a proportion of the entrepreneur's risk, which is added *twice* to the pure rate of interest to give the minimum prospective yield which will induce the investment."[16] But the net effect on investment demand is the same as previously stated.

Keynes devoted a brilliant chapter, one geared to a lower level of abstraction than most of the rest of the book, to "The State of Long-Term Expectation." Under this phrase he subsumes ". . . future events which can only be forecasted with more or less confidence," such as ". . . future changes in the type and quantity of the stock of capital assets and in the tastes of the consumer, the strength of effective demand from time to time during the life of the investment under consideration, and the changes in the wage unit in terms of money which may occur during its life."[17] The state of confidence as it affects long-term expectations must be considered not as relevant per se, but only because it is one of the major factors determining the marginal efficiency of capital.

INTEREST RATE THEORY

As we have seen, there are good reasons to expect fluctuations in the entrepreneurial estimation of the marginal efficiency of different types of capital to be greater than fluctuations in the market rate of interest. Two crucial questions thus were posed to Keynes: Is monetary policy capable of continuously stimulating the volume of investment necessary to maintain full employment? And, especially if not, is the government capable of both calculating the marginal efficiency of capital goods — in terms of social rather than individual advantage — and assuming the responsibility for organizing investment on its own initiative? While these questions are largely outside the realm of analysis proper, they acquire a singular significance within the framework of Keynes' general theory of the rate of interest. Expressed in the idiom of the new tools of analysis forged by Keynes, we can say that most economists of renown had seen the rate of interest as depending on the interaction of the schedules of the marginal efficiency of capital and the propensity to save. It is this notion of the rate of interest as a balance wheel bringing about equality between the demand for and the supply of saving to which the author of the *General Theory* takes most vigorous exception.

---

[16]*Ibid.*, pp. 144–45.
[17]*Ibid.*, p. 147.

In Keynes' view, psychological time preferences have two aspects. With the first, the propensity to consume, we are already familiar. For the second, which had hitherto been largely neglected, he coined the expression *liquidity preference*. The propensity to save, he points out, being the complement to the propensity to consume merely indicates that a certain portion of an individual's income will be held in *some* form of command over future consumption. In *what* form this command is to be reserved will be indicated, in part, by his liquidity preference — a schedule of the amounts of his unspent resources which, depending upon circumstances, he will want to retain in liquid (monetary, or money-like) form. The extent to which he is prepared to part with liquid command over future consumption will be determined by future market conditions under which he might convert his deferred command into immediate command over goods.

From these considerations, it follows that the rate of interest cannot be a return to saving as such; for cash hoards, a measure of liquidity preference even though they result from an act of saving, do not earn any interest. Instead, the interest rate now appears as a reward for parting with liquidity for a specified or indefinite period, or as a measure of the degree of unwillingness of savers to part with their control over perfectly liquid assets. It is the price which brings into equilibrium the desire to hold assets in the form of cash with the available quantity of cash. At a rate lower than the equilibrium rate the reward for parting with liquid funds would be diminished, and the public would want to hold an aggregate amount of cash which would exceed the available supply. The opposite would hold true if the rate were above the equilibrium level.

Combining these considerations with what we already know, we can say that it is liquidity preference in conjunction with the available quantity of cash that in a general way determines the actual rate of interest at any given time. In functional notation, we can write $M = L(r)$, where $L(r)$ is the liquidity preference as a function of the rate of interest, and M is the quantity of money.

The basic condition for the existence of liquidity preference is the existence of uncertainty as to the structure of interest rates in the future. What is more, expectations as to the future of interest rates are fixed by mass psychology and have their impact on liquidity preference. Should an individual believe that future rates of interest will be higher than the rates assumed by the market (the rates reflecting mass psychology), he would have a reason for keeping liquid cash.

The various motivations for liquidity preference are divided by Keynes into three groups: "transactions motive," "precautionary motive," and "speculative motive."

The *transactions motive* refers to the holding of cash to bridge the interval between the receipt and the disbursement of income. The strength of this so-called income motive will depend on both the amount of income and the length of time between its receipt and disbursement. On the other hand, liquid cash must be held also by firms, since they have to bridge the gap between the time when they incur business costs and when they receive sales proceeds.

The *precautionary motive* reflects the desire to provide for future contingencies requiring emergency spending or to take advantage of unforeseen buying opportunities, and to hold an asset fixed in terms of money to meet a subsequent liability likewise fixed in terms of money.

The *speculative motive* was implied when it was suggested that an individual might deem himself better qualified than the market to judge what the future interest rate will be. Monetary management, by "changing" the interest rate, can greatly influence the aggregate demand for money to satisfy the speculative motive. In Keynes' view, ". . . there is a continuous curve relating changes in the demand for money to satisfy the speculative motive and changes in the rate of interest as given by changes in the prices of bonds and debts of various maturities."[18] In practice, as illustrated in the accompanying diagram, it may be difficult to distinguish between an interest change (say, from r_1 to r_2) consequent upon a change in the supply of money available to satisfy the speculative motive (movement from A to B) and one which is the result of changes in expectation affecting the liquidity function itself (movement from A to C). Open market operations by the central bank will always influence the rate of interest by affecting the money supply; but in some cases they may, in addition, act upon the rate of interest through the other channel, that is, via changed expectations as to what the future

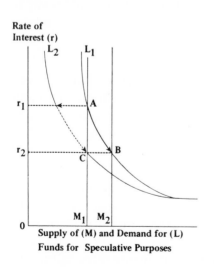

Supply of (M) and Demand for (L)
Funds for Speculative Purposes

[18]*Ibid.*, p. 197.

policy of the central bank will be. If people expect r to fall, i.e., bond prices to rise, they want to hold less cash — as illustrated by the leftward shift from L_1 to L_2 of the liquidity preference schedule.

While the existence of highly organized securities markets tends to accentuate fluctuations in liquidity preference due to the speculative motive, it also tends to diminish substantially liquidity preference due to the precautionary motive. Furthermore, both the transactions and the precautionary motives for liquidity preference are not likely to be very sensitive to changes in the rate of interest as such (apart from the reactions of the interest rate on the level of income). The opposite generally holds true for the speculative motive.

The general liquidity preference curve shows that the rate of interest and the quantity of money are closely related and that normally they change inversely: as the quantity of money is increased the interest rate will fall, and vice versa. But this need not be so. To discuss Keynes' reasons for the generally expected behavior would lead us too far afield, however.

The Keynesian analysis, as the reader will already have glimpsed, holds many potential lessons for the money managers. Perhaps the most impressive of all is that we cannot be *sure* that an increase in the quantity of money will reduce the interest rate; there may exist what later came to be called a "liquidity trap." While a reduction conforms to what we may expect under normal conditions, we should note that it will not happen if the liquidity preferences of the public are increasing more than the quantity of money.

Another lesson was suggested in the preceding section: Whereas a decline in the rate would normally increase the volume of investment, this will not happen in those rare cases in which the schedule of the marginal efficiency of capital is falling faster than the rate of interest.

If we wish, we may substitute the phrase "propensity to hoard" for "liquidity preference." But this will necessitate our discarding the view that interest is the reward for not spending and our recognizing it for what it properly is — reward for not hoarding.

SUMMARY

In *The General Theory of Employment, Interest, and Money*, Keynes subjected to critical examination the (neo)classical theory of the relationships between monetary and nonmonetary factors determining the flow of income, the volume of employment, the rate of interest, and the levels of consumption and investment. He undertook an elaborate analysis of the interrelations of these factors along lines, and with a set of tools, which differ sharply — though perhaps less so than he himself thought — from the (neo)classical approach.

The break from the past is highlighted by Keynes' denial of various firmly established propositions. He denied that the rate of interest is the price which equilibrates the supply of savings with investment demand, that unemployment is due merely to frictional disturbances coupled with an unwillingness to work at the prevailing wage rate, and that the lowering of money wages tends to increase the volume of employment and output (a point not made explicit in our preceding discussion). The book, while making no attempt at statistical verification, marked a strong advance in theoretical analysis and constituted the foundation on which, within the last twenty-five years, a large superstructure of thought has been erected.

Keynes' new theory was one of employment and of output in general, as well as one of shifting equilibrium. Perhaps more important, it was a theory of money, bringing the latter out of its isolated position as a separate subject into an integral relation with other branches of economic theory.

Departing from accepted definitions and authoring his own, Keynes proclaimed the necessary equality of saving and investment, stressing the dependent nature of the former as against the independent quality of the latter. His definitions of saving and investment, as contained in the *General Theory* but in contrast to the *Treatise on Money*, reflect a new and (in their practical implications) revolutionary point of view.

Keynes' equilibrium analysis was much influenced by the eminent place he assigned to the state of expectation, or to anticipations, if we please. In pursuing his main object, namely, to provide a theory of employment, he exercised his exceptionally clever mind intensively on such concepts as the average and the marginal propensities to consume, the marginal efficiency of capital, the multiplier, and liquidity preference. They refer, respectively, to the relation between demand for consumption goods and income (or changes therein); the rate of discount which would equate the present value of the net yields expected in future periods from an additional unit of a particular kind of capital good with its supply price; the ratio between the additional income created by a given increase in investment and that increase itself — or, the ratio between the total increase in employment and the addition to employment resulting from an increment in investment; and the schedule of the amounts of unspent resources which are retained in liquid form.

In discussing the aggregate amount of its income that a community will spend on consumption, he distinguished between objective and subjective factors and concluded that short-period changes in consumption do not depend on changes in the propensity to consume. He divided the various motivations for liquidity preference into three groups and concluded that the speculative motive is by far the most dynamic one. He viewed the determination of the rate of interest as a specifically monetary phenomenon related closely to liquidity preference, the rate being determined at that level which makes the demand for money equal to the supply. Changes in the activity of investment industries, and ultimately changes in the activity of the whole system, are basically the result of changes in the marginal efficiency of capital relative to the rate of interest. Keynes' startling theory of long-period unemployment rests on the proposition that (other things being equal) the greater the amount of capital goods already possessed, the lower the marginal efficiency of capital — a proposition with ominous implications for rich communities equipped with a large stock of capital goods.

In conclusion, Keynes' new conceptual framework has enabled the postdepression generation to transform completely its thinking about the level of output and employment as a whole.

BIOGRAPHICAL NOTES

A. — *John Maynard Keynes* (1883–1946) was perhaps the greatest Englishman of his age. Born in Cambridge, he remained firmly rooted in the parental home throughout his life; both of his parents survived him. In 1890 his father, John Neville Keynes, a logician by training, left a firm imprint and enhanced his reputation among such influential economists as Marshall by publishing a book entitled *The Scope and Method of Political Economy*, which for a number of years remained the standard British treatise on the subject. (The elder Keynes, like his incomparably more famous son, is to be remembered by future generations for his outstanding work as an administrator at Cambridge University.)

Prior to winning a highly competitive scholarship to Eton in 1897, Maynard Keynes received much of his mental training from his father. At Eton he quickly developed the qualities of a natural leader and cultivated a love of good literature, which was sustained through life. Here he was awarded many scholarships and prizes, which paved the way for King's College, Cambridge, where he studied from 1902 to 1905, graduating with the Mathematics Tripos. Not until then did he begin some serious reading in economics. "Fired up" by a study of Jevons, he soon went back to Cambridge to attend lectures by Marshall who, immediately recognizing his great potential, importuned him to turn professional economist. But

Keynes decided to take the Civil Service exam in the summer of 1906 and, having passed, to accept an assignment to the India Office.

For the next two years, finding little challenge in this type of government work, he devoted himself to the study of probability; *A Treatise on Probability* was published in 1921. In 1908, when Pigou was elected to the chair vacated by Marshall's retirement, Keynes accepted a lectureship for the Economics Tripos at Cambridge; three years later he became, at the age of only twenty-eight and with few publications to his credit, editor of the *Economic Journal* (jointly with Edgeworth until the latter's death in 1926). Keynes retained this position until 1945, when he was succeeded by Roy Harrod of Oxford, his main biographer. (For much of this note the author is indebted to R. F. Harrod's excellent study, *The Life of John Maynard Keynes.*)

In 1913 there appeared from Keynes' pen his first major work, entitled *Indian Currency and Finance*. It became a classic on the gold exchange standard and quickly established his reputation as a currency expert. In the same year but before the book's publication, he consented to serve as secretary for a Royal Commission with the mandate to inquire into Indian currency and finance.

In 1915 Keynes entered into Treasury service for the duration of World War I. He helped develop the system of allied war loans and occupied a key position with respect to guiding the interallied economic effort. This was the only great administrative (civil service) position he held during his life. Soon he began his lifelong career as a collector of modern paintings.

After the end of the war, still representing the Treasury, he participated in the preparation of the terms for the Peace Treaty with Germany. To his great chagrin, his clearheaded suggestions for a more just and practicable solution did not prevail — for which he never forgave Lloyd George — and in the summer of 1919 he left the Paris scene utterly frustrated about what appeared to him as a sorry mess fraught with the gravest consequences for Europe's future. Partly to assuage his anguished soul, but also to forewarn the world against the difficulties which the "impossible" Versailles Treaty would provoke, he wrote in two months' time *The Economic Consequences of the Peace*. Published in December of 1919, this masterpiece of polemics spread his fame to many lands, establishing him as a fearless flouter of prevailing opinion and making him an outlaw in British official circles for many years.

After this unhappy interlude, Keynes decided to put his Treasury experience to good personal account and began a new career, that of a speculator in buying and selling foreign exchange. He generally did well, but not without setbacks during the early years. His fortune, in excess of a half-million pounds sterling, reached its peak in 1937. In the 1920's, now able to dispense financial intelligence and knowhow, he began to manage the investments of a number of insurance companies and other institutions. His primary intellectual duties remained those connected with his Fellowship at King's College, Cambridge.

Keynes' second book on the reparations problem, *A Revision of the Treaty*, appeared in 1922, followed a year later by a book entitled *A Tract on Monetary Reform.* Here he attacked what was perhaps the most respected and sacrosanct of all the mechanisms of nineteenth-century capitalism, the gold standard, and argued cogently that it was not the best possible form of monetary standard, not a good thing in itself. He also cast his lot in favor of currency management so as to secure a stable internal price level, if necessary at the expense of external stability. The reception was extremely hostile. Almost a voice in the wilderness, with hardly any respectable opinion on his side, he preached that Britain's return to the gold standard, especially at prewar parity, would be a disastrous mistake. When, in the spring of 1925, the return became an accomplished fact, Keynes saw in it the triumph of unreasoning prejudice. As a matter of historical record, in the next five or so years Britain's industrial progress was markedly less than that in other advanced industrial countries.

In 1925 Keynes married a Russian ballerina, Lydia Lopokova, whom he had long admired for her artistic and personal qualities. His efforts to help the arts were not confined to ballet; they found many other outlets, such as the formation of the London Artists Association.

A Treatise on Money, largely the fruit of his thinking during the preceding five years, appeared in two volumes in 1930 and is generally ranked as the most mature of all his works. It was meant as a definitive contribution; but for Keynes this was an impossibility, since in his own restless mind doctrines were undergoing a continuous evolution. Furthermore, the appearance six years later of the *General Theory,* although not solely concerned with money, seemed to detract from interest in the *Treatise.* When, also in 1930, Keynes served on the Macmillan Committee on Finance and Industry, he deviated for the first time from his position as an unqualified free trader. Written between the *Treatise* and the *General Theory* were three smaller volumes: *Essays in Persuasion* (1931); *Essays in Biography* (1933); and *The Means to Prosperity* (1933), which foreshadowed many of the essential features of the International Monetary Fund.

In 1933 Keynes was encouraged by the activities of the newly elected President of the United States, Franklin D. Roosevelt, who, Keynes thought, was interpreting the duty of government in the way he had in mind. It was, however, more the spirit than the actual content of the New Deal that he deemed right. In June of 1934 he received the Honorary Degree of Doctor of Laws from Columbia University and had an interview with President Roosevelt. This event dated the tendency in the United States to lay at Keynes' door the blame for all that was most hated in the bureaucratic activities mushrooming on all sides under New Deal sponsorship. But evidence as to whether or not Roosevelt was profoundly influenced by this interview and thereafter framed his policy largely in the light of Keynes' theories is conflicting, although it is certain that Roosevelt had the highest regard for Keynes.

The next two years demanded Keynes' highest concentration as he approached the task of writing the *General Theory* with a perfectionist attitude. He relied heavily on the advice of his most outstanding pupil,

Richard F. Kahn, without neglecting his most ardent disciple, Mrs. Joan Robinson. D. H. Robertson, Ralph Hawtrey, R. F. Harrod, and others all had their say.

In the summer of 1937 Keynes suffered a heart attack due to a coronary thrombosis, and for many weeks his survival was in doubt. He recovered but was never the same man again; his life for the next nine years hung by a thread, as it were. In February, 1940, *How to Pay for the War* was published, a little book in which Keynes applied his technique of analysis to the economics of excessive (rather than of deficient, as in the 1936 volume) demand. He insisted on keeping the government interest rate at a low level, a course of action subsequently followed not only in England but also in the United States.

In June of 1940 Keynes became a member of a Consultative Council to advise the Chancellor of the Exchequer on questions of policy. Although he was not a civil servant and drew no salary, he remained attached to the Treasury in an advisory capacity till the end.

Between 1941 and 1946 Keynes paid six visits to the United States, all of great importance in furthering the understanding and cooperation between England and the country that had become the arsenal of democracy, especially in connection with the Lend-Lease program and planning for the postwar period. He was one of the staunchest laborers who helped make the Bretton Woods institutions a reality but saw many of the hopes he had nurtured for the technical arrangements of this new experiment in international cooperation shattered when American ideas prevailed in the Articles of Agreement for the Fund and the Bank, as finally adopted. Prior to his death, he served as chief negotiator of the large loan extended by the United States to Britain in 1946 and was elected a vice-president of the World Bank. Not long after his return from the United States in the spring of 1946, Keynes died of a heart attack.

Keynes was not without faults, the most persisting of all criticisms being that he was guilty of inconsistency — something more than just being flexible. In a sense he also was an incorrigible optimist, believing that by care and pains all our social and economic evils could be abolished — something of the "wild-eyed" liberal. Time and again he had a scheme, heartily believed in planning and contriving. But he was not a socialist, always had a high regard for the middle class, and felt himself closest to the Liberal Party.

He was first-rate in his logical capacity for developing a finespun theory, but he did so only when he believed his premises to be realistic and his conclusions applicable to life. His rapier-like intellect, his lightning speed of thought, and his inexhaustible capacity for work held a rare fascination for those who worked closely with him.

B. — *Richard F. Kahn* (see Biographical Note A) is one of the outstanding, though somewhat elusive, Cambridge economists. Born in 1905, he was one of Keynes' star students at King's College, Cambridge. He served in various government departments during World War II. Most of his publications are in the form of journal articles, the most famous of which he wrote at the age of twenty-six in the *Economic Journal* (June, 1931), pp. 173 ff., under the title "The Relation of Home Investment to Unemployment." He has been a professor of economics at Cambridge University since 1951.

Questions for Review and Research

1. Check the leading economic journal issues of the late 1930's for reviews of Keynes' *General Theory* and compare the evaluations it received some thirty years ago with later evaluations and/or with its treatment in modern textbooks.

2. Is Keynes' *General Theory* a logical extension of his earlier writings, or did it rather make some of the major conclusions contained therein obsolete? Explain.

3. Discuss the break with the classical tradition which Keynes' views on saving and investment represented.

4. Explain Keynes' concept of "effective demand." Did Keynes present most of the variables related thereto in diagrammatic form?

5. Given a country's aggregate propensity to consume, on what does the equilibrium level of aggregate employment depend? Does this constitute a situation of full employment?

6. What led Keynes to believe that as communities grow richer the gap between actual employment and full employment tends to widen?

7. Why does the sum of the propensity to consume and the propensity to save always equal 1?

8. Did Keynes regard the interest rate as the equilibrating factor between the supply of and the demand for savings? Explain.

9. Did Keynes have anything to say about the shape of the consumption function? Is it possible for the marginal propensity to consume to exceed (in numerical value) the average propensity to consume?

10. Explain the Keynesian equation $\triangle Y_w = k \triangle I_w$.

11. Define "marginal efficiency of capital."

12. Define "liquidity preference." Why is it not correct, according to Keynes, to regard the rate of interest as a return to saving as such?

Recommended Readings

Harrod, Roy F. *The Life of John Maynard Keynes.* London: Macmillan & Co., Ltd., 1951. Chapter XI, "The General Theory of Employment, Interest, and Money," pp. 432–486.

Hazlitt, Henry (ed.). *The Critics of Keynesian Economics.* Princeton, New Jersey: D. Van Nostrand Company, Inc., 1960. Chapter I, "Introduction," by Henry Hazlitt, pp. 1–10; Chapter VI, "Mr. Keynes' 'General Theory,'" by Etienne Mantoux, pp. 96–124; Chapter VII, "The Economics of Abundance," by F. A. von Hayek, pp. 125–130; Chapter XIII, "The Fallacies of Lord Keynes' 'General Theory,'" by Jacques Rueff, pp. 237–263; Chapter XIV, "Appraisal of Keynesian Economics," by John H. Williams, pp. 264–287; Chapter XVIII, "The Economics of Full

Employment," by Wilhelm Röpke, pp. 362–385; Chapter XX, "Keynes' Theory of Underemployment Equilibrium," by Arthur F. Burns, pp. 404–410; Chapter XXII, "Mr. Keynes and the 'Day of Judgment,' " by David McCord Wright, pp. 414–427.

Keynes, John Maynard. *The General Theory of Employment, Interest, and Money.* New York City: Harcourt, Brace & World, 1936.
Book I, "Introduction": Chapters 1–3, pp. 3–34.
Book II, "Definitions and Ideas": Chapter 6, "The Definition of Income, Saving and Investment," pp. 52–65.
Book III, "The Propensity to Consume": Chapters 8–10, pp. 89–131.
Book IV, "The Inducement to Invest": Chapter 11, "The Marginal Efficiency of Capital," pp. 135–146; Chapter 15, "The Psychological and Business Incentives to Liquidity," pp. 194–209; Chapter 18, "The General Theory of Employment Restated," pp. 245–254.
Book VI, "Short Notes Suggested by the General Theory": Chapter 24, "Concluding Notes on the Social Philosophy Towards Which the General Theory Might Lead," pp. 372–384.

Klein, Lawrence R. *The Keynesian Revolution,* 2d ed. New York City: The Macmillan Company, 1966. Chapter I, "Keynes as a Classical Economist," pp. 1–30; Chapter II, "The Birth of the *General Theory*," pp. 31–55; Chapter III, "The New and the Old," pp. 56–90.

Robinson, Joan. *Essays in the Theory of Employment.* Oxford: Basil Blackwell & Mott, Ltd., 1947. Part I, "4 Essays," pp. 1–74.

MACROECONOMICS

Extensions of Keynesian Macrotheory

The Keynesian thrust of the 1930's not only stimulated national income and related data-gathering activities — first in the industrially advanced countries and later, mostly under United Nations auspices, in less developed ones — but it also gave impetus to the formulation of hypotheses and, via econometric studies, to the accumulation and utilization of statistical knowledge. Much of this work has involved the testing of Keynesian-type theories built into ever more ambitious and refined models. Such efforts have been prompted, in part at least, by the hope of being able to implement Keynes' ideas in the formation of public economic policy. This, in turn, has justified undertakings designed to predict ever more accurately the level of strategic macroeconomic magnitudes. "Orthodox" built-in stabilizers (for example, progressive tax systems, transfer payments) were found useful still, yet increasingly less adequate, as standards for "fine-tuning" the economy were raised, especially by those leading economists who accepted advisory roles in the highest councils of government.

GENERAL THEORETICAL DEVELOPMENTS

Part of the trouble with a simple Keynesian model built on the three pillars of the marginal propensity to consume, the marginal efficiency of capital, and the liquidity preference function was that it could not be transformed from a theory of income determination to a theory of employment without making it considerably more complex. Employment was seen to be directly related to *real* income, not money income, necessitating an explanation of the price level. For this purpose, analysts had to include in their system production functions in general, and factor-demand and factor-supply functions in particular, as in these areas Keynes had fallen woefully short of rendering his model complete.

Even with these extensions the model could not serve as a fully satisfactory tool of economic policy. Klein,[1] who in his mid-twenties had already made a name for himself as an interpreter of Keynes' historical role and of the simple Keynesian structure, was one of the first to recognize that at least four other prerequisites had to be met before the *New Economics'* objective of maintaining adequate "effective demand" could be pursued in an operationally meaningful way: (1) a public sector had to be added; (2) the system had to be opened with respect to foreign trade; (3) the system had to be made dynamic; and (4) the system had to be disaggregated.[2]

As to the first point, doubts have had to be resolved concerning the extent to which the public sector is endogenous (responsive to changes in demand for day-to-day public services) rather than exogenous (requiring decisions relating to, for example, national defense and space exploration). In the realm of international economic relations, it was deemed not to be enough to allow for income effects via the foreign-trade multiplier, but terms of trade and the productivity of imports had to be reckoned with as well. Keynes' static model had to be replaced by one in which *dynamic relationships* are incorporated in a suitable lag structure and where the production function takes account of capital formation and its effects on the marginal productivity of labor. In disaggregating the system a compromise had to be struck between, on one hand, the need for realism by recognizing at least a few sectors with different behavior characteristics and, on the other, the imperative to keep the system from mushrooming to a size where the additional insights gained into the economy's *modus operandi* plainly do not justify the marginal costs involved.

Although the *General Theory* was an intellectual breakthrough, it had to be expanded in several directions to take into account neglected factors. For one, in order to test the implied linearity of the *consumption function*, sample surveys of consumer budgets, especially of income recipients in high brackets, had to be undertaken. Investigators have been cautioned not to draw, from the evidence of nonlinearity near the top, the conclusion that a change in the distribution of income could, in the short run, exert a major influence on aggregate consumption (or saving). Moreover, if greater equality in the distribution of income should be a more useful objective in the long run, there is still the perplexing question of whether the promotion of a *higher* rate of consumption in the present or near future is tenable in the light of the *lower*

---

[1]See Biographical Note A.

[2]Lawrence R. Klein, *The Keynesian Revolution*, (2d ed.; New York City: The Macmillan Company, 1966), pp. 194–196.

rate of consumption in the distant future (which is implied in the associated slower rate of economic growth). Here is where value judgments clash, while the evidence remains pitifully scant.

Turning to another challenging problem area, stock adjustment forms of lag distribution were applied by econometricians first to investment in fixed capital and later to consumer spending, and in the latter case it soon became evident that, as a minimum, total consumption should be broken down into durables and nondurables. In the process it was found that Keynes, who assumed consumption to adjust passively to the macro environment created by investment, had glossed over important differences; although consumption of nondurables and certain (convenience) services may be highly correlated with (i.e., passively adjusted to) income, spending on consumer durables and certain (luxury) services has — like the investment function in general — been correlated little with income. Because of the great influence of its relatively volatile components, consumption as a whole has come to be recognized as fairly autonomous by those aiming at a balanced view of consumer behavior.

The influence of *wealth* on the shape of the consumption function was originally suggested by Pigou, one of Keynes' major critics, and following Pigou's line of argument was later elaborated by Patinkin[3] in his real balance effect and by Friedman[4] in his permanent income hypothesis.

In brief, then, the simplistic view of the consumption function in the Keynesian model has been replaced by a sophisticated one which makes allowance for (1) fiscal effects (taxes, transfers, etc.), (2) lags, (3) effects of disaggregation, and (4) relative prices, wealth, and — occasionally — income redistribution.

Leaving refinements relating to the consumption (saving) function behind, what — it may be asked next — happened to Keynes' *propensity to invest* at the hands of modern economic "technicians"? Since Keynes' marginal efficiency of capital concept is not susceptible to testing, later work on the role of business investment by econometricians concentrated on stock adjustment forms of investment functions, modified by the inclusion of an interest rate variable, business cash flow, business liquidity, and measures of capacity utilization. Also, disaggregation of investment has opened new vistas neglected by Keynes. In particular, residential construction has come to be viewed as meriting, for various reasons, separate treatment in disaggregation,

---

[3]See Chapter 11.
[4]See Chapter 11.

while inventory investment is seen as influenced by speculation concerning price level and interest rate changes and as characterized by a reaction lag very different from that of other investment components.

Keynes' pessimistic views concerning the long-run prospects of the marginal efficiency of capital many years ago already gave way to agnosticism, or even outright optimism, what with a lengthening chain of technological advances being systematically and successfully achieved by an impressive array of firms blessed with generous budgets for research and development.

Keynes' doctrine of *liquidity preference*, viewed as a situation in which people choose between only two possible types of assets, money or bonds, was "softened" first by a largely fruitless debate between loanable funds theorists and liquidity preference theorists, to give way later to an increasingly pragmatic view of the many faceted money market. Such modern analyses attempt to account for many alternative assets or debt instruments (including goods as well as claims against nonbank financial intermediaries) and for the existence of many classes of wealth holders. They have abandoned the facile assumption that the supply of money is exogenously controlled by the monetary authorities and have grappled with the need for a supply theory of money. These points will be expanded in the last section of Chapter 11.

While Keynes did not tie his theory to any particular type of *production function* and thus evaded the criticism of too narrow a view of overall relationships on the supply side of the goods market, he made himself vulnerable by suggesting that labor supply is a function of the money wage and not the real wage. The idea of money illusion in labor supply has been discredited by the inflationary waves of the postwar period during which foresighted labor unions have sought effective protection against the erosion of the value of money by escalator clauses in collective bargaining contracts. While attempts to set up empirical equations of labor supply as a function of real wages have been hardly successful, statistical studies of wage determination have been found to be more fruitful, especially where they have taken the form of making money wage rate changes a joint function of unemployment (excess supply in the labor market) and previous changes in the price level. Such relationships have with increasing frequency been approximated by Phillips[5] curves. As has come to be known now even by undergraduate students, these curves are a graphic tool used to focus on the poten-

---

[5] A. W. Phillips, a British economist, started this with a widely noted article, "The Relation between Unemployment and the Rate of Change of Money Wage Rates in the United Kingdom, 1861–1959," *Economica*, N.S. Vol. XXV, 1958, pp. 283–300.

tial trade-offs between relative wage-rate stability and unemployment, or, more broadly, the compatibility of a relatively stable price level and full employment. (For example, a 4 percent rate of unemployment may have to be accepted if the increase in the general price level is to be held to 2 percent; with 3 percent unemployment, the unavoidable price level increase may be 3 percent or more.) Wage push theories, which may be regarded as a special variant of the dynamized Keynesian model containing Phillips curves, shift the focus of attention in wage and labor market analysis of inflation from the money market to the labor market. They are, of course, as one-sided in their view of the causal mechanism as are the arguments about administered price inflation in certain key sectors of the economy. The fact must not be lost sight of that it is a whole group of labor market equations which, along with savings-investment and money market equations, *jointly* determine the absolute levels of wages and prices.

Methodologically speaking, it is by no means a foregone conclusion that the systems which have been built by econometricians in the 1960's to describe and forecast economic activity in the United States and a few other (mostly advanced) countries can be considered as lineal descendants of Keynes' three-equation model involving the propensity to consume, the marginal efficiency of capital, and liquidity preference. Certainly, their resemblance to the "parent" system has largely vanished, and at least as far as the effects of real balances on spending and the analysis of wage determination are concerned, they cannot be regarded as simple extensions of the original model.

Advanced models, in contradistinction to the Keynesian matrix, lend themselves equally well to the analysis of inflation and of economic growth as they do to the analysis of depression or stagnation. Unbiased observers have had to admit that countries vary a great deal as far as the relationship between their growth rate and the rate of price change is concerned — a priori there is very little correlation between the two — and all combinations are possible, though not all are equally frequent (for example, Brazil's case of a high rate of inflation coupled with a high rate of real growth per capita is not a common one).

The bulk of the remainder of this chapter explores two related extensions of the Keynesian system. They have become standard fare, so to speak, in intermediate macro courses while requiring relatively little training in quantitative methods. These versions of the same theme were an outgrowth of the thinking of sympathetic Keynesians, one a Britisher, the other an American, and were nearly completed, as far as the durable skeleton is concerned, at the time of the master's death. They do reflect, however, the early dissatisfaction with the static nature of Keynes' approach. Although their shortcomings have been widely discussed, and sometimes unfairly enlarged, in the literature of the last twenty years, they continue to occupy a special place in the economist's vastly more spacious tool box. Their principal contribution has been that of dynamizing the Keynesian model by dwelling on the relationship between capital stock and investment in relation to income growth, while retaining the Keynesian concept of saving-investment balance. Specifically, they ask: Under what conditions will planned investment be continuously equated with a growing volume of planned saving, and how can full employment be sustained in a growing economy?

ROY F. HARROD[6]

Early Groping for a New Departure (Harrod I)

In an article published on the eve of World War II in *The Economic Journal*[7] Keynes' friend and biographer attempted to link together the acceleration principle and multiplier analysis. For this purpose, Harrod first distinguished between G, the actual geometric rate of growth of income (output), and G_w, the warranted rate of growth, namely, the rate at which all "parties" are satisfied that they have produced just the right amount and which will therefore cause them to attempt to maintain that rate of growth. He conceded that even under ideal conditions the actual rate of growth will diverge from time to time from the warranted one.

Harrod then introduced the symbol s to designate the fraction of total output saved (a magnitude likely to vary somewhat over time), and the symbol C for the value of capital goods required for the production of one more unit of output per time period. He then assembled these variables into a "fundamental equation," namely,

$$G_w = \frac{s}{C}$$

which is independent of the time period chosen since the value of G_w is assumed to vary directly, and that of C inversely, with the time span elapsed, while the fraction s is independent of time (in any direct way). Clearly, the unknown term, G_w, is a function of the propensity to save, the state of production possibilities, and other underlying conditions.

---

[6]See Biographical Note B.

[7]Roy F. Harrod, "An Essay in Dynamic Theory," *The Economic Journal* (March, 1939), pp. 14–33.

By assuming that (1) circulating and fixed capital are lumped together, (2) actual saving in a period is equal to the addition to the capital stock in that period, (3) the symbol C_p stands for the *actual incremental* capital/output ratio, and (4) the symbols x_0 and x_1 designate output in period 0 and period 1, respectively, Harrod can establish the following relations:

(1) addition to capital stock = incremental capital/output ratio times change in output, and

(2) total saving = fraction of income represented by personal and institutional saving times income (output) in period 0.

In equilibrium, (1) equals (2), or symbolically, equating their right-hand sides:

$$C_p (x_1 - x_0) = s \, x_0.$$

Thus the rate of growth of output G, $\dfrac{(x_1 - x_0)}{x_0}$, is equal to the saving rate divided by the incremental capital/output ratio. When C_p, the value of additional capital per unit increment of output *actually produced*, is equal to C, the incremental capital/output ratio required by technological and other — objective and subjective — conditions, then the sum of the decisions to produce has been justified on balance, according to Harrod. This means that the actual growth rate of output coincides with the warranted rate.

Harrod noted that the truism $G = \dfrac{s}{C_p}$ corresponds to Keynes' proposition that saving is necessarily equal to ex post investment. He is aware of the importance of lags, but these are deliberately neglected in his argument for the sake of clarity and a feasible division of labor. He correctly added that it is immaterial in the case of a steady advance in the rate of growth being maintained whether the increment of capital is being regarded as required to support the increment of total output in the *same* period or in the one immediately *following*.

Harrod also considered the possibility that a discrepancy between G and G_w is caused by ex post saving deviating from ex ante saving, but he deemed this not to affect the validity of the argument since such a discrepancy will have the same effect on growth as a divergence of C_p from C. For example, if G exceeds G_w, then $\dfrac{s}{C_p}$ must exceed $\dfrac{s}{C}$, and it makes no difference whether actual s *exceeds* ex ante s, with C_p equal to C, or whether actual s *equals* ex ante s, with C_p less than C. In either case, there is a stimulus to expansion, and firms caught short of inventory or equipment will increase their orders.

A major point in Harrod's line of reasoning is that normally dynamic equilibrium ($G_w = G$) is *unstable*, whereas static equilibrium is stable. The instability of the former was said to derive from the fact that when as a result of "excessive" output ($G > G_w$) the actual increase of capital goods per unit of output (C_p) falls below that necessary to stay on the moving equilibrium path (C), there will be an unwanted depletion of stock or a shortage of equipment, and consequently the system will be pushed to expand further. As a result, in the following period, G will exceed G_w by more than before, and the greater the upward divergence, the greater the stimulus to expansion will be. Growing instability of the opposite kind, i.e., cumulative downward divergence, would develop from an initial shortfall of G relative to G_w. "Thus in the dynamic field . . . a departure from equilibrium, instead of being self-righting, will be self-aggravating."[8] To illustrate, an increase in the propensity to save entails, *ceteris paribus*, a higher rate of warranted growth, but if the warranted rate was previously equal to the actual rate, the actual one now falls below the warranted one. This means a depressing influence which will drag the realized rate further and further below the warranted rate.

Harrod concluded that on either side of the unique warranted line of growth "is a 'field' in which centrifugal forces operate, the magnitude of which varies directly as the distance of any point in it from the warranted line."[9] As long as G_w corresponds to G, general overproduction is not taking place, although particular overproduction is not only possible but likely. Rather the enterprises with surpluses are balanced with those running short of stock, those which have underproduced. Contrasting with this case, in general overproduction excess outputs predominate over output deficiencies; but paradoxically this is the result of production having been *below* the warranted level.

After having established the razor's edge nature of the warranted growth path, Harrod added various modifications or refinements to the analysis. The instability theory is amplified by considering, among other things, the fact that *some* capital outlays have no direct relation to the current increase in output, be it as a result of changes in the state of confidence, in the rate of interest, or for other reasons. He attempted, as a first approximation to reality, to segregate that part of capital

[8]Roy F. Harrod, *Economic Essays* (New York City: Harcourt, Brace & World, Inc., 1952), p. 264.
    [9]*Ibid.*, p. 265.

outlays conceived to be independent of both the current level of income and its current rate of growth, and to conceive of the other part as varying with the current level of income (as distinct from its rate of growth). The basic formula is further complicated when foreign trade is taken into account.

Finally, Harrod introduced the *natural* rate of growth. It presupposes the existence of full employment (in some vaguely defined sense) and is the maximum rate made possible by the increase in primary and produced inputs, allowance being made for technological improvements affecting their use. The principal reason why there is no inherent tendency for the warranted and the natural rates to coincide is that the warranted rate varies with fluctuations in the level of business activity, while the natural rate does not. For the latter is the highest rate at which the economic system can advance in the long run. Unfortunately, Harrod then unnecessarily complicated the discussion by adding a warranted rate said to be *proper* to the economy — by which he designated that warranted rate which would obtain under conditions of full employment — and then permitting the warranted rate "proper" to be above or below the natural rate, which — the reader was told — *is* the full employment rate! This contradiction, real or apparent, does not recur in Harrod's later work.

The Model with the Finishing Touches (Harrod II)

The somewhat unfinished quality of Harrod's 1939 article on dynamic theory becomes evident when one examines the outcome of the postwar resumption of his pursuit of the same theme. This he did in one of a series of lectures presented in early 1947 at the University of London.[10] The problem, to wit: under what conditions can there be a steady rate of progress with full employment, was of undiminished relevance to economic policy makers as the forced draft on resources caused by World War II was ebbing away. Surely, coping with unemployment on a month-to-month basis would be at odds with attaining that sustained level of capital outlay necessary for a smooth advance of the economy in harmony with its expanding full employment capacity.

Harrod recalls that, as an economy moves from unemployment to full employment, there is usually a strong tendency for capital outlay to exceed the normal level compatible with the fundamental conditions

---

[10]Entitled "Fundamental Dynamic Theorems," this lecture, along with four others, was later published in book form. See Harrod's *Towards a Dynamic Economics* (London: Macmillan & Co. Ltd., 1952).

of a steadily advancing economy, and vice versa for an economy in a recession or depression. This bespeaks his conviction that it is not possible to divorce problems of long-run equilibrium growth from the business cycle problem. In sorting out the factors involved, Harrod again uses the method of analysis adopted eight years earlier and — as in *The Economic Journal* article — proposes to bypass problems of lag structure.

He first states the truism $G\,C\ =\ s$, where

G has the same meaning as before (increment of output in a period, expressed as a fraction of total output),

C is the addition to capital, or investment broadly defined (specifically, increase in volume of goods "outstanding" and in process, i.e., increase in those goods not in the hands of final users), and

s also has the same meaning as before (fraction of income saved). This fraction is assumed to be subject to change, but on the whole tends to be fairly constant, especially when compared to G.

Next, in order to counter the criticism that the equation gives too much emphasis to the acceleration principle, Harrod refines it to read:

$$G\,C\ =\ s\ -\ k$$

where k designates those additions to capital (expressed as a fraction of current income) which are not directly related to current requirements. However, the author fails to draw a useful boundary line between capital outlay of a "long-range character" (included in k) and that justified within a "fairly short period." On the assumption that in the long run all capital expenditures are justified by the use to which the capital goods are put, there would be no room for k any longer in the equation.[11] The truism $G\,C\ =\ s$ can be further analyzed to illuminate some important relationships. From

$$G\ =\ \frac{\Delta Y}{Y},\ C\ =\ \frac{I}{\Delta Y},\ \text{and}\ s\ =\ \frac{S}{Y}\text{, it follows that}$$

$$\frac{\Delta Y}{Y}\cdot\frac{I}{\Delta Y}\ =\ \frac{S}{Y}\text{, or}\ \frac{I}{Y}\ =\ \frac{S}{Y}\text{, or}\ I\ =\ S,$$

the Keynesian ex post equality of (realized) saving and investment.

Harrod confesses to the imperfection attaching to a dynamic principle of such great generality, but it is to his credit that he correctly anticipated the widespread use of his suggestive framework.

---

[11]Units of capital included in k must of course be excluded from C.

To be set off from the refined identity above is the corresponding refined equilibrium equation, which reads:

$$G_w\, C_r = s, \text{ where}$$

G_w has the same meaning as before (i.e., a rate of growth may be said to be warranted in the sense that it expresses the condition in which producers as a whole are satisfied with what they are doing and consequently are prepared to carry on a similar advance),

C_r is defined analogous to C, constituting the requirement for new capital relative to the increment of output which it sustains, and

s also has unchanged meaning.

The equilibrium of steady advance for the economy as a whole does not, of course, preclude more rapid advance in certain sectors and less rapid advance elsewhere.

Note, too, that the definition of C_r hinges on the assumption that additional capital is *required* to sustain additional output, but is required *only* for that purpose. The assumption of a constant capital/output ratio, overall and incremental, can in turn be justified only by stipulating that, in Harrod's words, "inventions" are neutral and the rate of interest is constant. Where this is not the case, the equation must be modified. For example, it cannot hold in a recession or depression: with redundant capacity C_r, the marginal requirement for new capital, must be lower than C. It is only for a condition of steady advance that C_r has to be assumed as constant. As to neutrality of inventions, it makes sense only where innovations requiring more capital per unit of output balance the effect of those which require less — capital using and capital saving innovations are counterpoised.

In sum, while the truistic equation must be satisfied whether the economy is expanding or contracting, the equilibrium equation expresses the idea that if an advance is to be *maintained*, the quantity of additional capital *actually* accruing must be just what is needed, both in terms of plant and equipment and of inventories. In an advancing economy, Harrod argues, goods in the "pipeline" must increase in proportion to turnover, hence are part of capital (the numerator of C_r).

It also follows that the greater G, the lower C, and that if G is larger than G_w, C will be smaller than C_r. The latter condition means that on balance entrepreneurs find their stocks in trade and/or equipment insufficient to sustain existing sales. (Recall that if the actual rate of growth exceeds the warranted rate, the system will be under pressure to expand, and vice versa.) Only in the unlikely case that variations in G caused equally large variations in s could the "centrifugal forces" making for instability be held in check.

Finally, Harrod relates the two equations to the steady rate of advance determined by fundamental conditions, namely, the natural growth rate permitted by increase in population and technological improvements. He writes:

$$G_n\, C_r = \text{ or } \neq s.$$

The principal difference between G_n and G_w is that G_n, representing (in Harrod's words) "a correct balance between work and leisure" (*Towards a Dynamic Economics*, page 87), rules out involuntary unemployment, whereas G_w, being purely an entrepreneurial, or profit taker's, equilibrium, is incompatible with the kind of (involuntary) unemployment equilibrium contemplated by Keynes.

Actual G may, of course, deviate from G_w, and both may deviate from G_n. In a sense, G is more closely related to G_n, the rate of advance permitted by population increase and technological improvements, than it is to G_w. Recall that in the long run G cannot exceed G_n, although after a recession, as unemployment dwindles, it may be larger than G_n. Since G can exceed G_w, it is, of course, also possible for G_n to exceed G_w. Now if both G_n and G exceed G_w most of the time, the economy is characterized by a recurrent tendency to develop booms. On the other hand, if G_w exceeds G_n most of the time, we know that, on an average, G_w must also exceed G, since G in the long run cannot exceed G_n. These, of course, are the conditions making for a prevailingly depressed economy. Thus saving is a "virtue" in the Keynesian sense when G_n exceeds G_w rather consistently (a case of secular exhilaration), but it is a "vice" when G_n falls persistently short of G_w (secular stagnation).

In *conclusion*, Harrod brought together in a novel way Keynesian short-run static analysis and (neo)classical long-run dynamic considerations. It is not surprising that he also put the analytical distinctions expressed in his equations to use in refining business cycle theory, but these collateral endeavors are beyond the scope of a résumé focusing on long-run equilibrium growth.

EVSEY D. DOMAR[12]

The rationale for assigning prior and more copious space to Harrod lies not in greater clarity of treatment but rather in the fact that, while Domar was still an undergraduate student, the Englishman had already worked on, and pushed considerably nearer a solution, the kind of problem which fascinated them both. Exemplifying another one of

---

[12]See Biographical Note C.

those freaks in the history of economics, Domar until after his article "Expansion and Employment"[13] had been sent to the printer remained unaware of Harrod's 1939 article, which, as will become clear instantly, contained a number of ideas similar to his own.　This article, still Domar's most durable contribution to economic thought, presents in essentially nonmathematical form many concepts incorporated in an article of his published a year earlier and entitled, "Capital Expansion, Rate of Growth, and Employment."[14]　Common to both is Domar's objective of closing a gap in income and employment theory, attributed by him to Keynes' having ignored the effect of investment on capacity to produce in the short run as well as its income generating effect in the long run.

In order to close the gap, light had to be shed on the dual character of the investment process.　Specifically, the problem was to identify and explain that rate of investment and of national income necessary to keep the two effects of investment in balance.　Although the contrary is often implied in critical studies, it was not Domar's purpose "to derive an empirically meaningful rate of growth, but to show that there exists a rate of growth of income, however vaguely defined, which if achieved will *not* lead to diminishing profit rates, scarcity of investment opportunities, chronic unemployment, and similar calamities."[15]　Such calamities had been analyzed by a series of writers from Malthus via Marx to Keynes.

The Framework

Domar's starting point is the question of whether the absence of hoarding is only a *necessary* condition for maintaining full employment, or whether it is at the same time also a *sufficient* condition.　His negative answer to the latter question concentrates on the dual character of investment as a generator of income on one hand, and as a means to increase productive capacity on the other.　The salient portion of the answer concerns the rate of growth of national income which continued full employment requires.

Domar's simplifying assumptions (or definitions) include the following: (1) There are no lags. (2) Income, investment, and saving are defined net of depreciation, the latter being equated with the cost of replacing a depreciated asset by another of equal productive capacity. (3) The price level remains constant. (4) The fraction of the labor force

---

[13]*The American Economic Review*, Vol. 37 (March, 1947), pp. 34–55.
[14]*Econometrica*, Vol. 14 (April, 1946), pp. 137–147.
[15]Evsey D. Domar, *Essays in the Theory of Economic Growth* (New York City: Oxford University Press, 1957), Foreward, p. 8.

employed is a function of the ratio between national income and productive capacity. (5) The marginal propensity to save remains constant, and consequently so does the average propensity to save. (6) The average productivity of investment remains constant.

In Domar's scheme, capital formation can have one or more of several possible effects. First, if capital remains unused, resources have simply been wasted. Second, if new capital displaces previously constructed capital (by assumption 2 above before the latter is worn out), some losses are likely to be sustained by capital owners and workers; yet such capital formation is, within limits, economically justified in a dynamic society. Third, if new capital is simply substituted for labor, and possibly for other factors, and this substitution results in a voluntary reduction in the labor force, it is unobjectionable; but if the substitution is involuntary, unemployment will result, possibly with grave social consequences. Although in most cases all three effects are likely to be present to some degree, it is, of course, the third one that calls for a remedy, and this must be sought in an expansion of income.

Domar, in full awareness of the difficulties of interpretation of the definition of productive capacity as the full employment output of the economy, notes that changes in such capacity may be a function of changes in a country's natural resources, its labor force, and its state of technique. Because of difficulties of measuring changes in resources and techniques, for practical purposes we can express changes in capacity either via changes in the quantity and productivity of labor, or else alterations in the quantity and productivity of capital. In both cases the remaining three of the four factors are assumed to be reflected — however they themselves may change — in changes in the productivity of the one factor one attempts to measure.

Of the two options, Domar chooses the one that puts capital to the center of the stage, the reason being its previously mentioned dual effect. What, then, he asks, is the nature of an equation, one side of which measures increases in productive capacity while the other side measures the generation of income?

Before setting up such an equation, Domar discusses the significant distinction between the net value added annually to productive capacity per dollar of newly created capital (which depends on the nature of such capital and varies among firms and industries), and what he calls the potential social average productivity of investment. The latter is the more meaningful concept, as it is concerned with the increase in productive capacity of the economy as a whole. That this is not necessarily the same as the productive capacity per dollar invested in the new plants, etc., taken by themselves becomes plausible when one recalls that frequently the output of existing plants must be *reduced* because of the effective competition of the new productive facilities in goods markets as well as those for factors of production. At any rate, in Domar's scheme, as a result of investment the productive capacity of the whole economy has increased by an amount equal to the value of that investment multiplied by a factor σ (sigma) which measures the potential social average productivity of investment. The fraction represented by σ may be equal to only one fourth of the value of I, rather than the, say, one third which constitutes the fraction of annual productive capacity per dollar of newly created capital per se.

Why, it may be wondered, does σ not denote the same concept as the familiar "marginal productivity of capital"? Simply because the latter implies — while σ does not — that labor, natural resources, and technology remain fixed.   Also note that the increase in productive capacity, $I\sigma$, is not tantamount to an increase in net national product, for σ merely indicates that the economy is *capable* of increasing its output by a certain amount.

Having "established" the supply side, viewed as the increase in output which the economy can produce, what, asks Domar, constitutes the matching demand side? We know that with Keynes it came to be expressed as the total increase in income brought about, via the multiplier, by an increment of investment. Thus, with the absolute annual increase in investment being symbolized by ΔI, the absolute annual increase in income by ΔY, and the multiplier by $\frac{1}{\alpha}$ (α being the marginal propensity to save), the demand equation reads:

$$\Delta Y = \Delta I \frac{1}{\alpha}.$$

Getting to the heart of the matter, what conditions must be met in order that

$$I\sigma = \Delta I \frac{1}{\alpha},$$

i.e., that the annual increase in productive capacity matches the annual increase in actual income?

First, the economy must be in full employment equilibrium to begin with, that is, the overall level of productive capacity must be equal to the level of effective demand, or $K\sigma = Y_s = Y_d = C + I$, where

K = total capital stock,
Y_s = total output produced (income generated),
Y_d = total effective demand,
C = consumption expenditures,
I = investment expenditures.

Second, only if capacity to produce and income generated increase *at the same rate* can this equilibrium position be maintained.

When the two conditions are met, we can rewrite the fundamental equation, $I\sigma = \Delta I \frac{1}{\alpha}$, by multiplying both sides by α and dividing them by I, in order to identify the equilibrium annual rate of growth of investment, i.e.,

$$\frac{I\sigma\alpha}{I} = \frac{\Delta I 1\alpha}{I\alpha}, \text{ and hence}$$

$$\sigma\alpha = \frac{\Delta I}{I}.$$

Thus, in order to maintain full employment, investment must grow at an annual rate equal to the product of the potential social average productivity of investment and the marginal propensity to save. For example, if the former equals one fourth and the marginal propensity to save equals .12, $\frac{\Delta I}{I}$ will be .03, or 3 percent per year. In this case, income must also grow at the same rate (or $\frac{\Delta Y}{Y} = \sigma\alpha = 3\%$) because the marginal propensity to save equals the average propensity to save, and the average productivity of (new) investment (after adjustments) equals the average productivity of the capital stock before the analyzed change.[16]

Two corollaries of the fundamental equation are: (1) saving and investment must grow in absolute amount from year to year, and (2) on the assumption of a constant income velocity, money must be injected into the system in increasing absolute amounts, thus allowing the economy to expand at a given percentage rate.

Some Qualifications

Domar reexamined and refined the argument in the light of a quite complex world of reality, touching on the interpretation that can be given to the propensity to save when a portion of resources is disposed of by government; the fact that the definition of depreciation does injustice to one or another of businessmen's depreciation practices; the fact that productive capacity had better be viewed as a range than as a single number; the deleterious influence which monetary and fiscal policy might have in giving investment such a push that a shortage of

---

[16]Domar showed elsewhere that these two assumptions are not vital for the validity of the argument. Stipulating them, however, facilitates understanding of the fundamental principle.

other factors relative to capital develops; the fact that new plants are not operated to capacity because of too high a propensity to save; and the fact that the multiplier effect and the increase in capacity do not take place instantaneously and simultaneously, but are affected by lags.

Not the least of the merits of Domar's article is the versatility of the fundamental equation, i.e., the variety of uses to which it can be put under proper safeguards. At the very least, it can shed light on the problem of growth from various points of view. Rather than inquiring what the equilibrium rate of growth is with given α and σ, one may ask: Given a target rate of growth and expected average social productivity of investment, what rate of saving, in the absence of both inflation and unemployment, will make the growth objective attainable? Or: Given the growth rate and the saving rate, what is the value of σ?

Conclusions

To return to the starting point, Domar's fundamental equation suggests that investment *does* have a dual effect since it appears on both sides of the equation: on the demand side as a rate of increase via the multiplier effect, and on the supply side as an absolute amount via the σ effect. While only the increment of investment raises net national product, the whole body of investment increases productive capacity.

A corollary of this analysis is that if investment and hence income grow at less than the required rate, unused capacity develops, inducing idleness of capital and/or labor, and perhaps substitutions of capital for labor, or vice versa. Now while unemployed manpower is almost universally deplored, Domar fears that idleness of plant and equipment, or of consumer durables such as dwellings, is potentially just as harmful because such idleness inhibits new investment. The extent to which this is the case depends on both the competitive structure of industry and the character of the economy in general, including the state of expectations.

In this view, although a high α endangers the maintenance of full employment, it is not the magnitude of α taken by itself that matters, but its relation to the growth of natural resources, technology, and labor. Thus, instead of artificially lowering α, the problem of maintaining full employment growth can be attacked by speeding up the rate of technological progress through research and development, which makes it at least *possible* for the economy to grow.

If it is neither feasible to change α nor to open up new investment opportunities, it is still possible to elevate income and reduce unemployment through increasing conventional investment, although this puts the economy on the horns of a dilemma. With enough being invested today for full employment today, still more needs to be invested to maintain full employment tomorrow; or, as Domar puts it:

> It is a remarkable characteristic of a private capitalist economy that while, on the whole, unemployment is a function of the difference between its actual income and its productive capacity, the standard measure, i.e., investment, directed toward raising national income also enlarges productive capacity. . . . As far as unemployment is concerned, investment is at the same time a cure for the disease and the cause of even greater ills in the future.[17]

It might be countered, however, that the notion of investment of today digging the grave of the investment of tomorrow loses some of its drama if it can be shown how this very investment, by pressing against a less rapidly increasing labor force, can propel the economy toward a new production function and thus generate investment opportunities in excess of what a mere sliding along the old one could provide.

SIMON KUZNETS[18]

The preceding pages of this chapter have been intended to convey to the reader that, although Keynes' *General Theory* is strictly static in form, he opened the door for a great outburst of research on dynamic problems. From his inner circle, Joan Robinson was one of the first to shift the direction of dynamic analysis to the economics of the *less developed countries,* inspiring others, notably Nurkse[19], to stress the causal importance of investment demand as well as of capital accumulation for these economies. For many years, Keynes' national income analysis also served as a first approximation base of reference for development programming and thus the estimation of important parameters and operationally significant variables in economic development. By now, post-Keynesian economics has long outgrown the modest framework used by econometricians of *General Theory* vintage.

It is appropriate to round out this chapter by reference to a man who built bridges between national income analysis in general and the macro aspects of development economics. Kuznets at an early date became prominent in the United States by heeding Keynes' plea for an improvement of quantitative analysis both through the collection of statistical data and the refinement of measuring techniques. In the process he contributed notably to theory, with much of his later work

---

[17]*Essays in the Theory of Economic Growth*, p. 101.
[18]See Biographical Note D.
[19]See, e.g., his *Problems of Capital Formation in Underdeveloped Countries* (Oxford: Basil Blackwell, 1953). A few additional data may be found in Biographical Note E.

bearing the imprint of his interest in development and growth on a *worldwide* basis. (Many of his profound essays evolved as a by-product of quantitative analysis of the modern growth of nations.)

Thoroughly at home in the major theories of economic growth spanning virtually the entire history of systematic thought from Adam Smith to the present, Kuznets in much of his work during the last twenty years has explored the basic causes of the vast differences in levels of economic performance among different countries and regions. In particular, he has been concerned with the structural characteristics of countries in various stages of advance and the changes in these characteristics occurring during the process of growth. In a similar vein, he has undertaken pioneering efforts to discover trends in personal income distribution in the growth process. And perhaps better than any other single economist, Kuznets has grasped the difficulties of problems associated with defining and measuring comprehensive aggregates (e.g., national income) in such a way as to make them suitable for international comparisons. By the same token, he has also averted to the limitations inherent in any of a number of more circumscribed measures (whose meaning can be more readily specified) as indices of economic growth.

Outline of the General Framework

A combination of economic historian and economic theorist at their best, both in a quantitative and qualitative sense, Kuznets has been particularly interested in economic growth within the last two centuries, a span of time which he considers as a distinctive economic epoch. By this expression he means "a relatively long period (extending well over a century) possessing distinctive characteristics that give it unity and differentiate it from the epochs that precede or follow it."[20] By the same token, he views "an epochal innovation as a major addition to the stock of human knowledge which provides a potential for sustained economic growth. . . ."[21] Hence throughout an economic epoch a specified set of forces is dominant, which has a close bearing on the distinctive characteristics of economic growth during that span of time.

That epochal innovations are not just figments of the scholarly imagination is evidenced by the fact that people living during the era of merchant capitalism (from about 1500 to 1750) realized that overseas expansion and the resulting network of trade with the New World was

---

[20]Simon Kuznets, *Modern Economic Growth* (New Haven, Conn., and London: Yale University Press, 1966), p. 2.

[21]*Ibid.*

the major source of more rapid economic growth in Western Europe. Contemporaries of that period became aware of the widely ramifying growth impulses emanating from an epochal innovation. According to Kuznets, the exploitation of the potential of growth provided by epochal *technological* innovations requires *social* invention, while epochal innovations in the nature of social inventions in turn call for a variety of technological changes. Thus Kuznets views the "interplay of technological and institutional changes" as the essence of economic growth taking place within the framework of an epochal innovation. From this interplay derives the importance of stressing, not just aggregative change, but shifts and modifications of the institutional structure.

In addition to the direct technological and economic consequences, and the institutional changes elicited thereby, epochal innovations, such as the discovery of the New World, also affect the systems of *views* (and beliefs) that govern the societies participating in the discovery. It follows that "the time and effort required to overcome the resistance of old beliefs and to evolve the new . . . framework . . . partially account for the length of epochs."[22] Kuznets assigns to the comparative study of economic growth the twin tasks of considering the internal pattern of growth as well as the spread of an epochal innovation from pioneering societies to the followers in the utilization of its growth potential. In order to understand the mechanism and pattern of spread of economic growth, it is necessary not only to study the specific sequence it follows among nations, but also the diverse patterns of adaptation.

In his analysis of epochal innovations in the modern growth period, Kuznets found that since roughly the middle of the last century the major source of economic growth in the developed countries has been science-based technology, but the application of science presupposed a proper climate of opinion, or the formation of a *Weltanschauung* conducive to the fostering of its pursuit. He characterizes the dominant views associated with the modern economic epoch as secularism, egalitarianism, and nationalism, all nonquantifiable to be sure but deserving nonetheless of even denser exploration to give more meaning to quantitative measures of economic growth.

Kuznets' approach cannot avoid the fuzziness of institutionalism, and he is the first to admit that in reality there are no sharp breaks between economic epochs. He still insists though, and irrefutably so, that science-based technology, together with the broad views that helped to

---

[22]*Ibid.*, p. 7.

sustain its momentum, have been the dominant and distinctive features of the modern economic epoch. Perhaps its end has come dimly into view although, to paraphrase Kuznets, a new economic epoch could not be said to have started until further progress in the application of science has resulted in mass communication with, and use of, other planets.

Finally, for any given period problems of definition and measurement of economic growth relate, according to Kuznets, to four items: (1) the unit whose growth is being studied, (2) the inclusion in its definition of increases in population, (3) the meaning of product, and (4) the specifications of sustained increase.[23] The interested student is referred to the recommended readings in *Modern Economic Growth*.

Conclusions

Kuznets set himself a lofty task: to review the aggregative, structural, and international characteristics of the economic growth of nations in modern times, no less. While the intellectual powers of no single man suffice to perform such a task exhaustively and to perfection, Kuznets has perhaps progressed further than any other living economist on the arduous road to its distant completion. Nevertheless, he seems to have realized that modern work of this kind, though vastly enriched by a refined technical apparatus, still shares basically the same fate as was suffered by the German Historical School a hundred years ago, to wit:

> . . . The contribution of theories of the type that employs a sufficient number of variables *with tested empirical coefficients* has lagged far behind the accumulation of empirical findings.[24]

If Kuznets had used simple, consistent, and closed models of the Harrod-Domar type, he could have escaped the vague nature of his hypotheses concerning economic growth; but he would then also have failed to establish any determinate relationship to observed or observable economic growth.

Be that as it may, Kuznets' postwar writings blend the qualitative with the quantitative aspects of growth in a most thoughtful fashion. Even if they were bare of other merits, they would still serve as a valuable antidote to that tendency which in the late 1950's and early 1960's began to be ridiculed by being given the somewhat contemptible epithet "growthmanship."

---

[23]*Ibid.*, p. 16.
[24]*Ibid.*, p. 32 (emphasis added).

SUMMARY

This chapter has dealt with various approaches to dynamic process analysis. After mentioning the principal features of post-Keynesian macrotheory, attention was given to two models with many common characteristics, a fact which explains why the literature generally refers to the Harrod-Domar model, rather than singling out, as a source of reference, one or the other of the two authors. The last portion of the chapter brought into the limelight Kuznets, whose contribution has been of a different though no less significant nature.

In the discussion of general theoretical developments, four general prerequisites for pursuing the study of "effective demand" over time and in an operationally meaningful way were listed. Much of the expansion of dynamized Keynes-type models has to do with (1) introducing additional variables, especially on the supply side of product and factor markets, and (2) specifying a suitable lag structure. Notice was taken of amendments relating to the consumption function and the influence of wealth thereon; the disaggregation of both consumption and investment flows; liquidity preference; and the role of labor in the production function.

The Englishman Harrod was one of the first to appreciate the importance of making Keynes' employment theory dynamic. He did so essentially by combining the acceleration principle and the multiplier, but without introducing time lags. Shortly after the end of World War II, he elaborated and improved upon his earlier "Essay in Dynamic Theory." Common to what was here called Harrod I and Harrod II was the drawing of a distinction between actual, warranted, and natural rates of growth, and the analysis of their relationship to each other during the business cycle as well as — of interest here — over long periods of time. Throughout his treatment, Harrod placed emphasis on the instability generated by deviations of the actual from the warranted rate of growth.

Domar, an American, effectively demonstrated that in order to determine the full employment rate of growth of the national product it is essential to take the dual character of the investment process, as increasing productive capacity and generating income, into account. The principal difference in approach between Harrod and Domar concerns the relationship between investment and national income (broadly defined), Harrod's C_r being approximately the reverse of Domar's σ. Domar stressed more (and in a different way) than Harrod did the need for investment today always to exceed saving of yesterday if the economy is to stay on the equilibrium growth path.

Although Domar and Harrod treat investment expenditures differently, both base their analysis on a continuing equality between the average and the marginal propensity to save. Harrod's variable s corresponds fully to α in Domar's model. Furthermore, both accorded to investment a strategic role in the investment process, and both built into their models fairly rigid assumptions concerning the output/capital (capital/output) ratio. They are agreed on the capacity creating effect of net investment.

The American Kuznets has usually been regarded as a statistically oriented institutionalist; but his roots in Keynesian aggregative economics are unmistakable. Long before his interest turned to comparative international economic growth — which, incidentally, combines micro and macro features — he had aroused the interest of economists by publishing data, covering several decades of United States economic history, which suggest something like long-run stability of the consumption function. Kuznets' continuing concern has been with the structural characteristics of countries in various stages of advance and changes in those characteristics occurring during the growth process.

It might be hypothesized that economic theorists turning to economic history later in life do better than economic historians acquiring subsequently an interest in economic theory. In the case of Kuznets, a man possessed of a far-ranging and powerful intellect mastering modern techniques of analysis and graced with a rare sense for *balance*, the particular sequence of fields of concentration may well have made no appreciable difference.

BIOGRAPHICAL NOTES

A.—*Lawrence R. Klein* (1920–   ) was born in Omaha, Nebraska, and received his BA from the University of California in 1942. Only two years later, he obtained his PhD degree from the Massachusetts Institute of Technology, being one of Samuelson's — who was then himself only 29 — precocious and most prolific students. Between his association with the faculty of the University of Chicago (1944–1947) and his position as a research associate at the National Bureau of Economic Research (1948–1950) Klein married and now has four children.

He joined the faculty of the University of Michigan in 1949, contributing to the work of the Survey Research Center there until 1954, when he accepted a position with the Oxford Institute of Statistics. Four years later he joined the faculty of the University of Pennsylvania as a full professor.

Klein has been a visiting professor with numerous academic institutions, including Osaka University, Hebrew University, and Princeton University. He has also been in demand as a consultant for several organizations, both public and private. But perhaps his greatest fame, aside from publication of *The Keynesian Revolution,* has stemmed from his role as the principal investigator of the econometric model project of the Brookings Institution.

His academic honors include the past presidency of the Econometric Society, membership in the Social Science Research Council, and receipt of the John Bates Clark medal of the American Economic Association. The latter has also enjoyed his services as a member of the Executive Committee. He has been an editor of the *International Economic Review.* In addition to the above-mentioned item, his most substantial publications include *Textbook of Econometrics* (1953) and *An Econometric Model of the United States, 1929–1952* (1955).

B.—*Roy F. Harrod* (1900–   ) was educated at Westminster School and New College, Oxford, England. He has been in a lifelong association with Christ Church: from 1922 to 1924 as a Lecturer, from 1924 to 1967 as a Student, and since 1967 as an Honorary Student. He has served in a great many different (partly administrative) capacities at Christ Church. For fifteen years (1952–1967) he was Nuffield Reader in International Economics at Oxford University. He has been awarded honorary Doctor of Law or LLD degrees from Poitiers (France), Pennsylvania University, and Aberdeen (Scotland).

Harrod was also honored by the presidency of Section F of the British Association in 1938 and that of the Royal Economic Society from 1962–1964, and in between (1952) he served as an Advisor to the International Monetary Fund. During World Was II he accepted positions as Statistical Adviser in the British Admiralty under Churchill and also a position in the Prime Minister's Office. Following the end of the war he was Joint Editor of *The Economic Journal* until 1961.

Harrod began to publish in 1933. In addition to macro and international economics, his specialties have been business cycles and monetary policy (both national and international). His latest in a long series of works in book and article form include these volumes: *International Trade Theory in a Developing World* (1963), *Reforming the World's Money* (1965), and *Towards a New Economic Policy* (1967). Among Keynesians he has probably been most prized for his *The Life of John Maynard Keynes* (1951), reference to which was made in the last chapter.

C.—*Evsey D. Domar* (1914–   ) was born in Poland but immigrated to the United States in 1936 and became a naturalized citizen in 1942. He earned degrees from the University of California at Los Angeles (BA, 1939); the University of Michigan (MA, 1941); and Harvard University (MA, 1943; PhD, 1947). He also was a teaching fellow at the two last-named institutions. After having held various temporary positions, including a three-year stint with the Board of Governors of the Federal Reserve System, he joined Johns Hopkins University in 1948, where he taught — first as an associate professor and after 1955 as a full professor — until 1958. A visiting professorship at M.I.T. in 1957 led to his permanent appointment there in the following year.

Professor Domar has had opportunities to lecture at many leading universities both in the United States and abroad. For four years he was a visiting associate professor of the Russian Institute at Columbia University from 1951–1955, and has been a research associate at the Harvard Russian Research Center since 1958. He has been used as a consultant for the Ford Foundation and the American Council of Learned Societies.

He is a holder of the John R. Commons Award of Omicron Delta Epsilon and is also a trustee of this fraternal professional organization. He served on the Board of Editors of the *American Economic Review* (1957–1959) and on the Executive Committee of the American Economic Association (1963–1965). Most of his published work is in the form of articles in first-rate professional journals. (In his publications, he appears to have favored quality over quantity.)

D.—*Simon Kuznets* (1901–   ) was born in Kharkov, Russia, but — like Domar — immigrated to the United States at a relatively early age. All his earned degrees — with the exception of one, a 1959 DSc from Harvard University — are from Columbia University (BS, 1923; MA, 1924; PhD, 1926); but he has been awarded at least as many honorary PhD or DSc degrees from leading academic institutions.

Kuznets is best known for his long-time association (since 1927) with the National Bureau of Economic Research. His second longest tenure of office was begun in 1930 at the University of Pennsylvania, where he advanced from assistant to full professor in six years, teaching at the latter rank from 1936 to 1954. At this time he accepted a call from Johns Hopkins University, and six years later (1960) he went to Harvard.

Kuznets served as president of the American Statistical Association in 1949 and of the American Economic Association in 1954. He also holds memberships in, among others, the Royal Statistical Society, the Econometric Society, and the American Philosophical Society.

Three of his early (1926–1933) published works belong to the field of economic fluctuations analysis. Then came several pacesetting volumes related to national income and capital formation (1938–1946). Among Kuznets' more recent publications are: *Shares of Upper Income Groups in Income and Savings* (1953), *Six Lectures on Economic Growth* (1959), *Capital in the American Economy* (1961), *Postwar Economic Growth* (1964), *Economic Growth and Structure, Selected Essays* (1965), and *Modern Economic Growth: Rate, Structure, and Spread* (1966).

E.—*Ragnar Nurkse* (1907–1959) was born in Estonia and from 1926 to 1934 studied at the Universities of Tartu (Estonia), Edinburgh, and Vienna. He then joined the Economic and Financial Department of the League of Nations in Geneva. During his tenure, and partly under League auspices, he published a work in German on international capital movements (1935) and two in English, *International Currency Experience* (1944) and *Conditions of International Monetary Equilibrium* (1945).

Invited as a visiting lecturer in economics to Columbia University for the academic year 1945–1946, Nurkse a year later (1947) was appointed a regular professor at Columbia. For three years (1946–1948) he was also a member of Princeton's Institute for Advanced Study. In addition, he lectured widely, and during the year before his premature death served as a Ford Foundation research professor at Geneva, his former abode when a League of Nations international civil servant.

Nurkse's postwar publications include, in addition to *Capital Formation in Underdeveloped Countries* (several editions), a work entitled *Cause and Control of Inflation* (1946).

Questions for Review and Research

1. Briefly state the elements of the formal Keynesian model in terms of two functional equations.

2. How can the Keynesian system be disaggregated on the demand side?

3. Since Keynes' marginal efficiency of capital concept is not testable, how have econometricians proceeded in coming to grips with business firms' propensity to invest?

4. Explain the difference between $G_w = \dfrac{s}{C}$ and $G = \dfrac{s}{C_p}$.

5. Is $G_w = \dfrac{s}{C_p}$ a truism? Why or why not?

6. Explain Harrod's natural rate of growth. Why can the actual rate of growth not be above the natural rate, except temporarily?

7. What does Harrod's neutrality of "inventions" have to do with the value of C_r?

8. Why is it unlikely that variations in G are accompanied by equally large variations in s, and what bearing does this have on the degree of instability of the economy, according to Harrod?

9. State the simplifying assumptions underlying Domar's model.

10. Explain the difference between the potential social average productivity of investment and the net value added annually to productive capacity per dollar of newly created capital.

11. Discuss and illustrate the notion of an epochal innovation, as used by Kuznets. Are all epochal innovations of a technological nature?

12. How did Kuznets characterize the dominant views associated with what he calls the modern economic epoch?

Recommended Readings

Domar, Evsey D. *Essays in the Theory of Economic Growth.* New York City: Oxford University Press, 1957. Chapter IV, "Expansion and Employment," pp. 83–108. This is a reprint from *The American Economic Review*, Vol. 37 (March, 1947), pp. 34–55.

Harrod, Roy F. *Economic Essays.* New York City: Harcourt, Brace & World, Inc., 1952. Essay No. 13, "An Essay in Dynamic Theory," pp. 254–277. This is a reprint from *The Economic Journal* (March, 1939), pp. 14–33.

———————. *Towards a Dynamic Economics.* London: Macmillan & Co., Ltd., 1948. Lecture 3, "Fundamental Dynamic Theorems," pp. 63–100.

Klein, Lawrence R. *The Keynesian Revolution*, 2d ed. New York City: The Macmillan Company, 1966. Chapter VIII, "The Keynesian Revolution Revisited," pp. 191–226.

Kuznets, Simon. *Economic Growth and Structure*. New York City: W. W. Norton & Company, Inc., 1965. "Toward a Theory of Economic Growth," pp. 1–81.

——————. *Modern Economic Growth*. New Haven, Conn., and London: Yale University Press, 1966. Chapter 1, "The General Framework," pp. 1–33.

Peterson, Wallace C. *Income, Employment, and Economic Growth*, 2d ed. New York City: W. W. Norton & Company, Inc., 1967. Chapter 15, "Post-Keynesian Theories of Economic Growth," pp. 411–440.

Samuelson, Paul A. "Interactions between the Multiplier Analysis and the Principle of Acceleration," *The Review of Economic Statistics*, Vol. 21 (May, 1939), pp. 75–78.

MONETARY AND BANKING THEORY

Developments through the Mid-1800's

FROM ARISTOTLE TO ADAM SMITH

What some of the early writers had to say on the topic to which we turn next may not justify the attribution to them of any definite view on the nature of money. Some of them, as will become clear in the first section, nevertheless spelled out certain canons of monetary policy which stimulated analytic work.

Preeighteenth-Century Writers

Aristotle.—The first coherent exposition of the nature and functions of money stems from Aristotle, who was much concerned with what he called the improper uses of this human invention. He condemned *chrematistics*, or the acquisition of money for its own sake, because such a practice conflicted with his philosophical view of an ideal human society. Money, properly used, appeared to him as essentially a standard of value and a medium of exchange, facilitating the distribution of goods produced from natural resources. Its role as a simple intermediary appeared to him as thwarted, however, when it became a means to buy cheap and to sell dear, or — worse yet — when it merely served to propagate itself, as when lent at interest. Both of these roles Aristotle viewed as abuses, since in both the acquisition of money is made an end in itself. He asserted that money is barren, inasmuch as one piece of it cannot beget another piece. If this view is interpreted to mean that loans cannot be productive, Aristotle's approach was definitely erroneous; if it is charitably taken to mean that money — as money — is not true wealth, then there is nothing about which to quibble.

Aristotle was, indeed, remarkably cognizant of the evolution of money. In his outline he pointed to the fact that the bulkiness of many necessities of life makes them inconvenient for use as media of exchange; yet exchange media, he felt, had to be useful for nonmonetary purposes as well. Iron and silver, adaptable to many purposes, soon came to be preferred. A laborsaving device had been discovered, but its potential was not fully realized while the value of money was still measured by size and weight. The next logical step was to stamp the metal, giving birth to coins which, in turn, stimulated the "art of money-making" (retail trade). Aristotle observed that things used as money are not inherently superior to things not so used, because both are subject to changes in value. Monetary media are only better in degree, because their value remains relatively more constant.

Oresme (*Oresmius*).[1]—Oresme, a fourteenth-century writer, in his *Treatise on the First Invention of Money,* expounded similarly. In distinguishing between natural and artificial wealth, he placed money in the latter category, because it does not satisfy human needs directly: it is a means of exchange of natural wealth. Money does not have to be useful in itself but must satisfy certain requirements: scarcity, uniformity, durability, and transportability (great value relative to weight) are clearly identified in the *Treatise.* In delineating these prerequisites, Oresme sticks to a commodity theory of money, which was entirely in harmony with the general point of view of that stage of economic development.

His assessment of wise monetary management as a prime desideratum for the orderly functioning of a monetary system may be considered as an early venture into "welfare economics." He observed that money, since it serves the common welfare, must be coined by the sovereign. This involves the exercise of a trusteeship function, so to speak, and does in no way invest the sovereign with ownership rights; these are vested in all those who have acquired money in exchange for natural wealth. Furthermore, the exercise of administrative functions of a monetary nature must not be made a cloak for taxing the people: what the sovereign retains of a metal entrusted to him for coinage must correspond to the true cost of this operation; any additional levy would be an impairment of public welfare.

A large portion of the *Treatise* was dictated by a desire to promote the common good through an inductive proof of the harmfulness of *mutations* (alterations of the commodity value) of money and reverberates the precept that these alterations must be based on the consent of the people. Laws relating to money must not be changed except in cases where the orderly functioning of the system hinges on such a change; for instance, when the relative supplies of the monetary metals

---

[1]See Biographical Note A.

no longer conform to the existing mint ratio. Devaluations are unmasked by Oresme as schemes for violent and deceitful exploitation. Uncertainty and chaos, poverty (through the exportation of good money and the retention in circulation of bad money), hazardousness and unprofitability of lending, encouragement of counterfeiting — these are some of the harmful consequences of monetary malpractice.

Oresme's pioneering, though given little notice for centuries, can hardly be overestimated. His *Treatise* represents a bold step in the direction of making economics an autonomous science and freeing it from the ethical rules of medieval scholasticism.

Bodin (Bodinus).[2]—Bodin, writing some two hundred years later, is usually named as the first exponent of the quantity theory of money. His grasp of the elements that determine the level of prices in a given country at a given time, however, was much wider than such a representation suggests. It is true that he singled out as the principal reason for price rises in general ". . . the abundance of that which governs the appraisal & price of things."[3] In the case of France's inflation in the sixteenth century, the influx of precious metals, mostly from Spain, demonstrably goes a long way toward explaining that phenomenon. However, he also pays due heed to a number of other elements which potentially can be just as powerful in raising the prices of goods and services. Bodin specifically mentions these: monopolies, scarcity brought on by excessive exports (adding to the inflow of circulating media) or by waste, the pleasure of the mighty to raise the prices of things, and debasement of the monetary standard. Bodin was the first to supply his contemporaries with a detailed explanation of the price revolution of the sixteenth century.

Petty.—With Petty, the somewhat unenlightened spirit which governed the discussion of monetary matters by mercantilist writers was largely left behind. For one, he was not a victim of the fairly widespread confusion between money and capital. Secondly, he hinted at the idea that there might be too much as well as too little money and that between these extremes there would be a theoretical optimum. In determining this optimum, the velocity of circulation of money has to be taken into account. Thirdly, throughout his discussion the view of money as a stimulus to trade and industry is dominant. Fourthly, he suggested that a nation, in groping its way to the "right" amount of money, should not see anything wrong in exporting excess bullion.

---

[2] See Biographical Note B.
[3] A. E. Monroe, *Early Economic Thought* (Cambridge, Mass.: Harvard University Press, 1930), p. 127.

Fifthly, Petty further refined Oresme's ideas on the effects of debasement, specifically by pointing out that such practices—resulting in a general price rise — are a burden upon all who live on pensions, rents, annuities, or other similarly fixed sources of income. The truth of this insight has lost none of its timeliness in the twentieth century.

Locke.[4]—The foundations of a more realistic statement of the relationships between the elements bearing on the price level were simultaneously enlarged by Locke. In his essay, "Consequences of Lowering the Interest and Raising the Value of Money" (1692), not only did he enunciate the fact that prices vary — along with the quantity of money — with the velocity of circulating media, but also he introduced into monetary theory the variable now known as the volume of trade. Moreover, he excluded from the effective quantity of money that portion which is hoarded and is thus prevented from influencing the prices of goods. He hinted at Fisher's[5] solution of two centuries later: that the price level is directly proportional to the amount of money and the velocity of money, and inversely proportional to the amount of goods to be exchanged. Perhaps most interesting, he was prepared to look at money as having a purely imaginary value created by common consent, but unfortunately he did not pursue this point.

Law.[6]—John Law, perhaps the most colorful of the world's financiers and in a class by himself, had a mind in which brilliance and recklessness were fatally fused. On the one hand, he supplied one of the most impressive justifications for the use of paper money and the productivity potential inherent in its creation. On the other hand, carried away by his early triumphs, he eventually led France down the road to financial disaster, and his daring schemes eventuated in miserable failure. Although he taught an unmistakable object lesson for all who are tempted to equate money with wealth and credit with capital, inflationists have again and again, though on a smaller scale, compounded Law's error into colossal fiascos.

In his *Money and Trade Considered; with a Proposal for Supplying the Nation with Money* (1705), he discussed several reasons why paper money is preferable to metallic money. He mentioned the relatively high cost of coinage as compared with the nominal cost of printing bills; the fact that metallic coins can be melted down and the metals used for industrial and other purposes, whereas the paper in bills is hardly competitive with other productive uses; that the transportation

---

[4]See Biographical Note C.
[5]See Chapter 11, Biographical Note E.
[6]See Biographical Note D.

of coins and their storage are much more costly than those of paper money; and that metallic money is not stable in value, being subject to fluctuations in the market supply of and demand for the commodities of which it is made. Paper money issued with real estate as backing, Law held, would be much more stable, since real estate would tend to rise in value roughly in proportion to the rise in value of goods in general.

He further argued that an increase in the quantity of money in circulation would tend to depress interest rates, and, assuming that loans are used for productive rather than for consumptive purposes, output would tend to expand and assure prosperity. Alas, Law was not aware that his theory would tend to support a runaway inflation, which would collapse whenever the wiser of the speculators realized that such a ridiculous price rise could not continue indefinitely and a sufficient number of them would dispose of their holdings. With the inability of the note-issuing agency to redeem paper money in specie, the spell would be broken, prices would tumble, and the bulk of the previously issued paper money would become redundant. Law's extravaganza proved a point which barely sixty years later, during the American Revolution, would be forgotten: that no government can force a nation to accept as money something which the people believe to be worthless.

Eighteenth-Century Writers

Cantillon.—If Law's ruinous "power play" tended to discredit the banking profession, Cantillon's sound and sober analysis tended to restore it to a position of respectability. Like Law's, his contribution to the theory of money was supported by a great wealth of practical observations, but success did not turn his head. He applied his distinction between the intrinsic price (value) and the market price of goods to the money commodity. The intrinsic price of the precious metals, as that of all things, stands in proportion to the land and labor necessary to produce them; whereas their market price, like that of other goods, fluctuates in value. Among the qualities of gold and silver that make them superior as money media (in addition to those already enumerated by Oresme), Cantillon includes divisibility without loss, the absence of a storage problem, and long-run stability of value. He considered copper as being more suitable than gold and silver for the making of small payments but pointed out that whatever the monetary metals in use, they did not become money through convention but because of their natural usefulness.

He considered the velocity of turnover of money from a different angle than his predecessors and correctly pointed out that the quantity of money required to accomplish a given number of transactions varies in inverse proportion to the speed with which it is spent. A quite modern ring emanates from his discussion of the factors determining the quantity of money "needed" in circulation, among which he included the minimum amount of cash a person insists on holding at any time, confidence in the banks, and the extent of barter.

Cantillon exhibits exceptionally remarkable perception in tracing what has come to be called a *profit inflation* (the inflationary effects of an increase in the money supply), based in Cantillon's case on an increase in the production of the precious metals and the consequent change in the distribution of income, as well as shifts in foreign trade flows resulting from the new price-supply-demand structure. In developing his extraordinarily advanced analysis, he is not oblivious of the fact that an increase in the supply of money may also be attributable to external causes, for example, a change in spending by foreigners in the home country.

A corollary of profit inflation, Cantillon observed, is the fact that an expansion in the amount of money available for spending does not have the same effect on the prices of all commodities. For instance, goods that are not freely imported will rise in price much more than those that can be brought in without impediments. Hence, a rise in real income will not lead to a uniform rise in consumption spending but will affect it unevenly.

The influence of foreign markets on the prices of goods in a given country is, according to Cantillon, more pronounced in the case of gold and silver than it is for other commodities, because the precious metals are uniquely endowed with the prerequisites for easy transfer between countries. It follows that, given complete freedom to export and import the precious metals, the value ratios between them would have to be approximately the same except for discrepancies caused by transportation costs. Gresham's Law (that "bad" money drives "good" money out of circulation) is illuminated by Cantillon when he describes the disorder, manifested by the exportation of undervalued money, which will follow a deviation of the market from the mint ratio under bimetallism without there being anything done to adjust the mint to the market ratio.

Finally, in his chapter on banks Cantillon successfully explains, in terms of communal custom and confidence enjoyed by the banks, what to many a layman is still a riddle today: how the banks can lend out various portions of funds received on deposit without running any great risk of being unable to meet their obligations to the original depositors.

Hume.—Hume, whose *Discourses* were written after Cantillon's *Essay* although published before, may or may not have seen a copy of Cantillon's manuscript. At any rate, he conveyed an impression of originality which might have flowered into a work of the dimensions of Smith's *Wealth of Nations* if he had systematically set out to produce a well-balanced and comprehensive treatise on economic thought. His most lasting contribution, contained in the *Discourse of Money* (1752), was probably his observation that the quantity of money in circulation is, in itself, of no consequence to the economic welfare of a country. For all practical purposes, any quantity of money can achieve the turnover of any quantity of goods; prices will simply adjust to the given volume of circulating media. However, as Hume recognized, this proposition loses some of its practical validity in an international economy: here an abundance of money and high prices may well create short-term difficulties. In this connection he observes some of the advantages of a central bank. When a country with a relatively low price level seeks to preserve its competitive advantage (as reflected in its export surplus), the bank might lock up the metal flowing in from abroad and thus keep down the price of labor (with which Hume was most concerned). However, it appears that such a sterilization policy in his view would be justified only if it provided a country's national treasury with a buffer for future emergencies.

Hume is also cognizant of the fact that the inflow of money may, through raising domestic prices, have a stimulating effect on the economy. Like Cantillon, he is aware of the time lag between the rise of some prices and incomes and that of others. But whereas Cantillon presented the economics of a profit inflation per se without revealing the problems it creates for national economic policy, Hume seems to have looked with favor upon such a development. He was perhaps the first of a long list of writers to suggest that a little inflation tends to insure lasting prosperity. This impression is corroborated by his statement regarding the consequences of an opposite course. He points out that a nation whose money decreases is actually, at that time, much weaker and more miserable than another nation which possesses no more money but experiences an increase in it.

Despite such qualifications as the ones discussed, Hume remains convinced of the subsidiary role of money as an economic magnitude, emphasizing repeatedly that men and commodities are the real strength of a country. Since the quantity of money in circulation will be self-regulatory, any artificial expansion of the money supply through credit inflation will be nugatory.

Quesnay.—Quesnay, as well as most of the other Physiocrats, became oblivious of the dynamic effects of money and thereby started a trend that was continued by the Classical school, to the detriment of its stature in the long run. Not that these writers underrated the medium-of-exchange function of money; in fact, their primary emphasis on the flow of goods through the economy helped to offset the mercantilist monetary bias. But, by the same token, their constructive contributions to the advance of monetary theory were distinctly minor.

Quesnay's critical restatements can be dealt with summarily. First, since the advantages of foreign commerce do not consist of an increase in pecuniary wealth — which may, however, be a by-product of it — injunctions on the outflow of money from a country, as advocated by the less enlightened Mercantilists, can only be founded upon prejudice. Second, money in itself not being equivalent to wealth, it would be a mistake to judge the opulence of nations by the greater or lesser amount of money at their disposal. Echoes of Hume!

Turgot.—Turgot's broad, philosophical outlook enables him to grasp a fact that may be registered as self-evident but which apparently had escaped previous thinkers: that every commodity may be looked at as money inasmuch as it possesses the two essential qualities of money — to measure the value of, and to represent, every other commodity. There is no good with such inherent qualities as would predestine it for monetary functions and for nothing else. On the other hand — and here Turgot was lacking in vision — he believed that every type of money is essentially a commodity. He ruled out the existence of a purely conventional money, money without "real" value. Within the confines of this unnecessarily restrictive viewpoint, he correctly analyzed those properties of gold and silver which qualified them par excellence to become a universally accepted standard of value, and he foreshadowed Smith in expounding how the use of money has greatly accelerated and facilitated the division of labor among the members of society. He underscored the clear-cut distinction between these two different roles of money: to purchase goods and services, and to be lent out at interest. Since these operations are carried out independently of each other, Turgot thought it would be foolish to expect that a larger quantity of money in circulation should depress the rate of interest. (But much more remained to be said on this score.)

Smith.—Smith, the ingenious summarizer, added little that was truly novel to the previous discussion. He did manage to present a very logical analysis of the developing need of an economically advancing society for coined money. Noting that the use of metals in a primitive state of society was attended by two considerable inconveniences — namely, the trouble of weighing and the burden of assaying, without which people were constantly in danger of being defrauded — he convincingly points out the advantages of a mint, designed ". . . to affix a public stamp upon certain quantities of such particular metals as were in those countries commonly made use of to purchase goods."[7] This stamp eventually authenticated both the weight and the fineness of the metal(s). What really matters, however, is not that such an institution relieved producers as well as consumers of a nuisance but that it facilitated exchanges, thereby encouraging industry and commerce to engage in specialization. Smith called money the "great wheel of circulation," the "great instrument of commerce." He considered it as part of the capital of society, but warned lest it be looked upon as part of the "revenue" of society. The fact that the revenue of a country's inhabitants is frequently paid to them in money should not obscure something more important: that their real riches are always in proportion to the quantity of consumable goods which can be purchased with money. But, the fact that the metal pieces (of which a society's stock of money is composed), in the course of their circulation, distribute to each member of society the revenue that belongs to him does not mean that they are therefore themselves part of that revenue.

Smith was substantially a theoretical metallist, that is, he believed that money essentially consists of, or must at least be backed by, a commodity or several commodities whose exchange value as commodities is the logical basis of their value as money. The substitution of paper for the precious metals appeared to him as merely a matter of convenience or cheapness. What is the prerequisite for such a substitution? Confidence of the people in the issuing banker so as to believe in his preparedness to exchange, on demand, their promissory notes for gold and silver. If this condition is met, the whole circulation may be conducted with only a fraction of the precious metals which would otherwise have to be provided.

---

[7]Adam Smith, *An Inquiry into the Nature and Causes of the Wealth of Nations* (New York City: E. P. Dutton & Co., Inc., 1776), p. 19.

In the first chapter of Book IV (in which Smith exposes the mercantilist fallacies), he exhibits his awareness of what we nowadays call the primary functions of money: to serve as an instrument of commerce (means of exchange) and as a measure of value. Other functions which played a major role in mercantilist policy, such as that of serving as a store of value, are not distinguished. Without detailing Smith's attempts to invalidate erroneous popular notions fostered by the advocates of the "mercantile system" — they have been intentionally suppressed in the present chapter of this text — it may be worthwhile in bringing the first section to a close to recall a basic truth which Smith pointed out and on which even an enlightened twentieth-century reader needs occasionally to refresh his mind. It is simply this: that the expense of acquiring an unnecessary quantity of gold and silver must always diminish the wealth available for consumption, be it food, clothing, shelter, or what not.

DEVELOPMENTS DURING THE CLASSICAL PERIOD

Introduction

Monetary, credit, and banking theory was in continuous ferment during the six decades or so between the death of Adam Smith and the California gold discoveries. Many of the previously laid foundations were firmed by writers who were still near the cradle of the Industrial Revolution and had to come to grips with its aftermath. As in value theory, English thinkers dominated the periodic debates on monetary issues. Moving on a fairly high level of abstraction, they did distinctly more than their counterparts on the continent and in the United States to clarify and spell out emerging issues and propose solutions thereto. Although most of the writers were men of practical affairs, there were few who could not hold their own in formulating generalizations derived from an increasingly complex "real world" situation. To see practitioners thrust themselves into the lead in the economic discussion was of course not unprecedented; the Mercantilists more often than not had been men of affairs. But to witness a group of bankers and financiers push back the theoretical frontiers and form the vanguard of analytic advance had never been commonplace — nor was it to become again. This is not to deny that the practitioners received varied support from the academicians who, for one, assisted in translating crudely formulated propositions into more elegant statements; this resulted, however, in their getting more credit than was due them.

Henry Thornton,[8] for example, was grossly overshadowed by David Ricardo. But Thornton was a man who towered above all others as far as scope of comprehension and analytic power in monetary matters was concerned, a man who anticipated the developments of several decades. Mill, the armchair economist, did an excellent job of summing up the work of the trailblazers, and it was primarily through his formulations that the work of the first half of the nineteenth century was transmitted to writers in the second half. Since the overall performance cannot be adequately appreciated without some familiarity with the special conditions forming its matrix, it will be necessary to review the institutional setting.

In 1797 the English Parliament passed the so-called Restriction Act, which suspended the obligation of the Bank of England to redeem its notes in gold. In spite of pressures imposed by the Napoleonic Wars, the subsequent inflation was relatively mild and the English currency never became seriously endangered. While war demands forced some lavish spending by the government, the introduction of the income tax, among other devices, kept inflationary financing to a minimum. All the same, the Bank of England became a convenient "whipping boy" for economic consequences that were generally disliked. But the Bank had a few courageous defenders, and — what makes a study of this period doubly rewarding — the differences in viewpoint nourished a controversy which contributed richly to monetary analysis. Those who indicted inflation and sought to locate the responsibility for it with the Bank scored a limited victory when, in 1810, the famous Bullion Report was published; its writers and supporters subsequently became known as Bullionists.

England had been on a de facto gold standard when restriction was decreed in 1797, and during the ensuing years sentiment grew in favor of de jure adoption of it. This action was taken a year after the end of the Napoleonic Wars, in 1816, although another five years passed before specie payments at the prewar par, based on Peel's Resumption Act of 1819, were actually resumed. Ricardo's recommendation, according to which the Bank should stand ready to redeem its notes in bullion rather than in coin, was actually embodied in the Resumption Act, although the relevant permissive clause did not become operative. Meanwhile the British economy, having lapsed from war prosperity, remained mostly depressed during the 1820's and a portion of the 1830's. What was more natural than to blame the slightly restrictive effect of resumption for the bad times? Only with the gold discoveries toward the

_____
[8]See Biographical Note E.

middle of the nineteenth century did the advocates of an unfettered
gold standard recover some of their lost prestige.

Another law of significance, giving rise to a new controversy, was
the Bank Charter Act (Peel Act) of 1844. In essence, this legislation
tried to implement the theory that banking ought to be separated from
currency control, and it enforced something like a 100 percent reserve
plan for bank notes. The man in the street this time had been told to
find his scapegoat for economic ills in the note-issuing banks; he, as well
as many well-informed persons, remained oblivious to a new trend
which would soon render the 1844 law obsolete: bank deposits were in
the process of becoming generally accepted means of payment. Those
who voted for the new law hoped, somewhat prematurely as it turned
out, that it would put a stop to misconduct and irresponsibility on the
part of note-issuing banks.

It should also be noted that the advocates of the Bank Charter Act
looked upon the notes of the Bank of England merely as a kind of
reserve currency, whereas its opponents regarded them as instruments
of credit, that is, as means of payment that originate in commodity
trade. The former became subsequently known as the Currency school,
the latter as the Banking school. Eventually the Banking school, for
whom the bank note originating in the discount of a trade bill remained
the backbone for any sound monetary policy, won out — especially in
the United States and on the European Continent. Their victory was
accelerated by the spreading practice of traders using bills of exchange
as actual means of payment.

Major Contributions

Ricardo and Others.— Most authors of this period defined money
as it had been previously defined: a commodity serving primarily as a
means of payment and a measure of value. Many of them also fought
against the conceptual merger of bank notes and deposits, and Peel's
Act of 1844 reflected the prevailing sentiment that there was an
essential difference between these payment instruments. A majority
of them, especially Ricardo, were metallists in the sense that they advocated fluctuations in the value of the monetary unit in accordance
with fluctuations in the value of gold. Indeed, they viewed the essential
problem of monetary theory as the *value of money*, which they identified
with the exchange ratios between money and goods. But they did not
develop any articulate theory of the price level and distrusted the method of index numbers — had they grasped its possibilities in the first
place. For instance, while the term "price level" occurs in Ricardo's

correspondence, he refused to recognize it as a meaningful or measurable concept. He therefore had to rely on the premium on gold bullion for the "proof" that bank notes had depreciated during the Napoleonic Wars and for a measure of that depreciation. He, as well as others, distinguished between a natural (or long-run normal) value of money and a short-run value, explaining the former by the cost of producing or obtaining the precious metals and the latter by supply and demand. Ricardo, especially, recognized that because of its great durability the total stock of gold varies but slowly in response to annual output; consequently, short-run equilibrium will, in the case of gold, be of greater importance relative to long-run equilibrium than it is in the case of other commodities.

With respect to the *quantity theory of money*, the position of various writers differed considerably. Ricardo seems to have adhered to a strict quantity theory, in the sense that he regarded an increase in the volume of money as causing a *proportionate* decrease in its purchasing power. Not only did he view the quantity of money as an independent variable, but he took the velocity of circulation as an institutional datum and regarded transactions as unrelated to the quantity of money.

Mill.—In contrast, J. Stuart Mill, after initially committing himself to a quantity theory of money akin to Ricardo's, made so many qualifications that he can no longer be viewed as an adherent of it. He felt that the emergence of credit made a world of difference; and even in the case of societies using only coin and irredeemable paper, the validity of such a theory could not be upheld unless it was restricted to the quantity of money actually circulating. And — taking another step in the right direction — he saw not only that the circulating quantity of money is dependent on output and employment but also that money may be hoarded. In his analytic schema, then, it is no longer the quantity of money per se that acts upon prices but a combination of quantity and velocity of turnover, or money spending. While he did not elevate velocity to the status of an explicit independent variable, Mill made clear that money spending is neither uniquely nor even closely related to the quantity of coin or paper money in existence.

Thornton.—Of the contributions of Thornton, which were of the first order of importance in the history of monetary analysis, two are especially worthy of mention: his treatment of the "rapidity of circulation" as a variable fluctuating with the state of confidence, and the introduction of interest into the theory of the monetary process. With respect to the rapidity of circulation, he specifically noted the methods of payment which economize the use of money, the volume of credit, and the amounts hoarded by individuals and by banks. He took great pains to show that such different means of payment as bank notes, commercial drafts, and metallic money usually have different velocities of circulation. Perhaps his most original contribution was that the velocity of circulation of the same kind of money (for example, bank notes) varies considerably according to general business conditions. A more methodical and clearer account was not given of the part played by velocity in the formation of the price level until, almost a century later, Irving Fisher dealt with this question in his *The Purchasing Power of Money*. Furthermore, as a first-rate economic diagnostician, Thornton was the only one among the leading writers who kept the Bank's note issue in proper perspective, that is, regarded it as only one among many influences that shaped the English monetary situation around the end of the eighteenth century.

Tooke.[9]—Among the opponents of Ricardo in the bullion controversy, there was one who stated more authoritatively and convincingly than all the others the case against a speedy return to redemption. Thomas Tooke pointed out that, in an inflation as mild as that of England during the first two decades of the nineteenth century, the influence of nonmonetary factors must necessarily account for a relatively much greater part of observed phenomena than would be true in cases of more vigorous rises in the general level of prices. In his *A History of Prices*, he analyzed economic data — year by year and month by month — from several decades beginning with 1792 and pointed out the influence of good and bad harvests as well as other "business" factors. He largely succeeded in invalidating Ricardo's theory as far as its application to the situation prevailing in the early 1800's was concerned, but he did not prove equal to the task when he attacked Ricardo's theory qua theory. For instance, he went so far as to declare that prices of commodities do not depend upon the quantity of money in circulation and, contrariwise, regarded the amount of circulating media as the consequence of prices. In his theory of general prices he reasoned that the quantity of money is not a useful datum for two reasons: commodities may be purchased without the use of money, and money need not all become active (a portion may be neutral in its "action" on prices). Tooke formulated an *income theory of prices* and saw in the various income shares (rents, profits, salaries, wages) the

[9] See Biographical Note F.

ultimate regulating principle of money prices. This income approach
to the problem of the value of money foreshadowed a line of thought
which was fully developed in Keynes' *General Theory*, as readers of
Chapter 8 may well have realized. But the approach was open to the
objection that prices determine these income shares as much as the
latter determine prices and that in the complex of factors that act upon
prices there is, after all, room for the quantity of money.

Some Further Characterizations

Mill's role can be viewed as that of an eclectic whose teaching was a
blend between those of Tooke and Ricardo. He assembled and combined what he found to be sound in each of them while regarding their
deficiencies as extraneous matter. Mill qualified the Ricardian proposition that an increase in money will, *ceteris paribus*, raise prices in the
same proportion — the *ceteris paribus* clause he recognized as too sweeping an assumption. Nevertheless he could not free himself from the
Ricardian doctrine that variations in the physical volume of output and
variations in the quantity of money are not related to each other. He
thus in effect denied the possibility of monetary stimulation as a depression remedy.

As far as *monetary management* is concerned, Mill remained on the
sidelines; he seems to have distrusted, for good or bad reasons, the
ability and independence of agencies that might have been placed in
charge of it. He simply refused to consider the theory of managed
money and to cope with facts and problems associated with the idea.
In the sponsorship of bimetallism he saw a thinly disguised attempt to
depress the purchasing power of money, and, disapproving of bimetallism, he failed to discuss the interesting analytical problems to which
this form of monetary standard gives rise. Other writers, too, seemed
to be largely impervious to this phenomenon, which had its repercussions in several countries. Ricardo, for one, was aware of the operation
of Gresham's Law, whose effect under bimetallism is for the system to
absorb the overvalued money and to set free the undervalued money
so that a country might wind up with a de facto gold standard or a
de facto silver standard. But he saw in this nothing more than an
inconvenience which should be remedied, the sooner the better.

The *theory of credit* was by no means neglected by the writers of the
period under review. They made some discoveries that substantially
contributed to monetary analysis, but they failed to construct a
systematic credit theory of money largely because they assigned to

legal tender money a logically privileged position. They did not recognize that demand supported by credit extension acts upon prices in essentially the same manner as does demand supported by legal tender — that the two are essentially on the same footing. Perhaps the most important reason for this attitude was the fact that the law treats these different types of means of payment differently. Thornton was the only genuine exception, because he perceived that the different means of payment may, on a certain level of abstraction, be treated as essentially alike.

We have already mentioned that Thornton was something of a pioneer on the subject of the relations between prices and interest. He was the first to call attention to the fact that a high rate of interest (discount) tends to attract gold from abroad. More important, having analyzed the market for loanable funds, he came close to stating the fundamental equilibrium theorem that the money rate of interest tends to equal the expected marginal profits on investment. He saw that there is no restriction inherent in the credit mechanism per se that will prevent bank credit, if extended far enough, from causing an inflationary increase in prices. He traced the connections leading from an initial expansion of loans via an increase in money incomes to increased demand schedules for goods and services. He pointed out that such lending can go on as long as there are offers to lend at a rate which is below the expected marginal profits, with the possibility of profits being regenerated by an increase in prices of goods and services. To prevent such a cumulative process from getting very far it would be necessary for means to enforce stability to come into play. Convertibility of notes and deposits in gold would be a prime necessity. This practical conclusion was also accepted by Ricardo, Senior, and J. Stuart Mill, among others. Nor did Thornton overlook the fact that such an inflationary process could take place only if the expansion of loans was not accompanied by a compensating reduction of expenditure by people other than the borrowers, that is, if not compensated by saving.

He further pinned down two observations that were, to say the least, far from commonplace a century and a half ago (though they are now basic tools of income and employment theory): in an underemployed economy, bank loans which add to the means of payment may stimulate output rather than raise prices; and, after full employment has been achieved, credit expansion will result largely in higher prices — largely, that is, because even in full employment output may be "stretched" somewhat further under extraordinary circumstances, such as a war.

Finally, Thornton anticipated Wicksell's doctrine of "forced saving" by focusing on cases in which money incomes do not increase in step with prices, so that recipients of such incomes may be forced to reduce their purchases of goods and services. And, he indicated, such involuntary saving would facilitate real capital formation just as meaningfully as does ordinary saving. The less flexible, though vastly more famous, Ricardo failed to face this issue squarely even after it was repeatedly brought to his attention. J. Stuart Mill, in turn, was too much under Ricardo's influence to accord the concept of forced saving more than passing notice, and it then remained buried until almost the turn of the twentieth century.

In the controversy about *Peel's Act of 1844*, most economists — and particularly Mill — ranged themselves with the Banking school. Both sides, however, were quite loath to monetary management and any comprehensive control of banking and credit. The Banking school fought the law without any substitute method of control, while the Currency school wanted to secure the necessary freedom of action for bankers by making the issue of currency automatic (removing it from the realm of human discretion). Since both groups were also firm supporters of the gold standard, in the still young laissez-faire tradition, there were probably more beliefs which they held in common than views that disunited them. Among the latter, only two were really relevant. First, the Banking school believed that convertibility of notes could be maintained under competent leadership by the Bank of England and would go a long way toward securing monetary stability, whereas the Currency school held that convertibility of notes could not be assured without specified restrictions on their issue. Second, the Banking school asserted that regulating the note issue, even *if* it were necessary, would remain meaningless as long as the creation of deposits were uncontrolled. The Currency school was blind to this argument, insisting as it did that only bank notes and coin were money; if deposits were not a medium of payment, they obviously could not affect the value of money. The Currency school felt that the monetary system could be tied directly to gold; the notes of the Bank of England should be treated as gold certificates, merely representing an equivalent amount of coin or bullion held as reserve. According to the "currency principle," then, gold plus notes should and could be made to behave as gold alone would behave.

Robert Torrens,[10] the principal exponent of the Currency school, met the graver of the above-mentioned objections of the Banking

---

[10]See Biographical Note G.

school by asserting that regulation of the note issue would in effect regulate also the creation of deposits. For he held that the amount of deposits which banks are able to create is closely geared to the existing amount of hand-to-hand money (notes and coin).

Apart from this, the only real disagreement between the two schools centered about whether there was a need for a special *guarantee* of the convertibility — since on both the importance and desirability of convertibility they were already agreed. Generalizing further, we can say that they saw "eye to eye" on fundamental objectives and were merely split on their practical implementation. As it turned out, the effects on policy brought about by the Bank Charter Act of 1844 were of little importance. The law was anachronistic in that it attempted to regulate the money supply by regulating currency at the very time when currency was becoming the less important constituent of the money supply.

In closing, it was also during the period under review that the *commercial bill theory of banking* came into its own. According to it, the financing of current commodity trade is the *differentia specifica* of a commercial bank. It implies that these banks derive the funds with which they discount commercial paper from public deposits and that in the satisfaction of the needs of commodity trade they do not influence prices. Thornton, however, revealed the erroneousness of the proposition that sound principles of discounting are sufficient to keep the economy on an even keel.

SUMMARY

Aristotle was the first to discourse on the nature and functions of money and to lay a (still tenuous) foundation for theorizing. Oresme began to list the desirable properties of monetary media. He inveighed against the numerous abuses to which the management of money lends itself. Bodin, in the course of investigating the causes of the European price revolution of the sixteenth century, emerged as the first exponent of a quantity theory of money. Petty rose above the unenlightened spirit that governed the discussion of monetary issues by most of the Mercantilists and was the first to account for the velocity of circulation of money. Locke introduced into monetary theory the influence of the volume of trade and took into consideration the possibility of hoarding. Law conceived the idea of substituting for specie paper money, secured by the value of land and placed in circulation by a government bank. His insight into the stimulating effects on trade of monetary expansion was sound, but its application was marred by his reckless experimenting.

Cantillon had a number of original and advanced ideas on economic issues in general and monetary matters in particular. An unusually keen student and practitioner, he reconciled his clear knowledge of the quantity theory of money with his balance-of-trade theory and originated the concept of "profit inflation," tracing some of its income effects.

Hume became famous for his observation that the quantity of money in circulation is per se of no consequence to the economic welfare of a nation. The Physiocrats, as well as Adam Smith, made few constructive contributions to the advance of monetary theory; their service consisted mainly in exposing mercantilist fallacies. Turgot distinguished himself by pointing out that money may take many different forms and that there is no one thing with such inherent qualities as would predestine it to serve as money.

By the end of the eighteenth century, the British banking system was, relatively, the most advanced. It is not surprising, therefore, that English thinkers, many of them men of affairs, were the ones to give content to the discussion of the increasingly complex monetary problems conjured up by the Industrial Revolution. They were almost solely responsible for the construction of more sophisticated theorems in the field of money and banking during the first half of the nineteenth century.

Henry Thornton occupies a place of honor as a man with an imaginative and fertile mind enabling him to blaze many a new trail. In several respects he was ahead of Ricardo as well as of academic political economists. Especially noteworthy were his treatment of the velocity of circulation of money and his fusion of interest theory and monetary theory. He was the first to observe that high interest rates tend to attract gold from abroad. He clearly perceived the relationship between the money rate of interest and the expected marginal profits on investment and of the inflationary consequences of credit expansion, which in turn he related to the level of employment. And he anticipated the major strands of Wicksell's doctrine of forced saving.

Ricardo was closely associated with the findings incorporated in the Bullion Report and with the analysis of the relation between gold prices and the depreciation of paper money during the Napoleonic Wars. He, like the majority of the leading authors of this period as well as practically all of the earlier writers, was still a metallist. He was an adherent of a strict quantity theory of money and showed awareness of

Gresham's Law as applied to bimetallism, without seeing in its effects anything more than an inconvenience. J. Stuart Mill, besides ably summing up the theoretical advances in the half century prior to publication of his *Principles*, substantially qualified the quantity theory of money. He observed that money spending is neither uniquely nor closely related to the quantity of hand-to-hand money in existence. At the same time he denied, in effect, the possibility of monetary stimulation of the economy and generally distrusted monetary management. Tooke was opposed to Ricardo in the bullion controversy. He gave reasons for his belief as to why the quantity of money in existence is not a useful datum for the formulation of a theory of prices. Instead, he framed such a theory in terms of income shares, anticipating an approach which a century later was taken by Keynes in his *General Theory*. He also was a vigorous spokesman for the Banking school. Torrens was the principal advocate of the currency principle and ably defended the reasons underlying the Bank Charter Act of 1844. While the difference between the positions taken by the two schools was of some practical importance, as far as analysis and basic policy objectives are concerned it involved only minor disagreements. While the Currency school carried the day in 1844, the basic arguments of the Banking school sound more convincing today; too, they have been vindicated by subsequent historical developments.

BIOGRAPHICAL NOTES

A. — *Nicole Oresme* (1320?-1382) was one of the outstanding French churchmen of the fourteenth century. Born in or near Caen, he was educated mostly in Paris. At the age of thirty-six he became grandmaster of the College of Navarre, and in 1362 he was made dean of Rouen. During the last five years of his life he filled the office of Bishop of Lisieux. He was a man of polyhistoric interests who wrote in many fields, especially theology and the sciences. He acquired fame as a translator, from Latin into French, of several works of Aristotle. His celebrated work *Tractatus de origine, natura, jure et mutationibus monetarum* (usually translated, for short, as "Treatise on the First Invention of Money") was written between 1350 and 1360 and is thought to reflect the principal views of his teacher, Buridanus. Regardless of the degree of originality incorporated in this work, it may be considered a milestone in the history of economic thought. It discusses economic questions no longer within the framework of canonistic theology but is oriented toward secular concerns and is characterized by a secular point of view. It may therefore be questionable to consider it as a summary of scholastic thought. Its translation from Latin into French was undertaken at the request of King Charles V, one of Oresme's early pupils. It met with great success in its own time but then fell into oblivion until it was rediscovered by nineteenth-century economists.

B. — *Jean Bodin* (1530–1596) wrote primarily what are now called treatises on political science, with the economics of public policy and administration being just one branch of political knowledge. Born at Angers, France, he studied law at the university there. Before going to Paris, he spent twelve years as a lecturer on law in Toulouse. His lack of success at the bar prompted his entering government service, where he incurred the king's displeasure by opposing his financial schemes; thereafter he was watched with suspicion.

A man of vast erudition mainly outside the field with which we are concerned (he formulated an ingenious theory of sovereignty), Bodin is better known for his *The Six Books of the Republic* (1576) and *Method for the Easy Learning of History* (1566) than for his *Answers to the Paradoxes of Mr. Malestroit* (1566). But it is the latter which contains his only significant contribution to economic analysis. Malestroit, who was comptroller of the mint, argued that the rise in prices was due to the lower intrinsic value of the debased coinage. Bodin countered with the *Answers*, which represent perhaps the most interesting discussion evoked by the European price revolution of the sixteenth century, an aftermath of the inflow of precious metals from the Western Hemisphere.

C. — *John Locke* (1632–1704) was the son of a small landowner and fought for the parliamentary system during the English Civil War. A product of Oxford, he started his career by tutoring and lecturing there. He then entered civil service, eventually rising to a seat on the Board of Trade. As a supporter of the opposition to King James II, he lived in exile for some time, returning to England after William III had assumed the crown following the Revolution of 1688–89. Locke's work was of first-rate importance on a number of counts. As a philosopher, he broke with the scholastic tradition and in his *Essay concerning Human Understanding* (1690) led empiricism (and hedonism) to victory in England. His advocacy of tolerance, liberty of the press, and extended education paved the way for the ascendancy of political liberalism and modern type representative democracy. With his *Two Treatises of Government* (1690) he established himself as a political theorist, drawing on the philosophy of natural law. As an economist, he made his most significant contributions in *Some Considerations of the Consequences of Lowering the Interest and Raising the Value of Money*, published in 1692.

D. — *John Law* (1671–1729) lived in the era of the "great bubbles." His name is intimately associated with the "Mississippi Bubble," a French adventure which served as a model for the "South Sea Bubble," of English origin. Both were of short duration, culminating around 1720.

Law, the son of an Edinburgh goldsmith, was well educated, widely traveled, and closely acquainted with the financial institutions of his time. After his monetary proposals had been rejected in England and Scotland — and after he had killed one of his countrymen in a duel — he found in France not only a political haven but also receptive ears for his pet schemes. His host country was on the verge of bankruptcy, its finances in a chaotic state.

Given the green light in 1715, Law promptly put into practice his
... *Proposal for Supplying the Nation with Money* (1705) by setting up an
incorporated bank with a monopoly of note circulation.   Despite some
dubious stock financing, his *Banque Générale* followed perfectly orthodox
methods and was on the way to achieving spectacular success in terms of
sound currency, credit availability, and restored confidence.   If Law had
confined himself to what he accomplished in these first two years, he would
have been one of the greatest benefactors any nation ever had.   It was the
conversion of the *Banque Générale* into the *Banque Royale* in 1718, accompanied by the buying out of private stockholders and a new provision
that bank notes were no longer to be redeemed in silver but rather in old
depreciated *billets d'Etat*, that set the stage for a reversal of fortunes two
years later.   With the setting up of a colonization scheme — the newly
established *Compagnie d'Occident*, headed by Law, first obtained a monopoly of France's whole foreign commerce and then spread its tentacles
to include almost all domestic governmental enterprises — speculative
fever went rampant and a singular height of frenzy was reached in 1720.

Then the bubble burst, touched off by no single event but rather the
gradual encroachment of common sense upon irrationality.   A few far-
sighted individuals were able to save their skins (or even make a fortune),
but the masses were utterly defrauded in the complete collapse of prices
and the forced removal of precious metals, in any form, from circulation.
When, during a bank run, a dozen or so people were trampled to death,
Law was barely able to escape the pent-up fury of the populace.   A few
years later the brilliant promoter died in ignominy.

E.—*Henry Thornton* (1760–1815) was the second son of John Thornton,
an eminent British merchant.   The younger Thornton followed in his father's
footsteps but, in addition, became a banker and — for over thirty years —
a member of Parliament.   He also was a leading figure in an influential
group of Evangelicals known as the Clapham Sect.   He inherited from his
father a passionate desire to relieve distress wherever he found it; his
unbounded benevolence made him a dedicated philanthropist.   He judged
that his inherited estate ought never to be increased by accumulation nor
diminished by sumptuousness, and he rigidly adhered to this decision until
his premature death.   Broadly speaking, his avocation was to investigate
the great controversies of his own and of all former times.   He was an
earnest and relentless seeker after unadorned truth.   As a legislator he
condemned the unequal pressure of direct taxes on the rich and the poor,
but none of the contending factions ever won his favor.   He was an infre-
quent and unimpressive speaker, and what influence he exercised over the
measures taken during his lifetime was due almost entirely to his writings.
His piety, reserved and unobtrusive, was the perennial source of his
mental health and energy.

His principal work in political economy, *Enquiry into the Nature and
Effects of the Paper Credit of Great Britain*, was published in 1802 and constitutes an amazing performance, considering his competing business and
political pursuits; Thornton himself did not seem to have been fully aware
of the book's potential.   All his numerous religious writings were published
after his death.

F. — *Thomas Tooke* (1774–1858) was born in St. Petersburg and was from early life until about his sixtieth year largely engaged in Russian trade in London. In 1821 he became one of the principal founders of the Political Economy Club — along with Ricardo, Malthus, the elder Mill, Torrens, and others. This association afforded its members an opportunity for discussion of political and economic subjects; it played a unique role in the dissemination of doctrine. Tooke, an authoritarian of sorts, at times dominated its proceedings, to the intense dislike of others.

He was regularly called upon to testify before parliamentary committees and was himself chairman of at least two commissions. He was the promoter of many public enterprises connected with the industrial reforms of Great Britain during the first half of the nineteenth century. Not negligible were his services to the cause of free trade, notably as the draftsman of a celebrated Petition of the London Merchants in 1820.

The one work, monumental in scope, which secured for him a permanent place in historiography was entitled *A History of Prices and of the State of the Circulation from 1792 to 1856*, published in six volumes between 1838 and 1857. While writing it Tooke enjoyed a higher social standing and more opportunities for leisured reflection than his much younger collaborator, William Newmarch (1820–1882). This enormous series contains over three thousand pages in print and embodies not only a continuous narrative but also a number of specialized inquiries involving Herculean labors. (The first two volumes, which appeared in 1838, covered the longest span, namely 1792 to 1837. The first four volumes carried only Tooke's name on the title page; the last two were mainly the work of Newmarch.)

Tooke was far from a "pure" historian; his purpose was to pursue and, if possible, to invalidate the economic theses to which he was opposed. The special appeal which *A History of Prices* has retained to the present day is that it constitutes the first panoramic utilization by an economist of historical material for the systematic statement of economic propositions. "Systematic" in this case does not imply orderly: the *History*, being an analysis of England's economic processes over more than six decades, is extremely prolix and repetitious; it is wanting in organic balance and sharp theoretical edge and was written in a florid, heavy, and somewhat tedious style. Nevertheless, it has merit as a unique type of analysis that combines presentation and explanation of facts in such a way that the two are no longer distinct but mutually condition each other throughout.

Many of Tooke's earlier writings were pressed into service again as the *History* proceeded; of his later writings the only piece that deserves independent scrutiny is his *Inquiry into the Currency Principle* (1844), probably the most able tract in opposition to the Peel Act passed in the same year.

G.—*Colonel Robert Torrens* (1780–1864), an Irishman, did not have an interpreter until 1958 when Lionel Robbins from the University of London published a book-length study, *Robert Torrens and the Evolution of Classical Economics*. A minor figure among the founders of the Classical school, this son of a clergyman spent his early career as a professional soldier in the Marines and was in active service during the Napoleonic Wars. Before he returned to civilian life in 1812, he began to display literary tendencies and a developing interest in political economy.

He started out as an anti-Bullionist with an *Essay on Money and Paper Currency*. Three years later, after he had met Ricardo, he established his position among the members of the profession with his *Essay on the External Corn Trade*. He differed with Ricardo on several issues including the question of resumption, but apparently, after his publication of the *Essay on the Production of Wealth* in 1821, enjoyed substantial prestige: he was chosen to occupy the chair at the opening meeting of the London Political Economy Club the same year.

Beginning in 1826, he was elected Member of Parliament several times. Just before he resigned, in order to promote in a pioneering way the colonization of South Australia, he had published his *Letters on Commercial Policy* (1833) and his *On Wages and Combinations* (1834). His interest in emigration was evidenced in a major work entitled *On the Colonization of South Australia* (1835). *The Budget* (1844) was a collection of public letters dealing with commercial and colonial policy, in which he emerged as an advocate of reciprocal tariff reduction.

Following his first published suggestion for the separation of the Issue and Banking Departments of the Bank of England in 1837, he was active (almost the only economist of some standing) in propagandizing the "currency principle" which resulted in the Bank Act of 1844, but not without having challenged both Tooke and J. Stuart Mill on this issue. His pen remained active until the late 1850's. Unfortunately, Torrens was somewhat careless in formulation and — perhaps for lack of sufficient training — not a good technician. He died, not as a man of outstanding eminence, but unduly neglected for many decades thereafter.

Questions for Review and Research

1. Who was Oresme? When was his famous treatise on money written? What did he mean by "mutations" of money?
2. What did Bodin regard as the principal reason for price rises in general? To what extent, if any, was this conclusion based on empirical evidence?
3. What writer(s) was (were) the first to take cognizance of (a) the velocity of circulation of money, and (b) the volume of trade, as explicit variables in monetary theory?
4. Discuss the reasons why, according to Law, paper money is preferable to metallic money.
5. In what respects did Cantillon's environmental situation resemble Law's? Were they contemporaries?
6. Trace the effects of a "profit inflation" as seen through Cantillon's eyes.
7. Was Hume aware of the need for qualifying the proposition that the quantity of money in circulation is of itself of no consequence to the economic welfare of a country? Explain.
8. What do you consider Turgot's leading contribution to the widening of the horizon of monetary theory?
9. What is meant by saying that Smith was still a "theoretical metallist"?

10. What important laws affecting the English monetary system were passed by the British Parliament between 1795 and 1845?
11. What were the positions of Ricardo and J. Stuart Mill in regard to the so-called quantity theory of money?
12. Give three reasons why Thornton deserves a place of honor in a history of monetary theory. On which side was Thornton in the controversy between the Banking school and the Currency school?

Recommended Readings

Monroe, Arthur Eli (ed.). *Early Economic Thought*. Cambridge: Harvard University Press, 1924. The selections IV, "Nicole Oresme," pp. 79–102, and VI, "Jean Bodin," pp. 121–141.

Newman, Philip C., Arthur D. Gayer, and Milton H. Spencer (eds.). *Source Readings in Economic Thought*. New York: W. W. Norton & Company, Inc., 1954. The selection "Of Money" in *Political Discourses*, by David Hume, pp. 86–90.

Robbins, Lionel. *Robert Torrens and the Evolution of Classical Economics*. London: Macmillan & Co., Ltd., 1958. Chapters IV and V, "The Theory of Money and Banking," pp. 73–143.

Thornton, Henry. *An Enquiry into the Nature and Effects of the Paper Credit of Great Britain* (1802), edited with an introduction by F. A. von Hayek. New York: Farrar & Rinehart Inc., 1939. "Introduction," pp. 11–58 and Chapters VIII and IX, pp. 193–229.

Tooke, Thomas, and William Newmarch. *A History of Prices and of the State of the Circulation from 1792 to 1856*. New York: Adelphi Co., 1928. Introduction by T. E. Gregory; Vols. 1 and 2, pp. 5–120.

Vickers, Douglas. *Studies in the Theory of Money 1690–1776*. Philadelphia: Chilton Book Company, 1959. Pp. 111–140 (Law) and pp. 186–216 (Cantillon).

11

MONETARY AND BANKING THEORY

From 1850 Onward

THE SETTING

Sifting out contributions of enduring value becomes more difficult as we move into the decades following J. Stuart Mill's restatement of classical doctrine. This observation applies especially to writings in the field of money and banking — quantity prevailed, rather than quality and originality. Nevertheless, the period did produce a few peak achievements which are far from uninteresting or expendable from the standpoint of analytical advancement. We will subject these to close scrutiny, after first surveying the practical problems with which the new literature tried to cope.

We may recall that the half century prior to World War I witnessed the rise of the international gold standard to a place of prominence and the concomitant decline of silver and bimetallic standards in the monetary arrangements of the leading industrial countries. There was, as always, a literary reflex of this trend. On the other hand, without the academic support forthcoming for this system of virtually stable exchange rates, many governments might have continued the arrangements which they found satisfactory prior to switching to the yellow metal as the international standard of value and medium of exchange. There arose many valiant defenders of the gold standard, people who were often strongly opposed to bimetallism. On the battleground of practical politics their rivals, the silverites and bimetallists, fought an uphill struggle that sometimes did not lack in tragicomic aspects.[1] But hardly any of those leaders of scientific economics in this period with whom we are already familiar — Jevons, Walras, Wieser, Marshall, Wicksell — lent their unqualified support to the use of gold. The

---

[1] Probably the best expression of the popular agitation in the United States in favor of "cheaper" money was William Jennings Bryan's slogan of the heated 1896 Presidential campaign: "You shall not press down upon the brow of labor this crown of thorns; you shall not crucify mankind upon a cross of gold." Quoted in Walter W. Haines, *Money, Prices, and Policy* (New York: McGraw-Hill Book Co., Inc., 1961), p. 143.

fact, moreover, that from the 1870's to the 1890's prices fell with few interruptions repeatedly brought to the forefront the general question of the adequacy of a single metal as a monetary base, and specifically of gold's responsibility for the price trend. Also, sponsorship of international bimetallism was by no means confined to monetary monomaniacs; some respected academic economists (as, for example, Francis Walker in the United States) vigorously rallied to its cause. Bimetallism itself was not a completely automatic system as long as only a limited number of countries were willing to adhere to its rules.

This era also marked the beginning of conscious international monetary cooperation, as reflected in a growing number of conferences and a few regional associations of more than ephemeral nature (as illustrated by the Latin Monetary Union). And inasmuch as the stabilization of price levels, employment, and money rates was occasionally mentioned as a goal of economic policy, the discussions in the decades preceding World War I already foreshadowed experiments in monetary management that proliferated during the Depression decade. Finally, the idea of open market operations, designed primarily to safeguard a nation's gold stock, appeared in several forms in those countries that had gained a measure of experience in central banking, notably England. We can see, then, that the gold-standard game was never played entirely for its own sake.

In the field of monetary reform, scientific leaders proffered several suggestions: abandonment of gold, not as a medium of exchange and common denominator of value, but as a standard of deferred payments; introduction of symmetallism, that is, having the monetary unit constitute a claim to both gold and silver in fixed proportions; varying the gold content of the monetary unit according to the variations of an official price index so as to make that unit represent a constant quantity of purchasing power (compensated dollar); and retaining gold as the standard monetary metal to be coined for private account without limit, while degrading silver to the status of token money — to be used expressly for the purpose of controlling the price level. These examples show that respectable monetary reform proposals have a more venerable history than is likely to be assumed by the student who is told about the free reign of the gold standard prior to the debacles of the twentieth century.

AVENUES OF THEORETICAL ADVANCE

Whereas in value and distribution theory one may, if he chooses, speak of a revolution as far as the theoretical advances between 1870 and 1914 are concerned, the purely analytic work in the field of monetary and banking theory was more in the nature of vigorous evolution. New theses grew mainly out of existing knowledge and were accretions to, rather than replacements of, received doctrine. All the same, the main conquests that resulted in our present-day structure of monetary analysis were made during the period under review, and not before. As exemplified by the findings of the United States Monetary Commission leading to the establishment of the Federal Reserve System, factual work was far from negligible: it supplied the underpinnings for that imposing structure, no less. Above all, the infiltration of modern statistical methods was largely responsible for adding precision to theoretical propositions. But due to the evolutionary quality of the methods developed during the period up to about 1920, as well as to the fact that the researchers largely failed to systematize their insights in a form readily accessible to the nonspecialist, the results of front-line work did not filter down into the textbook literature to a degree commensurate with its intrinsic merits. It was not until the 1930's that the major theoretical conquests really penetrated the textbooks on money and banking and gave them a badly needed new look.

What, then, were the principal avenues of theoretical advance? (1) Perhaps of most importance, the theory of money was made a part of the general theory of economic equilibrium — in other words, the analysis of money was built into the system of general theory, instead of developing the former independently and grafting it upon the latter. Prior to World War I, monetary theory and the value and distribution theory were treated as belonging in separate compartments. Also, models of the economic process were essentially still ones of barter exchange, with inflations and deflations merely disturbing phenomena.

(2) Economic theorists realized the importance of distinguishing between the real and the monetary rate of interest and exploring, in detail, the mechanism by which changes in the amount of money in circulation affect the functioning of the economic system.

(3) The majority of the writers, in referring to the nature and functions of money, distinguished between what they merely called money (sometimes primary money) and credit (sometimes fiduciary money). In the former category they always included coin, usually government fiat, not infrequently the notes of central banks, and at least occasionally commercial bank notes. Credit they viewed as comprising means of payment arising out of loan transactions. To this distinction many attributed an exaggerated importance right down to World War II. Only in the last three decades or so has the term *money* been

unhesitatingly applied to demand deposits subject to check. Furthermore, most writers developed their theory of money in terms of four functions: measure of value, medium of exchange, store of value, and standard of deferred payments. Although it is questionable that many of the pre-1930 writers were aware of liquidity preference in the Keynesian sense of this term, a number of them emphasized the store-of-value function of money. Several of them noticed the role that hoarding plays in the self-generating process of deflation, but few attached critical importance to it as a cause of unemployment.

(4) The concept of "neutral money" was formalized. This is money that would behave so as to leave the *real* processes of an exchange economy unaffected. Once it was recognized that money *could* influence economic processes autonomously, it became important to state how and under what circumstances money could be prevented from causing miscellaneous havoc. However, the neutral money concept proved largely unworkable in this sense: no constellation of conditions could be formulated under which money would be merely a contrivance for sparing time and labor (to use Mill's phrase) and would not interfere with the operation of the laws of value.

(5) Progress in the development of the method of index numbers was remarkable, and the method was brought to a degree of perfection from which little further refinement seemed possible. In fact, advances in the field of price index numbers constituted the most important strides beyond a merely quantitative economics, that is, toward economic theory that was also numerical. After price index numbers had "proved" their serviceability, the concept was gradually applied to production, wages, and employment. For some, the use of indices held a rare fascination which encouraged efforts toward systematizing findings into a semiindependent specialty. Although the most outstanding index number theorists warned that there is no such thing as an absolutely reliable formula for measuring change (only degrees of approximation to the theoretical ideal), index numbers were used with few qualms — especially in the United States, where many authors did not hesitate to define the value of money as the reciprocal of whatever price level happened to captivate their fancy. On the European Continent, especially among the followers of the Austrian Trio (Carl Menger, Friedrich von Wieser, and Eugen von Böhm-Bawerk), acceptance was far from wholehearted. The Austrians, you recall, emphasized the behavior of individuals and therefore tended to define the exchange value of money with respect to individual commodity prices, rather than with respect to a general level of prices. In other words,

marginal utility analysis did not readily apply to the case of the exchange value of money itself, although it could be applied easily to the significance which individuals attached to their money income.

(6) In Germany a singular and awkward attempt was made to explain the value of money in terms of the sanction money receives from the government. This was associated with the name of Georg Friedrich Knapp,[2] who in 1905 published his *State Theory of Money,* a vigorous and in some sense ingenious work but controversial even across international boundaries. Knapp decided that monetary questions originate in the history of law — not in political economy. Money is a creation of law, and it appears in the course of history under the most diverse forms. If only the *validity* conferred upon it by the state counts, the question of the *value* of money is really secondary. Since Knapp's theory of money was of such a limited construction, it had to come to grief eventually. But, as a healthy side effect, it accelerated the trend toward obliterating the distinction between paper money and metallic money; and it enhanced the popularity of state-managed money. Conceived as the only possible alternative to theoretical metallism — which is perhaps its principal weakness — the theory captured the imagination of many second-rate economists and was popularly successful out of all proportion to its scientific merits. And, having been proffered a few years before World War I, it helped to assuage some of the misgivings caused by the currency inflation associated with that war and its aftermath.

(7) As a result of the attention devoted to the refinement of the equation of exchange, much of the discussion of the theory of money assumed the form of arguments for and against the so-called quantity theory. The price level now came to be linked more closely with the quantity of money in circulation, its velocity of turnover, and the physical volume of trade. The concepts behind the symbols M, V, T, and P in the equation $MV = TP$ were being accurately defined, and through skillful marshalling of statistical materials these concepts became operationally significant. Those who worked most intensively at this task overcame their reluctance to calling checking deposits money since a more meaningful formulation of the equation of exchange imperatively demanded inclusion of the quantitatively most important (in England and the United States) type of credit instrument, namely, checking deposits. (Some went so far as to speak of deposit "currency," although on the whole this term has been confined to the hand-to-hand portion of the total money supply.) M was thus extended to include

[2]See Biographical Note A.

all the means of payment. Inasmuch as checking deposits (M') were elevated to separate status in the equation, it became necessary to assign to them a separate velocity of turnover (V'). It was realized that certain components of M, such as cash reserves of banks and cash hoards, were not active; but rather than subtract these noncirculating elements from M itself, they were as a rule simply assigned a velocity of zero. While this was substantially the position taken by American economists, their European counterparts who still stressed the difference between money and credit — that is, confined M to metallic money (and possibly fiat paper money) — interpreted the notes and deposit liabilities of commercial banks as devices for increasing the velocity of "money" (as they defined M). Viewed in this light, commercial bank reserves did of course have a very high velocity. It should now be clear that the appropriate velocity concept depends entirely upon the quantity concept one chooses to accept.

Not much progress was made in the analysis of the factors behind the velocity of money until the 1920's when various *types* of velocity began to be distinguished by thoughtful students. Of these, *income velocity* became subsequently the most familiar. The charge, however, that pre-World War I monetary economists generally considered velocity to be a constant is largely unfounded; several of them viewed its variability as a function of general business conditions, although they did not get beyond a pioneer stage in assigning numerical values to it.

(8) The more enlightened among the authors who wrote around the turn of the century did make a distinction between the equation of exchange per se and the quantity theory of money, although some spoke of the latter when they really meant the former. Certainly, few who gave this matter serious attention would take issue with the statement of the formal equilibrium relation $MV = PT$. But many, unfortunately, described themselves as in agreement with the quantity theory when all they meant was that they looked with favor on the use of some such equilibrium relationship as the above. It has been said many times, but bears repeating in this context, that the latter merely brings into an orderly and meaningful arrangement the principal causes by which the value of money is determined. In view of the vagueness of interpretation to which the quantity theory lends itself, it is, indeed, difficult to pinpoint writers who can without doubt be dubbed adherents of it. If we exclude only those who actually denied that autonomous variations in M have influence on the value of money, the great bulk of all writers were quantity theorists; whereas, if we

exclude all those who deny that the quantity of money in circulation is, under all conditions, the *only* significant determinant of the price level, few quantity theorists will be left. Some of those who held the middle ground between these extreme positions would simply say that the price level is, under *normal* conditions, a passive element in the equation of exchange. Others who went a little further would say that M is, under *normal* conditions, the most important "active" variable, with V and T, and especially P, performing a secondary role. Whether we should extend the label "quantity theorists" to the group taking this moderately bold stand or apply it only to those who took the still more rigid, but untenable, position that the value of money is always inversely proportional to its quantity must remain a matter of individual judgment. Whatever the choice, there are great interpretative difficulties in drawing a convincing boundary line between economists who adhered to and those who rejected what *we* may agree to call the quantity theory of money.

Generally speaking, those who professed to be outright enemies of it did not undertake a very serious effort in factual research to show that the relationships between M and P were less close than was alleged, or believed to have been alleged, by their opponents.

(9) The study of the value of money in this period utilized other avenues than the equation of exchange in standard form. Worthy of mention are especially two: the cash-balance approach and the income approach. They are fundamentally equivalent to the $MV = PT$ formula but suggest advance in a different direction, thereby commending themselves to economists with slightly different tastes.

The starting point of the *cash-balance approach* is the amount of money that individuals may desire to hold at any given point in time. The so-called Cambridge (England) equation states that if we let n be the amount of "cash in circulation" with the public, p the index number of the cost of living, k the number of "consumption units" representing the physical complement of the public's holdings of hand-to-hand money, k' the number of "consumption units" representing the physical complement of the public's checking deposits, and r the fraction of k' that banks keep as a cash reserve against k', then:

$$n = p\,(k + rk').\text{[3]}$$

In other words, at any given time the public — which, incidentally, includes business firms — chooses to keep in cash and bank balances

<hr />

[3] J. M. Keynes, *Monetary Reform* (New York: Harcourt, Brace & Company, 1924), p. 85.

an *amount* equal to the product of p and the sum of k and rk'. This formulation stressed the public's behavior in holding liquid assets and paved the way for the subsequent Keynesian analysis of motives for this behavior, especially liquidity preference, with which we familiarized ourselves in Chapter 8.

The *income approach* suggests that the explanation of money prices should take as its point of departure consumer incomes. It shares with the Cambridge cash-balance approach the idea that what really matters is individual behavior; it differs from the former by removing the quantity of money from the position of an immediate determinant of the price level and substituting for it income or — if we please — consumer expenditure. This approach has the important advantage of skirting the vexing question of what is to be considered as money. It calls our attention to such questions as: Who are the recipients of additional money? What is done with this money? In a period of inflation, for example, it is important that we gain clarity about the *mechanisms* through which an increased quantity of money becomes operative.

(10) There was some, but astonishingly little, progress in the academic analysis of credit and banking as the stock of ideas inherited from the preceding period was further clarified and refined. The *commercial loan theory of banking*, which was designed to provide protection against inflation while at the same time insuring that there would be enough money available, gained a further lease on life. It emphasized that the proper quantity of money is that amount sufficient to equal the quantity of goods currently available in the market at current prices and that this amount will be forthcoming if banks make loans only for commercial purposes, thus enabling merchants to buy additional goods for sale. Financing of fixed capital requirements is thereby considered outside the banks' proper domain.

Adherence to the commercial theory prevented most economists from rapidly enlarging their conception of the functions of central banking, that is, from recognizing the potential of monetary management. Instead of developing the idea of central banks as lenders of last resort, they viewed the role of such institutions as primarily, if not exclusively, one of control through changes in the discount rate. They debated the question of whether central banks actually had the power to regulate market rates of interest, or whether their own rate, called "bank rate" in England, could in effect only follow the market — be "declaratory," as they termed this passive adaptation to conditions in the credit market. Only gradually did economists outgrow the opinion that if commercial banks simply finance (with or without help from the central bank) the current needs of trade, M and T would necessarily move in step and, implying a constant V, inflationary forces would be held in abeyance. As they began to realize that discounting of sound commercial paper by banks does not guarantee price stability and insure continued prosperity, they also became aware that there is no such thing as a predetermined need for bank accommodation; actual borrowing depends on the rates charged by the banks, which in turn partly reflect their propensity to lend.

There is a corollary worth noting: the slow maturing of a realistic conception of the nature of bank credit. For years following World War I, some famous economists still viewed commercial bankers as essentially middlemen who borrow liquid funds from many small pools and lend them to trade. They had not yet adopted the much more realistic view that banks in the act of lending create deposits (money) but still maintained that the banks merely lend the deposits entrusted to them. Once they had sloughed off this old-fashioned viewpoint, they ceased to regard depositors merely as savers (which they may, but need not, be) and to attribute to them an influence on the supply of loanable funds which they do not in fact have. Today we take such things for granted, not realizing that this analytic victory was achieved only against stubborn, if uninformed, resistance. Perhaps we should not judge the profession too harshly since, the above case being of the nature of an either-or proposition, it required not only a thorough reorientation but also the jettisoning of a time-honored pet theory. And, we might add, after it had finally been conceded that bank loans create deposits (new money), it still proved quite difficult for economists to recognize that bank *investments* do likewise create deposits. The curious note about all this is that the facts of credit creation in the form of bank notes had long been familiar to economists, and some had even emphasized the truth that deposits and bank notes are fundamentally the same thing. It is a matter of historical record that as early as the 1850's the Scotsman Henry Dunning Macleod[4] had begun to lay the foundations of the modern theory of banks as manufacturers of (credit) money, but his pioneering efforts attracted little attention. Even when, some seventy years later, a German, Albert Hahn,[5] gave an exhaustive account of money creation by banks, the profession still had many holdouts. Some of them saw in this activity

---

[4] See Biographical Note B.
[5] His *Economic Theory of Bank Credit* (*Volkswirtschaftliche Theorie des Bankkredits*) went through the third edition in 1930 but left many economists (especially on this side of the Atlantic) unconvinced.

of banks something akin to unethical behavior — John Law had never been forgotten. Others feared, from acceptance of the new doctrine, a confusion of money and credit. But we have already moved into a discussion of individual contributions, which properly belongs to the next section.

PERSONALITIES

More so than in the previous chapters, the matter of selection here becomes rather difficult. There was a profusion of output, and the filiation of scientific ideas is now far from obvious. At the risk of committing injustice by omission, we will look at a handful of economists whose positive contributions to monetary and banking theory are no longer, if they ever were, a matter of doubt — with one possible exception.

Léon Walras

In the *Elements of Pure Economics* (1874, 1877), which went through several editions during his lifetime, Walras over a period of more than 20 years worked out a pure theory of money, fully integrated with his general equilibrium analysis. Like the rest of his system, this most difficult accomplishment did not find a hospitable reception — highly abstract formulations have seldom aroused favorable response, as exemplified by Cournot and Gossen a few decades earlier. Choosing a lonely but potentially promising route, Walras was able to fulfill, on a broader basis, the same desideratum that was met by Keynes' *General Theory*: the building of monetary analysis into a system of general theory. Seldom included in economics textbooks, Walras' theory of money discredited the idea that money adds nothing new to the exchange system, in other words, that the system would work in the same way if all exchanges were on the basis of barter. In the absence of a *numéraire* (Walras), or *tertium comparationis*, no general equilibrium could be established, because it would not be possible to make judgments with respect to two commodities of different price *and* a third commodity. Among the few who by the bent of their mind were capable of a measure of appreciation for Walras' work on money was Wicksell, but the other of Walras' followers in this area remained largely unknown.

Walras' work on monetary reform, contained in his *Studies of Applied Economics*, was less felicitous. He recognized the clear fact, but only in the case of bank notes, that banks can create means of payment. Disapproving of this method of financing which he considered an abuse, Walras suggested that additional silver tokens be coined in the amount of bank notes outstanding. This proposal made him a forerunner of full reserve, or 100 percent, plans. Positing that the value of money is inversely proportional to quantity, Walras proposed that practical control of the price level can be achieved by controlling the quantity of money — a rather crude piece of applied reasoning, and hardly expected of a man with his lofty vistas.

Alfred Marshall and the Cambridge Tradition

Marshall's monetary analysis was developed early in his life and may be viewed as an extension of late classical teaching, particularly the work of John Stuart Mill. Unfortunately, apart from his testimonies before various commissions in the 1880's and the 1890's, he did not systematically expound his views until he had reached extreme old age — at which time most of what he had to contribute had already been said by others. Nevertheless, for a rounded presentation of his mature views on monetary theory, *Money, Credit, and Commerce* (1923) is still worth consulting, especially when the book is studied in conjunction with his *Official Papers*.

Marshall agreed with Walras that monetary problems can only be discussed meaningfully in the context of a general analysis of the economic process. He saw more clearly than Walras the importance of the distinction between "real" and "money" interest rates. By virtue of this emphasis he was, as we shall see shortly, a close intellectual kin to Wicksell, though less explicit. For the overall advance of economics as a science, this was more unfortunate than it might seem. Here was Marshall, in possession of all the basic insights but hesitant to take that decisive step forward which by virtue of his authority he could have taken successfully. And then there was Wicksell, largely unknown in the Anglo-Saxon world, who did take the step, but with far greater obstacles in the way to international recognition. It was only through his successors and pupils at Cambridge that most of Marshall's ideas on money bore fruit. It was especially Ralph Hawtrey[6] who, on lines and in directions of his own, developed the Marshallian analysis. Keynes himself did not formally renounce his allegiance to Marshall on monetary matters until he wrote the *General Theory*. Even Dennis Robertson,[7] who went further beyond Marshall than any of the

---

[6]See Biographical Note C.
[7]See Biographical Note D.

Cambridge economists in the first half of the twentieth century, evinces deep Marshallian roots.

Marshall, the originator of the Cambridge tradition, was aware of the phenomenon of hoarding and sensed its role as an element in the mechanism of cyclical downswings. He was in sympathy with the equation of exchange, but merely as an expository device for the analysis of causes which determine the value of money. He took the lead in developing the Cambridge variant of the equation. Having examined in detail the concept of cash balances, he suggested that people find it worthwhile to keep some fraction of their income in the form of "ready purchasing power." Designating this fraction by the symbol k, the average individual cash balance (currency plus demand deposits) by m, and the annual income of the individual by y, he derived the equation $k = \dfrac{m}{y}$. Applying this concept to the nation as a whole, and letting M_c equal the quantity of money held by consumers and Y_c the aggregate personal income, we get $k = \dfrac{M_c}{Y_c}$. If we take into consideration the additional fact that businesses, too, hold cash, we can let K equal the proportion of the national product which a country desires to hold in cash. We then get what is usually called an "income K." Designating the latter as K_y, we can write

$$K_y = \frac{M}{Y},$$

which means that the total money supply held by the economy is a certain fraction of its income.

Writing the equation of exchange in its *income* form, rather than in its more usual transactions form, we have

$$MV_y = P_y T_y, \text{ where}$$

M = the quantity of money in circulation,

V_y = the income velocity of money, that is, the number of times money moves from one income recipient to another,

P_y = the price level at the point of final sale (primarily at retail), and

T_y = the physical volume of sales to final users (primarily at retail).

Thus $P_y T_y$ is the value of *final* product only. It excludes sales between businesses and is essentially the same as income, Y.

It is now easy to show through substitutions that the so-called "income K" (as distinguished from the "transactions K") is merely the *reciprocal* of the income velocity of money. For if

$$K_y = \frac{M}{Y}$$

while $Y = P_y T_y = MV_y$,

then $K_y = \dfrac{M}{P_y T_y} = \dfrac{M}{MV_y}$ and (cancelling M in numerator and denominator)

$$K_y = \frac{1}{V_y}.$$

In nonmathematical language, this amounts to the common-sense statement that the larger the proportion of their income that people hold in money, the more slowly money moves from one income recipient to another; or, any reduction in cash balances held speeds up monetary circulation.

Not all of the above implications were fully worked out by Marshall, and not all are found in his *Money, Credit, and Commerce*. Aside from Robertson, who at times went considerably beyond Marshall, Pigou worked most closely in the Marshallian tradition.[8]

Knut Wicksell

It was intimated in Chapter 6 that Wicksell took an important step in bridging the gap between price theory and monetary theory. Like Marshall, he started from J. Stuart Mill, whose treatment of the theory of money he found less than satisfactory, however. As was remarked earlier in the text, his reception in the English-speaking world was slow; only after his death in 1926 did his international reputation reach its zenith, and the latter would have been considerably lower if his disciples (Swedish school) had not worked so ardently at disseminating his message. Until the late 1930's the development originated by Wicksell paralleled and in certain respects anticipated the Keynesian variant of monetary theory, but this was largely unknown to Keynes and his disciples.

Wicksell's most famous idea centered around the monetary conditions that trigger a cumulative process, given a certain factor endowment. This contribution, a borderline case in our compartmentalized treatment, could equally well be discussed in Chapter 14, "Business Cycle Theory." At an early stage in his career, Wicksell decided that a concept of monetary demand for output as a whole was needed. Prior

---

[8]On Pigou, see Biographical Note B, Chapter 6. His chief contribution to monetary theory per se, an article entitled "The Value of Money" (*Quarterly Journal of Economics*, November, 1917), is unconditionally Marshallian.

to his *Interest and Prices* (1898, in German, which unfortunately was not translated into English until 1936), practically all economists regarded the rate of interest as a return to physical capital and the money rate as merely derived from the physical rate. Wicksell made the divergence of the money rate from what Marshall called the "real" rate the pivot of his theory on the value of money. He pointed out that if commercial banks keep their loan rate below the "natural" rate — the rate which would be determined by supply and demand if money were dispensed with and all lending were effected in the form of real capital goods — they will stimulate an expansion of production, especially in the form of investment in durable plant and equipment. Sooner or later, with the demand for goods and services increasing, the prices of commodities will rise. As long as the discrepancy between the loan rate and the natural rate is maintained — and this time span in turn depends on the elasticity of the monetary system — there will be no limit to the upward movement of commodity prices. If the banks have large excess reserves and these reserves can be diminished without endangering their solvency, there is no compelling reason for the two rates to move together rapidly. However, the rates will eventually coincide, or tend to coincide. The natural rate, Wicksell pointed out, is not fixed or unalterable, because it depends upon the efficiency of production, the ratio of capital to other factors of production, etc., and it fluctuates along with these magnitudes. The crucial question for Wicksell was whether the catching up of the money rate with the real rate can be achieved rapidly enough to prevent the process of cumulative inflation from getting out of hand — only to be followed by an inevitable, violent downswing. As to the answer he was doubtful, although he felt that bank managers, people of habit and routine, are conscientious individuals who do not unnecessarily engage in reckless ventures. Nevertheless, "during the period of transition, the deviation between the two rates has full play, resulting in that phenomenon. . . which on a superficial view appears to contradict our theory but in reality is in complete accordance with it: prices rise when the rate of interest (the capital rate and *consequently* the money rate) is high and rising, and in the contrary case they fall."[9]

Since Wicksell's theory, with appropriate modifications of assumptions, also explains a cumulative deflation, his fundamental ideas can be broadly paraphrased as follows: At any given time and place, the *normal* rate of interest is such a rate that the general price level has no

---

[9]Knut Wicksell, *Interest and Prices* (London: Macmillan and Co., Ltd., 1936), p. 119.

tendency to move upward or downward. This rate, ultimately determined in its magnitude by the current level of the *natural* rate, tends
to rise and fall with it. If the *money* rate of interest is set and maintained below the normal rate, prices will rise, or fall more slowly and
then rise; whereas if the money rate of interest is set and maintained
above the normal rate, prices will fall, or rise more slowly and then fall.
He realized that both the money and the natural rates, but especially
the latter, are vague conceptions and not subject to statistical verification. For him, however, "the essential point is that the maintenance of
a constant level of prices depends, other things remaining equal, on the
maintenance of a certain rate of interest on loans, and that a permanent
discrepancy between the actual rate and this rate exerts a *progressive
and cumulative* influence on prices."[10]

Unfortunately, Wicksell's concept of a natural rate of interest
proved to be of little use in dynamic analysis, largely because the
fundamental concepts of the purchasing power of income, of savings
and investments, as well as other aggregates, had not been defined with
sufficient clarity. But despite the deficiency of his tools Wicksell must
be credited with a substantial scientific achievement, especially as far
as the structure and character of the price system are concerned. This
achievement rests on the fact that natural (real) rate and money rate,
even though they are equal in equilibrium, could no longer be regarded
as essentially the same thing. While the natural rate may still be
regarded as determined by factors that govern the net return to physical capital, the money rate would henceforth have to be treated as a
distinct variable in its own right, depending only partly on the factors
governing the natural rate. We can express the same idea by saying
that the variable "money interest" thus had to be recognized as something that is not only monetary in *form* but monetary in *nature*. In this
view, the loan policy of banks, and possibly other factors, would appear
as perhaps equally fundamental. Economists now had clear sailing, as
it were, toward a purely monetary, as distinguished from a real, theory
of interest. That Keynes traveled a similar road we already know from
our review of the *General Theory*.

In the wake of analyzing the effects upon prices of interest rates
charged by banks, Wicksell could not help but recognize certain aspects of credit creation, especially the phenomenon of "forced saving,"
which was briefly discussed in the preceding chapter. Whenever bank
credit extension leads to general price increases, as it necessarily will
under conditions of full employment, people whose incomes have not

---

[10]*Ibid.*, pp. 120–121.

risen in proportion will be forced to sacrifice consumption if they are determined to maintain their customary rate of saving. This may be called a form of involuntary saving, although, strictly speaking, forced saving could only be said to take place where, in addition to full employment, there was no margin of saving on the part of fixed income recipients prior to their being confronted with a general price increase.

As far as definition of concepts is concerned, Wicksell was representative of those many Europeans who confined M to metallic money and presumably paper money issued by the government, while interpreting bank notes and deposits as devices for increasing the velocity of "money" (as he used the term in that narrow sense). With regard to the influence upon price levels of autonomous variations in the quantity of money, there was little room in his scheme for *direct* influences of such variations. They would act, for the most part, indirectly, that is, through interest rates, on whose role he placed so much emphasis.

Irving Fisher[11]

Fisher, a native American and perhaps equal in professional stature to another turn-of-the century leader, J. B. Clark, reached the height of his influence around World War I. Generally speaking, his body of original work on money is related to that of Walras and Wicksell. His preeminence was firmly established with *The Purchasing Power of Money* (1911), whose success obscured for some time Fisher's pioneering work on index numbers, published in 1922.

The first one of these two volumes stamped him as a sponsor of one of the more rigid forms of the quantity theory discussed in the preceding section. In *The Purchasing Power of Money* he proposed the famous "compensated dollar," which would combine adoption of the gold-exchange standard with the device of varying the gold content of the monetary unit in accordance with variations of an official price index. As a result, the monetary unit (say, a dollar) would represent a constant quantity of purchasing power instead of a constant quantity of gold. This probably constitutes the most famous among the many proposals that have been advanced in the interest of price stabilization and of mitigation of business cycle fluctuations. Fisher's theory of the purchasing power of money represents the outstanding achievement in marshalling a system of aggregates containing the value of money. He was the first to state the age-old functional relation $P = f(MVT)$

---

[11]See Biographical Note E.

by writing it in the form $P = \dfrac{MV}{T}$, or $MV = PT$. In itself, there was nothing new in linking the price level with the quantity of money in circulation, its velocity, and the physical volume of trade. What Fisher meant, however, was more than just a truism; he stressed the fact that given values of M, V, and T tend to bring about a determined value of P.

The first problem with which he was confronted was an accurate and, if possible, statistically operational definition of the concepts of P, and consequently T. In this respect Fisher's statistical work did not always harmonize with his theoretical preconceptions. As a first-rate mathematician he did not shy away, however, from the heavy work that enabled him to do something more; he introduced checking deposits (M'), with a distinct velocity (V'), separately into his equation, instead of making M bear the burden of everything that buys: coin, government fiat, bank notes, and demand deposits. Nevertheless, he emphasized that deposits and bank notes are fundamentally the same thing. In his refined version the equation of exchange then reads: $MV + M'V' = PT$.

He further assumed a very stable relation between hand-to-hand (or pocket) money and demand (or checking) deposits. He suggested that the variation in the amount of the latter was governed by the variation in the quantity of *primary currency*, that is, that portion of hand-to-hand money which under the then prevailing gold standard was identified with gold. Under assumptions such as these, his compensated-dollar plan made a lot more sense than it does in an age when the link between a nation's monetary gold stock and the amount of deposit "currency" has become extremely tenuous. We must not forget that the compensated-dollar plan was aimed at controlling the price level by appropriate changes in the gold content of the dollar via the control of checking deposits — the most important component of the money supply. Fisher introduced the further hypothesis that in equilibrium there exists a stable relation between bank reserves and the sum total of checking deposits, by which he gave auxiliary support to the compensated-dollar plan.

Fisher admitted the influence of T on both M and V and pointed out that the quantity theory does not hold in what he called "transition periods" between equilibrium positions. If it should be true, as is often argued, that the economic system is practically always in a state of transition (disequilibrium), Fisher for all practical purposes had to abandon his quantity theory, though he may not have been conscious of this.

Further qualifying, he emphasized that M, V, and T are only the "proximate causes" of the price level. He mentioned nearly a dozen indirect influences on purchasing power acting through M, V, and T, such as the division of labor, productive techniques, capital accumulation, and the banking system. There arises the legitimate question of what, if anything, is gained by forcing these indirect causes of price level fluctuations into the straitjacket of three aggregative, independent variables. But in spite of these critical objections, there can be no doubt that Fisher's observations represented the clearest attempt ever made by economists to elucidate the relations between M, V, T, and P.

No less than in the theoretical discussion on the purchasing power of money, Fisher was a leader in working on its statistical complement, the construction of price index numbers. In 1922 he published a monumental work, *The Making of Index Numbers*, methodologically the best that has ever been written on this subject in the United States. It served as a signpost and established guidelines for much of the later work. Growing out of a paper read at a meeting of the American Statistical Association, it assembled the results of a large number of painstaking calculations and presented a more or less exhaustive survey of possible formulae, including the "ideal" formula, $\sqrt{\dfrac{\Sigma p_1 q_0}{\Sigma p_0 q_0} \cdot \dfrac{\Sigma p_1 q_1}{\Sigma p_0 q_1}}$, for which Fisher claimed accuracy within less than one eighth of 1 percent. He also devised a number of "tests" by which he could analyze and classify existing and potential methods, and by which the appropriate index number(s) could be determined for specified conditions. Primarily inductive rather than deductive, his work on index numbers went a long way toward settling the question of how widely the results reached by different possible methods diverged and the reasons for discrepancies.

Fisher was much more than an economist. He commanded a vast realm of knowledge and fostered the intellectual climate of empirical verification which gave American economics a distinctive character.

Gustav Cassel[12]

Cassel, a foremost economist of the Swedish school, deserves brief mention mainly because he undertook a statistical verification for the quantity theory in one of its boldest variants. It revolves about the alleged direct action of gold upon prices. At the end of World War I, the problem of a stable price level assumed a new urgency because

---

[12]See Biographical Note F.

world currencies had been badly upset by the disruption of normal economic intercourse and differing degrees of domestic inflation. In his *Theory of Social Economy* (1923), he first expounded a strict quantity theory for the imaginary case of two disconnected states of an economy equal in all respects except for a difference in M, and hence in P. He stated that nothing can be said a priori about the effects of changes in the quantity of M in the real world; but after investigating the facts, he found that for 1850–1910 the quantity theory holds true. Specifically, according to the Sauerbeck index figures (best known index at that time), the general level of prices was nearly the same in 1850 as in 1910. Since the world's gold stock had approximately increased at an annual rate of 2.8 percent during that sixty-year span, Cassel boldly concluded that T must have a tendency to increase at approximately the same rate. And from this it was only a short step to conclude that there is what he called a "Law of 3 percent," according to which the price level will increase or decrease depending on whether gold production increases the world's gold stock by more or less than 2.8 percent per year. Operating with the concept of a "normal gold supply," he held that ". . . for the period under consideration (1850–1910) *the main cause of the secular variations of the general price level lies in the changes of the relative gold supply* and . . . the quantity theory is right to the extent that the general price level, though it is also influenced by other factors, is directly proportional to the relative gold supply."[13]

This was indeed a peculiar and unconventional application of the quantity theory. His somewhat glib generalization about the relationship between M and T may be countered by the objection that a great number of combinations of the elements entering the equation of exchange is possible, all of which have the same net effect (zero) on the price level as does a given increase in M accompanied by an equal increase in T. For instance, constant P will also result if, with a given increase in M *and* a given increase in V, T increases at the rate corresponding to the *combined* increase in M and V. Or T might not expand, in which case the price level remains the same if the increase in M is offset by an equal decrease in V.

Although the demise of the gold standard in the 1930's would make it futile to try to give further empirical support to the "Law of 3 percent," even if this could be done it would prove little concerning the most desirable international monetary standard. It is not uninteresting

---

[13]Gustav Cassel, *Theory of Social Economy* (New York: Harcourt, Brace & Company, 1923), p. 447.

to note that in the early 1930's Cassel argued for a permanently managed currency system. He claimed that the world's gold supply had failed to keep up with the general increase in production and trade; hence, under a free gold standard, chronic deflation might well result.

Cassel's line of reasoning has more defects than could be conveniently discussed here. Suffice it to say that Wicksell, who died three years after its publication in English, had a rather low opinion of the scientific quality of Cassel's *Theory of Social Economy*.

SALIENT POSTWAR DEVELOPMENTS — A SKETCH

The years falling approximately between the publication of Keynes' *General Theory* (1936) and the conclusion of the Federal Reserve-Treasury Accord (1951) were marked by a relative neglect of monetary theory and a largely passive monetary policy. These developments are attributable in part to the overpowering intellectual impact of the *General Theory* per se and in part to the major role which a fiscal policy come into its own was called upon to play in the circumstances of (1) a lingering depression and (2) the problems of wartime finance and postwar reconstruction.

During the 1950's academic interest in monetary theory was stimulated not only by the rise of nonbank financial intermediaries, but also by legislative hearings and investigations into the working of the financial system of some advanced countries. Some rather exhaustive studies were undertaken, especially in England and the United States, by special commissions of experts representing a broad spectrum of the academic and business world.

Although the recent revival of interest in monetary theory and policy has not been sustained by a unifying theme, such as the collapse of the world economy provided for national fiscal policy, the Walrasian and Wicksellian concern for integration of monetary theory with value theory has continued to dominate the labors of recent years. Wicksell's hint (in his *Interest and Prices*) at what later came to be called the "real balance effect," had first been taken up by Pigou, who in effect pointed out that the volume of money, measured in terms of the general price level, can affect "real" phenomena not only through the rate of interest but also through its effect on desired wealth portfolios. The integration of monetary and value theory through the explicit introduction of real balances as a determinant of behavior became a challenge eliciting a monumentally scholarly contribution from Don Patinkin.[14]   In his

---

[14]See Biographical Note G.

attempt to reformulate Keynesian theory on the basis of classical assumptions, Patinkin demonstrated that money would be neutral if one postulated wage and price flexibility, inelastic expectations, and the absence of money illusion.

Recognition of the problems posed for monetary theory and policy by certain institutional characteristics of the economy and by potential conflicts between diverse governmental policy objectives fired the imagination of others. In particular, they have grappled with the issue of whether monetary authorities have the policy instruments to achieve the expanded range of objectives that they must nowadays consider in fulfilling the mandate of keeping the economy on an even keel but growing rapidly — and if not, whether rules might be superior to discretion. Fruitful advance along this line has necessitated the kind of disaggregation of time series touched upon briefly in the first section of Chapter 9. Specifically, it is asked, how does monetary policy affect the spending and saving decisions of various groups and sectors in the economy?

From the viewpoint of *supply*, one of the lasting institutional transformations of the postwar economy has been the proliferation (and widespread holding) of liquid assets, or money substitutes. Coupled with the idea that there are differences in the behavior between various debtors and creditors and that the financial structure might have some influence on the types of debt issued and held by various groups, this led Gurley and Shaw[15] to inquire anew into the store-of-value function of money. In their well-known book, *Money in a Theory of Finance* (1960), they explore the extent to which various financial intermediaries may issue debts serving as substitutes for money in its store-of-value function. These substitute financial assets, they point out, make possible economies in the use of money, given the need for money to maintain a certain level of income and prices. A corollary of Gurley and Shaw's work was that the determinants of the rate of interest on the supply side included, in addition to the rate of growth of the money stock, the rate of growth of nonbank financial intermediaries. Another corollary concerns the extent to which an increase in the velocity of money, caused by the role played by the intermediaries, may at times offset a central bank's policy of restraint in the growth of the money stock.

Interested alike in *supply and demand*, empirical monetary analysis in the form of accounts for the flow of funds through the economy was also forthcoming in the 1950's. The Federal Reserve System, in

---

[15]See Biographical Note H.

pursuing a line of advance suggested by previous work done at the National Bureau of Economic Research, has produced and revised statistical tables which promise to do for monetary analysis what national income accounts have done for the analysis of real flows. Subdivided by type of asset-debt holders, the flow-of-funds accounts are capable of further extension and refinement.

As to the *demand* side for money, Professor Tobin[16] developed a portfolio approach in which, as in the Keynesian model, saving is largely determined by income, but the types of assets in which savings are held are determined by the relative certainty equivalent yields of these assets. In answer to the question of why any interest balances should be held in cash (rather than in the form of interest-bearing monetary assets), Tobin distinguished two possible sources of liquidity preference: (1) the inelasticity of expectations of future interest rates and (2) the uncertainty about the future of interest rates. Tobin's risk aversion theory of liquidity preference was intended to explain diversification by the same individual between cash and bonds ("consols"), whereas Keynes' liquidity preference theory implies that each investor will hold only one or the other of these assets. Thus Tobin has laid the groundwork for modern theories of portfolio selection in which average return and risk are separately considered.

Tobin's is not the only approach which rationalizes the liquidity preference theory in a multiple asset economy. Milton Friedman[17] developed a neoquantity theory of money that shares with Tobin's analysis the focus on the determinants of the demand for money. The main difference is that Friedman's asset preference theory also comprises the stock of human capital. Treating all factor income as emanating from capital, Friedman made the demand for money depend on the real rate of interest on financial assets, the rate of return on nominal money (which is equated to the rate of change in the price level), real income, the ratio of nonhuman to human capital, and a taste variable. This approach is based in part on the empirical evidence for the United States as elaborated in Friedman's monumental work (coauthored by Anna J. Schwartz) entitled *A Monetary History of the United States, 1867–1960,* published in 1963. Friedman found that over long periods of time the stock of money rises at a higher rate than does money income. He showed that this secular decline in income velocity as real income rises is quite compatible with a rise in income velocity during cyclical expansions as real income rises.

---

[16]See Biographical Note I.
[17]See Biographical Note J.

SUMMARY

In this chapter, after familiarizing ourselves with some of the practical monetary and banking problems that cropped up in the half century before World War I, we pursued the study of the main lines of theoretical advance up to the 1930's. We then examined a few of the peak achievements, most of which were produced by professional economists rather than — as during the first half of the nineteenth century — by outstanding representatives of the world of business. The period under review was one during which the gold standard displaced silver and bimetallic standards in the leading industrial countries. World War I led to its suspension, but it experienced a brief revival in the latter 1920's, only to eventuate in utter collapse during the 1930's.

The analytical work performed in the field of monetary and banking theory was evolutionary in nature rather than — as in value and distribution theory — revolutionary. It was supplemented and supported by numerous factual studies, some of which led to incisive reforms in the institutional structure of society, e.g., the establishment of the Federal Reserve System in the United States. The use of statistics to illuminate and make more precise the important quantitative relationships was pushed vigorously, especially under the leadership of Irving Fisher. His work in the areas of purchasing power and its determinants, as well as the setting up and testing of formulae for the computation of index numbers, was crowned by substantial success and greatly contributed to the enhancement of the international standing of American economics.

Building the analysis of money into a system of general equilibrium was Walras' unique, but at the same time little appreciated, contribution to theoretical advance. Realization of the importance of the distinction between the real (natural) and the money (loan) rate of interest is due to Marshall in England and, more fundamentally, to Wicksell in Sweden. Their disciples in many ways improved upon the findings of these late nineteenth and early twentieth-century masters. Wicksell's theory of the cumulative process triggered by rate discrepancies proved of great value as a catalyst for further research.

Until recently, the classification and treatment of the various components of the total money supply left much to be desired. Especially painful, retrospectively, was the slow maturing and crystallization of thought relative to the nature of checking deposits and to the role of commercial banks as genuine creators of money. There was much confusion as to the nature of the quantity theory of money in relation to the equation of exchange. The latter was expressed in several different ways or variants and, in time, the cash-balance and income approaches drew more attention than the transactions approach. It was Fisher's merit to expand the transactions formula so as to accommodate explicitly checking deposits (M') and their velocity of turnover (V'). Except for providing more detail, $\dfrac{MV + M'V'}{PT}$ is equivalent to $\dfrac{MV}{PT}$. Several important propositions emerged which have been gradually incorporated into the textbooks of the last thirty or so years. Essentially, these are:

(1) In modern complex society, money is not merely a passive agent whose only task is to facilitate the exchange of goods.

(2) The commodity theory of money, especially metallism, has outlived its usefulness because it no longer accurately describes the value of money — though it once did. Specifically, there is no such simple relation between gold and prices as the commodity theory suggests.

(3) The State theory of money, associated with the name of G. F. Knapp, is untenable: fundamentally, money is not what the State says it is.

(4) The equation of exchange — not itself a theory at all but a statement of fact — is the key to whatever may be called the quantity theory of money. It is the basis for various approaches to the study of the value of money.

(5) It is more common for the four terms M, V, T, and P to move together than for some to remain constant while others change.

(6) In its core (but with many possible ramifications or modifications), the quantity theory of money suggests that in the equation of exchange, changes in V and T can safely be ignored, while changes in P are passive. This theory is correct if it no more than purports that the quantity of money (M) is an important factor in determining prices. It is wrong if it purports that M is the *only* important factor and especially if it ignores the fact that price rises may themselves force an increase in the money supply.

(7) The *income K* (Ky), that is, the proportion of its income (net national product) that a country desires to hold in cash, is merely the reciprocal of the income velocity of circulation (Vy) of money.

Finally, we noted that monetary theory went into a kind of eclipse in the 1940's. Revival of interest in it during the last twenty years has been due to the impact of the early postwar and Korean inflations, the persistence of inflation in the face of unemployment in the late 1950's, the recognition of the problems posed by certain institutional characteristics of the financial system, and the potential conflicts between the diverse objectives now accepted as responsibilities of governmental policy.   The general nature of the contributions of Patinkin, Gurley and Shaw, Tobin, and Friedman was briefly considered as representative of major lines of theoretical advance.

BIOGRAPHICAL NOTES

A. — *Georg Friedrich Knapp* (1842–1926) was born in Giessen, Germany. He studied in Munich, at the University of Goettingen, and at the University of Berlin, where he attended Ernst Engel's famous statistical seminar. At the age of twenty-five he was appointed head of the Municipal Statistical Office of Leipzig; his scientific prowess was soon rewarded academically by his being appointed professor extraordinary at the university in the same city.   In 1874 he was appointed full professor of economics at the University of Strasbourg, where he remained until 1919.

Knapp was as much a statistician as he was an economist.   His first focus of professional interest was the methodological principles of population statistics.   Viewing statistics merely as a tool in the realistic study of the most diverse phenomena, he was at the same time acutely conscious of the limitations of statistical observations.   In 1869 he published a systematic theory of mortality measurement, based on empirical research in the province of Saxonia.   Five years later appeared his *Theory of Population Change*.   But his masterpiece was a two-volume work of "institutionalist" complexion entitled *Emancipation of Peasants and the Origin of the Rural Workers in the Older Parts of Prussia* (1887).

In about 1895, he began to devote himself to the study of money, but it was not until 1905 that his *State Theory of Money*, which raised him to international fame, was published. He was not truly at home in economic theory; the influence of the book on monetary theory and practice in Germany was far greater than was merited.   It was enough of a popular success, however, to be translated into English in 1924.

B. — *Henry Dunning Macleod* (1821–1902) was a self-taught economist who, upon discovering certain problems that had been neglected by orthodox economists, felt it to be his task to rebuild the science from its foundations.

The son of a Scottish landowner, he was trained as a lawyer. At an early age he recommended and successfully established the first poor law union in Scotland. In 1854 he accepted a directorship of the Royal British Bank. It was then that he began to display a more than peripheral interest in economics and, through extensive historical and theoretical studies, began to make up for the lack of a formal education in the subject. Strangely enough, his most important in a series of writings on economics, *The Theory and Practice of Banking*, appeared in the following year. Its major focus was an exposition of the historical development of the policy of the Bank of England. In it he revealed himself as an adherent of the Bullion Report and as very discerning with respect to the role of discount policy. In this work, he became the first to give a detailed account of the process by which bank credit is created; however, he did not advocate unsound maxims of monetary policy.

Subsequently, he attempted to reconstruct economics and to obtain a university chair, but his ability proved insufficient — he was unable to put his many good ideas in a professionally acceptable form. Unfortunately, the leading economists of the day did not give him credit even for his real contribution in *The Theory and Practice of Banking*. Barred from their circles, his distaste for the Classical school became even more acute. (Failure of his bank in 1856 had made his position more vulnerable.) He managed to get one of two projected volumes of a *Dictionary of Political Economy* published between 1858 and 1863. He further extended the foundations of the theory of money and banking in his *Lectures on Credit and Banking* (1882) and *The Theory of Credit* (1889–91).

Even these later works remained completely outside the bounds of recognized economics. Yet his perseverance must have been remarkable, for his *Elements of Political Economy*, first published in 1858, went through two additional editions before his death. Though his reception in England was poor, Macleod did find some recognition abroad, especially in France.

C. — *Sir Ralph Hawtrey* (1879–   ), who was knighted in 1956, is another star in the galaxy of the few still-living Cambridge economists who were at their best in the interwar period. He was educated at Eton and Trinity College, Cambridge, and entered the Admiralty in 1903. During most of his professionally active life, he served with the British Treasury (1904 to 1945); he was Director of Financial Enquiries roughly between the end of the first and the end of the second world wars. On special leave from the Treasury, he lectured on economics at Harvard University in 1928–29. He was Price Professor of International Economics at the Royal Institute of International Affairs from 1947 to 1952. At the time he was appointed, he had served the first year of a two-year term as President of the Royal Economic Society. He was made an Honorary Fellow of Trinity College, Cambridge, in 1959.

Hawtrey may well have been the most prolific author among the Cambridge graduates of Keynes' generation. The approximately half of his works that have gone through two or more editions include the following: *Currency and Credit* (1919), *Monetary Reconstruction* (1923), *The Gold Standard in Theory and Practice* (1927), *Economic Aspects of Sovereignty* (1930), *Trade Depression and the Way Out* (1931), *The Art of Central Banking* (1932), and *Capital and Employment* (1937). Hawtrey has an honorary D.Sc. degree in economics from the University of London.

D. — *Sir Dennis H. Robertson* (1890–1963), famous for his witty and entertaining style, studied at the same institutions of higher education as Hawtrey, was knighted three years before the latter, and served as Hawtrey's successor in the presidency of the Royal Economic Society from 1948 to 1950.

Robertson received about a half-dozen honorary degrees from institutions in almost as many countries. He was a Reader in Economics at Cambridge University from 1930–38, then occupied an endowed chair for six years at the University of London; from 1944 to 1957, when he retired, he was professor of political economy at Cambridge. During World War II he served as Treasury Advisor and has assisted on various governmental commissions. He was a Fellow of Trinity College, Cambridge, through most of his life.

His numerous book publications include: *A Study of Industrial Fluctuation* (1915), the best seller *Money* (1922), *Banking Policy and the Price Level* (1926), *Essays in Monetary Theory* (1940), *Britain in the World Economy* (1954), *Economic Commentaries* (1956), and *Lectures on Economic Principles* (3 vols., 1957–59).

E. — *Irving Fisher* (1867–1947) was a restless man, a man of voracious intellectual appetites and insatiable interests. Throughout a half century of assiduous striving he was too absorbed by urgent tasks to find opportunity for a synthesis, that is, to expound his thought in a systematic and comprehensive treatise. As a result, he founded no school, had no disciples.

Born in the state of New York, he entered Yale University as a mathematics student in 1884, won a number of prizes, and was deeply influenced by the famous William Graham Sumner, who suggested that he combine mathematics with economics. He graduated in 1888 and four years later had finished a Ph.D. thesis that was to prove of enduring worth: *Mathematical Investigations in the Theory of Value and Prices* (1892). At that time he had already joined the Yale staff as a tutor, and he remained associated with his Alma Mater until 1935, having become a full professor when only thirty-one years old. After his marriage in 1893, he spent a year in Europe and established contacts with the leading economists of the Old World. He was well received by Edgeworth and Pareto — indeed, no small compliment.

It was his sustained ambition to mold statistics into a better instrument toward making economics into a genuine science. Statistical method was to him part of economic theory and no longer a mere adjunct to it. In a sense he was the first econometrician of the Western Hemisphere. The success of his endeavor to fuse allied fields is manifested by the fact that, at one time or another, Fisher was president of the American Economic Association, the Econometric Society, and the American Statistical Association, that he was on the board of directors of numerous organizations, and that a number of his publications were translated into several foreign languages.

His *Mathematical Investigations* was a precocious and masterful presentation of Walrasian analysis and contained the fundaments of indifference curve analysis. In his *Nature of Capital and Income* (1906) he presented the first economic theory of accounting and the basis of modern income analysis: he distinguished between income as a flow of goods and services over time and capital as a stock of goods at a given time. In 1907 appeared his *The Rate of Interest* which, reworked, was published again in

1930 under the title, *The Theory of Interest*, a pedagogical masterpiece. It was highlighted by an exposition of the "impatience" theory of interest and the concept of the marginal efficiency of capital, which he called the "marginal rate of return over cost." *The Purchasing Power of Money* (1911) and *The Making of Index Numbers* (1922) have been noted in the text. *Booms and Depressions* featured his monetary theory of the business cycle. These are the more important of his works oriented to the specialist. In addition to numerous articles he also wrote a number of books addressed to the general public, including undergraduate students in economics.

His manifold reformist activities tended to divert attention from Fisher's genuinely scientific performance and, despite the above named honors, prevented him from attaining the stature of perhaps the greatest scientific economist in the United States during the first three decades of this century. Reaction to his "compensated dollar," "100% reserve against deposits," etc., was either lukewarm or hostile. His lively, dauntless, and evangelistic interest in social welfare projects was not incompatible with his capitalistic outlook; but his dabbling in eugenics, the temperance movement, and mental health (for example, a *Report on National Vitality* [1908]), was found odd, to say the least. He was a lifelong health faddist.

F.—*Gustav Cassel* (1866–1945), born in Sweden, earned the degree of doctor of philosophy in 1894 from the University of Stockholm. Only then was he drawn into economic studies. In 1898 he felt the need to go beyond autodidactic efforts but found the teaching at German universities rather barren — the Historical school, so-called, was paramount while Cassel was chiefly interested in economic theory. In 1901 he turned to England and took up contacts with Marshall, Edgeworth, and other leading British economists. The influence on him of Fabian socialists like Sidney and Beatrice Webb was reflected in a little book, *Social Policy*, published in Swedish in 1902. There appeared in the following year *Nature and Necessity of Interest*, in which his views on economic theory began to take definite shape. Much of his subsequent scientific interest was oriented to practical problems of the day, especially those of a monetary nature.

In 1907 he was appointed to a chair of political economy at the University of Stockholm and four years later began to devote himself intensively to his magnum opus, *Theory of Social Economy*, whose publication (in German) was delayed by the war until 1918. Its translation into English in revised form is dated 1923. Obsessed with the idea of giving his thoughts quantitative definiteness, he avoided some serious errors; and, thanks to his skills as a simplifier, he succeeded admirably in presenting his ideas in a clear and perspicuous way. This touch of lucidity was an important factor in the international acclaim of his writings. In contrast to Walras, whose work otherwise bore a striking resemblance to his own, Cassel purposely shied away from involved mathematical exposition; he even attempted to banish the concept of marginal utility from economic theory and advocated the scrapping of everything behind demand functions. The fundamental lines of Cassel's analytic structure were unmistakably Walrasian. The fact that Cassel owed to Walras more than he was inclined to admit was very unfavorably commented upon by Wicksell, Schumpeter, and others.

In the early 1920's, when he wrote *Money and Foreign Exchange after 1914*, Cassel attained the reputation of an expert for his ideas on monetary policy and for a few years became the most influential international leader of our science. At this time, when the foreign exchange markets were disrupted, he presented his purchasing power parity theory of exchange rates, which will be briefly discussed in Chapter 13. Cassel had a considerable share in the relative stabilization of the European economy which was attained in the mid-1920's. Unlike Keynes, he advocated return to the gold standard, though he was by no means blind to the objections to such a course of action. His somewhat one-sided explanation of the causes of the Great Depression — failure of gold supply to increase in about the same proportion as production and trade — caused his international prestige to recede. He was unable to present his ideas in a form in tune with the special problems of the 1930's.

Though his power as a theorist was spent, he remained what he had been for some forty years — a very frequent contributor to the *Svenska Dagbladet* (a Swedish newspaper) and a moulder of informed economic opinion in his home country. But he will be remembered mainly as a "system-builder" of strictly limited success.

G.—*Don Patinkin* (1922–   ), perhaps the most famous Jewish economist outside the United States, has been a full professor at the Eliezer Kaplan School of Economics and Social Sciences at Hebrew University since 1957. He has shouldered additional responsibilities as Director of the Maurice Falk Institute for Economic Research in Jerusalem, Israel.

Born in the United States and educated at the University of Chicago (Ph.D., 1947), he was first an assistant professor at his Alma Mater and then an associate professor at the University of Illinois, before becoming a lecturer at Hebrew University in 1949.

Patinkin is the author of a text widely used on the graduate level, *Money, Interest, and Prices* (1st ed., 1956; 2d ed., 1965) and of empirical works relating to the Israel economy, as well as of numerous articles in professional journals.

H.—*John G. Gurley* (1920–   ) received his A.B. and Ph.D. degrees from Stanford University in 1943 and 1951 respectively. After serving at Princeton University, the University of Maryland, and on the staff of the Brookings Institution, Gurley in 1961 returned to Stanford University, with the rank of full professor. Prior to publication of the jointly authored work mentioned in the text, Gurley also coauthored with Shaw an article published in the *American Economic Review* in 1955 ("Financial Aspects of Economic Development"). He was managing editor of the *American Economic Review* for several years.

Edward S. Shaw (1908–   ) also holds academic degrees from Stanford University (Ph.D., 1936). He has been a member of the faculty there ever since 1929 — a decade or so before Gurley became a student — has held full professor rank since 1941, and has served as head of the economics department on various occasions. He has been a consultant to the Board of Governors of the Federal Reserve System and to the United States Treasury Department, and a member of the advisory board of the Commission on Money and Credit. Shaw is the independent author of several works, including *Money, Income, and Monetary Policy* (1950). Along with Milton Friedman, of the University of Chicago (see Biographical Note J), Shaw has been a leading proponent of the "Chicago school" position — established earlier by the late Henry Simons of the University of Chicago — that monetary policy should be executed in accordance with a fixed rule. He thus represents the minority view in the dispute which has raged for a number of years regarding the question: Should human judgment determine the proper course of action of central bankers, or should a set of rules (formulas) be established which automatically indicate the direction monetary policy should take under differing circumstances?

I.—*James Tobin* (1918–   ) received his B.A., M.A., and Ph.D. degrees from Harvard University in the years 1939, 1940, and 1947. He was awarded an LL.D. degree from Syracuse University in 1967. After a few years as a teaching fellow and member of the Society of Fellows at Harvard University, Tobin became an associate professor of economics at Yale University in 1950, was promoted to full professor in 1955, and given an endowed chair in 1957.

Recipient of the John Bates Clark medal of the American Economic Association in 1955, Tobin was elected president of the Econometric Society in 1958 and vice president of the American Economic Association in 1964. He served on the Council of Economic Advisers during part (1961–62) of the Kennedy Administration. Author of *National Economic Policy* (1960) and of numerous articles in professional journals, Tobin also served as editor or associate editor of leading professional journals.

J.—*Milton Friedman* (1912–   ) earned B.A. and M.A. degrees from Rutgers University and the University of Chicago in 1932 and 1933, and a Ph.D. degree from Columbia University in 1946. He has been a member of the research staff of the National Bureau of Economic Research most of the time since 1937.

During World War II Friedman did research work for the United States Treasury Department and at Columbia University. In 1946 he joined the faculty of economics at the University of Chicago, where he became a full professor in 1948 and has held an endowed chair since 1962. Among many other honors, he was a recipient of the John Bates Clark medal of the American Economic Association in 1951 and president of this organization in 1967. His excellent academic credentials have earned him such deep respect that his reputation has not suffered from unpopular political views which he has occasionally embraced. (Friedman has been perhaps the strongest advocate of a return to free markets in an institutional framework which for a long time has been out of tune with old-fashioned liberal views.)

Friedman's best known works include *Essays in Positive Economics* (1953), *A Theory of the Consumption Function* (1957), *A Program for Monetary Stability* (1960), and *A Monetary History of the United States, 1867–1960* (1963). He served as editor of the famous *Studies in the Quantity Theory of Money* (1956).

Questions for Review and Research

1. Why, during the last three decades of the nineteenth century, was there an increasing number of economists and politicians who advocated (international) bimetallism?
2. Which economist(s) contributed most to making the theory of money simply a part of the theory of general economic equilibrium?
3. What is meant by the adjective "neutral" as applied to money?
4. Who explained the value of money in terms of the sanction which it receives from the government? When and where was this theory in vogue?
5. Since when (approximately) have checking (demand) deposits been regarded as a component of the total money supply? What, if anything, did the velocity concept have to do with the modernization of thought in this area?
6. Explain the differences between the quantity theory of money and the equation of exchange.
7. What do the cash-balance approach and the income approach to the study of the value of money have in common?
8. What do you know about the maturation of a realistic conception of the nature of bank credit?
9. Was Walras interested in practical monetary reform? Explain.
10. Show that the "income K" is merely the reciprocal of the income velocity of money.
11. Summarize Wicksell's interest rate theory.
12. In which works did Fisher present (a) his refined version of the equation of exchange? (b) his "ideal" index number formula?

Recommended Readings

American Economic Association. *Readings in Monetary Theory*. Blakiston series of republished articles on economics, Vol. 5. Homewood, Illinois: Richard D. Irwin, Inc., 1951. The selections "A Note on the Theory of Money," by D. H. Robertson, pp. 156–161, and "Money and Index Numbers," by R. G. Hawtrey, pp. 129–155.

Fisher, Irving. *The Making of Index Numbers, a Study of Their Varieties, Tests, and Reliability*. Boston: Houghton Mifflin Company, 1922. Chapter I, "Introduction," pp. 1–10; Chapter II, "Six Types of Index Numbers Compared," pp. 11–42; Chapter XVII, "Summary and Outlook," pp. 350–369.

——————. *The Purchasing Power of Money*, Rev. ed. New York City: The Macmillan Company, 1916. Chapter II, "Purchasing Power of

Money as Related to the Equation of Exchange," pp. 8–32; Chapter III, "Influence of Deposit Currency on the Equation and Therefore on Purchasing Power," pp. 33–54; Chapter IV, "Disturbance of Equation and of Purchasing Power During Transition Periods," pp. 55–73; Chapters V and VI, "Indirect Influences on Purchasing Power," pp. 74–111.

Friedman, Milton.   "The Quantity Theory of Money — A Restatement," *Studies in the Quantity Theory of Money*, edited by Milton Friedman. Chicago: University of Chicago Press, 1956. Chapter 1, pp. 3–21.

Gurley, John G., and Edward S. Shaw.   "Financial Intermediaries and the Saving-Investment Process." *Journal of Finance*, Vol. 11 (March, 1956), pp. 257–276.

Marshall, Alfred.   *Money, Credit, and Commerce*. London: Macmillan and Co., Ltd., 1923. Book I, "Money": Chapters I–IV, pp. 1–50.

Patinkin, Don.   "A Critique of Neoclassical Monetary Theory," from *Money, Interest, and Prices*, 2d ed. New York City: Harper & Row, Publishers, 1965.

Tobin, James.   "Liquidity Preference as Behavior towards Risk," *Review of Economic Studies*, Vol. 25 (February, 1958), pp. 65–86.

Wicksell, Knut.   *Interest and Prices, a Study of the Causes Regulating the Value of Money*, with an introduction by Bertil Ohlin.   Reprints of Economic Classics.   New York: Augustus M. Kelley, 1962.   Chapter 5, "The Quantity Theory and Its Opponents," pp. 38–50; Chapter 7, "The Rate of Interest as Regulator of Commodity Prices," pp. 81–101; Chapter 8, "The Natural Rate of Interest on Capital and the Rate of Interest on Loans," pp. 102–121; Chapter 9, "Systematic Exposition of the Theory," pp. 122–156.

INTERNATIONAL TRADE THEORY

Mercantilists and Classicists

Perhaps more so than any of the other topical areas that eventually constituted a hard core of economic principles, the field of international trade was first closely studied, reflected upon, and written about by men of affairs, in private or governmental employment, as part of an effort to increase the wealth and power of the nation with which these men tended to identify their own welfare. Adam Smith, critical and contemptuous of their beliefs, dubbed the body of doctrines worked out by them the "mercantile system," and its exponents are generally known as *Mercantilists*.

Attempts to trace modern ideas on foreign trade to ancient writings can easily be pushed too far. In a vague sense, the idea that trade takes place according to natural advantages was already understood by the educated of Plato's and Aristotle's generations. But in view of the tendency of these philosophers to subordinate economic affairs to "higher" interests, we should not expect to, and cannot, find more than a few hints to indicate the general direction that the discussion of foreign trade issues would take at the dawn of the New Era — the period, beginning at the turn of the sixteenth century, witnessing the rapid expansion of Western Europe's trade horizon — and especially following the Commercial Revolution of the sixteenth century. For the economic thought of the Middle Ages, when life was marked by a high degree of self-sufficiency, had not been favorable to a substantial accretion of analytic conquests either. If domestic trade lent itself to the practice of usury, there is no reason why this should not also hold true for foreign trade and why the latter, therefore, should not also be regarded with suspicion. (Remember that for St. Thomas usury was not merely what modern economists call "pure interest"; it also covered any injustice in trade, any violation of the "just price.")

With the emergence of mercantilism in the sixteenth century, an extensive body of literature dealing with our subject matter appeared, although we must add immediately that it yielded relatively few *lasting* contributions to international trade theory.

FOREIGN TRADE IN THE MERCANTILIST SCHEME OF THOUGHT

We will first attempt to catch the basic flavor of mercantilist reasoning and then turn to a few "star performers."

In General

The most pervasive and most emphasized doctrine was the importance of bringing about and maintaining an *excess of exports over imports*, for that was the only way for a country without gold and silver mines to increase its stock of the precious metals. The evolution of trade was paralleled by the formation of a new *terminology* to denote both old and new concepts. For example, it was in the early part of the seventeenth century that the term "balance of trade" was coined for a concept that was already common in the sixteenth century; yet the term "favorable balance of trade," or its equivalent, did not pass into common usage until the eighteenth century. In the seventeenth century there was much controversy about the methods to be used to attain an accumulation of specie. The so-called Bullionists advocated restrictions on, or the prohibition of, the export of bullion, in other words, regulating transactions in the exchanges; whereas the more moderate among the Mercantilists sought the same results indirectly by controlling imports and exports of merchandise.

It should be noted that inasmuch as there was controversy about the state of balances with particular countries, it was always in terms of their bearing on a country's aggregate balance; that is, particular balances, such as that of England with the East Indies, were judged in terms of their contribution to the total balance. Most of the writers in the second half of the seventeenth century and in the eighteenth century pointed out that allowance must be made for noncommodity items in explaining the net balance payable in bullion (or coin). A clear distinction between the *balance of trade* and the *balance of payments*, as these terms are used today, was lacking until after the middle of the eighteenth century, and the term *balance of indebtedness* did not become part of the economics vocabulary until the nineteenth century.

The desire for a "favorable" balance of trade was never based by mercantilist writers on a desire to see their countries engage in capital export, to make investments abroad. This fact lends support to the widespread charge that many Mercantilists, even if they did not mean to attribute value to the precious metals *alone*, were at least confused as to the *difference between money and wealth*. Contrary to Adam Smith, however, there were a few among them who were never guilty of an identification of the two concepts. Generally, they did raise the precious metals to a status which gold and silver had never enjoyed before and would enjoy no longer after the onset of the Industrial Revolution. With varying emphases, they viewed these metals as performers of many different functions, among them: to build up a state treasure as an emergency reserve; to serve as the most practical form in which wealth could be accumulated, such wealth accumulation being the chief objective of economic activity; to serve as the material embodiment of thrift; to stimulate trade by increased circulation from hand to hand, with possibly an additional fillip from price increases.

While most of the mercantilist arguments for a "favorable" balance of trade rested on the desirability of more bullion, there was one, the *employment argument*, which was not so motivated. In the early part of the seventeenth century, it was already held by some that, since exports were the product of domestic labor, whereas imports displaced such labor, the maximization of employment could be attained by maximizing exports and minimizing imports. It was this line of reasoning which had the most staying power, inasmuch as it constitutes even today a by-no-means-negligible element of protectionism. Furthermore, the employment argument was conducive to an appraisal of exports and imports not only in terms of their value but in terms of the quantity of labor each represented. This is why exports of manufactured goods were rated most highly, or why imports of raw materials were considered less undesirable than imports of finished goods. The stress on employment led a few of the later writers to conceive of a *balance of labor* and to deemphasize the balance-of-trade concept, in which the amounts weighed against each other were the values of exports and the values of imports. Instead, to compute the balance of labor they would compare the amount of domestic labor embodied in exports with the amount of foreign labor represented by imports. While both the balance-of-trade doctrine and the balance-of-labor doctrine are unsound as long-run propositions, the latter explains better than does the former the mercantilist endorsement of rapid population growth and a low level of wages. Low wages were advocated specifically as a means of stimulating workers to greater effort and of increasing a country's competitive strength by lowering the money costs of its products. We will now move on to a few of the more prominent contributions to international trade theory — a term denoting a still embryonic fund of theoretical knowledge.

Individual Contributions

Mun.[1] — Thomas Mun was one of the first to deal extensively with the *balance of international trade*. Writing in the seventeenth century, he described in detail the ways and means by which to maximize commodity exports and to minimize the domestic consumption of commodities produced abroad, listing, for example, the need to moderate or abolish duties on the export of native commodities and to impose or increase duties on imported manufactures other than those for reexport.

More important, a beginning was made by Mun toward a description and conceptualization of the *balance of international payments*. Specifically, he was able to show that a nation's earnings were increased not only by the sale of material economic goods but also via the sale of numerous services — freight earnings, marine insurance payments, Catholic remittances to Rome, travelers' expenses, and many more — to foreign countries. In fact, he listed almost all of the "invisible items" which would be included in a representative balance-of-payments statement of today. Thus a nation which despite an all-out effort might not achieve a surplus in its balance of trade could still avoid a deficit in its balance of payments. To this end it would, for example, build a merchant marine to serve not only the needs of its own foreign traders but also those of third countries. We see, then, that the accumulation of gold and silver as an intermediate or ultimate objective could be attained in many ways, and Mun's flexibility enabled him to be open-minded concerning the available means. It is not surprising, therefore, that as a spokesman for the East India Company, which in the seventeenth century tended to import more from than it exported to the East Indies, Mun was one of the early anti-Bullionists. His defense of its practices was not entirely selfless, however, as it was also designed to ward off hostile measures against the company.

Mun was one of the few early writers who, in dealing with trade matters extensively, made use of the *employment argument*. To foster the reexport or entrepôt trade and to win the carrying trade away from the Dutch, he advocated specially favorable customs treatment of goods imported for reexport. On the constant complaint of many Mercantilists that England was suffering from "scarcity of money" he heaped ridicule.

---

[1]See Biographical Note A.

Misselden.[2]—Another English anti-Bullionist of renown, whose view in the controversy over the exchanges at the beginning of the seventeenth century eventually won a victory, was Edward Misselden. The term "balance of trade" probably made its first appearance in a pamphlet of his, published in 1623. He inveighed against customs duties imposed on English exports for fiscal reasons as inconsistent with mercantilist doctrine. He explained that foreign-exchange rates were established in the same way as the prices of any other goods, pointing out how they fluctuate around an equilibrium point — called *mint par* — according to changes in supply and demand for foreign exchange. And he anticipated Smith in the formulation of the principle that man in pursuing his own ends was at the same time promoting the general good, that unregulated trade was therefore fundamentally desirable.

Petty.—Petty, who perhaps better than any other writer of the late seventeenth century illustrates the tenacity with which mercantilist thought patterns attached themselves even to independent, progressive, and creative minds, viewed *export duties* primarily as a means to provide the sovereign with additional revenue. His line of reasoning is interesting because it provides the counterpart of the cost-of-production argument for protective import duties, advanced much later. He would recommend "outward customs" whenever the cost of production of an exportable commodity is much less than the competitive price at which it can be sold abroad. His argument is based on the further desideratum that domestic labor should not earn more than its bare subsistence. He was aware that a policy of heavy export duties might induce traders to smuggle and bribe but apparently did not assess this danger as overly great. With all his emphasis on exports, he was yet not unmindful of the fact that a continuing surplus, accompanied by an inflow of precious metals, could be harmful to a country's cost and price structure, and at one point he went so far as to recommend the sale of surplus gold abroad. He advocated freeing merchants engaged in re-exporting commodities from the inconvenience and expense of the *drawback system* — the procedure of making application for a refund of previously paid import duties — and thus to enable them to compete more effectively with foreign sellers. He stressed saving above all other means of acquiring wealth.

North.[3]—North undertook a vigorous attack aimed at ridding the discussion of foreign trade matters from mercantilist "superstitions."

[2]See Biographical Note B.
[3]See Biographical Note C.

He has fittingly been called the first *free trader* in the Smithian sense, for he identified private profit with the public good, suggesting that foreign commerce is not undertaken unless both trading parties have good reason to expect a betterment of their position as a result of trading transactions. Viewing the whole world rather than a single nation as an economic unit, he may, with respect to his discussion of international economic intercourse, be regarded as the outstanding predecessor of Adam Smith. North also presented a concise formulation of the automatic and self-regulating mechanism which provides a nation with that sum of money required for carrying on its trade. He failed to explain the international distribution of money, a task which was later taken on by Hume. But he pointed out, and helped overcome, the common confusion between money and what can be bought with it.

Cantillon.—Cantillon deflated mercantilist tenets by showing that if a country continues to sell more than it buys from abroad, money will successively flow into it and, as a first consequence, land and labor in the export-surplus country will become more expensive. Thus the advantage which it enjoyed by virtue of the fact that it could exchange a smaller quantity of land and labor for a larger one from abroad will in time have disappeared. By the same token, a country abounding in resources of gold and silver will see this natural wealth dissipated among many other trading nations as it buys more from abroad than it sells there. Cantillon brilliantly revealed not only why it is difficult for a country to maintain an active balance of trade, but also some of the *secondary income effects of a foreign trade balance,* a subject developed not much further until the twentieth century.

To be sure, Bodin had anticipated much of the price effects of the flow of precious metals across national boundaries; it remained for Cantillon, however, to weave the strands of value and foreign-trade theory into a consistent fabric.

He also made a significant start at explaining the exchange-rate mechanism. He pointed out that under conditions of unfettered international economic relations the exchange rate tends to be above or below par by the amount which it would cost to send money (precious metals) abroad or have it imported from foreign countries, foreshadowing the specie-point analysis by Torrens. He also recognized that a prohibition to export or import the precious metals would permit the rate of exchange to move much further away from the par of exchange than would otherwise be the case. Finally, he provided the first known example of a *triangular exchange,* that is, a set of commercial relations in which three countries owe and are owed, as between pairs of them, the same amount. Thus if country A owes country B the same amount as is owed to A by country C, which in turn is a creditor of country B, no metallic money need flow out of any of these nations, because bills of exchange can be used to cancel the various debts.

Hume.—Hume greatly helped to piece together the theory of self-regulating international trade, but he went beyond Cantillon in pointing out why a country could not permanently have a "favorable" or "unfavorable" balance of trade. Specifically, he stated the *theory of the self-regulating mechanism* with a much greater degree of clarity and incorporated it more consistently with the remainder of his work than was the case with any of the earlier or contemporary writers. He included the influence of exchange-rate fluctuations on commodity trade in the mechanism as an additional equilibrating factor.

Conceding the stimulating influence on manufacturing of an increasing amount of money in circulation, he was especially interested in the repercussions through time of an "unfavorable" balance of trade. In this case, the loss of some of its treasure by a country would in time pull down its domestic prices, whereas the inflow of treasure accompanying a "favorable" balance would not fail in time to push them up. An increase in paper money would not succeed in maintaining an import balance because, this money not being acceptable abroad, the country with the import balance would in time simply be drained of precious metals needed to pay for excess purchases. He spotted the fluctuations in the foreign exchanges within the limits of the specie points as an additional, though minor, factor operating to correct "a wrong balance of trade." Thus, if a country's trade balance was unfavorable, the exchanges would move against it (the exchange rate would rise), and this would again encourage exports. In sum, if any one man had to be designated as *the* originator of the classical theory of the mechanism of international trade, the honor would almost certainly fall to Hume.

Quesnay. — Although Quesnay was the founder of the Physiocratic school rather than an enlightened Mercantilist, we will discuss him, as well as Condillac, in the present section. In all probability heavily indebted to Cantillon, Quesnay brought out the fact that the state of the balance of trade between nations is no indicator of the advantages of foreign commerce nor of the wealth of nations. It may well be that poor countries have relatively less domestic trade and engage in relatively more trading with foreign lands than do wealthy nations. An assessment of a nation's wealth is possible only through a joint

study of its foreign *and* domestic commerce. Quesnay's assertion —
that in foreign trade nations which sell the most necessary or most
useful commodities are at an advantage over those that sell luxury
goods — was more significant because he was not inspired by a mere desire to further undermine mercantilist fallacies or shortcomings. Of
course, this proposition lacks the necessary precision. It further rests on
the farfetched assumption that only an *excess* supply of necessities over
the quantity that can be usefully consumed at home would be offered
for sale abroad, allowing the country to import luxuries in exchange.
Hence consumption of luxuries at home would be ultimately geared
to the ability of a country to produce beyond the requirements for the
satisfaction of basic needs. Unfortunately, Quesnay creates the impression that foreign commerce is prima facie disadvantageous because
the costs of goods sold to or bought from foreign countries will, *ceteris
paribus*, be higher than the costs of those bought or sold at home. The
trouble, of course, is that the *ceteris paribus* clause will be condemned
to a shadow-like existence in this context once countries awaken to the
potential for increasing real income all around through a stepped-up
international division of labor. In this respect Quesnay was not able
to build successfully on the foundations laid by Cantillon and Hume.

Condillac. — Condillac applied his utility theory to international
trade and demonstrated that what holds true for exchange between
two persons is largely applicable also to commerce between nations.
The inequality of subjective valuations he saw reflected, on a larger
scale, in the total exchange transactions between nations. He decried
the foolishness of establishing trade barriers because it is in the very
nature of exchange that both parties will benefit — what is offered for
sale always being valued less highly than what is acquired in return.
If each nation insisted on selling only, they would all eventually wind
up without foreign trade and deprive themselves of its benefits.
Condillac went beyond his predecessors Hume and Cantillon in showing
that even if other nations continue putting up obstacles to international
exchange it will be advantageous for a particular country to adhere to
free-trade principles. He concludes, somewhat optimistically, that
when trading enjoys complete and permanent liberty wealth is bound
to spread everywhere.

ADAM SMITH

We mentioned at the beginning of this chapter the *negative side* of
Smith's contribution to the topic under discussion. His was probably

the boldest attack on the "mercantile system," which was already tottering both because economic change had given some of its doctrines an antiquarian flavor and because the piecemeal invalidations of these doctrines by the many forerunners of economic liberalism hardly left it a "leg to stand on." All the same, without Smith's vigorous, forceful, and systematic statement of its weaknesses, it might have lingered on much longer than it did.

On the *positive side*, Smith was unfortunately not capable of precisely formulating a general theory of international trade. Apart from his building up an imposing structure of arguments in favor of freedom from restrictions on foreign-trade activities, his contributions to the subject matter under discussion were relatively minor. Smith somewhat lightly assumed that international trade required a producer of exports to have an *absolute* advantage in production. That this is not so should become amply clear from a study of the remaining sections of this chapter.

Much as Smith was aware of the benefits of free trade and was able to influence British economic thought and policy in the nineteenth century, he was *not an unqualified free trader*. He singled out two *primary* cases which in his view justified the imposition of barriers on imports for the purpose of encouraging domestic industry.

First, some particular industry or industries may be necessary for the defense of a country. From this point of view, the British Navigation Acts, inasmuch as they promoted the building up of a merchant marine to be used in peace and war alike, were perfectly sensible. Mid-twentieth century laws providing for subsidies for the construction and operation of a fleet of vessels may be viewed as a modern application of Smith's principle that "... defence ... is of much more importance than opulence."[4] The *second* case is an application of the principle that normally competitive conditions should not be distorted by government intervention. Consequently, it will be proper to place a burden on foreign industry if this merely neutralizes the disadvantage under which domestic industry operates because it is burdened with some tax from which foreign producers are exempt. After the imposition of a "matching" tariff duty, a form of equalizing adjustment, no larger portion of domestic labor and capital would be devoted to the particular domestic industry of a country than what would naturally go to it. "It would only hinder any part of what would naturally go to it from being turned away by the tax, into a less natural direction. . . ."[5] Smith does

---

[4]Adam Smith, *An Inquiry into the Nature and Causes of the Wealth of Nations* (New York: E. P. Dutton and Co., 1776), p. 352.
[5]*Ibid.*, p. 353.

not underrate the difficulty arising from the fact that imported commodities are seldom perfect equivalents of the domestically produced
variety. He warns of the danger that domestic interests will clamor for
the taxation of all those goods imported from abroad which can enter
into competition, however remote, with any products of domestic industry. Some of the extensions of the Reciprocal Trade Agreements
Act in this country bear vivid testimony to the apparent timelessness
of this truth.

The author of the *Wealth of Nations* took up two *secondary* cases in
which he held it to be a "matter of deliberation" whether or not to
follow a laissez-faire policy. The *first* deals with the advisability, pro
and con, of imposing a retaliatory duty designed to bring about the
repeal of a duty imposed by a foreign country. The success of taking
such a step, Smith holds, will always be open to guess; and, unless the
odds are distinctly in its favor, the ". . . transitory inconveniency of
paying dearer during a short time for some sorts of goods"[6] would not
be justified. The *second* possibility, where the issue is not the imposition
of a new tax but rather the return to free trade from the evils of protection, centers around the need of preventing a sudden painful shock
to a domestic industry. This will be largely a question of size: only
when a "great multitude of hands" would all at once be deprived of
their ordinary employment and livelihood by the removal of high duties
and prohibitions is some special regard to their welfare in order. Indeed, Smith feels, it becomes a matter of equity in this case that the
return to exposure to competition from foreigners be undertaken ". . .
slowly, gradually, and after a very long warning."[7]

The same rule which in the second of the two main cases justified
the levying of an import duty also operates in reverse. Again the
question is one of restoring equality of competition between domestic
and foreign producers. In this case the desired result is hoped for from
a drawback, that is, allowing a merchant to draw back upon exportation an excise or inland duty imposed on the output of a domestic
industry. Why? Because such a policy could never result in the
exportation of a greater quantity of goods than would have left the
country had no excise or inland duty been levied in the first place, and
thus would not ". . . turn towards any particular employment a greater
share of the capital of the country, than what would go to that employment of its own accord."[8] Smith never tires of emphasizing the

---

[6]*Ibid.*, p. 355.
[7]*Ibid.*
[8]*Ibid.*, p. 381.

desirability of *restoring the natural balance among the various employments of a society*, of preserving the natural division and distribution of society's labor force.

The same principle applies to transit trade: foreign goods having been taxed upon their importation should be restored to their previous condition by enjoying an equivalent drawback upon their reexportation.

Bounties on exports, that is, government payments to exporters of goods who could not otherwise effectively compete with their foreign rivals, were, as we might expect, another device of the "mercantile system" scorned by Smith. They can only warp the natural allocation of resources. Since a country cannot *force* the buying of its exports on other countries, the next best expedient may be found in one country *paying* another for the buying of exports! But doing so, through bounties, will force a country's trade into less advantageous channels than those in which it would go if left alone. Domestic consumers will be the losers: under conditions of full employment they would pay a higher price for a smaller portion of the total supply, and in addition they would have to foot the bill for government payments to exporters. Such are the highlights of the attack on the absurdities of mercantilist restrictions, which had flowered too long to suit Smith's disposition.

DAVID RICARDO

Many regard this man, whose labor theory of value led some into blind alleys, as the true founder of modern international trade theory.

The Ricardian Framework

Ricardo's theory of international trade was a new departure. We may recall from Chapter 2 that he did not base his theoretical explanations of value upon extensive empirical research but mainly engaged in abstract reasoning. In working out his international trade theory, he also founded his conclusions upon a set of postulates which he considered as first approximations of the real world. The conclusions he drew, being valid within the framework of his assumptions only, had of course to be modified before they could be applied to actual circumstances. The same is also true for J. Stuart Mill, whose studies in international trade theory completed the framework built by Ricardo. In spite of many attacks and emendations, *the main structure of the Ricardo-Mill theory of international trade remained basically unimpaired until well into the twentieth century.*

The basic questions these Classicists sought to answer were the following: Why does trade take place between nations? How are international prices established; specifically, how are the terms of trade between nations determined? By what mechanism is equilibrium in the balance of payments achieved and maintained?

In his theory of domestic values, Ricardo pointed out that the value of commodities is determined by the comparative quantities of commodities that labor will produce. If in region A of a country a certain quantity of commodity X could be produced at a cost of 60 days' labor and in region B at a cost of 100 days, while in region A the labor cost of commodity Y was 30 days and in region B 90 days, then both commodities would be produced in region A. The real costs there are lower for both than in region B, and the commodities would exchange in the proportions of 1 unit of X for 2 units of Y. Labor and capital would desert region B and find employment in region A. This is the labor-cost principle which, according to Ricardo, governs exchange *within* a country. In other words, so far as domestic trade is concerned, Ricardo held that trade takes place on the basis of *absolute* differences in labor costs.

In international trade, however, this principle does not govern value in exchange; that is, the quantity of commodity X which country A will give in exchange for commodity Y of country B is not determined by the respective quantities of labor devoted to the production of each, as it would be if both X and Y were manufactured in different regions of the same country. Ricardo wrote: "The same rule which regulates the relative value of commodities in one country does not regulate the value of the commodities exchanged between two or more countries."[9] This conclusion is based on the postulates that (1) capital and labor move freely and without friction within a nation, and (2) labor and capital are immobile between countries. Consequently, production would not necessarily take place where labor costs are *absolutely* lowest.

Comparative Costs and Comparative Advantage

What, then, does determine values in international exchange? In seeking the answer to this question Ricardo was led to the doctrine of comparative (or relative) costs, which he illustrates with the assumed figures shown in the chart on page 333:[10]

---

[9]David Ricardo, *The Principles of Political Economy and Taxation*, ed. Gonner (London: George Bell, 1891), p. 113.

[10]Ricardo did not use a tabular format to convey this numerical information. *Ibid.* (Everyman's Library ed.; New York: E. P. Dutton and Co., Inc., 1912), p. 82.

COUNTRY	NUMBER OF MEN REQUIRED TO PRODUCE IN ONE YEAR	
	Wine (x barrels)	Cloth (y yards)
Portugal	80	90
England	120	100

A given quantity of wine which requires for its production in England the labor of 120 men could be produced in Portugal with 80 men, while a given quantity of cloth which in England requires the labor of 100 men could be produced in Portugal by 90 men. In other words, costs of producing both commodities are lower in Portugal. Nevertheless, it will be advantageous for Portugal to specialize in the production of wine and to exchange it for cloth produced in England (rather than to continue producing both). For in so doing, Portugal would procure for an outlay of 80 man-years what would cost her 90 man-years to produce at home. England, on the other hand, by concentrating on the production of cloth and exchanging it for wine, could get for a cost of 100 man-years what would cost her 120 man-years if she had no commercial connections with Portugal. The reason why Portugal, though she could make the cloth with the labor of 90 men, would import it from England, where it required the labor of 100 men to produce it, is that she will do better for herself by putting all her productive effort into the commodity in which she enjoys the greatest differential advantage in terms of labor cost. To say that it would take Portugal only two thirds as much time as it does England to produce a *given* quantity of wine, as compared to nine tenths as much in the case of cloth, is of course equivalent to saying that with a *given* amount of labor she could produce half again as much wine as England, as compared to one ninth more cloth. For additional proof of greater overall productivity with trade, it could be pointed out that if in the absence of trade England and Portugal each produced y yards of cloth and x barrels of wine this would take 390 man-years in all; whereas after specialization and with free trade, the same four "units" (unit quantities) could be produced in only 360 man-years.

There cannot be any doubt, then, that *England will benefit by specializing in the production of cloth and that Portugal will be better off by specializing in the production of wine.* All that is required for beneficial international trade is comparative, or *relative*, cost differences; it is not necessary that each country have an *absolute* advantage in the production of one commodity. Since Portugal has a greater advantage in wine and England a smaller disadvantage in cloth, they will each concentrate on those productions in which they have what is called a *comparative advantage*. Now we must see that the expression "comparative advantage" in the case of two countries and two commodities may mean one of two things: a greater absolute advantage *or* a smaller absolute disadvantage. Contrariwise, "comparative disadvantage" may denote a smaller absolute advantage *or* a greater absolute disadvantage.

Ricardo did not elaborate his conclusions in this way, although he was aware of the implications stated so far. From his concepts has been derived what is nowadays called the *Law of Comparative Advantage* (Principle of Comparative Advantage), which can be stated without ambiguity for a *two-country two-commodity model:* A country should export that commodity in which it has a comparative advantage and import the commodity in which it has a comparative disadvantage. (That is, a country should import that commodity in which it has, as the case may be, a greater absolute disadvantage or a smaller absolute advantage.) But the statement of the Principle becomes fuzzy in the case of *many countries and many commodities*, where it might be expressed somewhat like this: A country should export those commodities in which it has the greatest absolute advantage or the smallest absolute disadvantage; it should import those in which it has the greatest absolute disadvantage or the smallest absolute advantage. The difficulty arises from the fact that, with thousands of commodities, it cannot be indicated, in the case of a particular country, which of them fall under greatest absolute advantage or smallest absolute disadvantage. To say, as is sometimes done, that a country should export those commodities in which it has the greatest comparative advantage or the smallest comparative disadvantage does not clarify matters any, it only tends to confuse. Generally, the terms "greatest" (greater) and "smallest" (smaller) should only be used in conjunction with *absolute* (dis)advantage.

While Ricardo did not attempt any definition of the Principle, his development of the concept of comparative advantage was a genuine contribution to economic theory. (It is one of those relatively rare cases where a significant contribution is clearly identifiable.) Whereas Smith had extolled the virtues of territorial division of labor and specialization in terms of absolute advantage, Ricardo was able to argue on broader grounds. His formulation explains situations not covered by Smith's and includes the latter as a special case, the case where a country's comparative advantage is also an absolute advantage.

He left, however, much unfinished business for his successors, since *his statements did not explain how the actual ratios of international exchange determine international prices.* He was not particularly concerned with the terms of trade, although he stated that English cloth would exchange for Portuguese wine in the ratio of 1 cloth for 1 wine, which would be the case if England gave the product of the labor of 100 men (= 1 cloth) for the product of the labor of 80 men (= 1 wine). At this ratio the gain would be almost evenly divided between the two countries. It may already have been perceived intuitively by the reader that the ratio *could* fall anywhere between 9/8 unit of wine for 1 unit of cloth and 5/6 unit of wine for 1 unit of cloth without depriving either country of a net gain from trading. As will become clearer in the next section, at the ratio of 1 cloth for 9/8 wine, all the gain would go to England; and Portugal would be indifferent as between producing both cloth and wine to meet her entire domestic requirements and relying on England to satisfy her cloth requirement. (England would actually have 7/24 of a unit of wine more for each unit of cloth produced than she would have if she shifted 100 men out of cloth and into wine production, because $9/8 - 5/6 = 27/24 - 20/24 = 7/24$.) On the other hand, at the ratio of 1 cloth for 5/6 of wine, all the gain would be reaped by Portugal, with England being indifferent as between trading and not trading. (In this case Portugal would gain at the rate of 7/24 of a unit of wine per unit of cloth.)

Ricardo did not point out that comparative costs set maximum and minimum rates for the terms of trade and what the forces are which, within these limits, fix the equilibrium terms of trade. He was aware, however, that in the case of two countries each of which had a comparative advantage in the production of one of the commodities it might be more advantageous for one to engage in partial, rather than complete, specialization; in other words, he did not stress complete specialization as a result of division of labor in accordance with comparative advantage.

It should also be noted that Torrens preceded Ricardo in publishing a fairly satisfactory statement of the doctrine of comparative costs. But Torrens failed to give it much emphasis and did not make it an integral part of his presentation. It is nevertheless interesting to quote a passage he wrote in his *Essay on the External Corn Trade* (1815):

> If England should have acquired such a degree of skill in manufactures, that, with any given portion of her capital, she could prepare a quantity of cloth, for which the Polish cultivator would give a greater quantity of corn than she could, with the same portion of capital, raise

from her own soil, then tracts of her territory, though they should be equal, nay, even though they should be superior, to the lands in Poland, will be neglected; and a part of her supply of corn will be imported from that country. For, though the capital employed in cultivating at home might bring an excess of profit over the capital employed in cultivating abroad, yet, under the supposition, the capital which should be employed in manufacturing would obtain a still greater excess of profit; and this greater excess of profit would determine the direction of our industry.[11]

Ricardo has been attacked on many grounds: his statement of the doctrine in terms of labor costs only; his assumption of constant cost of production; and, of course, his artificial assumptions of perfect factor mobility within a nation as against complete factor immobility internationally. Many feel that these demerits are minor and are overshadowed by the fact that his novel approach opened up entirely new vistas for further research, for example, a restatement of the principle in terms of opportunity costs.

JOHN STUART MILL

From Ricardo to Mill

The main problem to which Mill addressed himself in discussing international trade was the determination of the *terms of trade*. He not only recognized that the value of a foreign commodity for a particular country depended on the quantity of the home product which had to be given in exchange for it, but he identified the "brackets" within which trade would take place. As applied to the Ricardian example, which he did not take as a starting point, he would have said that trade is advantageous to both countries as long as one unit of cloth is valued at more than 5/6 and at less than 9/8 of wine. It may be worthwhile for us to transform Ricardo's example and state it in output terms, à la Mill. Referring to the following table:

(1) As long as Portugal can get more than 10/9 of cloth for 5/4 of wine in trading with England, she will gain.

(2) As long as England has to give less than 9/9 of cloth for 5/6 of wine in trading with Portugal, she will gain.

From (1), since $10/9 : 5/4 = 9/9 : x$, Portugal will value one unit (9/9) of cloth at less than 9/8 of wine. (In solving for x we get: $10/9x =$

---

[11]Quoted in J. Viner, *Studies in the Theory of International Trade* (Harper and Brothers, 1937), p. 442; from Torrens' *An Essay on the External Corn Trade* (1815), pp. 264–65.

$45/36; x = \dfrac{45 \cdot 9}{36 \cdot 10} = \dfrac{9}{8}$.) Having established a common denominator in terms of cloth, we find that:

(3) As long as Portugal can get more than 9/9 of cloth for 9/8 of wine, she will gain.

From (2) and (3) we conclude that the area of profitable exchange for both nations lies between 5/6 and 9/8 barrels of wine for one yard of cloth.

PRODUCTION OF WINE AND CLOTH IN PORTUGAL AND
ENGLAND WITH AN EXPENDITURE OF
100 MAN-YEARS OF LABOR

COUNTRY	OUTPUT "UNITS"	
	Wine	Cloth
Portugal	5/4	10/9
England	5/6	9/9

Instead, then, of taking as *given* the output of each commodity in two countries with labor costs different — as Ricardo had done — Mill assumed a *given* amount of labor in each country but differing outputs. He thus arrived at the comparative effectiveness of labor, as contrasted with Ricardo's comparative labor costs.

Terms of Trade and Reciprocal Demand

Having proved that either of the two approaches leads to the same result, we may now look at the new example used by Mill. He assumed that with equal labor costs the output of two goods in two countries might be as follows:[12]

COUNTRY	BROADCLOTH	LINEN
England	10 yards	15 yards
Germany	10	20

In this case Germany has an absolute advantage in linen and England an absolute disadvantage in linen, whereas in broadcloth they are equally efficient. Since cost (output) ratios differ, we still have a comparative advantage situation, with Germany enjoying a comparative advantage in linen and England a comparative advantage in cloth.

If the two countries do not trade, 10 units of cloth will exchange in England for 15 yards of linen, in Germany for 20 yards of linen. Clearly,

[12]Mill did not use a tabular format to convey this numerical information. *Principles of Political Economy* (New York: D. Appleton and Company, 1884), pp. 396-7.

however, it would pay England to exchange her cloth for German linen as long as she could get more than 15 yards of linen for her 10 yards of cloth. By the same token, trade will be profitable for Germany if she could attain 10 yards of cloth for anything less than 20 yards of linen. The limits to the possible ratios of exchange are set by the comparative cost structures, and a relatively wide margin exists within which trade between the two countries would be mutually advantageous. The more closely the ratio approaches 10 yards of cloth for 20 yards of linen, the more of the total gain will go to England (in the limiting case of 10 for 20, Germany would no longer gain); the more closely it approaches 10 of cloth for 15 of linen, the smaller the share of the total gain that goes to England (in the limiting case of 10 for 15, Germany would reap the entire gain).

The actual ratio of exchange, or terms of trade, would be determined, according to Mill, by the demand of each country for the product of the other. This relationship he called "reciprocal demand." If, in the given illustration, the demand of England for German linen were strong, while the demand of Germany for English cloth were weak, a ratio would be established in which most of the gain would accrue to Germany, as would be the case, for example, if the ratio should settle at 15½ linen for 10 of cloth. On the other hand, if Germany were badly in need of cloth while England felt much less dependent on linen, a ratio of, say, 19½ linen for 10 cloth would be established and most of the gain would accrue to England.

Having fallen back on the law of supply and demand, Mill then perceived that the *equilibrium exchange ratio* would be determined by the condition that the quantity of each of the two products that the importing country is willing to take at this ratio be equal to the quantity that the exporting country is willing to give at this ratio. This so-called *Equation of International Demand,* at which Mill arrived under very restrictive assumptions, can also be stated by saying that the equilibrium exchange ratio is that which equalizes the values of exports and imports for each country. Mill implicitly assumed that if one country is willing to take more or less at a given ratio than the other is willing to give, competition will adjust the exchange ratio until it fulfills the equality condition.

Mill realized, of course, that trade is normally not conducted by barter, but this did not impair his reasoning because the equilibrium condition can be stated also in terms of foreign exchange earned from exports and owed for imports. His implicit assumption that trade takes place between nations approximately equal in size has been criticized.

But it was logically correct and, although it may not have been realistic enough, it did not invalidate his conclusions. We will take up this question in the next chapter.

The just mentioned criticism strikes the reader of the *Principles* as somewhat unfair because Mill in the same chapter outlined more complex cases than the one illustrated above. He introduced, first, the element of transportation costs; second, a greater number of commodities traded between the same two countries; third, additional countries; and fourth, changes in cost of production (for instance as a result of improvements in the manufacturing process). He emphasized that the sharing of the benefits of trade will always be in proportion to the degree of intensity of demand. The greater the intensity of demand in foreign countries for a given country's exports and the less intensive its own demand for the exports of other countries, the cheaper it will get its imports, that is, the greater the share of the total benefits from trade that will accrue to it.

SUMMARY

The first intensive preoccupation with theoretical questions relative to foreign trade occurred at the dawn of the New Era, when the trading horizon of Western Europe expanded rapidly. The Mercantilists, often associated with trading companies operating under monopoly charter from the government, embodied their economic ideas in a host of pamphlets and books which appeared intermittently from the early sixteenth down to about the middle of the eighteenth century. These writers for the most part remained captives of their own restricted outlook, which suggested to them that the gain of one nation must necessarily be at the expense of another. In particular, many missed these important insights: (1) International trade can be mutually advantageous. (2) The hoarding of gold and silver for its own sake is senseless, especially when achieved at the cost of a drain on the nation's productive resources. (3) The accumulation of precious metals may be self-defeating: price inflation may be attended by loss of competitive advantage and tends to lead to the reversal of an active balance of trade. (4) It is impossible for all nations simultaneously to pursue with any degree of success a policy of maintaining an excess of exports over imports.

Thomas Mun, who like his compatriot Misselden was an anti-Bullionist, had a formidable grasp of the transactions that enter into a nation's balance of trade and was particularly keen in his comprehension of the role of "invisible items." Petty, in discussing export duties as a fiscal source, set forth an argument that may be viewed as the counterpart of the cost-of-production argument for protective tariffs. North was the first full-fledged "free trader." Cantillon discussed both the price and income effects of a foreign trade balance and ably wove the strands of value and foreign-trade theory into a smooth fabric. Hume did more than any other writer of the period in describing and explaining the mechanism of self-regulating international trade. Condillac showed the application of the utility principle to transactions across national boundaries and the advantage to a nation of embracing free trade even as other nations follow protectionist policies.

Smith launched the most systematic attack against, and dealt a deathblow to, the already weakened "mercantile system." His chief positive contribution to the theory of international trade was an impressive exposition of the benefits of international specialization and division of labor, but he failed to see that a seller of export goods need not have an absolute cost advantage vis-à-vis the buyer. Smith singled out several cases in which deviations from the principle of free international trade would promote the general good.

Ricardo and Mill worked out a general theory of international trade on the basis of certain postulates which simplified their analysis. Ricardo found that his labor theory of value was not compatible with his assumption of factor immobility between nations. He discovered that the terms of exchange in foreign trade are determined by comparative costs of production. While he did not use this term, he elaborated the concept of comparative costs (which had already been introduced by Torrens) on the basis of which later writers formulated the Law (Principle) of Comparative Advantage.

Ricardo's contribution left unanswered the question of how the actual ratios at which goods exchange are determined. It was J. Stuart Mill who explained the determination of the terms of trade and did so with great skill. He found that they are dependent on reciprocal demand and that the equilibrium exchange ratio is the ratio that equalizes the values of exports and imports for each country in a two-country two-commodity situation. With the "Equation of International Demand" as a tool, he proceeded to envisage more complicated situations and to explain what modifications in assumptions their analysis necessitated. His work helped greatly in clarifying the intricate problems connected with the theory of international values and strengthened the foundations on which others could build.

BIOGRAPHICAL NOTES

A.—*Thomas Mun* (1571–1641) was a prominent businessman and the foremost English exponent of mercantilism. Son of a mercer, he was from his youth conversant with trade. Having acquired experience as a merchant in Italy and in the Levant, he was elected in 1615 as a director of the East India Company, which exported bullion, importing oriental goods greater in value than the goods exported from England to the Orient. This led to numerous attacks, and Mun felt the need to defend his company against criticism.

He did so in two books: *A Discourse of Trade, from England into the East-Indies* (1621) and *England's Treasure by Forraign Trade or, the Ballance of our Forraign Trade is the Rule of our Treasure* (written about 1630 and posthumously published by his son, John Mun, in 1664). Although it was essentially a collection of unproved assertions, the first of these books was an important contribution to the controversies about the East India Company. While still sympathetic to the bullionist doctrine, Mun in the *Discourse* crudely explained the reasons (lower prices, reexport of imports) why he thought the East India trade was profitable to England. His second book, much more skillful and diplomatic, and rich in analysis, constitutes a definite break with the bullionist theories. He criticized interference with individual transactions of merchants and the prohibition of the export of bullion as costly and ineffective. But he remained convinced of the beneficial effects of an augmentation of England's stock of bullion. To this end he recommended domestic production of goods formerly imported, laws to restrain the consumption of foreign luxuries, charging for exports what the traffic would bear, moderation of duties on exports and heavy duties on imports intended for home consumption, as well as a number of other measures.

B.—*Edward Misselden* (*fl.* 1608–1654) was a leading member of the Merchant Adventurers, whom he served as deputy-governor for ten years. In his first economic publication, *Free Trade: or the Meanes to Make Trade Flourish* (1622), he defended the Merchant Adventurers against a rival trading organization. By "free trade" he merely meant the removal of certain monopolistic restrictions, especially by the great trading companies. He was one of those who attacked the exportation of specie by the East India Company, which he later represented in its negotiations with the Dutch. When another Mercantilist, Gerard de Malynes, accused him of distorted views concerning England's economic situation, Misselden developed, and in 1623 published, a counterattack in *The Circle of Commerce; or the Ballance of Trade.* . . . He set up a theory of exchange based on this concept, which he placed in the center of his argument. He reversed his earlier position concerning the East India Company and now defended the exportation of specie on the reexportation theory which we have already encountered in Mun.

Misselden was relatively progressive but a less profound thinker than Mun, and his outlook was more sharply colored by the interests of the company he served.

C.—*Sir Dudley North* (1641–1691) was a self-made man who grew wealthy as a merchant. As a civil servant (after 1683) he attended to customs administration, and as a politician he served the cause of the Tories. In the year of his death his only work, a pamphlet entitled *Discourses upon Trade*, was published. It was lost soon thereafter and only rediscovered in 1822. It was characterized by rejection of many of the most fundamental mercantilist doctrines. He identified the private trader's good with the public good and condemned government restrictions on trade as injurious to the public. According to North, there is no fundamental difference between foreign and domestic trade — competition does not properly end at the water's edge, as American free-trade advocates would put it today — and no reason why the two should be dealt with differently.

Questions for Review and Research

1. Why were the Middle Ages not favorable to analytic conquests in the field of international trade theory?
2. Did Thomas Mun distinguish between the "balance of trade" and the "balance of payments"? Explain.
3. Did Adam Smith accurately portray the thinking of the most prominent mercantilist writers? Explain.
4. What were the two principal arguments advanced by the Mercantilists for (the desirability of) a "favorable" balance of trade?
5. Are there any parallels between Misselden's and North's views on foreign trade?
6. What rationale underlay Petty's conditional recommendation of "outward customs"?
7. Which pre-classical continental writer most ably deflated mercantilist tenets on foreign trade?
8. Discuss Hume's outstanding merits in the advance of international trade theory. In which respects did he surpass Cantillon?
9. How did Condillac apply his subjective utility theory to international trade?
10. Show in some detail why Smith was far from being an unqualified free trader.
11. What basis is there for the claim that Ricardo was the true founder of modern international trade theory? Was Ricardo aware of the foreign-trade multiplier?
12. What was the main problem to which J. Stuart Mill addressed himself in pushing out the theoretical frontiers in the field of international trade?

Recommended Readings

Einzig, Paul. *The History of Foreign Exchange.* London: Macmillan & Co., Ltd., 1962. Selected chapters.

Ellsworth, P. T. *The International Economy, Its Structure and Operation.* New York: The Macmillan Company, 1950. Chapter 5, "The Development of International Trade Theory," pp. 111–143.

Mill, John Stuart. *Principles of Political Economy, with Some of Their Applications to Social Philosophy*, 5th ed. 2 vols. New York: D. Appleton and Company, 1866. Vol. II, Chapter XVII, "Of International Trade," pp. 126–135; Chapter XVIII, "Of International Values," pp. 137–165.

Monroe, Arthur Eli (ed.). *Early Economic Thought*. Cambridge: Harvard University Press, 1924. The selection on Thomas Mun, pp. 169–197.

Newman, Philip C., Arthur D. Gayer, and Milton H. Spencer (eds.). *Source Readings in Economic Thought*. New York: W. W. Norton & Company, Inc., 1954. The selections "England's Treasure by Forraign Trade," by Thomas Mun, pp. 24–37, and "Of Exchanges in Generall," pp. 43–48.

Ricardo, David. *The Principles of Political Economy and Taxation*. Everyman's Library ed. New York: E. P. Dutton & Co., Inc., 1912. Chapter 7, "On Foreign Trade," pp. 77–93.

Spiegel, Henry William (ed.). *The Development of Economic Thought*. New York: John Wiley & Sons, Inc., 1952. The selection "Heckscher on Mercantilism," pp. 31–41.

INTERNATIONAL TRADE THEORY

From 1850 Onward

REFINEMENTS OF CLASSICAL DOCTRINES

Senior

This contemporary of J. Stuart Mill was probably the first to offer a contribution to the understanding of *international wage-level relationships*. He started from the premise that the level of money wages in all occupations in a given country is determined by the wages which labor can earn in the export industries. This position may have been defensible for midnineteenth-century England; it could hardly be correct for countries with a small stake in foreign trade. In his *Three Lectures on the Cost of Obtaining Money* (1830), Senior pointed out that the comparative levels of wages in the export industries of a given country are determined by the comparative prices which its export products can command in the world markets.

Senior did not try to answer the question of which industries would be export industries. But he showed that if labor in a country's export industries is more productive than such labor abroad, its level of money wages will exceed money-wage levels abroad, and vice versa; and that, under equilibrium conditions, wages in the industries producing only for domestic consumption must be equal to wages in the export industries. He condemned as false the notion — still occasionally encountered today — that high money-wage rates prevent a country from exporting. Instead, *he viewed a high rate of wages* as a necessary consequence of high labor efficiency and consequently *as a boon to a country's export capacity*. His reasoning remained defective, however, inasmuch as he did not point out that wages in both export and nonexport industries are jointly the result of a number of other variables, such as the distribution of natural resources, transport facilities, etc.

Cairnes[1]

A pupil of J. Stuart Mill, Cairnes strongly endorsed Senior's criticism of the "notion" that a high money-wage level prevents a country from competing abroad and is inimical to a thriving foreign trade. He considered "the rate of wages prevailing in a country and. . .the course of its external trade" as ". . . coordinate effects of a common cause, that cause being the degree and direction in which a nation's industry happens to be productive."[2] High money wages need not be paralleled by high real wages; the former are sometimes merely indicative of the possession of rich mines of gold and silver. Though he also considered as entirely without foundation the notion that a country's high wage level is incompatible with large exports, he was somewhat vague about the precise nature of the interrelationships between productivities, wage levels, and international specialization.

Much more important, because of greater originality, was his introduction of the concept of *noncompeting groups*, denoting groups of workers the members of which can or will not normally move among their occupations. This vertical immobility concept helped him to direct attention to the significance of differences in wages in different occupations. He explored the question of the extent to which effective competition among those engaged in industrial pursuits is actually realized. To secure this competition, he did not think it necessary that *every* worker should at all times be capable of turning to any selected occupation. But for effective competition to be realized there must be present in a community ". . . a certain quantity of those instruments of production existing in disposable form, ready to be turned toward the more lucrative pursuits, and sufficiently large to correct inequalities as they arise."[3] He regarded the capabilities of young generations as still in disposable form and likely to be turned towards the pursuits that promised the highest rewards. Meanwhile, the ranks of the less remunerative occupations would not be replenished as their occupants retired or died.

However, there are certain limitations on the action of competition in the labor market. Both financial conditions and social positions may bar some people from securing the education which will enable them to enter the occupation of their choice. Furthermore, a man trained as a carpenter might with equal ease have become a mason or a smith and may relatively easily switch from one to the other while at the same

---

[1]See Biographical Note A.
[2]J. E. Cairnes, *Some Leading Principles of Political Economy Newly Expounded* (New York: Harper & Brothers, 1874), p. 339.
[3]*Ibid.*, p. 63.

time being powerless to compete in higher departments of skilled labor, such as mechancial or electrical engineering. This vertical immobility is of course far from absolute; by virtue of extraordinary qualities, including willpower and a capacity to sacrifice, some people will always escape from their position into higher ranks. What we find is, in Cairnes' words, ". . . not a whole population competing indiscriminately for all occupations, but a series of industrial layers, superposed on one another, within each of which the various candidates for employment possess a real and effective power of selection, while those occupying the several strata are, for all purposes of effective competition, practically isolated from each other."[4] He mentioned four groups of occupations within which he considered movement to be feasible but among which it was difficult or impossible. Far from offering an exhaustive occupational classification or from suggesting any hard and fast lines of demarcation between the various strata, he merely made a case for a more sophisticated concept of industrial competition.

By now this question may have become pressing: In discussing international trade, what is the importance of recognizing the existence of noncompeting industrial groups in modern economic life? Mainly, that the formation of domestic prices has much more in common with the formation of international prices than might be supposed at first blush; and particularly that the supply *and demand* approach, stressed by Mill for international goods but not for domestic goods, also applies substantially to the latter. Just as there is no effective competition domestically *between* unskilled laborers on one hand and professional workers on the other as far as their chosen occupations are concerned, so there is little or no competition *among* unskilled laborers or *among* professional workers when they reside in different countries. Consequently, there is *little likelihood that international values will correspond with cost of production.* Yet in both cases there is a controlling force which restrains the fluctuations of exchanges between noncompeting groups. Following Mill, Cairnes sees this force in reciprocal demand, that is, international values tend to be regulated by the demand of, say, country A for the productions of all other countries coupled with their demand for what A produces. Analogous to the international case, reciprocal demand as applied to noncompeting groups (within nations) merely means the demand of a given group for the products of all other groups in conjunction with their demand for what the given group produces. In a similar way, Mill's "Equation of International Demand" could be so reformulated as to cover the equality between pur-

---

[4]*Ibid.*, p. 66.

chases and sales of all groups from and to each other, with relative prices of the products exchanged reflecting changes in reciprocal demand. For instance, an increase in the demand of a given group for the products of noncompeting industries will tend to depress the prices of its products relative to the prices of the products of noncompeting industries, and increases in the demand of the "outside" industries for the products of the given group will have the opposite effect. Finally, both noncompeting groups in domestic industry on the one hand and independent nations on the other have in common the fact that the prices of the products exchanged between these bodies are much less subject to large fluctuations than are the prices of *particular* commodities, whether traded internationally or in domestic markets only. In this manner *Cairnes brought reasoning with respect to domestic price formation into harmony with the more advanced price analysis that Mill had developed in his theory of international values.* Cairnes' conclusion was that the prices of all goods produced under conditions other than free competition are determined by reciprocal demand and that the gap between domestic and international price theory was closed.

In parting from Cairnes we might note that, like his teacher, he was convinced that **free trade** has the potential of substantially enhancing the real national income of the trading countries, but he saw no way in which the gain can in practice be measured concretely.

Bastable[5]

The Irish economist Bastable, in a short work entitled *Theory of International Trade* (1893), attempted to make the Ricardo-Mill theory of international trade more realistic by modifying some of the heroic assumptions underlying the classical analysis. For one among many examples, he included situations involving more than two countries and more than two commodities — which Mill had already vaguely attempted. It may be safer if we confine ourselves to the relatively simple case study of his model of two countries (only) and three commodities, because this can still be managed without too many *ifs* and *buts*.

We will assume with Bastable that without trade

$10x$ exchange for $20y$ and for $100z$ in country A, and
$10x$ exchange for $15y$ and for $90z$ in country B,

with no limit on substitutability between x, y, and z in either country.

---

[5]See Biographical Note B.

As far as commodities x and y are concerned, A has clearly a comparative advantage in y, and B a comparative advantage in x. They would profitably trade as long as $10x$ exchange for anywhere between $15y$ and $20y$. With regard to commodities x and z, B's comparative advantage is likewise with x, and A's is therefore with z. Does it follow, therefore, that when all three commodities are traded, A will export y and z, and B will export x only? Not necessarily. Commodity z could be an export of either A or B, depending on the terms of interchange between x and y. At $10x = 16y$, A sacrifices the equivalent of $80z$ (since $20y : 100z = 16y : 80z$). But the $10x$ exported from B to A are the equivalent of $90z$ — hence B could export $90z$ for $16y$. Anything over $80z$ received by A for $16y$ would be a net gain for A, and anything short of $90z$ exported by B would result in a net gain for B.

On the other hand, with the terms $10x$ for $19y$ (still favorable for both A and B as far as commodities x and y are concerned) A in exporting y would sacrifice the equivalent of $95z$ (since $20y : 100z = 19y : 95z$). But since B could never "give" more than $90z$ — the equivalent of $10x$ — commodity z would obviously be imported by B, rather than exported, as in the previous case.

Perhaps it has occurred to the reader that *at $10x = 18y = 90z$ the nature of commodity z as an export or import is indeterminate.* For if country B exports $10x$ and gets from A $18y$, y will have cost country A the equivalent of $90z$ ($20y : 100z = 18y : 90z$), which country A could have produced in lieu of $18y$. It follows that at anything less than $18y$ to $10x$ commodity z is an export commodity of B, whereas at anything more than $18y$ to $10x$ it is an export commodity of A. The comparative advantage in z will thus be enjoyed by A or B, depending on whether the terms of trade between x and y are closer to A's or closer to B's domestic cost ratios. In other words, *the less the share of the gain from trade accruing to a given country resulting from the exchange of x for y, the greater the likelihood that it will export the third commodity.* In more general terms, if two countries trade in more than two commodities, any commodity — except the pair (in our case: x and y) which is characterized by the greatest difference in relative costs between them — may be either an export or an import of either country.

Bastable arbitrarily assumed that the terms of trade would settle at $10x = 17y = 90z$ in the above example; but in the absence of further assumptions there is really no telling what they will be. Much depends on the respective size (total production) of the two countries and the economic importance of — intensity of demand for, according to Mill's expression — the commodities to them. Furthermore, whether B will export z to A, or A will export z to B, when both countries are producing z at what we may call the "neutral" ratio of $10x = 18y = 90z$, will depend on the degree in which the production of x absorbs B's productive power relative to that absorbed in A by the production of y. Bastable clearly asserted the possibility that *in the special case of trade between a large and a small country, the larger country will only partially specialize in the production of the commodity or commodities in which it has a comparative advantage.*

While the above illustrative example, like those of Ricardo and Mill, was based on the assumption of constant (unit) cost, in which case two countries will tend to specialize completely in the production of those commodities in which they "always" have a comparative advantage, Bastable also operated with the assumption of increasing and decreasing cost industries. He saw that *increasing unit cost* tends to limit the area of specialization and exchange — one of the two countries may produce part of its total requirements in a commodity and import the rest — while *decreasing unit cost* tends to lead to complete specialization.

Bastable anticipated Ohlin[6] when he toyed with the idea of substituting "interregional" for "international" as a label for trade between different areas. He decided to desist from adopting this new terminology, fearing that confusion might result. It is interesting, also, that he followed Cairnes in rejecting the assumption of perfect competition within each country, another defection from "pure" classicism.

Marshall

Although he was more skilled in the use of mathematical tools, Marshall, like Cairnes and Bastable, on the whole *leaned heavily on classical foundations.* In international economics he tried to avoid the unreality of situations involving only two commodities by introducing the concept of a *representative bale of goods.* (Do you remember his concept of the "representative firm"?) This would embody a constant quantity of a country's labor and capital, but the commodity composition of a bale could vary. Unfortunately, his ideas did not become available to a large number of readers until the publication of his *Money, Credit, and Commerce* (1923), notwithstanding the fact that he had aired some views as early as 1879 in a privately printed volume entitled *The Pure Theory of Foreign Trade.*

---

[6]See Biographical Note E.

Marshall proceeded on the following assumptions: (1) Two countries, E(ngland) and G(ermany), trade exclusively with each other. (2) No credit extension and no foreign investment. (3) No transportation costs. (4) Exporters are also importers, a merchant in E exporting those of his country's goods which he thinks will bring the greatest returns abroad and importing those goods from G estimated to bring the greatest returns when marketed in E. (5) Trade between the two countries to be on a pure barter basis, with the demand of each country stimulating the supply of the other and being made effective by its own supply.

Marshall suggests that the equilibrium condition of international trade might have been equally well summarized in an *Equation of International Supply* rather than the Equation of International Demand. He points out that while changes in international demand may be the dominant force, supply creates demand almost as certainly as demand backed by purchasing power calls forth supply. When he speaks of "supply and demand," this is merely another expression for "reciprocal demand."

He illustrated, both numerically and with diagrams, the possible relations of demand and value in the exclusive trade between two countries. We will summarize both of these approaches.

Numerical Analysis. — A summary of Marshall's first approach is shown in the chart on the following page.

The essentials of Marshall's development of the example could be shown without columns (*2*) and (*4*). Comparing columns (*1*) and (*3*) we see that because of the diminishing rate at which E is willing to substitute G bales for her own bales, the quantity of G bales E insists on acquiring for *every additional 10,000* bales of her own must increase. (E is willing to part with 10,000 bales for the first 1,000 bales of G; to induce E to part with an additional 10,000, G would have to offer an additional 3,000 G bales; the next 10,000 E bales command an additional 5,000 G bales, etc.)

Comparing columns (*1*) and (*5*) we see that G is willing to give as much as 23,000 of her own bales to acquire 10,000 E bales; but for the next 10,000 E bales G is willing to sacrifice only an additional 12,000 bales, and for the following 10,000 E bales only 7,900.

Eventually a point will be reached at which a given number of E bales (90,000) is worth the same in terms of G bales (70,200) to both E and G. To convince ourselves that this is an *equilibrium ratio of exchange*, we look at the closest alternatives. First, for 80,000 E bales

RELATIONS OF SUPPLY AND DEMAND IN INTERNATIONAL TRADE

(1) NUMBER OF E BALES	SCHEDULE OF TERMS ON WHICH E IS WILLING TO TRADE		SCHEDULE OF TERMS ON WHICH G IS WILLING TO TRADE	
	(2) Number of G bales *per 100* E bales at which E will part with those in (1)	(3) *Total* number of G bales for which E is willing to part with those in (1)	(4) Number of G bales *per 100* E bales at which G will buy those in (1)	(5) *Total* number of G bales which G is willing to give for those in (1)
10,000	10	1,000	230	23,000
20,000	20	4,000	175	35,000
30,000	30	9,000	143	42,900
40,000	35	14,000	122	48,800
50,000	40	20,000	108	54,000
60,000	46	27,600	95	57,000
70,000	55	38,500	86	60,200
80,000	68	54,400	82½	66,000
90,000	**78**	**70,200**	**78**	**70,200**
100,000	83	83,000	76	76,000
110,000	86	94,600	74½	81,950
120,000	88½	106,200	73¾	88,500

Source: Alfred Marshall. *Money, Credit, and Commerce.* London: Macmillan & Co., Ltd., 1923, p. 162.

G would be willing to sacrifice more of her own bales (66,000) than E is asking (54,400); second, for 100,000 E bales G would not be willing to sacrifice as many of her own bales (76,000) as E is asking (83,000). The forces of supply and demand will thus operate to bring about an equilibrium exchange ratio of 90,000 E bales for 70,200 G bales.

Another way of interpreting E's and G's "trading schedules" is a statement to the effect

> . . . that, if G's specialties generally were very scarce in E's markets, they would be bought up at very high costs by wealthy persons who had an urgent desire for them. If their supply increased greatly some of them would need to attract other persons, who were less wealthy, or had a less urgent desire for them. . . . If their quantities became very large, relatively to the population of E, they would have to be forced at still less advantageous rates to the importers: and at these low rates it might be possible to find a market in E for some other goods, for making which G had no very great differential advantage, and which had not been exported previously.[7]

Column (2) indicates the rate at which G bales exchange for 100 E bales; that rate increases in accordance with the *Law of Diminishing*

[7] Alfred Marshall, *Money, Credit, and Commerce* (London: Macmillan & Co., Ltd., 1923), pp. 161–2.

Marginal Utility as applied to *G* bales, from the viewpoint of *E*. Column (*4*) gives the same information from the viewpoint of *G*, the rate decreasing in accordance with the diminishing marginal utility of *E* bales as *G* sacrifices more and more of her own bales.

As to the *gains from trade*, Marshall adopted changes in the supposed equivalent of "consumer's surplus" as a better index of change in the amount of gain from foreign trade than the movement in the commodity terms of trade. Analogous to consumer's surplus, the gain from trade can be computed by adding up what a country would have been willing to pay if it had bought foreign bales separately on a market rising against it. For instance, according to column (*4*) *G* would have been willing to give 230 + 175 + 143 + ... + 78 = 1,119½ bales per hundred *E* bales, or a total of 111,950 *G* bales for 90,000 *E* bales. Since she got the same 90,000 *E* bales for 70,200 *G* bales (column [*5*]), the net benefit of trade to *G* is therefore 111,950 − 70,200 = 41,750 unit products of her labor and capital.

Graphical Analysis.—The information contained in the table on page 351 is brought out more lucidly in the following diagram.

RELATIONS OF DEMAND AND SUPPLY IN INTERNATIONAL TRADE

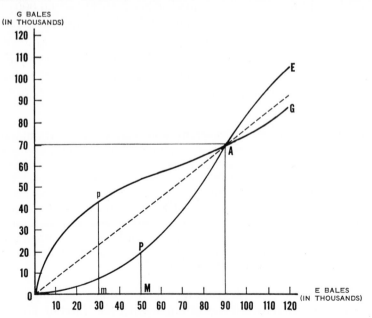

Source: Adapted from Alfred Marshall. *Money, Credit, and Commerce.* London: Macmillan & Co., Ltd., 1923, p. 331.

It will be seen that the quantity of E bales is measured along the horizontal axis, the quantity of G bales along the vertical axis. Country E's reciprocal demand function is denoted by the curve OE, country G's by the line OG. They show how many of its own bales each country is willing to give up in order to obtain various amounts of the other country's products. At any point on either the OE or OG curve it is possible to determine the number of E bales (G bales) country E (G) is willing to relinquish for a specified number of G (E) bales. For instance, if OM represents 50,000 E bales (column [1]), PM will measure 20,000 G bales (column [3]); and if Om represents 30,000 E bales (column [1]), then pm will measure 42,900 G bales (column [5]). The fact that the OE curve is convex towards the x-axis shows that greater quantities of G bales can be sold in E only under less favorable conditions.

It is important to distinguish clearly between the countries' external and internal equilibria. For *external equilibrium* p and P must merge and the quantities of G bales must become the same for country E and for country G. At point A country E is willing to surrender 90,000 E bales to obtain 70,200 G bales and country G gives up 70,200 G bales to obtain 90,000 E bales. *Internal equilibrium* is represented for each country by any given point on its reciprocal-demand (demand-and-supply) curve. Hence a movement along the curve merely indicates that a country's domestic production has changed to correspond with a different level of imports.

The *terms of trade*, not separately shown by Marshall, would be indicated by the slope of the dotted line from the origin through A. An increase in demand by consumers in E for G bales results in a shift of line OA downward and to the right (more E bales would be relinquished for a given number of G bales); and a decrease in the demand by E for G bales would be indicated by a shift of OA upward and to the left (fewer E bales being offered for a given number of G bales). In other words, the greater the angle between the dotted line OA and the x-axis, the more favorable will be the exchange ratio to E and the less favorable will it be to G.

Conclusions. — It was Marshall's merit to get away completely from the labor theory of value. His *real-cost analysis* includes both labor and capital as costs of production and shows the bearing of domestic production on the attainment of external equilibrium. But it is still true that his treatment of the relation of reciprocal demand to the terms of trade was in the main an exposition and elaboration in geometrical form of Mill's analysis.

It might be asked why Marshall dealt with international value problems in nonmonetary terms, as distinguished from the monetary approach of his general value theory. He gave as the principal reason the fact that an attempt to make an allowance for the change in value of money internationally results in unmanageable complications if one proceeds some distance into the pure theory of foreign trade. However, his theory of international value, although it abstracted from absolute money prices, was more than a theory of barter applied to foreign trade. Purely as a matter of convenience, Marshall took for granted the existence of money and its functions, confining his analysis to the nonmonetary manifestations of the equilibrium process.

It should also be mentioned that during the first half of the twentieth century, *Frank D. Graham*[8] penned what is perhaps the most scathing but not necessarily the most fair indictment of the Classicists. He lashed away at (1) the two-country two-commodity approach (especially in Mill's version), and (2) the assumption of a fixed comparative advantage situation. Graham's analysis, being more realistic than Mill's in regard to the nature of commodities traded and the relative importance of trading countries, gave a precision to the terms of trade which was lacking in nineteenth-century writings.

Taussig[9]

For many decades prior to his death in 1940, Taussig was the most highly respected among American international trade theorists; in particular, he was the country's great authority on the tariff. His empirical studies were of large dimensions, and they generally preceded his formulations of theoretical propositions. Although it was published as late as 1928, his most comprehensive statement of these propositions, which appeared under the title *International Trade*, followed in the main the lines of analysis and exposition initiated by Ricardo. Although he did not claim to have made contributions of large significance, he greatly enriched the discussion and filled in many chinks left by his predecessors. His work was lacking in acrobatic constructions. Instead, it was always geared to the *practical significance of the leading principles* to which Taussig drew attention: its keynote was a realistic evaluation of the possibility of subjecting it to test, verification, and correction. He was truly a master of the art of welding factual and theoretical analysis.

---

[8]See Biographical Note C.
[9]See Biographical Note D.

Taussig introduced several *new concepts*. He distinguished, for example, between the *gross barter terms of trade* and the *net barter terms of trade*. By the former he meant the ratio of the physical quantity of imports to the physical quantity of exports. The greater this ratio, the more favorable the gross barter terms. The net barter terms of trade, the more familiar of the two concepts, is the ratio of export prices to import prices.

Along with many earlier critics, Taussig regretted the use of the mercantilist expressions "favorable" and "unfavorable" to designate, respectively, a balance of trade in which merchandise exports exceed imports in money value, and vice versa. Now if there were no other than merchandise transactions to account for, the fact that there is nothing inherently favorable about receiving a specie flow would be the only matter of concern. But the mercantilist terminology has become increasingly misleading in proportion as nonmerchandise transactions have gained in relative importance. In other words, the relations of imports and exports in themselves may no longer give a clue to the determinants of the specie flow. This observation of Taussig's applies with even greater force to present-day circumstances: the United States has had a considerable excess of merchandise exports over imports throughout the post-World War II period, but its monetary gold stock in the late 1960's was only about half of what it had been at the end of World War II. Taussig pointed out that it is the balance of payments, rather than the balance of trade, which determines the specie flow. He gave examples of how the barter terms of trade, both net and gross, are changed to the advantage or disadvantage of a country, how they depend on the conditions (elasticities) of demand, and especially on the degree to which unilateral transactions (exports or imports which are surrendered without compensation or received without counterpayment) alter the terms. He described specific circumstances under which the commodity terms of trade would be a misleading index of gain from trade. He indicated that in the absence of countervailing factors, for example, a decrease in desire, an increase in imports obtained *per unit* of exports established a presumption for an increase in the amount of gain from trade.

With respect to differences in *wages in different occupations*, Taussig demonstrated how they may cause relative prices to diverge from relative labor-quantity costs and how, as a result, international specialization under free trade may not conform with comparative advantage in terms of labor-time costs. Except for this qualification — which he made in recognition of the objections raised against the labor-cost theory of value — Taussig remained an adherent of it, almost the only one among twentieth-century writers to take this position. He conceded that differences between countries in the hierarchy of occupations tend to deflect the course of trade from what it would be if prices were regulated by labor-time costs. He gave some concrete arithmetical examples based on somewhat different types of assumptions with respect to the nature of noncompeting groups, pointing out that differences of wages in different occupations may be what he called "equalizing" differences. By this he meant wage differences entirely attributable to and proportional to differences in the attractiveness or irksomeness, respectively, of the occupations, and not to the absence of complete mobility between them. He also analyzed differences in wages due to labor monopolies in the high-wage groups, as well as other cases, examining in each case to what extent the doctrine of comparative real costs holds in spite of wage differences between occupations. His main conclusion was that the existence of these differences does not suffice to overturn the doctrine of comparative costs.

Taussig admitted that the real costs of capital and labor, the two sacrifices represented by "abstinence" and work, are in their nature incommensurable. But this logical difficulty is not as paralyzing as one might expect because, according to Taussig, there are many cases in which the introduction of capital cost (interest) leaves comparative money costs the same as they would be in the absence of capital costs. Furthermore, he did not deem the quantitative importance of the capital charge factor to be great.

In sum, Taussig has given us a thorough treatment of the balance of trade, the balance of payments, the terms of trade, international wage and price levels, noncompeting groups, and capital and interest, much of it designed to substantiate the modified and more realistic labor-cost theory of value underlying his international trade theory.

CASSEL'S PURCHASING-POWER-PARITY THEORY

One of the most widely accepted theoretical contributions of the post-World War I period was the purchasing-power-parity doctrine already referred to in Chapter 11, formulated by the Swedish economist Gustav Cassel. It constitutes an attempt to formulate a theory of *international* price relationships in terms of simple quantitative relationships between average *domestic* price levels. It is a *theory of the equilibrium rate of exchange* which holds that under freely fluctuating rate systems there is a basic rate of exchange to which the actual rate constantly tends to conform. This basic exchange rate is the one which constantly reestablishes the relative purchasing power which a currency possessed (relative to some other currency) in a base period, when equilibrium is assumed to have prevailed. We must note that Cassel abstracted from relative changes in transportation costs of goods or in tariff rates. In his earliest pronouncement (the most widely noted) he said:

> Given a normal freedom of trade between two countries, A and B, a rate of exchange will establish itself between them and this rate will, smaller fluctuations apart, remain unaltered as long as no alterations in the purchasing power of either currency are made and no special hindrances are imposed upon the trade. But as soon as an inflation takes place in the money of A, and the purchasing power of this money is, therefore, diminished, the value of the A-money in B must necessarily be reduced in the same proportion. . . . Hence the following rule: when two currencies have been inflated, the new normal rate of exchange will be equal to the old rate multiplied by the quotient between the degrees of inflation of both countries. There will, of course, always be fluctuations from this new normal rate, and in a period of transition these fluctuations are apt to be rather wide. But the rate calculated in the way indicated must be regarded as the new parity between the currencies. This parity may be called the *purchasing power parity*, as it is determined by the quotients of the purchasing powers of the different currencies.[10]

Let us illustrate Cassel's "rule." Assume that during a base period the equilibrium rate of exchange between the dollar and the pound was £1 = $4. Suppose that since then the index of consumer prices in the U.S. has risen to 300 (base period = 100), and in England to 400. In other words, the internal value of the dollar has declined to one third its base-period value, and the internal value of the pound has fallen to one fourth its former level. In terms of dollars, the pound is now worth three fourths as much as in the base period, or

$$\$4 \cdot \frac{300}{400} = \$3 \text{ (base-period rate multiplied by the ratio of the price index in the U.S. to the British price index).}$$

Notice that if the price levels in the two countries had risen together at the same rate, the exchange rate for pounds would, according to Cassel, have remained the same — as it also would have if price levels had fallen at the same rate, or if they had not changed at all. On the other hand, if only one of the price levels was changing, or if both were changing (up or down, or both) but at different rates, the

---

[10]Gustav Cassel, "Memorandum on the World's Monetary Problems," International Financial Conference, Brussels, 1920, *Documents of the Conference*, V, 44–45; quoted in Jacob Viner, *Studies in the Theory of International Trade* (New York: Harper & Brothers Publishers, 1937), p. 380.

exchange rate between the two countries would be altered, tending to move in such a way as to reflect the new value relationship between the two monetary units.

Are there any basic objections that impair or invalidate the applicability of this rule? Specifically, are movements in the relative price levels of different countries the chief (or only) determinant of exchange rates and thus of balance-of-payments relationships?

Perhaps the most incisive *criticisms* can be summarized under three points. (1) Trade between countries may change as a result of various factors — changes in tastes, for example — without causing price changes. (2) Exchange rates are affected by capital movements, but these are not reflected in the consumer price index. (3) The index of prices on which calculations must be based always comprises goods which are not, and because of high transportation costs or for other reasons probably never will be, traded internationally.

Even if the purchasing-power-parity theory, instead of being applied to *general* price levels, were confined to the price levels of commodities entering international trade, it would still remain vulnerable. Cassel may be granted this much, however: The comparative domestic purchasing power of two paper currencies is ordinarily the *most important* single factor in determining the exchange rate between them. And for countries on an international gold standard, the exchange rate — which can never move far from the mint par — is ordinarily the most important single factor determining their price levels. (Strictly speaking, this observation does not constitute a defense of Cassel's theory, since the latter purported to explain exchange rates as determined by relative price levels, rather than vice versa.)

Cassel defended his failure to give attention to long-run factors that create divergencies between actual exchange rates and purchasing-power-parity rates by stating that his theory tended to emphasize in the postwar period of extreme currency inflation (internal depreciation) what is undoubtedly the most important outward manifestation of internal inflation, namely, exchange depreciation.

THE GENERAL EQUILIBRIUM APPROACH

Ohlin[11]

In his *Interregional and International Trade* (1933), this famous representative of the Swedish school set out to contribute to the attainment of the following objectives: (1) "To build up a theory of inter-

---

[11]See Biographical Note E.

national trade in harmony with the mutual-interdependence theory of pricing . . . and thus independent of the classical labor theory of value." (2) "To demonstrate that the theory of international trade is only a part of a general localisation theory. . . ." (3) "To analyse the domestic and international movements of the factors of production, and particularly their relation to commodity movements." (4) "To describe the mechanism of international trade variations and international capital movements under conditions of fixed foreign exchanges. . . ."[12] We will be concerned mainly with (1) and (3).

Ohlin takes as a premise the widespread acceptance of the general equilibrium theory of value, prices, and distribution, and aims at *restating the theory of international trade in terms of this modern value theory.* (Recall that general equilibrium analysis, in contrast with partial equilibrium analysis, includes all the relevant variables.) He believes that the *space element* has been unduly neglected, that the geographical distribution of the factors of production is important, and that, in view of the immobility of natural resources, the space aspects of the price mechanism need to be stressed. As the title of his book suggests, Ohlin is not concerned with international trade per se; a theory dealing with it alone he deems inadequate because space plays a role in pricing *within* countries also. He maintains that trade between nations is merely a special case of trade between regions, and views as the task of interregional and international trade theory the giving of full consideration to the element of space through its extension from one market to a number of related markets. His work deals with all those aspects of the existence of several markets which relate to the difficulties of moving factors of production and moving commodities between places — the former being to some extent confined to certain localities, the latter being hampered by costs of transport and other impediments (tariffs, quotas, etc.).

Ohlin defined a *region* as a district separated from other districts by some kind of natural border line more important than those between parts of the same district. In simpler language we may term a region any area endowed with a unique set of productive factors. He shows how interregional variations in the proportions of the factors of production result in different adaptations of regions for the same type of production. He states the important principle that ". . . each region is best equipped to produce the goods which require large proportions of the factors relatively abundant there; it is, on the other hand, least

---

[12]Bertil Gotthard Ohlin, *Interregional and International Trade* (Cambridge, Mass.: Harvard University Press, 1933), pp. vii and viii.

fit to produce goods requiring large proportions of factors existing within its borders in small quantities or not at all."[13]

How do these differences come to be expressed in different money costs and prices? According to Ohlin, the *price mechanism* in each region rests upon four basic elements: (1) wants and desires of consumers, (2) conditions of ownership of factors of production, (3) supply of productive factors, (4) physical conditions of production. The first two elements determine the demand for, and the last two determine the supply of, goods.

According to the general equilibrium theory, the price mechanism resting on these elements determines simultaneously factor prices and commodity prices. Whenever the latter differ in two isolated regions, there is a basis for interregional trade. In the unlikely case that differences between regions as to endowment with productive agents are just balanced by corresponding differences in the demand for commodities, no trade can arise because the *relative* scarcity of all factors and the *relative* commodity prices will be the same. Consequently, inequality in the relative prices of the factors of production in the isolated state is a necessary, but not a sufficient, condition for the establishment of trade. Generally, differences in the conditions of supply of factors are more important than differences in demand in bringing about variations in relative scarcity between two regions in an isolated state.

If region A has a relatively large supply of some factors, which are therefore — as a rule — comparatively cheap, and a relatively small supply of other factors, which are therefore comparatively dear, A will be able to produce cheaply those commodities requiring for their production a large quantity of cheap factors, while the production of other commodities would be relatively dear. The same holds, *mutatis mutandis*, for B with its different factor supply. But if interregional trade is also international trade, only after exchange rates have been established can prices and costs of production be compared directly. And the exchange rate, in turn, is not determined exclusively by relative factor scarcities in the isolated state but also by reciprocal demand when trade has been opened up. It should be clear, then, that the mutual interdependence of all pricing elements forbids unqualified reasoning in one direction from cause to effect.

If there are *several trading regions* instead of only two, the main features of the analysis remain the same, except that it is more difficult to say a priori which factors are relatively abundant and cheap, or

---

[13]*Ibid.*, p. 12.

relatively scarce and dear, that is, which goods each region will export and which it will import respectively. Ohlin enlivens his exposition by giving many concrete examples of the influence of differences in the equipment with productive factors. By themselves, however, the latter will never adequately explain the real nature of interregional trade: a mutual interdependence system of pricing must always be modified and completed through the introduction of demand from abroad.

Ohlin also brings out that trade has a far-reaching influence on the combinations and the prices of the factors of production, mainly in the sense that it tends to promote *equalization of factor prices*. This is a result of the fact that when specialization and trade begin each region will tend to produce goods requiring large quantities of the factors with which it is well endowed and to produce few, if any, goods requiring large quantities of the factors which are scarce. Consequently, both the relative abundance of the abundant factors and the relative scarcity of the scarce factors in each region tend to diminish, raising the prices of cheap and lowering the prices of expensive factors. In this fashion the relative scarcity of factors of production is made less different in the various regions, and their price differentials narrow.

While trade will thus give rise to a tendency not only towards an equalization of commodity prices but also towards equalization of factor prices, for various reasons complete interregional price equalization cannot come about. However, the relatively greater ". . . mobility of goods to some extent compensates the lack of interregional mobility of the factors . . ."[14] or, as we may also put it, *interregional trade serves to some extent as a substitute for interregional factor movements*. Incidentally, Ohlin also envisaged circumstances in which factor movements serve to stimulate commodity trade instead of replacing it.

This comprehensive statement of the equilibrium position, of which only the bare outlines have been sketched, has done much to promote a wider understanding of equilibrium reasoning as applied to the international field.

Haberler[15]

Although steeped in the tradition of the nonmathematically oriented Austrian school, Haberler in his *The Theory of International Trade* adopted for his contribution to international trade theory the framework of general equilibrium theory. He branded as a major

[14]*Ibid.*, p. 42.
[15]See Biographical Note F.

weakness of the principle of comparative advantage its use of a labor theory of value; he substituted for labor costs *opportunity costs* as the basis for trade according to comparative advantage. Let us briefly examine the nature of his analysis.

Haberler takes as his point of departure two facts: first, the technical impossibility of measuring the diverse factors of production in terms of a common quantity unit, and, second, the "specificity" of many factors of production, which may arise from their immobility — inherent or otherwise — or from their technical unsuitability for different uses. He shows diagrammatically, first under the assumption of constant costs, then under the assumption of increasing costs, all the possible combinations for producing two commodities, A and B, by utilizing a *given* labor supply.

In the first case these combinations lie on a straight line, with the constant exchange ratio between A and B being determined by their respective labor requirements. If each unit of commodity A requires the expenditure of one unit of labor and each unit of B requires the expenditure of two units, then two units of A can be substituted for one unit of B. Under the assumption of increasing costs for both A and B, the *substitution*, or production-possibility, *curve* will be concave to the origin. This means that as the output of one commodity is expanded, an increasing number of units of the second must be foregone for each additional unit of the first produced. Whereas under constant costs demand does not affect the exchange ratio, under increasing costs it does, because the substitution ratio varies with the relative demand for A and for B. For any combination in which A and B are demanded, the exchange ratio between them equals the substitution ratio at that point; and for every point on the substitution curve the exchange ratio will be different.

Haberler made use of Wieser's "opportunity cost" concept, according to which costs are measured, not by the absolute amount required of a given factor but by the alternatives foregone. "Thus the marginal cost of a given quantity x of commodity A must be regarded as that quantity of commodity B which must be foregone in order that x, instead of x-*1*, units of A can be produced."[16] Depending on the relative quantities of A and B which are produced, factor combinations will vary, with those factors especially suitable for B being used more fully as more of B and less of A is produced, and vice versa. Haberler proves that the proposition that the exchange ratio between two

---

[16]Gottfried von Haberler, *Theory of International Trade with its Applications to Commercial Policy* (New York: The Macmillan Company, 1936), p. 177.

commodities will be determined by their substitution costs applies to a modern money economy as much as it does to a barter economy. He shows that the *shape* of the substitution curve depends on the degree of "specificity" of the factors of production and on the length of time — short run v. long run — which elapses while production adapts itself to a situation of, say, more A and less B. Haberler concludes that if certain rigorous assumptions are met, a unit of a given commodity will exchange for that quantity of another commodity which at the margin requires "an equally valuable collection of factors" to produce it.

What are the implications of Haberler's analysis for the principle of comparative costs? He felt that the labor theory of value could be discarded, but for the rest the principle of comparative costs would remain intact. If, for example, on the basis of opportunity costs in country I one unit of A exchanges for 2 units of B, and in country II one unit of A exchanges for 3 units of B, then these exchange ratios would be substituted for those based upon, or expressed in terms of, the single factor labor.

Jacob Viner,[17] in his *Studies in the Theory of International Trade* (1937), discussed the application of commodity indifference curves to Haberler's opportunity-cost approach and expressed doubt about the feasibility of replacing real-cost analysis with opportunity-cost analysis. He felt, for instance, that the opportunity-cost theory in effect had to ignore the difficulties connected with certain alternative preferences, such as leisure v. employment or employment x v. employment y.

CONCLUSION

In the foregoing pages little attention has been given to the fact that throughout its history the classical approach to international trade theory was the target of severe attack much of which was being directed against the labor theory of value in crude or refined versions. The basic objection has been to its supply orientation and the consequent neglect of demand factors.

It must also be noted that the general equilibrium theory and the modern classical theory of international trade lead to basic conclusions which are not so far apart as might appear from a study of their fundamental differences. In a nutshell, and considerably simplifying: (1) The equilibrium theory recognizes not only cost as a determinant of price but also price as a determinant of cost, whereas modern classical theory has (over)emphasized the cost-to-price sequence of causation. (2) In

---

[17]See Biographical Note G.

contrast to modern classical theory, equilibrium theory does not count on free competition to bring prices in harmony with costs, and it asserts that demand is equally as important as is supply. (3) Modern classical theory emphasizes cost differences and equilibrium theory emphasizes price differences as the driving force behind trade. All the same, no reasonably enlightened Classicist would deny the essentials of the equilibrating process, nor would an open-minded equilibrium theorist deny the significance of cost analysis.

CONTEMPORARY INTERNATIONAL TRADE THEORY

For many topics of international economics discussed during the post-World War II period, there is no simple, generally accepted explanation of fundamental issues — no validated theory. While new basic constructs continue to be formed, in perhaps the majority of cases it is still too early to tell what will ultimately be acknowledged as accepted doctrine. It is mainly for this reason that only one more among many illustrious names will be dignified by special mention, the exception being justified by special considerations.

Keeping in mind the tentative, evolutionary nature of postwar theory, it is nevertheless appropriate to take stock of academic "growth points," so to speak. Perhaps the most fertile mind in the broad area covered has been that of *Harry G. Johnson*,[18] a cosmopolitan economist in outlook and living habits alike, with deepest roots in Canada, England, and the United States. A prodigious author of books and journal articles — some highly technical and narrowly focused, others in the nature of sovereign surveys of broad fields — coupling elegance with depth of thought, he recently assisted in the selection of the second series of *Readings in International Economics*[19] presented by the American Economic Association.

In what subject matter areas within the field of international economics does one find the seminal ideas which, by stimulating further thought and research, are likely to be assured of a permanent place in the history of economic thought? Johnson, whose own contributions cover most of them, found this to be the case in each of the following subdivisions into which he and his collaborator organized the material:

---

[18]See Biographical Note H.

[19]Published by Richard D. Irwin, Inc. (Homewood, Ill. 1968), this is Volume XI in a series of republished articles on economics under the sponsorship of the AEA. Johnson's collaborator on the selection committee was Richard E. Caves, of Harvard University. Its predecessor volume, *Readings in the Theory of International Trade*, was published in 1949 (Philadelphia: Blakiston Division of McGraw-Hill Book Co.) under the editorship of Howard Ellis and Lloyd Metzler.

(1) theory of comparative advantage, (2) international factor movements, (3) trade policy and welfare, (4) trade, growth, and development, (5) balance-of-payments and exchange stability, (6) international payments and national income, and (7) empirical investigations of international trade and payments.

Research in the pure theory of international trade has continued to converge on the popular Heckscher[20]-Ohlin model based on the assumption of two countries, two goods, and two factors of production, but has covered additional functional relations so as to make the model (more?) determinate. The related study of international factor movements has been more closely integrated with other aspects of international economics than was accomplished by Ohlin himself in his *Interregional and International Trade*.

In the wake of applying normative criteria to international trade, concepts of welfare economics have been used, especially in the evaluation of alternative trade policies, and the so-called theory of the second best has been conjoined with problems arising out of tariff and subsidy policies, balance-of-payments restrictions, and the formation of customs unions. The latter are, of course, only the most important aspect of regional economic integration, which has become the subject of a fast-growing literature.

Although it is somewhat artificial to distinguish between work on growth and work on development, the latter has attempted to incorporate assumptions thought to be particularly appropriate to the economies of the presently less developed countries. A number of models and hypotheses about international trade in the context of "underdevelopment" has been formulated, spawning geographically widespread controversy over the gains from trade in primary products and — as far as resource allocation in, and income transfers to, less developed countries are concerned — confronting adherents of "balanced" growth with advocates of "unbalanced" growth.

Stress on monetary aspects of trade theory has served to sharpen analysis of the balance of payments and the related issue of exchange-rate (in)stability. Much effort has been concentrated on the incorporation of Keynesian income-adjustment theory into the analysis of effects of exchange-rate variations. Specifically, the effects of currency devaluation on the trade balance have been analyzed in terms of the concepts of (price) "elasticity" and (income) "absorption," and their

---

[20]Eli F. Heckscher (1879–1952) was an outstanding economic historian and the highest authority on mercantilism. He also did distinguished pioneer work on the role of factor proportions in international trade and inspired his countryman, Ohlin, to pursue this subject in greater depth.

integration is hoped to provide a complete account of all the underlying economic adjustments.

The theoretical discussion of the supposed advantages and disadvantages of exchange-rate flexibility (a term of far from uniform coverage in the literature) has been mainly inspired by the continuing demand to insulate domestic income and employment levels against exogenous changes in the trade balance and has brought forth the notion of "optimum currency areas."

As happened before, a large amount of postwar theoretical work has been animated by the changing terms in which the issues of public policy are being conceived. They have been highlighted by the phenomenon of dollar shortage and dollar glut, the related but larger question of the effects on the international financial system of the revival of international capital markets and the greater fluidity (mobility) of funds, and — most ominous of all — the nightmare of a collapse of that system because of inadequate overall liquidity. Most likely to be of enduring value has been research showing how to attain "consistency between international and domestic policy and employing available policy instruments to attain multiple objectives."[21] Needless to say, the continuing controversy over reform of international monetary institutions has also elicited some fundamental theoretical work.

SUMMARY

Wage-level relationships within and between countries in their bearing on international trade, a subject which had been largely neglected by Ricardo and Mill, were dealt with extensively by Senior and especially by Cairnes. Both criticized the notion that a high money-wage level prevents a country from competing in foreign markets. Cairnes introduced the concept of noncompeting industrial groups, which brought reasoning with respect to domestic price formation into some harmony with the more advanced analysis embodied in Mill's theory of international values. Bastable modified the rigorous assumptions underlying the Ricardo-Mill analysis by examining increasing and decreasing unit cost conditions, viewing the nature of domestic competition more realistically, and including situations involving more than two countries and two commodities. Marshall, relying heavily on classical foundations but using more sophisticated tools, introduced the concept of the "representative bale of goods," embody-

---

[21]American Economic Association, op. cit., Preface, p. x.

ing a constant quantity of labor and capital. Having freed himself from the labor theory of value, he achieved a more generalized exposition of international trade theory and viewed the gains from trade in a new light. Taussig, the most famous and a universally respected American international trade theorist before World War II, held that although the comparative labor cost doctrine of the classical writers is only a rough approximation to reality, it is nevertheless a useful analytical tool. He erected an elaborate system of defenses for the modified labor-cost theory of value underlying his international economics. His performance in the areas of money wages, real wages, and price level relationships constituted a further refinement of the doctrines of the British economists discussed in this chapter. Whenever possible, especially in exploring the terms of trade, he made extensive use of statistical material, which kept his theoretical work closely attuned to the problems of the real world.

Cassel's purchasing-power-parity theory attracted considerable attention at the end of World War I in the circles of internationally oriented economists and statesmen. It related international and domestic price levels to exchange rates in a formula that greatly oversimplified the workings of the world economy, but it served to arouse attention to the penalties inflicted in foreign markets on a country pursuing a policy of heedless domestic inflation.

Although general equilibrium analysis had long been applied to domestic economics, its widespread acceptance in international trade theory dates only from the 1930's. Ohlin's work stressed the mutual interdependence of factor and commodity prices, trade and factor movements, and incomes. Whereas Ricardo had assumed factor immobility between nations, Ohlin recognized the existence of at least partial mobility. His broadly conceived scheme was in the nature of an international localization theory. His mutual interdependence approach has now largely displaced patched-up versions of classical international trade theory. But judicious midtwentieth-century economists agree that the two approaches are not as incompatible as their ardent exponents would have had us believe. Haberler helped to develop the equilibrium approach further by substituting opportunity costs for labor costs or — more broadly — for real costs as the basis for trade according to comparative advantage. In his two-commodity model, he explained the nature of substitution curves under various cost conditions and showed that for any combination in which the commodities may be demanded, the exchange ratio between them equals the substitution ratio.

The last section of this chapter was devoted to a bird's-eye view of the nature and the main directions of postwar work in international trade theory.

BIOGRAPHICAL NOTES

A. — *John Elliot Cairnes* (1823–1875) graduated from Trinity College, Dublin, Ireland, in 1848, and, as a member of the Irish bar, practiced law for a few years. In 1856 he was appointed professor of political economy at Dublin University. He was a member of the faculty at Queens College, Galway, from 1859 to 1866 and taught at University College, London, from 1866 to 1872.

Important among Cairnes' works, although not primarily an economic writing, is *The Slave Power* (1862), a powerful defense of the North in the American Civil War. Five years earlier, *The Character and Logical Method of Political Economy* had been published; it advocated use of the deductive and abstract method in economics. In 1873 *Political Essays* and *Essays in Political Economy Theoretical and Applied* appeared. His chief work, *Some Leading Principles of Political Economy Newly Expounded*, was published one year before his death, which was hastened by ill health. Cairnes regarded himself as a faithful Millian, but he survived the master by only two years, during which Jevons struggled in vain to undermine Mill's authority as personified by Cairnes. Trying to strengthen the classical edifice, Cairnes may in fact have made it more vulnerable to attack. Unwittingly and unintentionally, he slipped away from the tenets of the "orthodox" school, but he never embraced Jevons' doctrine of final utility.

B.—*Charles Francis Bastable* (1855–1945), born in County Cork, Ireland, was educated at Fermoy College and at Trinity College, Dublin. For a fifty-year period (1882–1932) he was professor of political economy at Dublin University. He also taught political economy at Queens College, Galway, from 1883 to 1903, and international law at Dublin in 1902. He served as Examiner at many universities on the British Isles and as Visiting Lecturer at the University of North Wales and the University of Manchester. In 1894 he was President of Section F of the British Association. His publications include: *The Commerce of Nations* (1892), *Theory of International Trade* (1893), and *Public Finance* (1892).

C. — *Frank Dunstone Graham* (1890–1949) was born in Halifax, N.S. He received his M.A. and Ph.D. degrees in 1917 and 1920 from Harvard University. He went from instructor in economics at Rutgers College (1917–1920) to assistant professor at Dartmouth College (1920–1921). He was on the faculty of Princeton University from 1921 until his death, holding the rank of full professor after 1930. He was an economic advisor to the Federal Farm Board from 1930 to 1931 and a professor of international economics at the Institut Universitaire de Hautes Etudes Internationales at Geneva, Switzerland, for the next two years. He served on the special War Department Commission on Nazi preparation and conduct of the war in 1945. His publications include: *Exchange, Prices, and Production in Hyper-Inflation, Germany (1920–23)* (1930); *The Abolition of Unemployment* (1932); *Protective Tariffs* (1934); *Golden Avalanche* (with C.R. Whittlesey, 1939); *Social Goals and Economic Institutions* (1942); *Planning and Paying for Full Employment* (with Abba P. Lerner and others, 1946); *The Theory of International Values* (1948).

D. — *Frank William Taussig* (1859–1940) was the son of European immigrants of great business ability. Young Taussig studied at Washington University, St. Louis, and at Harvard University, from which he was graduated in 1879, achieving "highest honors" in history. After a European tour and studies at the University of Berlin, he returned in 1880 to enter Harvard Law School, but soon thereafter committed himself to the study of economics. His Ph.D. thesis dealt with the history of American tariff legislation, especially the problem of infant-industry protection. He revealed himself as neither a protectionist in the ordinary sense of the term nor a free trader but as an advocate of economic development judiciously pursued. He happily blended economic theory with institutionalism, evidencing a great ability to view problems in their sociological settings.

The first one of eight editions of his standard work, *The Tariff History of the United States*, was published in 1888. In 1891 he produced a book, *The Silver Question in the United States*, in which he fought against free silver. When during the 1890's he developed more strongly theoretical leanings, he looked to Ricardo and Böhm-Bawerk as his models, but soon Marshall appealed to him most.

By 1886 he had been promoted from instructor to assistant professor at Harvard University, and six years later followed his promotion to full professor. In 1896, when he published *Wages and Capital*, he was appointed to the editorial chair of the *Quarterly Journal of Economics*, a position he filled until 1935, interrupted only by a two-year leave (1901–1903) during which he recovered in Europe from a nervous breakdown caused by overwork. In 1904 and 1905 he was President of the American Economic Association; although he did not embrace marginal analysis until a few years later, this fact did not preclude his attainment of this high honor! In 1915 the fruit of many years' research was published under the title *Some Aspects of the Tariff Question*. Four years earlier he had offered his *Principles of Economics*, which became one of the most widely used textbooks in economics; it was last revised in the year before his death.

Taussig did not shrink from judging public policy in the classroom nor from shaping it in positions of public service. The latter was evidenced by his efforts from 1917 to 1919 while serving as chairman of the newly created United States Tariff Commission. During this time he did much to shape its spirit and to create the nucleus of a tradition: fact-finding as a responsibility of the Commission. It was under his leadership that a systematic study of all important commodities listed in the Tariff Act was undertaken. After the end of World War I, he served as a member of President Wilson's Advisory Committee on the Peace. He returned from these public duties to the classroom with enhanced reputation and authority.

A book of collected essays was published in 1920 under the title *Free Trade, the Tariff, and Reciprocity*, and in 1927 appeared his masterpiece, *International Trade*. His interest in economic sociology achieved a conquest through the publication of a collaborative work, *Origin of American Business Leaders* (1932). Except for revisions of his earlier works, his career as a writer was then at an end, but he retained his teaching chair at Harvard for another three years.

E.—*Bertil Gotthard Ohlin* (1899–   ) is a leading member of the Swedish school. He studied under Cassel at the University of Stockholm (Ph.D., 1924) and first set forth his ideas on general price equilibrium in 1924 in *Theory of Trade*. He was a professor of economics at the University of Copenhagen from 1924–1929 and at Stockholm University's College of Commerce after 1929. He holds honorary doctor's degrees from many European universities. His magnum opus has been *Interregional and International Trade* (1st ed., 1933; rev. ed., 1967).

Ohlin worked on a number of government investigating committees set up during the Great Depression to study unemployment and related problems. After a controversy developed between the Swedish school and Keynes, he actively participated in the debate centering around the problem of the presumed equality between saving and investment, which projected into the international limelight the Swedish economists' distinction between *ex ante* and *ex post* analysis. He helped greatly in clearing the air through his article, "Some Notes on the Stockholm Theory of Savings and Investment," published in the March and June, 1937, issues of the *Economic Journal*. In 1936 he had written the major portion of a volume published by the Joint Committee of the Carnegie Endowment for International Peace and the International Chamber of Commerce entitled *International Economic Reconstruction*. The fruits of his research on interest theory were incorporated in the volume *The Capital Market and Interest Rate Policy*, published in 1941.

Member of Parliament beginning in 1938, Ohlin in 1944 became head of Sweden's Liberal party and in 1944–1945 served as Minister of Commerce. In the postwar years, Ohlin has been an internationally sought-after lecturer. Lectures he delivered at Columbia University and Oxford University were given wider circulation through the publication in 1949 of *The Problem of Employment Stabilization*.

F. — *Gottfried von Haberler* (1900–   ) was born near Vienna and educated in the Austrian capital. He acquired the degrees of Dr. rer. pol. and J.D. at the University of Vienna in 1923 and 1925. From 1927 to 1929, he pursued graduate studies at the University of London and Harvard University. Between 1928 and 1936, he was first lecturer and later professor of economics and statistics at the University of Vienna; in 1931–32, he appeared as visiting lecturer at Harvard University, whose staff of economists he joined permanently in 1936. For two years prior to this honorable appointment, he had been an expert attached to the Financial Section of the League of Nations at Geneva. Haberler has been a member of the American Economic Association, which he served as president in

1963; the Royal Economic Society; the Econometric Society; and the International Economic Association, which he served as its first president from 1950 to 1953. Since 1956 he has been chairman of the Board of the National Bureau of Economic Research.

Haberler's numerous publications include: *The Theory of International Trade* (1936, German edition 1933); *Prosperity and Depression* (1937); *Consumer Instalment Credit and Economic Fluctuations* (1942); *Quantitative Trade Controls, Their Causes and Nature* (1943); *Currency Convertibility* (1954); *Inflation, Its Causes and Cures* (1961; rev. and enl. ed., 1966); *A Survey of International Trade Theory* (1961); *Money in the International Economy* . . . (1965); *United States Balance of Payments Policies and International Monetary Reform: A Critical Analysis* (1968).

G.—*Jacob Viner* (1892–   ) received his B.A. degree from McGill University, Toronto, in 1914, and his M.A. and Ph.D. degrees from Harvard University in 1915 and 1922. He is now the holder of a long series of honorary degrees testifying to the fact that he has worn with distinction the mantle which fell upon his shoulders after Taussig's death.

A Canadian, Viner came to the United States in 1914 and was naturalized ten years later. His career as an economics teacher at the University of Chicago included an instructorship from 1916 to 1917, an assistant professorship from 1919 to 1923, an associate professorship for the next two years, and a full professorship from 1925 until 1946, when he transferred to Princeton University. There he held the Walker chair of economics and international finance from 1950 to 1960, and has been a professor emeritus since then. He has been a visiting professor or lecturer both in the United States and abroad. The United States Tariff Commission, the Treasury Department, and the State Department on many occasions between 1917 and 1952 utilized his services as an expert, consultant, or special assistant. Numerous awards have been conferred upon Viner. His membership in various learned societies includes the American Economic Association, of which he was president in 1939. His publications comprise: *Dumping, A Problem in International Trade* (1923); *Canada's Balance of International Indebtedness* (1924); *Studies in the Theory of International Trade* (1937); *Trade Relations between Freemarket and Controlled Economies* (1943); *The Customs Union Issue* (1950); *International Economics* (1951); *International Trade and Economic Development* (1952); *The Long View and the Short* (a collection of his essays published in 1958 by students and friends on the occasion of his sixty-fifth birthday).

H.—*Harry Gordon Johnson* (1923–   ) is another bright star in the firmament of Canadian international trade theorists. (In addition to the deceased Graham and the retired Viner, there is young [born 1932] Robert A. Mundell [editor since 1967 of the *Journal of Political Economy*], who at the age of less than thirty had already made a name for himself as a superbly skilled and imaginative scholar.)

Born in Toronto, Johnson received B.A. and M.A. degrees from the University of Toronto in 1943 and 1947, and from the University of Cambridge (England) in 1946 and 1951 respectively. Add to these the

A.M. (1949) and Ph.D. (1958) degrees from Harvard University, an M.A. from Manchester University in England (1960) and LL.D. degrees from St. Francis Xavier University in Nova Scotia (1965), the University of Windsor (1966), and Queens University, also in Canada (1967), and you begin to appreciate the meteoric rise in recognition, based on unusually solid academic credentials, which Johnson has earned.

He was a lecturer at Cambridge University and a fellow of King's College from 1949–1956, then became professor of economic theory at the University of Manchester for three years. Johnson "immigrated" to the United States in 1959, the year he was appointed professor of economics at the University of Chicago. Since 1966 he has doubled as a professor at the London School of Economics and Political Science!

Johnson belongs to the leading professional associations in Canada and the United States, has been president of the Canadian Political Science Association (1965–1966) and a member of the executive committee of the American Economic Association. From 1963–1965 he served as a member of the government-sponsored United States Review Committee on the Balance of Payments and from 1961–1966 was editor of the *Journal of Political Economy*.

His main publications in book form include: *International Trade and Economic Growth* (1958); *Money, Trade, and Economic Growth* (1962); *The World Economy at the Cross Roads* (1965); *Economic Policies toward Less Developed Countries* (1967); and *Essays in Monetary Economics* (1967).

Questions for Review and Research

1. According to Senior, what determines the comparative level of money wages in various occupations in a given country? Criticize. Did he deem high money-wage rates inimical to exporting? Explain.
2. What bearing does Cairnes' concept of "noncompeting groups" have on the international division of labor and on the relationship between international values and cost of production?
3. Was Cairnes able to advance beyond his teacher J. Stuart Mill in showing how the gains from international trade can be measured?
4. How did Bastable propose to make the Ricardo-Mill theory of comparative cost and reciprocal demand more realistic?
5. Explain Marshall's concept of a "representative bale of goods."
6. In his two-country, pure barter model, how did Marshall arrive at the equilibrium ratio of exchange?
7. What did Taussig mean when he spoke of (a) the "gross barter terms of trade"? (b) the "net barter terms of trade"?
8. Did his study of differences in wages in different occupations lead Taussig to the conclusion that the classical doctrine of comparative cost was faulty? Explain.
9. On what type of exchange-rate system is Cassel's purchasing-power-parity theory premised?
10. According to Ohlin, how do differences in the supply of factors of production in various regions influence trade among them?

11. What did Haberler find unsatisfactory in the traditional formulation of the principle of comparative advantage, and how did he propose to remedy this deficiency?
12. Look up Viner's *Studies in the Theory of International Trade* and evaluate his criticisms of Haberler's approach.

Recommended Readings

American Economic Association. *Readings in the Theory of International Trade.* Blakiston series of republished articles on economics, Vol. 4. Homewood, Illinois: Richard D. Irwin, Inc., 1949. The selection "The Theory of International Values Reexamined," by Frank D. Graham, pp. 301–330.

————. *Readings in International Economics,* edited by Richard E. Caves and Harry G. Johnson. Series of republished articles on economics. Homewood, Ill.: Richard D. Irwin, Inc., 1968. Vol. XI. Preface, pp. v–xii.

Bastable, Charles Francis. *The Theory of International Trade with Some of Its Applications to Economic Policy,* 3d ed. Rev. New York: The Macmillan Company, 1900. Chapter 2, "The Theory of International Values," pp. 22–48.

Cairnes, J. E. *Some Leading Principles of Political Economy Newly Expounded.* New York: Harper & Brothers, 1874.
Part I, "Value": Chapter III, "Normal Value," pp. 43–96.
Part III, "International Trade": Chapter II, "International Trade in Its Relation to the Rate of Wages," pp. 319–341.

Haberler, Gottfried von. *The Theory of International Trade with its Applications to Commercial Policy,* translated by Alfred Stonier and Frederic Benham. New York: The Macmillan Company, 1936. Chapter XII, "International Trade and General Equilibrium," pp. 175–208.

Marshall, Alfred. *Money, Credit, and Commerce.* London: Macmillan & Co., Ltd., 1923. Book III, "International Trade": Chapters 6–8, pp. 155–190.

Ohlin, Bertil. *Interregional and International Trade.* Cambridge: Harvard University Press, 1933.
Part I, "Interregional Trade Simplified": "Introduction," and Chapters I–IV, pp. 3–64.
Part II, "International Trade Simplified": Chapters V–VII, pp. 67–138.

Taussig, F. W. *International Trade.* New York: The Macmillan Co., 1927.
Part I, "Theory": Chapter 1, "Three Cases," pp. 3–6; Chapter 5, "Wages and Prices in Different Countries. Domestic Prices and International Prices," pp. 34–42; Chapter 9, "Varying Advantages," pp. 88–96; Chapter 10, "Two Countries Competing in a Third," pp. 97–107; Chapter 11, "Nonmerchandise Transactions. Tributes, Indemnities, Tourist Expenses," pp. 108–122; Chapter 13, "Duties on Imports and the Barter Terms of Trade," pp. 141–148.

Wasserman, Max J., and Charles W. Hultman. *Modern International Economics, a Balance of Payments Approach.* New York: Simmons-Boardman Publishing Corporation, 1962. Part V, "The Theory and Analysis of International Economics," pp. 256–295.

BUSINESS CYCLE THEORY

Until about the middle of the nineteenth century, business cycles were generally regarded as disturbances of the "normal course" of events which presented no challenge to theoretical ingenuity. Crises and depressions appeared to be associated with causes lying outside the area of economic science; these tended to divert trade only momentarily from its "normal" channels, and no more. It was not until the regularity of the business cycle had impressed itself upon the minds of many investigators during the second half of the nineteenth century that fluctuations in business activity came to be regarded as something more than temporary deviations from the smooth course of events. Even then, business cycle problems were given no systematic attention in standard treatises of political economy (economics).

The discovery and *preliminary analysis* of business cycles may be said to have occurred during the first half of the nineteenth century. Recall that in 1803 *J. B. Say* had stated his "Law of Markets" by which he argued that, however large the phenomenon of overproduction may loom in the historical picture of business crises, it would be wrong to argue that the latter were the result of general overproduction.

> It is worthwhile to remark that a product is no sooner created than it, from that instant, affords a market for other products to the full extent of its own value. When the producer has put the finishing hand to his product, he is most anxious to sell it immediately, lest its value should vanish in his hands. Nor is he less anxious to dispose of the money he may get for it; for the value of money is also perishable. But the only way of getting rid of money is in the purchase of some product or other. Thus, the mere circumstance of the creation of one product immediately opens a vent for other products.[1]

In a sense, Say hereby made a very important *negative contribution* to business cycle theory, with two possible results: his pronouncements either tended to lull the profession into complacency or else they necessitated a rebuttal which would tax the resourcefulness of the most

---

[1] J. B. Say, *A Treatise on Political Economy*, translated from the 4th ed. by C. R. Prinsep (London: Longman, Hurst, Rees, Orme, and Brown, 1821), I, 167.

gifted. Since Say *did* admit the existence of partial overproduction (and underproduction), he may be said to have inspired one variant or another of the disproportionality theory of crises.

By World War I just about all the essential facts and ideas relative to business cycle analysis had been mentioned in the professional literature; afterwards hardly any pioneering principle was added. Furthermore, in the decades immediately preceding that war, the concept "cycle" had definitely ousted the concept "crisis" from the minds of analytical workers, although many of them continued to use the latter term in their writings. The task which economists faced immediately after the war was to clarify and expand the subject into a recognized branch of economics.

The years just before fateful 1914 had been pregnant with new departures. In 1913 *W. C. Mitchell* (see pages 391–393) gave the problem of business cycles a comprehensive and empirically novel treatment which soon opened up entirely new vistas for factual research. Shortly before that event, a twenty-eight-year-old Austrian, *J. A. Schumpeter* (see pages 393–396) had established an intimate relation between traditional value theory and business cycle theory, something vastly greater in scope than just another explanatory hypothesis. The immediate effect of these pioneering feats was quite small, however. During the 1920's there continued to be a cleavage between economic theory and the facts developed in business cycle research. This was partly because Mitchell, the great intellectual innovator, did not aspire to determine how the fact of cyclical oscillations in economic activity could be reconciled with the general theory of equilibrium; he confined himself to an analytic description.

It was only after the onset of the Great Depression that the *relation of business cycle theory to traditional analysis* was subjected to searching scrutiny. During the late 1930's and the 1940's, dynamic analyses were developed which aimed at explaining business fluctuations and unemployment as part of the economic system and no longer regarded them as a consequence of "frictions." Indeed, what has come to be called macrodynamics was propelled by a strong preoccupation with business cycle problems, as a changing philosophy of the role of government made it incumbent upon the latter to mitigate cyclical fluctuations with a view to maintaining permanently high levels of employment. On one hand, the methods, materials, and results of business cycle research encompassed more and more of general economics; on the other, the methods, materials, and results of post-Keynesian macrodynamics evolved mainly with a view to serving business cycle research.

This work, which — regretfully — has to be omitted from our survey, developed more and more along econometric lines; in fact, *econometrics* (that is, statistically operational economic theory) may be viewed as a complement to macrodynamics (see Chapter 10). In essence, it has been the *interaction of macrodynamics and business cycle research* which, roughly since the publication of Keynes' *General Theory*, has been responsible for the bulk of advances on the frontiers of economic knowledge. Certainly, today the theory of business cycles means a vast apparatus of theoretical and statistical tools of analysis, undreamt of in the nineteenth century.

ANALYSIS IN THE CLASSICAL PERIOD

In General

During the classical period a few *hypotheses* concerning the causes of crises and cycles were ventured forth, and these hypotheses constituted the main contents of analytic work. To most of the classical writers, a theory of general overproduction appeared as a heresy which they sought to eradicate by demonstrating that the supply of goods of one sort necessarily constitutes demand for goods of other sorts. Say typically stood for the orthodoxy of this period, an orthodoxy which neglected *unemployment of resources* because it *was viewed as a peripheral problem.* This position of complacency rested on the classical preoccupation with long-run tendencies and the prevailing belief that the business cycle was a short-run phenomenon. Crises like those in 1815, 1825, and the late thirties, forties, and fifties had occurred with similar regularity in the nineteenth century; but nobody then found it worthwhile to distinguish these breakdowns clearly from external disturbances and to see in them anything but chance misfortunes (droughts, earthquakes, and other acts of God) and the results of unmitigated human folly (speculation manias such as the Mississippi and the South Sea bubbles). Whatever suggestions can be found in the literature of the Mercantilists to the effect that there might be deeper causes of economic breakdowns, these suggestions were not made explicit enough to justify our dwelling upon them.

Major Contributions

Sismondi and Malthus were the leaders of a rebellion against Say's Law — a tempest in a teapot. While neither of their theories was systematized enough to permit our labeling them, they were in the general nature of depression (stagnation) rather than crisis theories. Let us examine them briefly.

Sismondi.[2] — Sismondi, who had won European prominence as a historian, in his early years was an ardent admirer of Adam Smith, but the evidence of widespread economic distress following the end of the Napoleonic Wars shook his optimistic attitude. In his *New Principles of Political Economy* (1819), he set himself to finding out what was wrong with the philosophy of laissez-faire. He suggested that the businessman has to operate in a sea of uncertainty as to tastes and incomes of potential customers and the prices which his output will bring in the market. A comparison of present prices and present costs, he held, is an inadequate guide to enlightened business policy. In general he made much of the *anarchy of capitalist production*, the lack of knowledge of what other producers do, and of what buyers want. He also pointed out that in certain periods the income available for buying consumer goods falls short of the value of the goods sent to markets — the markets become glutted. While, moreover, he hinted at an oversaving theory of crises, he laid much stress upon the inequality of income distribution as the fundamental cause of crises. And although he deemed the desire for luxuries unlimited, he argued that due to the propensities of the wealthy for foreign wares domestic producers of luxury goods must seek foreign outlets for their production, and these foreign markets often prove to be undependable. Sismondi thus offered a *multiplicity of factors* responsible for the breakdown, but nobody seems to have been able to classify these factors in a satisfactory way. In sum, his writings constitute a sharp indictment but are somewhat lacking in constructive and clear analysis.

Malthus.—Malthus came considerably nearer to definiteness. A dissenter from orthodox opinion, he expounded an *oversaving type of underconsumption theory*, pointing out that stagnation ensues when people save and invest to such an extent that, owing to the consequent fall in prices and profits in consumer goods industries, producers have no motive to increase production further. He was primarily concerned with short-run forces and the explanation of market prices (rather than normal prices), arguing against Ricardo that only through a consideration of these do we come to grips with the real problem of business cycles. He maintained that there might be a voluntary failure of effective demand on the part of the rich (who had the "power but not the will"), or an involuntary failure of effective demand on the

[2]See Biographical Note A.

part of the poor (who had the "will but not the power"). For instance, the situation of a rich landed proprietor surrounded by very poor peasants represented a distribution of property very unfavorable to "effectual demand." But, in contrast to Sismondi, Malthus *rejected the idea that workers be given higher wages*, holding that the effect of higher wages during a depression would be merely to increase the cost of production and destroy the motive to accumulate before the economy had again reached a level of prosperity. He suggested as an immediate antidepression measure that workers be given employment in the construction of roads and other public works. But with Sismondi as his only reasonably competent ally, Malthus faced an uphill battle in which he gained little ground against the devastating arguments of Ricardo and his cohorts. Only in this century has the principal merit of Malthus' argument, namely, locating the source of stagnation in the saving-investment process, been recognized and has his still crude "business cycle theory" finally recuperated.

Tooke and Overstone.[3]—On a still higher level were the cycle analyses of Tooke and Overstone. We recall Tooke as one of the principal spokesmen of the Banking school; Overstone, along with the familiar Torrens, was an advocate of the Currency Principle. Tooke and Overstone not only influenced members of their own circles but also, despite their antagonism in matters of central bank policy, each other. The results of their probings in the field of business cycles were, in fact, quite similar. Although they gave expression to their visions of cyclical variations in different terms, in their understanding of this phenomenon they displayed a fundamental affinity.

Tooke arrived at his findings through a study of individual situations. In his *History of Prices* he showed awareness of a definite cyclical mechanism; he described the developments from 1818 to 1837 in terms of a lag of supply behind consumption during the upswing on one hand, and of a lag of consumption behind supply during the downswing on the other. He noted phases during which optimism prevails and others when despondency spreads and paralyzes the spirit of enterprise. Whereas Tooke followed the inductive path, Overstone took the deductive route — his deductions being tempered by his broad experiences as a banker. He spoke of the state of trade as revolving in an established cycle and loosely distinguished a large number of phases, as the following passage shows:

> The history of what we are in the habit of calling the "state of trade"
> is an instructive lesson. We find it subject to various conditions which

---

[3]See Biographical Note B.

are periodically returning; *it revolves apparently in an established cycle* [emphasis added]. First, we find it in a state of quiescence — next improvement — growing confidence — prosperity — excitement — overtrading — convulsion — pressure — stagnation — distress — ending again in quiescence.[4]

While the number of "phases" listed may strike the reader as excessive, especially since Overstone did not indicate their typical properties, their *sequence* still makes it possible to visualize the cycle in its entirety.

Both Tooke and Overstone knew that there were certain relations between prices, interest, credit, gold movements, speculation, and investment on one hand and the state of business activity on the other. His preoccupation with historical facts enabled Tooke to unfold a rich panorama of relevant characteristics. His constant emphasis on the importance of the trade in grains might incidentally suggest that he came close to stating a harvest theory of the business cycle, or at least has influenced later writers in this direction. Tooke also saw the significance of fixed capital investment in periods of prosperity and the propelling power of technological change (for example, railroad construction).

The analysis of Tooke and Overstone was forward-looking inasmuch as *they were aware that the cycle is largely self-generating in nature,* that each phase is induced by conditions prevailing in the preceding phase. Whether this makes their cycle theory an endogenous[5] one is open to question, because neither of them specified the relative importance attributed to exogenous factors, such as war or gold discoveries. However that may be, notwithstanding their special competence in monetary and banking matters, they veered away (Tooke more so than Overstone) from a purely monetary theory of the cycle, such as came to be expounded in the twenties and thirties of this century.

Overstone believed that an expansion of bank loans — whether represented by notes or deposits — that went beyond the supply of voluntary savings had something to do with prosperity and depression,

---

[4]Quoted by W. C. Mitchell, *Business Cycles, The Problem and Its Setting* (National Bureau of Economic Research, Inc., 1928), p. 11.

[5]Endogenous forces are responses shaped by the reaction of the whole business structure (economic system) to impulses coming from the outside. These impulses acting upon the economic system from outside are called exogenous factors, and theories that place primary reliance upon such factors are called exogenous theories. A clear distinction between exogenous and endogenous theories is often frustrated by lack of consensus as to what should be included in the economic system. "Politics" would typically constitute a border line case. Exogenous forces are perhaps best exemplified by changes in crops brought about by uncontrollable natural events, endogenous forces by expansion of bank loans, under gold-standard rules, on the basis of additional legal reserves.

although ups and downs in business activity would not be ruled out even if lending always remained within the boundaries of purchasing power not currently expended for consumer goods. He recognized that *inflationary credit extension* leads to a distortion of the structure of production and to violent readjustments. Recession was to him primarily a reaction to the credit expansion in the preceding boom. He looked upon the threat to the convertibility of bank notes resulting from cash drains as a cause of the rise in interest rates. This rise, he thought, may not only stop expansion but induce a contraction of deposits and a consequent fall in prices. The instability of money and credit was thus viewed by Overstone as a nonnegligible factor in unstabilizing economic progress. No wonder that he looked to the kind of moderate bank reform to which the Currency school committed itself as a means of mitigating cyclical fluctuations.

As a member of the Banking school, Tooke did not believe in the importance of special restrictions on the issue of notes since, under proper leadership by the Bank of England, convertibility of notes was enough to secure the kind of monetary stability of which a capitalist economy is capable. Minimizing the role of interest in the cycle, Tooke did not deem the contraction of credit to be the element triggering the downturn.

Mill.—John Stuart Mill offered a kind of synthesis of the many elements that had previously been mentioned by various writers as *sine qua non*'s in their particular explanation of the cycle phenomenon. This *synthesis* was not forceful, however, and has to be pieced together from many different passages in his *Principles*. He paid but incidental attention to the rhythmical oscillations of business activity because — like Smith and Ricardo — he was concerned primarily with elucidating principles which hold in the long run (or "normal" state). And, like most of the other Classicists, he subordinated the pecuniary aspect of economic behavior on the ground that money is merely a symbol the use of which makes no difference (except as a labor-saving device) so long as the system is functioning in an orderly fashion — that is, most of the time, as he saw it. Mill gathered many building blocks for a comprehensive theoretical structure — profit expectations acting upon dealers' stocks and hence upon prices, role of credit in aggravating fluctuations, external and internal cash drains, interest, periodicity, etc.— but he did not arrange these blocks in a unifying and logical way.

It would be tempting to look at the possibilities of interpretation which *Marx* (see Chapter 16), who never systematized his ideas on the subject of cycles, left open in his writings. However, in view of the fact that we lack the background information to understand his reasoning concerning, for example, the "falling rate of profit" or the "increasing severity of crises" in a capitalist economy and its eventual breakdown, we will move on to a consideration of developments in business cycle theory that are less closely associated with the classical structure of thought.

ANALYSIS IN THE NEOCLASSICAL ERA

Monetary Theories[6]

We recall from Chapter 11 that *Wicksell's* interest rate theory was at the same time a hypothesis concerning the forces that produce self-generating upward and downward movements in business activity. Wicksell's influence was twofold: he helped Malthus' idea of effective demand belatedly win a measure of recognition, and he anticipated much of the Keynesian concept of monetary demand for output as a whole. Few of the monetary economists in the early years of the twentieth century consciously arrived at their conclusions by working out the implications of the position that the net return to physical goods is the *fundamental* fact about the interest rate in the loan market. Neither did any of them deny that the rate of net return to physical capital (real rate) is at least one of the factors in the demand for loans. They would simply agree that it is incomplete to say that interest is the factor limiting investment expenditures. Some English economists, as well as many of the second-generation Austrians, built on Wicksell's foundation of the cumulative process. We will have to confine ourselves to a consideration of the contribution by the most representative monetary theorist from each of the two countries.

Hawtrey.—Hawtrey's analysis makes business cycles a *purely monetary phenomenon*: fluctuations in the flow of money income are the sole cause of general cyclical fluctuations in trade and employment. Since the elasticity of the money supply in modern industrialized communities is substantially equivalent to the elasticity of bank credit, any explanation of how monetary theory relates to fluctuations in business activity must focus on the potential elasticity of bank credit. Hawtrey views variations in effective demand as the substance of the

---

[6]The juxtaposition in two separate subsections of monetary and nonmonetary theories necessitates our abandoning the chronological procedure as far as the section "Analysis in the Neoclassical Era" as a whole is concerned.

trade cycle (as the business cycle is often called in England) and traces them to *changes in bank credit*. Effective demand is constituted by "consumers' outlay," that is, the total money payments made out of income. Hawtrey refers to total cash balances as the "unspent margin," which at any time must be equal to the total money supply of the community. This unspent margin will rise as a result of imports of gold or increases of bank credit on the basis of excess reserves; it will decrease when gold leaves the country or bank credit is contracted.

An *expansion* of business activity can originate in an increase of gold flowing in from abroad, an increased willingness of banks to make loans, a propensity of traders to increase their stocks of goods because of an improvement in expectations, as well as in a number of other conditions. When banks seek to increase their loans, they are usually willing to lower their interest rates; and, according to Hawtrey, these lower rates will ineluctably increase commercial borrowings. As this additional money is spent by the firms, consumers' incomes somewhere in the economy will rise. As a further result, consumers' outlay — barring the unlikely addition to cash balances of the full amount of additional income — will increase. The expansion becomes cumulative when this increase in effective demand on the part of consumers leads to further releases of cash both by traders adding to their stocks of goods and by banks satisfying the need for additional balances; and these releases, in turn, augment consumers' income and outlay. More and more dealers will use up their idle balances and become dependent for further inventory accumulation on additional bank credit, with this credit expansion increasing the total money income still more.

A price increase, caused by total spending rising at a faster rate than the volume of transactions effectuated by money, will begin in those places where output cannot be readily expanded and gradually will spread as more numerous plants reach the level of capacity operations. But this very price rise will add still further strength to the forces of the boom. As it becomes less advantageous to hold idle balances, velocity of money will increase also, adding its share to the upward pressure on prices.

In principle, nothing will stop this process of enlarging the money income and outlay of society — except the unwillingness and/or inability (under the gold standard) of the banks to accommodate further requests for loans. Indeed, the external and internal cash drain will put a brake on credit expansion by endangering the banks' legal or conventional reserve ratios. When they eventually raise their interest rates, the expansion may already have resulted in pronounced inflation and have caused frictions between various economic classes. Also, when action is taken this late, any check upon credit expansion may trigger a drastic and cumulative reaction.

In the phase of *contraction*, effective demand drops off as high interest rates discourage dealers from augmenting commodity stocks and the calling of loans by banks forces dealers to trim their inventories. As a result of slim orders, manufacturers have to curtail operations and will then pay less to wage earners, raw materials suppliers, and so on. With falling income, consumers' outlay (effective demand) will contract. For consumers to maintain spending by drawing down their cash balances becomes uneconomical as falling prices will enhance the real value of those balances. With falling prices, profits will shrink, particularly because some costs cannot be lowered in step with the fall in prices. As the velocity of turnover of money drops, prices will be weakened further.

Eventually, forces halting the decline in effective demand for goods will get under way. The fall in the volume of bank credit, coupled with the return flow of cash to the banks, will increase the reserve ratios and replenish bank reserves. Falling domestic prices in the meantime will have boosted exports and reduced imports, resulting in an inflow of gold. All this will make banks more willing to lend and to lower the interest rates charged on loans. As stocks of goods reach minimum size, new orders will be placed. Increased investment by dealers spells additional income payments, and consumers' outlay will again follow suit. As the revival develops into a new boom, the whole cycle begins to repeat itself.

Hawtrey is not blind to the fact that nonmonetary causes may affect production; but in his view, their effect on general productive activity is an indirect one, that is, it impinges on the economy through monetary media. Also, the periodicity of the trade cycle is due to the *monetary* effects of nonmonetary causes. If cumulative variations in bank credit could be avoided (through the stipulation of fixed reserves, for example), the trade cycle could be reduced to a minimum. In sum, the major relationships that account for the business cycle are not to be found in producers' goods industries but in the way that bank rates affect inventory holdings (commodities held for resale) of wholesale and retail traders.

While detailed criticism of Hawtrey's theory will be found in many places, we should bear in mind at least one *basic objection:* in the circumstances that have generally prevailed since the 1940's, it is questionable that monetary manipulation alone could control the business cycle. Businessmen no longer react as readily as they formerly did to interest rate movements, and their inventory policies have become a great deal more restrained.

Hayek.[7]—Another objection to Hawtrey's purely monetary cycle theory is that it bypasses the disproportionate variation in the production of capital goods which many of its students regard as the most striking feature of the business cycle. Hayek's analysis is a monetary one, but with emphasis on the phenomenon of overinvestment; hence it is often referred to as a *monetary overinvestment theory*.

Hayek rests his explanation on the Austrian distinction between higher and lower stages of production, with which we familiarized ourselves in Chapter 4. Together the many existing stages constitute what Hayek calls the *structure of production*. Changes in the relative volume of saving and spending tend to bring about appropriate changes in the structure of production. To Hayek there appears to be no reason why these adjustments should not be brought about with a minimum of friction — if it were not for the behavior of the banking system. With a fixed money supply, savings would be the only source for financing investments. But with an elastic money supply, investment can be altered without any increase in saving and will depend on the relation between the market rate of interest and the equilibrium rate.

Following Hayek, the course of events set in motion by changes in the rate of investment relative to the rate of saving can be summarized as follows. If, starting from an equilibrium position, entrepreneurs add to productive equipment (favor the higher stages of production), they expect to depend on a supply of funds for a considerable period of time, since, he argues, further investments will be called for after the first have been completed. It is the assumption that the present supply of money capital and the present rate of interest will continue, which justifies the use of any additional capital to begin new roundabout methods of production. Large fluctuations in saving might cause extensive losses on investments made during the preceding period and lead to an economic crisis. But experience tells us that there is

> ... no ground for assuming that such violent fluctuations in the rate of saving will occur otherwise than *in consequence* [emphasis added] of crises. If it were not for the crises ... the assumption of the entrepreneurs that the supply of saving will continue at about the present level for some time would probably prove to be justified. The decisions of the entrepreneurs as to the dates and quantities of consumers' goods for which they provide by their present investments would coincide

---

[7]See Biographical Note C.

with the intention of the consumers as to the parts of their incomes
which they want to consume at the various dates.[8]

How, then, can crises be explained? Hayek refers to the fact that
all kinds of monetary disturbances may change the supply of money
capital *independently* of the supply of savings. Entrepreneurs therefore
gear their investment decisions to criteria other than the current
willingness of consumers to save. In other words, entrepreneurs will
distribute their resources between production for the near future and
production for the distant future in a proportion different from that in
which consumers want to divide their current income between present
and future consumption. This *conflict between consumer and entrepreneurial intentions* constitutes a disequilibrium situation. If, as a
result of bank-created additions to the supply of money capital, the
market rate of interest is lowered below the equilibrium rate, relatively
too large a part of existing resources is devoted to production for the
more distant future. The investment of these bank-created funds will
in time be added to total income, regardless of whether wages are
raised to attract workers away from consumer goods industries toward
capital goods industries (in the case of full employment) or whether
the funds are used to employ formerly unemployed workers. How far
either alternative will tend to increase the demand for consumer goods
will depend on how consumers distribute their additional money income
between consumption spending and saving. And since the supply of
consumer goods will either remain the same or will actually fall, real
income will be the same or will be smaller. In fact, prices of consumer
goods will rise except in the most unlikely case where, with an undiminished supply of consumer goods, all the additional money income
will be saved.

Next we observe that the increased demand for consumer goods
need not discourage investment activity as long as credit expansion
enables entrepreneurs in capital goods industries to hire away from
consumer goods industries such increasing shares of the available
productive resources as are required to complete the new processes
already under way. The crucial question is: What will happen when
the demand for consumer goods begins to rise not only absolutely but
also relatively to the funds available for investment? Entrepreneurs
who have counted on a continuation of the original low rate of interest
and an ample supply of money will see their expectations disappointed
when, under gold-standard rules, banks are forced to tighten credit.

[8]F. A. Hayek, "Price Expectations, Monetary Disturbances and Maladjustments,"
Profits, Interest, and Investment; in *Readings in Business Cycle Theory* (Philadelphia:
Blakiston Division of McGraw-Hill Book Co., 1944), p. 356.

In the absence of a further increase in bank credit, a good deal of capital goods production will have to be abandoned, and a reversal of the changes in the structure of production is bound to begin.   Hence, Hayek concludes, the real trouble lies in a scarcity of capital which makes it impossible to use the newly created equipment designed to produce other capital goods (and consumer goods). Or, from another point of view, there is overinvestment brought about by "forced saving"; the crisis erupts because of a shortage of voluntary savings. Although we are already acquainted with the concept of "forced savings" from a brief consideration of Wicksell's *cumulative process*, it needs to be underscored that "forced savings" does not refer to a sum of money. It refers to a stock of durable capital (buildings, machinery, equipment, etc.) which is forced upon the community as a whole because of the action of entrepreneurs using bank credit in lieu of (voluntary) savings as a source of investment funds.

The difficulties involved in readjusting the structure of production so as to make it conform to voluntary savings may cause *depression*, where depression is conceived as the state of affairs in a period during which the structure of production is shortened to appropriate length. We see now that Hayek's theory of the cycle leads to conclusions diametrically opposed to those arrived at by economists who hold that *excessive* saving (relative to investment demand) is the fundamental cause of the downswing.

In perspective, it appears that the *similarities* between Hawtrey's and Hayek's cycle theories are sufficiently strong to permit us to consider them as members of the same family: they are both monetary theories — Hayek's being a semimonetary theory, if we please. Their adherents may be said to disagree on one basic issue only, namely, whether interest rates act primarily on durable capital (Hayek's higher stages) or via the stocks of traders.

Nonmonetary Theories

To avoid misunderstanding, note this: When we speak of nonmonetary cycle analysis we do not preclude the notion that the demand for money in one form or another plays a role in cyclical fluctuations; we simply mean that the elasticity of the money supply is not a *sine qua non* for the kind of fluctuations observed in the world of reality.

Juglar.[9]—The most distinguished pioneer worker striving for more exact observation and description of cyclical phenomena was the French

---

[9]See Biographical Note D.

economist Clément Juglar. His *Of Commercial Crises and their Periodic Return in France, England, and the United States* won the plaudits of the French Academy of Moral and Political Sciences in 1860 and was published in book form two years later. His elaborate treatise was a decisive performance that looked beyond "crises" or "gluts" and considered these merely as incidents or phases of a larger process. Juglar was the first to make systematic use of such time series as prices, interest rates, and bank balances for the purpose of analyzing a phenomenon that was only vaguely understood. His "book of facts" hastened the arrival of the time when economists passed on from the theory of crises to the theory of business cycles. His factual investigations involved long labors and were supplemented by a history of crises since the late seventeenth century.

Juglar sought to show the interrelations between three phases, called "prosperity," "crisis," and "liquidation," which, he said, follow one another always in the same order. But he did not realize clearly that the intervals between crises, which he estimated at roughly ten years' duration, often contain shorter alternations of prosperity and depression (minor cycles), which are not marked off by financial stringencies. Later investigators, who were aware of these shorter cycles, substituted the less specific term "recession" for the term "crisis" to designate the phase following prosperity.

Although Juglar used the term "periodic" in the title of his book, his own history of crises in France, England, and the United States showed that in none of them have the crises been regular. As long as it is borne in mind that "periodic" may refer to variable periods, Juglar's usage — followed by many later writers — is unobjectionable. In the interest of avoiding misunderstanding it might have been preferable to use the term "recurrent." In other words, what may be found regular is the recurrence of prosperity, recession, depression, and revival. However, as far as the post-World War II years are concerned, even this kind of regularity is scarcely found. Nowadays, many hold that we may have "licked" the Juglar cycle and no longer face anything more serious than alternations of prosperity and recession, with an occasional stock market collapse reminding us of the pre-World War II "periodic" crises. Qualifications aside, the twentieth-century morphology of cycles definitely dates from Juglar.

In explaining the periodic return of "crisis" (that is, the major or intercrisis cycles) *Juglar blended facts and theory in an ideal way*, arriving at his "law of crises" without any preconceived hypothesis. He diagnosed depressions as nothing but adaptations of the economic system to unbalanced situations created by the preceding prosperities and reduced the basic problem of cycle analysis to the question of what causes prosperities. Although he failed to give a satisfactory answer to this question, he set up a method for later research workers to arrive at answers. They were slow to take up the challenge; the first to proceed entirely in Juglar's spirit was W. C. Mitchell, whose contributions set the tone for much of the factual and theoretical analysis that has been pursued during the last half century.

Other Pre-World War I Analysts.—By the time Mitchell set another landmark, scientific workers agreed on the basic features or symptoms that characterize cyclical phases and at least tacitly took for granted that the fundamental fact about cyclical fluctuations was a rather violent variation in the rate of spending for plant and equipment. Observe, too, that, although the monetary theories we discussed seek the causes of the cyclical movement in the monetary sphere, they concede effects of the monetary phenomena on the plant-and-equipment industries. *There was no agreement, however, as to the relations of the basic features of the cycle to one another;* and it is differences in the interpretation of these relations which gave rise to the bewildering variety of so-called cycle theories — illustrated in the "monetary field" by Hawtrey and Hayek, for example. However, disagreement and antagonism between writers was less fundamental than they led their readers to believe. It was the endeavor to individuate their pet schemes, to "get credit" for a theory of their own, that led them to unreasonable lengths in attacking each other.

Among those who linked the phenomenon of business cycles with *fluctuations in additions to fixed assets*, the Russian *Tugan-Baranowsky*[10] occupies a prominent place. This thinker was fully aware of the pivotal importance of the relatively large amplitude of the movements of constructional as compared with consumption industries, recognizing it as one of the general characteristics of industrial fluctuations. He undertook an intensive study of *The Industrial Crises in England in the 19th Century*, first published in 1894. In this work, which made quite a mark in Western Europe, he distinguished between loan funds (individual and business savings) and capital invested in production. Not only the latter but also the former generally decline during depression; but there are some savers, such as bondholders, landlords, etc., whose incomes are little affected by the downswing, and the real value of whose savings is actually augmented. Tugan-Baranowsky

---

[10]See Biographical Note E.

brought out the vital point that aggregate saving, though it declines below prosperity levels, declines *less* than aggregate investment. Hence depression manifests itself in the gradual accumulation of a huge uninvested fund of loan capital, which is reflected in swollen bank reserves and low interest rates. A time will come, however, when savers, irrespective of these low rates, will become eager to get their funds into profitable use, and then large purchases made with borrowed funds will pave the way for prosperity. Eventually investment, feeding on itself, will attain a scale so large as to exceed current saving, it being now only a matter of time until the "uninvested loan fund" is exhausted. As this fund shrinks, interest rates will rise until, when bank reserves have fallen to the danger point, they are prohibitively high. A crisis is ushered in, and the cycle will repeat itself. Tugan-Baranowsky held that the alternate accumulation and exhaustion of the loan fund, the *differentia specifica* of his explanatory hypothesis, could not occur if income were more evenly distributed, in particular if labor were more amply rewarded.

Spiethoff[11] spun out this line of thought and presented his insights first to a professional association in Berlin around the turn of the century. Not until the mid-1920's, when they were incorporated in the leading social science encyclopedia in the German-speaking world, did his views on business cycles become accessible to the educated public.

Spiethoff placed great emphasis on the *difference between the roles played in the cyclical process by industrial equipment and by consumer goods*. He held that crises become inevitable when people put their savings on a large scale into industrial equipment, thus creating a relative scarcity of consumer goods.

In the first stage of the upswing, previously idle productive facilities are called into use; somewhat later, existing plants are expanded and new ones are erected. With the rise in consumer income because of increased payments for the use of factor services, pressure is exerted on consumer goods industries, which have difficulty in competing resources away from capital goods industries. But eventually the expanded production facilities will spout forth a large stream of consumer goods, whose "supply" now exceeds current "demand." In the absence of sufficient demand to absorb this plethora at cost-covering prices, production becomes unprofitable, and the stage is set for contraction.

Spiethoff used the consumption of iron as a fundamental index of the expansion of plant and equipment. His broadly conceived model

---

[11]See Biographical Note F.

left plenty of room for the accommodation of psychological factors, monetary factors, the principle of acceleration, and so on. It came as close as we may reasonably expect to an *organic synthesis of relevant forces conditioning the ups and downs of business activity*. Moreover, Spiethoff was one of the first to express in print that cycles are not merely a by-product of capitalist evolution, but that they are the essential form of a capitalist economy. And he did not fail to observe what he called "spans of prosperity" and "spans of depression," that is, long periods during which prosperity phases tend to be especially pronounced and others during which depression phases tend to predominate. He did not suggest, however, that "Juglar cycles" might be "overlaid" by long cycles; that hypothesis was ventured later by Schumpeter.

Aftalion.[12] — Aftalion, a French economist, following a series of articles in 1913 authored a book entitled *The Periodic Crises of Overproduction*, in which he gave a clear exposition of *generalized overproduction*, a further development of Spiethoff's main idea. It relates to errors of forecasting which are magnified by what Robertson was the first to call the *period of gestation* — the time period covered by any given process of production. For durable capital goods such as steel mills, railroads, and office buildings, this period may be very long, whereas for certain consumer goods it may be measured in weeks or days. The magnitude of the error of forecasting obviously depends on the length of this period, during which a powerful tendency to produce is at work in response to an initial increase in consumer (or producer) demand. If the gestation period is short, the boom itself will be short-lived; but if the former is long, the latter may get out of hand. A boom centering in demand for nondurable consumer goods or services would represent one extreme, a boom caused by an increased demand for long-lived producer goods the other extreme. Long or short, the euphoria will end when the average period of gestation is over and producers are faced with the reality of a sharp discrepancy between available output at current prices and the quantity demanded at those prices.

The crucial point to bear in mind is that during the period of gestation the supply of, say, consumer goods continues inadequate, and prices keep rising in step with fuller employment and the larger incomes disbursed, thus inducing entrepreneurs to start additional plants. These entrepreneurs fail to realize that, when the plants already under construction will begin production, the output of finished goods will be

---

[12]See Biographical Note G.

greater than the amount that can be absorbed by the market at profitable prices. As price reductions spread from one field to another in the wake of the crisis, depression becomes general. Recovery can come only because production tends to fall behind consumption when prices are falling. Eventually businessmen will have to step up their output rate and to begin ordering equipment more freely. This will initiate a new rise in prices and another round of prosperity.

Aftalion emphasized more compellingly than did others the phenomenon of a *lag between the time when new investment takes place and the time it becomes productive.* He was also the first to analyze in detail the relationship known as the *acceleration principle.*[13]

It would lead us too far afield to discuss those theories which in one way or another hark back to Sismondi and Malthus, that is, which impute responsibility for downswings to the inadequacy of money income in general, or to the inadequacy of the incomes of some classes, or to people's saving habits. For a representative sample of this kind of theory you may with benefit study the ideas espoused by *John A. Hobson.*[14] Most frequently referred to as underconsumption or oversaving theory, it is the kind with the greatest popular and political appeal, although in their analytic foundation these theories seldom represented a notable advance.

As we conclude our survey of nonmonetary explanations of the business cycle, we should note that most of the economists around the turn of the century were ardent "theorists," enamored of their own ideas and favoring one explanation or another of either crises or cycles. Few would confess to a belief that perhaps there was no general explanation of such phenomena, that every cycle is historically unique to some extent, and that unique combinations of circumstances must largely govern the analysis of every particular case. As Mitchell's work progressed, single factor explanations became more and more discredited, though they turned out to be hardy plants. To that work we now turn.

W. C. MITCHELL[15]

Mitchell ushered in an era characterized by a new wealth of data and new statistical methods of handling them. Alone or in cooperation with others, he published studies on the business cycle which have become classics. His first book, already a masterpiece with a profound

---

[13]This term was introduced in 1917 by J. M. Clark, the son of J. B. Clark. See Erich Schneider, *Money, Income, and Employment* (London: George Allen and Unwin, 1962), p. 175.
[14]See Biographical Note H.
[15]See Biographical Note I.

impact on economic research and analysis, appeared in 1913 under the title *Business Cycles*. For much of the remaining half of his life, associated with a trained staff at the National Bureau of Economic Research, Mitchell identified himself with the subject that was the major focus of his far-flung interests.

Mitchell's creative efforts were not simply directed toward the cyclical phenomena per se, but rather toward a new genre of economic theory, to be sustained by the ideas developed in the study of business fluctuations and representing an *analytic description of interrelated processes*. At the back of his factual work stood the theory that the economic process is essentially wavelike, that cycles are a form of capitalist evolution. He recognized that the capitalist economy is one in which economic activity depends upon the factors which affect present or prospective pecuniary profits — he saw in profits the clue to business fluctuations.

Mitchell started out with a succinct and detached survey of existing explanations, then traced the connections between economic organization (both past and present) and business cycles, and followed this up by the explanatory contribution which he could derive from statistics and business annals. He looked upon existing explanations as so many statements of partial truths, none particularly outstanding, each to be tested in the crossfire of facts. Possessed with an exemplary sense of impartiality, he did not rule out any theory before it came up for factual trial. His chapters on the modern money economy were in effect introductory treatises on general economic theory, in which he anticipated much of what has become incorporated in modern income accounting and aggregative analysis. His pioneer achievement, however, relates to his *use and development of statistical material*. Having perceived a need for such material, he diagnosed the available means to satisfy the need, and then attacked the problem head-on and with ingenuity.

To test the comparability of various statistical indices of business cycles, he compared those five among the available indices whose time coverage was most extensive, around fifty years in the case of three of them. He discovered that they have a number of similarities: their "saw-tooth" contour, their amplitude of month-to-month changes, their marking off peaks and durations of major cycles, etc. He did not suppress the fact that in some respects they lacked uniformity in results, but the conclusions at which he arrived by this comparative method helped to establish confidence in the validity of his procedure and the usefulness of the evidence he obtained. The results he derived from the use of business annals confirm the impression that the statistical picture of business fluctuations available in modern times is a reasonably faithful one.

It should be added that Mitchell's investigations into the subject of price and production index numbers for the most part followed rather than preceded the publication of *Business Cycles*. Similar in scope, that is, in the nature of a survey of work done and a program of work to be done, his second book entitled *Business Cycles, the Problem and Its Setting* was published in 1927. In writing it he availed himself of a team of fellow workers who had gathered under the wings of the National Bureau of Economic Research, of which he had been a cofounder in 1920. Even today the Bureau bears the stamp that Mitchell, its gifted research director, gently impressed upon it during more than a quarter century of close association with it. *Measuring Business Cycles* came from the press in 1946, and in it are analyzed the more than a thousand time series which the united forces of the Bureau were able to unearth and digest. Two years later the Bureau lost its guiding spirit, a technician of superior skill and craftsmanship and a man of singular devotion to scientific advance.

J. A. SCHUMPETER[16]

Digression: A Value Judgment

Schumpeter's economics occupies a unique place in the history of economic thought. The product of a rare and phenomenal mind, rivaled by few in its tremendous grasp, his business cycle theory, to which we turn in the following subsection, must be understood as part of a grand vision of the capitalist process taking place in historic time. *Extremely erudite as an economist*, Schumpeter was equally sovereign in all the sciences on which his specialty had to draw; he was a skilled mathematician and linguist. He has been called the last of the great polymaths, the *most widely read and versatile of the social scientists of his generation*.

He achieved his peak performance as a historian of economic theory and as a biographer, in which capacities he displayed an unsurpassed gift of analysis and understanding, a quality which has awed friend and foe alike. Of Austrian descent, professor at Harvard University for the last seventeen years of his life, he founded no school, but his critical acumen penetrated the remotest nooks and crannies of economic science. His genius had so many facets that he was a master of almost

---

[16]See Biographical Note J.

all variants of economics. For this reason, and also because his temperament would have rebelled against the idea, it is fruitless to place him in any school of economic thought. This suggests above all that Schumpeter was a *complex* personality which cannot be fathomed except by the most sincere and assiduous researchers — people without an "axe to grind" and only interested in the maintenance of the highest of scientific standards. Verily, no self-respecting student of the history of economic thought can afford to go without the inspiration that a perusal of his incomplete and posthumously published maximum opus, *History of Economic Analysis*, effuses lavishly.

Schumpeter's place as a twentieth-century giant is hardly disputed any longer. His stature may, or may not, overshadow that of Keynes by the end of this century. That he will always be mentioned alongside the all-time greats — Smith, Ricardo, J. Stuart Mill, Marshall — is to this writer beyond any doubt. For Schumpeter was also *genuinely creative*. If originality consists of the achievement of new combinations, Schumpeter was original in the highest degree.

Such an unabashed personal commitment must be understood as a parenthetical value judgment only, flowing from a large debt of gratitude for inspiration received. Let us now consider a few of Schumpeter's leading ideas.

Leading Ideas

Like Mitchell, Schumpeter held that the study of cycles was the best way of comprehending the capitalist process in its totality. Two of his works have a close bearing on advance in business cycle analysis: *The Theory of Economic Development* (1911) and *Business Cycles* (1939). In the first he traced the circular flow of economic life as conditioned by the social process in terms of a series of relationships modeled on the Walrasian equilibrium concept. (For Schumpeter, Walras was the greatest economist that ever lived.) A key role in his dynamic model is assigned to the *entrepreneur*, who carries out new combinations in production, which makes him an "innovator." Chapter VI of *The Theory of Economic Development* forms the bridge to the two-volume *Business Cycles*, which captured in fascinating detail the vast historical and analytical literature on the subject.

In his *business cycle model*, Schumpeter started with the assumption of general economic equilibrium and then let intrude an innovation, that is, a new production function in which certain entrepreneurs see the promise of money profits. These entrepreneurs are individuals possessed of a rare combination of capacities to originate new schemes and carry them to successful conclusion. Under the concept of a new production function can be subsumed such things as new techniques of production, new markets, new products, and new forms of organization. According to Schumpeter, there is a tendency for innovations to appear in clusters as success of the leaders smooths the path for imitators or followers — the mass of routine entrepreneurs. Schumpeter is aware of the fact that inventions are continually being made, but he held as sporadic the actual introduction into the economy of new combinations, hence the concept of clusters or swarms.

The *clustering of innovations* will tend to convert recovery into prosperity (in the four-phase cycle). It is assumed that innovation is financed by bank credit. In time factor scarcities will make their appearance, and as the boom continues credit will become tighter. The former innovations begin to turn out an ever-increasing supply of goods, which tends to flood the market and lower prices. Some profits are converted into losses, and the outlook becomes very doubtful. As innovators (are forced to) pay off their bank loans, credit will contract and the downswing gets under way. Errors of calculation with respect to the success of innovations are being "rectified." This means that considerable numbers of enterprises which did not manage to adapt themselves to the novel conditions brought about by the innovation will fail.

Overall, Schumpeter's business cycle appears as an ebb and flow of innovations and subsequent adaptations. *Recessions and depressions are the price the economy has to pay for dynamic progress.* In Schumpeter's scheme innovators are basically responsible for two primary waves — a two-phase cycle of prosperity and recession — without any definite periodicity. By introducing the concept of "secondary waves" of business activity as well as some other elements, Schumpeter gets the "Second Approximation" which converts the two-phase cycle into one of four phases, consisting of prosperity, recession, depression, and revival. (A depression will last until the readjustments have been worked out, and with the return to more stable conditions entrepreneurs regain confidence in the future.) Although the four-phase cycle model is more "realistic" than the two-phase one, it cannot do full justice to reality. Schumpeter recognizes that, historically, depression will not always follow recession — he is aware of the inventory cycle, for example — and that revival will not always lead to prosperity. While he attributed a considerable role to errors bred by uncertainty, he did not say that crises and depressions would be eliminated if it were possible to avoid miscalculation. This, in utmost brevity, suggests some of the vital ingredients of Schumpeter's cycle theory.

In rounding out our survey, it is of interest to observe that he attempted to systematize cycles by distinguishing three main types: (1) a Juglar cycle of about 10 years' duration, (2) a Kitchin cycle of 3 to 4 years in length, and (3) a Kondratieff cycle lasting for 50 to 60 years. The names under (2) and (3) are those of economists who were responsible for the "discovery" and description of these shorter and longer movements, which, according to Schumpeter, interact with the Juglar type. The Kitchin cycle was especially emphasized in the work carried out by the National Bureau of Economic Research. In Schumpeter's scheme, there were roughly three Kitchin cycles to a Juglar, and six Juglars to a Kondratieff.

Let us cast a glance back at the beginning of this chapter. It turns out that, along with Mitchell, Schumpeter was one of those few pre-World War I[17] writers who did not treat business cycles as a pathological phenomenon superimposed upon the normal course of capitalist life but looked to business cycles for the very stuff with which to build the fundamental theory of capitalist society.

SUMMARY

The main tradition of political economy, classicism and neoclassicism, assumed that capitalist economies tended toward equilibrium at full employment. Following Say's lead as symbolized in the Law of Markets, the exponents of the mainstream of economic thought from Smith to Marshall concentrated on problems of value and distribution theory and ignored the challenge to ingenuity presented by the phenomena of the cycle. Early rebels against the attitude of complacency prompted by this frame of mind were Sismondi and Malthus. A century later their diagnosis was confirmed by Hobson and made vastly more effective — thanks to a sophisticated technical armor — by Keynes.

All attempts prior to Juglar's to cope scientifically with problems of business fluctuations were in the nature of preliminary analysis. Among the forerunners of modern cycle theory, Tooke and Overstone excelled: Tooke by his painstaking study of individual situations which led him to awareness of a definite cyclical mechanism, Overstone by his holistic view of the state of trade passing through phases. No

---

[17]The Schumpeterian system had already been conceived in outline form in 1911. Fleshing out the skeleton was his life work.

mean feat, they grasped the self-generating nature of the business cycle. Mill's suggestive comments lacked organic integration and illustrate the fact that the whole — which he missed — is often more than the sum of its parts.

Wicksell pointed the way to monetary theories of the business cycle and in particular to the cumulative process of expansion and contraction of bank credit based on discrepancies between the real and the market rates of interest. Hawtrey expounded a purely monetary variant of cycle explanation which hinged on the expansibility of the money supply; he discussed the repercussions — in terms of prices, incomes, and spending — of a cyclical starter in the monetary sphere. Hayek acknowledged the crucial importance of the mechanisms described by Hawtrey, but he rested his main explanation on distortions in the structure of production relative to voluntary saving. Whereas in Hawtrey's view interest rates affect primarily the investment decisions of traders, Hayek sees them as acting mainly on entrepreneurial outlays for plant and equipment.

Nonmonetary theories do not deny that the demand for money plays a role in cyclical fluctuations, but they look to a real variable for the principal explanation of the turns and twists of business activity. Common to most is the crucial role attributed to variations in the rate of spending for plant and equipment, but they disagree in their interpretation of the relations of the basic features and symptoms that characterize cyclical phases. In Tugan-Baranowsky's explanatory hypothesis, the alternate accumulation and exhaustion of the loan fund appears as the villain; Spiethoff's emphasis was on the difference between the roles played by industrial equipment and consumer goods but left ample room for other factors; Aftalion focused on the period of gestation and its responsibility for overproduction.

In the empirically oriented development of business cycle theory, the peak performers were Juglar and Mitchell, whose remarkable attainments were widely separated in time and place. Juglar was the first to avail himself in systematic fashion of time series for the purpose of business cycle analysis. He hastened the transition from "crisis" theory to "cycle" theory, and stressed the periodicity of cyclical movements. Mitchell, basing his interpretation of the cycle on even more solid information, sought demonstrable statements and saw in brilliant hypotheses partial truths at best. As cofounder of the National Bureau of Economic Research, he did more than any other American economist (except possibly Fisher) to refine the techniques of investigation and statistical measurement, thereby greatly indebting the economic profession.   The offshoots of his pioneering investigations have grown too numerous to account for.

Schumpeter's feats exhibit the marks of lonely virtuosity.   His ambitious work combined statistical, theoretical, and historical techniques in a perfect blend.   The result: a theory of capitalism itself, that is, of a system in which (1) the innovating entrepreneur is the mainspring of dynamic change, (2) there is room for an economic elite, (3) miscalculations in the competitive struggle for a better tomorrow jeopardize the survival of firms.

BIOGRAPHICAL NOTES

A. — *Jean Charles Léonard de Sismondi* (1773–1842), whose real name was Simonde, was born in Geneva, Switzerland, the scion of an aristocratic Italian family which had settled in France long ago, after their native city of Pisa had changed hands.   During the French Revolution in the late eighteenth century, Simonde's family fled to England, having escaped from prison in 1793.   Previously, Sismondi had shown great acumen in business affairs and had accumulated much of the knowledge which enabled him later to write economic treatises.   In England he became an enthusiastic observer of his host country's political institutions.   Before the turn of the century, he returned to Geneva and afterwards settled on a farm in Tuscany.   His experience as a practical farmer enabled him to write the *Table of Tuscan Agriculture* (1801).   Two years later, when he expounded Adam Smith's doctrines for continental readers in a *Treatise of Commercial Wealth*, he showed that his conceptualization of political economy was much more English than French.   He then turned to research on medieval history and, extending over a period of twelve years beginning in 1807, published sixteen volumes on the *History of the Italian Republics in the Middle Ages.*

In the meantime he had returned to Geneva for good.   An invitation to write an article on political economy for the new *Edinburgh Encyclopaedia* recalled him to the theme of his *Treatise* in 1818.   As he studied current developments, especially the depression following the end of the Napoleonic Wars, he was struck by doubts concerning the theories he had accepted from Adam Smith and was moved to write the work on which his reputation as an economist rests, namely, *New Principles of Political Economy*, published in 1819.

For the remainder of his life, he was mostly occupied with writing a thirty-one volume *History of the French*, which came off the press between 1821 and 1844.   Although bulk never tells the whole story and may be deceptive, his greater achievement was indeed in the field of political-historical, rather than economic, analysis; his *Studies on Political Economy* (1837–38) did not add anything essentially new to his earlier theses.

B. — *Lord Overstone* (1796–1883), whose real name was Samuel Jones Lloyd, was a banker of inherited wealth and position, a brilliant personality and quite influential with politicians.   Overstone did not write a systematic work on economics. One of his outstanding contributions was *Reflections suggested by a perusal of Mr. J. Horsley Palmer's pamphlet on the Causes and Consequences of the Pressure on the Money Market,* published in 1837. Most of his writings were edited in 1857 by John Ramsay Mc-Culloch, the dedicated Ricardian, under the title *Tracts and other Publications on Metallic and Paper Currency.* McCulloch in 1858 also edited Lord Overstone's *Evidence before the House of Commons Select Committee on Bank Acts,* 1857.

C. — *Friedrich August von Hayek* (1899–　　) was born in Vienna, studied law and economics at the University of Vienna, and obtained his doctorate (rer. pol.) in 1923. The University of London awarded him a D. Sc. degree in economics in 1943.

After a term in the Austrian Federal Service from 1921 to 1926, he became a director of the Austrian Institute of Economic Research (1927–1931). He pursued research work in New York in 1923 and 1924 and was a lecturer at the University of Vienna from 1929 to 1931. From then until the end of the 1940's, he held the Tooke professorship of economic science and statistics at the London School of Economics. He was professor of social and moral science at the University of Chicago from 1950 to 1962 and has been a professor of economics at the University of Freiburg, Germany, since then. Hayek has been a naturalized British subject since 1938.

His voluminous scientific production in book form includes: *Prices and Production* (1931); *Monetary Theory and the Trade Cycle* (1933); *Collectivist Economic Planning* (1935); *Profit, Interest, and Investment* (1939); *The Pure Theory of Capital* (1941); *The Road to Serfdom* (1944, a best seller); *Individualism and the Economic Order* (1948); *John Stuart Mill and Harriet Taylor* (1951); *The Counter-Revolution of Science* (1952); *The Sensory Order* (1952); *Capitalism and the Historians* (1954); *The Constitution of Liberty* (1960); *Studies in Philosophy, Politics, and Economics* (1967).

Hayek is perhaps at his best as a historian of economic doctrine, but his impact on political philosophy has been much more powerful. He has refreshingly upheld the ideals of individual liberty and scathingly condemned "big government" and all forms of collectivism.

D. — *Clément Juglar* (1819–1905) had been a student and practitioner of medicine when, at the age of 29, he switched to economics. He did not undergo any formal training in the new subject of his interest and may have had only contempt for formal theory. But his aloofness from the accepted corpus of economic theory did not prevent him from making an original contribution to it. Of his many publications only the one mentioned in the body of the text is of interest to us.

E. — *Mikhail Ivanovich Tugan-Baranowsky* (1865–1919) was a remarkable Russian economist who was much interested in both theory and history. In this he may have been strongly influenced by Marx, although he was by no means a Marxist — he was not in sympathy with the Marxian theory of exploitation. He drew heavily from the English classical as well as the Austrian literature and was somehow able to blend Ricardo's labor theory of value with marginal utility theory. His most important work was the one mentioned in the body of the text. It was first published in Russian in 1894, its German version appeared in 1901, and a French edition came off the press in 1913. Among his many other works, the following are at least worthy of mention: *Theoretical Foundations of Marxism* (1905), *Modern Socialism in Its Historical Development* (1906), and *Social Theory of Distribution* (1913). In his political philosophy, Tugan-Baranowsky was a moderate socialist who emphasized cooperation and ethics. Although of great ability, he was often deficient in rigorous thinking, which explains that only few of his many books achieved success.

F. — *Arthur Spiethoff* (1873–1957) was a German economist in close relationship with Germany's Historical school, which for many years was "headed" by the then Rector of the University of Berlin, the redoubtable Gustav Schmoller (see Chapter 4, Biographical Note A). During the twelve years by which Spiethoff survived the defeat of Germany in World War II, he was probably the last of the great figures in his country's historical tradition.

He had been an assistant editor for *Schmoller's Jahrbuch*, a famous quarterly journal of economics, from 1899 to 1908; and it was during this period that he completed his doctoral work, which dealt with crises. He lectured at the universities in Berlin, Prague, and Bonn; in Bonn he was Schumpeter's colleague before the latter emigrated to the United States in 1932 (Biographical Note J, below).

As a result of his work in the field of business cycles, Spiethoff acquired an international reputation. He became most famous for his article on crises (1925) in the *Handwörterbuch der Staatswissenschaften*, reprinted under the title "Business Cycles" in *International Economic Papers*, No. 3, London, 1953. In his empirical investigations, Spiethoff employed a conceptual framework that was historically oriented. He recognized a large number of historical "styles" of economic life, each calling for its own theory, although he did not rule out such a thing as "timeless" theory. He wrote a number of articles for *Schmoller's Jahrbuch* and contributed to collectively authored works.

G. — *Albert Aftalion* (1874–1956) is a French economist who for many years taught at the University of Paris. In 1899 he published an account of Sismondi's contribution to economic science under the title *The Economic Work of Simonde de Sismondi*. His specialty has been monetary and business cycle theory, rather than the history of economic doctrines. In 1927 his *Money, Price, and Exchange* was published, mostly concerned with the value (purchasing power) of money; in 1932 a work entitled *Gold and its Distribution over the World* appeared. Finally, in 1937 he wrote *Equilibrium in International Economic Relations*. None of these works had the impact of *The Periodic Crises of Overproduction*, which is notable for strict adherence to Juglar's methodological principles.

H. — In *John A. Hobson* (1858–1940) we recognize the maturing of a crosscurrent of thought which rebelled against both the facile analysis of the Classicists and the reaction in the form of the marginal analysis offered by Jevons and the Austrians. Perhaps he belonged to what Keynes occasionally referred to as the "underworld of economics."

Born of middle-class parents, Hobson studied the classics at Oxford. Such historians as Ruskin and Toynbee aroused in him an interest in social reform and thus in economics. Haunted by the evils that had been generated by the Industrial Revolution, he could not discover in the erstwhile writings of economists a path to social justice. Not finding in teaching of the classics an outlet for his pent-up aspirations to be instrumental in social reform, he sought to obtain a teaching post in economics. Alas, as with George in the United States, the academic powers rejected his views, and Hobson had to be satisfied with university extension lecture assignments instead of being able to become a resident professor. As it turned out, he managed to reach a much greater number of people, many of them actually members of the working class. He reinforced his impact on the masses when, shortly before the turn of the century, he became a journalist. During the remaining four decades of his life, he frequently contributed to liberal periodicals.

Hobson published some three dozen books dealing with economic questions, many of which were not tightly enough reasoned to find a place on the bookshelf of academic economists. Those of relatively high quality include *The Physiology of Industry* (1889), *The Evolution of Modern Capitalism* (1894), *Work and Wealth: A Human Evaluation* (1914), and *The Economics of Unemployment* (1922). In all of his major writings he was concerned not so much with wealth per se as he was with welfare as conditioned by man's biological and psychological traits.

At the center of his business cycle theory — mainly a theory of extended business depressions — is his analysis of the unequal distribution of wealth between capital and labor. Some have considered it as a milder version of Marx's exploitation theory (see Chapter 16). In times of prosperity, members of the upper-income classes, unable to spend all they currently receive on consumer goods, invest a portion of their income in productive capital. But a portion of the currently produced supply of consumer goods remains unsold because it cannot be absorbed at cost-covering prices. The excess of production over consumption disappears when prices have to be lowered and losses take the place of profits. Oversaving, the root cause of the collapse, gradually vanishes as consumption catches up with production at the low prices prevailing during depression. With the revival of business, profits reappear; more generally, there is room again for an economic surplus. It is interesting to note that in one of his later works (*Taxation in the New State*, 1919) Hobson set forth a plan for taxing away economic surpluses — an extension of George's idea of taxing away land rent.

I. — *Wesley Clair Mitchell* (1874–1948) was one of Veblen's outstanding students although he was of a different temperament and never a follower of Veblen's unorthodox ways. Thanks to Mitchell, the institutionalist tradition has been not only kept alive but greatly enriched. Born in Illinois, he was of New England stock and, because of his father's poor health, soon had to learn how to handle family responsibilities. After completing high school, he enrolled in 1893 at the newly founded University of Chicago, which had been able to draw some of the country's top scholars into its fold. Here he came under the influence, above all, of Veblen and John Dewey, the first imparting to him a certain skepticism, the latter teaching him the merits of a pragmatic and operational philosophy. Veblen's and Dewey's emphasis on human behavior led Mitchell into a study of ethnology, anthropology, and psychology. Under the influence of J. Laurance Laughlin, he became intrigued with monetary problems. Perhaps as a backdrop for a fuller understanding of the burning issues of the 1890's — free silver, declining gold reserves — he chose as topic for his doctoral dissertation the issue of greenbacks during the Civil War. It was published in 1903 as the *History of the Greenbacks*.

After having received his Chicago degree *summa cum laude*, he briefly joined the Census Bureau. The favorable reception of his *History* may have helped him secure a teaching position at the University of California (Berkeley) in 1903. He occupied a still more prominent place in the profession when, ten years later, he joined the faculty of Columbia University, with which he was associated during the remainder of his teaching career. One of his favorite courses there was the History of Economic Thought, but he never published his notes on the subject. Thanks to the initiative of assiduous students, *Lecture Notes on Types of Economic Theory* found its way into print in 1949, after his death.

Gold Prices and Wages, published in 1908, also dealt with the economic experience of the Civil War. The volume *Business Cycles*, published in 1913, was the fruit of three years' work at an intense pace. In his written and oral pronouncements, Mitchell was always loath to deal with the mechanical laws of supply and demand; under Veblen's influence, he had become much more fascinated with man's habits, cultural patterns, and the like. At the beginning of World War I, he went to Washington as Chief of the Price Section of the War Industries Board. When he returned to New York in 1918, he joined with other intellectual leaders in creating the New School of Social Research, returning to Columbia University only three years later. Comparatively speaking, his work with the National Bureau of Economic Research has been of much greater significance in the long run. Reflecting a typical facet of Mitchell's own mind, the Bureau made no recommendations and offered no judgments on policy. Besides the books mentioned in the body of the text, Mitchell authored or coauthored many of the Bureau's numerous projects. We should add to the three main works on business cycles published during his lifetime one that appeared posthumously in 1951, *What Happens during Business Cycles*, a progress report on his latest investigations, and *The Backward Art of Spending Money* (1937).

J. — *Joseph Alois Schumpeter* (1883–1950) was born in Moravia (now part of Czechoslovakia) and spent his boyhood in Vienna. In 1906 he obtained his law degree, vouchsafing intensive training in economics, at the University of Vienna. This institution, under the influence of the Austrian Trio, was at that time the leading center in Europe for the study of economics, Menger and Böhm-Bawerk being the most eminent of Schumpeter's teachers.

He established his credentials with the publication, at the age of twenty-five, of a book entitled *Nature and Contents of Economic Theory*. This helped him get an appointment as professor at Czernowitz, an eastern outpost of the Austro-Hungarian monarchy. In 1912, a year after he had been called to the University of Graz, he published his *Theory of Economic Development*, conceived by a precocious mind and constituting a pathbreaking study of the process of economic change.

When he was thirty years old, Schumpeter visited Columbia University as Austrian Exchange Professor, returning to his native country on the eve of World War I. After the war he briefly and unhappily served as Minister of Finance in Austria's first Republican government. His subsequent foray into the banking business also ended on a sour note. In 1925 he settled down to a teaching position at the University of Bonn, Germany. Having been a Visiting Professor at Harvard University in 1927 and 1931, he was invited to join the faculty of that eminent institution permanently in 1932.

The last twenty-five years of his career, beginning with his return to academic life, were immensely productive for the Austrian expatriate. In addition to a long list of articles, he published his monumental *Business Cycles* in 1939, and his stimulating and widely debated *Capitalism, Socialism, and Democracy* in 1942. By the time of his death, he had nearly completed his *History of Economic Analysis* (published under the editorship of his wife in 1954), a treasure chest that Schumpeter's surviving colleagues, regardless of objections to detail, are apt to rave about for years.

Schumpeter was one of the founders of the Econometric Society and served as its president for several years. In 1948 the long-overdue honor of being elected to the presidency of the American Economic Association was bestowed on him. Death overtook Schumpeter before he could serve as the first president of the newly formed International Economic Association; instead, his countryman, colleague, and admirer Haberler filled that office. A man of boundless energy and sparkling vitality, Schumpeter was cosmopolitan in his outlook and a beacon for young scholars all over the world.

Questions for Review and Research

1. Say is said to have made a very important contribution to the exploration of cyclical phenomena. Explain.
2. Which theoretical work probably gave the greatest impetus to the interpenetration, on the macro level, of general economics and business cycle research?
3. Which early nineteenth-century writers questioned the validity of Say's Law and took the first important steps in the preliminary analysis of the business cycle?
4. Examine Tooke's and Overstone's contributions to cycle analysis from the point of view of scientific method.

5. Was Juglar the first to exhibit an awareness of the fact that the business cycle is largely self-generating in nature? Explain.
6. Evaluate J. Stuart Mill as a summarizer and synthesizer of previous work in the field under discussion.
7. What would you consider as indispensable elements in Hawtrey's purely monetary analysis of the business cycle? Has his theory gained or lost acceptance since the 1930's?
8. Explain how, according to Hayek, the conflict between consumer and entrepreneurial intentions, in conjunction with the structure of production, may lead to economic disequilibrium.
9. Assess the meaning of the adjective "periodic" as it appears in Juglar's account of crises during the nineteenth century.
10. Cite any features you can think of that are common to Tugan-Baranowsky's, Spiethoff's, and Aftalion's cycle theories.
11. What role did Mitchell assign to statistics as a tool in business cycle research?
12 Examine the role of the entrepreneur as depicted in Schumpeter's business cycle model.

Recommended Readings

Clemence, Richard V., and Francis S. Doody. *The Schumpeterian System.* Reading, Massachusetts: Addison-Wesley, International Division, 1950. Part I "Introduction," pp. 1–6; Part II, "Exposition," pp. 7–21; Part IV, "Conclusion," pp. 95–101.

Haberler, Gottfried von. *Prosperity and Depression,* 3d ed. Geneva: League of Nations, 1941. Part I, "Systematic Analysis of the Theories of the Business Cycle," Chapters 2–5, pp. 14–141.

Lee, Maurice W. *Macroeconomics: Fluctuations, Growth and Stability,* 4th ed. Homewood, Ill.: Richard D. Irwin, Inc., 1967. Chapter 11, "The Origins of Modern Cycle Theory: Smith to Hobson," pp. 251–269; Chapter 12, "Cycle Theory: The Origins of Modern Macroeconomics," pp. 270–303.

Mitchell, Wesley C. *Business Cycles, the Problem and Its Setting.* New York: National Bureau of Economic Research, 1927. Chapter I, "The Processes Involved in Business Cycles," pp. 1–60; Chapter II, "Economic Organization and Business Cycles," Sections I and II, pp. 61–107, and Section VIII, pp. 180–188.

Say, Jean-Baptiste. *A Treatise on Political Economy; or the Production, Distribution, and Consumption of Wealth,* translated by C. R. Prinsep, 2 vols. London: Longman, Hurst, Rees, Orme, and Brown, 1821. Vol. 2: Book I, "Of the Production of Wealth": Chapter 15, "Of the Vent or Demand for Products," pp. 162–182.

Schumpeter, Joseph A. *Ten Great Economists from Marx to Keynes.* New York: Oxford University Press, 1951. The biographical essay "Wesley Clair Mitchell (1874–1948)," pp. 239–259.

Spiegel, William Henry (ed.). *The Development of Economic Thought.* New York: John Wiley & Sons, Inc., 1952. The selections "Halévy on Sismondi," pp. 253–268, and "Haberler on Schumpeter," pp. 734–762.

PUBLIC FINANCE

THE FORMATIVE PERIOD

Some of the phenomena that accompanied the rise of the national states in Europe at the dawn of the New Era had already attracted the critical attention of *scholastic writers*. Among these phenomena was fiscal policy. Thomas Aquinas, for example, held that taxation should be reserved for emergencies. Medieval writers hardly scrutinized the specifically economic problems of public finance, in which we include as typical the incidence of taxation and the economic effects of government expenditure. They dealt only superficially with the relative merits of different kinds of taxes or with government borrowing. As far as taxation goes, they were primarily interested in its "justice" in the broadest sense of the term. They took up questions like these: May a given tax be rightfully imposed, and under what circumstances? Who may levy a tax and on whom may it be imposed? How heavy a tax burden is economically feasible? Much of their normative analysis dealt with the relation between state and citizen, and this analysis furnished a starting platform for the work of their laical successors.

Public finance in the modern sense first developed in the fifteenth century in the Italian city states and in the German free towns. More important, however, was the *development of the fiscal systems of the national states*, which depended on a growing awareness by the masses of the existence of some interests that were common to all members of a political unit. When, in the sixteenth century, the military service owed to territorial rulers by their subordinates proved increasingly less adequate, these rulers were forced to finance wars more and more from their own means, which included the feudal income from their lands and such customary fiscal rights as seigniorage, tolls, customs duties, etc. But these sources of revenue did not bring in enough to meet the rapidly mounting fiscal requirements caused by the spectacular price rise, the cost of mercenaries or of standing armies, and the lavish expenditure on court nobilities and bureaucracies, among others. The result was a swelling burden of debt. To mitigate this burden, the princes first appealed to their estates, pleading that wars were not just their own private affairs, whereupon the estates would generally grant subsidies levied upon their own feudal income (dues owed to them by the peasants). While these payments were initially in the nature of voluntary contributions to a common cause and expected to meet particular emergencies only, their regular recurrence soon gave them the character of direct taxes. Largely against the will of the princes, the estates set up their own administrations for the purpose of levying taxes and expending the proceeds thereof. Princes then tried to wrest control of the new fiscal apparatus from the estates, but did not succeed in all cases. The English parliament, for instance, representing the interests of the former vassals, did not surrender the purse strings, and, in the second half of the seventeenth century, it successfully throttled the power of the king.

In most other countries, the central government was able to conquer the fiscal stronghold of the estates, and, in the process, they began to develop forms of indirect taxation, especially excise and turnover taxes, and to neglect direct taxes. The preference for indirect taxes during the seventeenth and eighteenth centuries was partly a result of their being considered more just: indirect taxes had to be borne by all (including the nobility and the clergy), whereas the privileged classes contributed hardly anything to the proceeds of direct taxation. The resulting fiscal system was very disorderly, however. Since the proceeds from indirect taxation were far from sufficient to meet all the needs, the old fiscal rights had to be retained, and the whole apparatus was vexatiously complicated and burdensome to the taxpayers.

The Preclassical Literature

The wasteful tug of war between the princes and their bureaucracies on one hand and the estates on the other challenged the ingenuity of enlightened thinkers. It produced a flood of books and pamphlets dealing with such questions as were mentioned at the beginning of the chapter and with which scholastic writers had dealt in a preliminary fashion only. The tendency of seventeenth century laical writers on the European Continent was to side with the central government, whereas the majority of the English writers made a forceful stand for liberty and expounded the principle of "no taxation without representation." Much of the public finance literature, especially on the continent, continued to be purely descriptive in nature and was entirely lacking in depth; other writings, more sophisticated, constituted *fiscal juris-*

prudence, that is, consisted of writings of lawyers who saw as their task the safeguarding, expanding, and systematizing of existing fiscal rights by appropriate interpretation. There were also numerous writers who advocated schemes of fiscal reform — some did genuinely analytic work, especially in the field of taxation.

The most notable treatise on public finance before the close of the Middle Ages was written in the 1470's by a Neapolitan councilor, *Diomede Carafa*.[1] His interesting piece of work on statecraft, entitled "About the Office of the King and the Good Prince" (*De regis et boni principis officio*) gave financial questions more serious treatment than they probably had ever received before. His book consists of four parts, very systematically arranged. The third is a little treatise on public finance and foreshadows the Fifth Book of Adam Smith's *Wealth of Nations*. In general, Carafa held that income from domains should be the basis of state finance and that taxes had a place as a secondary source of revenue only. He divided public expenditures into three classes: (1) those for the defense of the state, (2) those for the support of the prince, and (3) those for contingencies. He recommended a balanced budget that would have room for welfare emergency expenditures. He abhorred forced loans, comparing them with robbery and theft. Economy in spending would make it possible to use the best kinds of taxes only and to dispense with the bad — such, for example, as would drive capital from the country or oppress labor. He argued that taxes should be stable and certain, letting people know beforehand what they have to pay. Business should be left alone, except as it may be advantageous to encourage agriculture, industry, and commerce by money loans and in other ways. (It is tempting to ask whether American lawmakers during the nineteenth century took a leaf from Carafa's book.) In sum, while the Italian did not plow very deep, he ably expounded the common-sense principle that the "Good Prince" should regard the wealth of his subjects as the real foundation of a prosperous condition of his own finances.

Bodin's economics of public policy and administration, as contained in the last book of his *The Six Books of the Republic* (1576), did not go far beyond Carafa's, although his principles of taxation advanced somewhat more closely toward Smith's Fifth Book. Better than does Carafa's work, these principles testify to the continental roots of

---

[1]*Diomede Carafa* (1406–1487), a Neapolitan count and duke, wrote the original of his work on the "Good Prince" in Italian. Carafa was a contemporary of Mattheo Palmieri and covered the same ground, but Palmieri was not able to produce a piece of writing of as high overall quality although he may have been superior to Carafa in developing special aspects of taxation.

Smith's ideas on public finance.   Bodin's book for many years also exercised a wide influence upon writers in the other continental countries.

He considered the proper management of government finances as "the nerves of the state." He mentioned the following prerequisites for such management: raising revenues by honest means; employing revenues for the profit and honor of the state; saving some portions of these revenues for emergencies.   While he deemed domains to be the most honest and assured sources of revenue, he approved of customs duties, and admitted the propriety of direct taxes levied upon the subjects. He attached the provisos that these taxes be levied with the consent of the payers, that all other means be insufficient, and that there be urgent necessity for additional revenue.   Relative to the second of the three prerequisites, he granted the desirability of several types of public works, but condemned extravagance and advised that the condition of the finances be shown by an annual account.   As to the third, the availability of emergency reserves would make it unnecessary for the state to borrow at interest — which Bodin believed to be the ruin of princes and their finances.

In the mass of literature published during the second half of the seventeenth century, some hundred years after Bodin, there was perhaps only one work of first-rate importance that professed to deal primarily with public finance: Petty's, *A Treatise of Taxes and Contributions* (1662). The superior quality of his mind, to which reference has already been made in Chapter 1, also shows in his comments and suggestions on public expenditures and revenues.   In a state of economic development when feudal methods of raising revenue had become inadequate, he regarded taxation as the *sine qua non* for providing the wherewithal required to keep government finances in balance.   Like Bodin, he argued for the need to create a revenue surplus in order to meet national emergencies, while at the same time frowning upon costly wars and wasteful employment of court and other supernumeraries.

His principal defense of taxing the subjects was the state function of property protection. Petty's notions of how the tax burden should be apportioned were crude by present-day standards: he believed that levies should be in proportion to the value of property holdings, leaving the relative distribution of wealth unchanged.   In other words, he advocated proportional rates. Accurate assessment of the tax base he considered an indispensable prerequisite of sound taxation, emphasizing the need for employing statistical methods to get the job done properly.

"Instead of using only comparative and superlative Words, and intellectual Arguments, I have taken the course . . . to express myself in Terms of *Number, Weight,* or *Measure;* to use only Arguments of Sense, and to consider only such Causes, as have visible Foundations in Nature."[2]

Having examined the various types of taxes from diverse angles, he concluded that *rent taxes and excise taxes* should be given priority, the former being especially appropriate for countries in which settlement had not yet advanced far. Future buyers of land would make an allowance for a rent tax, which through the increase in the prices of agricultural products would be shifted to the population as a whole. On the other hand, the imposition of a rent tax in an old and settled country would create inequities since new leases would have to make allowance for it, whereas old leases would continue at the contractual rent. He specified the advantages of excise taxes as follows: (1) People pay in accordance with what they actually enjoy. (2) These taxes stimulate thrift — for Petty, the only way to enrich a nation. (3) They avoid the evil of double taxation. (4) They provide a simple way for taking account of the wealth, growth, trade, and strength of the nation. Although under the last point he lumped together many disparate items, not all of which are reflected in the excise tax yield, Petty nevertheless laid bare significant considerations which a scientific approach to problems of taxation must not ignore.

During the eighteenth century, significant contributions to the study of public finance were made in France, Germany, Austria, and England. In France, after the time of Bodin, relatively little attention was given to the study of finance until disorders and abuses in the household of the government had become so grave as to cry out for reform. In the first decade of the eighteenth century the soldier-engineer *Marshal Vauban*[3] proposed a thorough *overhauling of the existing tax arrangements.* In 1695 he had first suggested the project which he published in 1707 under the title *Projet d'une dixme royale.* A man sparked by a passion for collecting and arranging economic facts and figures, he recommended a tax upon all incomes, though at varying rates—of which the highest was to be ten percent ("dixme"). This would be supplemented by various duties upon imports and articles of consumption.

Vauban's was an exemplary performance in the field of public finance, not matched until Adam Smith. It was based on a forthright

[2]C. H. Hull (ed.), *The Economic Writings of Sir William Petty* (2 vols.; London: Cambridge University Press, 1899), I, 244.
[3]See Biographical Note A.

diagnosis of France's fiscal disease, the unwieldy and irrational welter of taxes that had proliferated in a wholly unsystematic way. To assess the merits of Vauban's principal recommendation is not possible without a prior discussion of France's needs and resources at the beginning of the eighteenth century, and this is clearly beyond our scope. Although Vauban contributed nothing to the theoretical apparatus of economics, he was an excellent economist in the sense that he knew how to summon the available data for the purpose of meaningful and forceful analysis.

Some forty years after the publication of the Frenchman's work, a Neapolitan, *Broggia*[4] by name, published a work entitled *Treatise on Taxes, Money, and the Policy of Public Health* (1743). In a sense it was an *extension of Vauban's reform ideas*, for it outlined an "ideal" system of taxation. In the *Treatise* we find canons of taxation à la Smith (see pages 411–415). Lacking in the chief merit of Vauban's *Project*, an array of freshly mined facts and figures, it has instead the virtue of systematic completeness. It developed the implications of the principle that direct and indirect taxation are necessary complements of each other. Specifically, Broggia combined a proportional and nonshiftable tax on incomes that are certain with a system of indirect and shiftable taxes on other incomes that are also certain, but he wanted to leave free all uncertain incomes (for example, profits and the bulk of wage incomes). His scheme was designed to foster the increase of wealth through manufacturing and commercial activities and to penalize income from unearned wealth. This, he thought, might nudge people into business pursuits, either as wage earners or employers. When it is further realized that Broggia also would leave money loans to business untaxed, it seems likely that he had some vision of ideal economic conditions and was exceptionally capable of analyzing economic causes and effects.

With so many elements that can be worked into a theory of taxation now lying in the open, as it were, the Physiocratic school, in particular Quesnay, certainly did not have to build an edifice of taxation theory from scratch. It is true, however, that Quesnay, its founder, correlated a theory of taxation with his *Economic Table* (1758), in which he developed the first integrated theory of the production and distribution of wealth. Foreshadowing Henry George more than a century later

---

[4]*Carlo Antonio Broggia* (1683–1763) was a Neapolitan merchant of whose personal life very little is known. He was interested not only in combining direct and indirect taxation with a view to distributing the burden in proportion to ability to pay but also in greater simplicity and less arbitrariness in the assessment and collection of taxes. At one time he was exiled as a result of a pamphlet in which he criticized the Neapolitan ministry.

(see Chapter 5), he took the lead in proposing a single tax on land to replace all existing indirect taxes which, the Physiocrats believed, were always shifted to the landowners anyway. This was in harmony with their familiar doctrine that the produce of land is the only source from which the wealth of society can be increased. Beyond this, the only notable contribution of the Physiocrats was their urging that governments should exercise economy in spending and confine their activity within those limits suggested by the "natural order."

Eighteenth-century German and Austrian writers on public finance were chamberlains and ministers of the reigning petty kings and nobility. They were most interested in the practical technique of raising revenue for their royal masters. Sometimes referred to as "consultant administrators," they were often teachers and writers of more or less systematic and ponderous treatises. Their viewpoint was that of officials of the royal chamber, and hence they were given the group name *Cameralists*. In the course of the eighteenth century, professorial chairs began to be provided for the teaching of cameral science, that is, of the principles of economic administration and policy. *Von Justi*,[5] author of *System of Public Finance* (1766) and other works, may merely be mentioned as representative of this group of writers. The subject of his inquiries was always one or another aspect of the welfare state (in the comprehensive meaning of this term in eighteenth-century central Europe). He pinned his faith to a principle of all-embracing public planning. Economic problems, mainly those of public finance, were dealt with from the standpoint of a government that accepts responsibility for the moral and economic conditions of life. It is not amiss to regard the Cameralists as an offshoot of the Mercantilists and their contributions as overlapping the subject matter areas of international trade and public finance.

THE CLASSICAL PERIOD

As we reach the last quarter of the eighteenth century again, we observe in the field of public finance the same consolidation of materials and crystallization of principles that characterize the evolution in related branches of economic thought.

English Developments

For about three quarters of a century, that is, approximately until the middle of the nineteenth century, there were no stark contrasts

---

[5]See Biographical Note B.

between English and continental writings in the field of public finance; afterwards, diverging trends began to assert themselves.

Adam Smith.—A new era may be said to have begun with Adam Smith's *Wealth of Nations*. (This is not to gainsay the continuity of thought; it merely refers to a milestone in the "codification" of thought.) The fifth and longest book of this work was practically a self-contained treatise on public finance. It became the basis of nearly all the nineteenth-century treatises on the subject until a new viewpoint asserted itself, first in Germany and gradually elsewhere: that of taxation as an instrument of reform. As was typical of Smith's general approach, in the Fifth Book he introduced masses of material that were primarily historical. What we find, therefore, is far from a pure theory of public finance but rather a body of observations and ripe reflection which depict, in order, public expenditures, public revenues, and public debts. *Smith succeeded admirably in welding facts and theoretical technique together*.

He approached the subject of how *public expenditure* should be defrayed in a tentative fashion, betraying the fact that there were as yet few, if any, well-established principles to guide governments. One such principle set forth by Smith was that expenditures incurred for the benefit of society as a whole, that is, designed to meet social wants, should be paid by all parts of society. Therefore, individuals should contribute as nearly as possible in proportion to their abilities. He did not specify how this ability might be ascertained. In light of the twentieth-century trend to appeal to the national government for various kinds of assistance that could equally well or better be supplied by lesser governments, Smith's canon that expenditures benefiting such limited geographical areas only should be defrayed from local and provincial revenues has not lost its timeliness. Why, he argues, burden the general revenue of society with contributions which benefit only a limited portion of society? Smith thus expounded a philosophy of history that attached unique significance to the nature and distribution of property, and which defined the legitimacy of public expenditure in conformity with his general view of the functions of government.

His discussion of the ways in which *public revenue* is to be raised formed the starting point for all the subsequent liberal (in the nineteenth-century sense) theories of taxation. Most famous here are his *four maxims or canons of taxation: equality, certainty, convenience, and economy*. (1) All subjects (citizens) of a state should contribute towards the support of the government in proportion to the "revenue" which they enjoy under the protection of the state. But, in the chapter dealing with "Taxes upon the Rents of Households," he asserts that it would not be unreasonable to demand that the rich contribute to the public expense something more than in proportion to their "revenue," a faint hint of the propriety of progressive taxation. (2) The requisite that each tax should be certain rather than arbitrary covers such particulars as time of payment, manner of payment, and amount to be paid. Everything possible should be done to prevent arbitrariness on the part of tax collectors whose very unpopularity puts them under temptation to choose the path of least resistance. The great weight Smith attributed to this maxim is illustrated by his claim that a very small degree of uncertainty is a much greater evil — because it damages incentives— than a very considerable degree of inequality. (3) Smith's regard for the welfare of the taxpayer is reflected also in the third maxim, according to which taxes ought to be levied at the time and in the manner most likely to be convenient for the debtor. This principle is relatively most easily satisfied in the case of taxes on consumer goods which are included in their price. (4) The last maxim is more clearly suggested by the label "economy of administration," reference being made to the desirability of keeping the difference between what is taken or kept out of the pockets of the people and what goes into the public treasury at a minimum. The unadorned statement of this maxim conceals a great wealth of pertinent observation relative to such things as bureaucratic redundancy or featherbedding (supernumerary tax officers), undermining of private incentives to application and thrift, invitation to commit tax frauds coupled with ruinous penalties inflicted on convicted criminals, causing vexation which may paralyze the will and determination to forge ahead, etc. The maxim may be illustrated, for example, by saying that if import duties were widely evaded by smugglers, and the costs of policing ports of entry exceeded gross customs revenue, a death sentence on this kind of duty would be dictated by common sense.

Smith was skeptical of the taxation of profits. We recall that he included in this term interest on stock, an element which he thought not suitable as an object of taxation, because, first, the quantity of stock a person owned was very difficult to ascertain, and, second, stock could easily be removed by its owner if the tax proved to be burdensome. That part of profit which constituted a compensation for risk was likewise unsuited for taxation because, it being generally only moderate in amount, capitalists could not pay such a tax and continue to employ their capital. There is no doubt that *Smith subscribed without hesitation only to taxes on rent.* Broadening the path already delineated by the Physiocrats, he proclaimed that rental income is often enjoyed without any care and attention from the owner of land. If he were deprived of part of this income, there is no reason to assume that he would be less willing to use the land productively.

Smith's chapter on public debts unabashedly reflects the classical presumption against public expenditures and the view that such expenditures, if financed by the sale of government bonds, necessarily divert productive labor into unproductive employment.

Ricardo and Mill.—In Great Britain after the departure of Smith the systematic study of public finance languished until — and to some extent again after — Ricardo made important contributions to the *theory of shifting and incidence of taxes.* He did so in that part of his standard work (*Principles of Political Economy and Taxation*) suggested by its title. It largely complemented *The Wealth of Nations* since it developed a line of thought relatively neglected by Smith.

Ricardo put forth an impressive — yet, as we shall see, not invincible — argument to the effect that income or revenue, and not the accumulated wealth of society, should be the normal source of taxation. Whatever taxes are imposed, they should avoid penalizing capital. This desideratum would be fulfilled if government spending, when increased by the levy of additional taxes, is met either by increased production or by diminished private consumption, because in either case the nation's capital stock would remain unimpaired. Ricardo did not take into consideration the possibility of a government spending the proceeds of additional taxes for additions to the capital stock of the nation; he believed that all taxes have a tendency to lessen the power to accumulate capital and that they are unequivocably a burden. This burden can be minimized, Ricardo held, if taxes are so levied as to press on all equally, because in this case the natural equilibrium would be least disturbed. Direct taxes on wages or taxes on the products bought by labor would tend to be shifted to profits whenever wages are at the subsistence level. But shrinking profits imply a weakening of the motive for capital accumulation, and consequently the wages fund would suffer. Unfortunately, the concept of a wages fund, as we remember from Chapter 5, is a weak one.

J. Stuart Mill agreed with Ricardo that taxes should not fall on capital. He did not associate this potential effect with any particular mode of taxation but held that it would simply result from "overtaxation." He discounted the possibility that any country in Europe had already increased its taxes to such a high level as to deprive itself of a portion of its capital.　He further believed that no government could devise a tax system which would guarantee that the burden falls entirely on income rather than on capital.

Mill was not entirely consistent.　On the one hand, he asserted that all taxes are at least partly paid from what otherwise would have been saved; on the other hand, he held that rich, capital-exporting countries like England defrayed all public expenditures from funds which otherwise would have been spent on consumption, so that their wealth was actually no smaller than what it would have been in the absence of any kind of tax.　We may note that England's case, as viewed by Mill, accorded with one of the two possibilities that Ricardo envisaged for those taxes that fall on revenue only.　It may be surmised that what Ricardo actually meant by "revenue" was that portion of income which is spent on consumption — although he failed to make this clear.

Ricardo and Mill differed with regard to the question of whether or not capital formation in England would have been greater in the absence of taxes, Ricardo believing that it would have, Mill holding that it would not.　Mill conjectured that "capital" (saving) displayed a tendency to outrun improvements in production and that there would be stagnation — he did not use this modern term, but he seems to imply its meaning — if it were not for investment outlets abroad or for the periodic destruction of capital in commercial crises.　In a nutshell, Mill held that taxation in his day merely made additional room for an equivalent amount of saving, a curiously optimistic interpretation of trends.

Mill drew one of the logical conclusions from this line of reasoning, however, when he advocated the taxation of legacies and inheritances. He saw in this device a means of promoting equality without damaging incentives.　He nevertheless opposed the taxation of incomes at progressive rates, because this mode appeared to him to impose a penalty on some people for having worked harder and saved more than others. We may counter by saying, however, that the inheritance tax would hardly appear to be radically or fundamentally different: in this case the penalty may simply be imposed on other members of the family. Mill's position may strike many present-day Americans, who have lived with inheritance and progressive income taxes as far back as they can remember, as ambivalent.　Let us recall, however, that only fifty years ago the average American might have felt entirely different; and furthermore, that there probably has never been, among the leading economists, a stranger blend of conservatism and liberalism (in the modern sense) than was found in Mill.

Gladstonian Public Finance.—Even as late a writer as Bastable[6] continued essentially within the traditions established by Smith and Ricardo. What accounted for the perseverance with which new generations clung to the old precepts with little trace of a desire to innovate? Were they in tune with their times?

Around the middle of the nineteenth century, the English Prime Minister Gladstone witnessed the *triumph of the principle of laissez-faire* both in England's domestic and foreign affairs. He himself viewed as one of the foremost imperatives of his government the removal of fiscal obstructions to private activity. In order to keep public expenditures low, he advocated retrenchment in a double sense: first, by reducing the functions of the state to those of a "night watchman," to use an apt phrase coined by the Germans; and second, by rationalizing its absolutely essential functions, such as the maintenance of a military establishment (of minimum size). Expenditures by the state for the promotion of the arts would in this view be completely out of order. For, the argument went, what the state did not take away people had the power of spending themselves, and if the arts found their special favor they would get results by casting their sterling ballots for artistic productions. A second rationalization flowing from the attitude of thoroughgoing laissez-faire was the idea that private industry, given free play, would so boost national productivity and income as to make social expenditures, to all intents and purposes, superfluous. Furthermore, what little revenue was still to be raised in order to permit government to discharge its absolutely essential tasks should be provided without disturbing private economic behavior to an appreciable degree. Since the bulk of all savings was derived from the net earnings of business, the profit motive should be left unimpaired. By letting business leaders embark upon ventures holding the promise of greater productivity (lower cost), their ability to earn would be so strengthened as to permit a gradual increase in real wages, from which additional savings would in time be derived — a "trickled-down" variant of schemes to promote the welfare of all classes.

Translated into fiscal policy terms this meant: little reliance on direct taxation and, to the extent this revenue source was still needed, no progressive taxation of incomes; concentration of indirect taxes on a few important articles, mainly those of luxury consumption. To tax necessities would have been self-defeating, because it would have

---

[6]See Chapter 13, Biographical Note B, where reference is made to Bastable's *Public Finance.* Published as late as 1892, it seems to have held almost exclusive possession of the field for at least a decade.

necessitated a rise in wages for the great masses whose means of purchasing were barely sufficient to defray their subsistence needs.

As far as the Gladstonian budget was concerned, the most commendable policy was that of balancing income and outgo or, better yet, of achieving a surplus; deficit spending was clearly incompatible with the desire to minimize budget requirements in the long run.

Continental Writings

We may without loss omit consideration of nineteenth-century financial studies in *France,* because they followed a course scarcely different from that in England. General treatises of economics contained little analytical material in the field of public finance, this subject being for the most part downgraded and relegated to a subordinate position. There were exceptions to this general rule, the most important being the holder of the Chair at the Collège de France, *Leroy-Beaulieu,*[7] third successor in spirit and doctrine of J. B. Say. His *Treatise of the Science of Finance* was an encyclopaedic presentation of contemporaneous scholarship in public finance, a superior work which for decades ranked with the leading manuals in the field. Most of the other writers concentrated upon financial history and administration, budgetary matters, and other special subjects, yet some of these studies were quite meritorious. Germany, in the second half of the nineteenth century, was the seat of several new and important departures by fiscal scholars. Public finance was a subject of extensive research by members of the Historical school. Many of them treated it as a branch of political science and tended to look to the Cameralists, rather than to Adam Smith, for inspiration and ultimate authority. While *K. H. Rau,*[8] who in 1832 wrote *Principles of the Science of Finance,* was still strongly influenced by the English classical writers, this was definitely no longer true of *Adolf Wagner,*[9] who catapulted into prominence the social aspects of public finance.

Wagner was a leader in the fight for *Sozialpolitik,* that is, for policies designed to counter the tendencies of midnineteenth-century English liberalism, for policies that placed particular emphasis on assistance to the downtrodden masses. (Note that advocates of *Sozialpolitik* were not necessarily what we today vaguely refer to as "wild-eyed" liberals, but they were valiant fighters for social policies many of which half a century later became incorporated in the American New Deal.)

---

[7] See Biographical Note C.
[8] See Biographical Note D.
[9] See Biographical Note E.

Wagner's reputation rested mainly on his four-volume work in public finance. Encyclopaedic in scope, it appeared between 1877 and 1901. It did not exhibit the fiscal-administrative character which previous German financial literature had inherited from cameralism, but attempted to integrate fiscal phenomena with the totality of economic and social conditions. Wagner, moreover, represented a new spirit and trend diametrically opposed to the Gladstonian vision of the economic process, and which in the field of finance can be summarized by saying that he approved of a policy that went beyond taxing for revenue and aimed at taxing designed to "equalize" income distribution. Wagner admitted that one's views on the subject of justice in taxation depend on what one thinks of that distribution of wealth which free competition would bring about on the basis of the existing order. The argument pointing to possible harmful effects of high and progressive taxation on effort and capital formation had lost much of its force in Germany. To Wagner, then, the *science of finance appeared as a vehicle for effecting a redistribution of wealth and income*. A reformer rather than a revolutionary, he believed that public ownership would have to displace private ownership in some areas of capitalistic production. A conservative socialist of sorts, Wagner, in his work at least, provided an intellectual justification for many of the social reform measures of the regime of Chancellor Bismarck. Wagner was never strong as an economic analyst and left no devoted following to carry on his doctrines, although he inspired many shorter works and one or two handbooks (compendia) which brought theory and practice up to date and contained a valuable collection of monographs on public finance.

As an aside, it is interesting to note that Wagner acquired some fame for a not very profound but practically very important statement, which was subsequently referred to as "Wagner's Law," more tellingly as the "law of the increase of state activities." He observed that in industrially advancing countries the activities of both the central and the local governments tend to expand, extensively as well as intensively: extensively, because these governments constantly assume new functions; intensively, because they perform all functions more efficiently and completely. He welcomed this trend in which he saw proof that the economic needs of the people were being met to an increasing extent and more satisfactorily by government.

Italian fiscal scholars derived their inspiration mostly from German writers; they devoted their attention largely to historical studies and the social aspects of taxation. There were no truly outstanding performances, however.

SUBSEQUENT DEVELOPMENTS:
THE AMERICAN CONTRIBUTION

While financial problems demanded and received considerable attention in the United States ever since the country became an independent nation, *systematic study of public finance began only toward the close of the nineteenth century.* Until then, American textbooks on economics accorded financial topics distinctly superficial treatment. As long as the federal government achieved revenue surpluses, having occasionally a difficult time in disposing of them, scholarship in public finance was not felt to be a pressing matter. This changed when, beginning in the 1880's, an increasing number of states followed New York's lead in appointing commissions to consider current problems of an urgent nature, and these commissions issued more or less elaborate reports on taxation and related subjects.

Among the general treatises written during the last two decades of the nineteenth century, some showed a close kinship to the English school of fiscal thought, while others clearly evinced the influence of German doctrines in their emphasis on a historical approach and on the social aspects of taxation. Until the beginning of the 1930's American fiscal scholarship was oriented closely to the immediate and practical. Theoretical tenets were at first taken over from the classical sources with a minimum of careful reexamination. Factual problems on all levels of government claimed a great deal of attention, and little opportunity was found for extensive study in the general history and theory of taxation.

Seligman[10]

The leading writer in the field around the turn of the century was E. R. A. Seligman. He contributed many still useful *studies on income taxes and on the problems of shifting and incidence.* In his major works, *The Shifting and Incidence of Taxation* (1892) and *Progressive Taxation in Theory and Practice* (1894), he elaborated the ability-to-pay criterion and developed a persuasive theoretical justification for progressive income taxes. He found the compensatory, benefit, and equal-sacrifice theories all wanting in some respects. He held that while equality of sacrifice can never be completely attained because of the diversity of individual wants, it is possible in a majority of normal and typical cases to get closer to that ideal by some departure from proportionality. Whereas a proportional tax would normally curtail the enjoyments of

---

[10]See Biographical Note F.

low-income classes relatively more than those of people at the other end of the income scale, a progressive tax would reduce this dispropor- tionality of sacrifice. Yet it is still true, Seligman admitted, that the ability-to-pay doctrine cannot specify any definite rate of progression as the ideally just rate. He stressed the fact that the function of a progressive tax is not so much to raise the amount of revenue collected as to apportion the burden more equitably. He did not claim superi- ority of the principle of progression for all types of taxes.

Seligman made an important distinction between tax incidence, that is, where the tax burden comes finally to rest, and the incidental burden which accompanied the process of shifting. He laid much stress on the ultimate effects of a tax. He noted "transformation" as a way of escaping a tax burden: a tax may impel such changes in the methods of production, thereby increasing efficiency, as make it possible for firms to absorb the tax without shifting. Essentially, taxation would cease to be a burden if entrepreneurs undertook the proper output adjustments.

Recent Trends

Beginning with the 1930's, public finance came to be more closely integrated with other areas of economics as well as with other social sciences. National income theory, as developed by Keynes and his followers, became a handmaiden of fiscal policy; and fiscal policy itself came to be based on such concepts as *functional finance*,[11] compensatory spending, and the like. More and more, fiscal policy has been made subservient to resource allocation in accordance with new welfare concepts. The attempt to gear fiscal policy more emphatically to the requirements of economic stabilization has been — to judge from the United States experience in the 1960's — a qualified success at best. Once again the temptation to subordinate sound economic principles to political expediency, however misguided it may turn out to be, has

---

[11]This term, now widely accepted even by those who refuse to embrace the value judgments on which it is based, was coined by *Abba P. Lerner* (1903–   ), a graduate of the London School of Economics. A highly competent technician, Lerner has had a varied career; since 1959 he has been professor of economics at Michigan State University.

Lerner advocates a policy of full employment at all costs (except inflation), carried out within the framework of a "controlled economy" (welfare state). By "functional finance" he means "the principle of disregarding all traditional conceptions of what is 'sound' in finance and judging fiscal measures only by their effects or the way they *function* in society. . . ." (See his *The Economics of Control* [New York: The Macmillan Company, 1944], p. 302, Footnote 1.) In this book he discusses an elaborate set of instruments designed to place public finance on a new footing — going in his reform proposals far beyond Keynes. Here is a representative sample of Lerner's principles, principles that are clearly at odds with traditional notions of sound finance:
(1) The size of an internally held national debt is practically of no significance relative to the importance of maintaining full employment. (2) National debt in itself is neither

proved irresistible. While fiscal policy may have displaced monetary policy from its position as the primary means of smoothing out cyclical troughs — if not altogether to prevent these — monetary policy, itself not entirely aloof from political currents, has had to strain to rescue the economy from the fiscal excesses of prolonged prosperity. Although on the policy level coordination is still more fancy than fact, on the level of pure theory bridges have been built between public finance and monetary theory.

Many pressing problems are still found in the fields of state and local finance and have continued to absorb a great deal of scholarly energy. Tax theorists have striven for a closer working relationship with legal and accounting experts as the widespread ramifications of tax issues have become more generally recognized. Partly as a result of increasing specialization, students of public finance now must often cross the boundary lines between disciplines in an attempt to secure adequate information on a particular issue.

Among those who have most successfully labored to expand the theoretical horizon of, and to apply the general body of value theory rigorously to, the field of public finance, *Richard Musgrave*[12] of Princeton University stands out prominently. Musgrave's principal contributions relate to the theory of public wants. He has also helped to integrate the classical and the Keynesian aspects of public finance, having explored in particular the role of budget policy in macroeconomic theory. He recognizes that there is no simple set of principles that can be applied to the operations of the public budget; rather, there is a multiplicity of objectives. Musgrave discusses these objectives under the headings of (1) adjustments in the allocation of resources, (2) adjustments in the distribution of income and wealth, and (3) pursuit of economic stabilization.

---

good nor bad. (3) The national debt is a tool by which the proper division of a nation's resources between consumption and investment can be accomplished. (4) Taxes should never be imposed when the government merely needs additional money; to this end, use of the printing press will be fully adequate. (5) By the same token, the government should never borrow merely as a means of raising money. (6) The government can affect consumption (investment) and the rate of interest in any way it likes by making intelligent use of these six instruments: taxing and spending, borrowing and lending, buying and selling. (The printing of money is merely ancillary to the carrying out of government policies.) (7) The principle of balancing the budget should be completely disregarded — although, in achieving full employment, the budget may tend to balance itself, and may thus assuage popular fears even while nothing is done to uproot popular "prejudice."

These and similar principles, which Lerner deems wholly compatible with the maintenance of democratic forms of society, have never been tested. Many students of public finance are concerned that experimenting with them might result in a transformation to a society in which government plays the role of a master rather than a servant.

[12]See Biographical Note G.

His theory of social wants — public wants are classified into "social" wants and "merit" wants — falls under the first of these headings. He defines social wants as "those wants satisfied by services that must be consumed in equal amounts by all."[13] He locates the crux of the allocation problem in two difficulties. The first is that the true consumer preferences are not known; and the second is that there is no single most efficient solution to the problem of the satisfaction of social wants, because they cannot be satisfied through the mechanism of the market. Since no direct payment is required to obtain the services that satisfy social wants (for example, protection from floods), the consumer need not reveal through market bids his evaluation of such services. The problem therefore becomes one of determining what kind of group decision approximates most closely the solution that would be chosen if true consumer preferences were known. Here the principal difficulty is to induce people to disclose their individual preferences with regard to social wants; in the absence of such disclosure, it is necessary to substitute some kind of a social preference function.

When the reason for budgetary action is not the technical difficulties arising because certain services are consumed in equal amounts by all, but is instead the *correction* of individual choice, the wants satisfied under such conditions are merit wants. In this case, want satisfaction is no longer subject to the principle of consumer sovereignty, as it is in the case of social wants. Yet merit wants often arise in areas where consumers still exercise some freedom of choice. For example, subsidized public housing and free education do not displace privately financed services of these kinds, although they may (as in the case of education) overshadow the latter. In a sense, then, merit wants are private wants that partake of the nature of public wants: they are "considered so meritorious that their satisfaction is provided for through the public budget, over and above what is provided for through the market and paid for by private buyers."[14] (Negative merit wants are those whose satisfaction is to be discouraged, as through penalty taxes on distilled spirits.)

In sum, while both merit wants and social wants are public wants — to be provided for through the public budget — the satisfaction of social wants by its very nature does not, while the satisfaction of merit wants by its very nature does, involve interference with consumer preferences. Musgrave justly observes that a normative theory of public economy

---

[13]Richard A. Musgrave, *The Theory of Public Finance* (New York: McGraw-Hill Book Company, Inc., 1959), p. 8.

[14]*Ibid.*, p. 13.

(a term he prefers to public "finance") based on the premise of "extreme individualism" would, of course, disallow all merit wants.

SUMMARY

The formative period in public finance, stretching from about the thirteenth century to the end of the eighteenth, comprised the works of many dozens of writers, who were mainly influenced by changing political circumstances. Principles of public finance in the modern sense were first developed in a tentative way toward the close of the Middle Ages when Italian city states and German free towns became independent political units. Also, as territorial rulers were forced to tap new sources of revenue to defray their rapidly mounting fiscal requirements, the subject of taxation gained ascendancy, and with many of the old fiscal rights continuing, the revenue structure became very unwieldy and burdensome.

The most remarkable piece of writing on public finance foreshadowing Adam Smith's analysis in the *Wealth of Nations* was done by the Italian Carafa during the second half of the fifteenth century. He advanced arguments for the superiority of income from domains to the levying of taxes and held that a prosperous condition of the people was the best guarantee for the solvency of the ruler. A century later Bodin developed the principles of taxation beyond the level attained by Carafa and discussed the prerequisites for the proper management of government finances. Petty, writing after the middle of the seventeenth century, had still fewer scruples about the use of taxes as a source of government revenue — he clearly explained his preference for rent and excise taxes. Petty followed Bodin in advocating the creation of emergency reserves to meet any extraordinary demands on the state treasure. At the beginning of the eighteenth century, Marshal Vauban made a significant contribution through his criticism of the French system of indirect taxes and through his reform proposal. Shortly before the middle of the eighteenth century, a searching analysis by the Italian Broggia resulted in a treatise whose systematic completeness and anticipation of Adam Smith in many particulars gave it a permanent place in the public finance literature of the formative period. Soon thereafter, Quesnay, the founder of the Physiocratic school, proposed a single tax on land to replace all existing indirect taxes and correlated this proposal with his theory of production and distribution, as developed in the *Economic Table*. Among the eighteenth century exponents of cameral science, which dealt with the principles of administering an authoritarian state to the presumed advantage of all the subjects, Von Justi was the most remarkable writer. He composed the first general treatise in German on the subject of government finance; in particular, he further developed rules concerning taxation.

Adam Smith devoted the longest book of his *Wealth of Nations* to public finance and especially to taxation. Broadly conceived and distinguished by keenness of argument, it became, both in England and on the continent, the basis for all subsequent study of public finance. Its gap relative to the shifting and incidence of taxes provided Ricardo with an opening wedge for a detailed exposition of this topic. Later English writers, of whom only Mill was mentioned, continued essentially within the tradition established by Smith and Ricardo. The prevalence of laissez-faire thinking, as reflected in Gladstonian finance, limited the range of problems that presented a challenge to the classical writers. Generally, they occupied themselves with the theories of the proper distribution and incidence of taxes, condemned both the abuse of the taxing power and the granting of subsidies to favored groups, and gave little attention to the social aspects of taxation. Nor were there many new vistas opened up by French and Italian writers of the nineteenth century. Only in Germany was a radically different viewpoint fostered, a viewpoint which helped to transform the main contents of public finance. It was through the far-reaching influence of Adolf Wagner that the seemingly unlimited possibilities of utilizing the fiscal elements of government as agencies for social reform came to be recognized.

Seligman, the pioneer in developing the subject in the United States and a contemporary of Wagner, was clearly influenced by the German writers in both the formal and substantive aspects of his scholarship. He made a persuasive case for progressive income taxation based on the ability-to-pay principle. Generally, however, theoretical contributions to the subject by American economists were meager well into the twentieth century as the bulk of their energy continued to be absorbed by the factual problems calling for quick solutions. While issues of state and local finance still require wide attention, an expanding group of American fiscal scholars have proceeded to apply highly abstract national income theory in order to demonstrate how public finance might be used to influence the national economy and make it less susceptible to business cycle fluctuations.

BIOGRAPHICAL NOTES

A.—*Sébastien le Prestre Seigneur de Vauban* (1633–1707) was a favorite with Louis XIV, in whose wars he served as military engineer. His career led from governor of Lille (1668), to general commissioner of fortifications (1678), to Marshal of France (1703). In the course of his engineering experiences he became interested in the economic and social conditions of various localities as a basis for their warfare potential. He wrote a tremendous number of memoirs on both civilian and war matters and their interrelationships. He was especially interested in fiscal and population surveys and in 1698 instigated orders for a census. His ideal was mercantilistic in nature: a strong, well-populated and prosperous country united under the highly centralized authority of a benevolent monarch. He ascribed the rapid deterioration of France toward the end of the seventeenth century mainly to the unfortunate fiscal conditions; and, after many proposals for piecemeal reform, he finally came up with the comprehensive plan of fiscal reorganization that revealed him as a first-rate economist. Although his *Project* was immediately proscribed, it nevertheless served as a discussion basis for later attempts at reform.

B.—*Johannes Heinrich Gottlob von Justi* (1717–1771), the leading representative of eighteenth-century cameralism, was born in Thuringia and studied law at several of the German universities. From 1750 to 1753, he taught cameral science at the Ritterakademie of Maria Theresa in Vienna. Beginning in 1755, he was for two years professor at Göttingen, where he was also a member of the council of mines and commissioner of police. In 1757, he became director of mines and superintendent of glass and steel work in Berlin; in 1765, he entered the service of Frederick the Great as administrator of mines. Later he was consigned to prison because of irregularities in his accounts. He died before his term expired.

Population growth was the dominating theme in Justi's writings. Of his numerous publications in German, the only one, in addition to the one mentioned in the text, which deserves close scrutiny is *The Groundwork of the Power and Welfare of States or Comprehensive Presentation of the Science of Public Policy* (2 volumes, 1760–61). Justi displayed a power of independent and sound judgment and — though he often arrived at his conclusions by a circuitous route — considerable talent for organization.

C.—*Paul Leroy-Beaulieu* (1843–1916) studied in Paris, Bonn, and Berlin, and traveled in England. He was a first-rate economic journalist who from an early age wrote with more clarity and brilliance than depth. He won his first prize at the age of twenty-four with an essay, *The Moral and Intellectual Condition of the Working Classes and Its Influence on Wage Rates.* From 1869 on he collaborated on the *Revue des deux mondes* and two years later became an editor of the *Journal des débats.* In 1872 he accepted the chair of public finance at the *Ecole Libre des Sciences Politiques.* In 1873 he became the founder, editor, and a regular contributor to a weekly, *Economiste français,* with which he remained associated until his death. In 1880 he replaced Chevalier, his father-in-law and sponsor of the famous Cobden-Chevalier Treaty, as professor of political economy at the Collège de France. Leroy-Beaulieu was a large landowner and practicing farmer with a keen interest in agriculture. A staunch representative of nineteenth-century economic liberalism, he offered the most detailed exposition of his views in the *Theoretical and Practical Treatise of Political Economy*, which between 1895 and 1910 went through five editions. In his *Essay on the Distribution of Riches*, he argued against the application in his time of Ricardo's law of rent.

D.—*Karl Heinrich Rau* (1792–1870) studied at the University of Erlangen, where, at the age of twenty-four, he became professor. Six years later, the successful teacher was called to the chair of economics at Heidelberg, where he remained the rest of his life. At times he was active in politics.

Not a very original thinker, Rau wrote the most widely used textbook, used for decades at German universities by generations of future lawyers and civil servants. His *Principles of the Science of Finance* was the third volume of his comprehensive *Textbook of Political Economy* (1826–1837), the others being devoted to economic laws and economic policy, respectively. Rau's influence declined somewhat after the middle of the century when the Historical school gained in prestige. His volume on public finance, however, inspired Wagner, who had a high opinion of it, to write a systematic treatise of the subject. Among Rau's other works the most interesting was his *Economic Views* (1821), which contains a discussion of the controversy between Malthus and Say over the causes of the depression following the Napoleonic Wars.

E.—*Adolf Heinrich Gotthilf Wagner* (1835–1917) had gained experience as a teacher of economics at a number of universities before he was appointed to the University of Berlin, where he taught from 1870 to 1916. He participated in the organization of a professional association of economists and social reformers, the *Verein für Sozialpolitik*. He was also active in the Christian Socialist party and the Protestant Social Congress. From 1882 to 1885, he was a member of the Prussian Diet, and in 1910 he was made a life member of the Prussian House of Lords.

Besides his standard work on public finance, he had to his credit a volume entitled *Foundations of Political Economy* (1876) and also a substantial performance in the field of money. As an analytic economist, he steered a middle course between the somewhat abstract approach initiated in Austria by Menger and the historical approach represented in Germany by Schmoller and his followers.

F.—*Edwin Robert Anderson Seligman* (1861–1939) was born into a well-to-do family. After he had graduated in Arts, Law, and Philosophy at Columbia University, he continued his studies at the Universities of Berlin, Heidelberg, Geneva, and Paris. The influence of Wagner and the German Historical school gave birth to his lifelong conviction that every economic theorist should be something of a historian and every student of the history of economic institutions should be something of a theorist.

At the age of twenty-four he was appointed a Lecturer on Economics at Columbia. At that time (1885), as one of the "young rebels," he became a cofounder of the American Economic Association. Advanced to Assistant Professor in 1888 and to Professor of Political Economy and Finance in 1891, he was appointed to the McVickar chair at Columbia in 1904. After his retirement in 1931, he stayed on as Professor Emeritus and began to put the capstone on his scientific career by serving as editor-in-chief of the fifteen-volume *Encyclopaedia of the Social Sciences,* published between 1930 and 1935. Besides coordinating the other work, he also wrote eight articles and eleven biographies for the *Encyclopaedia.*

As a man of affairs Seligman served, beginning in 1908, on a number of government commissions and committees on all levels. His assistance was frequently asked for by the League of Nations. He was also in the public limelight when he argued for the constitutionality of the income tax before the United States Supreme Court.

The first group of important publications from his pen came in the 1890's when, in addition to the two works mentioned in the body of the text, he wrote *Essays in Taxation* (1895). He will probably be best remembered for this trilogy, which ranks highest as far as his originality is concerned. In 1902 and 1905 were published his *The Economic Interpretation of History* and *The Principles of Economics.* The latter work did not contain any chapters on public finance because Seligman held that this subject, in which he was the leading authority in this country, should be treated as a quasi-independent science. He returned to it in *The Income Tax* (1911), a *locus classicus,* and cultivated it until the publication in 1925 of *Studies in Public Finance.* The writings of this fourteen-year period included a large number of papers on war finance. Also published in 1925 were his *Essays in Economics,* which contain a very remarkable paper (written in 1903), "On Some Neglected British Economists," and other contributions to the history of economic doctrines. During the late 1920's and early 1930's he wrote on diverse economic topics.

Seligman had no peer in his complete grasp of public finance combined with so extensive a knowledge of past and present economic literature. His library, which was sold to Columbia University, was his pride and the envy of his less munificent colleagues. At the time of his death, it contained many tens of thousands of volumes and numerous pamphlets, including much foreign literature.

G.—*Richard Abel Musgrave* (1910–   ) is one of the most gifted economists to emigrate from Germany within the last generation. He obtained his diploma from the University of Heidelberg in 1933 and then engaged in graduate work at Harvard University, from which he obtained his M.A. and Ph.D. degrees in 1936 and 1937. He was naturalized in 1940.

A tutor and instructor at Harvard University from 1936 to 1941, he subsequently served as research economist with the Board of Governors of the Federal Reserve System until 1947. He was a lecturer in economics at Swarthmore College in the following year and then joined the faculty at the University of Michigan as an associate professor, becoming a full professor in 1950. He was professor of political economy at Johns Hopkins University from 1959 to 1962 and professor of economics and public affairs at Princeton University from 1962 to 1965, when he joined the Harvard faculty.

Musgrave has been in heavy demand outside the classroom as chief of international economic missions, tax consultant, Fulbright visiting professor, and consultant to the Board of Governors as well as to various executive departments of the federal government. He was on the executive committee of the American Economic Association from 1956 to 1959 and a vice president in 1962.

His publications include *Public Finance and Full Employment* (1945) and *The Theory of Public Finance* (1959). He served on the Selection Committee of the American Economic Association's *Readings in the Economics of Taxation* (1959) and was editor of *Essays in Fiscal Federalism* (1965).

Questions for Review and Research

1. What tenets were typically held by medieval writers in the field of fiscal policy?

2. How did the emergence and the rise of national states at the end of the Middle Ages affect the financing of public expenditures?

3. By whom and when was the most notable treatise on public finance before the end of the Middle Ages written?

4. According to the last book of *The Six Books of the Republic,* what are the prerequisites for the proper management of government finances?

5. What was Petty's principal justification for the levying of taxes?

6. What qualities of mind made Marshall Vauban an excellent "economist" in his own day?

7. Did Henry George's and François Quesnay's single-tax proposals rest on the same philosophical presuppositions? Explain.

8. Discuss Adam Smith's canons of taxation.

9. What do you believe to be the main plank in Ricardo's theory of the shifting and incidence of taxes?

10. On what grounds did J. Stuart Mill oppose the taxation of incomes at progressive rates while at the same time advocating the taxation of legacies and inheritances?

11. Where, when, and by whom were social (income redistributional) aspects of public finance first ably expounded?

12. Discuss, against the background of Seligman's contribution to the theory of taxation, the ability-to-pay principle and its limitations.

Recommended Readings

Due, John F. *Government Finance: Economics of the Public Sector,* 4th ed. Homewood, Ill.: Richard D. Irwin, Inc., 1968. Chapter 1, "The Rationale of Governmental Activity," pp. 3–21; Chapter 3, "Budget Systems and Cost Benefit Analysis," pp. 48–70; Chapter 12, "Intergovernmental Fiscal Relationships," pp. 316–340; Chapter 14, "An Optimal Tax Structure," pp. 367–388.

Groves, Harold M. (ed.). *Viewpoints on Public Finance; a Book of Readings.* New York: Henry Holt & Company, Inc., 1947. Chapter 1, Nos. 1–10, pp. 2–38; Chapter 5, No. 44, pp. 237–243; Chapter 7, No. 58, pp. 327–331; Chapter 8, Nos. 75 and 76, pp. 414–420; Chapter 10, No. 92, pp. 526–532, and No. 101, pp. 566–568; Chapter 11, No. 108, pp. 610–619, and No. 109, pp. 619–629; Chapter 12, No. 123, pp. 698–699, and No. 124, pp. 699–707.

Musgrave, Richard A. *The Theory of Public Finance, a Study in Public Economy.* New York: McGraw-Hill Book Company, 1959.
Part One, "Statement of Issues": Chapter 1, pp. 3–27.
Part Four, "Compensatory Finance": Chapter 17, pp. 405–428; Chapter 23, pp. 556–580; Chapter 24, pp. 581–615.

Schultz, William John, and C. Lowell Harriss. *American Public Finance,* 7th ed. Englewood Cliffs, N.J.: Prentice-Hall, Inc., 1959. Appendix, "History of Public Finance," pp. 605–608.

THE "ISMS"

A Survey

The precursors of socialism from antiquity until the eighteenth century worked mainly in a religious or metaphysical atmosphere. Biblical prophets and — centuries later — Plato, when in *The Republic* he laid down a comprehensive system of aristocratic communism, held up ideals which were a source of inspiration to many subsequent thinkers. Almost without exception, these men enunciated certain great principles of justice and social organization that transcended the limitations of their environment. But many were social dreamers, toying with a variety of fantastic ideas that did not lend themselves to being translated into new patterns of living for large populations.

UTOPIAN SOCIALISM

During the nineteen centuries from the age of Plato to that of Sir Thomas More, equality and common ownership were urged by many — philosophers, theologists, poets — who believed that a communistic state of society was natural and who saw in civil law a debased substitute for the reign of God and nature.

Early Highlights

The spirit of the Renaissance, the Reformation, and the beginnings of capitalism brought into being a significant literature of which the *Utopia* of *Thomas More*[1] has become the classic model. This Englishman lived in the age of the great explorations and discoveries. Coiner of the term "utopia," he incorporated in his writings the view that the state of nature was a state of innocence. Agreeing with the early church fathers in their communistic principles, he analyzed the defects of the society in which he lived and worked out a scheme of social reform of a

---

[1]See Biographical Note A. I have no valid defense against the charge of readers that in the section on "Utopian Socialism" two principles underlying this text have been violated: concentration on economic *theory* and keeping the number of biographies to a readily remembered minimum.

communistic type. He pictured a commonwealth whose members are honored neither for wealth nor accidents of birth but for their service to society and in which the end was the good and happy life.

Nearly a century after More's *Utopia* (1516), *Francis Bacon,*[2] a philosopher and natural scientist, pinned his faith to the progress of science and its application to human life. Contrary to More, he was not concerned with reform of laws of property but rather with increased productivity. In his *New Atlantis* (1622), he described how on an imaginary island a wise lawgiver had organized a kingdom of prospering human beings on the basis of applied science, but he apparently failed to see that the art of social cooperation must go hand in hand with the power to produce, lest science become a dividing and destructive force. During the sixteenth century Germany and Italy also gave impetus to utopian writers; their impact, however, was decidedly smaller than that of the two Englishmen just mentioned.

When during the seventeenth century the old agrarian feudalism began to crumble and commerce was extended to hitherto unknown parts of the world, the possessors of wealth were seeking a philosophy which would justify the existence of private property and discredit the communist vision of property relationships. They found able spokesmen in *Hobbes*[3] and *Locke:* Hobbes formulated what came to be known as the "social contract theory"; Locke worked out a theory according to which title to property is acquired and justified by labor. It is especially Locke's "labor theory of value" that could serve as a starting point for the socialist movement of the nineteenth century.

With the coming of the eighteenth century, English utopian thought began to be eclipsed by French versions. The strains and stresses building up during the decades before the outbreak of the French Revolution caused growing resentment, and this resentment was voiced forcefully by *Voltaire*[4] and *Rousseau.*[5] Their writings encouraged those who would sweep away rather than patch up the institutions of the tottering monarchy. Equality of economic opportunity was envisaged as a distant goal.

From the French Revolution to the Revolutions of 1848

The philosophy of equality in its extreme form of absolute equality was wholeheartedly embraced by *Babeuf,*[6] who during the prime of his

[2]See Biographical Note B.
[3]See Biographical Note C.
[4]See Biographical Note D.
[5]See Biographical Note E.
[6]See Biographical Note F.

life became a victim of the age of terror following the Revolution of 1789. One of his compatriots, *Cabet*[7] (about twenty-five years younger), aligned himself on the side of absolute equality and gave vent to his ideas in *The Voyage to Icaria* (1840). Both were overshadowed, however, by *Saint-Simon*,[8] who veered away from the concept of mechanical equality and laid stress on the development of a social system wherein man would be rewarded according to his deeds. Although of noble birth, Saint-Simon chose a life of extreme hardship. Sustained by an enthusiasm bordering madness, he completed before his death three works of which *The New Christianity* was the most celebrated. His followers were led to their proposals by observing the discrepancy existing in the contemporary economic system between merit and reward. They advocated the transfer of industry from private to public ownership and the retention of private ownership in consumer goods. Following their master, they proposed the subordination of private enterprise to regulation and directive councils of experts to maintain the harmony of economic forces. They enunciated the principle of "from each according to his capacity, to each according to services rendered" (merit); but they depended upon the existing class structure rather than upon a mass movement to bring about the needed changes. Their bureaucratically administered industrial organization lacked democratic safeguards.

The new faith gained a number of distinguished disciples, but under the leadership of *Enfantin*,[9] who began to depart from the master's teachings in certain respects, a violent controversy, ending in schism, broke out. Nevertheless, some of Saint-Simon's ideas — for example, on the evil of inheritance — exerted a profound influence on the later socialist movement.

Whereas Saint-Simon had been a scion of nobility, his contemporary *Fourier*[10] was of the common people. A liberal cooperative socialist, Fourier worked out a detailed scheme for ideal living conditions in spontaneous cooperative associations, called "phalanxes," and strove to demonstrate through experiments on a small scale the practicability of his ideas. He spun out a weird and fantastic philosophy inspired by a belief in the all-pervading power of "attraction." He listed twelve different "passions" which all combined into the one supreme passion of love for others. Community living in the fundamental social units, called phalanxes, would lead to a harmonious

---

[7]See Biographical Note G.
[8]See Biographical Note H.
[9]See Biographical Note I.
[10]See Biographical Note J.

blending of passions. In each of these phalanxes there would live a
number of people — Fourier mentioned a minimum of about eight
hundred — sufficient for the representation of all talents. The living
quarters would be set up according to a common pattern, somewhat
comparable to a modern grand hotel. Meals would be prepared in a
common kitchen but would be sold at varying prices, to suit the varying
degrees of affluence among the members. Each phalanx would control
an amount of land adequate for the support of its members. But
Fourier also envisaged cooperation between members of different
phalanxes for the purpose of realizing what are now called economies of
large-scale production.

Fourier's teachings implied that marriage and family would gradually tend to disappear; Plato had already forcefully suggested the idea.
Income would be divided according to a certain formula in which labor,
capital, and talent would each get its reward. It is interesting to
observe that Fourier actually reserved for interest and profits larger
relative shares than they receive, on the long-run average, in capitalist
societies.

Like Saint-Simon, Fourier had a number of followers who after his
death organized themselves for the propagation and implementation of
his teachings. The latter found enthusiastic support among some
brilliant thinkers in the United States; but all the experiments, of
which those at Brook Farm, Massachusetts, and Red Bank, New
Jersey, were the most famous, eventually failed. The Frenchman
Fourier was perhaps his country's most famous representative of what
came to be called "Associationism," a current of thought relying on
voluntary association and education as the means par excellence in the
pursuit of social reform.

Meanwhile an English Associationist, *Robert Owen*,[11] had risen to
fame. As a cotton manufacturer he had become sorely impressed by the
deterioration of working conditions which the Industrial Revolution
had wrought in British manufacturing plants. In the early nineteenth
century, as superintendent of a cotton mill at New Lanark, he began to
experiment with different methods of production and distribution.
They were governed by his plans for making work agreeable, dignified,
and pleasurable, somewhat along the lines advocated by Fourier. As a
result of his innovations, a favorable change occurred in the lives of
his workers and their families, with no loss in productivity.

The main pillars of Owen's philosophy included happiness as the
goal of society, character as a product of the environment, and education

---

[11]See Biographical Note K.

as a powerful tool in shaping the perfect life. At first Owen did not have in mind a revolution in the relations of property; he was merely interested in the promotion of legislation that would alleviate some of the worst evils of the factory system. When his pleas, made immediately after the end of the Napoleonic Wars, fell upon unreceptive ears, he began to place himself squarely in the ranks of utopian writers. Private profit now appeared to him as an obstacle to keeping consumption in line with production. He saw a beginning toward remedying the existing situation in the formation of villages of "unity and cooperation" for the unemployed, each with a large variety of occupations, availing itself of the best possible production methods. But efforts to raise enough money to start his experiments failed. Eventually he took a completely communist position, ruling out any admixture of private property. In 1824 he bought a community at Harmony, Indiana, in which he tried to apply his ideas of an enlightened social system; but after struggling along for a few years, the experiment collapsed.

After his return to England, Owen fought for a system of "labor exchange" and "labor exchange banks," conceived the idea of uniting trade unions and cooperative societies into a single organization, and sponsored an organization designed to bring capital and labor together in a common effort at reform. Very little came of any of this, although Owen kept active until near the end of his long life. As he grew older, he simply lost touch with the industrial world. But despite his errors in judgment and the unimpressive showing of his concrete achievements, his ideas exerted a profound influence beyond the boundaries of his native country. We might note that the term "socialism" was first used in its modern sense in 1827 in Owen's *Cooperative Magazine* to denote tendencies opposed to liberal individualism.

About the time of the French Revolution of 1848, *Louis Blanc*,[12] a utopian socialist anxious to use the political machinery of the country for the implementation of his ideas, was beginning to gain recognition. Like Marx soon thereafter, Blanc appealed to the workers rather than the propertied classes to effect a social transformation. He espoused the erection of social workshops by the state as a means by which everybody would be guaranteed useful employment. These workshops, equipped and financed by the government, would free the laborer from dependence on the capitalist; in them, the principle of full workers' control gradually would be established. In time, Blanc assumed, the remaining private workshops would succumb to the competition of the state-sponsored ones or would be merged into the latter. His other

---

[12]See Biographical Note L.

main principles included service according to capacity — that is, placement of each individual in such employment as will permit him to do the most good — and reward according to *need*. Blanc thus subscribed to a new ideal of *distributive* justice.

As a member of the Provisional Government in 1848, Blanc repeatedly talked up his idea of national workshops on an experimental basis, but he had a majority of the politicians against him. To silence the agitator, the government went through the motions of experimenting with a semblance of his idea while doing everything possible to discredit it. After the sham workshops had made a brief appearance, the hope of an immediate start toward production for service vanished.

The last revolutionary French social thinker of the midnineteenth century justifying brief mention in this survey was *Proudhon*.[13] He is mostly remembered for his frontal attack on private property coupled with his militant leanings. Proudhon shared with Marx (see pages 440–445) bitter hostility against established government and vociferous ridiculing of the utopian plans of his predecessors and contemporaries. He gave vent to his basic ideas mainly in *System of Economic Contradictions or the Philosophy of Misery* (1846). He served two prison terms — the second one shortened by his escape to Belgium.

Proudhon urged not the suppression of capital but only the elimination of its role as an agent of exploitation. Like Marx, who thought little of him, Proudhon distinguished between the ultimate goal of a state founded on the principles of liberty, equality, and fraternity, and the transition to that goal. During the transitional stage, a great national bank would furnish workers with tools free of charge and would issue paper money in exchange for commodities surrendered by producers. This bank, financed from the proceeds of property taxes and of progressive income taxes on certain groups, would use labor time as a measure of value of things exchanged under its auspices. Interest, rent, and profit would gradually be eliminated. When, following the Revolution, Proudhon was for a short time influential in government circles, he had an opportunity to try such a bank. But the "Bank of the People," established in Paris in 1849, came to nought.

Proudhon viewed *anarchism* as the distant goal — he construed any control of man by man as oppression. Since "property is theft," all property in the ideal society would be abolished. Proudhon's labor cost theory of value suggested to him that goods sold by capitalists above their costs incorporated an element of robbery. Only private possession secured by labor would be inviolate. He even anticipated some future

[13]See Biographical Note M.

time in which inequality in the talents and capacities of men would be reduced to a negligible minimum. Unfortunately, Proudhon was highly unrealistic in visualizing the coexistence of a completely nonauthoritarian system on one hand, and absolute equality on the other. What, we may ask, will prevent some from working harder and/or more successfully than others? The world is not likely ever to see a social organization without government, without private property, *and* without inequality.

In rounding out this topic, we may observe that Proudhon had had precursors in his demand for political anarchy and abolition of private property. The most famous of these, *William Godwin*,[14] had attacked government some fifty years earlier in his *Enquiry Concerning Political Justice* (1793). But, in contrast to Proudhon, Godwin would depend on reason and persuasion as the sole means for bringing in the new order; he did not believe in legislative action or in revolution.

CAPITALISM

The purpose of this section is to paint in broad strokes a picture of the forward surge of capitalism as an economic (business) philosophy. From about the thirteenth century onward, capitalist enterprise slowly began to attack the framework of feudal institutions that had for centuries both fettered and sheltered farmers and craftsmen. By the time of Columbus' discovery of the New World, most of the phenomena that we habitually associate with the vague word "capitalism" were already discernible. There were the Bourses — institutions developed to facilitate the handling of both foreign and domestic bills of exchange. There were other manifestations of "high finance," such as negotiable paper. Commodity speculation was not unknown.

Much of this activity had originated in the Mediterranean countries, hotbed of the Renaissance. With the growth of capitalist enterprise, a bourgeoisie with new attitudes toward economic problems arose and acquired power to assert its interests. It saw business facts in a light entirely different from that which shone upon the Scholastics; it imparted to society as a whole an increasing dose of its outlook on life, its mental habits, its scheme of values. Laical intellectuals gained in stature — physicians, lawyers, artists, and classical scholars (Humanists). Although none of these groups contributed to technical economics, they influenced the general intellectual atmosphere of their age and thus indirectly the setting in which technical economics could

---

[14]See Biographical Note N.

thrive later. Capitalism, of course, never appeared full-blown on the scene; rather, the germs of the society of a capitalist age, already contained in the society of feudalism, developed by slow degrees and were nurtured by the spirit of free inquiry that led to triumphs along many other fronts.

It is sometimes overlooked that the European countries, whose economic development was quickening after about 1500, remained predominantly agrarian well into the nineteenth century. Agrarian revolution characterized this development. A long series of changes in the technologies of all branches of agriculture gained momentum from the sixteenth to the eighteenth centuries. Also, the old relations between lords and peasants or farmers were destroyed in that process of organizational change of which the Enclosure Movement in England was the most notorious manifestation. Manufacture and international trade, though gaining ground, remained comparatively insignificant. Manufacturing industry was, for the most part, left in the hands of artisans, merchant capitalists, and owner-managers of relatively small factories (the term "manufacture" could still be taken literally). Large-scale enterprise did not significantly spread beyond the financial and commercial sphere — where, indeed, it expanded rapidly, giving capitalism one of its basic flavors. This changed significantly only with the onset of the Industrial Revolution in the late eighteenth and early nineteenth centuries. Even to Adam Smith, "big business" — which he looked upon with resentful distrust — meant large producing units in commerce and finance, especially colonial enterprises.

The industrial and commercial evolution was marked by *monopolistic public policy and private business practice* and was thus inimical to the true spirit of capitalism. Monopolistic behavior was manifest in attempts to (1) keep foreigners out of national and international markets, (2) keep other nationals (than the favored group) out of trade, and (3) restrict the output of the favored group and regulate its distribution between markets. Let us look at a few implications of these statements.

Since risks of doing business were great in an environment in which most potential customers were still very poor, business firms adopted defensive tactics and sought protective restriction. Even if governments had been actuated by the sole motive of fostering industrial development, they would have had to grant monopolistic privileges in those cases in which enterprise would not have been possible without them. Furthermore, capitalism grew from a pattern dominated by the spirit, institutions, and practices of craft guilds. These guilds resisted the introduction of new products, new methods of production, and new forms of enterprise and put legislators and administrators under pressure to act in their interest by subjecting new enterprises to various regulations. Finally, national governments had particular motives of their own for fostering monopolistic organization. For one, during the second half of the seventeenth century, following the very devastating Thirty Years' War, they faced an immense reconstruction problem. In addition, they could hardly be immune to the prospect of personal gain. In other words, monopolistic organizations could be exploited for the personal aggrandizement of the ruling monarch. The public, resenting any kind of exploitation — direct or indirect — denounced favored individuals or organizations such as the East India Company and the Merchant Adventurers. Generally, as illustrated by these not entirely random examples, it found more ready-made targets — and its reaction to restrictive practice was much stronger — in England than on the continent. Although they are often referred to as trading monopolies, these chartered companies were not monopolies in the strict sense of the term, that is, single sellers of a commodity for which there was no reasonably close substitute. Nevertheless, the word "monopoly" was used quite freely by the average Englishman, and it became loaded for decades, if not centuries, with the presumption of royal prerogative, favoritism, and oppression. The "monopolist" was a public enemy number one, and "monopoly" came to denote anything that a disgruntled person might dislike about capitalist practices.

The ascent of the business class did not hit its most rapid stride until the nineteenth century, when it proceeded nearly unimpeded and unchallenged. Although in general the bourgeoisie did not rule politically, in most countries governments did not hesitate to back bourgeois economic interests and in some cases to lend a helping hand in strengthening these interests. Even autocratic governments adhered to the principle of economic liberalism, that is, they acted on the theory that the best way to promote economic development and general welfare was to remove shackles from the private-enterprise economy and to leave it alone. (We should, of course, remember that the term "economic liberalism" has in the course of the twentieth century acquired almost the opposite meaning.) It may be less obvious that economic and political liberalism need not go together: many countries of eastern Europe in the nineteenth century did not sponsor parliamentary government, the suffrage, freedom of the press, and so on, although their governments were just as interested as those of England or Holland in seeing capitalism prosper through an approximation of laissez-faire.

It was in the area of *international trade* that laissez-faire made the most significant conquests in the first half of the nineteenth century — free trade was far from an established policy at the beginning of it, but by the middle it had triumphed in the case of at least a few of the leading countries. In England, the country known for a laissez-faire policy par excellence, a group of intellectuals called the Philosophical Radicals,[15] to whom several of the leading economists belonged, gave unfettered capitalism their wholehearted support. They were helped by progressive governments which could, indeed, claim a decisive share in the advance toward economic liberalism.

In the long sweep of time, economic liberalism now appears to have been a brief interlude, but this interlude was associated with an unprecedented rate of economic development. How much of the economic success of the nineteenth century was due to the removal of fetters from the energies that sought an outlet in business pursuits and how much to other causes (such as freedom from major wars) will always be disputed — to say that the policy of economic liberalism was the only cause of that impressive sequence of successes that started with the first wave of railroad construction would be quite bigoted. But we must not forget that, at its height, capitalism was a system which guaranteed to the businessman secure enjoyment of success while at the same time leaving him in no doubt that he could not expect any help in case of failure! While the level of living of the masses remained low, it did rise steadily all the time. In fact the welfare policies beginning roughly with the 1870's would not have been possible without the rapid strides of (private) development in the preceding three quarters of a century and the policies that fostered them.

At any rate, in the eyes of contemporaneous observers, including economists, the system kept justifying itself, and it is unfair, or malicious, to discount the intellectual honesty of those economists and to attach to them the label of apologists of the ruling class. Furthermore, there can be no doubt that at least J. Stuart Mill was aware of the historical relativity of social institutions and of some of the "economic laws" he worked out. He hardly believed in the permanence of the capitalist order of things. Rare and insignificant are the instances of a belief in the unsurpassable excellencies of capitalism as it unfolded from decade to decade.

But the idea that the capitalist order is only a historical phase and by its own inherent logic is *bound* to develop into something else — that idea belonged to Marx alone, and to him we shall now turn.

---

[15]See Chapter 2, Biographical Note E.

MARXISM

Until about the middle of the nineteenth century, utopianism in one form or another was the only real competitor of capitalism as it evolved in the Western world under England's leadership. After the appearance of the *Communist Manifesto* in 1848, a definite decline in prestige was suffered by the advocates of utopian schemes. *Marx*,[16] the great revolutionizer of thinking, made it amply clear that he stood for real, or "scientific," socialism, a social philosophy which since his day has continued to exert a powerful influence on the minds of hundreds of millions who have never read Marx. Actually he is the titular head of a heterodoxy of theories, encouraged by the vagueness or incompleteness of some of his writings, that somehow all claim to be true Marxism.

Marx could not have created the complex system he did without the material assistance of *Friedrich Engels*,[17] his companion-in-arms and continuous friend during the second half of his life. Engels not only was in almost daily correspondence with Marx, but he gave him the all-around support that permitted Marx to carry through (to a degree), notwithstanding numerous difficulties that plagued him; and Engels, under whose auspices the second and third volumes of *Capital* were published, executed the Marxian legacy after the master's death.

The *Communist Manifesto* (1848) already was a joint product, although it undoubtedly owed more to Marx than to his coworker — and the modest Engels readily admitted this. The fundamental thought expressed in it was that the whole history of mankind has been a *history of class struggles*, that is, between exploiting and exploited classes separated by an irreconcilable clash of interests. It outlined the broad sweep of conclusions concerning the nature and future of the capitalist economy, but it required untold hours of additional labor at the British Museum in London for Marx to be able to substantiate those conclusions with closely reasoned analysis. The *Manifesto* contained the germs of the *materialist conception of history*, which was an integral part of Marxian doctrine. Its fundamental proposition is that the "mode of production" of the material means of existence conditions all other processes of man's intellectual life. It must be noted that by "mode of production" Marx meant something much broader than the technique of production, namely, the totality of production relationships including the innumerable interactions between them. All of the social organization, the whole superstructure of institutions and ideas, is thus determined directly *or indirectly* by economic relationships.

---

[16]See Biographical Note O.
[17]See Biographical Note P.

Marx's Value and Distribution Theory

As an economist, Marx had to analyze the processes at work in the capitalist economy of his day. In *Capital* (first volume, 1867), he distinguished at the outset between use value and exchange value, following the accepted terminology. Since he was for the most part only interested in exchange value, he dropped the prefix and spoke just of value when he meant the latter. Things which have both use value and exchange value he termed "commodities." Like Smith, Ricardo, and others before him, he made a distinction between normal value and market value, terming the former "natural" or "real" value. He viewed the natural price of a commodity as the central price to which the market price is continually gravitating. He then proceeded through a process of elimination to accept labor time as *the* value-determining element common to all commodities. He left no doubt that by the amount of labor embodied in a commodity he meant all the labor in all stages of production, including the labor incorporated in the raw materials, power, and machinery necessary for the production of a given commodity. But, qualifying further, he recognized only "socially necessary" labor as value-determining. For instance, the quantities of past labor which are embodied in an existing commodity no longer determine the normal value of that commodity if the socially necessary labor required to produce it has changed — due, perhaps, to technological advances or to better training of the workers. By making his theory of value hinge on this element of "socially necessary" labor time, Marx attempted to show that unless a good has use value in the first place, labor spent upon it cannot create exchange value. But by leaving the final determination of whether labor is socially useful or not to the buyer, Marx in effect gave up his pure labor theory of value and reverted, like economists before and after him, to *demand* as a co-determining element of value! He never recognized this concession to demand as a possibly fatal flaw of his theory.

In order to compare the labor content of commodities in time units, Marx conceived of all the kinds and degrees of skills in various occupations as being reducible to standard time units of unskilled labor. However, he was unable to explain just how many units of unskilled labor time correspond to (are equivalent to) a certain amount of clock time spent by a skilled laborer.

Whereas to Ricardo value was merely exchange value or relative value, to Marx it was, in addition, an intrinsic entity incorporated in a commodity, the substance of which is congealed labor. Also in contrast to Ricardo, he did not assign to man-made and nature-made instruments of production any *direct* part in value determination.

On the basis of his general theory of value, Marx then construed a theory of wages, which is merely an extension of the former. Wages are the price paid for labor power, a special category of commodities. Like any other commodity, labor power has an exchange value. This exchange value is determined by the content of labor time socially necessary to produce the means of subsistence required for the maintenance of the worker and his family. Labor power, too, has a normal price and a market price, with the latter continually gravitating to the former. Marx accounted for wage differentials between grades of labor skill on the basis of differences in the costs of producing the various categories of skill, as modified by education and training. But, he was not entirely consistent in defining the subsistence concept.

The heart of Marx's elaborate and intricate structure was his *theory of surplus value.* He fashioned it by merely putting together his general theory of value and his theory of wages. He started from the premise that the socially necessary labor time embodied in the commodities necessary to maintain the worker for a day is less than the socially necessary labor time embodied in the commodities which the worker produces during that day's labor time. Workers who sell to capitalists their labor power — with the capitalists getting the use value of labor power, or simply labor — have no say as to the number of hours during which their labor power will be actually used. Since the capitalist, who specifies the length of the working day, sets it at a greater number of hours than the number required to produce the equivalent of labor's subsistence, the wage paid to the worker will be less than the total value of commodities produced by that worker in a day. Surplus value consists of the values produced by the worker during "excess hours" and for which he does not get paid. To illustrate, if the average amount of daily necessaries of a worker requires six hours of average labor to produce, but the worker has to "put in" twelve hours, the difference between the two, or six hours, may be called hours of surplus labor. This surplus labor will realize itself in a surplus value or surplus produce. The *rate* of surplus value depends on the proportion between that part of the working day necessary to reproduce the value of the labor power and the surplus labor time; in the above example it is 100 percent.

According to Marx, surplus value will always be appropriated by the capitalist. He will therefore strive to widen the gap between the value of the labor power (subsistence) paid out by him and the total value produced. He can do this in two principal ways: by lengthening the working day, and by reducing the hours of labor time socially necessary to produce the worker's subsistence. Marx was emphatic in pointing out that surplus value is the inevitable accompaniment of competition in the capitalist economy, that it is not caused by the greed of the capitalist, and that it cannot be eliminated by the opposition of the workers. What is more, the existence of surplus value provides the key incentive to the production of commodities under this system. It may be noted that the rate of surplus value (rate of exploitation) is always higher than the rate of profit. Both rates have as their numerator the absolute amount of surplus value. But the denominator of the rate of profit is greater because it includes not only the wages paid for labor power — what Marx called "variable capital" — but also funds going into the purchase of fixed equipment, raw materials, etc. — what he termed "constant capital." In symbolic form, the rate of surplus value equals $\frac{s}{v}$ (surplus value divided by variable capital) and the rate of profit equals $\frac{s}{v+c}$ (surplus value divided by variable plus constant capital).

Surplus value to Marx was a heterogeneous fund. It included not only profit, but also rent and interest, the former being taken by the landlord, the latter being absorbed by the money-lending capitalist. Only if the employer also owned the land and supplied all the funds would surplus value in its entirety be pocketed by him alone. Rent, interest, and industrial profit to Marx were merely different names for different parts of the surplus value, all of course derived from unpaid labor.

Corollaries

Marx gave a detailed account of the accumulation of capital and the origin of surplus value, which he explained in terms of "primitive accumulation," that is, the taking of funds by force from expropriated peasant workers at the dawn of the capitalist economy. Once the period of "primitive accumulation" was past, capital began to be accumulated by accretions from surplus value. Marx ridiculed the claims of political economists like Senior, who held that capitalists in acquiring funds to hire more labor for the production process performed an act of abstinence. He maintained that the funds "saved" by them were merely stolen since they came from surplus value.

Marx gave a trenchant account of the nature of the class struggle, the composition and contributions of the bourgeoisie under the capitalist system, and the way in which the latter is continually adding to the proletariat.

The state he construed as an agency of oppression, that is, as a device controlled by the bourgeoisie to advance its own interest. He held that "democracy" in the bourgeois state is nothing but a sham.

He laid much stress on the cropping up from time to time of "contradictions" under the capitalist system of production. He marshalled these to explain various "laws" (tendencies), for example, the increasing misery of the proletariat. One of the contradictions is the declining rate of profit, despite the fact that workers are pressed ever deeper into misery. He did not advance a clear-cut business cycle theory, but explained how capital accumulation in conjunction with the secularly growing "industrial reserve army" ("overpopulation") operates to increase the severity of successive crises. These crises, in turn, foster the progressive concentration and centralization of capital, as competition — amounting to an internecine warfare among capitalists — weeds out the weaker members of the bourgeoisie. A process of *expropriation* is thus said to be going on within the capitalist class itself. Finally, Marx predicted that the spiral of ever more deadly competition among capitalist firms would culminate in "finance capital" and "capitalist imperialism."

The "contradictions" of a capitalist economy, which are ultimately rooted in its valuation processes, according to Marxian theory will lead to its eventual and inevitable downfall. The trouble with the system, as he perceived it, is that it cannot help but generate the very processes which will doom it to extinction.

However, *Marx gave only the bare outlines of the institutions and processes which may succeed capitalist production.* With the breaking up of the system, its handmaiden, the political state, also would be dissolved. It will be the mission of the proletariat to seize power at the opportune moment, establish its own dictatorship, and then proceed to crush out all capitalist employers and their class ideology. This stage he called "socialism," or "the first stage of communism."

Then, in proportion as a new communized psychology developed, the proletarian state and its agencies of oppression gradually could be liquidated — or, rather, they would wither away. Only when each person would be motivated to contribute to the common effort in accord with his full "capacity" and to consume from the common output merely in accord with his "needs" would "full communism" (second stage) become a reality. In this ideal form of human association, economic society will have reached its highest possible state of perfection.

Marx did not make entirely clear, however, what degree of force and violence would accompany the downfall of the capitalist economy and the assumption of all power by the proletariat.

FABIANISM AND REVISIONISM

Although Marx spent the second half of his life mostly in London, Marxism in England never became a guiding principle, whereas its influence on the European Continent was widespread. British trade unionism, able to obtain for its members many advantages, felt itself not an outcast of society but a group advancing in social power.

Fabianism

In 1884, a year after Marx's death, a group of writers, scientists, and propagandists founded the Fabian Society, which elaborated an opportunist type of socialism. Flexible and pragmatic, this school of thought differed in many respects from Marxian socialism.

The primary emphases of Fabianism were as follows: (1) The transition from capitalism to socialism was to be gradual, not cataclysmic. (2) Industry was to be socialized by the peaceful economic and political agencies already in existence. (3) The large middle class was to be utilized in developing the administrative techniques by which to implement the new visions. (4) An important aspect in the attainment of socialism was to be an aroused social conscience.

Perhaps most significant is *point (2)*: the Fabians felt that in a democratic society with an orderly and sophisticated law-making process there was no need for a revolution in order to create a new political mechanism; the one already in existence had only to be used.

The Fabian Society attracted some of the most brilliant of England's younger men, notably *George Bernard Shaw*[18] and the *Webbs.*[19] It developed a pamphlet literature which was considerably above the common run in intellectual stature. It not only aided in the organization of the Labor Party, but introduced many legislative measures and sought support for its ideas by arranging for lectures before groups of all sorts. The most comprehensive statement of principles and of the general point of view of its members is contained in the *Fabian Essays*. In part a survey of economic trends toward a cooperative commonwealth, these *Essays* called for the control by the people themselves of the principal material means of production and for the gradual substitution of organized cooperation for the alleged anarchy

[18]See Biographical Note Q.
[19]See Biographical Note R.

of the competitive struggle — a struggle fanned by the Industrial Revolution and manifested by a brutal reign of individualism. They viewed the most desirable evolution toward socialism as one of a democratic, gradual, and peaceful character.

In the sphere of *economic principles* the Fabians were most strongly influenced by Ricardo's law of rent and by the writings of Henry George. They were impressed by George's demonstration of the injustice caused by private appropriation of rent. They made a distinction between riches and wealth, holding that the two have moved in opposite directions. Purchasing power that commands luxuries in the hands of the rich would command true wealth in the hands of the masses. The private appropriation of land, mostly by absentees, more than anything else was viewed as the source of the unjust privileges which Fabianism was to eradicate.

The Fabians shared with Marx the anticipation of socialism as a result of great economic and social forces. But they had faith — as Marx did not — in progress flowing from the steady extension of the functions of the state, political action, the development of education, and the arousing of a social conscience in the propertied classes. Whereas Marx had emphasized the iniquities following from the appropriation of surplus value by capitalists, the Fabians located the principal iniquities in the private appropriation of economic rent. Since they had as their chief objective the conversion of the middle class, they failed to stir the worker into excitement and action, something the Marxians were able to do. While they avoided the far-out fancies of the utopian writers, they sought — with limited success — to inspire devotion to their cause by unfolding the possibilities of associated action.

One of the weaknesses of the first edition of the *Essays*, which Sidney Webb attempted to rectify after World War I, was that the Fabians had not realized the importance of the trade-union movement and of an international outlook. During the 1930's Webb became intensely interested in the Soviet experiment, visited Russia, and expressed sympathy with many aspects of the Soviet system. Later writings emphasized that socialism is not a set of fixed dogmas but a set of principles in continual need of reinterpretation in the light of the changing conditions of time and place.

Bernstein's Revisionism

In Germany, where it had found a relatively fertile field, the Marxian point of view in time stirred up opposition. Especially in the agricultural and relatively democratic areas of southern Germany, some socialist politicians became impatient and pressed for immediate reform instead of entrusting their fortunes to the workings of the "laws" of capitalist development. The cause of the Revisionists, as people of this general outlook later came to be called, was greatly helped by the publication of Bernstein's *Evolutionary Socialism: a Criticism and Affirmation* (1899).

A close and loyal friend of Engels, Bernstein[20] apparently felt constrained not to publicize his deviating opinions before Engels' death, although his views may well have crystallized many years earlier. His intimate acquaintanceship with the leaders of the Fabian Society helped shape his point of view. An exile of sorts with parallels to Marx, Bernstein also chose London for his headquarters in elaborating his theories. After the publication of his book he was able to return to Germany, gain a following, and influence directly the fate of the German Social Democratic Party. His main opponent was *Karl Kautsky*,[21] who after Engels' death became the main propagator of Marxian doctrine.

Bernstein took issue with Marx on six main points: the viability of the capitalist system, the time element in social evolution, the nature of the class struggle, the concentration of capital, the nature of the state, and the potentialities of a revolution. Let us clarify these points.

To the revisionist leader, the collapse of the capitalist system was by no means imminent. Only the general tendencies of social evolution were correctly anticipated by Marx. The opposition between classes has not become more acute, and the middle classes have not disappeared but merely changed their character. The concentration of productive industry is proceeding at an uneven pace and has been notably slow in agriculture. The exploiting tendencies of capital have been partially checked by social legislation. A catastrophic crash does not hold much promise, but steady advance does.

This last point more than any of the others underscores the difference in Bernstein's outlook and temperament: to him the socialist *movement* meant everything and the final aim of socialism nothing. Whereas Marx was certainly concerned with adequate preparation of the working class for taking over the reins from the capitalists on the day of reckoning, he was disinclined to underwrite piecemeal advance; the system had to fall of its own weight. According to Bernstein's vision, the working classes must work out step by step their emancipation by changing society in all departments to a real democracy. While

---

[20]See Biographical Note S.
[21]See Biographical Note T.

Marx and Engels had allowed for noneconomic factors in capitalist development, Bernstein believed they had underestimated their role.

Bernstein declared the Marxian theories of value, wages, and surplus value to be abstract concepts and too remote from actual conditions to serve a useful role in illuminating reality. Nevertheless, he viewed surplus value, unless it were interpreted dogmatically, as an empirical fact of great importance — he only objected to Marx's attempt to prove its existence deductively. Bernstein challenged the Marxian thesis that economic crises tend to become ever more violent in their nature, leading to a world catastrophe. He admitted that the capacity to produce in modern society tends to outrun its capacity to buy, but denied that anything can be said a priori about crises.

It should be noted that Marx's theoretical structure had undergone several refinements before his death. Many of Bernstein's criticisms were directed against the early, crude statement of Marxian principles; he found much less fault with their mature elaboration. Although many of Bernstein's contentions were vigorously attacked by Marxists under Kautsky's leadership, they left a profound imprint on the socialist movement during the years immediately preceding World War I, with many professed Marxists beginning to agitate for day-to-day social reform.

Before turning to the last major "ism," two lesser "isms" should at least be mentioned. Guild socialism and syndicalism are forms of cooperative socialism based upon the organization of independent producers. The former, found mainly in England, stood for peaceful methods; the latter, prevalent mostly in France, advocated the use of force.

LIBERAL SOCIALISM

Between the two World Wars, the growing importance of socialism as a political power stimulated the discussion by a group of economists with widely divergent ideologies of the compatibility of economic freedom and planning. The resulting body of doctrine is usually referred to as the economics of liberal (or market) socialism. In many respects it harks back to Fabianism. Although it now still is in much the same rudimentary state of "development" as it was at the beginning of the 1940's — with only a few countries having in fact moved some distance toward a realization of the blueprints of this social-economic order — it is nevertheless rewarding to concentrate briefly on the highlights of a debate which built up to its climax at the end of the Depression decade and served, if nothing else, the very useful purpose of clearing the air and staking out the disputed issues and occasionally irreconcilable assumptions.

Mises' Economic Calculation in Socialism

Ludwig von Mises,[22] one in the group of many Austrians who during the first half of the twentieth century came permanently to the United States, in a book published in German in the early 1920's in effect denied the possibility of economic calculation and rational resource allocation in socialism. Specifically, it cannot solve, he said, that important aspect of the economic problem concerned with the valuation of the means of production, although the economic administration may know exactly what commodities are needed most urgently. Though it need not dispense with money, and would only make matters worse if it did, socialism cannot subsume the satisfactions afforded indirectly by the instruments of production under a common price denominator as is possible in a system of economic freedom. Rather, according to Mises, we can make systematic economic decisions only when *all* commodities that have to be taken into account can be equally measured by the monetary yardstick.

Now the fact that a socialist community would have to base proposed undertakings on vague valuations would not matter if the economic system were stationary, because here economic calculations would merely repeat themselves. But since the stationary state has no counterpart in reality, no comfort can be derived from this fact.

How about the possibility, argued by some "younger socialists," that the problem of economic calculation can be solved by creating an *artificial* market for the means of production? In reply to this argument Mises pointed out that it is impossible to divorce the price-forming function of the market from the working of a society based on private ownership of the means of production and the profit motive, for if the prospect of profits disappears, the market mechanism will have lost its mainspring.

But couldn't the socialist managers act *as if* they were entrepreneurs, by sufficiently decentralizing the decision-making process? Not so, according to Mises. It is the operations of speculative shareholders under capitalism which determine what will be produced or will no longer be produced, but there is no equivalent for this under socialism. Specifically, the deficiency of socialist constructions of an "artificial market" (with "artificial competition") consists in their resting on the belief that the market for factors of production is

----

[22]See Biographical Note U.

affected only by producers buying and selling commodities, whereas in reality it is impossible to eliminate from a market the influence of the supply of capital (by owners of funds) and the demand for capital (by entrepreneurs) without destroying the market mechanism itself. Basically, the trouble is that a socialist government cannot leave to other hands the disposition over capital (as is the case under capitalism) which guides the expansion and contraction of firms and industries.

A related, but no less important, point is that capitalists and speculators under capitalism perform their economic functions because they act under the incentive of "preserving" their property, yet there simply is no equivalent for this under socialism. Mises is led by his analysis to the conclusion that the market is eliminated from the guidance of economic activity because, although it is still easy to decide what consumer goods shall be produced, the problem of ascertaining how the existing instruments of production can be used most effectively for that purpose cannot be solved without economic calculation, i.e., by means of money prices established in producers goods markets based on a society with private property in the means of production.

Lange's Economic Theory of Socialism

In a widely noted collaborative work, the Polish economist Oskar Lange,[23] shortly before the outbreak of World War II, set up a model of liberal (or market) socialism characterized by a sharing in the making of economic decisions among households, a central planning board, and (subordinate) socialist managers. In accordance with this type of model, Lange assumed freedom of choice in consumption and freedom of choice of occupation; but, through a process of trial and error, the central planning board will set the prices of producer goods, and perhaps even of consumer goods, striving in the process to equate the supply of and demand for each good. The managers of socialist enterprises are then guided in their production decisions in part by these "parametric" prices and in part by familiar microeconomic principles of costing.

In tracing how economic equilibrium is determined in such a system, Lange distinguished between *subjective* and *objective* equilibrium conditions. The former refer to the indices of alternatives in the form of market prices and accounting prices, as the case may be, and the latter to the fact that quantity demanded of each commodity must be equal to quantity supplied. Since consumers can derive income only from

---

[23]See Biographical Note V. The work referred to is Oskar Lange and Fred M. Taylor, *On the Economic Theory of Socialism*, ed. Benjamin E. Lippincott (Minneapolis: University of Minnesota Press, 1938).

their own labor, not from the ownership of other productive resources, it is, in the final analysis, the "social organization" which determines their economic position in society. Specifically, this organization will permit the central planning board to distribute a social dividend in such a way as to reduce the inequality of income resulting from market-determined wages. (It follows from the above that this dividend is, in turn, determined by the total yield of real capital and natural resources.) Furthermore, the (consumer-preference oriented) rules imposed by the central planning board on the decisions of production managers help to determine the combination of factors of production and the scale of output. Finally, with prices of factors and of products being given, both the supply of products and the demand for factors will be determined.

Lange makes a vigorous attempt to refute the view that prices fixed by a central planning board are necessarily arbitrary and that this deprives them of any economic significance as indices of the terms on which alternatives are offered, claiming that the same objective structure of prices prevailing under capitalism can be obtained in a socialist economy if the parametric function of prices is retained. This is possible, Lange claims, by following the rule that accounting be done as if prices were independent of the decisions taken, which is the same as saying that prices must be treated as constant. Prices deviating from the equilibrium level would be reflected, at the end of the accounting period, in a surplus or a deficiency of the particular commodities in question. Based on his belief that both the prices of products and costs are uniquely determined, Lange concluded that the determination of equilibrium prices in a socialist economy occurs through a process analogous to that in a competitive market. This is the same as saying that he viewed the central planning board as a substitute for the market.

The remainder of his theory relates to the determination of the optimal distribution of the social dividend (must be such as to have no influence on the distribution of labor services between different industries and occupations) and to the determination of the rate of interest (he admits that the rate of capital accumulation, influenced by the rate of interest, is quite arbitrary).

Hayek's Critique of Socialism's Competitive "Solution"

Hayek, who as editor of, and contributor to, *Collectivist Economic Planning* (1935) had helped to assemble a battery of arguments against socialism in any form, subsequently felt challenged by Lange's views as set forth in *On the Economic Theory of Socialism* and summarized in the preceding section. He therefore mounted a vigorous counterattack in an article published in *Economica*,[24] which left matters unsettled — at least in the eyes of those not willing to accept Hayek's stern verdict at face value. In part, Hayek rendered a valuable service, however, by showing how many problems had been glossed over or left untouched by Lange and his "school."[25] The dual aspects of his principal conclusion are: (A) Liberal socialism requires a great deal more detailed central planning and control than its exponents are willing to admit. (B) The difference between liberal socialism and the totalitarian variety is much less than the market socialists admit, meaning that this social order is much closer to a totalitarian regime than to capitalism. A few highlights of his argumentation must suffice.

(1) He pointed out that none of the socialist authors had proved how economic values could be established in a socialist economic order, referring to a statement in Pareto's *Manual* to the effect that the mathematical problems are so overwhelming that their determination by calculation (through a system of equations) is impossible.

(2) Hayek examined specifically how far a socialist system where prices are fixed by central authority still conforms to the hopes placed originally on the substitution of planning for the competitive system, how far the proposed procedure answers the main difficulty (the valuation problem), and how far this procedure is applicable. As to the first point, he claimed that the hopes had been largely disappointing.

(3) Echoing Mises, Hayek conceded that, if in the real world we had a stationary equilibrium, the proposal of liberal socialism would not be entirely unreasonable; through a trial-and-error process we could then approximate equilibrium values. In practice, however, the question is which method — adjustment of planning estimates or the spontaneous action of market participants — will secure more rapid and complete adjustment to changing economic circumstances, and the answer to it can't be in doubt.

(4) While in the case of standardized commodities it is conceivable that prices be decreed from above in advance for a certain period of time, the output of heavy industries, which typically are the first to be socialized, cannot be standardized. Consequently, there would be

---

[24]"Socialist Calculation: The Competitive 'Solution,'" *Economica*, New Series, Vol. VII, No. 26 (May, 1940), pp. 125–149. On Hayek, see also Chapter 14, p. xxxx ff.

[25]More than half the contents of Hayek's article was directed specifically against the arguments advanced by H. D. Dickinson in his work *Economics of Socialism* (London: Oxford University Press, 1939).

need in such cases for a tremendous amount of price-fixing by central authorities, which would in effect have to take on the function of entrepreneurs.

(5) There is a host of thorny subsidiary issues related to pricing: what techniques should be followed in announcing and changing particular prices; by what considerations should the central planning board be guided in the fixing of prices; economic efficiency demands that prices be changed as promptly as possible when the market changes, but, where real competition is missing, the result is a high degree of inflexibility — especially when purely local conditions change — and prices thus lose their function of indicator of alternative opportunities.

(6) Under socialism there is no room for a newcomer to enter an industry if he knows of a cheaper method of production and is prepared to underbid established firms. With prices being fixed, the newcomer would first have to convince the central planning board of the merits of his case, and the board would then have to take over the entrepreneurial function for which it is so ill equipped.

(7) As to the relations between managers of production on the plant or industry level and the central planning board, it would be impossible to hold the former responsible for anticipating future economic changes, since these changes depend largely on the decisions of the central authority itself.

(8) It does not make much sense to attempt to rely on the interest mechanism for the distribution of capital if the market for capital is not a free one.

(9) Further problems are posed by the lack of knowledge relative to the direction of investment and by the assessment of responsibility for mistakes.

(10) Perhaps the greatest danger, though, is that of authoritarian despotism. Since planning on an extensive scale requires much more pervasive agreement among the members of society about the relative importance of wants than will normally exist, it becomes necessary to bring about such agreement artificially, i.e., a common scale of values may be imposed by force and propaganda. (A skeptic can hardly suppress the objection, of course, that Hayek remains silent about the excesses of advertising propaganda in a free-market economy.)

In closing it should be noted that during the 1950's the question of more, or less, centralized models and of the degree to which planning and a market mechanism could be combined also began to occupy economic discussion in the socialist countries of Eastern Europe. This discussion was prompted both by the need to give more initiative to the individual industrial enterprises in regard to the choice of inputs and outputs and by an increasing use of linear programming methods for selecting an optimum plan from among a range of alternative and self-consistent plans.

SUMMARY

In this chapter we briefly discussed the highlights of development of six of the world's leading "isms." It should be clear that no attempt has been made to enclose in our capsule the main contents of the comparative systems course as taught at American universities. "Communism" as practiced in Russia since the seizure of power by the Bolsheviks in 1917, which furnishes the prime living example of totalitarian socialism, was not discussed; nor were the beliefs underlying fascism, which dominated the scene in various countries during the period since the first world war, even mentioned. Guild socialism and syndicalism were merely named.

A brief account was given of the variety of schemes falling under the heading of utopian socialism. The first articulate expression of utopian ideas, that served as a model for many subsequent schemes of social reform, was More's *Utopia*. The following centuries witnessed a growing crop of utopian proposals, with France during the first half of the nineteenth century occupying a place of distinction for having produced fertile minds — Saint-Simon, Fourier, Louis Blanc, and Proudhon illustrate this span of the history of economic thought. At the same time Robert Owen in England ably focused on the evils of the factory system in the wake of the Industrial Revolution, expending the bulk of his energies on translating his reform ideas into practice. Some writers, including Godwin and Proudhon, placed their faith in anarchism as a worthy goal for which to strive.

The roots of capitalism are buried in the medieval period of history. Gradually free enterprise, tinged by monopolistic practices, gained strength and developed those capitalistic institutions which were incompatible with the permanency of feudalism. Already a healthy shoot at the turn of the sixteenth century, capitalism had enveloped much of the Western world by the beginning of the nineteenth century.

Capitalism's fortune became less predictable when the ideas of "scientific" socialism began to encroach upon it and take possession of millions of minds. Karl Marx, the founder of this creed, was convinced of the inevitable downfall of the capitalist system. He fashioned his vision into an elaborate structure of thought which is topped by his theory of surplus value, resting on the twin pillars of his general value theory and the theory of wages. He enunciated "laws" of capitalist development that are closely related to alleged "contradictions" within the system, which he viewed simply as a passing phase in the history of class struggles.

Bernstein, spokesman for revisionism around the turn of the twentieth century, ably disclosed some of the principal weaknesses of the Marxian system. He discredited the theory of surplus value while recognizing the importance of the concept of unearned incomes. Kautsky undertook to defend Marxism against the revisionist attack.

In England the Fabian Society gained influence toward the close of the last century. The Fabians discounted the need for revolutionary activity in order to cleanse the capitalist system of defects and make it more serviceable for the attainment of the greatest good for the greatest number. They relied on the potentialities of the lawmaking process in a democratic society, by which they hoped to get at the injustices caused by the private appropriation of rent and other less glaring abuses.

The chapter was rounded out by a summary of the arguments against the feasibility of a socialist economic system with free markets, as first advanced by Von Mises soon after World War I and elaborated by Hayek and others in the 1930's and later. An extended controversy about the compatibility of economic freedom and planning gained momentum especially after Lange and Taylor in the late 1930's had done some original work in sketching the outlines of a closely reasoned economic theory of socialism.

BIOGRAPHICAL NOTES

A.—*Sir Thomas More* (1478–1535) was educated in the household of an archbishop, a counselor of King Henry VII. From an early age he was a devotee of Greek literature and culture. Persuaded to enter the service of Henry VIII, he embarked upon an eminently successful career as ambassador and lawyer. He became an arbitrator in trade disputes and eventually Lord Chancellor of England. He disapproved of much of the royal policy, and when it came to a showdown between the Pope and the English King, More, a devout Catholic, failed to renounce the head of his church. He then was executed by royal decree.

A warm-hearted humanist and intimate friend of the outstanding classical scholars of the Renaissance, he worked on a dialogue in which he defended Plato's *The Republic*. But he never neglected the pronouncements of the Church and was an able interpreter of St. Augustine.

B.—*Francis Bacon* (1561–1626) was intended for the ministry but actually was educated for the law. Before he was appointed Lord Chancellor of England in 1618 — becoming one of More's successors — Bacon had been solicitor general and attorney general. As Lord Chancellor he evinced a certain servility to the Crown, but in 1621 he was charged with corruption and deprived of office. Sentenced to life imprisonment, he was later released by the king, and during the remaining few years of his life devoted himself to science and philosophy. While he was preeminent in natural science and philosophy, his direct contributions to the social sciences were meager; he contributed indirectly, however, by stressing a generally applicable method of thinking. In addition to his *New Atlantis*, he wrote a *Life of Henry VIII*, which was a model biography in style and design.

C.—*Thomas Hobbes* (1588–1679), an English philosopher, in early life acted as an amanuensis to Francis Bacon. He spent most of his life as a tutor, in which capacity he traveled widely on the European Continent. He expounded a materialist and mechanistic philosophy and was strongly influenced by the contemporary advances in mathematics and the physical sciences. In his writings, notably the *Leviathan*, he laid much stress on the human impulse to self-preservation.

D.—*François-Marie Arouet de Voltaire* (1694–1778), a Frenchman, had a stormy life because of his propensity to lampoon established authority. He was a man of great wealth and wit, a man of letters, and a European celebrity. His main contributions were in the fields of letters and arts. He wholeheartedly embraced the spirit and outlook of the Enlightenment.

E.—*Jean-Jacques Rousseau* (1712–1778), a French contemporary of Voltaire, was a social and political philosopher of renown. During his early years he had been a dissolute and restless vagabond. Largely self-taught, he gained renown with his *Discourse on the Sciences and the Arts* (1750), in which he stressed the corrupting influence of civilization upon the masses and predicted a further deterioration of mankind as civilization advances.

F.—*François Noël Babeuf* (1760–1797) helped usher in the first episode in the history of socialism in France by participating in the conspiracy of the Equals. As leader of a plot to overthrow the government, with a view to enforcing the constitution of 1793, he was condemned to death and executed. He and others of a like mind advocated community of property and the suppression of inheritance rights. Failure of the plot frustrated the plan to institute a communist regime.

G.—*Etienne Cabet* (1788–1856) was educated as a lawyer and in 1830 was appointed Attorney General of Corsica. Within months his inflammatory denunciations against the government of France cost him this position. Shortly thereafter he was elected a member of the Chamber of Deputies; and in 1831 he became the founder and editor of *Le Populaire*, a journal of communist principles with a wide circulation among the working classes. Later he was condemned to imprisonment for an article, but escaped to England, where he became acquainted with More's *Utopia*.

Later he helped set up an "Icarian city" in the United States, which did not survive.

H.—*Claude-Henri de Rouvroy, comte de Saint-Simon* (1760–1825) was born in Paris, joined the military at an early age and fought in the battle of Yorktown. Although he was already a colonel at twenty-three, he left the army in order to devote himself entirely to lofty social aims. He sketched many tendencies in modern thought, including — in addition to socialism — positivism, technocracy, and internationalism. During the French Revolution he renounced his title. His career as an author and "missionary" began in 1803. Discouragement over lack of recognition caused him to attempt suicide in 1823.

I.—*Barthélemy Prosper Enfantin* (1796–1864) studied at the *Ecole Polytechnique* and shortly before Saint-Simon's death became one of his followers. Later he assumed a codirectorship of the *Ecole Saint-Simon*, and after the death of his colleague Bazard changed the school from an institution devoted to social science into a Saint-Simonian "monastery." In 1832, with a group of apostles, he retired to his estate where he hoped to demonstrate the possibility of harmonious social existence. Later in life he devoted himself to business pursuits.

J.—*François Marie Charles Fourier* (1772–1837) was the son of a cloth merchant. After distinguishing himself as a student, he entered business life. His sense of decency was outraged by instances of dishonesty and waste in industry, and he made up his mind to become a social reformer. For many years he received little public encouragement, but he continued his devotion to honesty, integrity, and self-sacrifice. He asserted the possibility of a social order governed by pure reason. Despite the fact that his thinking was far removed from contemporary life, he impressed a number of men who, beginning about 1815, became his disciples.

K.—*Robert Owen* (1771–1858) had little schooling. When still a young boy he acquired a wealth of business experience which enabled him at the age of eighteen to go into partnership with a mechanic. In 1799 he purchased the New Lanark mills in Scotland, where he set out to establish a model community. His novel ideas frequently brought him into conflict with his partners, and the business ventures he joined were characterized by instability of management. In the early 1820's he left for America, hoping his ideas would find a more favorable reception in the New World. His hopes were dashed, but the early 1830's saw him at the head of a rapidly growing working-class movement in England, determined to reorganize industry on the basis of cooperative self-government. But the regular government successfully repressed the movement. Disappointed but not discouraged, Owen during the remainder of his life continued to engage in active propaganda on behalf of his ideas. In the last years of his life, when he became involved in ineffectual spiritualist experiments, the once clearheaded and practical man offered a sorry spectacle.

L.—*Louis Blanc* (1811–1882), descendant of a royalist family, was born in Spain. After the Revolution of 1830 he came, as editor of periodicals, in contact with the political and social problems of the day. Having in 1847 joined the staff of a paper of the extreme left, he was nominated in the following year to the Provisional Government, in which he represented the socialist element. In the same year he was indicted for his alleged connection with an insurrectionary movement, but before the trial he fled to England where he resided as a correspondent until the overthrow of Napoleon III in 1870. On returning to France in 1871, he was elected to the National Assembly as a member of the extreme left; however, he did not condone the violence of the Paris Commune. In the last five years of his life he was a member of the Chamber of Deputies. A politician of rare integrity, Louis Blanc wrote a monumental *History of the French Revolution*, published between 1847 and 1862.

M.—*Pierre Joseph Proudhon* (1809–1865) was born of poor parents in Besançon, the birthplace of Fourier. He left college at the age of nineteen and became a printer, a profession which facilitated his self-teaching. In 1840 he deemed himself well enough grounded in political economy to write the book *What Is Property?*, a pioneer work in which he attempted to prove the iniquity of private property per se. None of the factions contending for power in the Revolution appeared to him worthy of support, and he did not take part in the upheaval. After the Revolution he became a member of the Assembly, but his introduction of a scheme for reorganizing the credit of France failed of winning the necessary support. His private banking schemes did not get off the ground either.

N.—*William Godwin* (1756–1836) was trained as a Calvinist minister but preferred to exercise his mind on matters of logic and system. The book mentioned in the body of the text presented an argument for the perfectibility of man and of the social and political conditions conducive to this perfection. He was of first-rate importance as an interpreter to England of the intellectual ferment of the French Revolution. See also Chapter 2, Biographical Note B.

O.—*Karl Marx* (1818–1883) was born in Trier, Germany, the son of a Jewish jurist and of a mother descended from a Dutch rabbi's family. When Karl was six years old, his family embraced Christianity. He entered the University of Bonn at age seventeen with the intent of studying law, as his father had wished. He transferred to the University of Berlin the following year and devoted himself to a variety of subjects, including philosophy, history, literature, and arts, renouncing the social life of a typical German student. He acquainted himself with Hegelian philosophy and found in its dialectic a principle which he applied, in modified form, to his own philosophy of history. Hoping for a later lectureship at Bonn, he went to Jena, where in 1841 he received his Doctor of Philosophy degree.

But his nonconformist attitude prevented him from pursuing an academic career, and he turned to free-lance journalism. After he had become editor of a newspaper in 1842, he began a serious study of political economy; he was disappointed with the writings of the French utopian socialists, which he resolved to replace with something superior. In 1843 he began to edit in Paris the Franco-German Year Books, which were to give vent to fearless criticism of all existing institutions. Only one issue appeared, containing among other contributions an article by Engels; on this occasion their lifelong friendship took root. At the behest of the German government Marx was forced to leave Paris in 1845. He took up quarters in Brussels and remained there until the outbreak of the Revolutions of 1848.

That same year Marx had accepted an invitation from the League of the Just, with headquarters in London (later to become the League of Communists), to prepare a platform. He joined forces with Engels, and out of their effort emerged the *Communist Manifesto* with its flamboyant appeal to the workingmen of the world. Forced to leave Belgium, Marx returned via France to Germany to take part in the German Revolution of the same year. He became editor of the *Neue Rheinische Zeitung*, but the paper had to be suspended after a year and a half of struggle. Back to Paris!

Finally in 1850, when he was banished from the French capital and went to London, the restless life of a fugitive gave way to that of a settled student of human affairs, for Marx remained in London practically the remainder of his life. He began to write articles for the New York Tribune on the German Revolution. Year after year he was an almost daily visitor to the British Museum, where he prepared the draft for his *Critique of Political Economy* (1859). During the 1850's Marx's family was in dire want. In 1864 he addressed a conference which gave birth to the International Workingmen's Association ("First International"). Three years after this address he published the first (German) edition of his monumental work *Capital* (*Das Kapital*). This book, whose initial reception was cool, eventually occupied a place of honor among all classics addressed to workingmen. The second volume of *Capital* was published by Engels two years and the third one eleven years after Marx's death. Engels edited both volumes from notes and unfinished manuscripts.

Marx's principal significance lies in his contribution to the working-class movement, not in his refinement of classical theory: Marxian value theory is not now part and parcel of the modern body of value and distribution theory.

P.—*Friedrich Engels* (1820–1895) was the son of a wealthy German manufacturer born into a conservative, intensely pietistic environment. He entered his father's business before having finished high school. In his early twenties he went to Manchester as an agent of his father's partnership firm. Having connected himself with the Chartist and Owenite movements, for whose paper he wrote articles, he began to work on his *Condition of the Working Classes in England in 1844*. In 1845 Engels gave up the mercantile business and joined Marx in his scientific work, making his own library available to the friend of whom he thought so highly. Out of their joint effort came, among other things, the *Communist Manifesto*.

In 1850 he reentered business in order to earn enough to permit Marx to continue his self-imposed task. For the following twenty years Engels helped Marx in numerous ways. In 1860, to his own chagrin, Engels had to step into his father's position as a partner upon the latter's death.

In 1869 he sold out his partnership and was henceforth able to support Marx more substantially. He devoted the rest of his life to literary and practical revolutionary activity.

Q.—*George Bernard Shaw* (1856–1950) was born in Dublin, Ireland. After attending various schools he went to London in 1876, where he developed into the foremost dramatist and art critic of the English speaking world. He was a member of the Executive of the Fabian Society from 1884 to 1911. He edited the *Fabian Essays* and a number of other volumes, maintaining his connection with the socialist movement until his death.

R.—*Sidney Webb* (1859–1947) and *Beatrice Webb* (1858–1943) were a husband-and-wife team of immense value to the Fabian Society. From 1894 to 1925 they were coauthors of more than twenty volumes. Sidney Webb held various government jobs, taught at the University of London, and was a Member of Parliament on the Labor Party ticket. Beatrice Webb held two honorary doctor degrees and served on several royal commissions.

S.—*Eduard Bernstein* (1850–1932) was born in Berlin and educated in a German Gymnasium, whereupon he became a bank clerk. He joined the Social Democratic Party in 1872. He wrote extensively for working-class organs both at home and abroad. During approximately the last two decades of the nineteenth century, he lived as a German exile in Switzerland and England. In London he was a close friend of Engels until the latter's death and knew personally the leaders of the Fabian Society. After his return to Germany in 1900, he led the revisionist movement, which was opposed by the country's Social Democratic Party.

T.—*Karl Kautsky* (1854–1938) was the chief protagonist of the Marxian point of view in Germany. He stubbornly clung to the opinion that socialism would be brought about as a result of revolution rather than of a series of peaceful reform measures.

U. — *Ludwig von Mises* (1881–   ) was born in Lemberg in the Austro-Hungarian Empire. He entered the University of Vienna at the turn of the century, shortly before Schumpeter, and the two jointly studied under Böhm-Bawerk.

In 1913 Von Mises became a professor of economics at the University of Vienna. When, in the early 1930's, turbulence on the political horizon appeared, he left his native country in 1934 to settle in Geneva for about six years, teaching at the Graduate Institute of International Studies there. Von Mises then emigrated to the Western Hemisphere and joined the National Bureau of Economic Research; at the end of four years, on grants from the NBER and the Rockefeller Foundation, he published two works, *Bureaucracy* (1944) and *Omnipotent Government* (1944).

From 1945 until recently, Von Mises taught at New York University, having become a United States citizen in 1946. Around that time he had also helped to found the Mont Pélerin Society, an international association of free-market economists and social philosophers. Some of his colleagues — Wilhelm Röpke in Germany, Jacques Rueff in France, and Luigi Einaudi in Italy — contributed to the shift in emphasis in their countries from central planning to the free market. Shortly before, Hayek's *Road to Serfdom* had helped to inaugurate an economic liberal revival in the United States.

It is fair to say that, along with Hayek, Mises has been the foremost still living exponent of the theories of the Austrian school. Among his prodigious writings are, in addition to those mentioned already in this Note, the following: *The Theory of Money and Credit* (1912, 1953); *Socialism: An Economic and Sociological Analysis* (1922, 1951); *Epistemological Problems of Economics* (1933, 1960); *Human Action: A Treatise on Economics* (1949, 1966); *Theory and History: An Interpretation of Social and Economic Evolution* (1957); *The Ultimate Foundation of Economic Science: An Essay on Method* (1962); plus a great many works in German that have not been translated into English.

V. — *Oskar Lange* (1904–1965) was born in Poland, attended the University of Poznan, and later was connected with the University of Krakow — first as a student (LL.M., 1927; LL.D., 1928) and then as a lecturer (1931–1935).

Having toured several American universities as a Rockefeller fellow in 1932, Lange in 1936 joined the University of Michigan as a lecturer. The following year he settled in the United States, and after a rapid rise through the academic ranks was appointed to a professorship at the University of Chicago in 1943, the year when he also became a United States citizen.

During the next two years Lange began to display the marks of an exile and to play an active part in Polish politics. After he had resumed his Polish citizenship in 1945, he was appointed ambassador to the United States by the newly elected, Soviet-backed Polish government. He was Poland's delegate to the United Nations from 1946 to 1949.

Upon his return to Poland in 1949, Lange resumed the academic career which had been interrupted by his four years of diplomatic service. Between 1952 and 1955 he was rector of the Central School of Planning and Statistics and from 1955 until his death, professor at the University of Warsaw. An additional honor came to him in the late 1950's, when he was appointed deputy chairman and then chairman of the State Economic Council, a body designed to provide expert professional advice on ways and means of improving the Polish economy.

Aside from research and teaching, Lange's intellectual pursuits included the propagation of Marxist socialist ideas. His major analytic works are *Say's Law: A Restatement and Critique* (1942); *Price Flexibility and Employment* (1944, 1952); and *Political Economy* (2 volumes, 1963 and 1966).

Questions for Review and Research

1. Were the motives underlying the utopian constructs of Thomas More and Francis Bacon the same, similar, or different? Explain.
2. Was Saint-Simon primarily interested in maximizing the social product or in bringing about its more equitable distribution? Examine his major writings.

3. Were the majority of the French utopian socialists of noble birth or were they descended from the common people? Do their writings always unmistakably reflect this fact?

4. Investigate the literature with a view to explaining the failure of Fourierist communities in the United States.

5. Did Robert Owen have any use for private profit as a key institution in a harmoniously functioning social system?

6. To what ideal of distributive justice did Louis Blanc subscribe?

7. Was Proudhon more or less radical than Marx? Did the two team up for the propagation of ideas which they held in common? Explain.

8. Why is the designation *trading monopolies* for the royally chartered companies of the sixteenth and seventeenth centuries misleading?

9. Present a somewhat detailed account of Marx's stormy life.

10. Explain the terms (a) *organic composition of capital,* (b) *rate of surplus value,* (c) *rate of profit,* and (d) *industrial reserve army,* as used in *Capital.*

11. Contrast Bernstein's revisionism with both Marxism and Fabianism. With which of the two does it share more common features?

12. (A) Who was (were) the first to attempt to prove that rational pricing of the factors of production is possible in a socialist economy? (B) Against whose arguments was this theory primarily directed? (C) Where and in what form had these arguments been published?

Recommended Readings

Bornstein, Morris (ed.). *Comparative Economic Systems; Models and Cases.* Homewood, Ill.: Richard D. Irwin, Inc., 1965. Part II, "Models of Economic Systems," the division on "Market Socialism" (Selections 6–8), pp. 79–115.

Gray, Alexander. *The Socialist Tradition; Moses to Lenin.* London: Longmans, Green and Co., Ltd., 1946. Selected chapters, as suggested by the author or by the curiosity of the reader (who may want to know that this witty Englishman also authored *The Development of Economic Doctrine* in 1931).

Halm, George N. *Economic Systems; a Comparative Analysis,* 3d ed. New York: Holt, Rinehart & Winston, Inc., 1968. Chapter 10, "An Outline of Marxian Economics," pp. 125–133; Chapter 14, "Introduction to the Economics of Socialism," pp. 173–184.

Hayek, Friedrich A. von, *et al. Collectivist Economic Planning: Critical Studies on the Possibilities of Socialism.* London: Routledge, 1935. Selected chapters, including the translation of Mises' 1920 article.

Laidler, Harry W. *History of Socialism.* New York: Thomas Y. Crowell Company, 1968. As its subtitle indicates, it presents "A Comparative Survey of Socialism, Communism, Trade Unionism, Cooperation, Utopianism, and Other Systems of Reform and Reconstruction." The student is invited to proceed in his selections according to special interests and tastes. As a minimum, it is suggested that he read the Introduction by Frank A. Warren and Part 8, "Contributions of Various Social and Economic Movements": Chapter 49, "General Summary," pp. 870–875.

REORIENTATION AND OVERVIEW

In the preceding pages of this book, we have concentrated our attention on the principal contributions of a limited number of eighteenth-to-twentieth-century economists and their major doctrinal predecessors. We have become familiar primarily, if not exclusively, with their significance from the viewpoint of the formation of a permanent corpus of theory. Apart from sidelights in the context of biographical notes, we have hardly glanced at their stature as thinkers about broad, contemporary economic (and social) issues. This methodological approach commends itself to those who accept the premise that it is preferable to remember a few major ideas — clearly defined and skillfully formulated — of the most remarkable of past laborers in the field of economics, rather than to gather some vague notions about hundreds of economists who have somehow left their mark to posterity.

In the chapters on value and distribution theory as well as those devoted to complementary avenues of theoretical advance, we have considered economic doctrines as building blocks in the erection of that imposing structure of principles which the introductory economics student is likely to encounter right from the start. In the interest of avoiding superficiality, we had to neglect many refinements which in a more extensive treatment of the evolution of economic thought one could not afford to bypass. This final chapter has three primary purposes, as follows: to bring the principal highlights of our survey once more into focus; to view with utmost brevity a miscellany of ideas which, without meriting the label "theory," have left such deep tracks in the annals of our science as to have at least a claim to honorable mention, even in a text that is theoretically oriented; and to become familiar with the names of a few more significant post-World War II economists, whose contributions — often a mixture of macro- and microeconomics — could not be conveniently classified under the topical headings of this textbook.[1]

---

[1]Only a scattering of illustrious authors will be mentioned, and no firmly established principle of selection underlies the attempt to steer clear of being purely arbitrary. Since a few sentences of exposition in the text will have to suffice to satisfy the requisites of ready identification, the Biographical Notes will be compressed into a few hints relative to age, career, professional affiliation, and perhaps the title of a famous publication or two.

FILLER AND TRIMMINGS

In the first section, we shall consider a few strong stands taken by certain people during the classical era; a methodological reaction to the classical heritage, historicism; and the contribution of a writer who was second only to Veblen as an exponent of that new climate of thought — institutionalism — for which the United States provided the most fertile preconditions. Historicism and institutionalism are intellectual kins, albeit their common denominator is negative rather than positive: rebellion against the allegedly arid classical and neoclassical thought patterns.

The Optimists and the Manchester School

England, before the middle of the nineteenth century, was not the only country in which the virtues of economic liberalism had a strong basis in the facts of the economy. The same was true, though for the time being to a lesser extent, of France and the United States. It was pointed out in Chapter 16 that capitalism in France had to overcome a strong critical current of utopian socialism, feeding on the memories of the Revolution. Nevertheless, there appeared on the French scene in the 1840's a man filled with intransigent optimism, *Frédéric Bastiat*,[2] with whose counterpart in the United States, Henry C. Carey, the biography inclined student became slightly familiar in Chapter 5.

A feverishly active journalist and politician during the last few years of his short life, Bastiat believed in a Providential harmony of economic interests and in the beneficence of unrestricted competition in production. He vigorously campaigned for free trade and, in a delightful manner, reduced to absurdities the clamors for protection. One of his parables, taking the form of a hypothetical petition of candle-makers against the competition of the sun, is treasured by connoisseurs as one of the truly superlative pieces of merciless satire. It was rooted in Bastiat's vigorous objection to all devices of exploitation, of which tariff protection is only one.

Laissez-faire minded in early life but turning protectionist later, the optimist Carey responded to the pessimistic conclusions to which Malthus' and Ricardo's laws of diminishing returns, of population, and of rent had led these authors; he also responded to the limitless horizons of America in a period of rapid economic growth. Perhaps more drastically than any other writer, Carey as an economist reflected his environment. He adamantly rejected these classical principles of value,

[2]See Biographical Note A.

distribution, and population theory. His ingenuous optimism culminated in the faith that there will always be wide-open spaces awaiting man's cultivation and there is a perfect harmony of interests among the various classes. Inasmuch as Carey was not free of the reproach which he steadfastly hurled against the English economists, namely, their being restricted in outlook by their environment, his writings did not mark an advance.

In England, during the first half of the nineteenth century, a controversy flowed and ebbed. It centered around the country's famous Corn Laws — laws specifying the heights of tariff duties on imported grains. Theoretically, these laws tended to stabilize prices in England by encouraging a variable minimum of domestic food production without making imports prohibitively expensive. The country was, alternatively, a net exporter and a net importer of grain, depending on harvests at home and abroad. In the wake of the Industrial Revolution, and with a growing number of mouths to feed, England became more and more typically a net importer. This development irked the landowners, who toward the end of the Napoleonic Wars successfully agitated for higher duties on grain imports. But their interest in protection from foreign competition in order to increase rents on agricultural lands was diametrically opposed by the interests of the factory workers and their employers in lower food prices. The more enlightened among these could buttress their case by reference to Adam Smith's, and later Ricardo's, arguments in favor of free trade. But the advocates of a strengthening of the Corn Laws found an eloquent spokesman in Malthus, who looked with disfavor on a contraction of British agriculture at the expense of a growth in manufacturing.

After Malthus' death, the so-called Anti-Corn Law League began to fight with determination and persistence for repeal of laws which were incompatible with production and trade according to the comparative cost principle. *Richard Cobden*[3] and *John Bright*,[4] the leaders of the League, enjoyed the financial backing of fellow manufacturers. Although they waged a spirited fight, the Corn Laws were not taken off the statutes book until 1846, year of the Irish potato famine, when the conservative Peel administration finally convinced a reluctant Parliament of the necessity of cheaper food for Britain's rapidly growing population. The term *Manchester School,* or *Manchesterism,* relates to the attitude of laissez-faire to which Cobden and Bright were dedicated adherents. Interestingly, but consistently, they looked

[3]See Biographical Note B.
[4]See Biographical Note C.

with disfavor upon the exploitation of its colonies by the mother country; colonies, they held, exist for themselves, should be self-governing, and should be given the same commercial treatment as any other country.

Issues of Economic Methodology : Historicism

Perhaps the most important among the intellectual antecedents of what in this book, without further clarification, has been referred to as the Historical school — a nineteenth-century plant growing in Germany, with significant offshoots in England — was Friedrich List.[5] His message, like that of Veblen and some other "institutionalists," was somewhat elusive and contrasts sharply with the relatively clear-cut analytical techniques of the Classical and Neoclassical schools.

Spanning the greater part of a century, historicism proposed in fact not a new theory, but rather a certain attitude toward, or outlook on, economic research. Since those who deal primarily with historical materials tend to be loquacious, the writings of the members of the Historical school generally lack the crispness and conciseness of the (purely) theoretical treatise; nor do historical monographs yield their kernels of truth very elegantly. As a result the reader, if not the author himself, may be hard put to identify just what constitutes in a particular case a scientific advance or innovation. For these and other reasons it would have been disturbing, if not incongruous, if we had interspersed in previous chapters reflections on the contributions of the Historical school to the growth of economic thought. Nevertheless, the various fields of economic theory dealt with in Parts I to III might have absorbed to their benefit more generous doses of the quality of thinking for which the Historical school fought its battles and suffered abuse. On the other hand, its members proved often strangely unsympathetic to anything that faintly smacked of the abstract, deductive quality of Ricardian or, for that matter, Jevonian propositions. If we add to this the fact that members of the Historical school considered the state as an agent to promote social improvement and economic growth, while members of the Classical and Neoclassical schools were basically noninterventionist, we need not be surprised that between them scientific intercourse tended to be acrimonious.

Friedrich List, fervent protagonist of emerging nationalism in Germany after the Napoleonic Wars, was — a generation after Hamilton in the United States — the first to present a carefully reasoned argument for qualified tariff protection: the famous infant-

---

[5]See Biographical Note D.

industry argument. The larger purpose he achieved thereby was a demonstration of the historical relativity of many economic principles— or, negatively, the presumption against the cosmopolitan validity of theoretical truths. His most famous work, *The National System of Political Economy*, was written in 1841 and represented an attack on British classical economists, especially Smith, on the grounds that they neglected national needs. It also contained a suggestive classification of historical stages through which a developing nation is likely to pass. List viewed the precepts appropriate for contemporary England as inapplicable to a backward and splintered Germany, and regarded manufacturing as a prerequisite for the full release of a nation's productive powers.

Even before List died in 1846 from a self-inflicted bullet wound, there appeared the first writings from a member of what is generally regarded as the founding generation (or triumvirate) of the Historical school: Roscher, Knies, and Hildebrand. *Wilhelm Roscher*[6] in 1843 published his *Foundations of Lectures on Political Economy, according to the Historical Method*. He embraced views that differed only little from those of English liberals, did not condemn theory just because it was arrived at deductively, and did not rely much on the state as an agent of economic welfare. Positively, he undertook without bias an awe-inspiring amount of detailed historical research. *Karl Knies,*[7] who attracted a number of American postgraduate students in economics to Heidelberg, is most famous for a book published in 1853 under the title of *Political Economy from the Standpoint of the Historical Method*. A great skeptic and profound thinker, he proclaimed in this book the impossibility of framing universally valid policies, but nevertheless revealed himself as an able theorist who did little to inculcate economic historicism. *Bruno Hildebrand's*[8] chief contribution may well have been the establishment in 1863 of the *Yearbooks for Economics and Statistics*. His *The Political Economy of the Present and Future* (1848) expressed hostility to the concept of natural law and emphasized the character of economics as a cultural science.

A second generation of protagonists of the historical method was led by *Gustav Schmoller,*[9] one-time rector at the University of Berlin, formidable opponent of Carl Menger in the *Methodenstreit* that pitted "theorists" against "historians" in the German-speaking part of Europe in the 1880's.[10] Rejecting the idea of economics as a deductive science

[6]See Biographical Note E.
[7]See Biographical Note F.
[8]See Biographical Note G.
[9]See Biographical Note H.
[10]See Chapter 4, Biographical Note A.

and relishing controversy, Schmoller aimed at the meticulously detailed monograph penetrating to the origin of economic institutions, their growth, and adaptation to changing circumstances. Although he tried to write history dispassionately, his fervent belief in social reform found its counterpart in his role as a leader of the *Verein für Sozialpolitik* (Association for Social Policy). Some of the second-line defenders of the historical method, such as *Karl Bücher*[11] of Leipzig, were more skillful in blending induction and deduction.

In the next generation we find two men whose scholarly idiosyncrasies, coupled with rare brilliance, secure them a permanent place in the annals of historical research: Werner Sombart and Max Weber. *Sombart*[12] achieved fame mainly for his *Modern Capitalism* (1902). This is a bold book, providing rare stimulus and an artistic vision of the historical process, but it unfortunately displays a large number of errors — mostly due to the author's reliance on secondary materials. Covering a much wider area than its title suggests, it represents a synthesis merging economics into a kind of grandiose sociology. *Weber*,[13] a highly original and vitalizing force in German academic circles, unlike Sombart, did much firsthand historical research. His short life was a tribute to excellent all-around scholarship, and his scientific legacy as a sociologist of economics and religion constitutes a monumental achievement. Best known for his *The Protestant Ethic and the Spirit of Capitalism* (1904), he formulated a hypothesis that gave much food for Sombart's speculations along similar lines; it has challenged many others to investigate the role of religion in the development of economic systems. His labors in the field of the history of scientific methodology led him to the fertile concept of the "ideal type."

English historical economics was characterized by moderation and, in general, by the absence of fiercely partisan attitudes. Many writers, foremost *Arnold Toynbee*[14] in his *Industrial Revolution*, saw at an early time that the historical (inductive) and the deductive methods complement each other and that emphasis on one *or* the other is largely determined by the nature of a given scientific problem.

Beginnings of an Economics of Labor Relations

Throughout the nineteenth century, the purposes of labor organizations were largely defensive, designed to overcome the enormous ad-

---

[11]See Biographical Note I.
[12]See Biographical Note J.
[13]See Biographical Note K.
[14]See Biographical Note L.

vantage which employers had in bargaining. Only during the Great Depression did organized labor begin to embrace wholeheartedly the military doctrine that the best defensive is often a vigorous offensive.

John R. Commons—Uncommon Friend of the Common Man.— A turn-of-the-century American economist whose impact as a theorist has remained small, although the reforms which he promoted have become enormously important institutions, was John R. Commons.[15] Among those with whom he shared a rebellious attitude against the prevailing doctrines of his day, the most famous was Thorstein Veblen. Commons was instrumental in transforming, in the minds of people in key positions in public life as well as of legislators, prevailing views of the role of government in society. As he saw it, some of the most sacred principles of a free economy had become hollow shibboleths in a society in which monopolistic currents had eroded the foundations of competition among equals. What Commons felt to be even worse was that economic instability was a latent threat engulfing the virtuous and industrious along with the ne'er-do-well, reducing masses of workers to periodic destitution.

Commons' theoretical formulations, slow in ripening, were not well received by his fellow economists. But this mattered little since many of his ideas had already been translated into social reforms, especially in the state of Wisconsin which pioneered in legislation serving as a model for national efforts along similar lines. The University of Wisconsin, with which he was associated as a teacher for many years, demonstrated the fruits of close cooperation between the government of a state and its leading institution of higher learning.

Commons helped to introduce the "administrative commission" and to make this innovation in the field of governmental bodies a success. He extended its scope from the regulation of public utilities to the administration of labor laws, including safety, child and woman labor, minimum wages, maximum hours, unemployment compensation, mediation of disputes, and so on. Many states modeled their laws authorizing industrial commissions after that of Wisconsin, which was drafted by Commons. His work at the University enabled him to train young men in research techniques whose mastery would permit them to do an effective job of economic regulation, while at the same time fostering welfare statism. (By spotlighting what appeared to him as injustices, he never refrained from bringing ethical and moral arguments to bear on economic subjects.)

---

[15]See Biographical Note M.

Depending on one's philosophy of individual v. social responsibility, one may welcome or abhor the developments on which Commons pinned his faith; it would be malevolent, however, to doubt his sincerity and effectiveness. In view of the individualistic outlook that generally prevailed prior to the Great Depression, it is not surprising that his contributions were not widely appreciated in his time; nor did he leave a school of thought to carry on his theoretical work, to which we now turn.

Commons' Approach to Economics. — He derived impetus for his work from the firm conviction that traditional theory with its focus on commodities was both mechanistic and somewhat unrealistic. He blamed orthodox economists for trying to compare economic with physical phenomena. For him the focus of interest was the process of bargaining and the psychology of the parties to a transaction. As an institutional economist, he was much concerned with collective action. In his view, economic institutions are adopted and adapted by men as they try to solve new economic problems, and as a writer he helped to explore solutions for economic problems. For fruitful exploration he deemed practical experience an indispensable prerequisite.

Definitely committed to the *inductive* approach, he viewed synthesis in a unified system of principles as the final step — characteristically his theoretical work *Institutional Economics* (1934) was not published until he was almost seventy-two. In stressing the legal as well as ethical principles underlying economic institutions, he often had to cross the boundaries of economics proper. That left him with little time to keep up on the economic theories of his orthodox colleagues, and outside of monetary theory he was poorly informed on current economic literature. No wonder, then, that he failed to achieve much influence on professional economists. His tendency to be unsystematic in exposition and to use unfamiliar terminology made matters worse.

Commons' theory of institutional development cannot be ignored without loss by those interested in the study of economic history. It is found for the most part in his *Legal Foundations of Capitalism* (1924) and *Institutional Economics*, works which belong together because they are merely two aspects of the same theme. In both of them his lively interest in legal aspects of economics and in monopoly is present. One constant issue he faced was the determination of "reasonable," an adjective he used very freely in order to influence the decisions of courts. He tried to construct an evolutionary theory of value out of the habits and customs of social life, as tested by common law court decisions. Often new forms of behavior, having grown up in response to new needs, give rise to conflicts which courts are called upon to adjudicate. Judges then form in their own minds standards of what practices are reasonable; common law thus produces standards for economic behavior.

Commons emphasized that in labor transactions involving collective bargaining the final outcome depends on many variables — powers of persuasion, coercion, hesitation, and other psychological elements that cannot be measured — the effects of which may not be foreseen. In a given institutional framework, rights established by custom will set limits to bargaining. By following certain methods until they have become habitual, both parties acquire ideas concerning what is "fair" or "unfair," as exemplified by "fair pay," a "just day's work," and the like. Customs that have become formalized into laws further narrow the scope of effective (legal) bargaining.

In bargaining, the role of the "transaction" is of strategic importance, and Commons used it as his unit of investigation. In his view ". . . transactions have become the meeting place of economics, physics, psychology, ethics, jurisprudence and politics."[16] Since transactions are the means by which people in effect determine the allocation of resources and the distribution of product, they perform the same regulatory role as does the price system. But Commons did not aim so much at finding precise, objective valuations as he did at forming judgments based on the probing of human wills in action.

He distinguished between bargaining transactions, managerial transactions, and rationing transactions. In a managerial transaction a legal superior determines certain conditions for a legal inferior, as in an employer-employee relationship (supervisor-subordinate relationship). A rationing transaction involves a *collective* superior and individuals who are inferiors, as in the cases of corporate declarations of dividends or of union collections of dues. At the center of Commons' analysis was the *going concern* (a group with working rules designed to bring order out of conflict), on which each of the three kinds of transaction converged. In his view, the totality of "these three units of activity exhaust all the activities of the science of economics."[17]

The transaction, then, is the means by which collective action creates institutions, and institutions are created by men in their attempts to solve problems. By their very nature, institutions are subject to never-ending change. A system of deductive economics based on unchanging human behavior appeared to Commons as unreal.

---

[16]J. R. Commons, *Institutional Economics* (New York: The Macmillan Company, 1934), p. 706.

[17]*Ibid.*, p. 65.

RECAPITULATION

The preceding section was designed to show that if we cease to insist on rigorous theoretical analysis as the hallmark of great economists, we must make room for dozens of writers who — in view of our limited set of objectives — could not be discussed in the preceding sixteen chapters of this book. By the same token, the concluding section of this chapter, entitled "A Glance at Miscellaneous Recent Developments," is intended to demonstrate that if we embolden ourselves to size up the import of current developments, we can hardly avoid listing still more names — names, incidentally, which before the end of the century may well rank among the all-time greats. To repeat, the self-restraint with which we charted our course through the evolution of economic thought was dictated by an estimate of what can be done without "chafing at the bit," yet in reasonable comfort: *if* preference is given to a measure of thoroughness in studying the most theoretically oriented economists of the past instead of "covering the entire waterfront" with a light touch only. In what follows, we will retrace our steps, trying to recapture in utmost brevity an expanding web spun coarsely from major propositions in value and distribution as well as other types of economic theory.

Value and Distribution Theory

One of the most basic distinctions in economics is that between value in use and value in exchange and their relationships to one another. From Aristotle onward, most writers who tried to give a fairly comprehensive roundup of economic issues occupied themselves with it. It experienced the most subtle elaborations from among the members of the Austrian school. Perhaps the decisive breakthrough in groping toward a subjective value concept came with Galiani and Condillac, who clearly recognized the role of utility and scarcity in the formation of subjective exchange value. To find the laws governing the relationship between scarcity and utility, Gossen labored in virtual isolation; it was not until Jevons rediscovered his pioneering feats that something was done to bring these intellectual conquests before the profession.

The Classicists and some of their precursors had already gained valuable insights of a different kind. Cantillon gave a remarkably enlightened account of the interaction between value, in the sense of cost of production, of a good and its market price, discovering a regulatory mechanism which keeps the two in close relation. Adam Smith advanced value theory a step further by showing the effects on the price of goods of reproducibility and competition and the consequent equality of average cost of production and average market price in the long run. Having pieced together other partial truths, he stated the fundamental principle that in any advanced society the price of a commodity can be resolved into its component parts — he recognized wages, rent, and "profit." Except for the fact that he used the latter term to denote a mixture of interest payment and compensation for risk, Smith came close to modern usage in his analysis of factor payments. Meanwhile, the taboo on interest payments, the legacy of Aristotle and the Scholastics, had long come to nought. But there was not as yet a full awareness of the relation between the payment of interest and the productivity of capital; and the potentially wealth-creating effects of borrowing for consumption purposes which Smith failed to see at all.

Jean-Baptiste Say, Smith's popularizer on the European Continent, is remembered for his grasp of the strategic role of entrepreneurship as a factor of production. Malthus enriched the discussion of what constitutes a productive contribution in the economic process by pointing out, against Smith, the "worth" of services — a strange sequel since Smith had already revealed the shortcomings of the Physiocrats who had conceived of only agricultural activities as productive. Ricardo, who thought he had found a universally valid law of value in the proposition that the exchange value of commodities is always proportional to the quantity of labor required for their production, moved too far from reality to make value theory more meaningful for the uninitiated. He did contribute acute observations concerning the still embryonic theory of rent and founded this factor return on the concept of the differential fertility of land, coupling it with Malthus' Law of Diminishing Returns. While Senior, in working out the implications of his four postulates, merely elaborated principles which had already been stated before him, he gave the term "abstinence" a technical economic meaning, thus shedding light on the fact that, in general, capital accumulation is not possible without sacrifice. J. Stuart Mill assumed, somewhat prematurely as it turned out, that in his work the laws of value had all been laid bare and (re)stated with finality. But he convincingly showed the futility of trying to attribute to any one factor a definite share in the value of a produced good, inasmuch as the latter always depends on the cooperation of two or more factors.

The mathematical approach to elucidating economic phenomena received its first significant impetus from the Frenchman Cournot. Starting from monopoly, he developed various models of price determination under conditions of partial equilibrium. Johann von Thünen, the German landowner and farmer, was also possessed of a mathematical bent of mind, but he pioneered in a different field, evolving in his *Isolated State* the rudiments of a marginal productivity theory of distribution. Gossen applied the mathematical method to the study of man's conduct as a consumer, viewed in terms of Bentham's hedonistic calculus; at the same time, as a classifier of goods, he anticipated a line from the Austrian school.

The utilitarian approach found an even more determined defender in the Englishman Jevons who, along with Walras and Menger on the continent, is credited with the full development of the subjective theory of value. In Jevons' view, cost of production was no longer the direct determinant of value which it had been in classical perspective; for, as a first approximation, "value depends entirely on utility." He also proved that in exchange equilibrium marginal utility for each party is proportional to price. He acknowledged his indebtedness to Senior in further developing the concept of disutility of labor (labor pain) as a determinant of supply. Walras, a first-rate mathematician, followed closely in Cournot's footsteps, but he adopted the general equilibrium approach, being the first economist to incorporate the various functional parts of the economy into an all-embracing system of equations.

Menger, like Walras, was not beholden to utilitarianism; but, unlike the Frenchman, he was not at home in the use of the tools of higher mathematics. He fully appreciated the concept of marginal utility and laid great stress on complementarity of goods (factor services) in the determination of value; in so doing he made a start toward "imputation" theory. Two other Austrians, Von Wieser and Von Böhm-Bawerk, joined Menger in broadening the application of the "marginal principle" in value and distribution theory. Wieser was largely responsible for firm establishment of the concepts of "opportunity cost" and "imputation." He further enriched microeconomics by his views on the "antinomy" between value and utility, by his statement of the "paradox of value," and by his development of the notion of a factor's "productive contribution." Böhm-Bawerk outshone his fellow economists in the field of capital theory, which he discussed in its historical as well as current context. He saw capital as both an instrument of production and a source of interest. In its former role, capital is the key to the increasing roundaboutness of the methods of production; in the latter, it compels an analysis of the basic causes underlying the different valuation of present and future goods. Böhm-Bawerk advanced subjective value theory by pursuing the implications of the gradation of wants by kinds and degrees and price theory by the notion of the two "marginal pairs."

American economists gained in stature under the leadership of people such as Francis A. Walker and — to the dismay of many staid members of the profession! — Henry George; but no great contribution in pure theory was made until the arrival on the scene of John Bates Clark, the outstanding leader of neoclassicism in the United States. Clark was concerned with the problems of the proper balance of production factors and of income distribution. Tracing the social product to its sources, he tried to prove that distribution is controlled by a natural law, in which, under ideal conditions, each factor would get an amount of income equal to that created by the factor. He worked out a unique distinction between "capital" on one hand and "capital goods" on the other.

Neoclassicism, the salvaging from classical doctrines of elements that were sound and combining them with the Jevons-Walras-Menger fundamentals, was advanced in Europe mainly by Marshall. A brilliant synthesizer and master builder, he did for his own generation what Mill had ably done for his a few decades earlier. Superior in technique, Marshall forged a great many new concepts or tools, among which long run v. short run, elasticity, internal v. external economies, representative firm, and consumer's surplus are the best known. The widespread use of diagrams for the purpose of throwing additional light on verbal analyses was largely inspired by him.

Pareto, successor to Walras at the University of Lausanne, attempted a complete mathematical formulation of the theory of general economic equilibrium in still broader terms. He (and Edgeworth in England) originated the modern apparatus of indifference curves; Pareto may also be regarded as a pioneer econometrician. The Swedish economist Wicksell added further technical improvements to the formulation of general equilibrium theory; his peak achievement was its integration with monetary theory. Thanks to Wicksell's judicious eclecticism, the contributions of the Austrian school to the "marginal principle" were being more firmly embedded in general economic theory.

A new approach to value (price) theory was simultaneously inaugurated three decades ago by E. H. Chamberlin in the United States and Joan Robinson in England. They developed the largely neglected idea of partial competition into a systematic set of market relationships. Chamberlin focused particularly on the facets of nonprice competition (product differentiation) among many sellers, while Mrs. Robinson undertook *inter alia* an abstract but highly ingenious analysis of the problems of price discrimination and monopsony and skillfully integrated the theories of competitive equilibrium and monopoly equilibrium.   Both writers showed convincingly that the general effect of partial monopoly is to restrict output and to raise price.

A few allusions regarding the direction which research has taken in the field of value theory since the Great Depression will be made in the concluding section.

Macroeconomics

Keynes wrote *The General Theory of Employment, Interest, and Money* (1936) in an environment that had challenged economists to reexamine their theories and to reconsider the roles that might be played in the economic process by the public and private sectors, respectively. In Keynes' view, the Depression waste of unemployed resources had begun to endanger the very survival of the private enterprise economy; it suggested to him government spending in amounts sufficient to realize a nation's productive potential.   Thus arose a new and ominous ideology concerning the locus of responsibility for keeping the economic machine in smooth running order.   The theoretical underpinnings for these revolutionary policy conclusions Keynes supplied mainly in the *General Theory*.   This book has spawned an output of technical and popular writings, good and bad, that was unprecedented in the history of economic thought.

Keynes probably exaggerated the differences between accepted (neo)classical theory and his own system concerning the relationships that determine the flow of income, the volume of employment, the rate of interest, and the levels of consumption and investment.   All the same — and aside from policy conclusions — his departure was more than the branching off of another stream of economic thought; rather, it marked a multipronged thrust of theory pregnant with refinements on many fronts. From the definitional equality of saving and investment, through the various propensities and the relationship between the marginal efficiency of capital and the interest rate, to the concept of liquidity preference — Keynes boldly fashioned a new armor appropriate to the purposes he had set out to attain.   But let this be remembered: Keynesian economics is not tantamount to the science of economics or even to midtwentieth-century economics.   While it may well have crowded out microeconomics in graduate seminars, only a grossly misled or an intellectually dishonest person would claim that what is euphemistically called the "new economics" has superseded the structure of thought painstakingly erected during the preceding century and a half. The latter stands unimpaired; but economics has been enriched by the new concepts Keynes developed.

This enrichment has found expression in a variety of forms. Many of these are variants of dynamic process analysis and make up what Klein has called "the econometrics of the 'General Theory.'" Others appear in the guise of collateral contributions to the theory of optimal behavior and welfare economics, thus further cementing the union between micro and macrotheory. In some instances the writers' aim has been to provide a theoretical basis for the operations of a central planning board, a subject touched on briefly in the last section of Chapter 16. In recent years the work of Oskar Lange has been extended by such writers as Abba P. Lerner and Abram Bergson (not mentioned in the text) who have aimed at restating the optimum conditions of production and exchange.

Much of the expansion of dynamized Keynes-type models has been due to the pioneer effort of Tinbergen, who in the late 1930's built a model for the Dutch economy and then undertook the statistical testing of business cycle theories by analyzing cyclical developments in the United States between the end of World War I and the bottom of the Great Depression. This type of work stimulated Klein soon after the end of World War II to build a Tinbergen-type model for the United States economy, and to experiment with a succession of models of varying size and geared to different intervals of calendar time. Subsequently, research teams of growing size began to collaborate to produce highly refined models which have enjoyed some success in forecasting and simulation. Best known perhaps has been the *Brookings Quarterly Model of the United States Economy*, which was described in a large volume published in 1965. Similar, if less ambitious, models have been built in the 1960's for more than half a dozen countries, confirming the impression that the thrust of technique in economics has become a world-spanning phenomenon.

Such work has been cross-fertilized by the cosmopolitan research interests of Simon Kuznets, an eminent statistician with strong roots in Keynesian economics. In his studies of comparative international economic growth Kuznets has been able to fuse his superlative analytical techniques with an institutional approach, permitting him to set a new and higher standard for balancing out quantitative with qualitative elements of economic theory. Greatly inspired by Mitchell's views on the relations between theory, data, and policy in economics, Simon Kuznets in his lifetime has gathered an immense amount of economic intelligence, attempting to project on the world scene the kind of national economic introspection which Mitchell made respectable in the United States a few decades earlier.

Complementary Avenues of Theoretical Advance

Serious analyses of the nature and functions of *money* were undertaken in the preclassical centuries by only a handful of people. The roster of penetrating performances contains such names as Oresme, Bodin, Petty, Cantillon, Hume, and — with qualifications — Law. Most of these writers contributed to a sharper focus on that set of relationships somewhat vaguely known as the quantity theory of money. Monetary matters became rapidly more complex during the Industrial Revolution and the Napoleonic Wars, and English thinkers outside of academic circles, notably Thornton, began to fructify the discussion of monetary problems and principles in important ways. Ricardo indirectly had much to do with the famous Bullion Report and directly with the analysis of the relation between the price of gold and the depreciation of paper money during the early part of the nineteenth century. However, most academic economists, including Mill, in effect denied the possibility of monetary stimulation of the economy and distrusted monetary management. An interesting controversy developed in the 1840's between the Currency school and the Banking school; while the latter's position was more soundly reasoned, the Currency school carried the day in the Bank Charter Act of 1844.

Only well after the middle of the nineteenth century did professional economists once again contribute the bulk to the further theoretical advances in matters of money and banking. An important development was the vigorous use of statistics to illuminate important quantitative relationships under the leadership of America's Irving Fisher, who also excelled in helping to solve the conceptual problems associated with the use of index numbers. Walras, Marshall, and Wicksell contributed much to the integration of monetary and equilibrium analysis, the distinction between various types of interest rates, and their relation to cyclical phenomena. The equation of exchange was critically examined by many, and, in addition to the traditional Transactions Approach, the Cash-Balance and Income Approaches were found useful as the twentieth century marched on. With the increasing sophistication of students of monetary affairs, the commodity theory of money has gradually become obsolete, although metallism still has not run out of defenders — a determined band at that. Meanwhile the econometric exploration of the demand for money has been much stimulated by the innovative theoretical constructs of people like James Tobin and Milton Friedman.

International trade theory received its first major impetus in the course of the Commercial Revolution following upon the age of discoveries. Although few principles developed by the Mercantilists have stood the test of critical examination, some of the more enlightened among the pamphlet-writing members of trading companies expressed valid and valuable insights into the nature of a country's balance of trade and, to a lesser extent, its balance of payments. Thomas Mun, in particular, had a comprehensive grasp of the role played by different types of international transactions. North, also in England, and Cantillon in France were beacons of enlightened reasoning — the former in anticipating the advantages of unfettered trade, the latter in expanding the theory of domestic into one of international values. Hume lucidly discussed the self-regulatory features of international trade under conditions of free competition. Smith gave an impressive account of the benefits of an international division of labor, but he was not blind to the need for certain safeguards (national defense).

A few decades later, Ricardo worked out, and Mill improved, a general theory of international trade on the basis of certain simplifying postulates. Both recognized the importance of comparative, as distinguished from absolute, cost differences. While Ricardo left unanswered the question of how actual ratios at which goods exchange between nations are determined, Mill explained the important elements in the formation of the terms of trade. In particular, he developed the tool known as the Equation of International Demand.

Both Senior and Cairnes devoted themselves to the study of wage-level relationships and their bearing on international trade. Bastable relaxed some of the rigorous assumptions underlying the Ricardo-Mill analysis and made the theory of international trade reflect more closely the multicountry, multicommodity situation found in the real world. Marshall showed the usefulness of the concept of a "representative bale of goods." The American Taussig modified the labor-cost theory of value underlying classical trade doctrine but defended its continued usefulness as an analytical tool.

Cassel's purchasing-power-parity theory was not devoid of useful pointers, but it related domestic price levels to exchange rates in a too mechanistic way. His countryman Ohlin succeeded in securing widespread acceptance of general equilibrium analysis for the further evolution of international trade theory and made penetrating observations relative to the complementary roles played by commodity and factor movements in international trade. Haberler showed the applicability of the Austrian concept of opportunity cost in the theory of trade between nations and explained the nature of substitution curves under various cost conditions. Harry Johnson's scientific output during the last twenty years exemplifies some of the many laterals off the mainstream of general equilibrium international economics.

In the field of *business cycle* analysis, Sismondi and Malthus, soon after the turn of the nineteenth century, expressed their dissatisfaction with the complacent view taken by members of the Classical school and groped for an explanation of the periodic depressions which visited Western Europe. But not until Juglar stressed periodicity about half a century later did a scientifically satisfying explanation of the cycle phenomenon as a whole emerge. Wicksell opened up a main avenue to monetary theories of the business cycle, which found their most extreme variant in Hawtrey's exposition. Hayek, while acknowledging the crucial importance of the mechanism of bank credit expansion and contraction, looked for the ultimate cause of the ups and downs in the structure of production. Most nonmonetary theories stress the crucial role played in the cycle by variations in the rate of spending in the investment sector, usually in relation to one or more other strategic variables.

Mitchell's empirical approach to business cycle research has proved in the end to be the most promising of all; the National Bureau of Economic Research has enjoyed worldwide fame for its refined techniques of investigation and statistical measurement. Schumpeter's excellence rests on the unique blend of statistical, theoretical, and historical techniques which he brought to bear on the various hypotheses, including his own.

Crude principles of *public finance* were first tentatively developed toward the close of the Middle Ages in the Italian city states and German free towns. After Carafa's remarkable performance in the second half of the fifteenth century, Bodin in France a century later and Petty in England after the middle of the seventeenth century continued to probe questions of how to make optimum use of the various sources of governmental revenue. Within the next century, Marshall Vauban in France became perhaps the first to advocate a scientific overhaul of a major country's tax system, and Broggia in Italy wrote a systematic treatise on public finance which in quality almost vies with Adam Smith's contribution to that literature. Quesnay in the 1750's (and George more than a century later in the United States) proposed with impressive but partly faulty arguments a single tax on land. Smith excelled by his careful statement of canons of taxation, and Ricardo took up the topic of the shifting and incidence of taxes.

In the second half of the nineteenth century, social aspects of taxation began to be emphasized in Germany, especially under the intrepid leadership of Adolf Wagner. In the United States, the onset of the Great Depression expedited the use of fiscal policy as a major instrumentality for social reform, especially via the redistribution of income. Decades earlier, Seligman in his writings had prepared the ground for radical changes by his advocacy of progressive income taxation based on the principle of ability-to-pay. The concept of "functional finance" was first proposed by Lerner in the 1940's. The theory of "public wants" has been greatly refined by Musgrave, perhaps the most creative of America's fiscal theorists at the beginning of the 1960's.

Selecting has been hardest in the field of the *"isms."* From Plato's *The Republic* to the various schemes of social reform developed during the first half of the nineteenth century, many utopian plans were sketched by imaginative thinkers; perhaps the most famous of them was More's *Utopia* of the early sixteenth century. Frenchmen designed a disproportionately large number of projects envisaging some new economic order, and for a while Associationism, represented in England by Owen, enjoyed considerable prestige both in Europe and in the United States. However, none of the experiments translating lofty ideas into new forms of community living proved durable enough to invite imitation on a large scale. Occasionally, anarchism has been advocated as an ideal for the full development of man's faculties, but aside from wars it has never had a fair trial.

The roots of capitalism reach way back into the medieval period of history. This form of economic organization gained in strength in the Western world until about the middle of the nineteenth century, or perhaps until World War I. It has since had to face the competition for the allegiance of the masses that comes from one or another variety of "scientific" (as distinguished from utopian) socialism. While the evolutionary type has met with varying fortunes, totalitarian socialism as it evolved under the Communist Party and the government of the Soviet Union has so far had only a few and temporary setbacks. Its workability can no longer be doubted; its efficiency in raising the levels of well-being of the masses has been hotly — and perhaps futilely — debated for some time. Karl Marx, who preached the gospel of the inevitable downfall of capitalism, is still invoked for the rationalization of economic decisions made by the planners of totalitarian socialist societies. His elaborate structure of economic doctrines culminating in his theory of surplus value, which in turn rests on the twin pillars of his theory of commodity prices and his theory of wages, tends to be regarded as a *curiosum* in Western circles, although there have been grains of truth in some of his prophecies. Bernstein and Kautsky in Germany around the turn of the century battled over the interpretation of the Marxian legacy; while in England the Fabian Society, which did not prepare for the violent overthrow of the capitalistic system, gained in influence under the guidance of the Webbs, George Bernard Shaw, and other famous intellectuals. During the 1930's Lange's constructs of scientific socialism of the liberal variety heated up professional debate over the compatibility of economic freedom and planning. It challenged the ingenuity of the defenders — Mises, Hayek, and others — of the proposition that capitalism is inherently superior to other forms of economic order.

A GLANCE AT MISCELLANEOUS
RECENT DEVELOPMENTS

It is hoped that the following discussion will give the reader some *feel* of additional exciting avenues that have recently been explored; no balanced or reasonably full treatment is intended.

Torchbearers of the Lausanne School: Hicks, Leontief, Samuelson

John R. Hicks,[18] one of the best known Oxford economists, in 1939 published a genuinely important work entitled *Value and Capital*. Hicks is one of those economists fascinated by the elegance and apparent precision of equilibrium theory in the Walrasian tradition. In *Value and Capital*, he presents, undiluted, a highly refined current version of doctrine in the fields of utility and equilibrium analysis. Obviously, his appeal is limited to those who can draw upon the fruits of equally rigorous (mathematical) training. Eager to dispense with the notion of measurable utility, he proceeds in terms of preference positions; but he has hardly been able to relegate subjective utility to a minor role. The old neoclassical notions now appear in new garb, and such concepts as the marginal rate of substitution and its declining rate take the place of marginal utility and diminishing marginal utility. Hicks exemplifies an approach which may in time largely displace Marshall's partial equilibrium analysis. It is still too early to tell, however, whether the older doctrine has been much enriched by Hicks' impressive body of thought; more likely than not, the basic framework of received value

---

[18]See Biographical Note N.

theory will stand. (In another vein, it is well known that Hicks brought all the elements of Keynesian interest rate theory together in the comprehensive manner depicted by the standard *IS* and *LM* schedules.)

In his *Economic Table*, François Quesnay tried to demonstrate the ways in which goods and money flowed between different sectors of the economy. He thus became the first to incorporate a rough, general picture of the economy into what we now call a model. Walras, who was first to attempt a precise theoretical formulation of the mutual interdependence of the principal sectors of an economy, was not in a position to make his model empirically useful because he did not have available the necessary statistical data. His approach would necessarily eventuate in millions of equations because he did not try to aggregate factors of production and commodities. It became *Wassily Leontief's*[19] goal, some three decades ago, to produce a "structural model" of a real-world economy, and since 1941 he has published at fairly regular intervals the results of his "input-output" analyses of the American economy. The widespread adoption and increasing capacity of electronic computers within the last decade or so have facilitated fulfillment of his aim: more sophisticated aggregation of production by industries and the inclusion of all "sectors" of the economy in the model. The effective handling of the empirical content of a system of general equilibrium has thus come within reach.

The Bureau of Labor Statistics of the U. S. Department of Labor has lent a helping hand in the building of large "input-output" tables. Technically, these tables represent a schematic framework or matrix showing output flows from each sector to all the others, where they become inputs. For example, outputs may be arranged horizontally across the matrix and inputs vertically, with each sector thus appearing twice, namely, as a producer of outputs and as a consumer of inputs. With the schedule so obtained it is then possible to determine the "structural" relationships between the various magnitudes. Under the assumption that the proportions of factor inputs do not change as output is increased, linear equations can be developed to represent the major relationships. In conclusion, input-output tables have allowed economists to make a significant start toward solution of various economic problems, including the allocation of an economy's resources for war production.

A more flexible quantitative approach than input-output tables is represented by *linear programming* which, like input-output analysis, was first developed during World War II, when the ever-recurring ques-

---

[19]See Biographical Note O.

tion was: How can the (scarce) inputs required for a particular output be minimized?

This technique calls for the preparation of interconnected linear equations, each of which represents a quantitative relationship between input items and the resulting volume of output (that is, each represents a partial production function). Although the tools provided by linear programming have been of substantial usefulness to firms — operations research is a direct descendent of this innovation — it is not clear yet whether linear programming can provide valuable new insights into the theory of an economy, for example, the feasibility of rational calculations in a centrally planned economy. Most of the problems treated thus far with this new mathematical technique have been linear; that is, constant (rather than increasing or decreasing) returns were postulated. As additional experience is gained, more attempts will be made to construct nonlinear models.

A striking symbol of the merging of different schools was the founding in 1930 of the Econometric Society, which has steadfastly worked toward the fusion of mathematical, statistical, and theoretical inquiry. Perhaps one of its outstanding members today is *Paul A. Samuelson*,[20] whose devotion to mathematics in the service of modern economics has been very successful and has perhaps not been rivalled. A prodigy in economics, he was not yet thirty-five years old when Schumpeter, who mentioned him at various points in his unfinished *History of Economic Analysis*, died! Three years before, in 1947, Samuelson had completed his *The Foundations of Economic Analysis*, one of the most profound and demanding works published during the postwar period. (The fact that about the same time he also wrote the most successful Principles textbook, whose first edition was unadulterated Keynesian fare, may also be noted with some astonishment in passing.)

In *Foundations*, Samuelson translated most of the important economic propositions into high-powered mathematical language. He worked toward a general conception which allowed him to tie together the special branches of economics, such as price theory, public finance, international trade; he viewed these merely as particular expressions of a general theory. In his study of equilibrium conditions he was concerned foremost with maximizing behavior and with the determination of stability conditions. He has clarified the concept of economic dynamics and has vigorously broached problems in this area, as evidenced by his early work on the interaction of the multiplier and the accelerator. Finally, Samuelson's economics in almost all areas abounds with

[20]See Biographical Note P.

welfare propositions and has stimulated explorations of that still wide-open territory by other powerful minds. Perhaps we need not be surprised that at the age of forty-six Samuelson was already past president of the American Economic Association!

Game Theory

An unresolved problem faced by economists for a long time has been that of defining rational economic behavior on the part of an individual when the very rationality of his actions depends on the probable behavior of other individuals. For example, in the case of oligopoly it cannot be simply assumed that every oligopolist has a definite idea as to what the others will do under given conditions. A way out of this difficulty lies in the rejection of the treatment of the maximization principle as synonymous with rational behavior. The new approach was pioneered by professors *John von Neumann*[21] and *Oskar Morgenstern*[22] in a book published in 1944 under the title *Theory of Games and Economic Behavior*. Several decades earlier, Edgeworth had already likened the duopolist to a chessplayer who takes account of his opponent's moves before moving himself. Pigou had suggested that if under oligopoly the relative probabilities of the various potential relationships between firms could be postulated, it might be possible to mark off a range within which the price level would tend to be situated. The Neumann-Morgenstern tome of over nine hundred pages was largely a response to the intellectual challenge posed by the problem.

The authors view business enterprisers as considering various plans of action that might be taken by them or their rivals. They liken economic behavior to games of military strategy and tactics, with the outcome being determined by the mutually interdependent entrepreneurial actions of opposing individuals.

The theory of games is a general theory, capable of treating problems of collusion as well as open competition. Unfortunately, it calls for a rather involved and lengthy exposition if more than the principal underlying ideas are to be grasped. However, there are now satisfactory introductions — in book and article form — available to the interested student.

Conclusion

To what does all of this lead? Perhaps the main suggestion has been implicit in the preceding pages: without a thorough mathematical

[21]See Biographical Note Q.
[22]See Biographical Note R.

background, the student of present-day developments on the frontiers of economic knowledge cannot hope to obtain more than a very vague idea of what is "going on." Even if, for example, the conclusions of a particular journal article are presented in nonsymbolic language, the reader will hardly be able to appreciate the limitations encountered in solving the problem(s) stated at the outset if he is mentally debarred from interpreting and weighing the argument as it advances step by step. The thrust toward technique has been especially pronounced in the United States, and aspirants to a Ph.D. degree in economics in this country will have done well if during undergraduate days they subjected themselves to a heavy dose of mathematical training. And if you, the reader, plan to become an academic economist, make no mistake: the outlook is — at least until a superior shorthand method of professional communication has been invented — for more of the same! You need not be lost without a good knowledge of mathematics; but with it, your path will be much smoother and your prospects brighter for academic recognition and honor.

BIOGRAPHICAL NOTES

A.—*Frédéric Bastiat* (1801–1850), a Frenchman, attempted to form in his country an organization resembling the British Anti-Corn Law League. His *Economic Sophisms* was published in 1846, and *Economic Harmonies* in 1850.

B.—*Richard Cobden* (1804–1865) early in life made a fortune as a cotton textile manufacturer, then traveled widely to study foreign economies; in 1841, he won a seat in the English Parliament. In fighting for repeal of the Corn Laws, to which he gave his all, he ruined his health.

C.—*John Bright* (1811–1889) had a career which in many ways resembled Cobden's. He did not begin active work for the Anti-Corn Law League until 1841, three years after Cobden was made a member of the executive committee of the Manchester Anti-Corn Law Association. Bright possessed a rare gift of oratory, which he used extensively while serving, for decades, in Parliament.

D.—*Friedrich List* (1789–1846) was a German who, holding a professorial position, spoke up for the unification of his country but became suspect in government circles for his views; for reasons of self-protection, he emigrated to America, where he went into business. He eventually returned to Germany as an American Consul.

E.—*Wilhelm Roscher* (1817–1894) was a founder par excellence of the German Historical school. He taught mostly at the University of Leipzig and turned out a large number of publications, including his extraordinarily successful five-volume *System of Political Economy* (1854–1894).

F.—*Karl Knies* (1821–1898), before establishing himself at Heidelberg and making its University a center of economic study and research, taught at Marburg and Freiburg. He also published his three-volume *Money and Credit* (1873–79).

G.—*Bruno Hildebrand* (1812–1878) taught at German and Swiss universities and was the sole editor of the *Yearbooks* during the first decade of existence of this periodical. He shared the outlook of the group that later gathered around Schmoller.

H.—*Gustav von Schmoller* (1838–1917) did more than the "triumvirate" to ground the Historical school firmly in actual historical research. Before he became its rector, he had already taught at the University of Berlin. He was a cofounder of the *Verein für Sozialpolitik* (1872), an editor of the *Yearbook for Legislation, Administration, and Political Economy* (known as "Schmoller's Jahrbuch"), and he authored *Outline of General Economic Theory* (two volumes, 1900–04).

I.—*Karl Bücher* (1847–1930) became famous for his theory of "stages" — of the same general type as List's theory — which he developed in his *Industrial Evolution* (1901). His somewhat mechanistic approach was attacked by Sombart, but he inspired greatly America's John R. Commons.

J.—*Werner Sombart* (1863–1941) in 1917 returned as teacher and successor of Adolf Wagner to the University of Berlin, where he had been a student. He was a Marx-Engels specialist with radical views, but he eventually broke with socialism. Among his other works we may note *The German Economy in the 19th Century* (1921).

K.—*Max Weber* (1864–1920) taught at several German universities, mainly at Heidelberg. In a broad view he appears as a sociologist, but his first love was economics — in a historical context. In spite of the shortness of his life he gave rise to a kind of Weber school. Most notable among his other works is *General Economic History*, which renders a course he gave at the University of Munich just before his death.

L.—*Arnold Toynbee* (1852–1883), a teacher at Oxford University, originated the term "Industrial Revolution." He did not survive a breakdown in the prime of his life, but his main ideas were posthumously (1884) published as *Lectures on the Industrial Revolution in England*.

M.—*John R. Commons* (1862–1945) became immersed in social reform ideas as a graduate student of Richard T. Ely, one of the founders of the American Economic Association. Between 1899 and 1904, following an unhappy teaching experience at Syracuse University (his chair was abolished), he served with the U. S. Industrial Commission, the National Civic Federation, and the U. S. Department of Labor. Returning to academic life, he went to the University of Wisconsin and, at the same time, entered into a close, advisory association with the newly elected reform governor, Robert M. LaFollette. He retired from teaching in 1932.

N.—*John R. Hicks* (1904–   ) was a lecturer at the London School of Economics, a fellow at Cambridge, and a teacher at Manchester before he returned to his Alma Mater, Oxford University, where he is holding the Drummond Chair in Political Economy. He made a name for himself with his *Theory of Wages* (1932); much of his applied work has been in the area of public finance.

O.—*Wassily Leontief* (1905–   ), of Russian descent (Leningrad), received his doctorate from the University of Berlin in 1928. He came to the United States in 1931 and joined the staff of the National Bureau of Economic Research as well as the economics faculty at Harvard. His first "input-output" table was published in *The Structure of the American Economy, 1919–1929: An Empirical Application of Equilibrium Analysis* (1941).

P.—*Paul A. Samuelson* (1915–   ) has been a full professor at Massachusetts Institute of Technology since 1940. For his work leading to the Ph.D. degree in 1941, he was awarded the David A. Wells prize; in 1947, the American Economic Association bestowed on him the John Bates Clark Medal, a singular professional distinction given only rarely — and only for the most significant contribution made by an economist under the age of forty. He became president of the Econometric Society at the age of thirty-six. *Economics, An Introductory Analysis*, has gone through five editions and, having been translated into at least a dozen languages, has become a cosmopolitan success.

Q.—*John von Neumann* (1903–1956) was born in Budapest, Hungary. Having obtained his doctorate in mathematics there in 1926, he was then engaged in teaching in Germany for a few years. In 1930 he came to Princeton University, where he joined forces with Morgenstern in 1938. He served on the Atomic Energy Commission, but was "at home" in both the natural and the social sciences.

R.—*Oskar Morgenstern* (1902–   ) first came to the United States in 1925, after he had earned his Dr. rer. pol. degree at the University of Vienna. Beginning in 1929, he taught at Vienna for nine years and has been a member of the economics faculty of Princeton University since 1938. He made a name for himself through his work in business cycle research and methodology before coming to America permanently.

Questions for Review and Research

1. Which two writers are representative of the group referred to as "Optimists" in the literature on the history of economic thought? Where did they live?

2. Were Cobden and Bright primarily (or exclusively) (a) Mercantilists? (b) Socialists? (c) Free Traders?

3. Did Friedrich List participate in (a) the *Methodenstreit*? (b) the activities of the Anti-Corn Law League? (c) the founding of the *Verein für Sozialpolitik*?

4. Which one of the three leaders in the first generation of the Historical school veered away least from the views held by midnineteenth-century English (liberal) economists?

5. Who was Germany's foremost representative of the Historical school in the closing decade of the nineteenth century? Where did this man teach?

6. How did Max Weber and Werner Sombart differ in their scientific methodology?

7. Commons had a rather checkered career as a teacher and encountered some difficulty in getting satisfactory appointments. Radiating from Wisconsin, there nevertheless developed a strong Commons school in this country. Try to explain this apparent contradiction.

8. Summarize Commons' theory of "transactions."

9. Who are at present the leading English and American economists perpetuating and building on the Walrasian tradition? Where do they teach?

10. With what name is the evolution of input-output analysis during the last twenty years most closely associated?

11. Who authored (a) *The Foundations of Economic Analysis?* (b) *Theory of Games and Economic Behavior?* When were these works published?

12. Is the Econometric Society (a) an outgrowth of post-World War II developments? (b) a national or an international professional association? (c) the successor to the American Economic Association?

Recommended Readings

Gruchy, Allan G. *Modern Economic Thought, the American Contribution.* Englewood Cliffs, N.J.: Prentice-Hall, Inc., 1947. Chapter 3, "The Collective Economics of John R. Commons," pp. 135–243.

Harter, Lafayette G., Jr. *John B. Commons, His Assault on Laissez-Faire.* Corvallis, Oregon: Oregon State University Press, 1962. "Introduction," pp. 1–6; Part III, Chapter 8, "Commons' Approach to Economics," pp. 205–239.

Newman, Philip C., Arthur D. Gayer, and Milton H. Spencer (eds.). *Source Readings in Economic Thought.* New York: W. W. Norton & Company, Inc., 1954. Part Twelve, "Reactions Against Orthodoxy: The German Historical School," pp. 489–522.

Seligman, Ben B. *Main Currents in Modern Economics, Economic Thought Since 1870.* New York: The Free Press of Glencoe, Inc., 1962.
Part Two, "The Reaffirmation of Tradition": Chapter 5, "Equilibrium Economics and the Unification of Theory," Sections iii–v, pp. 403–441.
Part Three, "The Thrust Toward Technique": Chapter 9, "From Realism to Technique," Section vi, pp. 771–784.

INDEX OF NAMES

INDEX OF SUBJECTS